United States Edition

201

Workbook for Lectors, Gospel Readers, and Proclaimers of the Word®

jsimutis @ rawbw.com

Graziano Marcheschi, MA, DMIN

with Nancy Seitz Marcheschi

Marielle Frigge, OSB

Daniel J. Scholz

LTP
LITURGY
TRAINING
PUBLICATIONS

WORKBOOK FOR LECTORS, GOSPEL READERS, AND PROCLAIMERS OF THE WORD® 2016, United States Edition © 2015 Archdiocese of Chicago. All rights reserved.

Liturgy Training Publications, 3949 South Racine Avenue, Chicago, IL 60609, 1-800-933-1800, fax 1-800-933-7094, orders@ltp.org, www.LTP.org.

Cover art: Barbara Simcoe

Printed in the United States of America.

ISBN: 978-1-61671-224-2
WL16

In accordance with c. 827, permission to publish was granted on May 4, 2015, by Most Reverend Francis J. Kane, DD, Vicar General of the Archdiocese of Chicago. Permission to publish is an official declaration of ecclesiastical authority that the material is free from doctrinal and moral error. No legal responsibility is assumed by the grant of this permission.

As a publisher, LTP works toward responsible stewardship of the environment. We printed the text of *Workbook for Lectors, Gospel Readers, and Proclaimers of the Word®*, with soy-based ink on paper certified to the SFI (Sustainable Forestry Initiative) Certified

(continues on next page)

CONTENTS

Ordinary Time

The Authors

Graziano Marcheschi has taught, spoken, and written nationally on Scripture, liturgy and the arts, and lay ecclesial ministry. He holds a DMin from the University of St. Mary of the Lake, Mundelein, Illinois. Director of lay ministry formation in the Archdiocese of Chicago for eighteen years, he is currently executive director, office for university mission and ministry, St. Xavier University, Chicago. Nancy Seitz Marcheschi is a choreographer and a teacher of music, performing arts, and religion in Evanston, Illinois.

Marielle Frigge, OSB, has taught Scripture and theology for thirty-three years at Mount Marty College in Yankton, South Dakota. She has a PhD in theology and education from Boston College. A Benedictine sister, she now directs ongoing formation for Sacred Heart Monastery and continues to teach in pastoral settings. Her most recent publication is Beginning Biblical Studies (Anselm Academic, 2009; revised 2013).

Daniel J. Scholz is dean of the College of Arts and Sciences at Cardinal Stritch University in Milwaukee. He has a PhD in biblical theology from Marquette University. Dan has taught Scripture for over twenty-five years in academic and pastoral settings. His most recent publication is The Pauline Letters, Introducing the New Testament (Anselm Academic, 2013).

(continued from previous page)

Sourcing Standard, and Chain-of-Custody, confirming that the paper manufacturer takes a responsible approach to obtaining and managing the fiber. The wood fiber required for the making of this paper includes recycled content and was obtained from 100% Responsible sources.Renewable and carbon-neutral biomass fuels are used for the energy needed in the paper manufacturing process, reducing the use of fossil fuels.

INTRODUCTION

The Role of the Reader

As readers of the Word, we share in a sacred process. "In Sacred Scripture, the Church constantly finds her nourishment and her strength, for she welcomes it not as a human word, but as what it really is, the Word of God" (1 Thessalonians 2:13; Second Vatican Council, *Dogmatic Constitution on Revelation [Dei Verbum]*, 24). "When the Sacred Scriptures are read in the Church, God himself speaks to his people, and Christ, present in his word, proclaims the Gospel. Therefore, the readings from the Word of God are to be listened to reverently by everyone, for they are an element of the greatest importance to the Liturgy" (*General Instruction of the Roman Missal*, 29). We who are privileged to read at the liturgy help to present the Word to the assembly.

We owe this privilege, as well as the insights just expressed, to the work of the Second Vatican Council, 1962–1965, which issued the *Dogmatic Constitution on Divine Revelation* (*Dei Verbum*, quoted above) and the document that has most shaped our liturgical experience: the *Constitution on the Sacred Liturgy* (*Sacrosanctum Concilium*). Among many contributions to the liturgy, it provided for a richer selection of Scripture to be read at Mass, it invited the laity into liturgical ministry, including the ministry of reader, and it urged everyone to listen attentively to the Word proclaimed, because "it is he [Christ] himself who speaks when the holy Scriptures are read in the Church" (7).

Our mission entails a great responsibility. At Mass, we serve as a bridge between the Scriptures and the faithful. In undertaking this sacred ministry, you are committing yourself to the preparation and discipline that enables Scripture to become a living Word. According to the Introduction to the *Lectionary for Mass*, this requires that "preparation must above all be spiritual, [though] . . . technical preparation is also needed" and "spiritual preparation presupposes at least a biblical and liturgical formation. . . . Biblical formation is to give readers the ability to understand the readings in context and to perceive . . . the central point of the revealed message. . . . Liturgical formation ought to equip readers to have some grasp of the meaning and structure of the liturgy of the word and of its connection with the Liturgy of the Eucharist. The technical preparation should make the readers more skilled in the art of reading publicly" (55). Obviously, this responsibility requires serious effort.

Using This Book

Proclaiming Scripture is a ministry that involves your whole life. So make Scripture a part of your life each week, especially the week prior to proclaiming.

(1) Using this book, read all four Scriptures for your assigned Sunday. All were chosen for this day, so read them together. The Responsorial Psalm and Gospel can teach much about how the First Reading

In the beginning was the Word, and the Word was with God, and the Word was God.

should be proclaimed. (2) Build your prayer for the week around the Scripture passage you will proclaim on Sunday. (3) As you are becoming familiar with your passage, read it directly from your Bible, reading also what comes before and after it to get a clear sense of its context. (4) Always read all three commentaries. Suggestions in each can help you with your own passage. As you read the commentaries, refer to the sections of the Scripture passage being discussed and make your own margin notations. (5) Read the Scriptures again using your margin notes and those printed in this book to remind you of the commentary suggestions. (6) Always read aloud, noticing suggestions for emphasis. After several readings, alter the emphasis markings to suit your own style and interpretation.

Workbook helps you prepare to *proclaim* your assigned reading, and it can also build your knowledge and skills when you use it every week to prepare to *hear* the readings. The commentaries deepen your understanding of Scripture and the proclamation advice in the margin notes helps you gradually absorb the skills you need to be a mature and seasoned proclaimer of the Word.

Using Additional Resources

The better you understand the meaning of your passage, the more effectively you will proclaim it and so help the assembly to understand it. Although the commentaries in this book will help you, readers may wish to dig deeper. Also, readers need to develop a lifelong habit of turning to the Scriptures for study and prayer. Additional resources that will help you to do this are listed in a downloadable file at http://www.ltp.org/t-productsupplements.aspx.

Appropriate Dramatic Technique

Good readers use techniques from the world of theater judiciously, not to draw attention to themselves, but to draw attention to the Word. When people experience good proclamation, they forget the reader in front of them and they hear the Scripture in a powerful way. That goal is best achieved by skillful use of all the available reading techniques. Of course, when readers are overly dramatic, and more focused on *how* they proclaim than on *what* they proclaim, listeners stop believing them. Artifice (an imitation of artfulness) can become an obstacle to good proclamation.

Avoiding artifice does not mean settling for colorless proclamation. Failing to use appropriate techniques can lead to mediocre reading that guarantees the Scripture will not be heard. Readers who cannot differentiate one character from another, who read too fast or too slowly, who have too little energy and don't use the colorful words of a passage, who read in a monotone without rising and falling dynamics and pacing—these readers only draw attention to themselves. The assembly cannot see beyond them. But really good proclaimers who utilize appropriate techniques draw the assembly into the reading.

True Humility. All readers need a model of true humility as they work toward excellence in proclamation. We look to Christ who "emptied himself, taking the form of a slave . . . [and] humbled himself, becoming obedient to death, even death on a cross" (Philippians 2:7–8). Jesus, the Word, humbles himself each Sunday by making himself dependent on us who proclaim him in the assembly. He depends on us to communicate him as a living and vital Word. Jesus, alive in every line of Scripture, is indeed obedient "unto death."

Reading as Interpretation

God's Word is "living and effective" (Hebrews 4:12) and it "goes forth from [God's] mouth . . . achieving the end for which [he] sent it" (Isaiah 55:11), yet we know that doesn't happen automatically. People must allow the Word to become a transforming influence in their lives. Before they can do that, readers must help them to hear it.

Reading is a form of interpretation. The same word spoken by two readers will not be "heard" in exactly the same way. Pacing, the words stressed, pauses, volume, tone color, and intensity are all elements that interpret the text. Your responsibility is to make sure your interpretation upholds the plain sense of the text, the author's clear intent, and that you enable the text to speak to everyone. God's Word can lose its power, beauty, and spiritual import if a reader fails to communicate the full content of a passage, which clearly consists of more than the words. Every text contains three kinds of content: intellectual-theological, emotional, and aesthetic.

Intellectual-theological content is what the text is about: the plot of the story, the points or details, behind which is a theological teaching or insight. Examples: Peter calls us to imitate Christ; Paul tells the Corinthians to stop feuding; Moses goes to Mt. Sinai to inaugurate the covenant; Jesus heals a blind man. **Emotional content** is how the author or characters "feel" (or want us to feel). When Juliet calls "O Romeo, Romeo! wherefore art thou, Romeo?" it is important to know she's not searching for him,

This is my commandment: love one another as I love you.

but lamenting that his name makes him one of her family's sworn enemies. The emotional content would be far different if she were searching for him. **Aesthetic content** refers to the artistic elements that make the writing pleasing, like metaphor, rhythm, repetition, suspense, picturesque language, and imagery. Shakespeare repeats Romeo's name as an aesthetic device to give emphasis. As readers, we must help our assemblies experience the beauty of the fine literature we call Scripture.

To acquire the intellectual-theological content, begin by reading the Scripture and the commentary. Next, search the text for the emotion the author is expressing: the emotional content. Finally, look for the author's aesthetic devices: repetition, simile, metaphor, irony, and so forth, the aesthetic content.

Tools of the Trade

Margin Notes serve as your coach, suggesting how to express the motivations of characters or author.

Build refers to increasing vocal intensity as you move toward a climactic point in the text. It calls for intensified emotional energy which can be communicated by an increase or decrease in volume, or by speaking faster or slower. The point is to show more passion, greater urgency, or concern.

Stress (Bold Print) identifies words that are more important or expressive than others and require more stress. Use your judgment about the amount of stress so as to avoid an artificial delivery.

Echoes. Some words "echo" words that went before. For example, "You shall be a glorious crown . . . a royal diadem" (Isaiah 62:3). Here "diadem" echoes "crown" so it needs no stress. In such cases, emphasize the new idea: royal.

Words That Sound Like What They Mean don't require us to imitate the sound but to suggest it by stretching the word a bit. "Pop," "fizz," and "gulp" are obvious. Some are more subtle: "smashed," "vast," "in haste," "implore," "gleamed." They were chosen to convey meaning; let them do their work.

Word Value. "Shock" is always a more interesting word than "bean." "Shock" sounds like what it means and immediately conjures up vivid images. "Bean" won't even make your mouth water. Word value is also determined by context. The words "one, two, three" are neutral by themselves, but put in context they intensify: "Three seconds until lift-off! Three . . . two . . . !" If, in reading that sentence, "Three, two . . . " sounds the same as when followed by "buckle my shoe" you've got work to do. Words are your medium, like a painter's brush or a sculptor's chisel. You must understand the words before you can communicate them. Most words have a dictionary meaning (denotative) and an associational meaning (connotative). "House" and "home" both mean "dwelling," yet they communicate different feelings. Be alert to subtle differences in connotative meanings and express them.

Separating Units of Thought with Pauses. Identify the units of thought in your text and use pauses to distinguish one from another. Running words together blurs meaning and fails to distinguish ideas. Punctuation does not always indicate clearly what words to group together or where to pause. The listener depends on you for this organization of ideas. With Paul, especially, carefully identify individual ideas and share them one at a time.

> God so loved the world that he gave his only Son, so that everyone who believes in him might not perish but might have eternal life.

Sense Lines. Scripture in this book is arranged (as in the Lectionary) in sense lines, one idea per line. Typically at least a slight pause should follow each line, but good reading requires you to recognize the need for other pauses within lines. Moving from one thought unit to another within a paragraph requires shifts in mood and pacing. Don't rush these transitions; honor them with a healthy pause.

Pauses are never "dead" moments. Something is always happening during a pause. Practice will teach you how often and how long to pause. Too many pauses make a reading choppy; too few cause ideas to run together. Too long a pause breaks the flow. If pauses are too short, your listeners will be struggling to keep up with you. A substantial pause always follows "A reading from . . ." and both precedes and follows "The word [Gospel] of the Lord."

Ritardando refers to the practice, common in music, of becoming gradually slower as you approach the end of a piece. On the final line of a song you automatically slow down and expand the words. Many readings end this way—with a decreased rate but increased intensity.

Characters. To distinguish the various characters that populate a passage, try to understand their thoughts, feelings, and motivations. Use subtle variations in pitch, pacing, and emotion to communicate them. But don't confuse proclamation with theatrics. Suggest characters, don't "become" them.

Narrator. Knowing the point of view the narrator is "rooting for" will help you more fully communicate the meaning of the text. The narrator always has a viewpoint, often speaking as a believer, not as an objective reporter. For this reason, the narrator is often the pivotal role in a passage. Using timbre, pitch, rate, and energy can help you convey the narrator's moods or meanings.

Openings and Closings are not part of the reading; they are liturgical dialogue between you and the assembly, so they differ in tone from the Scripture and require pauses, *after* the opening dialogue and *before* the closing dialogue. These formulas are prescribed, so don't vary the wording. **The opening:** First, establish eye contact and announce, from memory, "A reading from . . . ." Then take a pause (three full beats!) before starting the reading. The correct pronunciation is "A [uh] reading from . . . " instead of "A [ay] reading . . . ." **Character names** are often the first word of a reading, so lift out the names to ensure listeners don't miss who the subject is. **The closing:** Pause (three beats!) after ending the text, then, with sustained eye contact, announce from memory, "The word [Gospel] of the Lord." Always pronounce "the" as "thuh" except before words beginning with a vowel as in "thee Acts of the Apostles." Maintain eye contact while the assembly makes its response.

Follow the custom of your parish, but a substantial period of silence after each reading is recommended. Approach and depart from the ambo with reverence—neither too fast nor too slow.

Eye Contact and Eye Expression. Eye contact connects you with those to whom you minister. Look at the assembly during the middle and at the end of every thought or sentence. That means you look down at the beginning, look up in the middle, look down quickly as you approach the end, and then look up again as you finish the sentence. This "down, up, down, up" pattern must not appear mechanical or choppy. Keep a finger on the page to mark your position. Through meaningful "eye expression" you help the listeners enter the story.

Pace. The rate at which you read is influenced by the size of your church, the size of the congregation, and the complexity of the text. As each increases, rate decreases. Too slow is better than too fast. Your listeners have not spent time with this reading as you have. They need time to absorb it—to catch your words and comprehend what they mean.

However, too slow can also be deadly. Besides being boring and making every text sound the same, it erases the reading's natural cadences and makes it impossible to impart the passion of the author.

You'll read more naturally if you read ideas rather than words, if you share images rather than sentences. Dialogue imitates real conversation, so it often moves faster than the rest of the passage.

Lists. Whether proclaiming a genealogy or one of Paul's enumerations of virtues and sins, avoid the extremes of too much stress (slowly punctuating each word with equal stress) or too little (rushing through as if each item were the same).

Magnify the LORD with me; let us exalt his name together.

Using the Microphone. Know your public address system. If it echoes, speak even more slowly. If you hear "popping," you're probably standing too close to the microphone. If you are the first reader, go to the ambo before the start of Mass to adjust the height of the microphone. If you are proclaiming the second reading or Gospel, adjust the microphone position when you reach the ambo.

Gestures and Posture. Using gestures is not part of the task of proclamation; within the liturgy, gestures are an unnecessary distraction. However, your body language is always communicating. Avoid leaning on the ambo or standing on one foot. And don't let your face or body contradict the Good News you announce. Readers are allowed to smile!

Pronunciation. Mispronunciations can be distracting for your listeners. Pronunciation aids are provided in the margin notes (see the key at the end of this introduction). You may also want to consult the LTP publication, *Pronunciation Guide to the Lectionary.* Various Internet pronunciation guides allow you to hear the word spoken aloud. Do a simple search such as: "Bible pronunciation guide."

The Responsorial Psalm

Because preparation for proclamation requires familiarity with all the day's texts, *Workbook* includes the psalm. Reflecting on it helps you see the connections among the texts and discern what to stress in your reading. In Sunday worship, the psalm should be sung, and its inclusion here is not meant to encourage its proclamation.

Giving Voice to God's Word

It is helpful to identify the literary form or genre of your reading. Is it a narrative (story or history), letter, or poetry (such as parts of Genesis or the prophets; the Psalms)? Each form possesses distinct characteristics that will influence your approach to the

Blessed are the poor in spirit, for theirs is the kingdom of heaven.

reading: plotlines and characters in stories; rhythm and rhyme in poetry. But simply identifying the form won't tell you all you need to know about the reading. One key to better understanding Scripture is to know who is speaking within a particular text. Recognizing the form puts you in the right neighborhood; next you want to pinpoint the house—the person speaking. The answer may not be obvious.

For example, even knowing you're reading from a letter by Paul doesn't tell you all you need to know, for Paul may be in various states of mind, even within the same letter. The circumstances Paul writes about, his age and health at the time of writing, whether or not he is imprisoned at the time, and the emotions surrounding the situation he addresses all determine who the speaker is at that given moment. The Paul who writes to one community is not the same Paul who writes to another. That is also true of the prophets, and even of Jesus.

So determining that a text is a narrative, prophecy, or poetry is just your starting point. Next you must determine who the speaker is, why he or she is speaking, and how the speaker feels about what is spoken. By identifying the speaker, you automatically fine-tune your proclamation so that you avoid the all-too-common problem of delivering two different passages in the same way. You will adjust your tone, pacing, energy, and mood to fit the identity and mood of the speaker. With that in mind, read the following discussions of the "neighborhoods" we call stories, epistles, prophecy, and poetry. Remember that your goal is not simply finding the right neighborhood but entering the home of the one who speaks your text.

Stories. Stories must be "told," not "read." You don't have to memorize them, but you do have to tell them. You are the storyteller. Make the story yours, then share it with your listeners.

Know the story and its context—what precedes and follows it. Know the significance of the events for the characters involved. Understand the chronology of the plot. Identify the climax and employ your best energy there. Use the language. Don't throw away any good words.

Settings give context for the action and usually appear at the beginning. Don't rush the description.

Characters must be believable. Understand their motivation: why they feel, act, and speak as they do. Characters are often identified in relationship to another character: "the parents of the one who had gained his sight" (John 9:18). Stress those identifying words. Create the characters as distinct individuals, changing inflection and tone of voice for each one.

Dialogue reveals character. What a character says and how are nearly infallible clues to personality. Besides subtly distinguishing one character from another with your voice, learn to let the speakers listen to and answer one another as in real conversation. Bring the dialogue to life and build suspense in the story, revealing one detail at a time.

Epistles. Epistles are simply letters. Know who wrote the letter and who received it. Many biblical resources explain the circumstances in which the letter was written. Whether addressed to an individual or to a community, each epistle is also addressed to the faithful gathered in your church. *The tone* of each letter may vary, but the delivery is always direct. Letters are like conversations between the writer and the person or community addressed. *The purpose* or intent of each letter dictates the tone. Very often Paul is the writer. As teacher and spiritual leader, he is motivated by multiple concerns: to

The LORD's word is true; all his works are trustworthy.

instruct, console, encourage, chastise, warn, settle disputes, and more. When reading from one of his letters, be aware of what he's trying to accomplish and which hat he's wearing: teacher, coach, father-figure, disciplinarian, and so forth. Paul is always direct and earnest; even when he exhorts, he never stops loving his spiritual children.

Go slowly in the epistles. The assembly needs time to catch the ideas you toss at them. Paul's theology can be tricky, and the style is often a tangle of complex sentences. Many times his mood and purpose change within a single passage. Remembering how seriously Paul took his role will help keep you from rushing. Love your listeners and desire their good as much as Paul and the other letter-writers do.

Prophetic Writing. The intensity of emotion and degree of urgency required in proclaiming the writing of the prophets make some readers uncomfortable. But their urgency can't be compromised. A pervasive theme in the Old Testament is that we are chosen. With election comes responsibility. Prophets were to remind the Chosen People about those responsibilities—not a popular task. Though not shown in the text, prophetic words are spoken with vocal exclamation points. One must work up courage to tell people what they don't want to hear. With equal passion the great seers spoke threat and consolation, indictment and forgiveness. You must do the same for the Chosen People you call "parish." It is a grave disservice to the prophets and their ministry to fail to distinguish consolation from indictment, letting all their words sound the same.

As with the epistles, use resources to learn the situation in which a prophet ministers. Prophets vary; be attentive to style as well as content. Beware of fast transitions, instant climaxes, and the frequent lack of conclusions. Willingly or reluctantly, prophets were compelled to speak for God. Don't rob them of their intensity. We need to hear their words.

Poetry. The Old Testament contains much poetry—a marvelously effective and economical form of communication. Because the carefully crafted words and images are so rich and evocative, poetry makes special demands on the proclaimer.

Take time. Poetry is gourmet food, eaten slowly and savored. Go slowly with readings like this passage from Baruch for the Second Sunday of Advent, Year C (Baruch 5:8-9): "The forests and every fragrant kind of tree / have overshadowed Israel at God's command; / For God is leading Israel in joy / by the light of his glory, / with his mercy and justice for company." You need to respond to images by letting yourself "hear" and "feel" as well as "see." Word choice in poetry affects meaning because it affects sound and rhythm.

Sound and meaning go hand in hand in poetry. Even in a language you don't understand, the sound of well-recited poetry should touch your emotions.

Rhythm is what distinguishes poetry from prose. It's what makes words sound like music. Compare these two verses: "In times past, God spoke in partial and various ways to our ancestors through the prophets" (Hebrews 1:1), and "For Zion's sake I will not be silent, for Jerusalem's sake I will not be quiet" (Isaiah 62:1). The first line is smooth and flat, but the second has a rhythmic beat flowing through it that makes it exciting.

Repetition abounds in poetry. Yet instead of feeling redundant, repetitions intensify our emotional experience.

In Hebrew poetry, *parallelism* is a technique used to repeat, balance, and develop ideas in a poem. Consider this first verse of Psalm 19: "The heavens declare the glory of God; / the sky proclaims its builder's craft." Two parallel images express *one* idea. Since the two thoughts mean the same thing, this is *synonymous parallelism*. In *antithetic parallelism*, opposing images express one idea. Proverbs 15:15 says: "Every day is miserable for the depressed, / but a lighthearted person has a continual feast."

Contrasting ideas make a similar point. Identifying such parallelism helps you decide what words to stress or balance. Look for these and other forms of poetry. Enjoy the language and give it time to do its work.

Graziano Marcheschi

An Option to Consider

The third edition of *The Roman Missal* encourages ministers of the Word to chant the introduction and conclusion to the readings ("A reading from . . . "; "The word of the Lord."). For those parishes wishing to use these chants, they are demonstrated in audio files that may be accessed either through the QR codes given here (with a smart phone) or through the URL indicated beneath the code. (This URL is case sensitive, and be careful to distinguish between the letter l (lower case L) and the numeral 1.)

The first QR code contains the tones for the First Reading in both a male and a female voice.

http://bit.ly/l2mjeG

The second QR code contains the tones for the Second Reading in both a male and a female voice.

http://bit.ly/krwEYy

The third QR code contains the simple tone for the Gospel.

http://bit.ly/iZZvSg

The fourth QR code contains the solemn tone for the Gospel.

http://bit.ly/lwf6Hh

A fuller explanation of this new practice, along with musical notation for the chants, is provided in a downloadable PDF file found at http://www.ltp.org/t-productsupplements.aspx. Once you arrive at this web page, scroll until you find the image of the cover of *Workbook*, click on it, and the PDF file will appear.

Pronunciation Key

bait = bayt	thin = thin
cat = kat	vision = VIZH*n
sang = sang	ship = ship
father = FAH-ther	sir = ser
care = kayr	gloat = gloht
paw = paw	cot = kot
jar = jahr	noise = noyz
easy = EE-zee	poison = POY-z*n
her = her	plow = plow
let = let	although = ahl-THOH
queen = kween	church = cherch
delude = deh-LOOD	fun = fuhn
when = hwen	fur = fer
ice = īs	flute = floot
if = if	foot = foot
finesse = fih-NES	

Recommended Works

Find a list of recommended reading in a downloadable PDF file at http://www.ltp.org/t-product supplements.aspx.

FIRST SUNDAY OF ADVENT

LECTIONARY #3

READING I   Jeremiah 33:14–16

A reading from the Book of the Prophet Jeremiah

The days are **coming**, says the LORD,
    when I will fulfill the **promise**
    I made to the house of **Israel** and **Judah**.
In **those days**, in **that time**,
    I will **raise up** for **David** a **just shoot**;
    he shall do what is **right** and **just** in the land.
In **those days Judah** shall be **safe**
    and **Jerusalem** shall dwell **secure**;
    this is what they shall **call** her:
    "The LORD our justice."

RESPONSORIAL PSALM   Psalm 25:4–5, 8–9, 10, 14 (1b)

R. To you, O Lord, I lift my soul.

Your ways, O LORD, make known to me;
    teach me your paths,
guide me in your truth and teach me,
    for you are God my savior,
    and for you I wait all the day.

Good and upright is the LORD;
    thus he shows sinners the way.
He guides the humble to justice,
    and teaches the humble his way.

All the paths of the LORD are kindness and
        constancy
    toward those who keep his covenant and
        his decrees.
The friendship of the LORD is with those
        who fear him,
    and his covenant, for their instruction.

Jeremiah = jayr-uh-MĪ-uh

From the start, let your tone suggest the hope that permeates this prophecy. God's promise, made and remade throughout Israel's history, was an enduring source of identity and hope. Use the word "promise" to awaken that hope.

This is an intentional repetition meant to achieve emphasis; such constructions require greater emphasis on the second phrase Stress God's initiative in bringing about a new age and new reality.

As you speak "Israel" (IZ-ree-uhl) and "Judah" (JOO-duh) persuade your listeners the promise includes them.

Speak the final line with a sense of awed gratitude: the goodness of God brands us; we bear his name and become icons of his justice.

For meditation and context:

TO KEEP IN MIND
Proclaiming the **words of the prophets** requires intensity and urgency. With equal passion, they spoke threat and consolation, indictment and forgiveness. You must do the same for the chosen people you call "parish."

READING I   Biblical prophets criticized their people and culture for infidelities and injustice. But just as surely, they energized them with visions of what would be, visions of a future only God could create, a future beyond their dreaming, much less their making. It would come at the hands of God who is merciful and faithful to his promises made long before to the ancient kingdoms of Israel and Judah. So while your words are few, your sound must convey the hope that Jeremiah has packed into these lines, addressed to people facing the possible destruction of their land by foreign invaders from Babylon.

Jeremiah gives voice to God's own words of comfort and reassurance. The northern kingdom of Israel, which already had fallen to the Assyrians, and the southern kingdom of Judah, feeling Babylon's threat, both receive God's encouragement. Despite the past and despite present threats, the future will bring "what is right and just" in the land. It will come in the form of a "just shoot," a descendant of David who will establish peace and security. Faith persuades us that this prophecy was ultimately fulfilled in Jesus, the Messiah. His presence and ministry will name the city and nation: "the LORD our justice."

As we start Advent, Jeremiah's prophecy reminds us that hope is never lost, even when buried under the debris of destruction and corruption. But while David's just shoot has bloomed among us, like Israel, we await the time when justice and peace will permeate our world. We trust that our longing, expressed in lives rooted in God's love, will itself help bring it about.

Thessalonians = thes-uh-LOH-nee-uhnz

After the salutation, pause briefly and assume a prayerful tone.

Note that the Lord will return "with all his holy ones." Perhaps some of us will be in that number.
The word "finally" provides an opportunity to command attention with increased intensity.

Remember, Paul's message is simple: You learned from me how to behave. You're doing very well. Now, try even harder.

Communicate both ideas in the last sentence: (a) You know how to behave. (b) You learned it from the Lord Jesus.

TO KEEP IN MIND
Know who wrote the letter and who received it. Discover the circumstances. **The intent of each letter dictates the tone.** Often Paul is the writer; he is motivated by multiple concerns: to instruct, console, encourage, chastise, warn, settle disputes, and more. When reading from one of his letters, be aware of what he's trying to accomplish.

READING II   1 Thessalonians 3:12—4:2

A reading from the first Letter of Saint Paul to the Thessalonians

Brothers and sisters:
 May the Lord make you **increase** and **abound** in **love**
   for one **another and** for **all**,
   just as **we** have for **you**,
   so as to **strengthen** your **hearts**,
   to be **blameless** in **holiness** before our **God** and **Father**
   at the coming of our **Lord Jesus** with **all** his **holy** ones. Amen.

Finally, brothers and sisters,
   we earnestly **ask** and **exhort** you in the **Lord Jesus** that,
   as you received from **us**
   how you should conduct yourselves to please **God**
   —and as you **are** conducting yourselves—
   you do so **even more**.
For you **know** what **instructions** we **gave** you
      through the **Lord Jesus**.

READING II Paul's words to the Thessalonians comprise a heartfelt prayer and an earnest plea. First, Paul asks God to help the Thessalonians grow in love for one another, then that they grow in holiness to such a degree that they can stand blameless before God. Challenging prayers, indeed, but Paul asks of them only what he expects of himself. He wants their love for each other to mirror the abounding love he has for them. His prayer for their growth in holiness asks for the very growth Paul experienced in his own life through much trial and adversity.

Only God can answer those prayers. But his third request is entirely in the community's hands. He takes credit for teaching them *how* to "conduct [them]selves to please God, something they're already doing quite well, but he encourages them to try even harder. The translation is awkward because of the subordinate clauses you have to squeeze in between the start and end of the main thought, which is: "You learned from us how to please God, but now do even More!"

The final sentence names two important realities: Paul taught the Thessalonians all they need to know, and he entreats them to remember what they learned. But more importantly, he reminds them that their instruction came not *from* Paul but *through* him, because their real teacher was Christ himself.

GOSPEL The new liturgical year begins as the last one ended, with visions of cosmic events that presage the end of time. The sobering nature of today's Gospel advances Advent's less recognized purpose—to expand our focus from Jesus' first coming as a child

The storm rages throughout the first paragraph. The tone is solemn and threatening and the pace is measured.

You're not trying to frighten, but don't dilute the powerful imagery that's meant to remind us Christ is a cosmic and awesome Lord.

We have no present day equivalent for such an event. Speak of it with great solemnity.

For a moment, the storm subsides and the tone softens as you offer words of hope and redemption.

These words comprise true warning and they are offered to save us, even if at first they must frighten us.

The sudden and unexpected advent of these events must be stressed.

These words come right from Jesus as prescient advice meant to steel us for the storm that will surely come.

TO KEEP IN MIND
As you are becoming familiar with your passage, read it directly from your Bible, **reading also what comes before and after** it to get a clear sense of its context.

GOSPEL   Luke 21:25–28, 34–36

A reading from the holy Gospel according to Luke

Jesus said to his disciples:
"There will be **signs** in the **sun**, the **moon**, and the **stars**,
    and on **earth nations** will be in **dismay**,
    perplexed by the **roaring** of the sea and the waves.
People will **die** of **fright**
    in **anticipation** of what is **coming** upon the **world**,
    for the **powers** of the **heavens** will be **shaken**.
And then they will see the **Son of Man**
    coming in a **cloud** with **power** and **great glory**.
But when these signs **begin** to happen,
    stand erect and **raise** your heads
    because your **redemption** is at **hand**.

"**Beware** that your **hearts** do not become **drowsy**
    from **carousing** and **drunkenness**
    and the **anxieties** of daily life,
    and that day catch you by **surprise** like a **trap**.
For that day will assault **everyone**
    who lives on the face of the earth.
Be **vigilant** at **all** times
    and **pray** that you have the **strength**
    to **escape** the tribulations that are **imminent**
    and to **stand** before the **Son of Man**."

---

and remind us he will return on a cloud clothed with glory. The two figures of Advent—the babe of Bethlehem and the Son of Man—are but one person: the eternal Christ who judges us and sends us to the eternal destiny we've *chosen* through the way we've lived our lives. The choices are "carousing . . . and the anxieties of daily life" or the Gospel.

This will not be anyone's favorite Advent reading. But neither should it be seen as an incongruous text mistakenly placed within a season of joy and hope. For hope is at its center. While the end can be terrifying, it need not be for those who have persevered in faith. They can "stand erect and raise [their] heads," for what awaits them is "redemption." And it's the birth of redemption that we celebrate at Christmas. Christianity always holds opposing truths in tension, never compromising one for the sake of the other. Both must be acknowledged and honored. In Advent we can hear both the lullabies of Bethlehem and the foreboding storm that rages in this Gospel.

The reason we listen for the storm is that it will come unexpectedly. Even for the faithful the end times will be hard, hence we must pray for "strength"—not to endure, but to "escape" the hardships of that day. While pointing to that final time, Advent also reminds us that each day we greet the sun might be the last before we stand before the "Son of Man." G.M.

SECOND SUNDAY OF ADVENT

LECTIONARY #6

READING I Baruch 5:1–9

A reading from the Book of the Prophet Baruch

Baruch = buh-ROOK

You begin with imperatives that express Israel's wondrous reversal of fortune!

Visualize these tangible items; they are sacred, like a wedding dress or a child's baptismal gown.

Speak with energy and conviction of what God will do.

Imagine speaking the name of your city when you call "Jerusalem" to rise up.

Being "remembered" is the difference between life and death.
Contrast the sorrow of being led away with the joy of returning home.
This is not a news report; you are joyfully sharing poetic images meant to rouse the imagination.

Let the final sentence summarize the joyous good news that fills the entire reading.

> **Jerusalem**, **take off** your robe of **mourning** and **misery**;
>   **put on** the **splendor** of **glory** from **God forever**:
> **Wrapped** in the cloak of **justice** from God,
>   **bear** on your head the **mitre**
>   that **displays** the **glory** of the **eternal name**.
> For God will show **all** the **earth** your **splendor**:
>   **you** will be **named** by **God forever**
>   the **peace** of **justice**, the **glory** of God's **worship**.
>
> **Up, Jerusalem! stand** upon the **heights**;
>   **look** to the **east** and **see** your **children**
> gathered from the **east** and the **west**
>   at the **word** of the **Holy One**,
>   **rejoicing** that **they** are **remembered by God**.
> Led away on **foot** by their **enemies** they **left** you:
>   but **God** will bring them **back** to you
>   borne **aloft** in **glory** as on **royal thrones**.
> For God has **commanded**
>   that **every lofty mountain** be made **low**,
> and that the **age-old depths** and **gorges**
>   be **filled** to **level ground**,
>   that **Israel** may advance **secure** in the **glory** of **God**.
> The **forests** and every **fragrant** kind of tree
>   have **overshadowed Israel** at God's **command**;

READING I Israel's exile in Babylon left the people hopeless, questioning their identity. Had they taken their privileged relationship with God for granted? How could God so utterly abandon them? How could the covenant be voided and their holy city and temple be destroyed? In the midst of such disorientation and soul-searching the prophet Baruch, the scribe of the great prophet Jeremiah, utters this glorious promise of restoration.

He offers hope by painting compelling images of the impossible that make it seem assured. Speak from the depth of your own conviction that God can and does bring life out of death and hope from despair. Tap your own experiences of such grace.

Baruch's initial image—removing garments of gloom and replacing them with a "cloak of justice" portray a divine love we can touch and feel, a love that wraps itself around us. Baruch urges Israel to pay attention. A great miracle is unfolding: those who were "led away on foot" will be brought back "as on royal thrones." The words "remembered by God" evoke deep emotion. Those who thought themselves forgotten realize that the eternal God is mindful of them at every moment. In the last lines, God commands nature to express the outpouring of divine mercy.

READING II Ever the teacher, Paul instructs his beloved community, even from prison where he awaits word of his fate: release or execution. His ability to remain hopeful, staying focused on others' needs rather than his own, is itself instructive. Notice also how he identifies with Christ, whose "affection" for the Philippians he has made his own. Paul demonstrates in his own life the kind of hope

for **God** is **leading Israel** in **joy**
　　by the **light** of his **glory**,
　　with his **mercy** and **justice** for company.

For meditation and context:

TO KEEP IN MIND
Know who wrote the letter and who received it. Discover the circumstances. **The intent of each letter dictates the tone.** Often Paul is the writer; he is motivated by multiple concerns: to instruct, console, encourage, chastise, warn, settle disputes, and more. When reading from one of his letters, be aware of what he's trying to accomplish.

RESPONSORIAL PSALM   Psalm 126:1–2, 2–3, 4–5, 6 (3)

R. The Lord has done great things for us; we are filled with joy.

When the LORD brought back the captives
　　of Zion,
　we were like men dreaming.
Then our mouth was filled with laughter,
　　and our tongue with rejoicing.

Then they said among the nations,
　"The LORD has done great things for
　　them."
The LORD has done great things for us;
　we are glad indeed.

Restore our fortunes, O LORD,
　　like the torrents in the southern desert.
Those who sow in tears
　　shall reap rejoicing.

Although they go forth weeping,
　　carrying the seed to be sown,
they shall come back rejoicing,
　　carrying their sheaves.

Philippians = fih-LIP-ee-uhnz

Remember, this is Paul's "letter of joy." Be sure it sounds like it by establishing eye contact and speaking directly to your assembly.
Here is the reason Paul is so joyful: they are remaining faithful to the gospel.
The word "confident" sets the tone. Be as confident as Paul as you speak to your community.

Paul is speaking not like a teacher but as a loving friend or parent.
Don't report the "prayer"; pray it.

Pray for yourself as well as for your assembly.
Paul's prayer contains several "intentions." Don't rush them together.

READING II   Philippians 1:4–6, 8–11

A reading from the Letter of Saint Paul to the Philippians

Brothers and sisters:
I pray always with **joy** in my **every prayer** for **all** of you,
　　because of your **partnership** for the **gospel**
　　from the **first day** until **now.**
I am **confident** of this,
　　that the one who **began** a **good work** in you
　　will **continue** to **complete** it
　　until the day of **Christ Jesus.**
God is my **witness,**
　　how I **long** for **all** of you with the **affection** of **Christ Jesus.**
And **this** is my **prayer:**
　　that your **love** may **increase** ever **more** and **more**
　　in **knowledge** and **every kind** of **perception,**
　　to **discern** what is of **value,**
　　so that you may be **pure** and **blameless** for the day of **Christ, ≫**

---

that is possible in the midst of trials that Baruch announces in the First Reading.

Paul tells us that growth in matters of the spirit is progressive. God has *begun* a "good work" in them, says Paul, and he is confident that God will "continue to *complete* it." But this completion won't be immediate; it will continue until "the day of Christ Jesus"—an important lesson for us also, and the reason Catholic theology differs from a fundamentalist approach that suggests conversion is a moment rather than a journey.

Paul prays that their love may grow and mature. While salvation is through Christ, offered to us fully on the day of Baptism, we must allow that baptismal grace to transform us, to make us "pure and blameless" for the day when we stand in judgment before Christ.

Let Paul's gratitude to this community (that has been generous with him and faithful to his teaching) echo in every line. Then Paul's "letter of joy" will convey the love he speaks in Jesus' name.

GOSPEL   By deliberately listing the power players of Jesus' day, Luke sets the context—political and geographical—for the unfolding of Jesus' ministry and the dawning of the Kingdom of God. The sequence of royal, religious, and political personages leads from the centers of power (palace, fortress, and Temple), from which one might expect an announcement of the Messiah's advent, to a wilderness place where a strange hermit proclaims a centuries-old prophecy as if it were about himself and his own time. That the "word of God" comes to the animal-

filled with the fruit of **righteousness**
that **comes** through **Jesus Christ**
for the **glory** and **praise** of **God**.

GOSPEL   Luke 3:1–6

A reading from the holy Gospel according to Luke

In the fifteenth year of the reign **of Tiberius Caesar**,
    when **Pontius Pilate** was **governor of Judea**,
    and **Herod** was **tetrarch** of **Galilee**,
    and his brother **Philip tetrarch** of the region
        of **Ituraea** and **Trachonitis**,
    and **Lysanias** was **tetrarch** of **Abilene**,
    during the high **priesthood** of **Annas** and **Caiaphas**,
    the **word** of **God** came to **John** the son of **Zechariah**
        in the **desert**.
John went throughout the **whole region** of the **Jordan**,
    proclaiming a **baptism** of **repentance** for the **forgiveness**
        of **sins**,
    as it is **written** in the book of the words of the prophet **Isaiah**:
    *A **voice** of one **crying out** in the **desert**:*
    *"**Prepare** the **way** of the **Lord**,*
        *make **straight** his **paths**.*
    *Every **valley** shall be **filled***
        *and **every mountain** and **hill** shall be made **low**.*
    *The **winding roads** shall be made **straight**,*
        *and the **rough ways** made **smooth**,*
    *and **all flesh** shall **see** the **salvation** of **God**."*

Margin notes:

Use ritardando (gradually slowing your rate) as you end the sentence.

These characters' names are from different arenas of first-century life; don't rush them, and change tone slightly from civil to religious authorities.
Tiberius = tī-BEER-ee-uhs; Caesar = SEE-zer
Judea = joo-DEE-uh
Ituraea = ih-too-REE-ah
Trachonitis = trak-uh-NĪ-tis
Lysanias = lī-SAY-nee-uhs
Annas = AN-uhs
Caiaphas = KĪ-uh-fuhs
Zechariah = zek-uh-RĪ-uh

Pause briefly before announcing the beginning of John's ministry.

Don't gloss over John's important ministry. You might speak the line in his proclamatory tone.

Isaiah's poetry is familiar; slow it down to make it fresh and help your listeners hear it as new.

Let conviction ring in your voice.

Rejoice in this final declaration that God's mercy is for all.

---

skin-clad loner in the "desert" rather than to one of the powerful is consistent with the reversals typical of the Gospel.

John announces the dawn of a new world order, the coming of an invisible kingdom that will permeate and leaven the world of human affairs, changing them forever. He quotes Isaiah's ancient promise of a coming salvation. Such a promise we would want fulfilled in moments, but in God's plan it comes to fruition through centuries of seeming silence. Isaiah speaks of a transformation of the physical order that will make rough paths smooth and winding roads straight. But poetry sublime as this speaks on many levels and from John's lips it tells us that the world of the Messiah will bring the straightening of human ways of interacting, the filling of empty, wounded hearts, the removal of obstacles to healing and wholeness. The sun of reconciliation will dawn on that day and the Good News will tolerate no obstacles. "All flesh" will see the salvation John announces.

Though the text is divided into two parts, the tone should be joyful throughout. As you name those who will be Christ's antagonists, there is no need to color their names negatively. An even and eloquent tone will suggest that these are ultimately players in a divine drama in which even their best efforts to obstruct will ultimately yield to God's loving plan for humanity. G.M.

THE IMMACULATE CONCEPTION OF THE BLESSED VIRGIN MARY

LECTIONARY #689

READING I Genesis 3:9–15, 20

A reading from the Book of Genesis

After the **man**, **Adam**, had **eaten** of the **tree**,
the LORD God **called** to the man and **asked** him,
"**Where are you?**"
He answered, "I **heard** you in the garden;
but I was **afraid**, because I was **naked**,
so I **hid** myself."
Then he asked, "**Who told you** that you were naked?
You have **eaten**, then,
from the **tree** of which I had **forbidden** you to eat!"
The man replied, "The **woman** whom you put here with me—
she gave **me** fruit from the tree, and so **I ate it**."
The LORD God then asked the woman,
"**Why** did you **do such** a **thing?**"
The woman answered, "The **serpent tricked me** into it,
so I **ate** it."

Then the LORD **God** said to the **serpent**:
"**Because you have done this**, **you** shall be **banned**
from **all** the **animals**
and from **all** the **wild creatures**;
on your **belly** shall you **crawl**,
and **dirt** shall you **eat**
all the days of your **life**. »

From the start, signal that Adam's eating of the apple was a dire offense.
Adam and Eve are not children hiding from a parent, but adults who have chosen rebellion.

God is not the victim here; though he inquires, he is fully aware and in full control.

Sin results immediately in alienation and mistrust. Adam is fearful, so he blames the woman.

The woman brazenly rejects responsibility and blames the serpent.

God's rebuke of the serpent is hard-hitting and unequivocal. Your tone should reflect the harsher judgment God levies on the serpent.

This curse heaps humiliation on the serpent.

Because there is no direct biblical reference to Mary being conceived without original sin, today's readings must be understood in light of centuries of Christian reflection on Mary's character and role in the unfolding of salvation history. From earliest Christianity, Mary was viewed as a model of the ideal Christian and of the Church.

READING I The section of Genesis from which this reading comes focuses on fundamental human realities: choice, freedom (and its limits), and responsibility. In that creation account, all humankind is represented in the characters of Adam and Eve; the Hebrew word *adam* means "humankind," and the name Eve means "mother of all the living." Preceding this scene, God had told the pair that they were free to eat the fruit of any tree in the garden, except the tree of the knowledge of good and evil. Tempted by the serpent, both man and woman succumbed and ate of this very fruit, their action representing an attempt at divine status (see Genesis 3:22). Adam and Eve, the creatures intended to be God's image in the world (Genesis 1:27) chose to overreach this exalted purpose. Not content to become the living image of God in creation, they grasped at equality with the Creator.

Both man and woman transgressed, for which both must accept the consequences. God's words to the serpent and to the woman indicate that temptation to resist the divine purpose will continue to pursue Eve's offspring, "all the living." Her descendants will repeat their parents' choices and actions. The New Testament proclaims that Christ, the New Adam, fully realized God's purpose for humanity as the

This is a key verse often called the protoevangelium or "first Gospel" for it is Scripture's first assurance of God's intent to save humanity.

The Church sees Mary as the "woman" and Christ as her offspring who will "strike" at the serpent's "head."

Pause before announcing that Eve became the mother of all humanity (as Mary is the mother of all who live in Christ).

For meditation and context:

TO KEEP IN MIND

Tell the story: Make the story yours, then share it with your listeners. Use the language; don't throw away any good words. Settings give context; don't rush the description. Characters must be believable; understand their motivation. Dialogue reveals character; distinguish one character from another with your voice.

Ephesians = ee-FEE-zhuhnz

With energetic rhythm, the opening sentence calls us to praise. Don't rush or you'll blur the several ideas expressed here. Start praying and don't stop praying until the end.

Blessed = BLES-uhd
blessed = blesd

We existed in the mind of God from all eternity! Share that profound insight with gravity.

"In love" = "because of love." Our status as children ("adoption") was always God's plan for humanity.

Joy should resound in these lines.

I will put **enmity** between **you** and the **woman**,
    and between **your offspring** and **hers**;
he will **strike** at **your** head,
    while **you strike** at **his** heel."

The man called his wife **Eve**,
    because she became the **mother** of **all** the **living**.

RESPONSORIAL PSALM   Psalm 98:1, 2–3ab, 3cd–4 (1)

R. Sing to the Lord a new song, for he has done marvelous deeds.

Sing to the LORD a new song,
    for he has done wondrous deeds;
His right hand has won victory for him,
    his holy arm.

The LORD has made his salvation known:
    in the sight of the nations he has revealed
        his justice.
He has remembered his kindness and his
        faithfulness
    toward the house of Israel.

All the ends of the earth have seen
    the salvation by our God.
Sing joyfully to the LORD, all you lands;
    break into song; sing praise.

READING II   Ephesians 1:3–6, 11–12

A reading from the Letter of Saint Paul to the Ephesians

Brothers and sisters:
Blessed be the **God** and **Father** of our **Lord Jesus Christ**,
    who has **blessed** us in **Christ**
    with **every spiritual blessing** in the heavens,
    as he **chose** us **in him**, **before** the **foundation** of the **world**,
    to be **holy** and **without blemish** before him.
In **love** he **destined us** for **adoption** to himself
        through Jesus **Christ**,
    in accord with the **favor** of his **will**,
    for the **praise** of the **glory** of his **grace**

---

true and complete image of God. Over centuries of reflection, the Church came to believe that God anticipated this fullness of the Christ mystery in his mother, Mary, a new Eve.

READING II   Because many early manuscripts of this letter lack the specific address to Christians "in Ephesus," and the perspective of the letter is much broader than that of a specific local congregation, many scholars regard Ephesians as a circular letter intended for multiple churches in Asia Minor. It presents

views in line with Paul's about the universal church. The vocabulary and imagery strongly suggest that parts of it are drawn from early hymns and liturgy, and that is the case with the first part of today's reading.

Pauline letters usually begin with a customary naming of writer and addressee, followed by a prayer of thanksgiving. Here the author (whether Paul, or, as some scholars believe, a disciple of his) inserts a blessing or praise of God for the divine work of salvation in Christ, emphasizing God's eternal plan and intention to recreate humankind through Christ. The

writer particularly gives thanks for God's motive: gracious love, which offers believers the status of son or daughter by "adoption" through the saving work of Christ. It is this free, loving action of God that creates and unifies the Church as a community of faith whose very existence has one purpose: "the praise of his glory."

GOSPEL   This Gospel passage is patterned on a literary form used in both Testaments, a "call story." Luke follows the basic outline: the presence of God or a divine messenger is made

beloved = bee-LUHV-uhd

In Christ, God chose us to inherit the glory of the Kingdom.

Despite appearances, all things work toward the accomplishment of God's will.

Sustain eye contact with the assembly and slow your delivery on the final line. Then pause before, "The word . . . "

that he **granted us** in the **beloved**.

In him we were **also chosen**,
    destined in accord with the purpose of the One
    who accomplishes **all things** according to the **intention**
        of his **will**,
    so that we might exist for the **praise** of **his glory**,
    we who **first hoped** in **Christ**.

GOSPEL   Luke 1:26–38

A reading from the holy Gospel according to Luke

Though familiar, these lines carry significant information packed into one sentence. Lift out each detail.

Speak Mary's name with reverence and affection.
The angel's voice should be reassuring and gentle, not jarring.
This narration should convey Mary's confusion.

Aware that his words are unsettling, the angel soothes and informs at the same time.

The angel is fully aware of the great dignity and destiny of Mary's child.

Mary believes God will do this, but can't imagine how.

The angel **Gabriel** was sent from **God**
    to a town of **Galilee** called **Nazareth**,
    to a **virgin** betrothed to a man named **Joseph**,
    of the house of **David**,
    and the virgin's **name** was **Mary**.
And coming to her, he said,
    "**Hail, full of grace**! The **Lord** is **with you**."
But she was greatly **troubled** at what was said
    and **pondered** what sort of **greeting** this might be.
Then the angel **said** to her,
    "Do **not** be **afraid**, Mary,
    for **you** have found **favor** with **God**.
Behold, you will **conceive in your womb** and **bear a son**,
    and you shall **name** him **Jesus**.
He will be **great** and will be called **Son of the Most High**,
    and the **Lord God** will give him the throne of **David** his **father**,
    and he will **rule** over the house of **Jacob forever**,
    and of his **Kingdom** there will **be no end**."
But **Mary** said to the angel,
    "**How can this be**,
    since I have **no relations** with a **man**?" »

known to someone; the person addressed receives a commission or call; the one called responds, usually presenting objections meant to excuse a positive response; the call is repeated, with God's assurance of help in carrying out the divine directive.

Luke's account of the angel Gabriel's visit to Mary differs from that of Matthew in several ways, one of which is his emphasis on Mary rather than on Joseph. By the time Luke wrote his account of the Good News, fifty to sixty years after the Death and Resurrection of Jesus, the mother of Jesus was already considered the ideal disciple:

receptive to, and trusting in God's grace. Describing Gabriel's greeting to Mary, Luke uses an unusual Greek word, the root of which is *charis*, literally meaning "gift" but most commonly translated into English as "grace" or "favor." Paul in particular stresses that God's redeeming work through Christ is a totally unearned gift to humankind: grace. It seems that Luke, who shares a number of Paul's perspectives, wishes to present Mary as one who has been given grace because she is open and receptive to God's action in her. Luke repeats the word *charis* again as Gabriel

assures Mary that she has "found favor with God."

Describing Mary's call to bear the Savior, Luke presents a summary of who this child will be: Jesus, meaning "God saves"; Son of God ("the Most High"), Son of David, the one through whom the longed-for final Kingdom of God will begin. Mary's response to the awe-inspiring commission is less an objection or refusal than a logical question: how is it possible that a virgin will bear a child? Gabriel's response reassures rather than explains: the Holy Spirit, the powerful divine presence within

This is the climax of the passage and its most tender lines.

Don't change tone here: "And behold" extends the miraculous hand of God's love from Mary to her elder cousin.

Pause after "Mary said to the angel." Mary announces her decision with simplicity and strength.

TO KEEP IN MIND

Word value: Words are your medium, like a painter's brush or a sculptor's chisel. You must understand the words before you can communicate them. Most words have a dictionary meaning (denotative) and an associational meaning (connotative). "House" and "home" both mean "dwelling," yet they communicate different feelings. Be alert to subtle differences in connotative meanings and express them.

And the angel said to her in **reply**,
    "The **Holy Spirit** will come **upon you**,
    and the **power** of the **Most High** will **overshadow you**.
Therefore the **child** to be **born**
    will be called **holy**, the **Son of God**.
And **behold**, **Elizabeth**, your relative,
    has **also conceived** a **son** in her **old age**,
    and this is the **sixth month** for her who was called **barren**;
    for **nothing** will be **impossible** for **God**."
Mary said, "**Behold, I am the handmaid of the Lord.**
May it be done to **me** according to **your** word."
Then the angel departed from her.

THE 4 STEPS OF *LECTIO DIVINA* OR PRAYERFUL READING

1. *Lectio:* Read a Scripture passage aloud slowly. Notice what phrase captures your attention and be attentive to its meaning. Silent pause.

2. *Meditatio:* Read the passage aloud slowly again, reflecting on the passage, allowing God to speak to you through it. Silent pause.

3. *Oratio:* Read it aloud slowly a third time, allowing it to be your prayer or response to God's gift of insight to you. Silent pause.

4. *Contemplatio:* Read it aloud slowly a fourth time, now resting in God's word.

Mary, will bring about what seems humanly impossible. From the beginning of his account of the Good News, Luke stresses the continuing presence and action of the Holy Spirit. Jesus is conceived in a woman totally receptive to God's Spirit, foreshadowing how that same Spirit will continuously act in Jesus himself as he carries out his own divine commission.

For Mary, the angel's assurance that God's power will be at work in her dissolves any need for explanation. As a faith-filled Jewish woman, Mary accepts that the Word of God carries divine presence and power: "may it be done to me according to your word." Luke expresses Mary's attitude of total surrender to God by using a startling word softened in most translations. In Mary's self-description as "the handmaid of the Lord," Luke in fact uses the Greek word *doule*, "slave." In the Roman Empire of the time, a servant was a paid employee, while a slave was owned by someone else and received no compensation for doing the owner's bidding. Not only Luke, but many other New Testament authors frequently describe Christians as "slaves of Christ." In this sense, Mary represents the primordial Christian. She chooses to be "owned" by God, expecting no recompense; she chooses to belong totally to the one whose word she trusts utterly. M.F.

THIRD SUNDAY OF ADVENT

LECTIONARY #9

READING I Zephaniah 3:14–18a

A reading from the Book of the Prophet Zephaniah

Shout for **joy**, O daughter Zion!
    Sing **joyfully, O** Israel!
Be **glad** and **exult** with **all** your **heart**,
    O **daughter Jerusalem**!
The Lord has **removed** the **judgment against** you,
    he has **turned away** your **enemies**;
the **King of Israel**, the Lord, is in your **midst**,
    you have no further **misfortune** to fear.
On **that day**, it shall be said to **Jerusalem**:
    Fear not, O Zion, **be not discouraged**!
The Lord, your **God**, is in your **midst**,
    a **mighty savior**;
he will **rejoice** over you with **gladness**,
    and **renew** you in his **love**,
he will **sing joyfully** because of **you**,
    as one **sings** at **festivals**.

Zephaniah = zef-uh-NĪ-uh

"Shout for joy . . . sing joyfully" is a form of repetition that characterizes biblical poetry. To convey the emphasis it intends, you must increase energy in your voice from the first expression to the second.
Keep in mind the trials the nation has endured as you speak these comforting words.

Renew your energy here as if noticing a face that remains unconvinced. "Fear not" is a consistent and important biblical theme.

The tone becomes more personal and intimate, and perhaps softer.

Try to memorize this sentence and announce it looking directly at your assembly.

TO KEEP IN MIND
Read all three commentaries. Suggestions in each can give you insight into your own passage.

READING I Today's text from Zephaniah serves well Advent's dual themes of warning and consolation. We are consoled by the knowledge that God came among us in human flesh. We heed prophetic warnings that the one who came as a helpless infant will return clothed in glory to judge the living and the dead.

Prophecies of restoration and comfort always carry a dual message; while they speak of a future that will know peace and prosperity, they acknowledge a present time of trial and distress, typically brought on by the people's own obstinacy and infidelity. In Zephaniah's words we hear both about what will be and what has been. When we hear that "judgment" against Israel is being removed, we're told simultaneously that Israel has experienced the Lord's bitter yet cleansing judgment. When we hear Israel will have "no further misfortune to fear," we know that misfortune has been part of their recent history.

Awareness of what preceded will help you announce more convincingly the anticipated time of renewal. Your voice must convey the joyous tone of this Gaudete (Rejoice!) Sunday. Zephaniah begins with imperatives commanding hearts to sing! You can do no less, so speak persuasively to your assembly of the *need* to "exult with all your heart." Energy is more important than volume in a text like this. Volume can be raised mechanically, but intensity results from genuine emotion felt deeply. Can you persuade us that God himself will "sing joyfully" because of us?

READING II On Gaudete Sunday, Paul's voice twice commands us to rejoice, and so the *sound* of your voice

11

For meditation and context:

RESPONSORIAL PSALM   Isaiah 12:2–3, 4, 5–6 (6)

R. Cry out with joy and gladness: for among you is the great and Holy One of Israel.

God indeed is my savior;
  I am confident and unafraid.
My strength and my courage is the LORD,
  and he has been my savior.
With joy you will draw water
  at the fountain of salvation.

Give thanks to the LORD, acclaim his name;
  among the nations make known his
    deeds,
  proclaim how exalted is his name.

Sing praise to the LORD for his glorious
    achievement;
  let this be known throughout all the
    earth.
Shout with exultation, O city of Zion,
  for great in your midst
    is the Holy One of Israel!

READING II   Philippians 4:4–7

Philippians = fil-LIP-ee-uhnz

A reading from the Letter of Saint Paul to the Philippians

Offer Paul's command joyfully. Then repeat it with even greater energy.

Each short sentence conveys a new and distinct thought. Don't run them together.

Stress the "thanksgiving" that should characterize our prayers of petition.

Communicate all three ideas here:
(a) God's peace, (b) that's like no other,
(c) will protect us.

Brothers and sisters:
Rejoice in the **Lord always**.
I shall say it **again**: **rejoice!**
Your **kindness** should be known to **all**.
The **Lord** is **near**.
Have **no anxiety** at **all**, but in **everything**,
    by **prayer** and **petition**, with **thanksgiving**,
    make your **requests known** to **God**.
Then the **peace** of God that surpasses **all understanding**
    will **guard your hearts** and **minds** in **Christ Jesus**.

must convey the joy Paul requires of us! The heart of the text is also the reason for rejoicing: "The Lord is near." That's a truth worth raising our voices over. And it remains true in good times and in bad. Anyone can rejoice over good news and under happy circumstances. But it is the privilege and duty of believers to rejoice even when times are hard because their grounding reality remains unchanged—the Lord is near! After all, Paul was in prison when he wrote these words; he was a living testament that one can indeed rejoice even under the direst circumstances.

Paul and his disciples anticipated the Lord's imminent return. But even when that did not occur as expected, they continued to understand that "anxiety" is the realm of the unbeliever, because those grounded in faith know that the Lord is *always* "near," even if his return in glory is millennia away. The Lord is near in our community, in his Word, in the Eucharist. When we know that, we will have "no anxiety at all" because our hearts will be linked to Christ's.

In his encouragement to pray, note that Paul links "petition" with "thanksgiving," another reminder to be joyful and

grateful in all things. Even in our need we must be thankful. That the "peace" of God "surpasses all understanding" is a point worth stressing because God's is a peace that, in Christ, protects us from the anxiety of the world.

GOSPEL   As precursor to the Messiah, John is already brimming with "good news." In his ministry, that Good News took the form of a baptism of repentance and exhortations about just living. This is what John had to share and he shared it generously. But more than

GOSPEL   Luke 3:10–18

A reading from the holy Gospel according to Luke

The **crowds** asked John the **Baptist**,
  "**What** should we **do**?"
He said to them in **reply**,
  "Whoever has **two** cloaks
  should **share** with the person who has **none**.
And whoever has **food** should do **likewise**."
Even tax collectors came to be baptized and **they** said to him,
  "**Teacher**, **what** should **we do**?"
He answered them,
  "**Stop** collecting **more** than what is **prescribed**."
Soldiers also asked him,
  "And **what** is it that **we** should **do**?"
He told them,
  "**Do not** practice **extortion**,
  do not falsely accuse anyone,
  and be **satisfied** with your **wages**."

Now the **people** were filled with **expectation**,
  and **all** were asking in their **hearts**
  whether **John might** be the **Christ**.
John answered them **all**, saying,
  "I am **baptizing** you with **water**,
  but one **mightier than I** is **coming**.
I am **not worthy** to **loosen** the **thongs** of his **sandals**.
He will **baptize** you with the **Holy Spirit** and **fire**.
His **winnowing fan** is in his **hand** to **clear** his **threshing** floor
  and to **gather** the **wheat** into his **barn**,
  but the **chaff** he will **burn** with **unquenchable fire**."
Exhorting them in **many other ways**,
  he preached **good news** to the people.

Margin notes:

Be sure to stress that John is the baptizer, so your listeners don't assume it is Jesus.

Given what we know of John, his manner is likely not refined and his tone might sound abrupt.

The questions are asked with sincerity and urgency.
Though brief, John's replies provide a complete response to each questioner. Speak them with authority and an attitude of "This is all you need to do."

"And be satisfied . . . " might be delivered as a kind of afterthought.

Pause before starting this section that begins a new "beat" in the text.

John's tone should convey a desire to suffer no illusions about his identity. He's saying: "You're wondering who I am. Well, I'll tell you!"

Don't rush his reference to the "Holy Spirit and fire."

Pause briefly before this final, summary statement and let your tone suggest that John himself was "good news."

---

anyone, John is aware of the incomplete nature of what he has to offer. The Good News of "the Christ" won't be limited to advice about right living, for the one who will follow John will be "mightier" than John, and his baptism will be wholly transforming, the way fire changes dough into bread or purifies gold.

The Messiah will separate wheat from chaff and leave nothing unchanged. This awareness was planted so deep within John that he could proclaim it any time he

heard speculation that he might be "the Christ." John understood what he had no apparent human way of understanding because his knowledge came from the same Holy Spirit with which the Messiah would baptize and transform the world. John was announcing the Gospel before any Gospel account was written.

His authenticity and discernment drew unlikely devotees, like tax collectors and Roman soldiers. For each, he had a word of guidance or instruction, and his wisdom

filled them with hope that he was the answer to centuries of longing. It's a tribute to John that the crowds so admired him that they thought he might be the Messiah, but it is an even greater tribute that he had no such delusions about himself. G.M.

FOURTH SUNDAY OF ADVENT

LECTIONARY #12

READING I   Micah 5:1–4a

A reading from the Book of the Prophet Micah

Micah = MĪ-kuh

After the introductory line, shift to the voice of God.

Bethlehem-Ephrathah = BETH-luh-hem-EPH-ruh-thuh

These words, spoken as if to an insecure young person, are meant to encourage and embolden.

"Old . . . ancient times" evokes the regal dignity of King David.

This is good news of restoration; those scattered to the ends of the earth will return home.

He will be both strong and gentle, shepherding not with his own strength but God's.

The final line should be set off with a pause before and after. Speak each word with great conviction and joy.

> **Thus says** the Lᴏʀᴅ:
> **You, Bethlehem-Ephrathah**
>   **too small** to be among the **clans** of **Judah,**
> from **you** shall come **forth** for **me**
>   one who is to be **ruler** in **Israel**;
> whose **origin** is from of **old,**
>   from **ancient times**.
> **Therefore** the Lord will give them **up**, until the time
>   when **she** who is to give **birth** has **borne,**
> and the **rest** of his **kindred** shall **return**
>   to the **children** of **Israel**.
> He shall **stand firm** and **shepherd** his **flock**
>   by the **strength** of the Lᴏʀᴅ,
>   in the **majestic name** of the Lᴏʀᴅ, his **God**;
> and they shall **remain**, for **now his greatness**
>   shall reach to the **ends** of the **earth**;
> **he** shall be **peace.**

READING I   In the Gospels, Jesus says that the last will be first and the least will be greatest. Such is the fate of Bethlehem, the least of the cities of the Kingdom of Judah's clans, but the future birthplace of Israel's Messiah. It was also the birth and coronation place of King David, from whose line the Messiah would one day come. This prophecy of Micah is cited in Matthew's Gospel account in answer to King Herod's question about where the Messiah is to be born.

Together with other prophecies, this text kept alive the longing for the coming of the Christ, God's anointed who would rule over Israel, establishing peace and ruling his people like a good and faithful shepherd. These words were first proclaimed to the exiles after Jerusalem fell and her leading citizens were deported to Babylon. Not only did the people of Israel lose their city and its Temple, but they also lost hope when Jerusalem fell. Micah's task is to restore that hope, and he does it by announcing the grand role to be played by little Bethlehem. From her will spring one "whose origin is from of old," that is, from the line of David.

The reign of Micah's future king will see the scattered exiles return to their homeland. He will rule justly, caring for the sheep entrusted to him, and the nation will know such peace that peace will become the king's identity. Of course, Christian eyes recognize Jesus in this prophecy; only in him do the majesty and peace of God extend to the very "ends of the earth."

READING II   The author of the Letter to the Hebrews draws a sharp contrast between the once-for-always sacrifice of Christ and the repeated sacrifices

14

For meditation and context:

RESPONSORIAL PSALM   Psalm 80:2–3, 15–16, 18–19 (4)

R. Lord, make us turn to you; let us see your face and we shall be saved.

O shepherd of Israel, hearken,
   from your throne upon the cherubim,
      shine forth.
Rouse your power,
   and come to save us.

Once again, O LORD of hosts,
   look down from heaven, and see;
take care of this vine,
   and protect what your right hand has
      planted,
   the son of man whom you yourself made
      strong.

May your help be with the man of your right
      hand,
   with the son of man whom you yourself
      made strong.
Then we will no more withdraw from you;
   give us new life, and we will call upon
      your name.

READING II   Hebrews 10:5–10

A reading from the Letter to the Hebrews

Brothers and sisters:
When **Christ** came into the **world,** he said:
   "**Sacrifice** and **offering** you did **not** desire,
      but a **body** you **prepared** for me;
   in **holocausts** and **sin** offerings you took **no delight.**
   Then I said, 'As is **written** of me in the **scroll,**
   behold, I come to do **your will,** O **God.**'"

First he says, "**Sacrifices** and **offerings,**
   holocausts and **sin offerings,**
   you neither **desired** nor **delighted** in."
These are offered according to the **law.**
Then he says, "**Behold,** I come to do **your will.**"
He takes away the **first** to establish the **second.**
By this **"will,"** we have been **consecrated**
   through the offering of the **body** of **Jesus Christ** once for **all.**

This week you have to work doubly hard to take the meaning of the text to your listeners. Communicate thoughts, not just words.

"You" refers to God.

Suggest the greater value of obedience over sacrifice. Though this reads like a teacher presenting a lesson, emotion is not absent. The contrasts made are significant.

The author is reviewing here.

"According to the Law," in the author's view, means they are of less value.

The author's emotion is most evident here in what is a clear declaration of faith.

---

of the old Law. He places that conviction on the lips of Jesus in the form of a quotation from Psalm 40 that asserts that "sacrifice and offering . . . holocausts and sin offerings" do not please the Lord. Those sacrifices of the Law relied on the blood of animals to expiate human sin. Realizing that these offerings could not possibly achieve what they intended, Christ offered himself instead as a pure, fitting, and one-time sacrifice. And he did it in obedience to the "will" of God.

That's the theology presented here and it's not all that complex. But the struc-

ture and phrasing used to communicate it is complex and awkward. The author imagines Jesus citing Psalm 40 when he "came into the world." In the quotation of the psalm, the speaker addresses God saying (in other words): (1) "You've shown me you don't desire sacrifices and sin offerings," (2) "but I am here to do your will." The author of Hebrews uses these two statements to make his point. The first statement establishes the inadequacy of the burnt offerings of the old Law. The second statement asserts that obedience is far more pleasing to God than sacrifice. The reason Christ

was incarnated (assumed the body "prepared for me") was precisely to do God's will and that obedience became the perfectly pleasing sacrifice that has "consecrated" us "once for all."

GOSPEL   There are powerful human as well as theological dynamics at work in this text. Luke is clearly demonstrating the power of God at work in and controlling the events that surround Jesus' birth. Despite humble circumstances, divinity hovers over these events,

Mary has just experienced a stunning revelation from the angel Gabriel. Elizabeth's pregnancy provides assurance for Mary of Gabriel's promise.

Judah = JOO-duh

Zechariah = zek-uh-RĪ-uh

Creating a sense of "haste" doesn't require fast reading. Let your energy suggest her hurriedness.

Take delight in recounting this warm detail.

Blessed = BLES-uhd

Don't give Elizabeth's remark the sound of rote recitation as in the Hail Mary. It is a spontaneous and heart-felt exclamation!

Elizabeth is inspired by the Spirit; she's not looking for explanations, but marveling at her good fortune!

Repeat this detail with Elizabeth's apparent joy.

Elizabeth's best insight is last: Mary is blessed because she believed God's word so much that it took root within her.

> **TO KEEP IN MIND**
> **Names of characters:** Often the first word of a reading. Lift out the names to ensure listeners don't miss who the subject is.

GOSPEL   Luke 1:39–45

A reading from the holy Gospel according to Luke

Mary set out
  and **traveled** to the **hill** country in **haste**
  to a town of **Judah**,
  where she entered the house of **Zechariah**
  and greeted **Elizabeth**.
When **Elizabeth heard** Mary's greeting,
  the infant **leaped** in her womb,
  and Elizabeth, **filled** with the **Holy Spirit**,
  cried out in a **loud voice** and said,
  "**Blessed** are you among **women**,
  and **blessed** is the **fruit** of **your womb**.
And **how** does this **happen** to me,
  that the **mother** of my **Lord** should **come** to **me**?
For at the moment the sound of your greeting reached my **ears**,
  the **infant** in my **womb leaped** for **joy**.
Blessed are **you** who **believed**
  that what was spoken to you by the **Lord**
  would be **fulfilled**."

leaving Elizabeth to wonder how such blessings could come to her.

Mary hurries to Elizabeth, not only to minister to her older cousin, but also to bask in the miracle that confirms to Mary the angel's promise that "nothing will be impossible for God."

In Mary's greeting, Elizabeth hears more than the sound of her cousin. Filled with the Holy Spirit, she senses the arrival of "[her] Lord," a title that, in this Gospel, Jesus receives even before his birth. Mary's salutation even rouses the child in Elizabeth's womb who seems to leap with joy, establishing an early and intimate link between these cousins, whose destinies will remain closely aligned. The same Spirit leads Elizabeth to name her cousin and the child she carries "blessed." But most importantly, she names Mary a believer and in the process tells us *why* she is blessed. If we were to wonder why Zachariah was struck dumb for asking the angel essentially the same question as Mary, the answer would be that Mary never doubted when she asked "How can this be?" She trusts utterly, and is interested to know how these things will come to pass. And for that faith she is forever blessed. G.M.

THE NATIVITY OF THE LORD (CHRISTMAS): VIGIL

LECTIONARY #13

READING I   Isaiah 62:1–5

Isaiah = ī-ZAY-uh

Zion = Zī-ahn

Note the pattern of couplets in the second line that repeat what was stated in the first. Let your energy increase from the first line to the second.

These lines call for energetic proclamation and unmuted zeal.

A reading from the Book of the Prophet Isaiah

For **Zion's** sake I will not be **silent**,
    for **Jerusalem's** sake I will not be **quiet**,
until her **vindication** shines forth like the **dawn**
    and her **victory** like a burning **torch**.

Throughout, your tone must announce the Good News in these lines as surely as the words themselves.

Nations shall **behold** your vindication,
    and all the **kings** your **glory**;
you shall be called by a **new** name
    pronounced by the mouth of the **Lord**.

God's people are held tenderly in God's own hand like a crown of precious jewels.

You shall be a glorious **crown** in the hand of the Lord,
    a royal **diadem** held by your God.

God comes to reverse our fortunes. Former times when we were "forsaken" and "desolate" are forever gone!

No **more** shall people call you "**Forsaken**,"
    or your land "**Desolate**,"
but you shall be called "My **Delight**,"
    and your **land** "**Espoused**."

For the Lord **delights** in you
    and makes your land his **spouse**.

The imagery of lover and beloved conveys the profound intimacy between God and people. God will forgive infidelities and transform Israel into a "virgin" bride.

As a young **man** marries a **virgin**,
    your **Builder** shall marry **you**;
and as a **bridegroom** rejoices in his **bride**
    so shall your **God** rejoice in **you**.

Let your eye contact tell us "you" refers to all in the assembly.

READING I Appearing near the end of the Book of Isaiah, this reading is generally dated near the time when the people who had been abducted from the southern conquered Kingdom of Judah and survived Babylonian exile were allowed to return home around 539 BC. The third section of Isaiah, chapters 56–66, turns toward hope for the future, fulfillment of what several prophets had promised: a new covenant, new Israel, new Jerusalem, even new creation. As in the past, such hope was rooted entirely in God's faithfulness to the people of the covenant. They understood themselves as a people punished for numerous infidelities, but never abandoned by the God who delivered them from slavery and established with them an unbreakable covenant relationship. God had restored and renewed them in the past, and could be counted upon to do so again.

The prophet announces that God will not only bring the people back to their land, but their reestablishment will astound other nations and kingdoms. The powerful Word of God will bring about what it proclaims: Israel will be "called by a new name pronounced by the mouth of the Lord." In biblical thought, a name indicated one's very character and identity. Through Isaiah, God promises future renewal of the covenant people at its core; the names by which Israel was known in exile will be changed by divine action.

To appreciate the significance of the names given to the people in this prophecy, it's helpful to know how several major prophets spoke about the people in the past. Before the destruction of both Israelite kingdoms (Israel and Judah), prophets often likened the relationship between God and the covenant people to a

For meditation and context:

TO KEEP IN MIND

Echoes: Some words echo words that went before. For example, "You shall be a glorious crown . . . a royal diadem" (Isaiah 62:3). Here "diadem" echoes "crown" so it needs no stress. In such cases, emphasize the new idea: royal.

RESPONSORIAL PSALM Psalm 89:4–5, 16–17, 27, 29 (2a)

R. Forever I will sing the goodness of the Lord.

I have made a covenant with my chosen one,
    I have sworn to David my servant:
forever will I confirm your posterity
    and establish your throne for all
        generations.

Blessed the people who know the
        joyful shout;
    in the light of your countenance, O LORD,
        they walk.
At your name they rejoice all the day,
    and through your justice they are exalted.

He shall say of me, "You are my father,
    my God, the rock, my savior."
Forever I will maintain my kindness toward
        him,
    and my covenant with him stands firm.

READING II Acts of the Apostles 13:16–17, 22–25

A reading from the Acts of the Apostles

When **Paul** reached Antioch in Pisidia and entered the **synagogue**,
    he **stood** up, motioned with his **hand**, and said,
        "Fellow **Israelites** and you **others** who are God-fearing, **listen**.
The God of this people Israel chose our **ancestors**
    and **exalted** the people during their sojourn in the land
        of **Egypt**.
With uplifted **arm** he led them **out** of it.
Then he removed **Saul** and raised up **David** as king;
    of him he **testified**,
        'I have found **David**, son of **Jesse**, a man after my own **heart**;
    he will carry out my every **wish**.'

Paul is speaking in a setting similar to yours—the weekly gathering place for worship.

Paul is quite deliberate in securing people's attention before speaking. Do the same!

To gain their attention, Paul must speak with authority. He reviews their salvation history in order to arrive at Jesus, who culminates that history!

David is always a point of reference in Israelite history. But in Jesus, they have one even greater than David!

---

marriage. Various prophets described the people's frequent lapses into idolatry or other infidelities as adultery, or as seeking divorce from the Lord (see Jeremiah 3:6–10). Addressing the northern kingdom nearing its destruction, Hosea presented God as a husband abandoned by unfaithful Israel who was seeking out other lovers; that is, other gods. Like a jilted husband, the Lord vacillates between seeking ways to punish his adulterous wife and ways to win her back. In the destruction of the second Israelite kingdom, loss of the Promised Land, and return to captivity, the people

saw God "divorcing" the people he once called "my beloved" (Jeremiah 11:15).

What Isaiah proclaims in this passage is an unimaginable healing of this seemingly shattered bond. A renewed people will no longer be named "Forsaken." (The Hebrew word used here can also mean "divorced.") Rather, the Lord, like an ever-faithful husband, will completely erase Israel's infidelities and treat her as a virgin bride, rejoicing in a relationship not only restored but completely re-created.

READING II This reading is taken from one of several speeches in Acts in which Luke presents Peter or Paul proclaiming the Good News of Jesus as the expected Messiah. While Peter addresses fellow Jews, Paul preaches to a broader audience—fellow Israelites, non-Jews sympathetic to Judaism ("others who are God-fearing"), and Gentiles. Usually these early proclamations of faith strive to demonstrate that the life, Death, and Resurrection of Christ bring the Old Testament Scriptures and Jewish hopes to

From David came the "savior." This makes Jesus far greater than his ancestor.

Now he cites John, another hero superseded by Jesus. John insists they be clear about his identity.

Speak "one is coming after me . . ." with simple sincerity, as if John could see Jesus coming from a distance.

From this man's **descendants** God, according to his **promise**,
  has brought to Israel a **savior**, **Jesus**.
John **heralded** his coming by proclaiming a **baptism** of **repentance**
  to all the people of Israel;
  and as John was **completing** his course, he would say,
  'What do you suppose that I **am**? I am not **he**.
Behold, one is coming **after** me;
  I am not **worthy** to unfasten the **sandals** of his feet.'"

GOSPEL   Matthew 1:1–25

A reading from the holy Gospel according to Matthew

The book of the **genealogy** of Jesus **Christ**,
  the son of **David**, the son of **Abraham**.

Abraham became the father of **Isaac**,
  Isaac the father of **Jacob**,
  Jacob the father of **Judah** and his brothers.
Judah became the father of **Perez** and **Zerah**,
  whose **mother** was **Tamar**.
Perez became the father of **Hezron**,
  Hezron the father of **Ram**,
  Ram the father of **Amminadab**.
Amminadab became the father of **Nahshon**,
  Nahshon the father of **Salmon**,
  Salmon the father of **Boaz**,
  whose **mother** was **Rahab**.
Boaz became the father of **Obed**,
  whose **mother** was **Ruth**.
Obed became the father of **Jesse**,
  Jesse the father of **David** the **king**. »

Rehearse pronunciation of the names. Litanies like this make an impact through repetition, so don't rush this sacred listing. To sustain interest, renew your energy every few lines.

Abraham = AY-bruh-ham

Isaac = Ī-zik

Judah = JOO-duh

Perez = PAYR-ez

Zerah = ZEE-rah

Tamar = TAY-mahr: see Genesis 38.

Hezron = HEZ-ruhn

Ram = ram

Amminadab = uh-MIN-uh-dab

Nashon = NAH-shun

Salmon = SAL-muhn

Boaz = BOH-az

Rahab = RAY-hab: see Joshua 2:1–7

Obed = OH-bed

Ruth was the great-grandmother of King David.

Jesse = JES-ee

---

their fulfillment. Today's Second Reading serves this major purpose.

Paul points to Israel's very beginnings, when God brought an enslaved people through the wilderness to freedom. His reference to King David and his descendants alludes to Jewish hopes that in the age of salvation, God would complete the promise of a righteous descendant of David who would lead a new Israel to fulfill its destiny as a holy people. Paul proclaims that the unfolding story of salvation has been brought to completion through Jesus, Son of David and Savior.

GOSPEL This passage, Matthew's full genealogy of Jesus, is one of the most challenging for Gospel readers to proclaim. It is easy to lose sight of the power behind these names. When they are read simply as a long list, the congregation looks dazed and shifts restlessly. In fact, Matthew carefully constructed the opening of his account of the Good News to alert us to vital characteristics of the child who will bring God's salvation to the world. The evangelist presents not a biological family tree, but a biblical literary form intended to show significant elements of a

person's origins. While most English translations call Matthew's beginning a "genealogy," he uses the Greek word *genesis*, which also means "origins," and recalls the creation account that begins the Old Testament. In his first few words, the author indicates that the birth of this infant initiates a new creation story. Through this child, God will bring humankind and all creation to the fullness intended from the beginning.

From the beginning of his genealogy, Matthew establishes that Jesus is thoroughly Jewish: a "son of Abraham" and a descendant of David. The reference to

Uriah = yoo-RĪ-uh. His "wife" is Bathsheba: 2 Samuel 11:1–27.

Rehoboam = ree-huh-BOH-uhm

Abijah = uh-BĪ-juh

Asaph = AY-saf

Jehoshaphat = jeh-HOH-shuh-fat

Joram = JOHR-uhm

Uzziah = yuh-ZĪ-uh: Struck with leprosy for usurping role of priests: 2 Chronicles 26:16–20.

Jotham = JOH-thuhm

Ahaz = AY-haz

Hezekiah = hez-eh-KĪH-uh: One of the few "good" kings; a reformer.

Manasseh = muh-NAS-uh: The nation's worst king.

Josiah = joh-SĪ-uh: One of Judah's best kings; a reformer. Ascended the throne at age eight.

The exile was the nation's greatest trial.

Jechoniah = jek-oh-NĪ-uh

Shealtiel = shee-AL-tee-uhl

Zerubbabel = zuh-ROOB-uh-b*l

Abiud = uh-BĪ-uhd

Eliakim = ee-LĪ-uh-kim

Azor = AY-sohr

Zadok = ZAD-uhk

Achim = AH-kim

Eliud = ee-LĪ-uhd

Eleazar = el-ee-AY-zer

Matthan = MATH-uhn

"Fourteen" is a deliberate redundancy. Stress each recurrence.

David became the father of **Solomon,**
  whose **mother** had been the wife of **Uriah.**
Solomon became the father of **Rehoboam,**
  Rehoboam the father of **Abijah,**
  Abijah the father of **Asaph.**
Asaph became the father of **Jehoshaphat,**
  Jehoshaphat the father of **Joram,**
  Joram the father of **Uzziah.**
Uzziah became the father of **Jotham,**
  Jotham the father of **Ahaz,**
  Ahaz the father of **Hezekiah.**
Hezekiah became the father of **Manasseh,**
  Manasseh the father of **Amos,**
  Amos the father of **Josiah.**
Josiah became the father of **Jechoniah** and his brothers
  at the time of the Babylonian **exile.**

After the Babylonian exile,
  Jechoniah became the father of **Shealtiel,**
  Shealtiel the father of **Zerubbabel,**
  Zerubbabel the father of **Abiud.**
Abiud became the father of **Eliakim,**
  Eliakim the father of **Azor,**
  Azor the father of **Zadok.**
Zadok became the father of **Achim,**
  Achim the father of **Eliud,**
  Eliud the father of **Eleazar.**
Eleazar became the father of **Matthan,**
  Matthan the father of **Jacob,**
  Jacob the father of **Joseph,** the husband of **Mary.**
Of her was born **Jesus** who is called the **Christ.**

Thus the total number of **generations**
  from **Abraham** to **David**
  is **fourteen** generations;
  from **David** to the Babylonian **exile,**

David carries messianic connotations, since early first-century Judaism held strong hopes that the messiah would appear as a new and righteous king of David's line, a true "Son of David." In a carefully constructed pattern of three sets of fourteen generations each, the evangelist then highlights particular ancestors of Jesus. This threefold pattern outlines major segments of Israel's life in covenant with the Lord: Abraham to David, David to the Babylonian exile, and exile to the Christ. In Jewish number symbolism, the number fourteen points to the name of David.

Matthew thus suggests that God is about to bring Israel's salvation story to completion in this child, the true Son of David.

At the beginning of the last section of this reading ("Now this is how the birth . . . "), Matthew again uses the word *genesis* (translated in English as "birth"), indicating that this child's origins provide important clues about who he is and what he will accomplish. In this, Matthew twice stresses that the birth of Jesus came about through God's powerful action in the world, the Holy Spirit. The name Jesus begins to unfold his true character and identity, for it

means "God saves." Matthew further announces that his Nativity brings to fullness the prophetic word concerning a son to be called "Emmanuel," God's own presence in the world. This child who is of God will carry out God's work; through him the divine purpose of creation from the beginning will reach completion. This newborn infant is revealed as a true image of God, a human being in whom "God is with us." M.F.

fourteen generations;
from the Babylonian exile to the **Christ**,
fourteen generations.

Now this is how the **birth** of Jesus Christ came about.
When his mother **Mary** was betrothed to **Joseph**,
    but before they **lived** together,
    she was found with **child** through the Holy **Spirit**.
Joseph her **husband**, since he was a **righteous** man,
    yet unwilling to expose her to **shame**,
    decided to divorce her **quietly**.
Such was his **intention** when, **behold**,
    the **angel** of the Lord appeared to him in a **dream** and said,
    "**Joseph**, son of David,
    do not be **afraid** to take Mary your **wife** into your **home**.
For it is through the Holy **Spirit**
    that this child has been **conceived** in her.
She will bear a **son** and you are to name him **Jesus**,
    because he will **save** his people from their **sins**."
All this took place to **fulfill**
    what the Lord had said through the **prophet**:
        *Behold, the **virgin** shall **conceive** and bear a **son**,
            and they shall name him **Emmanuel**,*
    which means "**God** is **with** us."
When Joseph **awoke**,
    he **did** as the angel of the Lord had **commanded** him
    and took his **wife** into his **home**.
He had no **relations** with her until she bore a **son**,
    and he **named** him **Jesus**.

[Shorter: Matthew 1:18–25]

Matthew purposefully stresses details of Jesus' conception and the role of Joseph.

"Before they lived together" addresses the delicacy of the situation.

"Righteous man" should be stressed. Take a brief pause before the word "quietly."

The angel's role asserts Jesus' divine origin and his messianic destiny.

The word "Emmanuel" climaxes the reading. The name's translation should be vocally set apart.
Joseph is confident his dream has divine origin.

Again, this detail regarding marital "relations" bears emphasis.

Sustain eye contact with the assembly after speaking "Jesus" and when announcing "The Gospel of the Lord."

TO KEEP IN MIND

Lists: Whether proclaiming a genealogy or one of Paul's enumerations of virtues and sins, avoid the extremes of too much stress (slowly punctuating each word with equal stress) or too little (rushing through as if each item were the same).

THE NATIVITY OF THE LORD (CHRISTMAS): NIGHT

LECTIONARY #14

Isaiah = i-ZAY-uh

READING I Isaiah 9:1–6

A reading from the Book of the Prophet Isaiah

This is a reading of contrasts. Images of darkness and pain contrast with those of light and rejoicing. Greater energy goes to the positive images.

We all are among those who lived in "darkness." But we also are among those who have seen "light."

Your tone marvels at the goodness of God who has brought an abundance of joy.

Three negative images ("yoke," "pole," "rod") are offset by the single word "smashed." Take a slight pause between "smashed" and "as on the day . . . "

Even the refuse of war will be consumed and forgotten!

This is the reason that light is shining and oppression has ended: "a child"!

The four titles must each stand alone, as if spoken by four different voices. Don't rush.

Speak these closing lines with a sense of deep joy knowing you live securely under the authority of the Prince of Peace.

The people who walked in **darkness**
   have seen a great **light**;
upon those who dwelt in the land of **gloom**
   a light has **shone**.
You have brought them abundant **joy**
   and great **rejoicing**,
as they rejoice before you as at the **harvest**,
   as people make **merry** when dividing **spoils**.
For the **yoke** that **burdened** them,
   the **pole** on their **shoulder**,
and the **rod** of their **taskmaster**
   you have **smashed**, as on the day of **Midian**.
For every **boot** that tramped in **battle**,
   every **cloak** rolled in **blood**,
   will be **burned** as fuel for **flames**.
For a **child** is born to us, a **son** is given us;
   upon his shoulder **dominion** rests.
They name him **Wonder-Counselor**, **God-Hero**,
   Father-Forever, **Prince** of **Peace**.
His dominion is **vast**
   and forever **peaceful**,
from **David's** throne, and over his **kingdom**,
   which he **confirms** and **sustains**

READING I In the liturgy, we often hear from the great prophets. Through their writing the earliest disciples, who were Jews, came to understand who Jesus is. Judaism taught that God had implanted the fullness of the divine plan in the Scriptures; it was the task of the faith community to discover their unfolding meaning by continual reflection. For that reason, authors of the New Testament often used an earlier text (from what we call the Old Testament) to illuminate what they were writing for their own time and place. This is why the New Testament writers saw Jesus "fulfilling" Israel's Scriptures.

Chapter 9 reflects a time when the powerful Assyrian empire invaded territory north of the Israelite kingdoms. Given that threat, people in the kingdom of Judah longed for a mighty and righteous warrior-king. Their ideal was a political and military leader, but one who would establish right relationships and seek the good of all.

While the northern kingdom of Israel had its own succession of kings, the kings of Judah descended from David. In today's First Reading, Isaiah expresses Judah's hope that a true son of David would soon appear, bringing military victory, protecting against foreign powers, and embodying the ideal of Israelite kingship. The expected "child" of Isaiah 7:14, a sign that God was truly present among the people of Judah in dangerous times, is described in Isaiah 9 as the fullness of that ideal: he rules with "judgment and justice." The Hebrew words used describe one who is righteous and who labors to bring about right relationships among the people, supporting sincere worship of God and social justice throughout the kingdom.

The sense of this sentence is: His dominion, which he exercises from David's throne and over David's kingdom, and which he confirms and sustains by judgment and justice, both now and forever, is vast and forever peaceful.

This is a promise. Speak it with great conviction.

For meditation and context:

> **TO KEEP IN MIND**
> **Poetry** is gourmet food, eaten slowly and savored. Go slowly. Pay attention to the sounds, rhythms, and repetitions.

Beloved = bee-LUHV-uhd
The first line is a birth announcement! Take time to announce that "The grace of God / has appeared / bringing salvation . . . ." When filled with gratitude and joy, turning away from such darkness is less difficult.

blessed = BLESS-uhd
God's grace has once appeared; now we await a second "appearance."
Even on the night of Jesus' birth we contemplate how he gave himself that we might be cleansed.
The word "eager" is your guide to the tone of this reading. Doing good is our response to God's mercy.

Trust the simplicity of the story. You need no embellishment; just tell it simply and honestly.
The events recounted here touch "the whole world."

by **judgment** and **justice**,
　　both **now** and **forever**.
The **zeal** of the Lord of hosts will **do** this!

RESPONSORIAL PSALM　Psalm 96:1–2, 2–3, 11–12, 13 (Luke 2:11)

R. Today is born our Savior, Christ the Lord.

Sing to the Lord a new song;
　sing to the Lord, all you lands.
Sing to the Lord; bless his name.

Announce his salvation, day after day.
　Tell his glory among the nations;
　among all peoples, his wondrous deeds.

Let the heavens be glad and the
　earth rejoice;
　let the sea and what fills it resound;
　let the plains be joyful and all that is
　in them!
Then shall all the trees of the forest exult.

They shall exult before the Lord,
　for he comes;
　for he comes to rule the earth.
He shall rule the world with justice
　and the peoples with his constancy.

READING II　Titus 2:11–14

A reading from the Letter of Saint Paul to Titus

Beloved:
The grace of **God** has appeared, **saving** all
　and training us to **reject** godless ways and **worldly** desires
　and to live **temperately, justly,** and **devoutly** in this age,
　as we await the blessed **hope,**
　the **appearance** of the glory of our great **God**
　and **savior** Jesus **Christ,**
　who **gave** himself for us to **deliver** us from all **lawlessness**
　and to **cleanse** for himself a people as his **own,**
　eager to do what is **good.**

GOSPEL　Luke 2:1–14

A reading from the holy Gospel according to Luke

In those days a **decree** went out from Caesar **Augustus**
　　that the whole **world** should be **enrolled.** »

READING II　The brief letter of Titus, along with the two attributed to Timothy, form a group usually called the "pastoral letters." While scholars debate their authorship and dating, these texts give insight into the concerns and emerging structures of the early Christian Church. They discuss how Christians should live amidst cultures with values they oppose, the qualifications ministry requires, the distribution of ministers, and the structures of the Church.

In one of the shortest of New Testament writings, Titus deals primarily with Christian conduct. In today's reading, the author roots his admonitions in what God has done for us in Jesus Christ. Like Paul, Titus stresses that the Christ event is God's gracious gift, initiated solely by his love for us. Like Paul and many early Christians, he also seems to expect an imminent return of Christ in full glory. Emphasizing Christ's gift of himself to and for us, Titus encourages his hearers to live as a community saved by divine gift, eagerly responding to that gift by conduct befitting those who belong to God.

GOSPEL　Of the four Gospel accounts, only Matthew and Luke begin with Jesus' birth. Unlike modern Western culture, people in the biblical world did not think in terms of human growth and development; what a person was at birth represented what he or she would be throughout life. Thus an infancy narrative served to depict a person's character and role in the world; accuracy of historical detail was not the primary concern.

Scholars generally agree that Luke was a Greek-speaking Gentile convert to

Quirinius = kwih-RIN-ee-uhs

This requirement brings Joseph, through whom Jesus receives his royal lineage, to the city of his ancestor, David.

Engagement and pregnancy were not incompatible.

Each phrase tells an important detail, so share one phrase/thought at a time.

Don't overstate this detail, but let it linger momentarily.

Your pace can quicken and your energy climb on these lines describing the sudden and shocking appearance of angels.

"Do not be afraid" is one of the most common exhortations in the New Testament.

Slow your delivery for these significant details.

Fast or slow, louder or softer, these lines must echo joy.

This was the **first** enrollment,
    when **Quirinius** was governor of **Syria.**
So all went to be **enrolled**, **each** to his own **town.**
And **Joseph** too went up from **Galilee** from the town
    of **Nazareth**
    to **Judea,** to the city of **David** that is called **Bethlehem,**
    because he was of the **house** and **family** of David,
    to be enrolled with **Mary,** his **betrothed,** who was with **child.**
While they were there,
    the time came for her to **have** her child,
    and she gave **birth** to her firstborn **son.**
She wrapped him in **swaddling** clothes and laid him in a **manger,**
    because there was no **room** for them in the **inn.**

Now there were **shepherds** in that region living in the **fields**
    and keeping the **night** watch over their flock.
The **angel** of the Lord **appeared** to them
    and the **glory** of the Lord **shone** around them,
    and they were struck with great **fear.**
The angel **said** to them,
    "Do not be **afraid;**
    for **behold,** I proclaim to you good **news** of great **joy**
    that will be for **all** the people.
For **today** in the city of **David**
    a **savior** has been born for you who is **Christ** and **Lord.**
And this will be a **sign** for you:
    you will find an **infant** wrapped in **swaddling** clothes
    and lying in a **manger.**"
And **suddenly** there was a **multitude** of the heavenly host with
    the angel,
    praising God and saying:
      "**Glory** to God in the **highest**
        and on **earth peace** to those on whom his **favor** rests."

Christianity, addressing an audience of similar background.

This evangelist is the only one to place Jesus on the world stage of his time, locating the Savior's birth in the reign of Caesar Augustus and naming Quirinius, the Syrian governor. Luke describes a required "enrollment" as the reason for Joseph and Mary's journey to Bethlehem. No historical record of such a decree at this specific time has been found, though a census did occur at some point under Quirinius. The writer most likely uses such an event to locate Jesus' birth in Bethlehem, indicating the

fulfillment of Micah 5:1, which states that the expected messiah-king will arise from this traditional birthplace of King David.

Luke includes several details that underscore Jesus' outreach to the poor, as well as his true identity as Savior, Lord, and bringer of peace. The infant who comes to serve the poor and outcast is laid in a feeding trough for animals. Because Luke mentions the manger repeatedly, some scholars believe that he intends to foreshadow the ministry of Jesus that so often took place at a meal. Eventually, Jesus will give his own life as nourishment for the new life of all

humankind. Again stressing Jesus' ministry to the poor and marginalized, Luke presents a startling scene: the first to receive the Good News of dawning salvation are shepherds, generally despised and avoided as unclean sinners. The angelic proclamation contradicts the imperial cult, which proclaimed Caesar Augustus as divine Lord, Savior of the people, and bringer of peaceful order in the empire. Luke presents a different scenario; not the Roman emperor, but the infant lying in a feed trough is the true Savior and royal Son of God who establishes peace on earth. M.F.

THE NATIVITY OF THE LORD (CHRISTMAS): DAWN

LECTIONARY #15

READING I Isaiah 62:11–12

A reading from the Book of the Prophet Isaiah

> **See**, the LORD proclaims
>   to the **ends** of the **earth**:
> say to daughter **Zion**,
>   your **savior** comes!
> Here is his **reward** with him,
>   his **recompense** before him.
> They shall be called the **holy** people,
>   the **redeemed** of the LORD,
> and you shall be called "**Frequented**,"
>   a city that is **not forsaken**.

RESPONSORIAL PSALM Psalm 97:1, 6, 11–12

R. A light will shine on us this day: the Lord is born for us.

The LORD is king; let the earth rejoice;
    let the many isles be glad.
The heavens proclaim his justice,
    and all peoples see his glory.

Light dawns for the just;
    and gladness, for the upright of heart.
Be glad in the LORD, you just,
    and give thanks to his holy name.

READING II Titus 3:4–7

A reading from the Letter of Saint Paul to Titus

Beloved:
When the **kindness** and generous **love**
    of God our savior appeared, »

Isaiah = ī-ZAY-uh

Short readings require slower pacing.

The operative word here is "proclaims." Let your tone become expansive and regal for you proclaim news for the whole world to hear.

On this special night, this line must be savored. Establish eye contact with the assembly.

The Savior's coming changes everyone's fortunes. Speak these new names as if to someone you love whose face you hold in your hands.

For meditation and context:

> **TO KEEP IN MIND**
> **Read all three commentaries.**
> Suggestions in each can give you insight into your own passage.

Beloved = bee-LUHV-uhd

"Not" and "but" are the keys to the major contrast of the opening lines: Christ appeared "not" because of what we did, "but" because of God's mercy.

READING I This passage comes from a section of Isaiah dated after the Babylonian exile; after more than a half century of captivity in a foreign empire, Isaiah's prophecies of hope for restoration began to be realized. Today's reading closes chapter 62, which exults in God's renewal of covenant love with Israel. Through Isaiah, God proclaims to Zion (another name for Jerusalem) that now is the moment of her savior's coming. The root of the Hebrew word used here translated "savior" carries a range of meanings, including salvation, deliverance, rescue, safety, well-being, healing, and wholeness. The announcement that God is coming to save Jerusalem thus carries multiple layers of meaning. Rebuilding the city of Jerusalem implies restoring Davidic kingship and building a new dwelling place for God in Israel's midst; by extension, it points to the renewal of Israel's covenant relationship with God. New names for the people and their capital city signify new character and identity. The prophet Hosea, speaking to the kingdom of Israel before its destruction, was told to give his children names that symbolized God's view of the people at that time, names like "without compassion" and "not my people." But with a new act of divine salvation, the Lord's people will be called "the holy people, the redeemed of the LORD." By the power of Israel's Redeemer, Jerusalem, once known as a desolate heap of ruins, will also receive a new identity from its saving God.

READING II In this reading, the author presents a masterful summation of Christian faith in the first century. He stresses that human salvation is God's gracious love given as a completely

> not because of any righteous **deeds** we had done
>   but because of his **mercy**,
> he **saved** us through the **bath** of **rebirth**
>   and **renewal** by the Holy **Spirit**,
> whom he richly **poured** out on us
>   through Jesus **Christ** our **savior**,
> so that we might be **justified** by his grace
>   and become **heirs** in hope of eternal **life**.

"Bath of rebirth" is a reference to Baptism. Increase energy when you cite the work of the Holy Spirit.
Speak with both conviction and gratitude.

As in most of the lines, here you have more than one idea to share: (a) we are justified by grace; (b) we become heirs in hope.

GOSPEL   Luke 2:15–20

A reading from the holy Gospel according to Luke

When the **angels** went **away** from them to **heaven**,
  the **shepherds** said to one another,
  "Let us **go**, then, to **Bethlehem**
  to **see** this thing that has taken place,
  which the Lord has made **known** to us."
So they went in **haste** and found **Mary** and **Joseph**,
  and the **infant** lying in the **manger**.
When they **saw** this,
  they made known the **message**
  that had been **told** them about this child.
All who heard it were **amazed**
  by what had been **told** them by the shepherds.
And Mary **kept** all these things,
  reflecting on them in her **heart**.
Then the shepherds **returned**,
  glorifying and **praising** God
  for all they had **heard** and **seen**,
  just as it had been **told** to them.

The story reverberates with the sound of angel wings and the excitement of the shepherds. Sustain that joyful energy throughout.
The shepherds are full of belief and hurry to see the promise.
Though they go "in haste," don't race this important line.

Convey a sense of awe as they share the angels' message.

Take time with this classic line that speaks of Mary's own sense of wonder.

"Heard" refers to their expectation, "seen" to its fulfillment.

---

unearned gift, repeating the important point that we are made whole by divine grace (Greek *charis*, which literally means "gift"). This gift of "generous love" was poured out through Christ, received through Baptism, and continues to renew believers through the indwelling presence of the Holy Spirit.

| GOSPEL | This passage continues Luke's account of the angelic announcement of the Savior's birth to the most unexpected hearers; lowly shepherds, commonly avoided as ritually impure sinners. The shepherds may remind us of King David's humble origins, and they underscore one of Luke's favored themes: Jesus' preference for sinners and outcasts. Shepherds though they be, they immediately respond to God's Word proclaimed by heavenly messengers. Hurrying toward the Savior, they find him "lying in the manger." For the third time in his infancy narrative, Luke points out the manger. This humble child will be food for all who hunger for God's deliverance, nourishing first the poor, outcasts, sinners, and the marginalized.

In an interesting turn of events, the shepherds are witness to God's revelation, telling the angelic message to Mary and Joseph. Their testimony confirms and expands Gabriel's words to Mary about her child (Luke 1:31–33). She and the shepherds model a proper response to God's Word of salvation through this newborn child: reflection and gratitude. Mary seems aware that the full meaning of divine revelation takes place only gradually and with reflection. The shepherds display another response: they give joyful praise and thanks to God, the sole source of salvation. M.F.

THE NATIVITY OF THE LORD (CHRISTMAS): DAY

LECTIONARY #16

READING I Isaiah 52:7–10

A reading from the Book of the Prophet Isaiah

How **beautiful** upon the **mountains**
    are the **feet** of him who brings glad **tidings**,
announcing **peace**, bearing good **news**,
    announcing **salvation**, and saying to **Zion**,
    "Your **God** is **King!**"

Hark! Your sentinels raise a **cry**,
    together they shout for **joy**,
for they see **directly**, before their **eyes**,
    the Lord **restoring** Zion.
Break out together in **song**,
    O **ruins** of Jerusalem!
For the Lord **comforts** his people,
    he **redeems** Jerusalem.
The Lord has **bared** his holy arm
    in the sight of all the **nations**;
all the ends of the **earth** will behold
    the **salvation** of our **God**.

Isaiah = ī-ZAY-uh

The first part of the text marvels at the beauty of one who brings news of peace. Recall the instinct to embrace or kiss someone who brings great news and let that color your proclamation.
Pause briefly before announcing "Your God is King." Then pause again.

Sustain energy and joyous excitement, but don't speed through these elegant lines.

"Break out" is a command. Even the "ruins" will sing!

The final sentence both celebrates what God has done and promises God's mercy will extend to all the earth.

READING I Commentators usually divide the lengthy book of Isaiah into three sections, each reflecting a different time in the history of God's people. Today's reading is part of the second segment (Isaiah 50–55) often called "the book of consolation." These chapters seem to have been written in the later part of the Babylonian Captivity, a time when the people felt more hope and assurance that they would return to the Promised Land. The destruction of Judah, Jerusalem, and the magnificent temple of the Lord was a devastating event that called into question not only Israel's future, but its very identity as God's people. Several prophets, however, continued to proclaim that Israel would not simply return home; it would be renewed. God's new future would be more resplendent than anything that came before; all that had been destroyed would be created anew with divine glory.

In this reading, Isaiah imagines the day of deliverance as it draws near. A divine herald announces the arrival of peace and salvation, with God once again ruling in a new Jerusalem as Israel's true King. The Hebrew words translated here as "peace" and "salvation" are laden with significance. "Peace" means much more than absence of war, and "salvation" is not limited to heavenly reward. Together, these two terms evoke multiple meanings, including deliverance, rescue, security, wellbeing, health, wholeness, and completeness, all beginning in the present world. Similarly, the Hebrew word translated "redeems" derives from ancient tribal culture, in which the clan's "redeemer" was designated to restore to the family persons or property that had been captured. The prophet envisions Israel's God and King acting as

For meditation and context:

RESPONSORIAL PSALM   Psalm 98:1, 2–3, 3–4, 5–6 (3c)

R. All the ends of the earth have seen the saving power of God.

Sing to the LORD a new song,
  for he has done wondrous deeds;
his right hand has won victory for him,
  his holy arm.

The LORD has made his salvation known:
  in the sight of the nations he has revealed
    his justice.
He has remembered his kindness and his
  faithfulness
toward the house of Israel.

All the ends of the earth have seen
  the salvation by our God.
Sing joyfully to the LORD, all you lands;
  break into song; sing praise.

Sing praise to the LORD with the harp,
  with the harp and melodious song.
With trumpets and the sound of the horn
  sing joyfully before the King, the LORD.

READING II   Hebrews 1:1–6

A reading from the Letter to the Hebrews

You are contrasting God's past and "partial" dialogue with Israel with the full and climactic communication of God in Jesus.

Brothers and sisters:
In times **past**, God spoke in **partial** and **various** ways
  to our **ancestors** through the **prophets**;
  in these **last** days, he has spoken to us through the **Son**,
  whom he made **heir** of all things

The author focuses on the divine and preexistent nature of Christ. Don't let the theology obscure the joy!

These lines come from an early liturgical hymn making them a prayer of praise.

  and **through** whom he created the **universe**,
  who is the **refulgence** of his **glory**,
    the very **imprint** of his **being**,
  and who **sustains** all things by his mighty **word**.
When he had accomplished purification from **sins**,
  he took his **seat** at the **right** hand of the **Majesty** on high,
  as far **superior** to the **angels**
  as the **name** he has inherited is more **excellent** than theirs.

With authority, you declare that Christ is superior to every rank of angels.

For to **which** of the angels did God ever say:
  *You are my **son**; this day I have **begotten** you?*
Or again:

Christ is unique for he is not a creature but a "son." Speak the two affirmations not as a lawyer making a point but as a parent speaking of a beloved child.
Imagine the heavenly court and the angelic host being ordered to worship the "firstborn"!

  *I will be a **father** to him, and he shall be a **son** to me?*
And again, when he leads the **firstborn** into the world, he says:
  *Let all the **angels** of God **worship** him.*

redeemer, freeing her from captivity and restoring her as members of God's family.

READING II   Both authorship and dating of this letter are much debated, but clearly the writer is very familiar with the Old Testament, and addresses "the Hebrews." Like the Gospel account of John, Hebrews begins with a poetic introduction presenting Christ as the culmination of God's revelation: God's own Word in a human person, Jesus. Both writers draw upon the Old Testament personification of divine Wisdom, which in the early New

Testament period was virtually equivalent to God's self-revealing Word. Both authors allude to Old Testament Wisdom texts that describe the Wisdom/Word of God as coming from the mouth of God, existing with God from the beginning, assisting in the work of creation, radiating the glory of God in the world (Sirach 24:3; Proverbs 8:22–31; Wisdom 10:1–2; Wisdom 7:25–26).

The writer of Hebrews notes that in times past, partial revelation of God's Word came to Israel, particularly through the prophets. But in Jesus Christ, that self-revealing Word appears in all its fullness:

the Son is "the very imprint" of God's being. The Greek word used here is *charakter*, which originally meant an engraving tool, later a die or mold, still later a stamp for marking a seal or coin; in each case, a reality stood behind the image produced. Finally the term pointed to an exact impression or reproduction that also reveals inner character. In short, the writer indicates that anyone who wishes to know the very character of God has only to turn to the Son.

The image of "Son" also points to an exact representation of the "Father," because in Jewish culture a son could

GOSPEL   John 1:1–18

A reading from the holy Gospel according to John

Three distinct ideas that must be shared one at a time and each with great reverence.

This creed is the foundation for the narrative that follows. Speak each article of faith as both instruction and celebration.

> In the **beginning** was the **Word**,
>   and the **Word** was with **God**,
>   and the Word **was** God.
> He was in the **beginning** with God.
> All things came to be **through** him,
>   and without him **nothing** came to be.
> What came to be through him was **life**,
>   and this life was the **light** of the human race;
>   the light **shines** in the **darkness**,
>   and the darkness has not **overcome** it.

From the beginning, John is fascinated with the contrast between light and darkness.

The setting shifts from the cosmic realm to an earthly context. Your tone should signal the shift.

Note the repetitions that name John as witness to Christ.

> A man named **John** was sent from **God**.
> He came for **testimony**, to testify to the **light**,
>   so that all might **believe** through him.
> **He** was not the light,
>   but came to **testify** to the light.
> The **true** light, which enlightens **everyone**,
>   was coming into the world.
> He was **in** the world,
>   and the world came to **be** through him,
>   but the world did not **know** him.
> He came to what was his **own**,
>   but his own people did not **accept** him. »

There is a sense of regret in relating the blindness that kept "his own" from recognizing him.

TO KEEP IN MIND
Pray the Scriptures: Make reading these Scriptures a part of your prayer life every week, and especially during the week prior to the liturgy in which you will proclaim.

---

stand in the place of his father to communicate or to carry out a task. When a son thus represented the father, it was as if the father himself were present, speaking and acting.

In his Death and Resurrection, Jesus, exact representation and actual presence of God, is higher or greater than any other divine beings. Many followers of Judaism believed in the existence of divine beings other than the Lord, though none were ever on a par with him. To indicate that they were in some sense divine, angels were sometimes called "sons of God." Using several Old Testament references, the author of Hebrews takes pains to insist that "the Son," the exact representation of God, ranks high above any and all other sons of God.

GOSPEL   The import of John's prologue is similar to that of the Second Reading, though he has his unique perspective. John's poetic prologue, both introduction to and summary of his account of the Good News, most likely makes use of an already-existing Christological hymn. It is evident that he intersperses material concerning John the Baptist, but whether and how he might have edited the hymn otherwise cannot be determined precisely. Two interjections concerning John the Baptist emphasize that he functions as witness, giving testimony to "the light" that is Christ; in no way is he himself the one who reveals God. Many scholars think that John inserted this material to counteract claims that the Baptist, not Jesus, was the expected Messiah. This and other themes introduced in the prologue are repeated by John in subsequent chapters.

Adopt a more upbeat tone here to contrast with the previous lines.

Let your intensity grow as you move through the "not," "nor," and "but" phrases.

These sacred words conjure images of the birth of Bethlehem's child.

The voice of John penetrates without shattering the mood of awe in the previous lines.

John's voice returns, commenting on the gift of Christ on which we all have feasted.

Lift out John's contrast of "law" / "Moses" with "grace" / "Jesus Christ."

The intimacy between Father and Son is once again highlighted.

TO KEEP IN MIND
Who really proclaims: "When the Scriptures are read in the Church, God himself is speaking to his people, and Christ, present in his own word, is proclaiming the gospel" *(General Instruction of the Roman Missal, 29).*

But to those who **did** accept him
he gave power to become **children** of **God**,
to those who **believe** in his name,
who were born not by **natural** generation
nor by human **choice** nor by a **man's** decision
but of **God**.
And the **Word** became **flesh**
and made his **dwelling** among us,
and we saw his **glory**,
the glory as of the Father's only **Son**,
full of **grace** and **truth**.
John **testified** to him and cried out, saying,
"This was he of whom I said,
'The one who is coming **after** me ranks **ahead** of me
because he existed **before** me.'"
From his **fullness** we have all received,
grace in place of **grace**,
because while the **law** was given through **Moses**,
grace and **truth** came through Jesus **Christ**.
No one has ever **seen** God.
The only **Son**, **God**, who is at the Father's **side**,
has **revealed** him.

[Shorter: John 1:1–5, 9–14]

Like the author of Hebrews (see above), John draws upon Old Testament references to the Wisdom/Word of God to interpret Jesus to a late first-century audience. More than any other evangelist, John focuses on the identity of Jesus; for him, that identity is the divine Word totally united to full humanity, embodying and so revealing God in the world.

Opening the prologue, John uses the very same words that begin the Greek Old Testament (in the Book of Genesis), signaling a new creation begun in Christ. That he existed with God from the beginning, assisted God in creation, and radiated divine being into the world all recall the personification of the divine Wisdom/Word in the Old Testament. Still, John forewarns, not all adherents to that testament will accept Jesus; those who do will become children of God like the Word.

This Word of God, John graphically insists, "was made flesh"; the Greek word *sarx*, usually translated "flesh," means the entire human person in all its weakness and mortality. Precisely by taking on all that is human, including suffering and death, the Word reveals God and makes God present. Here John signals his interpretation of Jesus' Passion: it is the potent revelation of God's own life and love poured out for us (John 15:13; 10:1–18). This is the "fullness we have all received" through the divine Word made flesh. M.F.

THE HOLY FAMILY OF JESUS, MARY, AND JOSEPH

LECTIONARY #17

READING I 1 Samuel 1:20–22, 24–28

A reading from the first Book of Samuel

In those days **Hannah conceived**, and at the end of her **term**
  bore a **son**
whom she called **Samuel**, since she had **asked** the LORD
  for him.
The next time her husband **Elkanah** was going up
  with the rest of his **household**
  to offer the **customary sacrifice** to the LORD and to **fulfill**
  his **vows**,
  Hannah did **not** go, explaining to her husband,
  "Once the child is **weaned**,
  I will **take** him to **appear** before the LORD
  and to **remain** there **forever**;
  I will **offer** him as a **perpetual nazirite**."

Once Samuel was **weaned**, Hannah **brought him up** with her,
  along with a three-year-old **bull**,
  an **ephah** of flour, and a skin of **wine**,
  and **presented** him at the **temple** of the LORD in **Shiloh**.
After the boy's **father** had **sacrificed** the young **bull**,
  Hannah, his mother, approached **Eli** and said:
  "**Pardon, my lord!**
As you **live**, my lord,
  I am the **woman** who stood **near** you here, **praying** to the LORD. »

Hannah prayed earnestly at Shiloh the year before, but longed for a child through many years.

"Samuel" means "asked of God."

Elkanah = el-KAY-nah. You start a new beat here, so renew your energy.

Hannah has a plan, but will keep the child close for now.

Nazarite = NAZ-uh-right
Hannah is resolved, but it does not come without effort and pain.
These items ("flour," "bull") are sacrificial offerings, not traveling supplies.
Ephah = EE-fah

Shiloh = SHĪ-loh

Eli = EE-lĭ

Hannah identifies herself to Eli who had seen her praying the year before and mistook her for a drunkard, then prophesied her pregnancy.

Today options are given for the readings. Contact your parish staff to learn which readings will be used.

READING I Veneration of the Holy Family dates to the sixteenth century, but the feast was established only in 1893 by Pope Leo XIII to hold up Jesus' family as a model for our own.

1 Samuel 1:20–22, 24–28. The birth of Samuel was, for Hannah, a direct answer to prayer. In fact, the boy's name means "Asked of God." In her gratitude, Hannah resolves to give this child (for whom she'd longed) back to the God who answered her plea. Rather than join the pilgrimage to Shiloh for the annual celebration, she will wait until her son is weaned and then bring him to the Lord's house where he will spend his life. In today's Gospel we see Mary relieved to find Jesus in the Temple, from which she eagerly retrieves him to bring him home. That Hannah willingly leaves her boy behind may anticipate Jesus' words to his parents, who should have known his life would be centered on the Temple and on doing his father's business.

In answering Hannah's prayer, God did more than give her a child to love; he also removed from her the shame of sterility. This frees her to yield the child to God, who will use him mightily to bless the nation. He will be a Nazirite—a person set apart, consecrated to God's service in a life of strict asceticism. Hannah's words show no hesitancy in offering her son; she knows she leaves him in the hands of the only One who loves him even more than she does.

Sirach 3:2–6, 12–14. Sirach's words are as contemporary as the latest news about reverse mortgages or dementia.

31

Don't miss the blend of resolve, eloquence, and pain in Hannah's statement to Eli, especially in the poignancy of the final line.

"I **prayed** for this **child**, and **the** LORD **granted** my request.
Now **I**, in turn, **give him** to the LORD;
   as **long** as he **lives**, **he** shall be **dedicated** to the LORD."
Hannah **left** Samuel **there**.

Or:

READING I   Sirach 3:2–6, 12–14

A reading from the Book of Sirach

Sirach = SEER-ak
While these are independent proverbs, be sure to avoid a choppy delivery. The assertion of a mother's right is stated with greater force than a father's because, in biblical culture, it was far more significant to rank over "sons" (the "men" in the family) than over "children" (the "boys and girls").

Two distinct ideas here: sins are forgiven; prayers are heard. Stress both.

Slow your pacing on this reference to reverence for one's mother.
A second reminder that "honor" makes for efficacious prayer.

   God sets a **father** in **honor** over his **children**;
      a **mother's authority** he **confirms** over her **sons**.
   Whoever **honors** his father **atones** for sins,
      and **preserves** himself from them.
   When he **prays**, he is **heard**;
      he **stores up** riches who **reveres** his mother.
   Whoever **honors** his **father** is **gladdened** by children,
      and, when **he prays**, is **heard**.
   Whoever **reveres** his father will live a **long life**;
      he who **obeys** his father brings **comfort** to his mother.

While the first half of the text seems to refer to parents in their prime, these last lines speak of older parents in great need of care. Here is a warning against prideful neglect.

The last two lines modify "kindness to a father . . . ." Speak those lines as if each began with "It will be . . . ."

   My son, **take care** of your father when he is **old**;
      grieve him not as long as he **lives**.
   Even if his **mind fail**, be **considerate** of him;
      revile him not all the days of his life;
   kindness to a **father** will **not** be **forgotten**,
      firmly planted against the **debt** of your **sins**
      —a house **raised** in **justice** to you.

Reflected in this advice is a profound awareness that we make the culture in which we live and determine the quality of life that we and others will enjoy. Sirach's admonitions suggest both that society is structured on family life and that God designed it to work that way. The love and care we show our parents not only pleases God; it also determines the quality of our relationship with God. Respect and honor for parents is what all children *must* do if they expect their own lives to be blessed and their prayers to be heard.

Notice the poetic structure of the text, which is laid out in two-line couplets. Each couplet gives you an opportunity to renew your energy to make the new point being presented. While the word "honor" and its close synonym "revere" are repeated throughout, they don't need emphasis each time they recur; instead, emphasize the new idea introduced in that couplet.

We must hear this instruction as Jesus would have heard it (and probably did) from his own parents. Genuine honor flows in two directions and never demeans the one giving it, but lifts up both the one who renders and the one who receives it. Parents want to see each other respected by their children and every child must respect *both* parents if harmony is to dwell in their home. Sirach underscores that respect is not reserved for the "father." In fact, "he stores up riches who reveres his mother."

Though the final section speaks of care for "your father," the injunction applies to "parents" in their dotage, and the care of aging parents is made so important that it helps to expiate our sins. In a culture that tends to forget the elderly,

RESPONSORIAL PSALM   Psalm 84:2–3, 5–6, 9–10 (see 5a)

> **TO KEEP IN MIND**
>
> **Read all four Scriptures** for your assigned Sunday. Because all were chosen for this day, it is important to look at them together.

R. Blessed are they who dwell in your house, O Lord.

How lovely is your dwelling place, O Lord
  of hosts!
  My soul yearns and pines for the courts of
  the Lord.
My heart and my flesh cry out for the living
  God.

Happy they who dwell in your house!
  Continually they praise you.
Happy the men whose strength you are!
  Their hearts are set upon the pilgrimage.

O Lord of hosts, hear our prayer;
  hearken, O God of Jacob!
O God, behold our shield,
  and look upon the face of your anointed.

Or:

RESPONSORIAL PSALM   Psalm 128:1–2, 3, 4–5 (1)

> **TO KEEP IN MIND**
>
> As you are becoming familiar with your passage, read it directly from your Bible, **reading also what comes before and after** it to get a clear sense of its context.

R. Blessed are those who fear the Lord and walk in his ways.

Blessed is everyone who fears the Lord,
  who walks in his ways!
For you shall eat the fruit of your handiwork;
  blessed shall you be, and favored.

Your wife shall be like a fruitful vine
  in the recesses of your home;
your children like olive plants
  around your table.

Behold, thus is the man blessed
  who fears the Lord.
The Lord bless you from Zion:
  may you see the prosperity of Jerusalem
  all the days of your life.

READING II   1 John 3:1–2, 21–24

Beloved = bee-LUHV-uhd

The salutation is the key to the tone of the passage.
Let your gratitude for the love of God you've experienced in your life color these lines.

There is a sense of regret in this line.

A reading from the first Letter of Saint John

Beloved:
See what **love** the **Father** has **bestowed** on us
  that we may be called the **children of God**.
And **so we are**.
The reason the **world does not know us**
  is that **it did not know him**. **»**

Sirach's insistent lines require conviction and emphasis. You are telling us that for those who hope to reap rewards when they reach their own twilight, love of parents is not an option. But remember that this text addresses children of all ages in our assembly.

READING II | **1 John 3:1–2, 21–24.** On the face of it, there was not much to commend Christianity to its first adherents. After all, among those who first embraced it, many became outcasts, shunned by friends and family; some gave up their lives. The Gospel offered no assurance of wealth or power, so why did so many throw their arms around this faith and risk throwing their lives away with it? Part of the answer lies in these lines. Imagine a believer who's risked everything telling a curious nonbeliever about what God and Jesus mean in their life. Perhaps in some out-of-the-way place, they meet and, in hushed tones, calling the other "Beloved," the believer tells the nonbeliever, "See what love the Father has bestowed." "The reason the world does not know us is that it did not know him." There is a power in these words that touches the heart and compels belief!

Although sent in a letter, these words read like a spontaneous testimony; these sentences are filled with the love of which the author speaks; words that could sound hollow and rehearsed persuade us instead that they speak the truth and are meant for us. They testify to what is certain—"we are God's children . . . we shall be like him"—and they acknowledge that we don't yet know what awaits beyond this life.

Throughout, the author of this letter offers a formula for establishing here on

What we "are" is joy enough to hold us till we know what more will come!

This is a great truth: We will be like God and know God fully.

Beloved = bee-LUHV-uhd

Let your tone convey the "confidence" of which you speak.

Remember, repetition has a purpose and should never sound like careless redundancy.

Two expectations: believe and love.

Joyfully proclaim the indispensable role of the Spirit in the life of the community of faith.

Beloved, we are God's children now;
  what we **shall** be has **not yet** been **revealed**.
We **do know** that when it **is revealed** we shall be **like** him,
  for **we** shall **see** him **as he is**.

Beloved, if our **hearts do not condemn** us,
  we have **confidence** in **God** and **receive** from him
    whatever we **ask**,
  because we **keep** his **commandments** and **do** what **pleases** him.
And his **commandment** is **this**:
  we should **believe** in the **name** of his **Son**, Jesus **Christ**,
  and **love** one another just as he **commanded** us.
Those who **keep** his **commandments remain** in him,
    and **he** in **them**,
  and the **way** we **know** that he **remains** in us
  is from the **Spirit** he **gave** us.

Or:

READING II　Colossians 3:12–21

A reading from the Letter of Saint Paul to the Colossians

Brothers and **sisters**:
Put on, as God's **chosen** ones, **holy** and **beloved**,
  heartfelt **compassion**, **kindness**, **humility**, **gentleness**,
    and **patience**,
  bearing with one another and **forgiving** one another,
  if one has a **grievance** against another;
  as the **Lord** has forgiven **you**, **so must you also do**.
And over **all** these put on **love**,
  that is, the **bond** of **perfection**.
And let the **peace** of **Christ control** your **hearts**,
  the **peace** into which you were also **called** in **one body**.
And be **thankful**.

Colossians = kuh-LOSH-uhnz

Make eye contact as you speak the salutation.

beloved = bee-LUHV-uhd

Speak these admonitions to yourself as much as to your listeners, but don't let them sound like items on a shopping list.

Again, make eye contact as you encourage forgiveness and love.

The energy keeps building from one "and" to the next; each initiates a new idea that requires new energy.

earth the beloved community we are meant to become. The key is obedience to God's commandments; doing what "pleases" God. But we can't do it on our own; only through God's Spirit can we find our way, surrender our will to Christ, and "remain in him." Emboldened by our faith in God we can do what God expects of us: believe in his Son and love one another.

Colossians 3:12–21. There are appropriate clothes for every profession and occasion; from uniforms to formal wear, from armor to bathing suits. Life in the family, Paul tells us, is no exception. What fits

that time and place is not something we already carry within ourselves; rather, it is something we "put on" the way we would don a coat to shield us from the cold or a tank top to welcome the summer sun. The clothing imagery is instructive because it tells us, without having to use words, that harmony in the home is the result of grace that comes from outside ourselves. We don't manufacture "compassion, kindness, humility," and so forth; we put them on as we receive them from the Lord.

On top of those virtues we hear of another—and that virtue is love. Because

relationships are difficult to build and sustain and often become volatile, Paul also urges us to embrace "peace" that will rule our unruly hearts. Finally, he says, be "thankful." That statement stands alone without embellishment, suggesting the importance of a grateful heart in our homes and all our relationships.

The "word of Christ" shifts the mood and metaphor. We don't wear the "word"; it is to "dwell" in us and become a part of us. The "word," which is Christ himself, is to be a leaven within us, moving us to joyful song, to expressions of gratitude, and even

Your pace can slow a bit, but don't let the energy and enthusiasm wane.

Let the **word** of Christ **dwell** in you **richly**,
    as in all **wisdom** you **teach** and **admonish** one another,
    singing **psalms**, **hymns**, and **spiritual songs**
    with **gratitude** in your **hearts** to **God**.
And whatever you do, in **word** or in **deed**,
    do **everything** in the **name** of the **Lord Jesus**,
    giving **thanks** to **God** the **Father** through **him**.

Speak "do everything . . . " with conviction that says it's worth whatever price it costs.

Wives, be subordinate to your **husbands**,
    as is **proper** in the **Lord**.
Husbands, love your **wives**,
    and avoid **any bitterness** toward them.
Children, obey your **parents in everything**,
    for this is **pleasing** to the **Lord**.
Fathers, do **not** provoke your **children**,
    so they may not become **discouraged**.

You address three distinct groups within your congregation with three distinct messages. Pause before each sentence to focus and consider before you speak.

Take a three-beat pause before announcing the end of the reading.

[Shorter: Colossians 3:12–17]

GOSPEL   Luke 2:41–52

A reading from the holy Gospel according to Luke

The family faithfully observes the annual festival. At this point, this is just a prosaic family story of unremarkable events.

Each **year** Jesus' **parents** went to **Jerusalem** for the feast
    of **Passover**,
    and when he was **twelve** years **old**,
    they went **up** according to festival **custom**.
After they had **completed** its days, as they were **returning**,
    the boy **Jesus** remained **behind** in **Jerusalem**,
    but his **parents** did not **know** it.
Thinking that he was in the **caravan**,
    they **journeyed** for a **day**
    and **looked** for him among their **relatives** and **acquaintances**,
    but **not finding** him,
    they **returned** to **Jerusalem** to **look** for him. »

Your tone should suggest the unusual nature of this decision and the implication for the parents.
Your tone suggests their innocent assumption that all is well.

Here their concern is switched on. Quicken your pace on this sentence.

---

to words of admonition for each other because living the Christian life does not come naturally to our fallen nature; it is something we learn and put on.

The final lines, which at times in our history were misunderstood and misused, remain difficult in our culture. Derived from Stoic philosophy, they follow a Greek approach to family and marital relationships that is alien to us. But Paul is stressing mutuality between family members: children must "obey," but parents must not "provoke" and cause their children to lose hope. All is to be "done in the Lord" which means that obedience and submission

should never become oppressive or demeaning. "Love" brings its own requirements to a relationship and demands mutual submission from those who love each other. While it might be easy to see why some find this text troublesome, it is even easier to see why mutual love expresses the heart of the Gospel: Bear with one another, forgive "as the Lord has forgiven you," "put on" love. Families living by those standards will thrive in the Lord.

GOSPEL | There is an odd tension in this passage that wrestles between presenting Jesus as (1) a pious

Jewish youth who observes the Law and submits to the authority of his parents and (2) a self-assured young man who rather ominously suggests that his heavenly Father has a stronger claim upon him than the flesh and blood parents who breathlessly seek and find him in the Temple.

The details of this unique story, told only by Luke, are fascinating and revealing. The family has honored its religious duty to make a pilgrimage to Jerusalem for the annual Passover festival. Jesus is twelve, nearly a man in that culture, but also very much in the care of his parents. Remaining behind is clearly a choice Jesus makes

This scene is a flash-forward into his future, but his parents can't possibly know this and marvel along with the elders.

Consider the likely tone of Mary's voice: anger, disappointment, hurt, relief?

Jesus acknowledges no responsibility for her distress; instead he assumes the role of teacher even with his mother.

Don't rush this final section; all the information is important: Jesus obediently returned home, Mary held many things in her heart, Jesus advances toward his destiny.

After three days they **found** him in the **temple,**
   sitting in the **midst** of the **teachers,**
   listening to them and **asking** them **questions,**
   and **all** who **heard** him were **astounded**
   at his **understanding** and his **answers.**
When his **parents saw** him,
   they were **astonished,**
   and his **mother** said to him,
   "Son, why have you **done** this to **us?**
Your father and **I** have been **looking** for you with **great anxiety."**
And **he** said to **them,**
   "Why were you looking for **me?**
Did you not **know** that I **must** be in **my Father's house?"**
But they did not **understand** what he said to them.
He went **down** with them and came to **Nazareth,**
   and was **obedient** to them;
   and his **mother kept all these things** in her **heart.**
And **Jesus advanced** in **wisdom** and **age** and **favor**
   before **God** and **man.**

THE 4 STEPS OF *LECTIO DIVINA* OR PRAYERFUL READING

1. *Lectio:* Read a Scripture passage aloud slowly. Notice what phrase captures your attention and be attentive to its meaning. Silent pause.

2. *Meditatio:* Read the passage aloud slowly again, reflecting on the passage, allowing God to speak to you through it. Silent pause.

3. *Oratio:* Read it aloud slowly a third time, allowing it to be your prayer or response to God's gift of insight to you. Silent pause.

4. *Contemplatio:* Read it aloud slowly a fourth time, now resting in God's word.

---

without his parents' knowledge. It is a fascinating glimpse into that time and culture to read that, for an entire day, Mary and Joseph were comfortable in the assumption that their son was among relatives in the caravan. When they discover their mistake, they turn back and find him only after a search of "three days." While this detail is a likely anticipation of Jesus' dark sojourn in the tomb, it also suggests the distraught state of the parents when finally they find the boy in the Temple precincts.

The scene of which he is at the center is indeed remarkable: this boy, shy of his bar mitzvah, is nonetheless holding court among the scholars and teachers, astounding them with the insight he manifests, not only in his "questions," but also in his "understanding and his answers." He feels at home; he *is* home and seems as surprised that Joseph and Mary came looking as they are to find he'd stayed behind on purpose. Mary takes the lead and doesn't hide her disappointment and hurt as she asks what almost every mother has asked at some point, "How could you?"

Jesus replies with his own questions that seem to challenge his parents' assumptions about who is parenting whom. Jesus has another Father and his "house" and "work" have already laid claim to Jesus' heart. We sense Jesus has never spoken like this before. Mary and Joseph are left to wonder, as many parents do, about what awaits their remarkable child.

The sober final sentences tell us of Jesus' obedience, his mother's silent, prayerful musings, and of how Jesus, in his hidden, inner life grows into an impressive figure before both "God and man." G.M.

THE OCTAVE DAY OF THE NATIVITY OF THE LORD / SOLEMNITY OF MARY, THE HOLY MOTHER OF GOD

LECTIONARY #18

READING I   Numbers 6:22–27

A reading from the Book of Numbers

The *Lord* said to **Moses**:
　"**Speak** to **Aaron** and his sons and **tell** them:
　This is how you shall **bless** the **Israelites**.
Say to them:
　The Lord **bless** you and **keep** you!
　The Lord let his face **shine** upon
　　you, and be **gracious** to you!
　The Lord look upon you **kindly** and
　　give you **peace**!
So shall they invoke my **name** upon the **Israelites**,
　and I will **bless** them."

As always, take extra time with such a short reading. Don't rush the introduction, and distinguish the Lord, Moses, and Aaron and his sons.

You have two lines to introduce the blessing; take more time with the first line, speak faster on the second, and then slower again on the blessing itself.

Each invocation is a separate petition; don't run them together.

The key word here is "name," not "my." Remember, you are teaching us to pray. Do it prayerfully!

For meditation and context:

TO KEEP IN MIND
Read all three commentaries. Suggestions in each can give you insight into your own passage.

RESPONSORIAL PSALM   Psalm 67:2–3, 5, 6, 8 (2a)

R. May God bless us in his mercy.

May God have pity on us and bless us;
　may he let his face shine upon us.
So may your way be known upon earth;
　among all nations, your salvation.

May the nations be glad and exult
　because you rule the peoples in equity;
　the nations on the earth you guide.

May the peoples praise you, O God;
　may all the peoples praise you!
May God bless us,
　and may all the ends of the earth
　　fear him!

READING I　The Book of Numbers continues the great story of the Exodus journey, beginning with the departure from Sinai and ending with the arrival at the border of the Promised Land. As the book opens, the people prepare to move forward in their desert passage, and the author reviews rules and practices to ensure they maintain the purity of a community dedicated to the Lord.

This passage is commonly called "the priestly blessing," which was to be pronounced at the end of an act of ritual worship. In the Bible, a blessing is understood to transmit a beneficial power to the person or community receiving it. The Lord is the sole source of the blessing and its potency, so it is forever effective, and the blessing becomes effective when accompanied by some act that confirms the blessing. This act of blessing invokes God's name upon the people. In ancient Israel, a name expressed and conveyed the person's character, and so the name of God often represents the actual presence of God. Invoking God's name over the people calls upon the divine source of every blessing to bestow positive power upon them.

READING II　Paul wrote his letter to the Galatians about twenty-five years after the Resurrection. In this still-new Christian movement there were some conflicting interpretations of Christ and what God accomplished through him. In this letter, Paul clarifies his views of Christ in the face of those who opposed his preaching. Points of disagreement included salvation through the Law or through grace in Christ, and whether Gentiles could be included in Israel's final age of salvation.

Paul upholds both the divinity and humanity of Jesus the Messiah: "God sent

Galatians = guh-LAY-shunz

You can add weight to this text by surrounding it with silence. Pause after the salutation, after "Abba, Father," and at each comma in the final sentence.

The parenthetical phrases make important statements about Jesus. Stress them.

Share this truth with gratitude for what the "Son" did for us.

Quicken your pace, then increase your energy, but not your volume, on "Abba, Father" using the same inflection for both words.

Make eye contact as you tell your listeners they are heirs of the promises of God.

READING II   Galatians 4:4–7

A reading from the Letter of Saint Paul to the Galatians

Brothers and sisters:
When the **fullness** of time had **come**, **God** sent his **Son**,
   born of a **woman**, born under the law,
   to **ransom** those under the law,
   so that **we** might receive **adoption** as **sons**.
As **proof** that you are sons,
   God sent the **Spirit** of his **Son** into our **hearts**,
   crying out, "**Abba, Father**!"
So you are no longer a **slave** but a **son**,
   and if a **son** then also an **heir**, through **God**.

Let your tone suggest the haste and excitement of the shepherds.

They are filled with amazement and can't contain their enthusiasm.

A quieter tone tells us Mary is somewhat detached from the shepherd's exhilaration and turns inward to reflect.
The shepherd's joy won't be abated!

Employ slower pacing on this final section. This one sentence focuses us on both Jesus' humanity (circumcision) and his divine origin ("the name given him by the angel").

GOSPEL   Luke 2:16–21

A reading from the holy Gospel according to Luke

The **shepherds** went in **haste** to **Bethlehem** and found **Mary**
   and **Joseph**,
   and the **infant** lying in the **manger**.
When they saw this,
   they made **known** the message
   that had been **told** them about this child.
All who **heard** it were **amazed**
   by what had been **told** them by the **shepherds**.
And **Mary** kept all these things,
   reflecting on them in her **heart**.
Then the **shepherds** returned,
   glorifying and **praising** God
   for all they had **heard** and **seen**,
   just as it had been told to them.

When **eight** days were completed for his **circumcision**,
   he was named **Jesus**, the name given him by the **angel**
   before he was **conceived** in the womb.

his Son, born of a woman." The Christ came to free those bound by the Law of Moses and offer a relationship to God like his own. Through Christ, believers are adopted into God's own family as sons and daughters. As proof of this filial relationship, he points out that Christians participate in the powerful presence of the Crucified and Resurrected Christ, the Spirit, and so with Christ can address God as he did: "Abba, Father!" Further, the adopted sons and daughters of God then also share in Christ's inheritance: the fullness of life of the final age of salvation.

GOSPEL   In this final scene in Luke's account of the annunciation to the shepherds, we see their joyful response to the Good News. They immediately seek out the infant Jesus, telling Mary and Joseph of their revelation from heaven. Mary responds with a Jewish understanding of God's Word; it is to be received even if it cannot be understood in the moment. Then slowly, with time and reflection, the full meaning will unfold. Mary had surrendered to the message of Gabriel in this way, and now she receives confirmation of his words from a most unlikely source:

shepherds, despised as unclean sinners. She continues to hold the words in her heart. Trusting even when she cannot yet fully know, she names her son Jesus, which means "God saves." In time, the meaning of that powerful name and the character of her son as the One in whom God acts to save all humankind, will be revealed to her.

Meanwhile, the shepherds continue to rejoice, praising God. Luke thus raises up a theme he will repeat often: God has come in Jesus to save, first of all, to the lowly, the poor, the outcast, and the despised, including women and sinners. M.F.

THE EPIPHANY OF THE LORD

LECTIONARY #20

READING I Isaiah 60:1–6

A reading from the Book of the Prophet Isaiah

> Rise up in **splendor**, Jerusalem! Your **light** has **come**,
>   the **glory** of the Lord **shines** upon you.
> **See**, **darkness** covers the earth,
>   and thick **clouds** cover the **peoples**;
> but upon **you** the LORD **shines**,
>   and **over** you appears his **glory**.
> **Nations** shall walk by your **light**,
>   and **kings** by your shining radiance.
> Raise your **eyes** and **look** about;
>   they all **gather** and **come** to you:
> your **sons** come from **afar**,
>   and your **daughters** in the arms of their **nurses**.
>
> Then you shall be **radiant** at what you see,
>   your **heart** shall throb and **overflow**,
> for the **riches** of the sea shall be emptied out **before** you,
>   the **wealth** of nations shall be **brought** to you.
> **Caravans** of camels shall **fill** you,
>   **dromedaries** from **Midian** and **Ephah**;
> all from **Sheba** shall come
>   bearing **gold** and **frankincense**,
>   and proclaiming the **praises** of the *LORD*.

Isaiah = ī-ZAY-uh

You are reading poetry that conveys joy enough to celebrate the end of war, the coronation of a king, and the cure of a dread disease.

Each couplet repeats or develops in the second line what was said in the first. This characteristic of biblical poetry adds texture and color. Enjoy the repetitions and increase energy from the first line to the second. Dark and gloom give way to light! Imagine the countless visitors, from paupers to royalty, who have traveled to this land which Isaiah extols.
Isaiah addresses Jerusalem as if it were a person. Let your tone convey that intimacy.

Now, it is we, Christ's Body, who must radiate the light of his glory.

"Dromedaries" are single-humped camels.
Midian = MID-ee-uhn
Ephah = EE-fah
Sheba = SHEE-buh

"Gold and frankincense" will echo again in today's Gospel. The reading ends as it began, praising God.

READING I On this celebration of Christ's manifestation to all the world, the First Reading brims with light, brightness, radiance, and glory. This passage comes from the last section of Isaiah (chapters 56–66), most likely written about the time of Judah's release from exile in Babylon and the return to the Promised Land. The prophet looks forward to the fulfillment of divine promises to re-create the covenant people, the city of Zion, and God's dwelling place among them. Repeatedly, Isaiah stresses that God's act of restoration will be witnessed by foreign nations, who will thus recognize the saving work of the Lord.

Twice in the first two verses of today's reading, Isaiah uses the Hebrew word *kabod*, translated "glory." This significant term indicates an outward manifestation of divine presence, at times nearly equivalent to God himself. The earlier prophet Ezekiel, a Jerusalem priest taken into Babylon with the first wave of exiles, saw a vision of the glory of the Lord leaving the Temple (Ezekiel 10), a certain sign that Judah's final desolation had begun. Isaiah now announces that not only will the Lord's people return to their land, but more importantly, the "glory" of God will again dwell in their midst in a new Temple, in a new Jerusalem. The prophet further proclaims that the radiance of the Lord's saving act will be the marvel of other nations and their rulers. The Lord will again gather together a scattered people, drawing those from foreign lands to praise the God of Israel.

READING II Though commonly called "Ephesians," important early manuscripts of this Pauline letter do not carry that designation. The letter does

For meditation and context:

TO KEEP IN MIND

Sense lines: Scripture in this book is arranged (as in the Lectionary) in sense lines, one idea per line. Typically at least a slight pause should follow each line, but good reading requires you to recognize the need for other pauses within lines.

RESPONSORIAL PSALM   Psalm 72:1–2, 7–8, 10–11, 12–13 (11)

R. Lord, every nation on earth will adore you.

O God, with your judgment endow the king,
  and with your justice, the king's son;
he shall govern your people with justice
  and your afflicted ones with judgment.

Justice shall flower in his days,
  and profound peace, till the moon be no
    more.
May he rule from sea to sea,
  and from the River to the ends of the earth.

The kings of Tarshish and the Isles shall
    offer gifts;
  the kings of Arabia and Seba shall bring
    tribute.
All kings shall pay him homage,
  all nations shall serve him.

For he shall rescue the poor when he cries out,
  and the afflicted when he has no one to
    help him.
He shall have pity for the lowly and the poor;
  the lives of the poor he shall save.

READING II   Ephesians 3:2–3a, 5–6

A reading from the Letter of Saint Paul to the Ephesians

The language here is somewhat obscure. Paul is declaring that he was given a special "revelation," but what that is won't be shared until the end of the text.

Brothers and sisters:
You have heard of the **stewardship** of God's **grace**
  that was **given** to me for your **benefit**,
  namely, that the **mystery** was made **known** to me by **revelation**.

What was revealed to Paul was also kept hidden from former generations.
Stress the role of the Spirit in enlightening the "apostles and prophets."

It was not made known to people in **other** generations
  as it has **now** been revealed
  to his holy **apostles** and **prophets** by the **Spirit**:

Here we have the truth formerly hidden but now revealed! You tell us four things: Gentiles are "coheirs," "members," and "copartners," and it's the "gospel" that makes that possible.

that the **Gentiles** are **coheirs**, **members** of the same **body**,
  and **copartners** in the promise in Christ **Jesus** through
    the **gospel**.

GOSPEL   Matthew 2:1–12

A reading from the holy Gospel according to Matthew

This is a suspenseful story of menace averted through God's providence.
Don't rush the important details that provide the story's context.

When **Jesus** was born in **Bethlehem** of **Judea**,
  in the days of King **Herod**,
  behold, **magi** from the **east** arrived in **Jerusalem**, saying,
"Where is the newborn **king** of the **Jews**?

They've traveled far based solely on the testimony of a star.

not focus on a specific community, but on the unity of the entire Church, hence many scholars believe that it was written for circulation among a number of churches in Asia Minor. It is uncertain whether Paul himself authored the letter, but it clearly expresses the perspective of Paul, Apostle to the Gentiles. Here the writer stresses that the new Israel of the new age of salvation embraces both Jews and Gentiles. This insight, a gift of grace for the good of the entire Church, reveals the "mystery" of the Gospel of Christ. In New Testament usage, the Greek word, *mysterion,* points to much

more than something difficult to understand. The "mystery" encompasses God's plan of salvation, ultimately revealed through Jesus Christ. The author emphasizes several times that this mystery cannot be perceived by human effort, but only through divine revelation. In this passage, Ephesians strongly emphasizes that God's plan reaches completion in one united Body of Christ on earth, in which Jews and Gentiles equally participate in the culmination of God's plan for human salvation.

GOSPEL   Matthew, a Jew who came to faith in Jesus as Messiah, addressed a primarily Jewish Christian community that also seemed open to a Gentile mission. He frequently uses quotations or allusions to the Old Testament to illustrate for his audience how Jesus "fulfills" or brings these Scriptures to completion. This technique is particularly evident in his infancy narrative.

While many have debated the exact character of the magi, what is more important is that they come "from the east," indicating that they are Gentiles. In Matthew,

We saw his **star** at its **rising**
    and have **come** to do him **homage**."
When King Herod **heard** this,
    he was greatly **troubled**,
    and all **Jerusalem** with him.
Assembling all the chief **priests** and the **scribes** of the people,
    he **inquired** of them where the Christ was to be **born**.
They said to him, "In **Bethlehem** of **Judea**,
    for **thus** it has been written through the **prophet**:
        *And **you**, Bethlehem, land of **Judah**,*
            *are by no means **least** among the rulers of Judah;*
        *since from you shall come a **ruler**,*
            *who is to **shepherd** my people Israel*."
Then Herod called the magi **secretly**
    and **ascertained** from them the **time** of the star's appearance.
He sent them to **Bethlehem** and said,
    "**Go** and search **diligently** for the child.
When you have **found** him, bring me **word**,
    that I **too** may go and **do** him **homage**."
After their **audience** with the king they **set** out.
And **behold**, the **star** that they had seen at its rising
        preceded them,
    until it came and **stopped** over the place where the **child** was.
They were **overjoyed** at seeing the star,
    and on entering the **house**
    they saw the **child** with **Mary** his **mother**.
They **prostrated** themselves and did him **homage**.
Then they opened their **treasures**
    and **offered** him gifts of **gold**, **frankincense**, and **myrrh**.
And having been **warned** in a **dream** not to **return** to Herod,
    they **departed** for their country by another **way**.

Herod's fear soon turns to threat.

"And all Jerusalem with him": Does the city sense the upheaval Jesus will bring?

Is this the voice of an authority simply sharing expertise, or of a devout believer speaking with reverence?

Let your tone convey the conspiratorial plans Herod is brewing.

Herod laces his poison with honey.

The "star" brings comfort and reassurance.

Note, they enter a "house" not a cave or stable. The child is not mentioned without his mother.
First they pay him homage on their knees, then by opening their "treasures." Don't rush the naming of the three precious gifts.

Let your tone suggest the ominous nature of the dream that warned them.

these foreigners are the first to pay homage to the infant "king of the Jews." Like most in the ancient world, the magi understood the appearance of a great star to signal a ruler's birth; the evangelist also alludes to Balaam's oracle that "A star shall advance from Jacob" (Numbers 24:17). Giving a reason for the child's birth in tiny Bethlehem, Matthew quotes Micah 5:2, which states that Israel's messianic ruler will come from this town of David's birth. Reference to one who is to "shepherd" Israel may be a further allusion to the shepherd-king, David, and to Ezekiel 34:15, in which God promises that in the coming age of salvation, "I myself will pasture my sheep."

King Herod's instruction to the magi is in fact a ruse to discover the child so that Herod can destroy him. Appointed by Rome to rule the province of Judea, Herod received the title, "King of the Jews," and he was ruthless toward any possible rival. The guiding star leads the magi to the infant and his mother, and these Gentiles from a far country prostrate themselves before the true King of the Jews, Jesus the Messiah. Warned in a dream to ignore Herod's request, the magi foil his plan. Matthew makes apparent that God, not Rome, has designated Israel's true Messiah-King, and that though he first appears among the Jews, Gentiles also welcome the revelation of their true ruler. M.F.

THE BAPTISM OF THE LORD

LECTIONARY #21

Isaiah = Ī-ZAY-uh

READING I   Isaiah 40:1–5, 9–11

A reading from the Book of the Prophet Isaiah

Begin as instructed: with tenderness and comfort!

> **Comfort**, give **comfort** to my **people**,
>   says your God.
> Speak **tenderly** to Jerusalem, and **proclaim** to her
>   that her **service** is at an **end**,
>   her **guilt** is **expiated**;

Speak as if to wrongdoers who can't believe their crimes have been expunged.

> **indeed**, she has **received** from the **hand** of the LORD
>   **double** for all her **sins**.

> A **voice** cries out:
> In the desert **prepare** the **way** of the LORD!
>   Make **straight** in the wasteland a **highway** for our **God**!

This section calls for greater intensity. The prophet speaks God's command that we clear the clutter and throw open the doors of our hearts!

> **Every valley** shall be **filled** in,
>   **every mountain** and **hill** shall be **made low**;
> the **rugged land** shall be made a **plain**,
>   the **rough country**, a **broad valley**.

Keep in mind these are metaphors—images of the terrain in our hearts that must be cleared.

Paint clearly this ideal picture of what will be when our will and God's are one.

> **Then** the **glory** of the LORD shall be **revealed**,
>   and **all people** shall see it **together**;
>   for the **mouth** of the LORD has **spoken**.

"Zion . . . Jerusalem" are just another way of addressing your own assembly.

> Go **up** on to a **high** mountain,
>   **Zion**, **herald** of glad **tidings**;
> **cry out** at the **top** of your **voice**,
>   **Jerusalem**, **herald** of good **news**!

Today options are given for the readings. Contact your parish staff to learn which readings will be used.

The Baptism of the Lord continues the theme of *epiphany*. God is *manifest* in the incarnate Christ at the Jordan as he is manifest in the manger and to the magi.

READING I   **Isaiah 40.** While Israel's exile in Babylon ended more than two millennia ago, its spiritual significance is never exhausted because it speaks to the condition of the human heart that so regularly wanders from its God, languishes in self-imposed exile, and when it hears the promise of redemption, must choose whether to heed or to ignore it. Isaiah is speaking comforting words to exiles longing for liberation; but all we know from this text is that the prophet spoke on God's behalf. Whether the people listened, whether their souls were soothed and spirits lifted we do not know.

Two details in this text relate to today's liturgy. First, the prophet crying in the desert closely resembles John the Baptist, who baptizes Jesus in today's Gospel. Second, the hope and joyous expectation the prophet arouses as he speaks of God coming with "power" to restore Israel call to mind the strong yet gentle messiah, an expectation fulfilled in the one whom John baptizes today.

You have many cues for effective proclamation in the text: "Comfort . . . *comfort* to my people . . . . Speak *tenderly*"; ignore those cues and you'll contradict Isaiah as well as disappoint your assembly. "A voice cries out" is another cue that calls for energy and conviction: in

42

You must speak these lines from the depth of your own conviction that God is indeed a God of mercy and redemption!

Though shepherds live a hard and rugged life, their lambs and sheep survive only because of their care and even tenderness.

Fear not to cry out
 and **say** to the cities of **Judah**:
  Here is your **God**!
Here comes with **power**
 the Lord **GOD**,
  who **rules** by his **strong arm**;
here is his **reward** with him,
 his **recompense** before him.
Like a **shepherd** he **feeds** his **flock**;
 in his **arms** he **gathers** the **lambs**,
carrying them in his **bosom**,
 and **leading** the **ewes** with **care**.

Or:

READING I   Isaiah 42:1–4, 6–7

Isaiah = ī-ZAY-uh

The Lord's proud voice introduces the servant. Speak these lines as a blessing that will become a self-fulfilling prophecy.

He won't be like the prophets of old who often made a spectacle of themselves.

His ministry will incarnate gentleness and compassion. "Reed" and "wick" are metaphors for the bruised and faint-hearted among us.

Note the shift to speaking to the servant rather than about him. Imagine speaking these encouraging words to a young person in need of reassurance.

A reading from the Book of the Prophet Isaiah

Thus says the LORD:
Here is my **servant** whom I **uphold**,
 my **chosen one** with whom I am **pleased**,
upon whom I have put my **spirit**;
 he shall bring forth **justice** to the **nations**,
not **crying out**, not **shouting**,
 not making his **voice heard** in the street.
A **bruised reed** he shall not **break**,
 and a **smoldering wick** he shall **not quench**,
until he establishes **justice** on the **earth**;
 the **coastlands** will wait for his **teaching**.

I, the LORD, have called **you** for the victory **of justice**,
 I have grasped **you** by the **hand**; »

the deserts of our lives, we too are to clear the way for God to come and overwhelm us with his glory. "Cry out at the top of your voice" tells you that fainthearted proclamation will not serve this text or the God who inspired it, for this God of power is also a kind shepherd who leads lambs to safety.

Isaiah 42. In this first of Isaiah's four Songs of the Suffering Servant, God's own voice raises joyous expectation about the "servant" who walks in the Spirit of God, brings justice to the nations, and will minister among the people without harming even the most vulnerable. His manner

won't draw attention to itself, nor will he run roughshod over those who get in his way, treating them like collateral damage. Ancient prophets might roam the streets shouting their message, but this servant won't cry out; his service is characterized by compassion and mercy. A "smoldering wick" is one cut too short or leaning that burns too close to the wax, so its flame is small, dim, and easily extinguished. But even these souls too weak to glow with faith's light he will keep from going out.

The "suffering servant" is God's "chosen one" who will endure much sorrow,

ridicule, and pain in the service of the Lord. That title may refer to Israel as a nation, the prophet Isaiah, or perhaps the future Messiah, but juxtaposed with today's Gospel the Church reads this text in the light of Christ's own ministry and identifies this "servant" with Jesus the Lord.

The servant is sent to embolden the downtrodden and enflame those whose spirits have been overwhelmed by life's trials. His mandate to open the eyes of the blind and free prisoners resembles the words Jesus quotes in the Nazareth synagogue to describe his own ministry. This

I formed you, and **set you**
    as a **covenant** of the **people**,
    a **light** for the **nations**,
to **open** the **eyes** of the **blind**,
    to **bring out prisoners** from **confinement**,
    and from the **dungeon**, those who live in **darkness**.

It is God's grace working through the servant that will cause such transformative effects.

For meditation and context:

> **TO KEEP IN MIND**
> Proclaiming the **words of the prophets** requires intensity and urgency. With equal passion, they spoke threat and consolation, indictment and forgiveness. You must do the same for the chosen people you call "parish."

RESPONSORIAL PSALM   Psalm 104:1b–2, 3–4, 24–25, 27–28, 29–30 (1)

R. O bless the Lord, my soul.

O LORD, my God, you are great indeed!
    You are clothed with majesty and glory,
robed in light as with a cloak.
    You have spread out the heavens like
        a tent-cloth.

You have constructed your palace upon
        the waters.
    You make the clouds your chariot;
you travel on the wings of the wind.
    You make the winds your messengers,
and flaming fire your ministers.

How manifold are your works, O LORD!
    In wisdom you have wrought them all—
the earth is full of your creatures;
    the sea also, great and wide,
in which are schools without number
    of living things both small and great.

They look to you to give them food in
        due time.
    When you give it to them, they gather it;
when you open your hand, they are filled
    with good things.

If you take away their breath, they perish
    and return to the dust.
    When you send forth your spirit,
        they are created,
and you renew the face of the earth.

Or:

RESPONSORIAL PSALM   Psalm 29:1–2, 3–4, 3, 9–10 (11b)

For meditation and context:

R. The Lord will bless his people with peace.

Give to the LORD, you sons of God,
    give to the LORD glory and praise,
give to the LORD the glory due his name;
    adore the LORD in holy attire.

The voice of the LORD is over the waters,
    the LORD, over vast waters.
The voice of the LORD is mighty;
    the voice of the LORD is majestic.

The God of glory thunders,
    and in his temple all say, "Glory!"
The LORD is enthroned above the flood;
    the LORD is enthroned as king forever.

---

mandate comes directly from God and it propels the servant toward a ministry of liberation and healing. From the beginning of the text we hear the same parental voice that will speak on Jordan's shore in today's Gospel story. Speak the lines with pride, but not over the achievements the servant will accrue; rather, over his singular commitment to the will of God.

READING II **Titus.** The baptismal reference in this passage and its focus on the "appearance" of God's "grace" and "glory" evoke the manifestation of

Christ that this feast celebrates. Through our Baptism, Christ first came into our lives and became the driving force that configures us to the will of the living God. Baptism, we are taught, initiates a lifelong "training" for a life in the Spirit and cleanses us of those "godless ways and worldly desires" that impede growth in the Lord.

We're also reminded that we live in a middle time between Christ's first coming and his return. While that unique moment may be millennia away, it must also be a present reality we never forget or ignore. It should condition each day of our lives,

committing us to living so as to be ready to greet him whenever he might appear.

This time of waiting is not to be marked by fear, but by gratitude. We were initially saved, not because we earned or deserved it, but purely for love's sake! The bath of rebirth opened our hearts to God's Spirit whom God lavishly poured out on us. And now we are "justified" and we are "heirs" in hope to eternal life. While that language is not common to us, it expresses the great and unassailable truth of Christian faith. We belong now to God, who sought us out and made us his own.

READING II   Titus 2:11–14; 3:4–7

A reading from the Letter of Saint Paul to Titus

Beloved:
The **grace** of **God** has **appeared**, **saving all**
   and **training** us to reject **godless** ways
     and **worldly** desires
   and to live **temperately**, **justly** and **devoutly** in **this** age,
   as we **await** the **blessed hope**,
   the **appearance** of the **glory** of our great **God**
   and **savior Jesus Christ**,
   who **gave himself** for **us** to **deliver us** from **all lawlessness**
   and to **cleanse** for **himself** a **people** as his **own**,
   eager to do what is **good**.

   When the **kindness** and **generous love**
     of **God** our **savior appeared**,
   not because of any **righteous deeds** we had done
     but because of his **mercy**,
   he saved us through the **bath** of **rebirth**
     and **renewal** by the **Holy Spirit**,
   whom he **richly poured out** on us
     through **Jesus Christ** our **savior**,
   so that **we** might be **justified** by his **grace**
     and become **heirs** in **hope** of **eternal life**.

Or:

READING II   Acts 10:34–38

A reading from the Acts of the Apostles

Peter proceeded to **speak** to those gathered
   in the house of **Cornelius**, **saying**:
"In **truth**, I see that **God** shows **no partiality**. **»**

Margin notes

Titus = TĪ-tuhs
Beloved = bee-LUHV-uhd
Let the first word set your tone.
The "grace of God" appeared in Christ Jesus.
blessed = BLES-uhd

Be sure to distinguish the sinful ways and the virtues enumerated here. Each is distinct.

Our "blessed hope" is the "appearance" of Christ at his second coming.

Jesus' willing sacrifice is remembered here.

Renew your energy for this section that glows with gratitude.

This point requires extra emphasis: we were saved because of God's "mercy," not because we merited it.

These final lines encapsulate an entire theology of salvation. Through Baptism we received the Spirit and received justification and the promise of eternal life! Slowly progress from one concept to the next.

Remember that Peter is in the home of a Gentile where he has experienced a powerful and unexpected manifestation of the Holy Spirit.

    This entire text consists of only two sentences so we must communicate ideas rather than sentences, for a sentence can contain several equally important ideas. The concepts here are not complicated, but speak slowly and with conviction, reminding us that while the gift of Baptism was freely given, embracing the responsibilities it places upon us is not optional for those who hope to inherit the gift of eternal life.

    Acts. The Baptism of the Lord is one "epiphany" or manifestations of Christ—a step toward his full revelation, to both Jews and Gentiles. The truth prophesied, but often resisted by God's Chosen People, was that salvation would be offered to all lands and nations; God's mercy would extend to the ends of the earth.

    Here, Peter is speaking in the home of the Gentile Cornelius who, with his entire household, and although none of them is baptized, has just experienced a manifestation of the Holy Spirit. This was not supposed to happen, the disciples first thought. Jesus' message was for the Chosen People alone. But God shows otherwise and Peter gets the message. While others will resist his conclusion, he now understands that God really has no favorites and desires the good of all. God accepts all who "fear him and act uprightly," Jew or not, circumcised or not.

    The reason for this is Jesus. Through his ministry, Jesus not only transformed "Judea" but every land and every person privileged to hear the Gospel he preached. Jesus did good for "*all*" who were in need. That he drove out "the devil," who is lord of all this world, also suggests the universality of his mission. Through his Death and Resurrection Jesus broke the devil's hold

Peter has gone through a conversion experience; let us hear that what he's saying is something he never expected to say.

Rather, in **every** nation whoever **fears** him and **acts uprightly**
 is **acceptable** to him.
You know the word that he **sent** to the **Israelites**
 as he proclaimed **peace** through **Jesus Christ**, who is **Lord** of **all**,
 what has **happened all over Judea**,
 beginning in **Galilee** after the **baptism**
 that John **preached**,
 how God **anointed Jesus** of **Nazareth**
 with the **Holy Spirit** and **power**.

Paint these scenes of Jesus' ministry with vivid energy.

He went about doing **good**
 and **healing all** those **oppressed** by the **devil**,
 for **God** was **with him**."

Jesus conquered the prince of this world, therefore the whole world belongs to him.

GOSPEL   Luke 3:15–16, 21–22

A reading from the holy Gospel according to Luke

The people were **filled** with **expectation**,
 and **all** were **asking** in their **hearts**
 whether **John** might be the **Christ**.
John **answered** them all, saying,
 "I am **baptizing** you with **water**,
 but **one mightier** than I is coming.
I am **not worthy** to **loosen** the **thongs** of his **sandals**.
He will **baptize** you with the **Holy Spirit** and **fire**."

You begin in the middle, so don't rush the mention of the people's suspicions about John.

John speaks with deliberate intent to dispose of the people's misguided speculation.

Even without knowing who the Christ will be, John intuits the nature of his God-given ministry.

"And was praying" is a significant detail that must be heard. Pause first, then share that information.

The real, not metaphoric, nature of this event is highlighted by the word "bodily."

beloved = bee-LUHV-uhd

In Matthew the voice addresses the crowd, but here we have an intimate moment between Father and Son. Consider an encouraging and gentle tone for the divine voice.

After **all** the **people** had been **baptized**
 and **Jesus also** had been **baptized** and was **praying**,
 heaven was **opened** and the Holy Spirit
  descended upon him
 in **bodily form** like a **dove**.
And a **voice** came from **heaven**,
 "**You** are my beloved **Son**;
 with **you** I am well **pleased**."

---

on all people; thus all people can now reap the abundant harvest of grace.

 GOSPEL The remarkable relationship between Jesus and his cousin rests at the center of this brief Gospel text. John has so impressed the people with his teaching, his austere lifestyle, his preaching truth to power, that a profound question has been planted in their hearts: could this be the Messiah? Several pretenders had tried to claim the messianic mantle, and each was eventually exposed. But John is different. He makes no

claims about himself, he challenges people in every corner of society to live with integrity, and, unlike the priests, he derives no direct benefit from his ministry. Scholars generally believe that Jesus may have been a follower of his eccentric cousin who engaged, before him, in a ministry of baptism for the forgiveness of sins.

Despite all this, John has no delusions about himself and quickly acts to dispel any misunderstandings. With striking humility, he points to one who will be greater and mightier than he. We don't know if he's yet begun to wonder if this relative and former

disciple might be the one. It would take rare and generous vision to perceive truth under such circumstances.

But Luke relies less on John's testimony and more on the divine speaker who thunders from the sky. Despite John's protests, Jesus has asked to be baptized. After the baptism, as Jesus is immersed in deep communion with the Father, the heavens open and the Spirit descends upon him. The revelation of God in Christ takes a major step forward as the heavenly voice announces Jesus' divine sonship and God's favor. G.M.

SECOND SUNDAY IN ORDINARY TIME

LECTIONARY #66

READING I   Isaiah 62:1–5

Isaiah = ī-ZAY-uh

Declare newness and joy from the first lines!

The sound of the words is as important as the words themselves. Make this announcement personal, intended for each member of your assembly.

When an idea is stated twice ("silent"/quiet," "crown"/ "diadem") greater energy goes to the second term. That's what we call "build."

Again, the key is to make this a personal message directed at your listeners. It is a message for both the nation and the individual.

Slow down and soften your tone for this very intimate imagery. Convey the love, not just the words.

A reading from the Book of the Prophet Isaiah

For **Zion's sake** I will **not** be **silent**,
    for **Jerusalem's sake** I will **not be quiet**,
until her **vindication shines** forth like the **dawn**
    and her **victory** like a **burning torch**.

Nations shall **behold** your **vindication**,
    and all the **kings** your **glory**;
you shall be **called** by a **new name**
    pronounced by the **mouth** of the L ord.
You shall be a **glorious crown** in the **hand** of the L ord,
    a **royal diadem** held by your **God**.
No more shall people call you **"Forsaken,"**
    or your land **"Desolate,"**
but you shall be called **"My Delight,"**
    and your land **"Espoused."**
For the L ord **delights** in you
    and makes your land his **spouse**.
As a **young man marries a virgin**,
    your **Builder** shall **marry you**;
and as a **bridegroom rejoices** in his **bride**
    so shall your **God rejoice** in **you**.

READING I Repetition gives power to poetry. *Useless* repetition we call "redundant." But in poetry, repetition serves a *useful* purpose, deepening our experience of the idea or emotion the author is trying to convey. This text employs *synonymous parallelism*, a technique by which *two* parallel images express a *single* idea, like the two opening lines. Don't think, "I just said that," when you read the second line. Instead, use the new image to *emphasize* what you just said, and thus intensify your impact on the listener.

No longer languishing in exile, Israel basks in the mercy of the Lord. Her sin of idolatry is behind her and God speaks to her like a lover longing for his beloved. Though originally addressed to the Chosen People after the trauma of exile, these words convey a much larger message that extends to all people for all time. They name a reality known to us all: bad times don't last forever; "vindication" and "glory" follow times of hardship, even those we brought upon ourselves, because God is never stingy with mercy.

Though its marriage imagery links this text to today's Gospel, both passages speak of something more than weddings; God's ability to take a painful past and turn it into a glorious future, to transform lack into abundance—those are the real messages here. Knowing that no matter what we've done, God can remake and rename us is transformative.

Imagine a father's wedding toast and the energy and momentum it would develop as he looks on the bride and groom and paints with words the future he envisions for them: that's the energy that

For meditation and context:

RESPONSORIAL PSALM   Psalm 96:1–2, 2–3, 7–8, 9–10 (3)

R. Proclaim his marvelous deeds to all the nations.

Sing to the LORD a new song;
  sing to the LORD, all you lands.
Sing to the LORD; bless his name.

Announce his salvation, day after day.
Tell his glory among the nations;
  among all peoples, his wondrous deeds.

Give to the LORD, you families of nations,
  give to the LORD glory and praise;
  give to the LORD the glory due his name!

Worship the LORD in holy attire.
  Tremble before him, all the earth;
Say among the nations: The LORD is king.
  He governs the peoples with equity.

TO KEEP IN MIND

Pace: The rate at which you read is influenced by the size of your church, the size of the congregation, and the complexity of the text. As each increases, rate decreases.

READING II   1 Corinthians 12:4–11

A reading from the first Letter of Saint Paul to the Corinthians

Brothers and sisters:
There are **different** kinds of **spiritual gifts** but the **same Spirit**;
  there are **different** forms of **service** but the **same Lord**;
  there are **different workings** but the **same God**
  who **produces all** of them in **everyone**.
To **each** individual the **manifestation** of the **Spirit**
  is **given** for some **benefit**.
To **one** is given through the **Spirit** the expression of **wisdom**;
  to **another**, the expression of **knowledge** according
    to the **same Spirit**;
  to another, **faith** by the same **Spirit**;
  to another, **gifts** of **healing** by the **one Spirit**;
  to another, mighty **deeds**;
  to another, **prophecy**;
  to another, **discernment** of **spirits**;
  to another, **varieties** of **tongues**;
  to another, **interpretation** of **tongues**.
But **one** and **the same Spirit** produces **all** of these,
  distributing them **individually** to **each person** as **he wishes**.

Corinthians = kohr-IN-thee-uhnz

The salutation helps set the conciliatory tone of Paul's teaching.

Be aware of the reasons for sharing this teaching: to foster appreciation of each other's gifts and to heal division.

This summary sentence ends the opening section. Speak it with authority. Then elaborate with what follows.

In the listing of gifts, you need not emphasize "another" each time it recurs. However, the new gift named in each line must be stressed.

Speak each "gift" as a treasure that adds to the community's storehouse of grace. Don't rush the naming of gifts, but varying your pace can be helpful.

Pause before this important closing summary. Speak with awareness of Paul's authority to share this instruction.

---

pervades these lines. You must persuade, through the joy *you* clearly feel, that because God is in charge, hope and joy are not only possible but assured.

| READING II | As a family can lose its center and splinter, so some of the Christians in Corinth began to lose their way. Among those who had who viewed Paul as their spiritual father, disagreements abounded, even at this early stage of Christian life: over sacrificing to idols, issues of sexual morality, and perhaps most divisive of all, the role of various char-

ismatic gifts, like prophecy and speaking in tongues. While they had learned from Paul that the Holy Spirit endows the community with many gifts, all important and necessary, some members turned these very gifts into sources of competition and pride.

From across the sea, Paul writes his spiritual children to restore peace and right teaching. He reminds them that their gifts come from God for the good of all, not for the glory of the one who is the conduit of God's grace. He also reemphasizes the value of each gift and the community's *need* for a variety of charisms. His listing of

the gifts is not in rank order; quite the contrary. His intent is to persuade the dissenting members that every gift is necessary, for it contributes to the health of the body of Christ, which in their dissension they had been tearing apart. That charismatic gifts of prayer ("tongues [and] . . . interpretation of tongues") would be valued above charity to the poor was shocking to Paul. So he hammers two great truths: all the gifts are from the same Spirit so they're equally valuable; each person has something to offer, which makes him or her an indispensable member of the body.

GOSPEL   John 2:1–11

A reading from the holy Gospel according to John

Speak these details with energy.

There was a **wedding** at **Cana** in **Galilee**,
   and the **mother** of **Jesus** was there.

Mention of Jesus signals this will be no ordinary wedding feast.

Jesus and his **disciples** were **also** invited to the wedding.
When the **wine** ran **short**,
   the **mother** of **Jesus** said to him,
   "They have no **wine**."

Mary's tone suggests her concern and her expectations.

And **Jesus** said to her,
   "**Woman**, how does **your** concern affect **me**?

"Woman" is in no way disrespectful.

My **hour** has **not yet come**."
His mother said to the **servers**,
   "**Do whatever** he **tells** you."

Mary does not hear a "no" in his response. Her words contain a deeper level of meaning.

Now there were **six** stone **water** jars there for Jewish
      ceremonial **washings**,
   each holding **twenty** to **thirty gallons**.
Jesus **told** them,
   "**Fill** the jars with **water**."
So they **filled** them to the **brim**.
Then he told them,

Move briskly through this narration and speak with an upbeat tone.

   "**Draw** some out **now** and **take** it to the **headwaiter**."
So they **took** it.
And when the **headwaiter tasted** the **water** that had become **wine**,
   without knowing where it **came** from
   —although the **servers** who had **drawn** the water **knew**—,

Imagine the headwaiter drawing the groom aside for this hushed dialogue.

   the **headwaiter** called the **bridegroom** and said to him,
   "**Everyone** serves **good wine first**,
   and **then** when **people** have **drunk freely**, an **inferior** one;
   but **you** have **kept** the **good wine** until **now**."

A "sign" designates something that has greater witness value than Jesus' various miracles.
The belief of the disciples is a key outcome of this unique event.

Jesus did this as the **beginning** of his **signs** at **Cana** in **Galilee**
   and so **revealed** his **glory**,
   and his **disciples began** to **believe** in him.

GOSPEL   Although the Lectionary reading omits it, John opens this passage with the phrase, "On the third day." That cryptic designation, which both evokes the "first day" and the "Resurrection," signals that we should expect the unexpected, and we're not disappointed. We trust Jesus and his friends were not the reason for the wine running out, but Mary takes the matter to her son, who seems reluctant to inaugurate his messianic mission. Only twice does Jesus address his mother as "woman": here at the start of his ministry and from the Cross on Calvary when it ends. We can't determine whether Mary's request changed Jesus' mind about when to initiate his public ministry, but Mary doesn't hear a "no" in his response and boldly instructs the waiters to heed his instructions.

From Mary we may see a desire to spare the groom's family, responsible for providing wine, of this unique embarrassment, but this evangelist author always has a theological lesson behind the plot. When Jesus uses the water reserved for Jewish ceremonial washings to transform into wine, he shifts focus from ritual to the heart of the Gospel. Rather than slavish ties to rubrics of the old Law, Jesus introduces his disciples to the superabundance of God's grace and the freedom of God's Kingdom.

Mary's words to the servants—the last she speaks in all the Gospel accounts—echo down the centuries as sage advice to all who would be her son's disciples. This event transcends Jesus' other miracles to become one of John's seven *signs* that manifest the glory and power of Jesus and God's Kingdom. G.M.

THIRD SUNDAY IN ORDINARY TIME

LECTIONARY #69

READING I   Nehemiah 8:2–4a, 5–6, 8–10

A reading from the Book of Nehemiah

Nehemiah = nee-huh-MĪ-uh

Begin with a solemn tone that suggests the exalted nature of this event.

Don't rush the details of how long he read and how many people listened.

The repetition of
"men . . . women . . . children" is a mantra-like formula that lends greater dignity to the telling.

Ezra the **priest** brought the **law** before the **assembly**,
  which consisted of **men**, **women**,
  and those **children** old enough to **understand**.
Standing at one end of the open place that was before
    the Water **Gate**,
  he **read** out of the **book** from **daybreak** till **midday**,
  in the **presence** of the **men**, the **women**,
  and those **children** old enough to **understand**;
  and **all** the **people listened attentively** to the **book** of **the law**.
Ezra the scribe stood on a wooden **platform**
  that had been made for the occasion.
He **opened** the **scroll**
  so that **all** the **people** might **see** it
  —for he was standing **higher up** than any of the people—;
  and, as he **opened** it, **all** the people **rose**.
Ezra blessed the LORD, the **great God**,
  and **all** the **people**, their **hands** raised **high**, **answered**,
  "**Amen, amen!**"
Then they **bowed** down and **prostrated** themselves
    before the LORD,
  their faces to the **ground**.
Ezra read **plainly** from the **book** of the law of **God**,
  interpreting it so that **all** could **understand** what was **read**.

The "book" becomes a sacrament of God's presence and love, so the people show great reverence.
Take time with the telling of this sacred moment.

READING I The Book of Nehemiah narrates events following the Babylonian exile, when the Persian conquerors of Babylon are inspired by God to assist in the restoration of Israel. In successive waves, they send Jewish leaders back to the land of Judah, both to rebuild the city and Temple and to restore worship and fidelity to God's Law.

The first wave saw the rebuilding of the Temple under Zerubbabel and 40,000 former exiles sent to do the work. Next, Ezra is sent back to instruct in God's Law those who lack knowledge of it. Finally, Nehemiah is sent to rebuild Jerusalem's walls. Following completion of the walls and discovery of the list of workers who rebuilt the Temple with Zerubbabel, the people request that Ezra read for them the scroll of the Law of Moses. That history and context are unique and far removed from your experience. On the other hand, what's narrated here speaks powerfully of your ministry as proclaimer of the Word and of the assembly's role as those who receive it.

The people's request to hear the Law and their response to it speak powerfully of the Jewish nation's understanding of God's Word as a liberating gift that teaches the ways of life and thus saves us from our human instincts for selfishness and self-destruction. In response to their request, Ezra prepares a ritual in which he both reads and *interprets* God's word, which he proclaims from a platform built for the occasion.

Because the vast assembly has opened their hearts in prayer, the Word penetrates them deeply, moving them to tears. Its compelling truth opens their eyes and they realize anew that the Law was given not to condemn but to teach and lead

You are describing a unified experience of proclamation and preaching. "His excellency" = governor.

Then **Nehemiah**, that is, His **Excellency**, and **Ezra**
　　　the **priest-scribe**
　and the **Levites** who were **instructing** the **people**
　said to **all** the **people**:
　"**Today** is **holy** to the Lord your **God**.
Do **not** be **sad**, and do **not weep**"—
　for **all** the **people** were **weeping** as they **heard** the **words**
　　　of the **law**.

Speak these words with compassion, as you might address someone who's apologizing for arriving late to your wedding.

He said further: "**Go**, **eat** rich **foods** and **drink** sweet **drinks**,
　and **allot portions** to those who had **nothing prepared**;
　for **today** is **holy** to our Lord.
Do **not** be **saddened** this **day**,

As always, first believe what you are saying, then proclaim it boldly.

　for **rejoicing** in the Lord must be your **strength!**"

For meditation and context:

RESPONSORIAL PSALM　Psalm 19:8, 9, 10, 15 (see John 6:63c)

R. Your words, Lord, are Spirit and life.

The law of the Lord is perfect,
　refreshing the soul;
the decree of the Lord is trustworthy,
　giving wisdom to the simple.

The precepts of the Lord are right,
　rejoicing the heart;
the command of the Lord is clear,
　enlightening the eye.

The fear of the Lord is pure,
　enduring forever;
the ordinances of the Lord are true,
　all of them just.

Let the words of my mouth and the thought
　of my heart
　find favor before you,
O Lord, my rock and my redeemer.

> **TO KEEP IN MIND**
> **Context:** Who is speaking in this text? What are the circumstances?

READING II　1 Corinthians 12:12–30

A reading from the first Letter of Saint Paul to the Corinthians

Corinthians = kohr-IN-thee-uhnz

Brothers and **sisters**:
As a **body** is **one** though it has **many parts**,
　and **all** the **parts** of the **body**, though **many**, are **one** body,
　so also **Christ**. »

Start slowly using the first sentence to set the stage for the theological point you will make. You're saying: What's true of our bodies is true of Christ and his Body the Church.

---

them. Thus convicted by their own short-comings, they weep. But Ezra and Nehemiah encourage them to take heart. The people's desire for God's Word, the public proclamation, and their eager reception of its message have sanctified the day and made it an occasion of joy and celebration.

Since the text describes the very ritual action you are engaged in as you proclaim, this reading should have special significance for all lectors. In chapter 50:4 of the Book of Isaiah, the prophets says he was sent to "speak to the weary a word that will rouse them." Here we see the Word doing

just that. Every proclamation of God's Word is meant to waken us, stir within us a love of the Lord, and move us to tears of joy—or maybe both.

READING II　The Christian community in Corinth, founded by Paul himself, had become fractured and mired in various controversies. Factions had developed; some felt their God-given gifts were of greater value than those of others, and the single-mindedness of the community was in peril. When word of these troubles reaches Paul as he is traveling, he pens this

letter to his spiritual children. In last week's passage from Corinthians, Paul addressed a controversy over the gifts of the Spirit, reminding them each gift is important and equally necessary.

In today's passage he goes further, talking not about the gifts of the members, but about the members themselves. Paul was writing to citizens of an ancient culture enmeshed in pagan religious practices. He had introduced his converts to a new religion that challenged their old assumptions and called them to a demanding lifestyle. Two thousand years later, Christianity is

Stress the oneness that results from Baptism, which makes our differences less important than unity.

Be aware of the inherent humor in Paul's vivid analogy.

Varying your pace will help hold the listeners' attention. The details of the analogy ("If the ear should say . . . I am not an eye") can be spoken at a faster pace than Paul's points and conclusions: "there are many parts, yet one body . . . . Indeed, the parts of the body . . . . But God has so constructed the body."

Use eye contact to assure your listeners Paul is speaking about them as well.

Here Paul speaks of the "private" parts of the body that we cover with greater care. Don't belabor the point and keep the pace brisk.

Take a breath and renew your energy on this important line. You are reminding us that the seemingly less honorable parts can take on great importance.

This sentence and the next require a slower, more sober tone.

For in **one Spirit** we were **all baptized** into **one body**,
   whether **Jews** or **Greeks**, **slaves** or **free** persons,
   and **we** were **all** given to **drink** of **one Spirit**.

Now the **body** is not a **single part**, but **many**.
If a **foot** should say,
   "**Because I** am **not** a **hand I** do **not belong** to the **body**,"
   it does **not** for this reason **belong any less** to the body.
Or if an **ear** should say,
   "**Because I** am **not** an **eye I** do **not belong** to the **body**,"
   it does **not** for this reason **belong any less** to the body.
If the **whole body** were an **eye**, where would the **hearing** be?
If the **whole body** were **hearing**, where would the **sense**
   of **smell** be?
But as it **is**, **God** placed the **parts**,
   each one of them, in the **body** as he **intended**.
If they were **all one** part, **where** would the **body** be?
But as it **is**, there are **many parts**, yet **one** body.
The **eye** cannot say to the **hand**, "I do not **need** you,"
   nor again the **head** to the **feet**, "**I** do not **need you**."
Indeed, the **parts** of the body that seem to be **weaker**
   are all the more **necessary**,
   and those **parts** of the **body** that we consider less **honorable**
   we surround with **greater honor**,
   and our less **presentable** parts are treated with **greater propriety**,
   whereas our **more** presentable parts do not **need** this.
But **God** has so **constructed** the **body**
   as to give **greater honor** to a part that is **without** it,
   so that there may be **no division** in the body,
   but that the **parts** may have the **same concern** for **one another**.
If **on**e part **suffers**, **all** the parts **suffer** with it;
   if **one** part is **honored**, **all** the parts **share its joy**.

even more fractured than in Paul's day, and even within the Church we spend much time debating differences and judging others whose opinions differ from our own. So, under the Spirit's guidance, Paul addresses his Corinthian disciples and the countless generations since who have manifested the same weaknesses and the same tendency to come unglued.

    Paul invents the image of the community of believers as a "body" comprised of "many parts," and all of them necessary. It's a brilliant metaphor that illustrates the importance of all and the need for each.

Who hasn't been stopped in their tracks by a blister on a toe, or a nasty paper cut? When they're hurting, even these seemingly less significant parts of the body suddenly claim primacy. Paul dives into his analogy with vigor and not without humor. Having asserted our oneness in Baptism, the sacrament that washes away the differences that would divide, he invites us to imagine a haughty "hand" or a presumptuous "eye" speaking condescendingly to the rest of the body. Wise teachers know how to employ wit and humor to disarm the defensive student, and Paul is no excep-

tion. He uses carefully crafted progressive reasoning, worthy of the finest lawyer, to speak of body parts.

    Remember that you are reading an analogy that's meant to teach a lesson. Paul is adverting to common sense, not to lofty, esoteric ideas, so the tone is less formal and more direct, as in a conversation with a co-worker who doesn't understand office dynamics. After the lengthy analogy, Paul reasserts his theological point: together we are Christ's Body; as individuals we are its "parts." Save your lofty tone for that declaration. Then

Now **you** are **Christ's body**, and **individually parts** of it.
Some people **God** has designated in the **church**
    to be, **first**, **apostles**; **second**, **prophets**; **third**, **teachers**;
    then, **mighty deeds**;
    then **gifts** of **healing**, **assistance**, **administration**,
    and **varieties** of **tongues**.
Are **all apostles**? Are **all prophets**? Are **all teachers**?
Do **all** work **mighty deeds**? Do **all** have **gifts** of **healing**?
Do **all** speak in **tongues**? Do **all interpret**?

[Shorter: 1 Corinthians 12:12–14, 27]

GOSPEL Luke 1:1–4, 4:14–21

A reading from the holy Gospel according to Luke

Since **many** have **undertaken** to **compile** a **narrative** of the **events**
    that have been **fulfilled** among us,
    just as those who were **eyewitnesses** from **the beginning**
    and **ministers** of the **word** have **handed them down** to **us**,
    I too have **decided**,
    after **investigating everything** accurately **anew**,
    to **write** it down in an **orderly sequence** for you,
    most **excellent Theophilus**,
    so that you may **realize** the **certainty** of the teachings
    you have received.

Jesus returned **to Galilee** in the **power** of the **Spirit**,
    and **news** of him **spread** throughout the **whole region**.
He **taught** in their **synagogues** and was **praised** by **all**. »

A faster pace is appropriate for this listing of roles, but don't lose a sense of the dignity of these God-given offices.

One idea is communicated through these multiple rhetorical questions. Use a brisk pace, but slow down for the final question and give it a tone of finality.

Luke's prologue is one long sentence comprised of several main and subordinate clauses. Keep in mind where you're headed as you vary your pacing and your emphasis.

Luke's careful research is an important assertion.

Here, the text jumps from chapter 1 to chapter 4 of Luke. Renew your energy as you begin this section and emphasize the influence of the Spirit.

Jesus' initial acclaim and the spread of his fame are important to Luke.

---

remind us of the holy offices and roles God has given some and the equally important roles given to others.

GOSPEL Luke, not an Apostle, but a later disciple of Jesus, undertakes to tell his story and addresses it to "Theophilus," a "friend of God" who may be a contemporary of his or may be every one of us who also longs to hear the words of life he uttered and to experience the deeds of life he performed then and still performs today. In the Gospel's prologue that opens our reading, we learn that "many

have undertaken" to tell this story and that Luke has done due diligence in compiling a narrative that's orderly and accurate.

For Luke, an "accurate" portrayal of events means true to the *experience* of Jesus, so he takes an event that his source, Mark, places at the end of Jesus' ministry and uses it as Jesus' inaugural proclamation of the Good News. Familiar themes in Luke appear right from the start: the spread of Jesus' fame, the role of the Spirit, the fulfillment of prophecy, and great concern for the poor.

The Lectionary's use of this event leaves out its bad ending when Jesus is rejected by his friends and neighbors. Our portion tells only of his proclamation, truncated by Luke, of Isaiah's great prophecy regarding the ministry of the coming Messiah. Boldly, Jesus declares that in him, on that day, Isaiah's prophecy is fulfilled. He will say a good deal more before his words provoke their ire and turn initial approval into hostile rejection. But that's next week's passage. Today we hear and bask in the declaration of God's purposes in Jesus. He is the Anointed One sent to bring "glad

Several significant details here: Nazareth is home for Jesus; he regularly attends synagogue; it's the Sabbath day.

Jesus does not seem to choose the scroll, but he does select the passage.

He came to **Nazareth**, where he had grown **up**,
    and went according to his **custom**
    into the **synagogue** on the **sabbath** day.
He **stood up** to **read** and was handed **a scroll** of the prophet **Isaiah**.
He **unrolled** the **scroll** and found the **passage** where it was **written**:
    *The **Spirit** of the **Lord** is upon me,*
        *because **he** has anointed **me***
        *to bring **glad tidings** to the poor.*
    *He has sent me to proclaim **liberty** to captives*
        *and **recovery** of **sight** to the blind,*
        *to let the **oppressed** go free,*
        *and to proclaim a year **acceptable** to the Lord.*
Rolling up the **scroll**, he handed it back to the attendant
        and sat **down**,
    and the **eyes** of **all** in the **synagogue** looked **intently** at **him**.
He said to them,
    "**Today this** Scripture passage is **fulfilled** in your **hearing**."

Pause before narrating that he rolled up the scroll.

The narrative creates suspense as Jesus sits and all fix their eyes on him waiting for what will happen next. Jesus does not disappoint. Speak his final dialogue as Jesus' effort to make them understand what just happened.

TO KEEP IN MIND
Tell the story: Make the story yours, then share it with your listeners. Use the language; don't throw away any good words. Settings give context; don't rush the description. Characters must be believable; understand their motivation. Dialogue reveals character; distinguish one character from another with your voice.

tidings" not to the power brokers, not to the rich elite, not to the ritually pure, but to the "poor" and the "blind," to those imprisoned by forces outside them or enslaved by those within.

We see Jesus' respect for God's Word as he assumes the role of lector, seeks out the passage to read, then carefully rolls up the scroll again before sitting and declaring its fulfillment. The story requires a tone of authority, for Jesus makes no apology for his assertions. The awe-inspiring aspect of this text is that what happened then happens yet "today" as weekly the words of

Scripture fall upon us and actualize the sacred realities of which they speak. G.M.

FOURTH SUNDAY IN ORDINARY TIME

LECTIONARY #72

READING I   Jeremiah 1:4–5, 17–19

A reading from the Book of the Prophet Jeremiah

The **word** of the Lᴏʀᴅ came to me, saying:
   Before I formed you in the **womb** I **knew you**,
      before you were **born** I **dedicated you**,
      a **prophet** to the **nations** I **appointed** you.

But **do** you **gird** your **loins**;
   stand up and **tell** them
   all that I **command** you.
Be **not crushed** on their account,
   as **though** I would **leave** you **crushed** before **them**;
for it is **I** this **day**
   who have made **you** a **fortified city**,
a **pillar** of **iron**, a **wall** of **brass**,
   against the **whole land**:
against Judah's kings and **princes**,
   against its **priests** and **people**.
They will **fight** against **you** but **not prevail** over you,
   for **I** am **with you** to **deliver** you, says the Lᴏʀᴅ.

Jeremiah = jayr-uh-MĪ-uh

Only the first line is the prophet's. The balance is spoken by the Lord.

Always begin slowly; here it's especially important so these key declarations are clearly heard.

The text jumps ahead to God's "pep-talk." Don't rush, and speak like a teacher, coach, or parent encouraging an insecure youth who faces a great challenge.

"This is what I've done for you," God says. "I've made you like a city with thick walls and strong defenses."

Listed here are all those who will oppose Jeremiah.
Speak this promise with the love of a parent or spouse sending a loved one off to battle.

READING I   In a world that permits the taking of life from the womb, the words God speaks to Jeremiah are especially striking: "in the womb, I *knew* you." Those words suggest much more than God's early selection of Jeremiah as spokesperson "to the nations." It means even more than Jeremiah's being set apart, "dedicated," to the Lord before he was born. Significant as those realities are, they don't compare with being *known* by God and *chosen*. Before God gives Jeremiah any title or task, God already is in *relationship* with him.

God was loving Jeremiah, calling Jeremiah to himself, before the boy was born.

Today's portion from Jeremiah leaves out the boy's protest that he is "too young" to undertake this daunting role. But that dialogue is necessary prologue to the pep talk God gives this young recruit for his elite corps of reluctant prophets. Often, the sign of a true prophet is his or her unwillingness to accept the role because it is a thankless job that brings more suffering and sorrow than reward. Prophets often did suffer greatly, and usually at the hands of their own people.

In response to Jeremiah's hesitancy, God undertakes to reassure and steel him for the task he will surely embrace. Note the strong, almost military language of the text: "gird," "stand," "I command you," "crushed," "fortified city," "pillar of iron, a wall of brass." God speaks as if Jeremiah were being prepared for war. And in a sense, he is. Jeremiah will indeed fight: his own brothers, a faithless priest and false prophet, and Jewish officials. But God's promise that opposition will not destroy him is consistently fulfilled.

For meditation and context:

TO KEEP IN MIND
You'll read more naturally if you read **ideas rather than words**, and if you share **images rather than sentences**.

RESPONSORIAL PSALM   Psalm 71:1–2, 3–4, 5–6, 15, 17 (see 15ab)

R. I will sing of your salvation.

In you, O LORD, I take refuge;
    let me never be put to shame.
In your justice rescue me, and deliver me;
    incline your ear to me, and save me.

Be my rock of refuge,
    a stronghold to give me safety,
    for you are my rock and my fortress.
O my God, rescue me from the hand of the
    wicked.

For you are my hope, O Lord;
    my trust, O God, from my youth.
On you I depend from birth;
    from my mother's womb you are my
    strength.

My mouth shall declare your justice,
    day by day your salvation.
O God, you have taught me from my youth,
    and till the present I proclaim your
    wondrous deeds.

READING II   1 Corinthians 12:31—13:13

A reading from the first Letter of Saint Paul to the Corinthians

Corinthians = kohr-IN-thee-uhnz

From the start, let your tone suggest that this message will be extraordinary.

Pause after "excellent way" to breathe and renew your energy. Then launch into his exhortation.

Because he's speaking in the first person, he can use dismissive language about how these things amount to nothing.

In each successive example the level of excellence grows, and yet it all still amounts to nothing.

This section speaks truth to all our self-delusions, so deliver the lines with authority and conviction.

Brothers and **sisters**:
Strive **eagerly** for the **greatest** spiritual gifts.
But I shall **show** you a **still more excellent** way.

If I speak in **human** and **angelic** tongues,
    but do **not** have **love**,
    I am a resounding **gong** or a clashing **cymbal**.
And if I have the **gift** of **prophecy**,
    and **comprehend all mysteries** and **all knowledge**;
    if I have **all faith** so as to move **mountains**,
    but do **not have love**, I am **nothing**.
If I give away **everything** I **own**,
    and if **I hand** my **body over** so that I may **boast**,
    but do **not have love**, I **gain nothing**.

Love is **patient**, love is **kind**.
It is not **jealous**, it is not **pompous**,
    it is not **inflated**, it is not **rude**,
    it does **not** seek its own **interests**,
    it is not **quick-tempered**, it does not **brood** over **injury**,

The final line offers assurance in the form of an ancient formula that promises faithfulness, "I am with you." That formula became a bedrock, divine promise made to all Israel's prophets and its antecedent was God's unique self-identification to Moses, "I am." Trusting in God puts the impossible within reach. Knowing he is never alone, the prophet confidently faces hostility and peril. Today, remind your assembly that they, too, never walk alone.

READING II   Today's words from Paul are his most poetic and among the most poetic in all of Scripture. They are beloved words, often quoted, proclaimed at weddings and whenever people want to be reminded of our true calling and the true meaning of love.

Paul begins with an exhortation to seek the "greatest spiritual gifts," not just the showy, extraordinary gifts like "tongues" and "interpretation" that had become a source of division among the Corinthians. Without judgment or condescension, Paul alludes to those more sensational gifts and says that without love, those gifts amount to less than soot and ash. Speaking in tongues and uttering prophecies, even exemplary faith and extraordinary generosity, make nothing of us if we lack love.

Paul refuses to trivialize love; he rejects sentimentality and won't resort to stereotypes. And he understands that loving is hard to do. That's why he begins with what love is not. Relationships are difficult to sustain, so he paints no rosy picture of what it means to be in love or stay in love. He acknowledges that jealousy and anger can creep in, that lovers can be "rude" and

it does not **rejoice** over **wrongdoing**
    but **rejoices** with the **truth**.
It **bears all** things, **believes all** things,
    hopes all things, **endures all** things.

Love never fails.
If there are **prophecies**, they will be brought to **nothing**;
    if **tongues**, they will **cease**;
    if **knowledge**, it will be **brought** to **nothing**.
For we **know partially** and we **prophesy partially**,
    but when the **perfect** comes, the **partial** will pass **away**.
When **I** was a **child**, I used to **talk** as a **child**,
    think as a **child**, **reason** as a **child**;
    when I became a **man**, I put **aside childish** things.
At **present** we see **indistinctly**, as in a **mirror**,
    but **then face to face**.
At **present** I know **partially**;
    then I shall know **fully**, as I am **fully known**.
So **faith**, **hope**, **love** remain, these **three**;
    but the **greatest** of these is **love**.

[Shorter: 1 Corinthians 13:4–13]

GOSPEL   Luke 4:21–30

A reading from the holy Gospel according to Luke

Jesus began speaking in the **synagogue**, saying:
    "**Today** this **Scripture** passage is **fulfilled** in your **hearing**."
And **all** spoke **highly** of him
    and were **amazed** at the **gracious** words that came
        from his **mouth**.
They **also asked**, "Isn't this the **son** of **Joseph**?" **»**

Don't shy from these repetitions, but emphasize only the new verb in each phrase.

After slowly asserting that "Love never fails," move quickly through the listing of what will cease.

Prophesy = PROF-uh-sī

Make the case here with energy and brisk pacing.

This is a continuation of the point just made.

Pause before this climactic final line. Establish eye contact and then speak these compelling words with great sincerity.

Since there is no introduction to the scene, let your solemn tone suggest the impression Jesus has made on them.
Contrast the praise in this line with the skepticism implicit in the question that follows.

"pompous," irritable, and resentful. Those are not the ways of love.

Love's "more excellent way" gives life, heals hurts, sustains hopes, and endures slights and trials. Paul is famous for his lists, but this one is different. As you read his words, the love of which you speak is made present in your midst. These words become a sacrament, and they rely on your voice to do their work. Poetry must sound like what it means. So hear and convey the cadences of these lines. Most of all, fix in your minds' eye someone whose heart longs for these healing words, and speak the words for them.

Having made his point, Paul returns to the extraordinary gifts and tells us that in the end they won't matter. His famous words about the ways of a "child" and those of a "man" challenge us to consider whether we linger in youthful ignorance or have progressed to mature insight. Of the three great virtues, he says, only love endures because although faith and hope are the only paths to God, love *is* God.

GOSPEL   Jesus is home, led there by the Spirit, and he's just proclaimed an Isaian text declaring release to prisoners and sight to the blind. But his own neighbors will suffer from a peculiar kind of blindness that afflicts those who have lived alongside the fountain of truth without drinking deep from its refreshing waters. They respond well, glowingly in fact, to his initial utterance. Luke tells us they "were amazed" and commented on his "gracious words." But he also gives us a clue that acquits Jesus of intentionally provoking his neighbors with inflammatory

Sensing the doubt that's welling in their hearts ("Where does this son of Joseph get such wisdom?") Jesus launches into a strong rebuttal.
Capernaum = kuh-PER-nay-*m.

This much-quoted line should not be rushed.

No question that these words of his are provocative. He's challenging Israel's exclusive claim on God.

Jesus never fails to teach; his words are more instruction than indictment.
Zarephath = ZAYR-uh-fath
Sidon = SĪ-duhn
Elisha = ee-LĪ-shuh
Naaman = NAY-uh-muhn

Jesus begins to assert the freedom of God to choose and favor whomever God wills.

They're not only angry, but their righteous anger convinces them the law requires that they destroy this heretic.
Let your confident, serene tone suggest the inner power that enabled him to slice through the crowd unharmed.

TO KEEP IN MIND
The closing: Pause (three beats!) after ending the text. Then, with sustained eye contact, announce from memory, "The word [Gospel] of the Lord." Always pronounce "the" as "thuh" except before words beginning with a vowel, as in "thee Acts of the Apostles." Maintain eye contact while the assembly makes its response.

He said to them, "**Surely** you will quote me this **proverb**,
  '**Physician**, **cure** yourself,' and say,
    'Do **here** in your **native place**
      the things that we **heard** were **done** in **Capernaum**.'"
And he said, "**Amen**, I say to you,
  no **prophet** is **accepted** in his own **native place**.
Indeed, I tell you,
  there were many **widows** in **Israel** in the days of **Elijah**
    when the **sky** was **closed** for **three** and a **half years**
    and a severe **famine** spread over the entire **land**.
It was to **none** of these that **Elijah** was **sent**,
  but only to a widow in **Zarephath** in the land of **Sidon**.
Again, there were **many lepers** in Israel
  during the time of **Elisha** the prophet;
    yet not **one** of them was **cleansed**, but only **Naaman**
      the **Syrian**."
When the people in the **synagogue heard** this,
  they were all **filled** with **fury**.
They **rose** up, **drove** him out of the **town**,
  and **led** him to the **brow** of the **hill**
    on which their town had been **built**,
  to **hurl** him down **headlong**.
But Jesus **passed through** the **midst** of them and **went away**.

---

words about the thick blood of their ancestors running in their own veins.

They also asked, "Isn't this the son of Joseph?" Luke tells us. That's all that Jesus needed to read their hearts. Already some of them are wondering how a hometown boy could be so smart. After all, they've known him and his family. He's been away and now comes home with insight and authority beyond his stature. How could he suggest that Isaiah's words were, in that moment, being fulfilled? Perhaps Luke is preparing us for the inevitable and showing us, through adulation turned to violence,

what will be the pattern of Jesus' ministry. What happens in his hometown will be repeated in Jerusalem.

Because the liberation that Jesus was to bring would not be what his people expected, Jesus already understands that his message will not satisfy many. They seek signs and wonders, but not the truth that bubbles up within him. They're not willing to believe that he could be who he's just suggested that he is. So Jesus confronts them and cites two prophets who, because their message was rejected by their own people, took their ministry to

Gentiles. And like a match tossed among tumbleweeds, Jesus' words ignite their passions and they drive him from their midst. An ancient pattern is repeated and another prophet knows the burden of bearing God's word.

Proclaim Jesus' words with the strong feeling they possess and help us hear the raging animus of the crowd that would tear him to pieces. It's not his hour yet, so Jesus escapes unharmed. But the clock that will strike three on Calvary has already started ticking. G.M.

FIFTH SUNDAY IN ORDINARY TIME

LECTIONARY #75

READING I Isaiah 6:1–2a, 3–8

A reading from the Book of the Prophet Isaiah

In the year **King Uzziah** died,
   I **saw** the **Lord seated** on a **high** and **lofty throne**,
   with the **train** of his **garment filling** the **temple**.
Seraphim were stationed **above**.

They **cried** one to the other,
   "**Holy, holy, holy** is the LORD of hosts!
All the **earth** is **filled** with his **glory**!"
At the **sound** of that cry, the frame of the door **shook**
   and the house was **filled** with **smoke**.

Then I said, "**Woe** is me, I am **doomed**!
For I am a man of **unclean** lips,
   living among a **people** of **unclean lips**;
   yet my **eyes** have **seen** the **King**, the LORD of **hosts**!"
Then one of the **seraphim flew** to me,
   holding an **ember** that he had taken with tongs
     from the **altar**.

He **touched** my **mouth** with it, and said,
   "**See**, now that this has **touched** your **lips**,
   your **wickedness** is **removed**, your **sin purged**."

Then I **heard** the voice of the **Lord** saying,
   "**Whom** shall **I send**? **Who** will **go** for **us**?"
"**Here I** am," I said; "**send me**!"

Margin notes

Isaiah = ī-ZAY-uh

Uzziah = yuh-ZĪ-uh. He reigned fifty-two years during a period of prosperity, but was struck with leprosy for disobeying the Lord. He died in 740 BC.

Remember, you are about to narrate a unique and mystical experience.

Convey the angels' praise with energy and awe. Isaiah is awed and overwhelmed but unable to turn away.

Smoke is a biblical sign of God's presence.

Because humans are unworthy to stand before God, "seeing" God almost certainly ensured death. Isaiah's fear is real.

Let your tone suggest the remarkable nature of this event.

What is the tone of the angel: reassuring, comforting, rousing?

Pause to transition from hearing the angel to hearing God's own voice.

Try for a blend of determination and humility.

READING I Last week we read about the call of the prophet Jeremiah. Today we proclaim a similar text about the call of Isaiah to his prophetic ministry. Last week's first reading that assured Jeremiah of God's support in his difficult ministry was paired with the story of Jesus' rejection by his own townspeople. Today's text, in which Isaiah's fear and sense of unworthiness is overcome by visions of God enthroned in glory, is paired with the story of Jesus' call of the first disciples.

For various reasons, true prophets are typically reluctant to embrace their call.

Jeremiah thought he was too young. Isaiah believes he is unworthy. God intervenes with a powerful vision meant to reassure Isaiah so he can respond without reservation. The experience narrated here is mystical and mysterious, the kind of unique and life-changing event most of us never experience. Yet when we read it, we sense immediately that the Holy One who is totally other is also so gracious and compassionate as to enter lovingly into our lives. That's the challenge of this proclamation: to paint the terrifying yet fascinating nature of this experience of the divine.

The overwhelming aspects of the story are found in the majestic scene of God's presence filling the temple and angels singing God's praise. Earth and heaven meet when the heavenly song shakes the door frame and divine smoke fills the house. Isaiah responds in terror, as aware of his unworthiness as he is of God's glory. But God ministers to Isaiah through the angel who sears his lips with purifying fire. God's announcement to Isaiah is one we all long to hear: your "wickedness" and "sin" are blotted out!

For meditation and context:

RESPONSORIAL PSALM   Psalm 138:1–2, 2–3, 4–5, 7–8 (1c)

R. In the sight of the angels I will sing your praises, Lord.

I will give thanks to you, O LORD, with all
    my heart,
  for you have heard the words of my
    mouth;
  in the presence of the angels I will sing
    your praise;
I will worship at your holy temple
  and give thanks to your name.

Because of your kindness and your truth;
  for you have made great above all things
    your name and your promise.
When I called, you answered me;
  you built up strength within me.

All the kings of the earth shall give thanks
    to you, O LORD,
  when they hear the words of your mouth;
and they shall sing of the ways of the LORD:
  "Great is the glory of the LORD."

Your right hand saves me.
  The LORD will complete what he has done
    for me;
  your kindness, O LORD, endures forever;
    forsake not the work of your hands.

Corinthians = kohr-IN-thee-uhnz

Like Paul's community, yours has need of this reminder of the Gospel they "received" and on which they "stand." Remember, you are reminding them of "good news." Be sure you sound like it.

Nothing is automatic: We are being saved if we practice what we've been taught.

"In vain": let your tone say: You wouldn't be that foolish, would you?

Here is a review of the faith for which many have shed their blood. Make it sound that important.

READING II   1 Corinthians 15:1–11

A reading from the first Letter of Saint Paul to the Corinthians

I am **reminding** you, **brothers** and **sisters**,
  of the **gospel** I preached to you,
  which you indeed **received** and in which you also **stand**.
Through it you are also being **saved**,
  if you hold **fast** to the word I **preached** to you,
  unless you **believed** in **vain**.
For I **handed** on to you as of **first importance** what I also **received**:
  that **Christ died** for our **sins** in accordance with the **Scriptures**;
  that he was **buried**;
  that he was **raised** on the **third day**
    in accordance with the **Scriptures**;
  that he **appeared** to **Cephas**, then to the **Twelve**.
After that, Christ appeared to **more**
    than **five hundred** brothers **at once**,
  most of whom are still **living**,
  though some have **fallen asleep**.

This listing of appearances is meant to impress his readers.

Despite God's desire and remarkable initiative, Isaiah remains free to choose his response. God asks of him what he asks in every age and of every person: "Whom shall I send?" Isaiah's response, made possible not only by what God did but by his courage and generosity (or perhaps made possible not only by his courage and generosity but by what God did!), rings with daring and humility: "Send me!"

READING II The complex man we know as Paul comes to the fore today offering words of encouragement about what we've been taught, what we've embraced, and what has taken root in our hearts. He asserts the Resurrection of Jesus and alludes to numerous post-Resurrection appearances, which were all appropriate and predictable, all that is, except for the appearance to Paul himself. Paul was unique among the band of disciples: he never knew the Lord, he appropriated to himself the title of "Apostle," and he undertook to evangelize Gentiles instead of his fellow Jews. But none of that compares to the greatest difference between Paul and his brother Christians: he had sought to destroy the faith and put Christians to death. Thus he considers himself as born "abnormally" and remains keenly aware of God's mercy in his life. Paul is complex because he can assert both that he snuck in the back door *and* deserves a place at the table.

Because abuses have crept into the lives of his Corinthian converts, Paul writes to reassert the faith they had so eagerly given themselves to when he first preached it to them. So he does in this text what you do when you proclaim—reviews

After that he appeared to **James**,
  then to **all the apostles**.
Last of all, as to one born **abnormally**,
  he appeared to **me**.
For **I** am the **least** of the apostles,
  not fit to be **called** an apostle,
  because I **persecuted** the church of **God**.
But by the **grace** of God **I am** what **I am**,
  and his **grace** to me has not been **ineffective**.
Indeed, I have **toiled harder** than **all** of them;
  not I, however, but the **grace** of **God** that is **with** me.
Therefore, whether it be **I** or **they**,
  so we **preach** and so you **believed**.

[Shorter: 1 Corinthians 15:3–8, 11]

GOSPEL   Luke 5:1–11

A reading from the holy Gospel according to Luke

While the **crowd** was **pressing** in on **Jesus** and **listening**
  to the **word** of **God**,
he was standing by the **Lake** of **Gennesaret**.
He saw two **boats** there alongside the **lake**;
  the **fishermen** had **disembarked** and were **washing** their **nets**.
Getting into one of the boats, the one belonging to **Simon**,
  he asked him to **put out** a **short distance** from the **shore**.
Then he sat **down** and **taught** the crowds from the boat.
After he had finished **speaking**, he said to **Simon**,
  "Put out into **deep water** and **lower** your nets for a **catch**."
Simon said in reply,
  "**Master**, we have worked hard **all night** and have
    caught **nothing**,
  but at **your** command I **will** lower the nets." »

Sidenotes (left/margin):

Paul has already dealt with the incongruity of his past behavior. His focus is not on guilt but on saving grace.

Paul is saying: I'm "unfit" and yet "I am what I am," an Apostle. The reality of what he is is greater than his unworthiness.

This might sound like arrogance, were Paul not aware that even his labor was made possible by God's mercy.

The fishermen are just ending their night of work; Jesus is beginning his day of preaching.

Washing of nets signals the night's work is over.

Jesus does not ask to enter Peter's boat.

The metaphoric meaning of "into the deep" is significant.

His tone suggests, "I'm only doing this because you're asking."

---

the content of the faith and the solid reasons Christians have for clinging to it.

Unless you embraced the faith "in vain," he says, you are being saved by it even now; that is, if you haven't *lost* what you received! The basics of the early kerygma (proclamation of the Gospel) are all here: Jesus died, was buried, rose again, and appeared to many. It is this bedrock belief in the Resurrection, supported by the testimony of many reliable eyewitnesses, which brought non believers into the Church, so Paul's evidence requires your stress and conviction.

His discourse about his status as backdoor Apostle should not be dismissed as just an effort to overcome insecurity. Paul's true purpose is to manifest the goodness and mercy of God, who took an enemy of Christ like him and turned him into a champion of the Gospel through whose efforts they have come to believe.

GOSPEL   In both the Isaiah text and this Gospel, we hear a call story in which the one called is painfully aware of sinfulness. In each, the one called is overwhelmed, almost speechless, certain only he's unworthy to be in the presence of the divine power that's calling and healing him at the same time. But that's where the similarities end. While Isaiah's call fits the Oz-like stereotype of a majestic temple and a God of terrifying presence, in Luke, Peter encounters God on a seashore, tired from the night's labor and smelling of fish. What could be more appropriate in a post-Incarnation world? God has come to live among us, so we meet him mostly on the streets and in the alleys of our lives. It's when our

Narrate in the awed tone of the fishermen who are struggling with this unexpected haul.

Pause here to suggest the dawning awareness on Peter that he's in the presence of great mystery.

As he will many more times, Jesus has overturned their expectations and they're completely off-balance.

"Do not be afraid" is Jesus' formula for reassurance (especially following the Resurrection.)

Pause first, then announce their decision in a tone that suggests nothing will ever be the same for them.

TO KEEP IN MIND

Pray the Scriptures: Make reading these Scriptures a part of your prayer life every week, and especially during the week prior to the liturgy in which you will proclaim.

When they had done this, they caught a **great number** of fish
and their **nets** were **tearing.**
They signaled to their **partners** in the **other** boat
to come to **help** them.
They came and **filled both** boats
so that the boats were in danger of **sinking.**
When **Simon Peter** saw this, he **fell** at the **knees** of Jesus and said,
"**Depart** from me, **Lord,** for I am a **sinful man.**"
For **astonishment** at the catch of fish they had made **seized** him
and **all** those with him,
and **likewise James** and **John,** the sons of **Zebedee,**
who were **partners** of **Simon.**
Jesus said to **Simon,** "Do **not** be **afraid;**
from now on you will be **catching men.**"
When they brought their **boats** to the **shore,**
they **left everything** and **followed him.**

---

hands are full of fish, or diapers, or smartphones that Jesus comes and asks us to reorder our priorities and follow him.

Jesus enters uninvited into Peter's life. The crew is resigned to their night of empty nets, but Jesus steps into their boat and makes of it his pulpit. Then, not satisfied with this indulgence, Jesus asks the tired men to "go out into the deep." It's not reliance on Jesus' gifts as fisherman that forces Peter to comply. Expecting nothing, and perhaps sensing an alluring mystery within him, he acknowledges Jesus as "master" and accedes to the request.

It's the abundance of the Kingdom that soon overwhelms him, as later it will the crowds when bread and fish are multiplied. Peter is a businessman; he has "partners" in the other boat. These professionals know where and when to fish. Has Jesus shown them up? Hardly. Peter's reaction shows awareness that no mere man could have done what Jesus did. Like Isaiah, he knows he's in the presence of the holy, and he's terrified. Divinity and humanity are not supposed to mix. So he says, "Depart from me." Then gives the reason why: "I am a sinful man."

Peter doesn't yet know Jesus came specifically to draw *near* to "sinful man": after all, how could such goodness come near such imperfection as was their daily life? So Jesus speaks his saving refrain: Don't be afraid. With that injunction and the promise to catch people instead of fish, Jesus changes everything for them. They put away their boats, and their former lives, and set out to follow him. G.M.

ASH WEDNESDAY

LECTIONARY #219

READING I   Joel 2:12–18

This text consists of three sections that differ in mood. In this first section, the prophet passionately urges the people to abandon sin and return to God.

In the first lines we hear God's own voice urging remorse and conversion.

"Rend your hearts . . ." asks that they convert inwardly, not simply make an outward show.

Any possible threat is balanced with images of God's patience and mercy.

Your optimistic tone should suggest the possibility of God "relenting" and abandoning threats of punishment.

Here begins section two—it is a rousing call to every member of the community to ask forgiveness!

The tempo and energy are swelling as you give one command after another.

Neither children, nor infants, nor honeymooners are exempt from this call to repentance.

A reading from the Book of the Prophet Joel

Even **now**, says the LORD,
 return to me with your **whole heart**,
 with **fasting**, and **weeping**, and **mourning**;
Rend your hearts, not your **garments**,
 and **return** to the LORD, your God.
For **gracious** and **merciful** is he,
 slow to anger, **rich** in kindness,
 and **relenting** in **punishment**.
Perhaps he will **again** relent
 and leave behind him a **blessing**,
Offerings and **libations**
 for the LORD, your God.

Blow the **trumpet** in Zion!
 proclaim a **fast**,
 call an **assembly**;
Gather the people,
 notify the congregation;
Assemble the elders,
 gather the **children**
 and the **infants** at the **breast**;
Let the bridegroom **quit** his room
 and the bride her **chamber**. »

READING I Although the Book of Joel lacks a clear historical reference, internal clues indicate 450–400 BC as a likely time for this prophecy. Jerusalem and the Temple had been rebuilt, but now about a century after their return from exile in Babylon, the old issues had resurfaced: priestly corruption, social injustice, and lax observance of the Torah. The Old Testament books of Nehemiah and Ezra speak of their attempts at religious reform, probably near the time of Joel's prophecy. Although these reformers called for public recommitment to the way of life described in God's Torah, response was sometimes tepid at best.

At the time of Joel's prophecy in today's reading, too little winter rain, extreme summer heat, and locusts threatened Judah's grain fields, orchards, and vineyards. For the prophet, this agricultural disaster represented the voice of the Lord, calling the people to return to living as they had promised in the Sinai Covenant. In the Old Testament, "return" normally translates the Hebrew *shuv*, which literally means "to turn." Most often used to indicate a plea for true repentance or conversion, *shuv* calls for a complete reversal of attitude and behavior. The prophets often express the meaning of "turn/return" as a dual action: "Turn from evil and do good." Since in biblical times the heart represented the core of a human being, Joel demands that Judah's return to covenant faithfulness must originate in the heart. He emphasizes the point again by proclaiming that the ritual action of tearing garments as an outward sign of repentance remains meaningless without tearing open one's heart to God.

Using a familiar Old Testament phrase, Joel reminds the people that when they

Even the priests should be moved to tears.

You are telling the people what to say, not actually saying it, so don't overdramatize this line.

The people ask God not to make them a laughingstock among the nations.

The final lines comprise the third section, which is God's response to the people's repentance. Read slowly and imagine God quietly surveying the assembled masses bowed in humble contrition.

For meditation and context:

TO KEEP IN MIND
Proclaiming the **words of the prophets** requires intensity and urgency. With equal passion, they spoke threat and consolation, indictment and forgiveness. You must do the same for the chosen people you call "parish."

Corinthians = kohr-IN-thee-uhnz

Like Joel, Paul makes a passionate plea to get our attention and produce a response. Through our words and our lives, we are to call others to reconciliation with God.

Christ not only became like the rest of sinful humanity, he assumed all human sin upon himself.

Between the **porch** and the **altar**
    let the **priests**, the **ministers** of the LORD, **weep**,
And say, "**Spare**, O LORD, your people,
    and make not your **heritage** a **reproach**,
    with the nations **ruling** over them!
Why should they say among the peoples,
    '**Where** is their God?' "

Then the LORD was stirred to **concern** for his land
    and took **pity** on his people.

RESPONSORIAL PSALM   Psalm 51:3–4, 5–6ab, 12–13, 14 and 17 (3a)

R. Be merciful, O Lord, for we have sinned.

Have mercy on me, O God, in your goodness;
    in the greatness of your compassion wipe
        out my offense.
Thoroughly wash me from my guilt
    and of my sin cleanse me.

For I acknowledge my offense,
    and my sin is before me always:
"Against you only have I sinned,
    and done what is evil in your sight."

A clean heart create for me, O God,
    and a steadfast spirit renew within me.
Cast me not out from your presence,
    and your Holy Spirit take not from me.

Give me back the joy of your salvation,
    and a willing spirit sustain in me.
O Lord, open my lips,
    and my mouth shall proclaim your praise.

READING II   2 Corinthians 5:20—6:2

A reading from the second Letter of Saint Paul to the Corinthians

Brothers and sisters:
We are **ambassadors** for **Christ**,
    as if **God** were **appealing** through us.
We **implore** you on behalf of Christ,
    be **reconciled** to God.
For **our** sake he made him to **be** sin who did not **know** sin,
    so that we might become the **righteousness** of God in him.

repent sincerely, God always responds with gracious mercy and steadfast love. To this God all Judah must turn, fasting, praying, and offering proper sacrifices in the rebuilt Temple. All are called to repent—young and old, priest and people, and no other activity is more important. Joel ends his cry for repentance with a direct appeal to the Lord: if not for the people's true repentance, at least spare them for the sake of your own good name! If Israel truly belongs to God, then let God demonstrate that reality to other nations by sparing the Chosen People from disaster.

READING II   Second Corinthians is Paul's most personal letter, in which he passionately speaks of both the Good News of God in Christ and his own ministry of that Gospel, with its joys and sorrows. He uses "we" to refer to himself, possibly including his co-ministers of the Gospel. Immediately before today's reading, Paul speaks of human re-creation and reconciliation with God, brought about through the Death and Resurrection of Christ. Those who are united to Christ are then called to carry on his work of recon-

ciliation, so that God continues this saving work through Christian believers.

Paul continues to emphasize that God's work in Christ can and must continue through the Church, with Christian believers as conduits of ongoing reconciliation. Seeking to communicate the mystery of Christ, Paul uses a difficult and much-discussed statement. He describes Christ as "made . . . to be sin" so that believers might "become the righteousness of God." Many scholars view this as Paul's way of saying that as Christ took on full humanity, humankind, transformed in Christ, becomes

Worse than never knowing Christ is knowing him in vain; that is, seeing the light and then turning from it.

Working **together**, then,
> we **appeal** to you not to receive the grace of God in **vain**.
For he says:

> In an **acceptable** time I **heard** you,
> > and on the day of **salvation** I **helped** you.

This is Lent's main message: now—today—is the time to respond, before it's too late!

Behold, **now** is a very **acceptable** time;
> behold, **now** is the **day** of **salvation**.

GOSPEL   Matthew 6:1–6, 16–18

A reading from the holy Gospel according to Matthew

The contrast throughout is between the "hypocrites" and "you." When a discipline is introduced (giving alms, praying, fasting) stress the verb, but on the second mention of the discipline, stress the pronoun "you." Our good deeds are to be for the glory of God, not for our own glorification.

Jesus said to his **disciples**:
> "Take care not to perform righteous deeds
> in order that people may **see** them;
> > **otherwise**, you will have no **recompense** from your heavenly
> > > Father.
When you give **alms**,
> do not blow a **trumpet** before you,
> as the **hypocrites** do in the **synagogues** and in the **streets**
> to win the praise of **others**.

Don't over-articulate these instructions as if they were complicated directives. It's a simple message spoken in common sense tones.

Amen, I say to you,
> they have **received** their reward.
But when **you** give alms,
> do not let your **left** hand know what your **right** is doing,
> so that your almsgiving may be **secret**.

There is a dismissive tone in these judgments pronounced by Jesus.

And your **Father** who sees in secret will **repay** you. **»**

You will repeat this line twice more; employ the same inflection each time.

---

who Christ is: the "righteousness of God" incarnate. By living in communities of reconciliation, the Church embodies the God revealed in Christ. The Apostle urges the church at Corinth, which had struggled with various divisions, to waste no time in responding to God's gift of reconciliation. Referring to Isaiah, Paul indicates that the salvation the prophet proclaimed to God's people of old has now arrived in Christ; the time to accept and respond to that grace is also now.

GOSPEL   The Gospel Reading appears in the Sermon on the Mount, three chapters (5–7) that form the first of five teaching discourses of Jesus in Matthew. Since Matthew addresses a community of mostly Jewish Christians, near the beginning of this section Jesus stresses that he does not intend to abolish the Laws and Scriptures of Judaism, but to bring them to completion. In this way, Matthew reassures his hearers that their former way of life is not obliterated, but reaches its fullest development through Jesus, the Christ who inaugurates God's

final rule. More than any other, this evangelist presents Jesus as teacher and true interpreter of God's teaching given through Moses. The Torah or Law given on Mt. Sinai taught a way of righteousness, right relationships among God, human beings, and created things. In the Kingdom of God, righteousness as taught by Jesus surpasses that of previous interpreters of the Law (see Matthew 5:17–20).

In today's passage from the Sermon on the Mount, Jesus focuses on Judaism's three major spiritual disciplines: almsgiving, prayer, and fasting. These practices,

This is less mockery of their puffed-up arrogance and more a deep sense of regret over their self-deception.

Jesus' tone is rather ominous.

Even fasting must be done in joy, if we understand rightly why and for whom we're doing it.

Again, regret over their blindness.

Speak with an energetic, upbeat tone.

Go slowly on this final iteration; your punctuated stress should signal that this line culminates the reading.

TO KEEP IN MIND

Openings and Closings: differ in tone from the Scripture and require pauses, after the opening dialogue and before the closing dialogue. These formulas are prescribed, so don't vary the wording.

"When **you** pray,
do not be like the **hypocrites**,
who love to stand and pray in the **synagogues** and on **street** corners
so that others may **see** them.
Amen, I say to you,
they have **received** their reward.
But when **you** pray, go to your **inner** room,
close the door, and pray to your Father in **secret**.
And your Father who **sees** in secret will **repay** you.

"When **you** fast,
do not look **gloomy** like the **hypocrites**.
They **neglect** their appearance,
so that they may **appear** to others to be **fasting**.
Amen, I say to you, they have **received** their reward.
But when **you** fast,
anoint your head and **wash** your face,
so that you may not **appear** to be fasting,
except to your **Father** who is **hidden**.
And your Father who **sees** what is hidden will **repay** you."

---

especially associated with times of repentance (see Reading 1), were continued by the Christian community. Almsgiving, usually in the form of aid to the needy, was meant to arise from righteousness, which understood wealth as God's gift to be shared with the poor who also had a claim on divine bounty. Prayer, in both individual and communal forms, constituted proper response to divine initiative in rescuing and forming God's people. Judaism practiced fasting, a common religious practice in the ancient world, especially at times of mourning and repentance.

In his teaching on each of these religious disciplines, Jesus repeatedly counsels his followers to purify inner intentions and motivations. He warns his disciples against performing good actions as "hypocrites." (The Greek word *hypocrites* originally described an actor, and so came to designate someone who pretended to be something he or she was not.) True righteousness, Jesus emphasizes, springs from the heart; no one should perform religious practices in order to convince people (oneself included) of a genuine right relationship to God, others, and material things. Under

God's final rule, authentic righteousness springs from the heart, a heart responding to God. M.F.

FIRST SUNDAY OF LENT

LECTIONARY #24

READING I   Deuteronomy 26:4–10

Deuteronomy = doo-ter-AH-nuh-mee; dyoo-ter-AH-nuh-mee

A reading from the Book of Deuteronomy

Name Moses with the tone of dignity and respect his memory should evoke.

This procedural detail is followed by a dignified and lofty recitation of a very sacred history.
A shift in tone should signal the quote within a quote.
Aramean = ayr-uh-MEE-uhn

Recalling the enslavement in Egypt requires a different tone.

Let gratitude fill your voice as you describe God's mercy.

Part of what's remembered is God's awesome power and dignity.

"Milk and honey" does not imply a lack of hardship.

Moses spoke to the **people**, saying:
  "The **priest** shall **receive** the **basket** from **you**
  and shall set it in front of the **altar** of the Lord, your **God**.
Then you shall **declare** before the Lord, your **God**,
  'My **father** was a **wandering Aramean**
  who went down to **Egypt** with a **small household**
  and **lived** there as an **alien**.
But **there** he became **a nation**
  great, **strong**, and **numerous**.
When the **Egyptians maltreated** and **oppressed** us,
  imposing **hard labor upon** us,
  we **cried** to the Lord, the **God** of our **fathers**,
  and he **heard** our **cry**
  and **saw** our **affliction**, our **toil**, and our **oppression**.
He brought us **out** of **Egypt**
  with his **strong hand** and **outstretched arm**,
  with **terrifying power**, with **signs** and **wonders**;
  and **bringing** us into **this country**,
  he gave us **this land flowing** with **milk** and **honey**. »

READING I For the author of Deuteronomy, memory and identity are one. There can be no such thing as a "people" without "memory," because it is not enough to share a common history; that history must be kept alive in memory if it is to bind us together and fuel our imaginations. The same holds true for religion: it is our memory of what God has done for us in history that draws us together to celebrate and enables us to live in confidence and hope. That's precisely what is taking place in the ritual narrated in today's text.

The ritual action and speech described by Moses in this ancient text, one of the oldest in the Bible, are to be repeated by each successive generation. Those repeating the speech will remember those who lived the story it describes and thus experience a kinship that makes them one with those ancestors. In the ritual telling of a story, the tellers, the hearers, and the players in the original event are brought together in the present. The event that calls for the retelling of Israel's history in today's text is an annual harvest festival. The "basket" offered to the priest contains the ritual offering of "firstfruits" reserved for God as a sign of gratitude. It is in that spirit of gratitude that this story must be told.

This is a story of wandering ancestors whom God took and turned into a great nation. It is a story of deliverance from the clutches of Egypt's pharaoh, and a story of delivery to the borders of a rich new land "flowing" with abundance. The firstfruits offered to the Lord are given in *gratitude* for this history and for the good that God pours into their daily lives.

"'Therefore, I have now brought . . .'" should communicate deep gratitude for God's mercy. The quote within a quote ends here.

This is both a liturgical instruction and a call to humble worship.

Therefore, I have now brought you **the firstfruits**
  of the **products** of the **soil**
  which **you**, O LORD, have **given** me.'
And having **set** them before the LORD, your **God**,
  you shall **bow down** in his **presence**."

RESPONSORIAL PSALM   Psalm 91:1–2, 10–11, 12–13, 14–15 (see 15b)

R. Be with me, Lord, when I am in trouble.

You who dwell in the shelter of the Most
  High,
  who abide in the shadow of the Almighty,
say to the LORD, "My refuge and fortress,
  my God in whom I trust."

No evil shall befall you,
  nor affliction come near your tent,
for to his angels he has given command
    about you,
  that they guard you in all your ways.

Upon their hands they shall bear you up,
  lest you dash your foot against a stone.
You shall tread upon the asp and the viper;
  you shall trample down the lion and the
    dragon.

Because he clings to me, I will deliver him;
  I will set him on high because he
    acknowledges my name.
He shall call upon me, and I will answer
  him;
  I will be with him in distress;
I will deliver him and glorify him.

> **TO KEEP IN MIND**
> **Dialogue** imitates real conversation, so it often moves faster than the rest of the passage.

READING II   Romans 10:8–13

A reading from the Letter of Saint Paul to the Romans

Brothers and **sisters**:
What does **Scripture** say?
The **word** *is* **near** *you,*
  in your **mouth** *and in your* **heart**
  —**that** is, the **word of faith** that we **preach**—,
  for, if you **confess** with your **mouth** that Jesus is **Lord**
  and **believe** in your **heart** that **God raised** him from the **dead**,
  you **will** be **saved**.

Begin with energy and ask the question with an upbeat tone.

Here is the answer to Paul's own question. Announce it with joy.

Slow down to enunciate Paul's careful reasoning.

Be sure to contrast "believes" / "confesses" and "mouth" / "heart."

Let your telling suggest your own connection with this story of our faith ancestors. There is pride in Abraham, pain in the oppression of Egypt, delight in the gift of the Promised Land. As we begin Lent, we see in Christ the same deliverance prefigured here, for we escape the exile of sin through the saving waters of Baptism and dwell in the Promised Land of grace.

 READING II Here is a joyful declaration of faith, couched within a didactic piece of instruction, which should appeal to both sides of the brain because it uses both logic and the compelling influence of the heart to make its case. Paul is both teacher and evangelist, so he knows the need to appeal both to the head and to the heart. Some people respond better to the tugging of their hearts, but others need persuasive logic to draw them into the circle of faith.

Paul argues the need to both "believe" and "confess" in order to be saved. It is not enough to assent in our hearts to the mysteries of Christ; we must also be willing to *proclaim* those truths. And proclamation is not a rote recitation of facts, it is a declaration that we have committed our lives to those truths, that we will live them with integrity, that we will not be satisfied with lip service and would even give our lives for them.

Belief in Christ, Paul tells us, is transformative. It not only eliminates the distinctions between "Jew and Greek" but it also changes us from mere speakers to committed doers of God's Word. When what we speak with our lips and believe in our hearts turns into concrete action on behalf of others for the sake of Christ, then our salvation is manifest.

Declare this scriptural truth with conviction.

The generosity of God is emphasized in these closing lines. That Christ's salvation is available to all is a revolutionary declaration. Proclaim it persuasively.

For one **believes** with the **heart** and so is **justified**,
   and one **confesses** with the **mouth** and so is **saved**.
For the **Scripture** says,
   No one who **believes in him** *will be put to* **shame**.
For there is **no distinction** between **Jew** and **Greek**;
   the **same Lord** is **Lord** of **all**,
   enriching **all** who **call upon** him.
For **"everyone** who **calls** on the **name** of the **Lord will be saved."**

GOSPEL   Luke 4:1–13

A reading from the holy Gospel according to Luke

Let the *end* of the opening sentence suggest your tone; the seriousness of what's to unfold should be heard from the start.

Without overdoing it, keep in mind the physical state of Jesus and the barren desert context.
Avoid a stereotypical devil who drips with malice. Instead, make him reasonable, intelligent, and persuasive.

Don't rush any of Jesus' replies. Suggest, instead, his effort to come to his conclusions.

Don't fail to convey the settings to which the devil transports Jesus.

Pause after the devil's dialogue before giving Jesus' response.

Filled with the **Holy Spirit**, **Jesus returned** from the **Jordan**
   and was **led** by the **Spirit** into the **desert** for **forty days**,
   to be **tempted** by the **devil**.
He ate **nothing** during those days,
   and when they were **over** he was **hungry**.
The **devil said** to him,
"If you are the **Son** of **God**,
   command this **stone** to become **bread**."
Jesus answered him,
"It is **written**, *One does* **not live** *on* **bread alone**."
Then he took him up and **showed** him
   all the **kingdoms** of the **world** in a **single instant**.
The **devil said** to him,
"I shall **give** to you **all** this **power** and **glory**;
   for it has been **handed over to** me,
   and **I** may give it to **whomever** I **wish**.
All this will be **yours**, **if** you **worship** me."
Jesus said to him in **reply**,
"It is **written**:
   You shall **worship** *the* **Lord**, *your* **God**,
     and **him alone** *shall you* **serve**." »

From Paul's opening question to his closing declaration, joy pervades the text. Paul says that the "*word*," that is, the Truth and the Person of Christ, is "*near you*," that is, around us and within us. There is no denying it because, through Baptism, that "*word*" has become part of our very life. Paul's logical argumentation leads to his final, evangelistic proclamation that "'everyone who calls on . . . the Lord will be saved.'"

GOSPEL | Under the influence of the Spirit that descended upon him at his baptism, Jesus enters the desert to fast and pray and ends up doing battle with the "the devil." Here, Jesus as a faithful son is contrasted with the infidelity of Israel, the often faithless and disobedient son. The importance of this story is demonstrated by its presence in all three synoptics. Luke's and Matthew's telling greatly resemble each other, the main difference being the different ordering of the temptations. By putting last the temptation to put God to the test, Luke makes a strong theo-

logical point about our relationship with God and about Jesus' identity. Israel proved its infidelity by repeatedly putting God to the test. When the Lucan Jesus quotes Deuteronomy's admonition against testing God, "God" refers not only to God the Father but to Jesus as God's own Son. The devil is toying with someone much greater than he admits.

In the desert, a biblically consistent place of trial, the hungry Jesus now needs food for his body after having received food for his soul for the past forty days. Jesus is strengthened in his relationship with the

The heart of this temptation is "*If you are the Son of God . . .*" He wants to sow doubt in Jesus' heart that would require a sign from God to dispel.

Is Jesus informing the devil or warning him?

The end is not the end, for the devil will seek another opportunity.

TO KEEP IN MIND

Tell the story: Make the story yours, then share it with your listeners. Use the language; don't throw away any good words. Settings give context; don't rush the description. Characters must be believable; understand their motivation. Dialogue reveals character; distinguish one character from another with your voice.

Then he led him to **Jerusalem**,
   made him **stand** on the **parapet** of the **temple**, and said to him,
"**If you** are the **Son** of **God**,
   throw yourself down from here, for it is **written**:
      *He will command his **angels** concerning you, to **guard** you,*
   and:
      *With their **hands** they will **support** you,*
      *lest you dash your **foot** against a **stone**.*"
Jesus said to him in **reply**,
   "It **also** says,
   *You **shall not put** the **Lord**, your **God**, to the **test**.*"
When the **devil** had finished **every temptation**,
   he **departed** from him **for a time**.

Father, but physically weakened by his fasting, and the opportunistic devil seeks to take advantage. He offers subtle temptations, the only kind that could possibly ensnare Jesus. He invites Jesus to make his mission about himself, to enjoy the riches of this world rather than the rewards (and painful challenges!) of total fidelity to God's will. Jesus' repellent is God's Word, as articulated in Deuteronomy (8:3; 6:13; 6:16). With the Word of God, Jesus both rids himself of the tempter and steels himself for the hard work ahead. He reminds himself of what sustains us, who is worthy of our worship, and what is the nature of faith. Notice that the devil offers no rebuttals, only new temptations.

Relate the story without overdramatizing the narrative nor rushing through it as if it were merely a moralistic parable. Tell it as Luke does, presenting a real man engaged in genuine struggle with a real adversary. If Jesus was like us in all things but sin, then his experience of temptation must have been akin to ours. His responses, therefore, are not facile, but the culmination of an inward effort to resist becoming the easy messiah that the conniving devil proposes. Jesus wins the match, but only for a time; the devil will return. In the meantime, even he has deepened his understanding about sonship and true worship. G.M.

SECOND SUNDAY OF LENT

LECTIONARY #27

READING I   Genesis 15:5–12, 17–18

A reading from the Book of Genesis

The **Lord God** took **Abram outside** and said,
  "Look up at the **sky** and count the **stars**, if you can.
Just so," he added, "shall **your descendants** be."
Abram put his **faith** in the Lord,
  who **credited** it to him as an act of **righteousness**.

He then **said** to him,
  "I am the Lord who brought you from **Ur** of the **Chaldeans**
  to give you **this land** as a **possession**."
"O **Lord God**," he asked,
  "how am I to **know** that I shall **possess** it?"
He **answered** him,
  "Bring me a three-year-old **heifer**, a three-year-old **she-goat**,
  a three-year-old **ram**, a **turtledove**, and a young **pigeon**."
Abram brought him **all** these, **split** them in **two**,
  and placed **each half opposite** the **other**;
  but the **birds** he did **not** cut up.
Birds of prey **swooped** down on the carcasses,
  but Abram **stayed** with them.
As the **sun** was about to **set**, a **trance** fell upon Abram,
  and a **deep**, **terrifying darkness enveloped** him.

When the sun had **set** and it was **dark**,
  there **appeared** a **smoking fire pot** and a **flaming torch**,
  which **passed between** those pieces. **»**

Genesis = JEN-uh-sis

Keep in mind that Abram has just whined to the Lord that he has no son to inherit his wealth. God is saying, "Look. THAT'S how many 'sons' you will have!"
Pause before announcing this significant line. God immediately crowns him with "righteousness."

Abram is being reminded that this is the same God who called him to leave his homeland. Don't make Abram sound demanding. In the intimacy of the relationship, it is alright to ask.

The specifics are less important than the elaborateness and seriousness of the ritual.

The "birds of prey" require a negative tone that suggests they are omens of threat.

The "fire pot" and "torch" contrast with the "terrifying darkness" of the scene.

READING I   God had previously promised Abram that he would become a great nation, a blessing to all the families of the earth. In the verses before this reading begins, Abram laments that he has grown old and still has no heir. So God reassures him by comparing his future descendants to the number of stars in the sky. That promise is good enough for Abram, who immediately abandons his doubt and despondency and turns to faith.

But when God promises "land" as well as heirs, Abram asks for a sign that he will, in fact, possess it. God complies by enacting an ancient contract ritual that's as alien to us as it is bloody. Animals are cut in half and the halves placed opposite each other so those making the contract can walk between them to suggest their willingness to suffer the fate of the animals if either should break the agreement. The birds of prey represent threats to the covenant just enacted, but Abram stands guard to keep them at bay.

Then the "theophany," or divine encounter, deepens. Abram enters into a trance and experiences the Lord as a "smoking pot and flaming torch" (familiar biblical representations of God) that pass between the cleaved carcasses as if to sign the contract. In the "terrifying darkness," Abram's interaction with God has shifted from dialogue to immersion in awe-inspiring mystery. Your tone should suggest the wonder and terror of this sacred moment.

Abram emerges from this experience with no concrete *proof* of what God will do for him, but he has an even deeper faith. In that faith Abram walked until God's promise was fulfilled and in that same faith we, his descendants, are called to walk today.

Speak the divine promise slowly, with dignity and authority.

It was on **that** occasion that the LORD made a **covenant** with **Abram**,
>   saying: "To **your descendants** I give this **land**,
> from the **Wadi** of **Egypt** to the **Great River**, the **Euphrates**."

For meditation and context:

RESPONSORIAL PSALM   Psalm 27:1, 7–8, 8–9, 13–14 (1a)

R. The Lord is my light and my salvation.

The LORD is my light and my salvation;
>   whom should I fear?
The LORD is my life's refuge;
>   of whom should I be afraid?

Hear, O LORD, the sound of my call;
>   have pity on me, and answer me.
Of you my heart speaks; you my glance seeks.

Your presence, O LORD, I seek.
>   Hide not your face from me;
do not in anger repel your servant.
>   You are my helper: cast me not off.

I believe that I shall see the bounty
>   of the LORD
>   in the land of the living.
Wait for the LORD with courage;
>   be stouthearted, and wait for the LORD.

TO KEEP IN MIND
Eye contact connects you with those to whom you minister. Look at the assembly during the middle and at the end of every thought or sentence.

READING II   Philippians 3:17—4:1

A reading from the Letter of Saint Paul to the Philippians

Philippians = fih-LIP-ee-uhnz

This is an unusual opening declaration. Make sure it's heard, but put the stress on "imitators," not "me."

Join with **others** in being **imitators** of **me**, brothers and sisters,
>   and **observe those** who thus **conduct** themselves
> according to the model you have in **us**.
For **many**, as I have **often told** you
>   and **now** tell you even in **tears**,
>   **conduct** themselves as **enemies** of the **cross** of **Christ**.
Their **end** is **destruction**.
Their **God** is their **stomach**;
>   their **glory** is in their "**shame**."
Their **minds** are occupied with **earthly** things.
But **our** citizenship is in **heaven**,
>   and from **it** we **also** await a **savior**, the **Lord Jesus Christ**.
He will change our **lowly** body
>   to **conform** with his **glorified** body
>   by the **power** that enables him **also**
>   to bring **all things** into **subjection** to **himself**.

"Enemies of the cross" are those who think belief in Christ is not enough and require adherence to the old Law.
He fears for the salvation of those who deny the efficacy of the cross and weeps for them.

You need a shift in tone to contrast with what went before. You're saying: "*This* is who we are."
Let this sound like the Good News it is!

READING II   Paul has heard that his hard work among the Philippians is being threatened by false teachers and he writes urgently from prison to bring them back. Some among them have been arguing for the necessity of circumcision. For Paul there is no room for debate: if circumcision is necessary, then Christ is not. Those who argue for this ritual of the old Law are negating the efficacy of Christ, and Paul won't stand for it. So he holds himself up as a model, urging them to be like him. After all, Paul let go of his reliance on the Law and he now stands confidently on the rock that is Christ. They should do the same. But, instead, some have made a god out of their adherence to the old dietary laws and they "glory" in what Paul considers "shame[ful]" reliance on circumcision.

Paul wants to free the Philippians from focusing on the rigors of the Law, which are "earthly things" and turn their attention instead to the things of heaven, the place from whence will come the Savior, Jesus, to transform our "lowly" bodies into glorified bodies like his own. What's at stake in Paul's argument is salvation. He is not competing with other (false) teachers for the attention of the Philippians; no, he's competing for the souls of his beloved converts whom he himself won for Christ. Paul ends with a strong and moving declaration of love for the Philippians. Out of that love he calls them to imitate him in standing "firm in the Lord."

GOSPEL   Today we consider one of the most startling events in our faith story. The man the disciples knew as friend and rabbi is suddenly revealed to a privileged three as God's Son. Jesus leads the three up a mountain, Scripture's regular

Pause before this closing statement and look at your own assembly, then speak to them with the love Paul felt for the Philippians.

Therefore, my **brothers** and **sisters**,
  whom I **love** and **long for**, my **joy** and **crown**,
  in **this way stand firm** in the **Lord**.

[Shorter: Philippians 3:20—4:1]

GOSPEL   Luke 9:28b–36

A reading from the holy Gospel according to Luke

Jesus took **Peter**, **John**, and **James**
  and went up the **mountain** to **pray**.
While he was **praying**, his **face changed** in **appearance**
  and his **clothing** became **dazzling white**.
And **behold**, **two men** were **conversing** with him, **Moses**
    and **Elijah**,
  who **appeared** in **glory** and spoke of his **exodus**
  that he was going to **accomplish** in **Jerusalem**.
Peter and his **companions** had been **overcome** by **sleep**,
  but becoming **fully awake**,
  they saw his **glory** and the **two men standing** with him.
As they were about to **part** from him, **Peter** said to **Jesus**,
  "**Master**, it is **good** that we are **here**;
  let us make **three tents**,
  one for **you**, one for **Moses**, and one for **Elijah**."
But he did **not know** what he was **saying**.
While he was **still speaking**,
  a **cloud came** and **cast** a **shadow** over them,
  and they became **frightened** when they **entered** the **cloud**.
Then from the cloud came a **voice** that said,
  "**This** is my **chosen Son**; listen to **him**."
After the **voice** had **spoken**, **Jesus** was found **alone**.
They fell **silent** and did not at that time
  tell **anyone** what they had **seen**.

Since there are few words of narration, take extra time to suggest the special and sacred nature of this ascent.
Highlight the fact that Jesus is in the midst of prayer.
Let your tone suggest the significance of these giants of Israel's history.

Don't overdramatize, but let us hear the very special nature of this event.

Peter is eager to extend this sacred, privileged moment.

This is no ordinary "cloud." It signifies God's presence. See Exodus 24:16–18.

Only Jesus is left to embody both the Law and the Prophets.

Let your slowed delivery and your tone suggest the powerful impact made on the disciples.

place for divine encounter. As Jesus prays, his face is suddenly changed and his clothes begin to radiate with heavenly light. Jesus is already in deep communion with the Father when God decides to manifest his full identity.

Shaking off their sleepiness, the disciples discover Jesus talking with Moses and Elijah, (representing the Law and the Prophets), about his "exodus." The word evokes Israel's past deliverance from Egyptian enslavement and anticipates the freedom Jesus will win, but only through his suffering, Death, Resurrection, and

Ascension. A heavenly voice urges the frightened disciples to listen to Jesus, the "chosen Son," for in him the Law and the Prophets converge and are fulfilled. The disciples have glimpsed "his glory," that is, they have beheld as part of Jesus' own identity the splendor and wonder that belong only to God.

Luke characterizes Peter as unaware of "what he was saying," but perhaps Peter is so overcome with joy that he equates the present moment with the experience of the feast of Tabernacles, when families inhabit tents.

Just before this passage, in response to Peter's confession, Jesus told the disciples of his future Passion and declared that true discipleship consists in a willingness to deny oneself and carry one's cross. In light of those assertions, this transcendent moment serves to strengthen the three key disciples by declaring the divine sonship of the one whom they will follow to Jerusalem. The experience leaves them "silent," a most fitting response to the wonder and mystery of the infinite God. G.M.

THIRD SUNDAY OF LENT

LECTIONARY #30

READING I   Exodus 3:1–8a, 13–15

A reading from the Book of Exodus

Moses was tending the flock of his **father**-in-law **Jethro**,
   the **priest** of **Midian**.
Leading the flock across the **desert**, he came to **Horeb**,
   the **mountain** of **God**.
There an **angel** of the Lord **appeared** to **Moses** in **fire**
   flaming out of a **bush**.
As he **looked on**, he was **surprised** to see that the **bush**,
   though on **fire**, was **not consumed**.
So **Moses** decided,
   "I must go **over** to **look** at this **remarkable sight**,
   and see why the **bush** is **not burned**."

When the Lord saw him **coming over** to **look** at it more **closely**,
   God **called** out to him from the **bush**, **"Moses! Moses!"**
He answered, **"Here** I am."
God said, **"Come no nearer!**
Remove the **sandals** from your **feet**,
   for the **place** where you **stand** is **holy ground**.
I am the **God** of your **fathers**," he continued,
   "the God of **Abraham**, the God of **Isaac**, the God of **Jacob**."
Moses hid his **face**, for he was **afraid** to **look** at God.
But the Lord said,
   "I have **witnessed** the **affliction** of **my people** in **Egypt**

Margin notes (left column)

Exodus = EK-suh-duhs

Though the opening events are unremarkable, let your tone suggest something special is about to happen.
Jethro = JETH-roh
Midian = MID-ee-uhn
Horeb = HOHR-ebb

Communicate the bizarre nature of this sight.

He wants to solve this mystery.

The second "Moses" receives more emphasis.

God is making Moses aware of who has reached out to him.

Remember, God is reasserting his intimate relationship with the patriarchs. Speak of them tenderly.

No human could survive looking upon God.

These lines reveal the merciful compassion of God.

Today options are given for the readings: Year A or Year C. Contact your parish staff to learn which readings will be used.

READING I   A typical afternoon of tending sheep turns into a transformative event for Moses, the Israelites, and all of human history. In Moses' unexpected encounter with God we learn about who God is and how God interacts with people. Who God is comes later; but from the start we glimpse the ways of God. God takes people by surprise and calls those who least expect to become his instruments. God is both totally other *and* remarkably intimate with humanity, for while he warns Moses to come no closer and remove his sandals, he has also taken notice of "the affliction of my people."

God's promises are always fulfilled, but seldom according to human expectations. Only a few generations lived in the land promised to Abraham before a famine drove them to Egypt. There they spent nearly five hundred years, mostly as slaves, until God sent Moses to lead them back to their own land. Remarkably, this people will rely on a six-hundred-year-old promise to uproot themselves and follow Moses back to the Promised Land.

Although raised like a prince in Egypt's royal household, Moses is now an outcast because he killed an Egyptian. The remarkable bush that's blazing yet-not-consumed grabs his attention, but it is the divine voice issuing from the bush that convinces him he's in the presence of awe-inspiring mystery. Immediately, he hides his face, for one risked death, it was believed, if he dared to look at God.

and have **heard** their **cry** of **complaint**
> against their **slave drivers**,
so I **know well** what they are **suffering**.
Therefore I have come down to **rescue** them
> from the **hands** of the **Egyptians**
> and **lead** them **out** of **that** land into a **good** and **spacious** land,
> a land **flowing** with **milk** and **honey**."

Moses said to **God**, "But when I **go** to the **Israelites**
> and say to them, 'The **God** of your **fathers** has **sent** me to you,'
> if they **ask** me, '**What** is his **name?**' **what** am I to **tell** them?"
God replied, **"I am who am."**
Then he added, **"This** is what you shall tell the **Israelites:**
I AM sent me to **you."**

God spoke **further** to **Moses**, "**Thus** shall you **say**
> to the **Israelites:**
The **Lord**, the **God** of your **fathers**,
> the God of **Abraham**, the God **of Isaac**, the God of **Jacob**,
> has **sent me** to **you**.

"**This** is my **name forever;**
> thus am I to be **remembered** through **all generations**."

"I have come down" is a biblical figure of speech that signals an extraordinary divine intervention.

This special knowledge will give Moses confidence to approach his kinsmen.

This is a turning point in the history of salvation. Don't rush the moment.

Speak with authority and dignity. First God is "Lord," then God is the one who was in relationship with Abraham, Isaac, and Jacob!

Look directly at your assembly and let your tone stress the divine relationship God is asserting.

TO KEEP IN MIND

Names of characters: Often the first word of a reading. Lift out the names to ensure listeners don't miss who the subject is.

RESPONSORIAL PSALM   Psalm 103:1–2, 3–4, 6–7, 8, 11 (8a)

R. The Lord is kind and merciful.

Bless the Lord, O my soul;
> and all my being, bless his holy name.
Bless the Lord, O my soul,
> and forget not all his benefits.

He pardons all your iniquities,
> heals all your ills.
He redeems your life from destruction,
> crowns you with kindness and
> > compassion.

The Lord secures justice
> and the rights of all the oppressed.
He has made known his ways to Moses,
> and his deeds to the children of Israel.

Merciful and gracious is the Lord,
> slow to anger and abounding in kindness.
For as the heavens are high above the earth,
> so surpassing is his kindness toward
> > those who fear him.

By identifying himself as the God of "Abraham . . . Isaac . . . and Jacob," God names his enduring *relationship* with these children of the patriarchs. Today's text omits verses that reveal Moses' insecurity. He asks God's name because being able to cite it will give him credibility before his kinsmen in Egypt. In biblical times, something was considered real only if you could name it; knowing someone's name created a bond and a degree of control over that person. But here God is saying, my name is "You can't control me. "God will be in relationship with Moses, but his unique name

asserts God's absolute self-sufficiency and autonomy: he is the cause beyond all causes, beholding to no one. God acts with complete *freedom* and out of love and mercy for the Israelites. Communicate those certainties when you declare God's closing message to his Chosen People.

READING II   In the spiritual life, pride is as likely as, and even more deadly than in other arenas. Therefore, Paul cautions his readers to look at their ancestors. They were favored by God during their desert journey, yet they wound

up in destruction. He warns them that their knowledge of Christ is no guarantee that they won't "fall." Paul is teaching a lesson believers must learn and relearn in every generation.

During the Exodus, Paul asserts, their Jewish ancestors were guided through the desert by a "cloud" and escaped safely through the "sea" from Pharaoh's army. They dined on "spiritual food," (the Manna) miraculously provided by God during their wanderings, and even their thirst was miraculously sated by water that flowed from a rock that Moses struck at God's

Corinthians = kohr-IN-thee-uhnz

The opening calls for clear eye-contact and strong delivery. During the Exodus, a cloud and a pillar of fire led the Israelites through the desert.

Your tone is upbeat, for these are all positive experiences.

"All passed through . . . all . . . were baptized . . . all ate . . . all drank . . . ": *stress* these repetitions.

Paul links the rock that produced water in the desert to Christ, the source of living water.

"Yet" is the fulcrum on which your tone takes a turn.

Paul is very deliberate in drawing out his analogy. Let your tone do the same.

The Israelites, to their peril, grumbled mightily in the desert!

Here "us" also includes your assembly!

This last sentence is a blunt statement of warning. Don't dilute it.

READING II   1 Corinthians 10:1–6, 10–12

A reading from the first Letter of Saint Paul to the Corinthians

I do **not** want you to be **unaware**, **brothers** and **sisters**,
  that our **ancestors** were **all under** the **cloud**
  and all **passed through** the **sea**,
  and **all** of them were **baptized** into **Moses**
  in the **cloud** and in the **sea**.
All **ate** the **same spiritual food**,
  and all **drank** the **same spiritual drink**,
  for they **drank** from a **spiritual rock** that **followed** them,
  and the **rock** was the **Christ**.
Yet God was **not pleased** with **most** of them,
  for they were **struck down** in the **desert**.

These things **happened** as **examples** for **us**,
  so that **we** might not **desire evil** things, as **they** did.
Do not **grumble** as some of **them** did,
  and **suffered death** by the **destroyer**.
These things **happened** to **them** as an **example**,
  and they have been **written down** as a **warning** to **us**,
  upon whom the **end** of the **ages** has **come**.
Therefore, whoever **thinks** he is standing **secure**
  should **take care** not to **fall**.

GOSPEL   Luke 13:1–9

A reading from the holy Gospel according to Luke

Some people told **Jesus** about the **Galileans**
  whose **blood Pilate** had mingled with the **blood**
    of their **sacrifices**.

Jesus' point will be based on the details narrated in these opening lines. Share them simply but clearly.

Galileans = gal-ih-LEE-uhnz

---

command (and which Paul equates with Christ). Yet despite all this, very few survived the desert and entered the Promised Land.

Paul intends this allusion to their history to serve as an object lesson for the Corinthians. They, too, are being led by the "rock" that is Christ; they have passed through their own "sea" in the waters of Baptism and God provides them with spiritual food and drink in the Eucharist. But the analogy does not end with parallel blessings. Ancient mistakes are manifesting in the Corinthian community just as surely as

ancient blessings. And Paul does not want to see the same consequences. The grumblings and the "desire [for] evil things" of their ancestors brought them destruction and death. To spare his converts (and us!) from suffering this same fate, Paul firmly warns them to "take care not to fall."

| GOSPEL | Without a good familiarity with all of Scripture, we can end up stereotyping even God. An incomplete reading of the Old Testament can yield a stern and angry God that many contrast with "the God of the New

Testament." And an incomplete reading of the New Testament can yield a saccharine Jesus who doesn't seem to have a spine in his body. Of course, the reality, in both testaments, is quite different from the stereotype. And today's Gospel text helps make the point.

While it would be false to assume, as did those of Jesus' day, that all suffering results from sin, it would be just as false to assume that sin doesn't result in suffering. Even sin that's been forgiven leaves a mark on us. Here, Jesus is asserting two truths: those who suffer have not necessarily

Jesus' question is rhetorical; his tone makes a "no" response quite apparent.

The call for repentance is paramount.

Jesus uses a second illustration to reinforce his point.

Jerusalem = juh-ROO-suh-lem; juh-ROO-zuh-lem

The dialogue at the end of the second example is identical to that in the first. Don't waste it.
Pause and take a breath before launching into the parable.

The owner is both disappointed and angry.

Our sins affect more than just ourselves!

The gardener's call for mercy ends with a sober warning.

This final option should not sound vindictive.

Jesus said to them in reply,
  "Do you **think** that because these **Galileans suffered**
     in **this way**
  they were **greater sinners** than **all other** Galileans?
By no means!
But I **tell** you, if **you** do **not repent**,
  you will **all perish** as **they** did!
Or those **eighteen people** who were **killed**
  when the tower at **Siloam fell** on them—
  do you **think** they were **more guilty**
  than **everyone else** who lived in **Jerusalem**?
By no means!
But I **tell you**, if you do **not repent**,
  you will **all perish** as **they** did!"

And he told them this **parable**:
  "There once was a person who had a **fig tree** planted
     in his **orchard**,
  and when he **came** in search of **fruit** on it but found **none**,
  he said to the **gardener**,
  'For **three years** now I **have come** in search of **fruit**
     on this **fig tree**
  but have found **none**.
So **cut** it **down**.
Why should it **exhaust** the **soil**?'
He said to him in **reply**,
  '**Sir**, **leave** it for **this** year **also**,
  and I shall **cultivate** the ground around it and **fertilize** it;
  it **may** bear **fruit** in the **future**.
If not you can **cut** it **down**.'"

sinned; but those who sin will eventually reap the fruit they've sown. In the first century, it was common to believe that misfortune was a sign of God's disfavor. Jesus disputes that false notion by alluding to the victims of two well-known contemporary disasters. Neither those killed by Pilate nor those killed by a falling tower were greater sinners than the other citizens of Galilee Jesus asserts. Jesus' goal, like that of the season of Lent, is to awaken his listeners to an elusive truth: there's not as much time as we think! If we want to be right with God, today is the day and now is the hour to take the first step.

Twice Jesus sets the condition, "if you do not *repent*." Yes, God never tires of *forgiving*, but, as Pope Francis reminds us, we tire of *asking* forgiveness; we fail to repent, and then the consequences of our free choices fall upon us. Jesus even uses a parable to illustrate the point. In the tale, God is both the disappointed landowner *and* the gardener who asks for more time. The owner doesn't want the tree to "exhaust the soil" (a reminder that endless patience would do more harm than good) but agrees to yet another year. But even then the warning bell does not stop ringing in this cautionary tale. If it does not produce, says the gardener, "you can cut it down." But stern as it is, even that final caution is an expression of divine love that wants no one lost and nothing, not even a fruitless tree, cast into the fire. G.M.

THIRD SUNDAY
OF LENT, YEAR A

LECTIONARY #28

READING I   Exodus 17:3–7

A reading from the Book of Exodus

In those days, in their **thirst** for **water**,
the people **grumbled** against Moses,
saying, "**Why** did you ever make us **leave** Egypt?
Was it just to have us **die** here of **thirst**
with our **children** and our **livestock**?"
So Moses **cried** out to the LORD,
"What shall I **do** with this people?
A little **more** and they will **stone** me!"
The LORD **answered** Moses,
"Go over there in front of the **people**,
along with some of the **elders** of Israel,
holding in your hand, as you go,
the **staff** with which you struck the **river**.
I will be **standing** there in front of you on the rock in **Horeb**.
Strike the rock, and the **water** will flow from it
for the people to **drink**."
This Moses **did**, in the presence of the **elders** of Israel.
The place was called **Massah** and **Meribah**,
because the Israelites **quarreled** there
and **tested** the LORD, saying,
"Is the LORD in our **midst** or **not**?"

Start slowly. "Thirst for water" sets up the whole reading.

Moses is angry, but at whom—the people, God, both?

Like a frustrated parent, angry at first but then melting into a tone of loving reassurance.

"Staff . . . river" is a reference to the plague that changed the Nile river to blood. The staff that deprived Egypt of water will provide for Israel. The words, "in front of the people" convey the public nature of God's reassurance made "in the presence of the elders" who witness the saving miracle. Speak the words "This . . . did" in a tone that suggests the miracle occurred.

Massah = MAH-sah; Meribah = MAYR-ih-bah.

Massah means "the place of the test," and Meribah means "the place of the quarelling". The question can be read with the anxiety of the people or with the narrator's regret at their apparent lack of faith.

Today options are given for the readings: Year A or Year C. Contact your parish staff to learn which readings will be used.

READING I   Today's passage from Exodus continues the foundational Old Testament account of Israel's journey from Egyptian slavery to freedom in Canaan, the Promised Land. In the story of this wilderness trek, although Moses, Aaron, and Miriam appear as leaders, God is the warrior-hero who leads the people to new life. In the ancient world, hero and warrior imagery expressed the people's belief that the Lord was a powerful God who fought on their side against all odds to keep promises. This understanding of God also guided the choice of literary forms often used in the Exodus account, as in today's First Reading. Built around a historical core, this legend exaggerates various elements of the story to present the Lord God of Israel as a hero.

When the people can find no water at all, there are quarrels and demands that Moses provide it. For his part, Moses fears that the people are testing God, seeking to determine if the Lord is truly a mighty hero, able and willing to meet their need. (They should know better.) Yet in response to Moses' plea, God instructs him to use the same staff with which he struck the Red Sea to strike the rock at Horeb (another name for Sinai). It is abundantly clear whose power causes water to flow, for the Lord declares to Moses "I will be standing there in front of you on the rock." Once again, the Lord demonstrates that he is indeed Israel's hero while the place names given record the people's testing of their God.

For meditation and context:

RESPONSORIAL PSALM   Psalm 95:1–2, 6–7, 8–9 (8)

R. If today you hear his voice, harden not your hearts.

Come, let us sing joyfully to the LORD;
  let us acclaim the Rock of our salvation.
Let us come into his presence with
    thanksgiving;
  let us joyfully sing psalms to him.

Come, let us bow down in worship;
  let us kneel before the LORD who made us.
For he is our God,
  and we are the people he shepherds, the
    flock he guides.

Oh, that today you would hear his voice:
  "Harden not your hearts as at Meribah,
    as in the day of Massah in the desert.
Where your fathers tempted me;
  they tested me though they had seen
    my works."

TO KEEP IN MIND

Know who wrote the letter and who received it. Discover the circumstances. **The intent of each letter dictates the tone.** Often Paul is the writer; he is motivated by multiple concerns: to instruct, console, encourage, chastise, warn, settle disputes, and more. When reading from one of his letters, be aware of what he's trying to accomplish.

READING II   Romans 5:1–2, 5–8

A reading from the Letter of Saint Paul to the Romans

Brothers and sisters:
Since we have been **justified** by **faith**,
  we have **peace** with God through our Lord Jesus **Christ**,
  through whom we have gained **access** by faith
  to this **grace** in which we stand,
  and we boast in **hope** of the glory of **God**.

And hope does not **disappoint**,
  because the **love** of God has been poured out into our **hearts**
  through the Holy **Spirit** who has been **given** to us.
For **Christ**, while we were still **helpless**,
  died at the appointed time for the **ungodly**.
Indeed, only with **difficulty** does one die for a **just** person,
  though perhaps for a **good** person one might even find **courage**
    to die.
But God **proves** his love for us
  in that while we were still **sinners** Christ **died** for us.

Don't read this like abstract theology, for the text announces hope, love, and joy!
Paul describes the workings of faith, hope, and love, moving effortlessly from one to the other: faith brings peace and access to grace; this leads to a hope which will not disappoint. Note: we don't "speak" of hope; instead, we "boast" of it!

There are three distinct ideas in this sentence.

Assume the diction of a teacher making an important point.

Yes, it would be unusual to willingly die for a just person,

It would be unusual to willingly die for a righteous person, but more unusual is what God did—dying for us while we were still in sin! With joy and awe.

READING II   Generally thought to be written near the end of Paul's life, Romans represents his mature thought. Though usually called a letter, it is more of an essay on salvation through faith in Christ. Today's reading is part of the second section of Romans, which explains an important teaching. After summarizing his earlier discussion, that we are justified, or saved, by our faith rather than by our obedience to the Law, Paul turns to unfold several effects of this justification. As he often does in other writings, in today's reading Paul emphasizes the role of Christ in human salvation with a favored phrase, "through our Lord Jesus Christ."

Paul, a strictly observant Jew and Pharisee, came to believe that no human effort, including any and every attempt to observe the Law of Moses, could bring about a state of uprightness before God. Human justification could be accomplished only by means of an unearned gift of God. For Paul, faith is not a cause of, but a response to, the grace of justification. In biblical thought, "faith" usually means absolute trust in God, and precisely by such complete trust in God's work through Christ, believers participate in the gift (grace) freely given. For Paul, "grace" signifies God's own life-giving love given freely and abundantly, abiding as a continuous presence within and among those justified; this enduring divine presence in the "heart" or core of believers is the Holy Spirit.

It seems that Paul cannot repeat often enough the totally gracious, undeserved quality of justification through Christ. He stresses that "while we were still helpless," unable to do anything at all to secure our own justification, Christ gave his very life for us as a gift of love. One could, perhaps,

Narrate as if you were one of the Samaritans who is converted at the end of the story. It's your own town that you're describing; the woman is your neighbor, and this incident changed your life.
Samaria = suh-MAYR-ee-uh; Sychar = SĪ-kahr.
Slower pacing helps suggest his tiredness.

She is stunned that he would ask her for a favor.

Keep the dialogue conversational, not theological.

She bluntly challenges him and his *chutzpah*.

Contrast his tone with the woman's.

She's eager for this amazing water.
Speak evenly, with no hint of judgment.

GOSPEL   John 4:5–42

A reading from the holy Gospel according to John

Jesus came to a town of **Samaria** called **Sychar**,
near the plot of land that **Jacob** had given to his son **Joseph**.
Jacob's **well** was there.
Jesus, **tired** from his journey, sat down there at the well.
It was about **noon**.

A **woman** of Samaria came to draw **water**.
Jesus **said** to her,
"Give me a **drink**."
His **disciples** had gone into the **town** to buy **food**.
The **Samaritan** woman said to him,
"How can **you**, a **Jew**, ask me, a **Samaritan woman**, for a **drink**?"
—For **Jews** use nothing in **common** with Samaritans.—
Jesus **answered** and said to her,
"If you knew the **gift** of God
and **who** is saying to you, 'Give me a drink,'
you would have asked **him**
and he would have given you **living** water."
The woman **said** to him,
"**Sir**, you do not even have a **bucket** and the cistern is **deep**;
where then can you **get** this living water?
Are you **greater** than our father Jacob,
who **gave** us this cistern and drank from it himself
with his **children** and his **flocks**?"
Jesus **answered** and said to her,
"Everyone who drinks **this** water will be **thirsty** again;
but whoever drinks the water **I** shall give will **never** thirst;
the water I shall give will become in him
a **spring** of water **welling** up to eternal **life**."
The **woman** said to him,
"Sir, **give** me this water, so that I may not be **thirsty**
or have to keep **coming** here to draw water."

imagine dying for a truly good person; but only divine imagination could conceive of dying for those still immersed in sin.

GOSPEL   Today's reading from John presents one of several dramatic encounters with Jesus. This most symbolic of the Gospel accounts abounds with Old Testament references, layers of meaning, and unfolding insight into Jesus' true identity as God's self-revealing Word made flesh (John 1:1, 14). Throughout his Gospel account, John uses various literary techniques to suggest multiple aspects of

the mystery of Jesus. In encounter narratives such as today's passage, Jesus is addressed or described with numerous titles or phrases, implying that his identity cannot be fully expressed even in a flood of such descriptors. John further indicates an implied call in every encounter with Jesus: whoever engages with him and so comes to believe is thereby commissioned to bring others to Jesus, so he can reveal himself to them also.

"Believing" carries much spiritual weight in John; the evangelist uses the word ninety-eight times, always as a verb.

For John, the first stage of faith consists in openness to encounter and perceive Jesus; at this point, a person "*begins to* believe." Such openness can lead a person to recognize certain aspects of Jesus' identity and mission, and John indicates such recognition when someone "believes *that*" Jesus is or does this or that. Those who develop a personal relationship with Jesus arrive at the deepest level of faith and so "believe *in*" him (the Greek phrase literally means "believe into"). John often uses "hearing" and "seeing" as near equivalents to "believing."

Is her tone wholly transformed, or is this a final brusque reply?

Jesus is blunt here, but not harsh.

His prescient knowledge impresses her, but she abruptly changes subjects.

Here, too, despite the teaching, maintain a conversational tone.

TO KEEP IN MIND

Each text contains **three kinds of content**: intellectual-theological, emotional, and aesthetic. The plot and details of the story and the theological teaching behind them, comprise the intellectual-theological content. How the author or characters feel (or want us to feel) is the emotional content. Elements that make the writing pleasing—rhythm, repetition, suspense, and picturesque language—are the aesthetic content.

Jesus said to her,
"**Go** call your **husband** and come **back**."
The woman **answered** and said to him,
"I do not **have** a husband."
Jesus answered her,
"You are **right** in saying, 'I do not have a **husband**.'
For you have had **five** husbands,
and the one you have **now** is not your **husband**.
What you have said is **true**."
The woman said to him,
"Sir, I can see that you are a **prophet**.
Our **ancestors** worshiped on this **mountain**;
but you people say that the place to worship is in **Jerusalem**."
Jesus said to her,
"**Believe** me, woman, the hour is **coming**
when you will **worship** the Father
neither on this mountain **nor** in **Jerusalem**.
You people worship what you do not **understand**;
we worship what we **understand**,
because **salvation** is from the **Jews**.
But the hour is **coming**, and is now **here**,
when **true** worshipers will worship the Father in **Spirit**
and **truth**;
and **indeed** the Father **seeks** such people to worship him.
God is **Spirit**, and those who **worship** him
must worship in **Spirit** and **truth**."
The woman **said** to him,
"I know that the **Messiah** is coming, the one called the **Christ**;
when he **comes**, he will tell us **everything**."
Jesus said to her,
"I am **he**, the one **speaking** with you."

At that moment his disciples **returned**,
and were **amazed** that he was talking with a **woman**,
but still no one said, "What are you **looking** for?"
or "Why are you **talking** with her?" »

Initially, a woman of Samaria would seem a most unlikely candidate for an encounter with Jesus because, as John indicates, Samaritans and Jews avoided each other. Yet John will present her as the first missionary, the only person to whom Jesus directly identifies himself as Messiah and the one who first proclaims him to non-Jews. Because Jews considered Samaritans unclean, Jesus' request for a drink would elicit more than surprise; it is possible that the woman's first reference to Jesus, "a Jew," was said with curled lip. Jesus' words in reply begin to reveal aspects of who he is: "gift of God" and "living water." The woman then addresses Jesus as "Sir"; at this point in the encounter, this is a likely translation of the Greek word used, *kyrios*, which could mean "sir" but was also used to translate the name of God in the Old Testament. The dialogue implies that Jesus will indeed prove to be greater than the patriarch Jacob (renamed Israel). Taking Jesus' words too literally—a common technique of misunderstanding in John—she asks about "living water," understood to mean flowing water. But Jesus clarifies: he is the water of eternal life. John elsewhere associates water with the Spirit.

No satisfactory interpretation of the cryptic reference to five husbands has been given; the woman may have been testing whether Jesus is a seer. She does then move to another level of understanding, addressing Jesus as a prophet. Jews and Samaritans each had a temple in which they believed God dwelled, but Jesus tells her that a time draws near when God will not be localized in any building. At this point the reader should recall the preceding chapter, which indicates that in the

She begins to sense who she's talking to.

His self-identification is a gesture of love to the woman.

The second act begins here. The return of disciples shatters the mood. They seem suspicious.

The woman undertakes her missionary journey. Speak the phrase "Could he possibly be . . . ?": with expectant joy.

They're prodding: "Rabbi, eat!" His response summarizes his ministry.

Note the ample harvest imagery.

This is the final act. Maintain high energy when speaking "the word of the woman."

They are urging him to remain with them.

There should be joy and gratitude in their comment to the woman who is responsible for their faith. Place special emphasis on the title given to Jesus.

The woman **left** her water jar
    and went into the town and said to the people,
    "**Come** see a man who told me **everything** I have done.
Could he possibly be the **Christ**?"
They went out of the town and **came** to him.
Meanwhile, the disciples **urged** him, "Rabbi, **eat**."
But he said to them,
    "I have **food** to eat of which you do not **know**."
So the disciples **said** to one another,
    "Could someone have **brought** him something to eat?"
Jesus said to them,
    "My **food** is to do the will of the one who **sent** me
    and to **finish** his work.
Do you not **say**, 'In four months the **harvest** will be here'?
I tell you, look up and see the fields **ripe** for the harvest.
The reaper is **already** receiving **payment**
    and gathering crops for eternal **life**,
    so that the **sower** and **reaper** can rejoice **together**.
For here the saying is verified that 'One **sows** and another **reaps**.'
I sent you to **reap** what you have not **worked** for;
    others have done the work,
    and **you** are sharing the **fruits** of their work."

Many of the **Samaritans** of that town began to **believe** in him
    because of the word of the **woman** who testified,
    "He told me **everything** I have done."
When the Samaritans **came** to him,
    they invited him to **stay** with them;
    and he stayed there two **days**.
Many **more** began to believe in him because of his word,
    and they **said** to the woman,
    "We no longer believe because of **your** word;
    for we have heard for **ourselves**,
    and we **know** that this is **truly** the **savior** of the **world**."

[Shorter: John 4:5–15, 19b–26, 39a, 40–42]

future, God will be approached in the Crucified and Rsen Christ. The woman then speaks of an expected Messiah, a hope shared by Jews and Samaritans. With Greek wordplay difficult to capture in English, Jesus' response to her both affirms that he is the expected Messiah and adds a further revelation: God ("I AM") stands before you in the person of Jesus.

When the disciples re-enter the scene, the woman begins her missionary task, returning to her town to tell of her encounter with Jesus. Her question "Could he possibly be the Christ?" is rhetorical, implying an expected "Yes." The disciples turn to questions of food, but Jesus clarifies what truly nourishes him: carrying out the will of the God who sent him. He then speaks of the coming harvest, a New Testament image for God's work of completing the plan of salvation.

At this point the narrative returns to the Samaritan woman. Her missionary testimony already has had its effect, for some of the townspeople "began to believe" in Jesus. John's word choice suggests that the people were open to the meaning of Jesus, or they could not have entered this early stage of believing. John then uses a Greek word often translated as "stay," "remain," "dwell," or "abide"; he uses it to indicate a mutual indwelling of Jesus and the believer. When Jesus comes to "stay" with the Samaritans, they enter into their own deeply personal encounter with him. As a result, their believing no longer depends upon the woman's testimony, though her word was its beginning. Now that they themselves have dwelled with Jesus, divine Word of God in the flesh, they have come to know that he is "the savior of the world." M.F.

FOURTH SUNDAY OF LENT

LECTIONARY #33

READING I   Joshua 5:9a, 10–12

A reading from the Book of Joshua

The LORD said to **Joshua**,
>   "**Today** I have **removed** the **reproach** of **Egypt** from you."

While the **Israelites** were encamped at **Gilgal** on the plains
>   of **Jericho**,
>   they celebrated the **Passover**
>   on the evening of the **fourteenth** of the **month**.
On the day **after** the **Passover**,
>   they **ate** of the **produce** of the **land**
>   in the form of **unleavened cakes** and **parched grain**.
On that **same day after** the **Passover**,
>   on which they ate of the **produce** of the **land**, the **manna ceased**.
No **longer** was there **manna** for the **Israelites**,
>   who **that** year ate of the yield of the land of **Canaan**.

Pause briefly after "Today." Removal of "reproach" is an announcement of joy.

Gilgal = GIL-gahl
Jericho = JAYR-ih-koh

Speak of the Passover with reverence.

Eating food they've grown is occasion for joy.

The cessation of manna signifies the end of an era, but it is not sad news.

With God's help, Israel will now fend for herself; speak with a mix of pride and gratitude.

Canaan = KAY-n*n
                    For meditation and context:

RESPONSORIAL PSALM   Psalm 34:2–3, 4–5, 6–7 (9a)

R. Taste and see the goodness of the Lord.

I will bless the LORD at all times;
>   his praise shall be ever in my mouth.
Let my soul glory in the LORD;
>   the lowly will hear me and be glad.

Glorify the LORD with me,
>   let us together extol his name.
I sought the LORD, and he answered me
>   and delivered me from all my fears.

Look to him that you may be radiant with
>   joy,
>   and your faces may not blush with shame.
When the poor one called out, the LORD
>   heard,
>   and from all his distress he saved him.

TO KEEP IN MIND
Eye contact connects you with those to whom you minister. Look at the assembly during the middle and at the end of every thought or sentence.

Today options are given for the readings: Year A or Year B. Contact your parish staff to learn which readings will be used.

READING I   While the similarity may seem elusive, this text from Joshua bears resemblance to the Gospel story of the prodigal son. Both narratives proclaim the faithfulness of God who waits, merciful and forgiving, for the return of the one who lost his way and then returns home. In this text, it is Israel that returns. Having fled to Egypt during a time of famine early in their history, the Israelites were eventually enslaved—held captive for centuries—until Moses came to lead them back to the land of God's promise.

But because of disobedience and lack of faith, their escape included forty years of desert wandering. During that time, God fed the people with manna, but as punishment for their sins, none of the circumcised warriors who left Egypt were allowed to enter the Promised Land. Only those born in the desert would enter it. Just prior to the start of today's text, Joshua circumcises these younger men and then announces that the ritual has "removed the reproach of Egypt" from them. They have entered a new and significant moment in their life as a nation. While in the desert, the miraculous manna signified God's provident care; but in their new home, the manna ceases. Their wanderings are over; now they will rely not on God's direct intervention, but on the sweat of their brows and the fruit of their labor.

Today is Laetare Sunday, a Lenten day of rejoicing in the midst of our penitential journey toward the triumph of Easter. We rejoice because (among other reasons), like

Corinthians = kohr-IN-thee-uhnz

Use the greeting to win everyone's attention; then announce the joyous good news that follows.

You will need to believe this about yourself to proclaim with conviction.

Take time with this significant declaration of God's benign initiative.

That ministry is now ours!

Only if we believe that our "trespasses" are not held against *us* can we become true "ambassadors."

Don't ignore the strong word, "implore."

Pause before starting this final sentence. You are sharing a profound truth that, for us, is joyful good news. Stress the words "be" and "know."

READING II   2 Corinthians 5:17–21

A reading from the second Letter of Saint Paul to the Corinthians

Brothers and **sisters**:
Whoever is in **Christ** is a **new creation**:
   the **old** things have **passed away**;
   behold, **new** things have **come**.
And **all this** is from **God**,
   who has **reconciled** us to **himself through Christ**
   and given us the **ministry** of **reconciliation**,
   namely, God was **reconciling** the **world** to **himself** in **Christ**,
   not counting their **trespasses against** them
   and **entrusting** to **us** the **message** of **reconciliation**.
So we are **ambassadors** for **Christ**,
   as if **God** were **appealing through** us.
We **implore** you on **behalf** of **Christ**,
   be reconciled to **God**.
For **our sake** he made **him** to be **sin** who did **not know** sin,
   so that **we** might become the **righteousness** of **God** in **him**.

Jesus tells the story in the midst of the righteous and the outcast. He addresses the parable to the complainers: is he trying to chasten or to change hearts?

Pharisees = FAYR-uh-seez
The pacing of the dialogue should be brisk.

This too-soon division of property must be painful for the father.
You might narrate this with the naïve bravado of the son.

GOSPEL   Luke 15:1–3, 11–32

A reading from the holy Gospel according to Luke

Tax collectors and **sinners** were **all drawing near** to **listen** to **Jesus**,
   but the **Pharisees** and **scribes** began to **complain**, saying,
   "**This** man **welcomes sinners** and **eats** with them."
So to **them** Jesus addressed **this parable**:
"A man had **two sons**, and the **younger** son said to his father,
   '**Father** give me the **share** of your **estate** that should **come**
      to me.'
So the father **divided** the property **between** them.
After a few **days**, the **younger** son collected **all** his **belongings**

the Israelites, we realize that God has given us the means to live like adults, taking responsibility for our actions, making our home in God and the land of his promise—exactly what we will see the prodigal son do in today's Gospel.

Announce this milestone in Israel's history with joy and gratitude. There is no hint of arrogance in their new-found self-reliance. That, too, is a gift of God who enabled them to eat "of the yield of the land of Canaan." Stress the words and phrases that announce Israel's progress from dependence to grateful Indepen-

dence. In our success we can always find evidence of God's provident care.

READING II   The Israelites in today's First Reading start their new life as a nation when they reach the Promised Land. We begin a radically new life, Paul says, through our association with Christ. Ours is not the novelty of new land and self-sustenance celebrated in the text from Joshua, but a newness that is total and for always. We are "a new creation," Paul proclaims! God fashions a new Eden in each heart that gives itself to Christ. Our

old life is gone and forgotten because God has reached out to us to restore what was broken in the original Eden. Like the father of the prodigal son in today's Gospel, God is overeager to reconcile, for while we were steeped in our "trespasses," he sent Christ to reconcile "us to himself."

Strife is not uncommon, even among Christians, and the Christians at Corinth experienced their share of discord. So this message of reconciliation is especially poignant for them. If God has been so generous with them, how can they not take up the banner of reconciliation and proclaim it

and **set off** to a **distant country**
where he **squandered** his inheritance on a life of **dissipation**.

When he had **freely spent everything**,
a **severe famine struck** that country,
and he found himself in **dire need**.
So he **hired** himself **out** to one of the local **citizens**
who **sent** him to his **farm** to **tend** the swine.
And he **longed** to eat his **fill** of the **pods** on which the **swine fed**,
but **nobody gave** him any.
Coming to his **senses** he thought,
'How many of my father's hired **workers**
have **more** than enough food to eat,
but here am I, **dying** from **hunger**.
I shall **get up** and go to my **father** and I shall **say** to him,
"**Father**, I have **sinned** against **heaven** and against **you**.
I no longer **deserve** to be called your **son**;
treat me as **you** would **treat** one of your **hired workers**." '
So he **got up** and **went back** to his **father**.
While he was still a **long way off**,
his **father** caught **sight** of him, and was **filled** with **compassion**.
He **ran** to his son, **embraced** him and **kissed** him.
His **son said** to **him**,
'**Father**, I have **sinned** against **heaven** and against **you**;
I no longer **deserve** to be called your **son**.'
But his **father** ordered his **servants**,
'**Quickly** bring the **finest robe** and put it **on** him;
put a **ring** on his **finger** and **sandals** on his **feet**.
Take the **fattened calf** and **slaughter** it.
Then let us **celebrate** with a **feast**,
because this **son** of mine was **dead**, and has come to **life** again;
he was **lost**, and has been **found**.'
Then the **celebration began**.
Now the **older** son had been out in the **field**
and, on his way **back**, as he neared the **house**,
he heard the sound of **music** and **dancing**. ➤➤

The tone shifts here. Pick out the words that convey the son's degradation: "squandered," "dissipation," "longed," and especially "pods" and "swine."

The prodigal's humiliation is now complete.

His conversion has begun and he is willing to admit his selfishness.

His rehearsal is sincere, but leave out the emotion here and save it for his actual dialogue with the father.

This is a classic and critical line. God is always looking for us while we are still "a long way off."

The father won't even let him finish his rehearsed contrition. He is focused on welcome, healing, and celebration. The "ring" signifies household authority.

Another classic and revered line.
Here begins an unexpected new act of the drama. Your tone can signal the coming confrontation.

---

to each other and to the world? In his ministry to the Corinthians, Paul is himself an "ambassador" of this divine purpose. Despite their failings and their disagreements (even with Paul), the Apostle labors on their behalf calling them back to the purpose and destiny they embraced when they embraced Christ.

It is our purpose, he says, to allow God to appeal through us. And no sooner has he said that than he himself begins to plead on Christ's behalf to let nothing stand between us and God. Paul reminds us, as will the Gospel parable, that in our spiritual lives

God is not the only player. We, too, have freedom we can exercise. God stands always at the ready; but whether or not we are reconciled results from a decision only *we* can make.

Finally, Paul shares a sublime truth about Christ and his sacrifice. He who was sinless was made "to be sin," taking upon himself the consequence of all *our* sins and experiencing that alienation or distancing from God that is part of the human condition. Let that Good News infuse your entire proclamation with joy!

GOSPEL | This miraculous parable teaches us much about the Christian life. One of its truths is that there is no one who doesn't need to rely on God's mercy. Even the elder brother is a prodigal who finds his own, more subtle way, of leaving the father for the far country of righteousness and resentment.

Often, it is the forgiving, unconditionally loving father of the parable who steals the show. And because the father so well depicts the reality of God's love, it is possible to deal too simply with this parable. We cannot exhaust the mercy of God and

The servants, unaware of his displeasure, are in full celebration mode.

Stress the father's initiative. The angry son holds nothing back.

For this boy, the "far country" was in his own resentful heart.

The father understands the son's complaint but won't compromise his love and mercy. Remember, most of those in church are more like this son than the prodigal. Don't rush.

Speak the last line sustaining eye contact with assembly.

He **called** one of the **servants** and **asked** what this might **mean**.
The servant said to him,
  'Your **brother** has **returned**
  and your **father** has **slaughtered** the **fattened calf**
  because he has him **back safe** and **sound**.'
He became **angry**,
  and when he **refused** to enter the **house**,
  his **father** came **out** and **pleaded** with him.
He said to his father in reply,
  '**Look**, **all these years** I **served** you
  and **not once** did I **disobey** your **orders**;
  yet you **never** gave me even a young **goat**
    to **feast** on with my **friends**.
But when **your son** returns
  who **swallowed** up your **property** with **prostitutes**,
  for **him** you **slaughter** the **fattened calf**.'
He **said** to him,
  '**My son**, **you** are here with me **always**;
  everything I have is **yours**.
But **now** we must **celebrate** and **rejoice**,
  because your brother was **dead** and has come to **life** again;
  he was **lost** and has been **found**.' "

TO KEEP IN MIND

Characters: To distinguish the various characters that populate a passage, try to understand their thoughts, feelings, and motivations. Use subtle variations in pitch, pacing, and emotion to communicate them. But don't confuse proclamation with theatrics. Suggest characters, don't "become" them.

THE 4 STEPS OF *LECTIO DIVINA* OR PRAYERFUL READING

1. *Lectio:* Read a Scripture passage aloud slowly. Notice what phrase captures your attention and be attentive to its meaning. Silent pause.

2. *Meditatio:* Read the passage aloud slowly again, reflecting on the passage, allowing God to speak to you through it. Silent pause.

3. *Oratio:* Read it aloud slowly a third time, allowing it to be your prayer or response to God's gift of insight to you. Silent pause.

4. *Contemplatio:* Read it aloud slowly a fourth time, now resting in God's word.

we *can* rely on God to be the loving Father. But can we rely on ourselves to be as bold and humble as the prodigal, to pick ourselves up and find our way back home? From the elder son we learn it's possible to lose our willingness to return, our knowledge of the way back home. Had he not been willing to turn around and admit his failure, the younger boy would not have experienced the father's forgiveness. Yes, we can count on God's constancy, but our willingness to act like the courageous, brutally honest prodigal is not assured. That awareness, and the contrition it engen-

ders, are gifts from God that we might or might not accept.

The elder brother takes the stage just when the drama ought to end. The dialogue between father and son adds great texture to this story and reinforces a central message of the parable: the love of the father cannot penetrate a heart unwilling to receive it. We never learn of the elder boy's decision. Is it possible he spends the night in a den of anger rather than feasting with father, brother, and friends?

As the elder, the angry brother was entitled to a double share of the estate,

which was in fact set aside for him when the younger demanded his smaller portion. Customarily, a father deeded property to his sons and then collected rent until his death. The father reminds the elder of this when he says, "everything I have is yours." Note that in both instances, it is the father who goes out to the sons. With the younger, the sight of the boy brings him running; with the elder, his absence sparks the father's initiative. The father is ever ready, but the crucial question is, are we? G.M.

FOURTH SUNDAY OF LENT, YEAR A

LECTIONARY #31

READING I   1 Samuel 16:1b, 6–7, 10–13a

A reading from the first Book of Samuel

The Lord said to **Samuel**:
   "Fill your horn with **oil**, and be on your way.
I am sending you to **Jesse** of **Bethlehem**,
   for I have chosen my **king** from among his **sons**."

As Jesse and his sons came to the **sacrifice**,
   Samuel looked at **Eliab** and thought,
   "**Surely** the Lord's anointed is here before him."
But the Lord said to Samuel:
   "Do not judge from his **appearance** or from his lofty **stature**,
   because I have **rejected** him.
Not as **man** sees does **God** see,
   because man sees the **appearance**
   but the Lord looks into the **heart**."
In the **same** way Jesse presented **seven** sons before Samuel,
   but Samuel said to Jesse,
   "The Lord has not chosen any **one** of these."
Then Samuel **asked** Jesse,
   "Are these **all** the sons you have?"
Jesse replied,
   "There is still the **youngest**, who is tending the **sheep**."
Samuel said to Jesse,
   "**Send** for him;
   we will not **begin** the sacrificial banquet until he **arrives** here." »

The voice of God is authoritative and resolute.

Speak of Eliab with Samuel's conviction that this is God's anointed.
Eliab = ee-Lī-uhb.

Give God's dialogue the tone of a patient teacher rather than a disciplinarian. God uses this opportunity to teach a valuable lesson about God's ways and ours.
Suggest the tediousness of this lengthy process. Stress "seven."

Samuel is confused, perhaps worried, and somewhat exasperated.

Jesse is not hopeful that his youngest will be the one.

Today options are given for the readings: Year A or Year C. Contact your parish staff to learn which readings will be used.

READING I   The books of Samuel belong to an Old Testament genre called religious history, narratives that interpret historical figures and events in light of Israel's covenant with the Lord. Because the Lord was Israel's one true king, the human monarch was to act as God's representative. In the chapter preceding today's reading, the judge and prophet Samuel announced to the reigning king, Saul, that God has rejected him as ruler because of his disobedience. At the Lord's command, Samuel turns to Jesse, father of the one chosen to succeed Saul. Beginning with the oldest of his seven sons, Jesse presents them to the prophet, testing for God's approval. However, Samuel rejects the first seven sons one by one, stating that divine criteria often ignore those of humans. Above all, God takes into account the heart, the core of a human being, rather than age, status, or appearance.

Apparently Jesse considered his seventh son, David, too young to offer to Samuel, but on meeting the shepherd boy, the prophet announces God's judgment: here is the one chosen to lead Israel as a people in covenant relationship with the Lord. With the ritual designating a king, Samuel anoints David with oil, and he immediately receives the powerful presence of God, the "spirit of the Lord" that will empower him to carry out the divine commission.

Speak with great respect and admiration for David.

God is pleased with this choice!

Describe the anointing in a slow, stately way, but then emphasize the force of the Spirit that "rushed" upon David..

Jesse **sent** and had the young man **brought** to them.
He was **ruddy**, a youth **handsome** to behold
 and making a **splendid** appearance.
The LORD said,
 "**There**—**anoint** him, for **this** is the one!"
Then Samuel, with the horn of **oil** in hand,
 anointed David in the presence of his **brothers**;
 and from **that** day **on**, the **spirit** of the LORD **rushed**
 upon David.

For meditation and context:

RESPONSORIAL PSALM   Psalm 23:1–3a, 3b–4, 5, 6 (1)

R. The Lord is my shepherd; there is nothing I shall want.

The LORD is my shepherd; I shall not want.
 In verdant pastures he gives me repose;
beside restful waters he leads me;
 he refreshes my soul.

He guides me in right paths
 for his name's sake.
Even though I walk in the dark valley
 I fear no evil; for you are at my side
with your rod and your staff
 that give me courage.

You spread the table before me
 in the sight of my foes;
you anoint my head with oil;
 my cup overflows.

Only goodness and kindness follow me
 all the days of my life;
and I shall dwell in the house of the LORD
 for years to come.

> **TO KEEP IN MIND**
>
> **The opening:** Establish eye contact and announce, from memory, "A reading from . . . ." Then take a pause (three full beats!) before starting the reading. The correct pronunciation is "A [uh] reading from" instead of "A [ay] reading from."

READING II   Ephesians 5:8–14

A reading from the Letter of Saint Paul to the Ephesians

Brothers and sisters:
You were once **darkness**,
 but now you are **light** in the **Lord**.
Live as **children** of light,
 for **light** produces every kind of **goodness**
 and **righteousness** and **truth**.
Try to learn what is **pleasing** to the Lord.

Ephesians = ee-FEE-zhuhnz

The Good News of the opening and closing sentences undergirds the teaching tone in the body of the reading

Speak one line at a time. You must not blur these ideas..

"Goodness," "righteousness," and "truth" are three distinct virtues.

"Try" sets the tone of this line: exhortation softened by an understanding that doing right is not an easy process to learn.

READING II While Ephesians seems to be addressed to the Christian community in this cosmopolitan city, several important early manuscripts lack this designation in the opening verse. Tone and content of the letter strongly suggest that its message was intended for the universal Church and that the letter itself would circulate among various churches of Asia Minor. Scholars debate whether Paul himself wrote Ephesians, but at the least, the author shows familiarity with Pauline thought. In content, the letter focuses on the unity and mission of the Church, closing with admonitions for daily Christian life that express this unity. Today's reading belongs to the latter part of Ephesians.

The passage begins by emphasizing an appeal to the Church made in the preceding chapter: you have been given a new kind of life through Christ's self-giving love; now you must live that life! Using images of darkness and light, the author repeats the point that Christians are now "light in the Lord" and so must live in that light, which produces right living of every kind. To appreciate the implications of this imagery, today's hearers need to place themselves in the world of Ephesians. Ancient peoples depended upon the sun's light; they could not flick a switch to instantly imitate daylight. Hence they were much more conscious than the modern world that without that light, one can see little or nothing. The metaphor here suggests that what now enables Christians to see rightly is their oneness with Christ; seeing all things with his eyes leads to a way of life pleasing to God. Those who share Christ's risen life clearly recognize and so shun works of darkness. The reading ends with a plea taken from an early hymn, perhaps related

Imagine speaking these words to a beloved young person in your charge.

Take no part in the fruitless works of **darkness**;
  rather **expose** them, for it is shameful even to **mention**
  the things done by them in secret;
  but everything **exposed** by the light becomes **visible**,
  for everything that **becomes** visible is **light**.
Therefore, it says:
  "**Awake**, O sleeper,
  and **arise** from the **dead**,
  and **Christ** will give you **light**."

Hear the cadence in this line. Speak it with joyous hope.

GOSPEL   John 9:1–41

A reading from the holy Gospel according to John

Stress "blind from birth" for it is later questioned.

As **Jesus** passed by he **saw** a man **blind** from **birth**.
His **disciples** asked him,
  "**Rabbi**, who **sinned**, **this** man or his **parents**,
  that he was born **blind**?"
Jesus answered,
  "Neither **he** nor his **parents** sinned;
  it is so that the works of **God** might be made **visible**
    through him.

Jesus' answer is unexpected and new. Don't rush.

We have to do the works of the one who sent me while it is **day**.
Night is coming when **no** one can work.
While I am in the **world**, I am the **light** of the world."

Enjoy the graphic details!

When he had said this, he **spat** on the ground
  and made **clay** with the saliva,
  and **smeared** the clay on his **eyes**, and said to him,
  "Go **wash** in the **Pool** of **Siloam**"—which means **Sent**—.
So he **went** and **washed**, and came back able to **see**.

Siloam = sih-LOH-uhm

Relate the miracle with a sense of awe. Pause, to shift to a new scene.

His **neighbors** and those who had **seen** him earlier
    as a **beggar** said,
  "Isn't this the one who used to sit and **beg**?" ≫

---

to Baptism, again calling believers to accept new life in Christ, the true source of light that illumines the Church's thought and action.

GOSPEL   In John's account of the Good News, a simple healing story becomes one of several dramatic, revelatory encounters with Jesus. This most symbolic of Gospel accounts abounds with Old Testament references, layers of meaning, and unfolding insight into Jesus' true identity as God's self-revealing Word made flesh (John 1:1, 14). Throughout his

Gospel account, John uses various literary techniques to suggest multiple aspects of the mystery of Jesus. In several narratives such as today's reading, Jesus is addressed or described with numerous titles or phrases, implying that his identity always includes more than any human language can convey. John further indicates that anyone who truly engages with Jesus and so comes to believe is thereby commissioned to bring others to him, so he can reveal himself to them also.

In John, the word "believe" carries much spiritual weight; the term appears

ninety-eight times, always as a verb. For this evangelist, the first stage of faith consists in openness to encounter and perceive Jesus; at this point, a person *"begins to believe."* Such openness can lead someone to recognize certain aspects of Jesus' identity and mission, and John indicates such recognition when someone "believes *that*" Jesus is or does a particular thing. Those who develop a personal relationship with Jesus arrive at the deepest level of faith and so "believe *in*" him (the Greek phrase literally means "believe into"). Often, as in today's Gospel, John uses

The man is insistent: "I am!"

He relates the details joyfully.

It suddenly dawns on him that he doesn't know Jesus' whereabouts. Pause. New scene.

As you read "So then the Pharisees," your tone hints at where they're going with this.

Proclaim "He put clay . . . " in a matter-of-fact way, but joyfully.

One of the Pharisees is angry, the other reasonable.

He must decide if he will make this confession of faith, and he does it boldly.

Some said, "It **is**,"
  but **others** said, "**No**, he just **looks** like him."
He said, "**I am**."
So they said to him, "How were your eyes **opened**?"
He replied,
  "The man called **Jesus** made **clay** and **anointed** my eyes
  and told me, 'Go to **Siloam** and **wash**.'
So I went there and **washed** and was able to **see**."
And they said to him, "Where **is** he?"
He said, "I don't **know**."

They brought the one who was once blind to the **Pharisees**.
Now Jesus had made clay and opened his eyes on a **sabbath**.
So then the Pharisees **also** asked him how he was able to see.
He **said** to them,
  "He put **clay** on my eyes, and I **washed**, and now I can **see**."
So some of the **Pharisees** said,
  "This man is not from **God**,
  because he does not keep the **sabbath**."
But **others** said,
  "How can a **sinful** man do such **signs**?"
And there was a **division** among them.
So they said to the blind man **again**,
  "What do **you** have to say about him,
  since he opened **your** eyes?"
He said, "He is a **prophet**."

Now the Jews did not **believe**
  that he had been **blind** and gained his **sight**
  until they summoned the **parents** of the one who had gained
    his sight.
They **asked** them,
  "Is this your **son**, who you say was **born** blind?
How does he now **see**?"
His parents answered and said,
  "We **know** that this is our **son** and that he was born **blind**.

"seeing" and "hearing" as a near equivalent to "believing."

John, writing at a time of increasing debate among Jews about authentic Judaism, portrays growing opposition of Jewish leaders to Jesus and his claims. Such opposition to Jesus reflects intra-Jewish debates of the time, when Christianity was thought to be yet another Jewish sect. In chapter 9, John symbolizes such conflicts through the character of the blind man, open to learn from his own experience of Jesus, and the Pharisees, who continually insist upon what they already "know"

about him. The story unfolds in several interrogations of the man born blind by the Pharisees. Each time, the man refers to his own concrete experience, which brings him to increasing insight into Jesus' identity, while the Pharisees repeatedly cling to their current beliefs. The man who begins in darkness comes to see the light that heals him, while those who believe they already see remain in darkness.

Immediately before today's reading, Jesus has stated that he is "the light of the world," echoing the beginning of this Gospel account (John 1:3). As today's read-

ing opens, even Jesus' disciples display a rather low level of insight into his identity, addressing him simply as "Rabbi" when inquiring about the cause of the man's blindness. Jesus again announces that he is "the light of the world," and then, to heal the blind man, he smears a mud paste on his eyes and directs him to go and "wash in the Pool of Siloam." The Greek word *baptizo* used here can mean "to wash or immerse," and at the time of John's writing it also referred to Christian Baptism. Further, Siloam means "Sent," and John repeatedly refers to Jesus as the one sent

They feel they've been duped, so they look further.

Their speech is guarded. They say only what they must.

Offer this aside as an excuse for the parents' behavior.

Speak the narration as if through clenched teeth, suggesting the exasperation of the leaders.

The tone here should be: "Don't entangle me in your politics. All I know is that I'm healed!"

He's becoming impatient, and bold!

The leaders' anger is mounting.

We do **not** know how he **sees** now,
   nor do we know **who** opened his eyes.
Ask **him**, he is of **age**;
   he can speak for **himself**."
His parents said this because they were **afraid**
   of the Jews, for the Jews had already **agreed**
   that if anyone **acknowledged** him as the **Christ**,
   he would be **expelled** from the **synagogue**.
For this reason his **parents** said,
   "He is of **age**; question **him**."

So a **second** time they called the man who had been **blind**
   and said to him, "Give **God** the praise!
We **know** that this man is a **sinner**."
He replied,
   "If he is a **sinner**, I do not **know**.
One thing I **do** know is that I was **blind** and now I **see**."
So they said to him,
   "What did he **do** to you?
   How did he open your eyes?"
He answered them,
   "I told you **already** and you did not **listen**.
Why do you want to hear it **again**?
Do **you** want to become his disciples, **too**?"
They **ridiculed** him and said,
   "**You** are that man's disciple;
   we are disciples of **Moses**!
We **know** that God spoke to **Moses**,
   but we do **not** know where this one is from."
The man answered and said to them,
   "This is what is so **amazing**,
   that you do not know where he is **from**, yet he opened my **eyes**.
We **know** that God does not listen to **sinners**,
   but if one is **devout** and does his **will**, he **listens** to him.
It is **unheard** of that anyone ever **opened** the eyes of a person
      born blind. »

from God to reveal God. The blind man is thus admonished to immerse himself in Jesus if he wishes to see.

   Because Jesus kneaded clay to smear on the blind man's eyes, an act that by contemporary Jewish law constituted work, the Pharisees conclude that he is a sinner, evidenced by breaking the Sabbath. The Pharisees question the man with new sight about how he came to see, and he identifies Jesus by name—the name which means "God saves." The man responds further that surely God would not work through a sinful man, whom he now

describes as "a prophet." In a telling phrase, John states that the man's questioners "did not believe" that the man had actually been born blind, and so they next query his parents. Their response reflects the time of John's writing, when some synagogues barred Jewish Christians from fellowship with other Jews. Explaining their response, John adds the title "Messiah" to his narrative's unfolding insight into Jesus' identity.

   Beginning another interrogation, the Pharisees again rely on their already entrenched conclusion that "this man is a sinner." The healed blind man, however,

relies on his actual experience of Jesus. Facing the Pharisees' demand for further questions about how he came to see, the man responds with a devastating statement: I told you, but "you did not listen." In the Old Testament, the fundamental definition of a true Israelite was one who listened to and acted on God's Word, which scarcely describes the interrogators. Again using Jewish religious logic, the man replies that if Jesus were not from God, he would not have been able to bring sight to a blind man. The Pharisees, still relying on their own perspectives, reject the testimony of a

First he mocks them, and then he instructs them.

They take refuge in the false assumption that his blindness was the result of sin. Pause before the final scene with Jesus.

As yet, he has not seen Jesus. He's anxious to "see" him.

Pause after the words "he said" to suggest his moment of decision.

Jesus' tone attracts the attention of the Pharisees.

This is strong, uncompromising language, but it's motivated by his desire that they truly "see."

> **TO KEEP IN MIND**
> **Ritardando:** refers to the practice, common in music, of becoming gradually slower and expanding the words as you approach the end of a piece. Many readings end this way—with a decreased rate but increased intensity.

If this man were not from **God**,
  he would not be able to **do** anything."
They answered and said to him,
  "You were born totally in **sin**,
  and are you trying to teach **us**?"
Then they **threw** him out.

When Jesus **heard** that they had thrown him out,
  he **found** him and said, "Do you **believe** in the Son of Man?"
He answered and said,
  "Who **is** he, sir, that I may **believe** in him?"
Jesus said to him,
  "You have **seen** him,
  and the one **speaking** with you is **he**."
He said,
  "I **do** believe, Lord," and he **worshiped** him.
Then Jesus said,
  "I came into this world for **judgment**,
  so that those who do **not** see **might** see,
  and those who **do** see might become **blind**."

Some of the **Pharisees** who were with him **heard** this
  and said to him, "Surely **we** are not also blind, **are** we?"
Jesus said to them,
  "If you **were** blind, you would have no **sin**;
  but now you are saying, 'We **see**,' so your sin **remains**."

[Shorter: John 9:1, 6–9, 13–17, 34–38]

"sinner," and eject him from the synagogue. They reflect traditional Jewish belief that illness resulted from the sin of an afflicted person or his or her ancestors, a belief that Jesus set aside at the beginning of this narrative.

At this point Jesus reenters the story, asking the man who now sees if he believes in the "Son of Man," a messianic title, and the man, totally open to believing, asks Jesus to point out who that is, so that he may believe. Here the man addresses Jesus as *kyrios*, which can mean "sir" or "Lord," signifying both sovereignty and divinity.

John presents Jesus' double-meaning response, expressed in Greek word play: the one speaking to you—I AM [he]. On one level, Jesus says, "I'm the one"; on another level, he indicates that he is I AM, the divine presence incarnate in the man Jesus. The man prostrates himself in worship, addressing Jesus as "Lord." The encounter ends with the Pharisees' oblique recognition that they have refused to see the "light of the world" displayed before their eyes; Jesus states that this chosen blindness is their sin. M.F.

FIFTH SUNDAY OF LENT

LECTIONARY #36

READING I   Isaiah 43:16–21

Remember, these are not questions but poetic lines that describe how God saved Israel and destroyed Pharaoh's army. Stress the verbs "opens" and "leads."

A reading from the Book of the Prophet Isaiah

Thus says the LORD,
  who opens a **way** in the **sea**
  and a **path** in the **mighty waters**,
who **leads** out **chariots** and **horsemen**,
  a **powerful army**,
till they lie **prostrate** together, **never** to **rise**,
  snuffed out and **quenched** like a **wick**.
Remember **not** the events of the **past**,
  the things of **long ago** consider **not**;
see, I am doing something **new**!
  Now it **springs forth**, do you not **perceive** it?
In the **desert** I make a **way**,
  in the **wasteland**, **rivers**.
Wild beasts honor me,
  jackals and **ostriches**,
for I put **water** in the **desert**
  and **rivers** in the **wasteland**
  for my **chosen people** to **drink**,
the people whom I **formed** for **myself**,
  that they might **announce** my **praise**.

Your tone should signal that now we hear the voice of the Lord instead of the prophet. Use a slower, more solemn tone.

These words are meant to rouse hearts and engender hope.

All of nature will respond to God's saving initiative.

The natural response of a person of faith to God's mercy is overflowing praise.

Today options are given for the readings: Year A or Year C. Contact your parish staff to learn which readings will be used.

READING I   These words were meant to rouse disillusioned exiles who languished in a foreign land wondering whether God still loved them. But the words are just as rousing for people today whose lives have been turned upside down and are left wondering if God remembers them. The prophet begins by reminding the people of what God did in the past, insist-

ing that if God formerly worked wonders on their behalf, they should not doubt that he will do so again!

The wonder Isaiah cites is the exodus from Egypt. At that time, God not only opened up a path through the sea, he also destroyed Pharaoh's army that pursued the fleeing Israelites. Note that the six lines that follow "Thus says the Lord" are not questions; they comprise two relative clauses that *describe* God as one "who opens a way . . . [and] who leads out chariots." Cite this pivotal moment in

Israel's history as *joyful proof* of God's merciful love.

"Remember not" starts what God "says" to the people. He tells them these past events will no longer be the standard of God's love and fidelity. Right now, in the present, God will work new and more glorious wonders. "I am doing something new," says the Lord. "Do you not *perceive* it?" For Isaiah, this is not a distant, future promise but a present reality: "*now* it springs forth," he declares as if the desert were being transformed before his eyes. But the surest proof of God's love won't be roads rising in

For meditation and context:

RESPONSORIAL PSALM   Psalm 126:1–2, 2–3, 4–5, 6 (3)

R. The Lord has done great things for us; we are filled with joy.

When the LORD brought back the captives
     of Zion,
   we were like men dreaming.
Then our mouth was filled with laughter,
   and our tongue with rejoicing.

Then they said among the nations,
   "The LORD has done great things for them."
The LORD has done great things for us;
   we are glad indeed.

Restore our fortunes, O LORD,
   like the torrents in the southern desert.
Those that sow in tears
   shall reap rejoicing.

READING II   Philippians 3:8–14

A reading from the Letter of Saint Paul to the Philippians

Brothers and **sisters**:
I consider **everything** as a **loss**
     because of the **supreme good** of knowing **Christ Jesus** my **Lord**.
For **his** sake I have **accepted** the loss of **all things**
     and I **consider** them so much **rubbish**,
     that I may **gain Christ** and be **found** in **him**,
     not having any **righteousness** of my **own** based on the **law**
     but that which comes through **faith** in **Christ**,
     the **righteousness** from **God**,
     depending on **faith** to **know** him and the **power**
          of his **resurrection**
     and the **sharing of** his **sufferings** by being **conformed**
          to his **death**,
     if **somehow** I may **attain** the **resurrection** from the **dead**.

It is **not** that I have **already** taken hold of it
     or have already **attained perfect maturity**,
     but I **continue** my pursuit in **hope** that I **may possess** it,
     since I have **indeed been taken** possession **of** by **Christ Jesus**.

Philippians = fih-LIP-ee-uhnz

The Letter to the Philippians is known as the "Letter of Joy." Let that color your tone. "Everything" refers to his earlier efforts to achieve righteousness through the Law, which has lost its power and meaning for him.

Christ is the only prize worth seeking.

Paul can't speak of "resurrection" without also speaking of the necessary path there: "sufferings" and "death."

Paul speaks honestly of the progress he still must make. "Taken hold of it" refers to the resurrected life that comes only after death.

the desert or rivers in the wasteland; it will be the exiles themselves who will overflow with *praise* of the God who "formed [them] for myself."

READING II This difficult text makes several theological points not readily apparent within the confines of this brief excerpt from Paul's letter. Prior to these verses, Paul cites himself as one who was beyond reproach in observance of the old Law. He was circumcised accord-

ing to that Law, but in light of Christ, all that effort seems like so much "rubbish." Paul persecuted Christians for the sake of the Law; but Christ has taken the Law's place and whatever "righteousness" he possesses comes entirely from Christ, not from his own effort to observe the Law.

Paul gladly surrenders everything—even his freedom, for he writes this "Letter of Joy" (from a prison cell!)—to be one with Christ. We might say Paul has embraced Christ the way a lover embraces

a beloved, but Paul tells us it is the other way around: Christ has taken "possession" of him and he now enjoys a sublime solidarity with his Lord. From that oneness comes a desire to imitate Christ, even in his "sufferings," in order that he might share also in his "resurrection."

The second paragraph makes clear Paul has no delusions about his own spirituality. Unlike heretical Gnostics who think they "have already attained perfect maturity" he realizes he has far to go. An earlier

He has not yet reached the "goal," but nothing in his past (nor anything in ours!) will prevent further progress.

The "goal" and "prize" is eternal life with Christ.

Brothers and **sisters**, **I** for **my** part
   do **not** consider **myself** to have **taken** possession.
Just one thing: **forgetting** what lies **behind**
   but **straining forward** to what lies **ahead**,
   I **continue** my **pursuit** toward the **goal**,
   the **prize** of God's upward **calling**, in **Christ Jesus**.

GOSPEL   John 8:1–11

A reading from the holy Gospel according to John

As proclaimer, you are a faith-filled storyteller. Tell the story simply and naturally, aware that Jesus has love for *all* the players in this tense drama.

Jesus has probably been praying before this encounter.

Don't rush the details of how the crowds flocked to him.

Emphasize the treatment of the woman, exposed and humiliated before the crowd.

The leaders play their cards close so as all the better to snare Jesus.

This aside reveals your attitude as narrator—protective of Jesus or contemptuous of the leaders.

Slow your delivery as you share this enigmatic behavior.

Let Jesus speak without anger. The witnesses to the sin were to be the first to throw a stone.

Jesus' words and actions have undone them, so they cower away.

Jesus went to the **Mount** of **Olives**.
But **early** in the **morning** he arrived again in the **temple** area,
   and **all** the **people** started **coming** to him,
   and he **sat** down and **taught** them.
Then the **scribes** and the **Pharisees** brought a **woman**
   who had been **caught** in **adultery**
   and made her **stand** in the **middle**.
They said to him,
   "**Teacher**, **this woman** was **caught**
   in the **very act** of committing **adultery**.
Now in the **law**, **Moses** commanded us to **stone** such **women**.
So what do **you** say?"
They said this to **test** him,
   so that they could have some **charge** to bring against him.
Jesus bent down and began to **write** on the **ground** with his **finger**.
But when they continued **asking** him,
   he **straightened up** and said to them,
   "Let the **one among you** who is **without sin**
   be the **first** to throw a **stone** at her."
Again he **bent** down and **wrote** on the **ground**.
And in **response**, they went **away one** by **one**,
   beginning with the **elders**.
So he was left **alone** with the **woman before** him. »

---

translation used images of being in a "race" and reaching for the "finish line." Here we read that Paul "continue[s his] pursuit," aware that he has not yet "taken possession." Nothing in the past can hold him back, for his eyes are on the "goal." And his goal is worth everything he must sacrifice to attain it. Pause briefly before you announce it: "the prize of God's upward calling, in Christ Jesus."

GOSPEL   Sometimes the biggest divide between people is over the smallest points. In this story, no one disagrees about what the woman did, even Jesus recognizes it as "sin." He differs with the Pharisees not on exercising the human faculty to distinguish right from wrong, but on passing judgment, on standing in the place of God, presuming to read a person's heart and condemning them in a way that alienates them from the

community, rather than calling them to true repentance, as Jesus does.

The religious leaders hope to trap Jesus; the woman is just their pawn. Either Jesus will challenge Roman law that denied the vanquished Israelites authority to impose capital punishment, or he will negate the Law of Moses that requires it in this instance. But Jesus makes the woman more important than their gamesmanship. Before him he sees a real person gripped by sin and public shame, who needs liberation.

Shift tone for this new beat in the drama.

The woman must be mystified at all this.

TO KEEP IN MIND

Narrator: Knowing the point of view that the narrator is "rooting for" will help you more fully communicate the meaning of the text. The narrator always has a viewpoint, often speaking as a believer, not as an objective reporter. For this reason, the narrator is often the pivotal role in a passage. Using timbre, pitch, rate, and energy can help you convey the narrator's moods or meanings.

Then **Jesus straightened up** and **said** to her,
    "**Woman**, **where are** they?
Has **no one condemned** you?"
She replied, "**No one**, sir."
Then Jesus said, "**Neither** do **I condemn** you.
Go, and from now **on** do **not sin** any **more**."

She knows where she's gone wrong, but the Pharisees don't recognize their sins. So he teaches them. The enigmatic finger-writing is his means of opening their eyes to their own weaknesses. When they press him, he tells the sinless ones to cast the first stone. But, lest it bounce right back at them, they demure and wander away, elders first!

Alone with the woman, he does for her what the community declined to do. He opens her eyes. Neither he nor anyone else can condemn her. Our sins, those freely chosen acts of selfishness we make, condemn us, not God or man. Perhaps he reads contrition in her heart, perhaps he's praying for that grace for her. But his advice is clear: Don't do this anymore. G.M.

FIFTH SUNDAY
OF LENT, YEAR A

LECTIONARY #34

READING I   Ezekiel 37:12–14

A reading from the Book of the Prophet Ezekiel

Thus says the LORD **God**:
    O my **people**, I will **open** your **graves**
    and have you **rise** from them,
    and bring you **back** to the land of **Israel**.
Then you shall **know** that **I** am the LORD,
    when I **open** your graves and have you **rise** from them,
    O my people!
I will put my **spirit** in you that you may **live**,
    and I will **settle** you upon your land;
    thus you shall know that **I** am the LORD.
I have **promised**, and I will **do** it, says the LORD.

RESPONSORIAL PSALM   Psalm 130:1–2, 3–4, 5–6, 7–8 (7)

R. With the Lord there is mercy and fullness of redemption.

Out of the depths I cry to you, O LORD;
    LORD, hear my voice!
Let your ears be attentive
    to my voice in supplication.

If you, O LORD, mark iniquities,
    LORD, who can stand?
But with you is forgiveness,
    that you may be revered.

I trust in the LORD;
    my soul trusts in his word.
More than sentinels wait for the dawn,
    let Israel wait for the LORD.

For with the LORD is kindness
    and with him is plenteous redemption;
and he will redeem Israel
    from all their iniquities.

Ezekiel = ee-ZEE-kee-uhl

"Thus says the Lord" is meant to get our attention. Speak it with authority. Pause briefly before narrating the intense vision.

The same idea is stated twice, with word order reversed. This is a poetic technique meant to give emphasis. Enjoy the repetition and speak it boldly.

Use a quieter tone here. This is God's promise of restoration. The fulfillment of the promise will persuade Israel of God's great love for them. "And I will do it" must be spoken with strength and conviction.

For meditation and context:

TO KEEP IN MIND
Context: Who is speaking in this text? What are the circumstances?

Today options are given for the readings: Year A or Year C. Contact your parish staff to learn which readings will be used.

READING I Ezekiel was a prophet and priest of the Jerusalem Temple who was among the earliest Judean captives taken to Babylon. By the time of today's prophecy, the final dissolution of the kingdom and destruction of Jerusalem had recently taken place. In the land of exile, the prophet attempted to awaken the captive people to reasons for

their catastrophe, principally their continuing refusal to hear and obey God's teaching through the Law and numerous prophets. In the verses preceding those in today's reading, God has announced a future restoration of the people to their land. However, this divine regeneration will come about, not for their sake, but so that other nations can realize that the Lord is indeed God. The covenant people repeatedly failed to make the Lord known to other peoples and nations, but in days to come, God's own saving act will reveal his true character to all.

Today's reading is part of Ezekiel's well-known vision of scattered dry bones reconnected and enlivened by divine power, the "spirit" of God. Twice the captives are addressed as "my people," a two-edged sword reminding them of both their failure to act as the Lord's covenant people and God's promise to recreate them as such. Only the power that brought all creation into being in the beginning can bring about this new creation: the spirit of God. In the Book of Genesis, the Hebrew word *ruah*, which can mean wind, breath, or spirit, describes the creation of all things

READING II Romans 8:8–11

A reading from the Letter of Saint Paul to the Romans

Brothers and sisters:
Those who are in the **flesh** cannot **please** God.
But **you** are not in the flesh;
    on the **contrary**, you are in the **spirit**,
    if only the Spirit of God **dwells** in you.
Whoever does not **have** the Spirit of Christ does not **belong**
        to him.
But **if** Christ is **in** you,
    although the **body** is dead because of **sin**,
    the **spirit** is **alive** because of **righteousness**.
If the **Spirit** of the one who raised Jesus from the dead **dwells**
        in you,
    the **One** who raised Christ from the **dead**
    will give life to **your** mortal bodies also,
    through his **Spirit dwelling** in **you**.

GOSPEL John 11:1–45

A reading from the holy Gospel according to John

Now a man was **ill**, **Lazarus** from **Bethany**,
    the village of **Mary** and her sister **Martha**.
Mary was the one who had **anointed** the Lord with perfumed **oil**
    and dried his **feet** with her **hair**;
    it was her **brother** Lazarus who was ill.
So the sisters sent **word** to Jesus saying,
    "**Master**, the one you **love** is **ill**."
When Jesus **heard** this he said,
    "This illness is **not** to end in **death**,
    but is for the **glory** of **God**,
    that the **Son** of God may be **glorified** through it."

A short text calls for a slow reading. Paul's logic is filled with joy.

The negative tone of "Those who are in the flesh . . ." immediately turns positive on "But you are not . . . ."

The negative tone of "does not belong to him . . ." immediately turns positive on "But if Christ . . . ."
Contrast "dead/sin" with "alive/righteousness."
This is an "if-then" clause with an implied "then." Proclaim these words with joy.

For the narrator, these are familiar names and places. Speak of the anointing with tenderness.
Bethany = BETH-uh-nee

Say the word "Master" with anxiety in your tone.
Don't get philosophical here. Keep the tone low-key and conversational.

and of the human creature (Genesis 1:1–2; 2:7). Here translated "spirit," *ruah* signifies the powerful life-giving presence of the Lord at work, bringing about divine purposes. Even the people's repeated sin cannot frustrate the divine plan, which always seeks fullness of life. When God restores the Israelites as a people, returning them to their land, not only foreign nations but the Lord's own people will again know him as the powerful God of life, the God who fulfills promises.

READING II Written near the end of Paul's life, the Letter to the Romans contains his mature thought, some of which can be difficult to translate adequately. Today's reading includes his own attempt to present his native Hebrew thinking in the Greek language; when translated into English, the results can mislead. Some schools of Greek philosophy viewed a human being as composed of body and soul. Hebrew thought, however, understood the human person as an indivisible unity, though different words were employed to describe a human being from

various perspectives. To clarify the difference between a person oriented toward Christ and a person without Christ, Paul employed various Greek terms, including *sarx*, usually rendered in English as "flesh." In English, this word can signify only the physical reality of a human being, or suggest "sins of the flesh." But for Paul, a person "in the flesh" usually designates someone who is not turned toward Christ, while a person living "in the spirit" indicates someone enlivened by the powerful inner presence or "spirit" of the Risen Christ. (Early Christians did not yet draw

Proclaim the words "Jesus loved" slowly. Everything else builds on this.

The disciples are immediately anxious and incredulous.

Again, avoid a lofty tone and keep it conversational.

Here, speak as if you were really going to wake a sleeping friend.

The tone here should be "Master, you're not making sense!"

Speak with some gravity, but not sadness.

He's willing to pay the price of discipleship.

"Four days" reflects the Jewish belief that the spirit left the body after three days: hence Lazarus is "fully" dead.

Now Jesus **loved** Martha and her sister and Lazarus.
So when he **heard** that he was ill,
   he **remained** for two **days** in the place where he was.
Then **after** this he said to his disciples,
   "Let us go back to **Judea**."
The disciples said to him,
   "**Rabbi**, the Jews were just trying to **stone** you,
   and you want to go **back** there?"
Jesus answered,
   "Are there not **twelve** hours in a day?
If one walks during the **day**, he does not **stumble**,
   because he sees the **light** of this world.
But if one walks at **night**, he **stumbles**,
   because the light is not **in** him."
He said this, and then told them,
   "Our friend **Lazarus** is **asleep**,
   but I am going to **awaken** him."
So the disciples said to him,
   "Master, if he is **asleep**, he will be **saved**."
But Jesus was talking about his **death**,
   while **they** thought that he meant **ordinary** sleep.
So then Jesus said to them **clearly**,
   "**Lazarus** has **died**.
And I am **glad** for you that I was not there,
   that you may **believe**.
Let us **go** to him."
So **Thomas**, called **Didymus**, said to his fellow disciples,
   "Let us **also** go to **die** with him."

When Jesus **arrived**, he found that Lazarus
   had already been in the **tomb** for **four days**.
Now Bethany was **near** Jerusalem, only about two miles away.
And many of the **Jews** had come to Martha and Mary
   to **comfort** them about their brother.
When Martha **heard** that **Jesus** was coming,
   she went to **meet** him;
     but **Mary** sat at home. »

clear distinctions of "persons" of the Trinity, a dogma that would take centuries to articulate.) These aspects of Paul's thought underlie today's reading.

In the preceding verses, the Apostle notes that "the flesh" orients someone toward death, but "the spirit" directs a person toward life—the life of God. Paul then reminds his baptized hearers that they are not "in the flesh," but share in the life of Christ's Spirit, by which they belong to Christ. Because they belong to Christ, even physical death cannot deprive them of divine life, which never ends. As he often

does, Paul points out that Christians are formed in the pattern of Christ. As God's Spirit raised him from death, so also his followers are raised from death through the indwelling divine Spirit.

GOSPEL As with most stories from the Fourth Gospel, today's reading must be understood in light of the understandings about Jesus presented in the prologue. John's prologue serves as a summary-introduction to his account, which focuses on the identity of Jesus more than the synoptic Gospel accounts

(Matthew, Mark, and Luke). In his prologue, the evangelist proclaims that in the fullness of his humanity, Jesus reveals and makes present the very character or "glory" of God. Those who accept and respond to the divine Word made flesh in Jesus can share in the intimacy Jesus experiences with God as a child of God. Some, however, will not accept him (John 1:1–18).

Throughout his account, John reiterates that double message: that Jesus is sent from God precisely to reveal God, and that while some will open themselves to the revelation, others will remain closed.

Martha exhibits mixed emotions: disappointment and hopefulness.

Martha has missed his point. Jesus' explanation and self-identification are the key points of this Gospel passage.

Speak slowly here. This parallels the "light of the world" pronouncement in last week's Gospel.

Martha's confession is sincere and unreserved.

Use a quieter tone here. Martha may have been coaxing Mary to go, but now Mary goes eagerly.

Her line echoes Martha's, but vary the delivery for variety.

Martha said to Jesus,
  "Lord, if you had **been** here,
  my brother would not have **died**.
But even **now** I know that **whatever** you ask of God,
  God will **give** you."
Jesus said to her,
  "Your brother will **rise**."
Martha said to him,
  "I **know** he will rise,
  in the **resurrection** on the last **day**."
Jesus told her,
  "**I am the resurrection and the life**;
  whoever **believes** in me, even if he **dies**, will **live**,
  and everyone who **lives** and believes in me will **never** die.
Do **you** believe this?"
She said to him, "**Yes**, Lord.
I have come to believe that you are the **Christ**, the Son of **God**,
  the one who is **coming** into the **world**."

When she had **said** this,
  she went and called her sister Mary **secretly**, saying,
  "The **teacher** is here and is **asking** for you."
As soon as she **heard** this,
  she rose **quickly** and **went** to him.
For Jesus had not yet come into the **village**,
  but was still where Martha had **met** him.
So when the Jews who were with her in the house **comforting** her
  saw Mary get up quickly and go out,
  they **followed** her,
  presuming that she was going to the **tomb** to **weep** there.
When Mary came to where **Jesus** was and **saw** him,
  she fell at his **feet** and said to him,
  "**Lord**, if you had **been** here,
  my brother would not have **died**."
When Jesus saw her **weeping** and the **Jews** who had come with
  her weeping,

John presents a series of "signs" that reveal Jesus' identity, which meet with varying responses of believing or rejection. These different responses to Jesus most likely reflect the situation at the time the account was written, near the end of the first century, when Judaism was struggling to define itself in the face of differing views of the Law and the prophets. Some Jews considered the Christian movement one among other Jewish sects that needed to be corrected or rejected. That group is the one John means when he uses the term,

"the Jews." The term represents those Jews who opposed Jesus.

The raising of Lazarus is the last of John's signs and one that inspires faith even from many of "the Jews" in the story, thus escalating plans to kill Jesus (John 11:45–53). Although Lazarus and his sisters, Mary and Martha of Bethany, are presented as intimates of Jesus, he does not hurry immediately to his sick friend when he learns that Lazarus is ill. Jesus announces the true purpose of this sign: "for the glory of God," that is, to reveal concretely the

true character of God, who always wills fullness of life for humankind.

To emphasize that Lazarus is certainly dead when Jesus finally arrives, John states that the dead man has been entombed for four days. Some rabbis taught that the life force might hover about a tomb for up to four days, after which decay would surely set in. Thus this sign will demonstrate divine power over certain death, revealed and effective in Jesus.

Running to meet him, Martha chides Jesus for his tardiness, but still expresses her belief that God is truly present and at

he became **perturbed** and deeply **troubled**, and said,
"Where have you **laid** him?"
They said to him, "**Sir**, come and **see**."
And Jesus **wept**.
So the Jews said, "See how he **loved** him."
But some of them said,
"Could not the one who opened the eyes of the **blind** man
have **done** something so that this man would not have **died**?"

So Jesus, perturbed **again**, came to the **tomb**.
It was a **cave**, and a **stone** lay across it.
Jesus said, "Take away the **stone**."
Martha, the dead man's **sister**, said to him,
"Lord, by **now** there will be a **stench**;
he has been dead for **four days**."
Jesus said to her,
"Did I not tell you that if you **believe**
you will see the **glory** of **God**?"
So they **took** away the stone.
And Jesus raised his **eyes** and said,
"**Father**, I **thank** you for **hearing** me.
I know that you **always** hear me;
but because of the **crowd** here I have said this,
that they may believe that you **sent** me."
And when he had **said** this,
he cried out in a **loud** voice,
"**Lazarus**, come **out**!"
The **dead** man **came** out,
tied **hand** and **foot** with **burial** bands,
and his face was wrapped in a **cloth**.
So Jesus said to them,
"**Untie** him and let him **go**."

Now **many** of the Jews who had come to Mary
and **seen** what he had done began to **believe** in him.

[Shorter: John 11:3–7, 17, 20–27, 33b–45]

work in him: "whatever you ask . . . God will give you." The next few lines of Martha's conversation with Jesus develop John's point that God has completely overcome the evil of death through the Death and Resurrection of Jesus, who is himself the fullness of life that God wishes to share with humankind. For those who believe in Jesus, he is their "resurrection and life." John uses Greek *zoe* (fullness of life, or life in God) rather than *bios* (physical life).

In response to Jesus' question, "Do you believe this?" Martha proclaims and expands upon statements of faith uttered by Peter in Mark and Matthew (Mark 8:29; Matthew 16:16). She recognizes Jesus as Messiah/Christ and Son of God, the one sent to reveal the Father, repeating other affirmations about Jesus' identity that appear throughout John's Gospel account. Some in the crowd question Martha's confidence in Jesus, asking if one who healed a blind man could not have prevented this death; they do not seem to comprehend the true intent of the sign unfolding before them. After reminding his hearers that Lazarus has been dead for four full days, John again focuses on this purpose: to inspire belief that the glory of God is manifest in Jesus, who reveals God's character as life-giving love that overcomes death itself.

Fully confident of his sonship, Jesus prays to the Father for Lazarus' release from death and reiterates the reason for God's certain response: "that they may believe that you sent me." At the word of the Word made flesh, the dead man emerges from the tomb, bearing his burial wrappings. At this sign, even "many of the Jews . . . began to believe in him." M.F.

PALM SUNDAY OF THE PASSION OF THE LORD

LECTIONARY #37

Jerusalem = juh-ROO-suh-lem;
juh-ROO-zuh-lem
Bethphage = BETH-fuh-jee
Bethany = BETH-uh-nee

Suggest the fuller meaning of the movement toward Jerusalem.

His confident tone regarding the "colt" can be spoken with strength or with such matter-of-factness that no one would think to question it.

"Found everything . . . told them": is this what they expected or are they surprised? Owners' question could be either a challenge or a non-threatening request for an explanation.

"The Master has need of it": delivered with *confidence* in the adequacy of the rehearsed response, or parroted with *uncertainty* about its efficacy

GOSPEL AT THE PROCESSION   Luke 19:28–40

A reading from the holy Gospel according to Luke

Jesus proceeded on his **journey** up to **Jerusalem**.
As he drew near to **Bethphage** and **Bethany**
    at the place called the **Mount** of **Olives**,
    he sent **two** of his **disciples**.
He said, **"Go** into the **village opposite** you,
    and as you **enter** it you will **find** a **colt tethered**
    on which **no one** has **ever sat**.
Untie it and **bring** it here.
And if anyone should **ask** you,
    'Why are you **untying** it?'
    you will answer,
    'The **Master** has **need** of it.'"
So those who had been **sent** went **off**
    and found **everything just** as he had **told** them.
And as they were **untying** the **colt**, its **owners** said to them,
    "Why are you **untying** this **colt**?"
They answered,
    "The **Master** has **need** of it."
So they **brought** it to **Jesus**,
    threw their **cloaks** over the colt,
    and helped **Jesus** to **mount**.

<hr />

PROCESSION GOSPEL   Today's reading before the procession with palms marks a turning point in Luke's narrative. Previously, he has repeatedly shown Jesus moving toward Jerusalem with clear intention and great determination, for it is there that his mission will reach its climax. For Luke, Jesus' teaching ministry continues for some time in the city before his arrest and execution. From the beginning of his account, Luke has also demonstrated that Jesus' life and ministry fulfills prophecy, and his entry into Jerusalem continues in this vein. The manner of Jesus' entering the city appears as an action meant for further teaching about his purpose.

Several details of Luke's narrative suggest that Jesus' entrance signals the arrival of the Messiah in the city of David. Twice the evangelist states that Jesus approaches Jerusalem by way of the Mount of Olives. The prophet Zechariah proclaimed that on the day of the Lord's final coming, his feet would rest upon this very place (Zechariah 14:4). The manner of Jesus' entry also echoes Zechariah's description of Israel's humble King and Savior "riding on a donkey" (Zechariah 9:9). Among the Gospel accounts of this event, only Luke specifically calls Jesus a king, inserting the word into yet another Old Testament text that looks forward to God's coming as mighty savior (Psalm 118:25–26).

Describing the manner in which the disciples are to secure the donkey's colt for Jesus, Luke's word choice may be another allusion to royal status. Jesus instructs the disciples that if anyone questions their actions in acquiring the animal, they are to simply say, "The Master [Greek *kyrios*] has need of it." The owners of the colt do

Express the mounting excitement and joy. They spread "cloaks," not "palms."

As he **rode along**,
> the people were spreading their **cloaks** on the **road**;
> and **now** as he was approaching the **slope** of the **Mount**
> > of **Olives**,
> the **whole multitude** of his **disciples**
> began to **praise God aloud** with **joy**
> for **all** the **mighty deeds** they had seen.
They proclaimed:
> > "**Blessed** is the **king** who **comes**
> > > in the **name** of the **Lord**.
> > **Peace** in **heaven**
> > > and **glory** in the **highest**."
Some of the **Pharisees** in the crowd said to him,
> "**Teacher**, **rebuke** your **disciples**."
He said in reply,
> "I **tell** you, if **they keep silent**,
> the **stones** will **cry out**!"

Blessed = BLES-uhd

"Peace in heaven" is Luke's version of "hosannah."

They are fearful.

Jesus is saying: This is out of my hands. With energy.

LECTIONARY #38

READING I   Isaiah 50:4–7

A reading from the Book of the Prophet Isaiah

> The **Lord God** has **given** me
> > a **well-trained tongue**,
> that I might know how to **speak** to the **weary**
> > a **word** that will **rouse** them.
> **Morning** after **morning**
> > he **opens** my **ear** that I may **hear**;
> and I have **not rebelled**,
> > have **not turned back**.
> I **gave** my **back** to those who **beat** me,
> > my **cheeks** to those who **plucked** my **beard**;
> my **face** I did **not shield**
> > from **buffets** and **spitting**. »

Isaiah = ī-ZAY-uh

The Lord's servant is speaking with gratitude despite much suffering.

Be aware of the multivalent meaning of "weary" as you speak the word.

God has been persistent and faithful.

Communicate pride and gratitude for the God-given strength to endure.

Don't gloss over these graphic details. Give them their due. "Plucked my beard" is a grave insult in that culture. The past tense lessens the intensity of the pain described.

indeed challenge Jesus' followers, who repeat the statement. Luke uses the same Greek word to refer to both Jesus ("Master") and the owners. The word could simply indicate a person deserving respect or an owner of slaves or material goods, but by the time of Luke's writing it had become a title indicating divine status and royal authority conferred upon the crucified and Risen Christ. Luke thus suggests that the true king and owner of all things will soon be revealed as the story of Jesus unfolds in Jerusalem.

When Jesus' disciples proclaim him as king, the Pharisees object, most likely for fear of the Roman authorities, who were constantly on guard for any sign of resistance to their absolute rule. Later, charges against Jesus presented to Pilate include the very accusation that he claimed to be "the Messiah, a king" (Luke 23:2). Jesus' reply to the Pharisees' call for him to rebuke the disciples probably recalls Habbakuk 2:11. In this text, the prophet, witnessing Judah's final downfall, states that even the stones will call out the reasons for Jerusalem's destruction: the continuing

injustice of God's people and its kings. It is possible that Luke here hints at a reason for the Roman destruction of Jerusalem, which occurred a decade or two before the writing of his Gospel account: the city and its people rejected their true Messiah and King, Jesus.

READING I Today's passage from Isaiah is the third of four poems usually called the "Servant Songs." The prophet variously describes the unnamed "Servant of the Lord," sometimes called the "Suffering Servant," as both an

Here is the voice of hope in the face of adversity.

Speak with rock-like confidence and strength.

The **Lord God** is **my** help,
therefore I am **not disgraced**;
I have **set** my **face** like **flint**,
knowing that I shall **not** be put to **shame**.

For meditation and context:

TO KEEP IN MIND
Pauses are never "dead" moments. Something is always happening during a pause. Practice will teach you how often and how long to pause. Too many pauses make a reading choppy; too few cause ideas to run into one another.

RESPONSORIAL PSALM   Psalm 22:8–9, 17–18, 19–20, 23–24 (2a)

R. My God, my God, why have you abandoned me?

All who see me scoff at me;
    they mock me with parted lips, they wag
        their heads:
"He relied on the LORD; let him deliver him,
    let him rescue him, if he loves him."

Indeed, many dogs surround me,
    a pack of evildoers closes in upon me;
they have pierced my hands and my feet;
    I can count all my bones.

They divide my garments among them,
    and for my vesture they cast lots.
But you, O LORD, be not far from me;
    O my help, hasten to aid me.

I will proclaim your name to my brethren;
    in the midst of the assembly I will
        praise you:
"You who fear the LORD, praise him;
    all you descendants of Jacob, give glory
        to him;
    revere him, all you descendants of Israel!"

READING II   Philippians 2:6–11

Philippians = fih-LIP-ee-uhnz

Begin slowly, but with solid energy.
Speak the name of the Lord with reverence.

A reading from the Letter of Saint Paul to the Philippians

"Rather" signals a shift. As important as what he rejected, what Christ humbly embraced is even more important.

Christ Jesus, though he was in the **form** of **God**,
    did not regard **equality** with **God**
    something to be **grasped**.
Rather, he **emptied** himself,
    taking the **form** of a **slave**,
    coming in **human likeness**;
    and found **human** in **appearance**,
he **humbled** himself,
    becoming **obedient** to the point of **death**,
    even **death** on a **cross**.
Because of this, God **greatly exalted** him
    and **bestowed** on him the **name**
    which is **above every name**,
    that at the **name** of **Jesus**

Speak with gratitude that Christ became one of us, also of the great pain he endured.

Another significant shift: tempo quickens. You can get louder, or softer but more intense.

---

individual and a community. Many scholars believe the servant represents an ideal figure that embodies what is expected of those in covenant with the Lord: to hear and obey, or listen and respond to God's Word. Numerous prophets lamented the people's repeated failures to do so, and Isaiah looks forward to a time when the Chosen People will be able to fulfill God's intention for them.

The Servant of the Lord appears as a figure chosen and sent by God, filled with divine spirit in order to accomplish God's saving purpose. In the prophet's portrayal,

however, the servant sometimes suffers rejection, mental and physical abuse, and even death in carrying out God's commission. Ultimately, the servant is vindicated as one through whom divine purposes are accomplished. After the Death and Resurrection of Jesus, Christians understood Jesus as the final embodiment of the prophet's servant figure.

In today's First Reading, God gives the servant both the words and the skill to proclaim God's message to the people: "a well-trained tongue." Several characteristics mark the servant as a true member of

God's people. In ancient Israel, having an "open ear" was one way to describe an ideal slave or servant; a slave's pierced ear indicated that necessary quality. In other words, a true servant of God is one who continually hears and responds to the divine voice. The prophets often described the people's sinfulness as rebellion against God and his Torah, but the servant is free of such attitudes or actions. Although the servant suffers contemptuous treatment such as beard plucking and spitting, he places total trust in the God who gives him

Slowly—stress "heaven," "earth," and "under the earth." The hymn is citing Isaiah 45:23.

Your greatest energy goes to the acclamation of Christ, followed by a slightly lower key delivery of the final line.

every knee should **bend,**
of those in **heaven** and on **earth** and **under** the earth,
and **every tongue confess** that
Jesus Christ is **Lord,**
to the **glory** of **God** the **Father.**

PASSION   Luke 22:14—23:56

The Passion of our Lord Jesus Christ according to Luke

"Hour" refers to the hour of Jesus' Death, not the time of the meal. In other words, the time of fulfillment has been inaugurated.

Only Luke includes this line. Jesus anticipates the suffering ahead.

Intimate, yet solemn mood.

When the **hour came,**
   Jesus took his **place** at **table** with the **apostles.**
He **said** to them,
   "I have **eagerly desired** to eat this **Passover** with **you**
      before I **suffer,**
   for, I **tell you,** I **shall not eat** it **again**
   until there is **fulfillment** in the **kingdom** of **God."**
Then he took a **cup,** gave **thanks,** and said,
   "Take this and **share** it among yourselves;
   for I **tell** you that from **this time on**
   I shall **not drink** of the **fruit** of the **vine**
   until the **kingdom** of **God comes."**
Then he took the **bread,** said the **blessing,**
   broke it, and **gave** it to them, saying,
   "This is my **body,** which will be **given** for **you;**
   do this in **memory** of me."
And likewise the **cup** after they had **eaten,** saying,
   "This cup is the **new covenant** in my **blood,**
   which will be **shed** for **you.**

Take time with these sacred words. Don't speak them as a formula, but convey the love they embody.

The sense of betrayal is deep.

"And yet **behold,** the **hand** of the one who is to **betray** me
   is **with** me on the **table;**
   for the **Son of Man indeed goes** as it has been **determined;**
   but **woe to that man** by **whom** he is **betrayed."**
And they began to **debate** among themselves
   who among them would **do** such a **deed. »**

Shatter the mood.

---

a mission for salvation, "knowing" that he will ultimately enjoy divine vindication.

READING II The Second Reading, incorporated into Philippians about thirty years after the Death and Resurrection of Jesus, was most likely an already-existing hymn, an indication that it expresses very early understandings of the mystery of Christ. At the time of this letter, Paul is in prison, perhaps even facing death for preaching Christ. He exhorts the church at Philippi, and perhaps himself, to follow

the example of Jesus' passage through death to greater life.

Some scholars believe that this hymn reflects what Paul elsewhere names more specifically as a way of describing Christ: he is the Second Adam, or New Adam. This view uses typology, a Jewish way of interpreting Scripture in which an earlier figure appears as a "type" or foreshadowing that helps readers understand a person or event of the present time. As used by Christian writers, the earlier type could serve as a contrast to the present, or as an incomplete version of someone or something that now

fully reveals or embodies God's original intention. In the beginning, God created the human race (the Hebrew word *adam* normally means "humankind") to be an image, an exact representation of the Creator. However, the First Adam never fully realized this divine purpose; not content to be an image of God, the human creature attempted to seize divine status itself (see Genesis 3:22). In the life, Death, and Resurrection of Christ, however, God's purpose for humanity reaches completion: Christ is the Second Adam, the beginning

The Apostles' insensitivity turns into self-absorption.

Jesus continues his teaching ministry to the end.

Then an **argument** broke out among them
     about **which** of them should be **regarded** as the **greatest**.
He said to them,
     "The **kings** of the **Gentiles lord** it **over** them
     and those in **authority over** them are addressed as '**Benefactors**';
     but among **you** it shall **not be so**.
Rather, let the **greatest** among you be as the **youngest**,
     and the **leader** as the **servant**.
For **who** is **greater**:
     the one **seated** at table or the one who **serves**?
Is it not the **one seated** at **table**?
I am among you as the one who **serves**.
It is **you** who have **stood by** me in my **trials**;
     and I **confer** a **kingdom** on you,
     just as my **Father** has conferred **one** on **me**,
     that you may **eat** and **drink** at my **table** in my **kingdom**;
     and you will **sit** on **thrones**
     judging the **twelve** tribes of **Israel**.

Don't rush past this significant line.

Jesus speaks with gratitude and hope.

A sudden shift, as if Jesus responds to seeing Peter with this urgent caution.

"**Simon**, **Simon**, **behold Satan** has demanded
     to **sift** all of you like **wheat**,
     but I have **prayed** that your **own faith** may **not fail**;
     and once you have **turned back**,
     you must **strengthen** your **brothers**."
He said to him,
     "**Lord**, **I** am prepared to go to **prison** and to **die** with you."
But he replied,
     "I **tell** you, **Peter**, before the **cock crows this day**,
     you will deny **three times** that you **know** me."

A solemn instruction to Peter.

Peter is fully sincere.

Not judgmental. Jesus will forgive.

Mood shift. Instructing, but more urgent.

He said to them,
     "When I **sent you forth** without a **money bag** or a **sack**
          or **sandals**,
     were you in **need** of anything?"

or first fruits of new humanity as the perfect Image of God.

The hymn Paul employs follows the outline of this typology. The man Jesus, like every human being, bore the "form of God," but unlike the First Adam, did not grasp at equality with God. Instead, in humble obedience and self-giving love, he "emptied himself" of life itself, serving God's purpose like a slave. Precisely because of this, God raised him up to the status of "Lord." In the Roman world, it was common to acclaim the divinity and authority of the ruling Caesar with shouts of "Caesar is Lord!" For

Paul and for the Church, the self-emptying, exalted Jesus Christ alone merits such praise, which ultimately glorifies God.

PASSION   Luke's Passion narrative appears to draw from two major sources: the Gospel according to Mark, written perhaps two decades before Luke, and another body of material employed only by Luke. This account of the Good News was written by a Greek-speaking Gentile Christian for a community of similar background. By this time, most of the original disciples and Apostles had

died, and most Christians no longer expected Christ to return at any moment. At the time of Luke's composition in the late 80s, a majority of Christians came from the Gentile world, and the Church needed to understand Christ in ways that supported their present and future life as his disciples.

For such an audience, Luke frequently presents Jesus as a rejected and persecuted prophet who shares many characteristics of the Suffering Servant of the Lord (see Reading 1). Luke also refers to a similar Old Testament figure, the Suffering

"**No**, **nothing**," they replied.
He said to them,
    "But **now** one who has a **money bag** should **take** it,
    and likewise a **sack**,
    and one who does **not** have a **sword**
    should **sell** his **cloak** and **buy** one.
For I **tell** you that **this Scripture** must be **fulfilled** in me,
    namely, *He was counted among the* **wicked***;*
    and **indeed** what is written about **me** is coming to **fulfillment**."
Then they said,
    "**Lord**, **look**, there are **two** swords here."
But he replied, "**It is enough!**"

Then going **out**, he **went**, as was his **custom**, to the Mount
        of **Olives**,
    and the **disciples followed** him.
When he **arrived** at the place he **said** to them,
    "**Pray** that you may **not undergo** the **test**."
After withdrawing about a **stone's throw** from them and **kneeling**,
    he **prayed**, saying, "**Father**, if you are **willing**,
    take this cup away from me;
    still, not **my** will but **yours** be done."
And to **strengthen** him an **angel from heaven appeared** to him.
He was in **such agony** and he **prayed** so **fervently**
    that his **sweat** became like **drops** of **blood**
    falling on the **ground**.
When he **rose** from **prayer** and **returned** to his **disciples**,
    he found them **sleeping** from **grief**.
He **said** to them, "**Why** are you **sleeping?**
Get up and **pray** that you may **not undergo** the **test**."

While he was **still speaking**, a **crowd** approached
    and in **front** was **one** of the **Twelve**, a man named **Judas**.
He went up to **Jesus** to **kiss** him.
Jesus said to him,
    "**Judas**, are you **betraying** the **Son** of **Man** with a **kiss?**" »

He's urging them to be ready for anything, including hostile opposition.

As if saying: Lord, we're ready to fight! Jesus says, That's enough! They've missed his point.

The garden is a familiar place of prayer.

Jesus is not in anguish here.

Now the agony begins in earnest.

Luke makes excuses for disciples' lack of vigilance. Jesus is forceful in his urging.

The pain of betrayal is palpable.

Righteous One, who appears in several psalms and in other Wisdom books written in the few centuries before Jesus' birth. The Suffering Righteous (or Innocent) One appears as a person who hears and obeys God, is unjustly condemned, mistreated, and sometimes killed, but ultimately vindicated by God. In the Book of Wisdom, this vindication includes immortality (Wisdom 3:1–5). In addition to these interpretations of Jesus, Luke seeks to reassure his Gentile hearers that they who were once viewed as unclean sinners according to Jewish purity laws are now part of the new Israel of the final age of salvation. Hence he often emphasizes Jesus' inclusive forgiveness and mercy offered to all without condition.

Today's Gospel begins with Jesus' final meal with disciples before his arrest and execution. Rather than offering a strictly historical account, this section reflects Luke's community's understanding and practice of the Lord's Supper as well as the author's insights about Christ's identity. The meal is patterned loosely after a Palestinian Passover meal including three courses and sharing of three cups of wine. The Jesus who had often shared his life and his merciful compassion with sinners and outcasts continues to nourish all who come to him. In the words repeated to this day, "this is my body," Luke uses the Greek term *soma*, which designates not only the physical body but one's whole life and entire person. Blood, the source of life, similarly indicates life itself, "shed for you." The Jesus who welcomed all to table continues to share the fullness of his life and person at a meal, even with those who betray him.

Luke inserts a brief farewell discourse into the meal, including an incident Mark places elsewhere (Mark 10:35–45). In so

Eager to defend.

His disciples **realized** what was about to happen, and they asked,
　　"**Lord**, shall we **strike** with a **sword**?"
And **one** of them struck the high priest's **servant**
　　and **cut** off his right **ear**.
But **Jesus** said in reply,
　　"**Stop**, **no more** of this!"

Jesus says: Don't interfere. Only Luke records this compassionate healing.

There is judgment in his voice.

Then he **touched** the servant's ear and **healed** him.
And Jesus said to the **chief priests** and **temple guards**
　　and **elders** who had **come** for him,
　　"Have you come out as against a **robber**, with **swords**
　　　　and **clubs**?
Day after **day** I was **with** you in the **temple** area,
　　and you did **not seize** me;
　　but **this** is **your hour**, the time for the **power** of **darkness**."

After **arresting** him they **led** him **away**
　　and took him into the **house** of the **high priest**;
　　Peter was following at a **distance**.
They lit a **fire** in the **middle** of the **courtyard** and **sat around** it,
　　and **Peter** sat down **with** them.

She's too loud to ignore.

When a **maid** saw him **seated** in the **light**,
　　she looked **intently** at him and said,
　　"**This man too** was with him."
But he **denied** it saying,
　　"**Woman**, I **do not know** him."

Peter still remains calm.

A short while **later** someone **else** saw him and said,
　　"**You too** are **one** of them";
　　but **Peter** answered, "My **friend**, I am **not**."

Hostile. Through clenched teeth.

About an hour **later**, still **another** insisted,
　　"**Assuredly**, this man **too** was **with** him,
　　for he **also** is a **Galilean**."
But **Peter** said,
　　"My **friend**, I do **not know** what you are **talking** about."
Just as he was **saying** this, the **cock crowed**,
　　and the **Lord turned** and **looked** at **Peter**;
　　and **Peter remembered** the **word** of the **Lord**,

doing, Luke offers a Eucharistic theology similar to that expressed in John's foot washing scene (John 13:1–35). An argument about who is the greatest is hardly befitting followers of Jesus, let alone at the meal in which he calls them to imitate his self-giving for others, even to the point of death itself. Greatness in the Christian community consists not in worldly status but in service. Even after such instruction, Jesus must tell Peter, whom Luke describes in Acts as a leader of the early Church, that he will soon deny even knowing his master, who teaches with his life—and death.

As in all the Gospels accounts, Luke's narrative of Jesus' suffering and death is less an exposition of factual detail than a theological reflection on the meanings of these events. In comparison to Mark and Matthew, Luke alters several details in the scene at the Mount of Olives for his own purposes. Not only Peter, James, and John accompany Jesus, but "the disciples." By the time of Luke's writing, Christians had already faced the testing of their discipleship, and Luke asks them to consider their own response in such a situation. The reference to Jesus' sweat falling like drops of

blood do not appear in the original text of Luke; it may have been inserted in order to contrast Jesus' deep trust, even in great agony, with his followers' sleep. Still, Luke softens the disciples' failure by stating that they fell asleep "from grief," and only once, not three times as in Mark and Matthew. When the crowd arrives to seize Jesus, he maintains his steadfast mercy, allowing a kiss from his betrayer and healing the ear of an enemy. Soon Jesus' prediction of betrayal is fulfilled yet again, when Peter denies any knowledge of Jesus. Ironically, the mockery of those who arrest Jesus

Jesus' look releases bitter tears. Luke alone relates this detail.

Pause.
As narrator, you are angered by this treatment of Jesus.

Prophesy = PROF-uh-sī

"Sanhedrin" = san-HEE-druhn. There is tension throughout the scene.

Pilate comes across as sympathetic. His interest in Jesus grows steadily.

He's a blasphemer!
On the offensive, they accuse him of political crimes.

"Galilean" = gal-ih-LEE-uhn. Pilate is eager to be rid of Jesus.

how he had **said** to him,
"Before the **cock crows** today, you will **deny** me **three times**."
He **went out** and **began** to **weep bitterly**.

The men who held Jesus in **custody** were **ridiculing** and
      beating him.
They **blindfolded** him and **questioned** him, saying,
  "**Prophesy! Who is it** that **struck** you?"
And they **reviled** him in saying **many other things against** him.

When **day** came the council of **elders** of the people **met**,
    both **chief priests** and **scribes**,
and they brought him **before** their **Sanhedrin**.
They said, "If **you are** the **Christ, tell us**,"
  but he **replied** to them, "If **I tell you, you** will **not believe**,
  and if I **question**, you will **not respond**.
But from **this time on** the **Son** of **Man** will be **seated**
  at the **right hand** of the **power** of **God**."
They all asked, "**Are** you then the **Son** of **God**?"
He replied to them, "**You** say that I am."
Then they said, "What further **need** have **we** for **testimony**?
We have **heard** it from his **own mouth**."

Then the **whole assembly** of them **arose** and **brought** him
     before **Pilate**.
They brought **charges** against him, saying,
  "We found this man **misleading** our people;
  he **opposes** the payment of **taxes** to **Caesar**
  and **maintains** that **he** is the **Christ**, a **king**."
Pilate asked him, "**Are you** the **king** of the **Jews**?"
He said to him in reply, "**You** say so."
Pilate then addressed the **chief priests** and the **crowds**,
  "I find this man **not guilty**."
But they were **adamant** and said,
  "He is **inciting** the **people** with his **teaching**
    throughout **all Judea**,
    from **Galilee** where he **began even** to **here**." »

demands that he prove he is a prophet, though his word at the supper has just been fulfilled.

All of the Gospel accounts indicate that Jesus was brought before both Jewish religious leaders and Roman authorities, but in Luke these scenes contain several unique elements. The Jewish Sanhedrin demands to know if he is the "Son of God," both a title of the expected Jewish messiah and a claim to divinity and authority applied to several Roman emperors in the first century. When Jesus is brought before Pilate, he is accused of crimes against the state, including a claim to be Israel's Messiah, a king. Any attempt to resist the absolute power of Rome was a capital crime, and the charges against Jesus indicate that he is guilty of insurrection. Before both the Jewish court and the Roman governor, Jesus offers only an obliquely affirmative answer to those who interrogate him: "You say" I am a king. Neither court fully recognizes what Luke's hearers understand: the full meaning of Jesus' titles as royal Son of God and Messiah.

Only this evangelist includes an appearance before Herod, whom Luke has previously portrayed as curious about Jesus and his activities. But Herod is interested only in seeing Jesus perform a sign, not in what it might reveal of Jesus' true identity, and his mere curiosity is not satisfied. Presenting Jesus as the Suffering Righteous One, Luke describes Pilate's repeated pronouncement that he finds Jesus innocent of charges brought against him. The dissatisfied crowd shouts for the release of Barabbas, not Jesus. While it is unknown if Barabbas is a historical figure, Luke uses the character to make a point about both Jesus and those who persecute

Herod is expecting to be entertained.

On hearing **this** Pilate asked if the **man** was a **Galilean**;
  and upon learning that he was under **Herod's** jurisdiction,
  he sent him to **Herod**, who was in **Jerusalem** at that time.
Herod was **very glad** to see **Jesus**;
  he had been **wanting** to see him for a **long time**,
  for he had **heard** about him
  and had been **hoping** to **see** him perform some **sign**.
He **questioned** him at **length**,
  but he gave him **no answer**.
The **chief priests** and **scribes**, meanwhile,
  stood by **accusing** him **harshly**.

Again, you are not an impartial narrator.

Herod and his **soldiers** treated him **contemptuously**
    and **mocked** him,
  and after **clothing** him in **resplendent garb**,
  he **sent** him back to **Pilate**.

Don't rush this detail.

Herod and **Pilate** became **friends that very day**,
  even though they had been **enemies** formerly.
Pilate then summoned the **chief priests**, the **rulers**
    and the **people**
  and said to them, "**You** brought **this man** to **me**
  and **accused** him of **inciting** the **people** to **revolt**.

Pilate makes his best effort, arguing logically and convincingly.

I have conducted my investigation in **your presence**
  and have **not found** this man **guilty**
  of the **charges** you have brought **against** him,
  nor did **Herod**, for **he** sent him **back** to us.
So **no capital crime** has been **committed** by him.
Therefore I shall have him **flogged** and then **release** him."

The crowd turns ugly.

But **all together** they **shouted out**,
  "**Away** with this man!
  Release Barabbas to us."

Barabbas offers a glimmer of hope. Read as if hoping Pilate might persuade them.

—Now **Barabbas** had been **imprisoned** for a **rebellion**
  that had taken place in the **city** and for **murder**.—
Again Pilate **addressed** them, **still wishing** to **release** Jesus,
  but they **continued** their **shouting**,
  "**Crucify** him! **Crucify** him!"

him. The name means "son of the father," and the crowd chooses a false "son of the father" over the true Son of God. Though Pilate declares Jesus innocent a third time, the crowd prevails and Jesus is taken away for execution. Throughout various interrogations, Jesus says little; he behaves like the Suffering Servant of Isaiah: though mistreated and led like a lamb to slaughter, he "opened not his mouth" (Isaiah 53:7).

On the way to Crucifixion, Simon of Cyrene carries the cross "behind Jesus," indicating the action of a disciple imitating his master. Jesus' words to the women of Jerusalem amount to a statement of judgment on those of the city who have rejected and condemned God's innocent prophet. Still, the death of the Suffering Righteous One will not be God's final word.

Though Jesus' words of forgiveness for those who crucify him are not found in earliest manuscripts, this detail is consistent with Luke's emphasis on Jesus' mercy for all, even enemies. As in Mark, the jeering of bystanders and casting lots for the crucified one's clothing alludes to Psalm 22 (today's Responsorial Psalm), the lament-prayer of a suffering innocent person who expresses faith in God's ultimate vindication. In another detail unique to Luke, one of the crucified criminals further attests that Jesus suffers in innocence. With even his dying breath, Jesus offers life to a condemned man. Luke voices the theme of Jesus as Suffering Righteous One yet again in two further details. In contrast to Mark and Matthew, according to Luke, Jesus' last words express the utter trust of a suffering innocent one in a phrase from Psalm 31. He surrenders his life-breath (spirit) to the God who first breathed life into the human creature, and who will breathe everlasting

Pilate more emotional now.

Pilate addressed them a **third** time,
    "**What evil** has this man **done?**
    I found him **guilty** of **no capital crime.**
Therefore I shall have him **flogged** and then **release** him."
With **loud shouts**, however,
    they **persisted** in calling for his **crucifixion,**
    and **their** voices **prevailed.**

Their anger persuades him.
A very reluctant decision.

The **verdict** of **Pilate** was that their **demand** should be **granted.**
So he **released** the man who had been **imprisoned**
    for **rebellion** and **murder**, for whom they **asked,**
    and he **handed Jesus over** to them to **deal** with as they **wished.**

"Cyrenian" = sī-REE-nee-uhn

As they **led him away**
    they took hold of a certain **Simon**, a **Cyrenian,**
    who was coming in from the **country;**
    and after **laying** the **cross** on him,
    they **made** him **carry** it **behind Jesus.**
A **large crowd** of people **followed Jesus,**
    including **many women** who **mourned** and **lamented** him.
Jesus **turned** to them and **said,**
    "**Daughters of Jerusalem**, do **not** weep for **me;**
    weep instead for **yourselves** and for your **children**
    for **indeed**, the **days are coming** when **people** will **say,**

Blessed = BLES-uhd

    '**Blessed** are the **barren,**
    the **wombs** that never **bore**
    and the **breasts** that never **nursed.'**
At **that time** people will say to the **mountains,**
    '**Fall upon us!'**
    and to the **hills**, '**Cover us!'**
    for if these things are done when the **wood** is **green**
    what will **happen** when it is **dry?"**
Now **two others, both criminals,**
    were **led** away **with** him to be **executed.** »

divine life into Jesus and his disciples. On witnessing such a death the Gentile soldier speaks as a believer: he has witnessed the death of the Lord's chosen Suffering Innocent One, whom God will soon raise up.

As in the other Gospel accounts, several women and Joseph of Arimathea receive the body of Jesus for burial. The linen burial cloth befits a true king; at the time of Luke, linen also symbolized immortality, since it was made from a product of the fertile earth. In three days, Peter will find the linen burial cloth empty, giving testimony to its meaning (Luke 24:12). M.F.

When they came to the **place** called the **Skull**,
  they **crucified** him and the **criminals** there,
  one on his **right**, **the other** on his **left**.
Then **Jesus** said,
  "**Father**, **forgive** them, they **know not** what **they do**."
They **divided** his **garments** by **casting lots**.

Jesus ministers even as he goes to his death.
Speaking through exhaustion and pain.
Slowly.
Pause briefly after this poignant line.

The **people stood** by and **watched**;
  the **rulers**, meanwhile, **sneered** at him and said,
  "He **saved others**, let him **save himself**
  if he is the **chosen** one, the **Christ** of **God**."
Even the **soldiers** jeered at him.
As they **approached** to **offer** him **wine** they called **out**,
  "If **you** are King of the **Jews**, **save yourself**."
Above him there was an **inscription** that read,
  "**This** is the **King** of the **Jews**."

People watch. It's the leaders and soldiers
who jeer; speak with their voices.

Emphatic. Spoken in Pilate's voice.

Now **one** of the **criminals** hanging there **reviled** Jesus, saying,
  "Are you **not** the **Christ**?
  Save yourself and **us**."
The **other**, however, **rebuking** him, said in reply,
  "Have **you no fear** of **God**,
  for **you** are subject to the **same condemnation**?
And **indeed**, **we** have been **condemned justly**,
  for the sentence **we received corresponds** to our **crimes**,
  but **this** man has done **nothing criminal**."
Then he said,
  "**Jesus**, **remember** me when you **come** into your **kingdom**."
He replied to him,
  "**Amen**, **I say** to **you**,
  today you will be **with** me in **Paradise**."

Remember, he too is exhausted and dying,
but sincere.
A prayer. As if murmured over and over.
Take time with this.

The powers of darkness are raging.

It was **now** about **noon** and **darkness** came
    over the **whole land**
  until **three** in the **afternoon**
  because of an **eclipse** of the **sun**.
Then the **veil** of the **temple** was **torn** down the **middle**.

"Father / into your hands / I commend my spirit." Deliberate and peaceful.

Jesus cried out in a **loud voice**,
 "**Father**, into **your hands** I **commend** my **spirit**";
 and when he had **said** this he **breathed** his **last**.

[Here all kneel and pause for a short time.]

Jesus' innocence declared again. Crowd experiences change of heart. Women watch prayerfully.

The **centurion** who **witnessed** what had **happened glorified God**
  and said,
 "**This man** was **innocent beyond doubt**."
When **all** the **people** who had **gathered** for this spectacle **saw**
  what had **happened**,
 they returned **home beating** their **breasts**;
 but **all** his **acquaintances stood** at a **distance**,
 including the **women** who had **followed** him from **Galilee**
 and **saw** these events.

Joseph is obviously a believer.

Now there was a **virtuous** and **righteous** man
  named **Joseph**, who,
 though he was a **member** of the **council**,
 had **not consented** to their plan of action.

"Arimathea" = ayr-ih-muh-THEE-uh

He came from the **Jewish** town of **Arimathea**
 and was **awaiting** the **kingdom** of **God**.
He went to **Pilate** and **asked** for the **body** of **Jesus**.
After he had taken the **body down**,
 he **wrapped** it in a **linen cloth**
 and **laid** him in a **rock-hewn tomb**

Don't rush these many details.

 in which **no one** had **yet** been **buried**.
It was the **day** of **preparation**,
 and the **sabbath** was about to **begin**.

It is the women who take notice and prepare.

The **women** who had come from **Galilee** with him
  followed behind,
 and when they had **seen** the **tomb**
 and the **way** in which his **body** was **laid** in it,
 they **returned** and **prepared spices** and **perfumed oils**.
Then they **rested** on the **sabbath** according to the **commandment**.

[Shorter: Luke 23:1–49]

TO KEEP IN MIND
Pray the Scriptures: Make reading these Scriptures a part of your prayer life every week, and especially during the week prior to the liturgy in which you will proclaim.

THURSDAY OF HOLY WEEK (HOLY THURSDAY): EVENING MASS OF THE LORD'S SUPPER

LECTIONARY #39

READING I   Exodus 12:1–8, 11–14

A reading from the Book of Exodus

The Lord said to **Moses** and **Aaron** in the land of **Egypt**,
  "This **month** shall stand at the **head** of your **calendar**;
  you shall reckon it the **first** month of the year.
Tell the whole **community** of Israel:
  On the **tenth** of this month every one of your families
  must procure for itself a **lamb**, one apiece for each **household**.
If a family is too **small** for a whole lamb,
  it shall **join** the **nearest** household in procuring one
  and shall **share** in the lamb
  in **proportion** to the number of persons who **partake** of it.
The lamb must be a year-old **male** and without **blemish**.
You may **take** it from either the **sheep** or the **goats**.
You shall **keep** it until the **fourteenth** day of this month,
  and **then**, with the whole assembly of Israel **present**,
  it shall be **slaughtered** during the evening **twilight**.
They shall take some of its **blood**
  and apply it to the two **doorposts** and the **lintel**
  of every **house** in which they **partake** of the lamb.
That same **night** they shall **eat** its roasted **flesh**
  with **unleavened** bread and bitter **herbs**.

Through these many details regarding a ritual meal, you evoke the roots of our faith and help us be present to that original event and experience it tonight.

This sacred meal has bonded the Jewish people and united them to their ancestors for thousands of years. What you describe is of great significance.

Your tone must suggest these are not fussy details, but a means of sustaining the nation.

God is aware of the needs and the limits of his people.

This offering to the Lord must not be flawed, but the finest they have to offer.

The ritual draws the people together in community.

This blood will become a life-saving sign.

All is done in haste: no time for dough to rise, so "*unleavened* bread" is required. Bitter herbs will remind them of their bitter enslavement.

READING I   This description of the first Passover meal represents centuries of reflection on the meaning of Israel's Exodus and the rituals that developed to celebrate it. The account appears within the Pentateuch, in Hebrew called the Torah, comprising the five most important books of the Old Testament. The final editors, writing with centuries of hindsight, placed the account after the Lord pronounces the tenth and decisive plague upon Egypt; the death of the firstborn will finally convince Pharaoh to release God's people from slavery. Long after Israel's

passage from Egyptian captivity to a new life of freedom, the Lord's people continued to observe a religious festival in remembrance of this foundational event, as Jews do to this day.

As described in Exodus, the Passover meal appears as a meal-sacrifice, a ritual intended to strengthen bonds of unity between the Hebrew people and God, and among members of the community as well. In Israelite culture, a fellowship meal was a significant way to express and create mutual bonds and mutual commitment. As the ritual developed over

centuries, participants told the story of God's deliverance as an act of remembrance. In biblical thought, to "remember" does not merely mean to call to mind past events; recounting of events makes an ancient reality real, present, and active here and now.

The narrative intersperses description of the impending plague and Israel's escape with elements of the ritual meal. The Passover supper, a family celebration, required an unblemished offering to the Lord; here the lamb's blood marks Hebrew homes so that the plague will "pass over"

Speak in an authoritative tone that culminates in the weighty pronouncement: "It is the Passover . . . ."

Don't shy from these hard images of destruction: Israelites and Egyptians are in the hands of the all-powerful God.
"I, the LORD" is a declaration of God's singular sovereignty.
Again, blood, the sign of death, becomes a sign of new life.

In these lines we hear God's voice saying to Israel, I have chosen you and will let no harm come to you.
This is a solemn pronouncement; observing this commandment will help ensure Israel's future.

For meditation and context:

"This is **how** you are to **eat** it:
   with your loins **girt**, **sandals** on your feet and your **staff**
      in **hand**,
   you shall eat like those who are in **flight**.
It is the **Passover** of the _LORD_.
For on this **same** night I will go through **Egypt**,
   striking down every **firstborn** of the land, both **man** and **beast**,
   and executing **judgment** on all the **gods** of Egypt—**I**, the **LORD**!
But the **blood** will mark the houses where **you** are.
Seeing the blood, I will pass **over** you;
   thus, when I **strike** the land of Egypt,
   no destructive blow will come upon **you**.

"**This** day shall be a **memorial feast** for you,
   which all your generations shall **celebrate**
   with **pilgrimage** to the LORD, as a **perpetual** institution."

RESPONSORIAL PSALM   Psalm 116:12–13, 15–16bc, 17–18
(see 1 Corinthians 10:16)

R. Our blessing-cup is a communion with the Blood of Christ.

How shall I make a return to the LORD
   for all the good he has done for me?
The cup of salvation I will take up,
   and I will call upon the name of the LORD.

Precious in the eyes of the LORD
   is the death of his faithful ones.
I am your servant, the son of your handmaid;
   you have loosed my bonds.

To you will I offer sacrifice of thanksgiving,
   and I will call upon the name of the LORD.
My vows to the LORD I will pay
   in the presence of all his people.

TO KEEP IN MIND

Tell the story: Make the story yours, then share it with your listeners. Use the language; don't throw away any good words. Settings give context; don't rush the description. Characters must be believable; understand their motivation. Dialogue reveals character; distinguish one character from another with your voice.

---

them but strike the Egyptians with divine judgment. This dramatic event leads to the second and deepest meaning of "Passover": with the Lord leading them, the Chosen People will pass from slavery to freedom. Hence the author stipulates a perpetual celebration of this meal, to "remember" the saving acts of God.

READING II This oldest written account of the Lord's Supper was incorporated into Paul's letter less than thirty years after the Death and Resurrection of Jesus. However, the Apostle's use of particular terms for handing on authentic Christian tradition indicates that it dates from an even earlier time. Paul appeals to the original core of faith and practice to correct the Corinthian community, a community still struggling to shed its social and cultural divisions. Distinctions based on status, wealth, and even the minister from whom they learned of Christ have plagued the community. Most disturbing to Paul, divisions have appeared among members who gather to celebrate the Lord's Supper, the meal meant to unite believers to Christ and to one another.

Referring to the earliest faith proclamation, the Apostle links the supper to Jesus' meal with disciples before his Passion. This ancient tradition strove to communicate not simply Jesus' actions, but their meaning. The broken bread and outpoured wine recall and make present the very person of the Crucified and Risen Christ, who gave his entire person and life itself "for you." In New Testament times, "body and blood" signified the whole person as a unity. It is this complete self-sacrifice for the good of the other

Corinthians = kohr-IN-thee-uhnz

This short text is a precious condensation of Christ's institution of the Eucharist. Each detail is chosen, so all are significant.

Paul was not there, so his narrative came to him through revelation from Christ. Don't miss the poignant detail that it's "the night he was betrayed."
Note the verbs: "took," gave thanks, "broke."

Only Paul and Luke relate the command to "Do this . . . in remembrance of me."

This is an intimate moment of self-giving. It's Jesus' voice we hear.
Paul's voice returns underscoring the great significance of the ritual we are privileged to celebrate.

READING II   1 Corinthians 11:23–26

A reading from the first Letter of Saint Paul to the Corinthians

Brothers and sisters:
I **received** from the Lord what I also handed on to **you**,
    that the Lord **Jesus**, on the **night** he was handed **over**,
    took **bread**, and, after he had given **thanks**,
    broke it and said, "This is my **body** that is for **you**.
Do this in **remembrance** of me."
In the **same** way also the **cup**, after supper, saying,
    "This cup is the new **covenant** in my **blood**.
Do this, as often as you **drink** it, in **remembrance** of me."
For as often as you **eat** this bread and **drink** the cup,
    you proclaim the **death** of the **Lord** until he **comes**.

First you set the context—it is "before . . . the Passover" and when "his hour had come."
This reminder of his enduring love for them will be enacted shortly.
Don't miss the assertion of the devil's role in the imminent betrayal.

In John, Jesus is always fully aware and in control of what is happening around him.

Used to caring for and waiting on him, the disciples are thrown by this role-reversal.

GOSPEL   John 13:1–15

A reading from the holy Gospel according to John

Before the feast of **Passover**, Jesus knew that his hour had **come**
    to pass from **this** world to the **Father**.
He loved his **own** in the world and he loved them to the **end**.
The **devil** had already induced **Judas**, son of Simon the **Iscariot**,
     to hand him **over**.
So, during **supper**,
    fully **aware** that the Father had put **everything** into his power
    and that he had **come** from God and was **returning** to God,
    he **rose** from supper and took off his outer **garments**.
He took a **towel** and **tied** it around his **waist**.
Then he poured **water** into a **basin**
    and began to **wash** the disciples' **feet**
    and **dry** them with the towel around his waist.

that the community celebrating the Lord's Supper must carry out "in remembrance." (see Reading 1). To "proclaim the death of the Lord" means to make present and active here and now his gift of life for others, without exception.

| GOSPEL | Like the other evangelists, John places the Death of Jesus near the time of the Jewish Passover, indicating that his passage through death to new life represents God's new and final act of deliverance. However, John's account of Jesus' last meal with his disciples before

his execution differs from the synoptic Gospel accounts (Matthew, Mark, and Luke) in significant ways. Lacking an institution account, John instead presents a major aspect of his Eucharistic theology through Jesus' deeply symbolic teaching act at the supper. Like the entire Gospel account, this passage often carries multiple meanings.

In an earlier chapter, John presented Jesus as the Good Shepherd who would lay down his life for the sheep (John 10:1–18). At the supper, this supreme act of self-sacrificing love approaches, and it is here that disciples are commanded and strength-

ened to follow his example. The hour has come for Jesus to manifest love for his own "to the end"; in Greek the phrase can mean "to the utmost" or "to the point of death," and surely John intends both. In recounting Jesus laying aside his outer garment, the writer uses the same verb used to describe the Good Shepherd laying down life itself for the sheep. As John signaled at the very beginning of his Gospel account, some recognize who Jesus is and what he does, while some reject him; both, however, share in the supper.

Peter's discomfort is genuine.

He came to Simon **Peter**, who said to him,
>   "**Master**, are you going to wash **my** feet?"

Jesus responds gently and fails to persuade Peter.

Jesus **answered** and said to him,
>   "What I am **doing**, you do not understand **now**,
>   but you **will** understand **later**."

Again, Peter is sincerely asserting, "I can never let you humiliate yourself this way."

Peter said to him, "You will **never** wash my **feet**."

Jesus' stronger, clearer response causes a complete reversal in Peter.

Jesus answered him,
>   "Unless I **wash** you, you will have no **inheritance** with me."

Simon Peter said to him,
>   "**Master**, then not only my **feet**, but my **hands** and **head**
>   as well."

Jesus' gentle tone returns, assuring Peter he is already "clean."

Jesus said to him,
>   "Whoever has **bathed** has no **need** except to have his
>   **feet** washed,
>   for he is clean all **over**;
>   so **you** are clean, but not **all**."

"But not all . . . " must have elicited a twinge of pain in Jesus.

For he knew who would **betray** him;
>   for this **reason**, he said, "Not **all** of you are clean."

So when he had **washed** their **feet**
>   and put his **garments** back on and reclined at **table** again,
>   he **said** to them, "Do you **realize** what I have **done** for you?

Jesus' question is rhetorical and he immediately shares his prepared answer.

You call me '**teacher**' and '**master**,' and **rightly** so, for indeed I **am**.

Jesus' emphatic speech signals an awareness that this will be a hard teaching to adopt.

If **I**, therefore, the **master** and **teacher**, have washed **your** feet,
>   **you** ought to wash one **another's** feet.

Here is yet more emphasis from Jesus to do as he has done.

I have given you a **model** to follow,
>   so that as **I** have done for **you**, you should **also** do."

TO KEEP IN MIND
Eye contact connects you with those to whom you minister. Look at the assembly during the middle and at the end of every thought or sentence.

Assuming the role of a slave, Jesus demonstrates the depth of sharing in his life and mission that partaking in this meal implies, and begins to wash their feet. Resisting this astonishing role reversal, Peter protests, addressing Jesus as *kyrie*, "master" or "lord." Word and act present an astounding juxtaposition, especially in contemporary culture. A lord owned slaves, but most assuredly would never lower himself to behave like one, taking on a most demeaning task. Jesus replies that refusal to participate in this action will mean having no part with Jesus. Typically impetuous,

Peter then demands a more complete cleansing. Jesus responds that those who have bathed need no further washing, though not everyone present is clean. On the surface, John points to the presence of the betrayer, Judas. But the dialogue may also refer to the cleansing of Baptism, since John emphasizes that some accept life offered by Jesus, while others do not. A decision is required.

Lest the disciples miss the meaning of his symbolic act, Jesus teaches it again by word: the foot washing is a model for followers. By the standards of the prevailing

culture, one could lower himself no further in serving another than to do so as a slave, as one owned by the other. By all human standards, one can give nothing more than life itself. Jesus is about to give his whole self. and life itself, for those he loves—an act which those who share his supper "should also do." M.F.

FRIDAY OF THE PASSION OF THE LORD (GOOD FRIDAY)

LECTIONARY #40

READING I   Isaiah 52:13—53:12

Isaiah = ī-ZAY-uh

The voice of God, strong and proud.

Sudden mood shift to narrating the suffering of God's servant.

The sense of this verse is: In the way that many were amazed at him—because he was so disfigured he didn't even look human—in that same way others will be startled and astonished.

New voice: that of the people.

Much lamenting here. People hid their faces because he was not pleasing to look at.

A reading from the Book of the Prophet Isaiah

See, my servant shall **prosper**,
   he shall be raised **high** and greatly **exalted**.
Even as many were **amazed** at him—
   so **marred** was his look beyond human **semblance**
   and his **appearance** beyond that of the sons of **man**—
so shall he **startle** many **nations**,
   because of him **kings** shall stand **speechless**;
for those who have not been **told** shall **see**,
   those who have not **heard** shall **ponder** it.

Who would **believe** what we have heard?
   To **whom** has the **arm** of the LORD been **revealed**?
He grew up like a **sapling** before him,
   like a **shoot** from the parched **earth**;
there was in him no **stately** bearing to make us **look** at him,
   nor **appearance** that would **attract** us to him.
He was **spurned** and **avoided** by people,
   a man of **suffering**, accustomed to **infirmity**,
one of those from whom people **hide** their faces,
   spurned, and we held him in no **esteem**.

Yet it was **our** infirmities that he bore,
   our **sufferings** that he endured,
while we thought of him as **stricken**,
   as one **smitten** by God and **afflicted**.

READING I   Today's First Reading, the fourth "Suffering Servant" song of Isaiah, is one of the most discussed and debated texts in the entire Old Testament. The exact identity and occasion of the servant's suffering is far less important than the overall themes rendered here in poetry.

The "servant songs" appear in the second of three parts of Isaiah's prophecy, most likely dating from the later part of the Babylonian exile. At this time, the prophet looks toward God's release of the people. In four poems scattered through this sec-tion (chapters 40–55), the prophet describes the Servant of the Lord, or the Suffering Righteous One, as a figure chosen by God and anointed with divine spirit to carry out saving activity on behalf of the shattered covenant community. This last and longest poem often uses language and imagery of the psalms, especially those that express thanksgiving for God's rescue from debilitating or death-dealing situa-tions. While today many scholars believe the servant represents the covenant peo-ple, the Church's liturgy has followed New Testament interpretations that apply this poem to Jesus. In so doing, these Christian authors made use of Jewish methods of interpreting earlier Scriptures in order to clarify their meaning for the present.

The beginning of the reading seems to anticipate its ending, describing a complete reversal of the servant's fortunes brought about by God. Though the servant grew up under the divine gaze, by human standards there was nothing remarkable about him. In fact, as a person accustomed to suffering, he was avoided by others, because Jewish belief assumed that various human sor-rows resulted from sin.

"Stripes" meaning the marks left behind from a whipping.

But he was **pierced** for our **offenses**,
    crushed for our **sins**;
upon **him** was the chastisement that makes us **whole**,
    by his **stripes** we were **healed**.
We had all gone astray like **sheep**,
    each following his **own** way;
but the Lord laid upon **him**
    the guilt of us **all**.

Softer tone. The two images—"lamb," "sheep"—make the same point so the pace can be a bit quicker, though intensity should not wane.

Though he was **harshly** treated, he **submitted**
    and opened **not** his mouth;
like a **lamb** led to the **slaughter**
    or a **sheep** before the **shearers**,
    he was **silent** and opened not his mouth.

"Oppressed" and "condemned" are *two* distinct words; don't rush them together. Perhaps anger and regret over this indignity.

Oppressed and **condemned**, he was taken **away**,
    and who would have thought any more of his **destiny**?
When he was cut **off** from the land of the living,
    and **smitten** for the sin of his people,
a **grave** was assigned him among the **wicked**
    and a **burial** place with **evildoers**,
though he had done **no wrong**
    nor spoken any **falsehood**.

Resignation.

But the *Lord* was **pleased**
    to **crush** him in **infirmity**.

Voice of God returns—Energetic, proud, and proclaiming.

If he gives his **life** as an offering for **sin**,
    he shall see his **descendants** in a **long** life,
    and the **will** of the Lord shall be **accomplished**
        through him.

Quieter now, but persuasive.

Because of his **affliction**
    he shall see the **light** in fullness of days;
through his **suffering**, my servant shall justify **many**,
    and their **guilt** he shall **bear**.
Therefore I will give him his **portion** among the **great**,
    and **he** shall divide the **spoils** with the **mighty**, »

High point of the reading; Servant is honored; but notice *why*: he suffered willingly!

At this point in the poem, the servant begins to be described as "we," a corporate body that is somehow healed and restored to wholeness through the servant's sufferings. It appears that ancient Israel did have some level of belief that vicarious suffering could be redemptive. Reference to the people's guilt taken on by the servant may reflect an ancient scapegoat ritual that formed part of atonement rituals. In this symbolic act, the people's offenses were confessed and laid upon a goat that was then driven into the wilderness, taking away the community's sin and guilt (Leviticus 16:20–22).

Though mistreated, oppressed, and condemned, the servant bears all in silence, and though he is innocent, the view that suffering implies guilt prevails, and the servant is designated for burial among the wicked. Again the poem expresses belief that one person's suffering can ultimately bring about renewal for the community. Through the servant's self-offering, "the will of the Lord shall be accomplished." It is important to know that in biblical thought, God's will always ulti-mately desires human salvation, healing, and wholeness.

Like a psalm of thanksgiving, the poem shifts from lament to giving praise and thanks for divine reversal of the sufferer's plight, even before the fact. The prophet describes the most important effect of the servant's sacrificial suffering: the people will be justified, restored to right relationships with God and with all things. The servant who trusted in God's saving might is not disappointed: God purifies, renews, and justifies the people, and the servant himself is vindicated.

because he **surrendered** himself to **death**
and was counted among the **wicked**;
and he shall take **away** the sins of **many**,
and win **pardon** for their **offenses**.

Ritardando (slowing toward the end): "and win pardon . . . offenses."

For meditation and context:

RESPONSORIAL PSALM   Psalm 31:2, 6, 12–13, 15–16, 17, 25 (Luke 23:46)

R. Father, into your hands I commend my spirit.

In you, O LORD, I take refuge;
  let me never be put to shame.
In your justice rescue me.
Into your hands I commend my spirit;
  you will redeem me, O LORD,
    O faithful God.

For all my foes I am an object of reproach,
  a laughingstock to my neighbors, and a
    dread to my friends;
  they who see me abroad flee from me.
I am forgotten like the unremembered dead;
  I am like a dish that is broken.

But my trust is in you, O LORD;
  I say, "You are my God.
In your hands is my destiny; rescue me
  from the clutches of my enemies and my
    persecutors."

Let your face shine upon your servant;
  save me in your kindness.
Take courage and be stouthearted,
  all you who hope in the LORD.

> **TO KEEP IN MIND**
>
> **Narrator:** Knowing the point of view that the narrator is "rooting for" will help you more fully communicate the meaning of the text. The narrator always has a viewpoint, often speaking as a believer, not as an objective reporter. For this reason, the narrator is often the pivotal role in a passage. Using timbre, pitch, rate, and energy can help you convey the narrator's moods or meanings.

READING II   Hebrews 4:14–16; 5:7–9

A reading from the Letter to the Hebrews

Brothers and sisters:

Begin with confident rejoicing.

Since we have a great high **priest** who has passed through
  the **heavens**,
  Jesus, the Son of **God**,
  let us hold **fast** to our **confession**.
For we do not have a high priest

He was one of us. He can sympathize and knows our pain.

  who is unable to **sympathize** with our **weaknesses**,
  but one who has similarly been tested in every way,
  yet without **sin**.

Confidently persuade us of his sinlessness.

So let us **confidently** approach the throne of **grace**
  to receive **mercy** and to find grace for timely **help**.

In the days when Christ was in the **flesh**,

Christ truly suffered: That's why he understands our suffering.

  he offered **prayers** and **supplications** with loud **cries** and **tears**

READING II Because Hebrews is unique among New Testament books in presenting Christ as the perfect high priest, it is helpful to understand the high priestly role in Jewish religious practice. A major function of the high priest was to offer prayer and sacrifice on the Day of Atonement; only he could stand before God in the Temple's Holy of Holies to ask forgiveness for the sins of all the people during the preceding year. Note that the biblical view of atonement gives precedence to God's saving, renewing action; the

people's sacrifice confirms but does not cause wholeness and oneness with God.

More a sermon than a letter, Hebrews is designated as a "word of exhortation" (13:22). The author interweaves a call to persevere in faith and mutual love with his interpretation of Christ as both perfect high priest and the atonement sacrifice itself. As divine Son of God, Jesus is capable of bringing about atonement. But Christians called to imitate him should be reassured that their high priest is fully human, able to understand our weakness because he "has similarly been tested in every way."

Regardless of the depth of Jesus' suffering, he never chose to sin. In this he is the supreme example to emulate.

The writer refers to Christ's days "in the flesh," emphasizing his complete identification with humanity. The Greek word here translated "flesh" is *sarx*, which indicates the entire human being as susceptible to weakness, suffering, and death. Fully experiencing "the flesh," Jesus called upon divine help in reverent submission to God. Jesus' action and attitude provides the model for Christian imitation, for he "learned obedience" through his own

to the one who was able to **save** him from **death**,
and he was **heard** because of his **reverence**.
Son though he **was**, he learned **obedience** from what he suffered;
and when he was made **perfect**,
he became the **source** of eternal **salvation** for all who
obey him.

GOSPEL   John 18:1—19:42

The Passion of our Lord Jesus Christ according to John

Jesus went out with his **disciples** across the Kidron **valley**
to where there was a **garden**,
into which he and his disciples entered.
Judas his **betrayer also** knew the place,
because Jesus had **often** met there with his disciples.
So Judas got a band of **soldiers** and **guards**
from the chief **priests** and the **Pharisees**
and went there with **lanterns**, **torches**, and **weapons**.
Jesus, knowing **everything** that was going to happen to him,
went out and said to them, "Whom are you **looking** for?"
They **answered** him, "**Jesus** the **Nazorean**."
He said to them, "**I AM**."
Judas his betrayer was **also** with them.
When he said to them, "**I AM**,"
they turned away and fell to the **ground**.
So he **again** asked them,
"**Whom** are you looking for?"
They said, "**Jesus** the **Nazorean**."
Jesus answered,
"I **told** you that **I AM**.
So if you are looking for **me**, let these men **go**."
This was to **fulfill** what he had said,
"I have not lost **any** of those you gave me." »

Note: Jesus "learned" obedience through his suffering.

Jesus modeled obedience. We imitate him and find salvation. Ritardando (slowing toward the end): "for . . . obey him."

Kidron = KID-ruhn. The garden is a peaceful, familiar place.

Shadow of Judas suddenly shifts mood.

"Lanterns" are symbolic of the hour of darkness.
Jesus moves forward fully aware and in charge of his destiny.

Jesus' power overwhelms the guards. He'll be taken only when he permits it.

---

suffering. It is difficult to capture in translation the full meaning of the phrase rendered "when he was made perfect." The Greek term here can include several meanings: to reach a physical or chronological end, to reach a goal, or to achieve completion. It seems that the author wishes to reassure his readers that when God's plan reached its completion through Christ's Death and Resurrection, he became the source of God's own saving life for all who, like him, learn obedience in trusting surrender to God.

PASSION | This reading must be understood in light of the prologue, in which the author offers a summary-preview of his foundational understanding of Christ: he is God's own self-revealing Word "made flesh" (see Reading 2). In Jesus' full humanity, in his words, works, and passage through Death to Resurrection, God proclaims: This is who I am: self-giving love for the re-creation of humankind, my beloved. John's interpretation of Jesus, the Christ, reflects about seven decades of Christian reflection on his life, Passion, and Resurrection, and por-

trays above all the living, glorified Christ experienced in the present, alive within and among believers in the Spirit. Like the other Gospel accounts, this is a faith proclamation in narrative form; even more than the synoptic accounts (Matthew, Mark, and Luke), John focuses on the meaning of Jesus in and for the present. The author writes not simply to communicate factual details, but to inspire faith in Jesus as the Messiah and Son of God (John 21:30–31).

Being aware of other aspects of John's historical context and literary approach also aids in understanding his message. In

Violence expressed with "struck" and "cut off." Malchus = MAL-kuhs

Jesus rebukes Peter.

Annas = AN-uhs; Caiaphas = KĪ-uh-fuhs. This is a significant quote attributed to Caiaphas.

Is Peter kept out or staying out from fear?

Peter doesn't want to be overheard denying Jesus.
New scene. Renew energy.

Jesus is strong in his self-defense, showing the weakness of their "case."

Then Simon **Peter**, who had a **sword**, **drew** it,
    struck the high priest's slave, and **cut** off his right ear.
The slave's name was **Malchus**.
Jesus said to Peter,
    "Put your sword into its **scabbard**.
Shall I not **drink** the cup that the Father gave me?"

So the band of **soldiers**, the **tribune**, and the Jewish **guards**
    seized Jesus,
    bound him, and brought him to **Annas** first.
He was the **father-in-law** of **Caiaphas**,
    who was high **priest** that year.
It was **Caiaphas** who had **counseled** the Jews
    that it was better that **one** man should die rather than
        the **people**.

Simon **Peter** and **another** disciple **followed** Jesus.
Now the **other** disciple was **known** to the high **priest**,
    and he entered the **courtyard** of the high priest with **Jesus**.
But **Peter** stood at the gate **outside**.
So the other **disciple**, the **acquaintance** of the high priest,
    went out and spoke to the **gatekeeper** and brought Peter **in**.
Then the **maid** who was the gatekeeper said to Peter,
    "You are not one of this man's **disciples**, are you?"
He said, "I am **not**."
Now the slaves and the **guards** were standing around a char-
    coal **fire**
    that they had made, because it was **cold**,
    and were **warming** themselves.
Peter was **also** standing there keeping warm.

The high priest **questioned** Jesus
    about his **disciples** and about his **doctrine**.
Jesus **answered** him,
    "I have spoken **publicly** to the world.
I have always taught in a **synagogue**
    or in the **temple** area where all the Jews **gather**,
    and in **secret** I have said **nothing**. Why ask **me**?

the New Testament era, mainstream Judaism struggled to identify its most authentic form in a time of varying interpretations of the Law of Moses. Some proponents of mainstream Judaism viewed Jewish Christians as members of one among several misguided Jewish sects, and this antagonism surfaces frequently in John. The author repeatedly presents Jesus and "the Jews" in debate and opposition, a conflict which grows in intensity. This descriptor ("the Jews") does not condemn all Jews of all time, but represents strains of Judaism that resisted the Christian

movement at the end of the first century. John's interpretation of Christ sees Jewish thought, institutions, and observances as replaced by Jesus, divine Word made flesh. In John's Gospel account, Jesus does not speak the Word of God, he *is* that Word. One need not approach the Temple to meet God, one need only encounter Jesus. Jesus does not celebrate God's great saving act of Passover, he himself *is* a new Passover. To convey his message convincingly to those who remain in Judaism, John uses Jewish modes of interpreting the Scriptures, often making creative use of the

Old Testament to interpret the meaning of Jesus for his time and place (see Reading 1).

John presents Jesus' Passion and Death as the final and definitive self-revelation of God in Jesus, the divine Word made flesh. For John, Jesus freely chooses to lay down his life for those he loves, so that they may have fullness of life. In his Passion and Death, the Word Jesus himself spoke to "the Jews" (John 10:10–18) becomes a Word made flesh, a Word enacted. In John's account, Jesus appears to be the one in charge of all proceedings of his Passion, from arrest through his last breath.

Ask those who **heard** me what I said to them.
They know what I said."
When he had **said** this,
   one of the temple guards standing there **struck** Jesus and said,
   "Is this the way you answer the high **priest**?"
Jesus answered him,
   "If I have spoken **wrongly**, **testify** to the wrong;
   but if I have spoken **rightly**, why do you **strike** me?"
Then Annas sent him **bound** to **Caiaphas** the high priest.

Now Simon **Peter** was standing there keeping warm.
And they **said** to him,
   "**You** are not one of his disciples, **are** you?"
He **denied** it and said,
   "I am **not**."
One of the **slaves** of the high priest,
   a **relative** of the one whose **ear** Peter had cut **off**, said,
   "Didn't I see you in the **garden** with him?"
Again Peter denied it.
And **immediately** the **cock** crowed.

Then they brought Jesus from **Caiaphas** to the **praetorium**.
It was **morning**.
And they themselves did not **enter** the praetorium,
   in order not to be **defiled** so that they could eat the **Passover**.
So **Pilate** came out to **them** and said,
   "What **charge** do you bring against this man?"
They **answered** and said to him,
   "If he were not a **criminal**,
   we would not have handed him over to you."
At this, **Pilate** said to them,
   "Take him **yourselves**, and **judge** him according to your **law**."
The Jews **answered** him,
   "We do not have the right to **execute** anyone,"
   in order that the word of Jesus might be **fulfilled**
   that he said indicating the kind of **death** he would die. »

Deliver line like a slap—fast and hard.

Jesus holds his ground.

New scene.

Peter gets angry.
The denials are brief, but with this line suggest the lasting impact on Peter.

A spat among political adversaries. Each is annoyed with the other.

Scene shift. Pilate is "starting over." Pilate is not presented as a villain.

Only John names the place of Jesus' arrest as a garden. Just as the evangelist signaled in the opening words of his prologue ("In the beginning") that a new creation story originates with Jesus, so now he suggests that everything turned awry in the first garden will soon be set right. Unlike the synoptic accounts in which Jesus is seized, in John he steps forward to meet those who will lead him to death, with clear knowledge of what is about to happen. Taking an active role in his own capture, he asks those who confront him who they are looking for. To their reply, "Jesus the Nazorean," he responds three times, with dual meaning, "I AM." In Greek, his answer (*ego eimi*) can simply mean, "It is I" or "I am the one." However, the Greek Old Testament translated the revealed name of God, often rendered "I AM" or "I am who am," with the same words. John again indicates that the true character of the divine Word made flesh will soon be fully revealed, and it will be manifest in Jesus' chosen act of laying down life itself for those he loves. Preventing Peter from doing violence to ward off Jesus' arrest, Jesus does not ask the Father to let the cup of suffering pass, as in the synoptic accounts. Instead, he freely embraces it, again proclaiming his identity as divine Word made flesh.

Most scholars believe that a historical reality underlies the scenes of Jesus brought before Annas, Caiaphas, and Pilate. Ample evidence indicates that historically, some Jews, primarily those in religious leadership, colluded with Roman authorities to eliminate Jesus in order to protect their power and position. Throughout his narrative, John has portrayed growing antagonism between "the Jews" and Jesus, and now it reaches

Pilate becoming impatient again.

Stressing "are" or "king" changes the meaning of the question.
Jesus speaks with confidence.

So **Pilate** went back into the **praetorium**
   and **summoned** Jesus and said to him,
   "Are you the **King** of the **Jews**?"
Jesus answered,
   "Do you say this on your **own**
   or have **others** told you about me?"
Pilate answered,
   "I am not a **Jew**, am I?
Your own **nation** and the chief **priests** handed you over to me.
What have you **done**?"
Jesus answered,
   "My **kingdom** does not belong to **this** world.
If my kingdom **did** belong to this world,
   my attendants would be **fighting**
   to **keep** me from being handed over to the Jews.
But as it **is**, my kingdom is not **here**."
So Pilate said to him,
   "Then you **are** a king?"
Jesus answered,
   "**You** say I am a king.
For this I was **born** and for **this** I came into the **world**,
   to **testify** to the **truth**.
Everyone who **belongs** to the truth **listens** to my voice."
Pilate said to him, "What is **truth**?"

When he had **said** this,
   he **again** went out to the Jews and said to them,
   "I find no **guilt** in him.
But you have a custom that I release one **prisoner** to you
     at **Passover**.
Do you want me to release to you the **King** of the **Jews**?"
They cried out again,
   "Not **this** one but **Barabbas**!"
Now Barabbas was a **revolutionary**.

Seeking a quick resolution. Is he trying to put words in their mouths? Barabbas = buh-RAB-uhs

a crescendo; religious leaders in the story would be grateful to Rome for ridding them of Jesus. John intersperses the episodes of Peter's denial of Jesus among the scenes of Jesus' confrontation with Jewish and Roman authorities.

Among the canonical Gospel accounts, only John indicates a reason for the Jewish leadership to accuse Jesus of a capital crime before the Roman governor, Pilate. Although the religious laws of Judaism found Jesus guilty of an offense meriting death, execution itself could be carried out only by the ruling empire. The first scene involving Jesus and Pilate involves multilevel meanings, often ironic, which is typical of John. Pilate tests Jesus' response to his inquiry, "Are you the king of the Jews?" Any prisoner answering in the affirmative would be sentenced to death as an insurrectionist, and Jesus initially seems to sidestep the question. He then claims a Kingdom not of this world, and echoes John's assertion in the prologue: that he is sent from God as bearer of truth. Pilate can only respond with a question, "What is truth?", for he fails to recognize the truth of God in the prisoner before him. As in the synoptic Gospel accounts, not Jesus, but Barabbas is chosen for release; the name means "son of the father," and he is chosen over the true Son of the Father. In John it is not the crowds who call for Barabbas, but "the Jews," who cannot accept that Jesus is Son of God.

After Jesus is scourged and mocked, Pilate repeatedly states that he finds no guilt in his prisoner. "The Jews," however, respond that according to their Law he must die because he made himself "Son of God." This charge is not made in the Passion account, but appears earlier in the

A greatly understated scene, but the pain is real.

Perhaps he is saying: Look at what you made me do!

When a phrase is repeated, give greater stress to second utterance.

Pilate's frustration turns on Jesus.

Then Pilate took Jesus and had him **scourged**.
And the soldiers wove a **crown** out of **thorns** and placed it
    on his **head**,
  and clothed him in a **purple** cloak,
  and they came to him and said,
    "**Hail**, **King** of the **Jews**!"
And they **struck** him **repeatedly**.
Once **more** Pilate went out and said to them,
    "**Look**, I am bringing him out to you,
  so that you may **know** that I find no **guilt** in him."
So Jesus came out,
  wearing the crown of **thorns** and the purple **cloak**.
And he said to them, "**Behold**, the man!"
When the chief priests and the guards saw him they **cried** out,
    "**Crucify** him, **crucify** him!"
Pilate said to them,
  "Take him **yourselves** and crucify him.
I find no **guilt** in him."
The Jews **answered**,
  "We have a **law**, and according to that law he ought to **die**,
  because he made himself the **Son** of **God**."
Now when Pilate **heard** this statement,
  he became even **more** afraid,
    and went back into the praetorium and said to **Jesus**,
  "Where are you **from**?"
Jesus did not **answer** him.
So Pilate said to him,
  "Do you not speak to **me**?
Do you not know that I have power to **release** you
  and I have power to **crucify** you?"
Jesus answered him,
  "You would have **no** power over me
  if it had not been **given** to you from **above**.
For this reason the one who handed me **over** to you
  has the **greater** sin." »

account (John 5:18). Pilate threatens Jesus, claiming he has the power of life and death over him, but Jesus again speaks as no ordinary prisoner, as one who can claim a greater authority. When Pilate tries to release Jesus, "the Jews" remind him that such a decision would surely fail to earn him the honorific title "Friend of Caesar."

Finally, battered by continuing insistence of "the Jews," Pilate calls for Jesus' execution. John carefully notes the day and the hour: about noon on preparation day for the Sabbath. His chronology does not match that of the synoptic accounts, but

John is far less focused on historical detail than on Christological meaning. At this moment, the slaughter of lambs for the Jewish feast of Passover begins. With his chronology, John instructs his hearers that Jesus is even more than the Suffering Servant of Isaiah, led like a lamb to slaughter (see Reading 2); he himself is the new Passover for a New Israel of the final age.

Alone among the canonical Gospels accounts, John states that Jesus carries the Cross himself; the Word of God who is one with the Father relies only on divine assistance. The placard indicating the crucified

one's crime, usual Roman procedure, mockingly indicates that Jesus dies as an insurrectionist. But John adds another detail to proclaim Jesus' true kingship. When the chief priests demand that the inscription should not state "King of the Jews" but only that Jesus had made this claim, even the obtuse and unbelieving Pilate decrees, "What I have written, I have written."

Historically, Roman soldiers who carried out a crucifixion were allowed to take portions of the executed person's clothing, but the evangelist John notes deeper

"Friend of Caesar" is a title of honor bestowed by Rome on high-ranking officials—which Pilate might lose if he mishandles this situation.

Consequently, Pilate tried to **release** him; but the **Jews** cried **out**,
      "If you **release** him, you are not a **Friend** of **Caesar**.
Everyone who makes himself a **king** opposes Caesar."

Gabbatha = GAB-uh-thuh

When Pilate heard these words he brought Jesus out
      and **seated** him on the **judge's** bench
      in the place called **Stone Pavement**, in **Hebrew**, **Gabbatha**.
It was **preparation** day for **Passover**, and it was about **noon**.
And he said to the **Jews**,
      "**Behold**, your **king**!"
They **cried** out,
      "**Take** him away, **take** him away! **Crucify** him!"

A last effort to forestall.

Pilate said to them,
      "Shall I crucify your **king**?"
The chief priests answered,
      "We have no king but **Caesar**."
Then he **handed** him over to them to be **crucified**.

New scene. Slowly. Golgotha = GOL-guh-thh

So they **took** Jesus, and, **carrying** the cross **himself**,
      he went out to what is called the **Place** of the **Skull**,
      in **Hebrew**, **Golgotha**.
There they **crucified** him, and with him two **others**,
      one on either **side**, with Jesus in the **middle**.

Proclaim the inscription.

Pilate also had an **inscription** written and put on the cross.
It read,
      "**Jesus** the **Nazorean**, the **King** of the **Jews**."
Now many of the Jews **read** this inscription,
      because the place where Jesus was crucified was near the **city**;
      and it was written in **Hebrew**, **Latin**, and **Greek**.
So the chief **priests** of the Jews said to Pilate,
      "Do not write 'The **King** of the Jews,'
      but that he **said**, 'I am the King of the **Jews**.'"

"What I have written, I / have / written!"

Pilate answered,
      "What I have **written**, I have **written**."

---

meanings as fulfillment of Scripture, quoting Psalm 22. Only John speaks of Jesus providing for mutual care of his mother and the beloved disciple. Various interpretations of this act have been given; some believe it points to Jesus' care for those who belong to him to the end, and others see an indication that Jesus will soon hand over his work to those who do believe in him.

Jesus approaches the end of his earthly life and the work the Father has given him, aware that both are reaching completion. John emphasizes this sense of accomplishment, arriving at an intended

goal, with words here translated "finished" and "fulfilled." In Greek, the words share a single root which can carry both meanings. The evangelist portrays Jesus as fully conscious that his total self-gift will end his life in "the flesh" as it brings God's plan to its desired goal. John interprets Jesus' words "I thirst" as fulfilling Scripture; the author may be referring to Psalm 22:16 and/or 69:22. Both prayers present a faithful sufferer crying out to God in lament, yet expressing hope in ultimate divine deliverance.

Still, John's interpretation of Jesus reaches beyond this Old Testament theme

of the vindicated Suffering Servant or Suffering Righteous One. In response to his cry of thirst, someone offers a sponge soaked with wine, using "a sprig of hyssop." With this detail, John alludes to the first Passover, when the Lord instructed the Hebrews to mark their door posts with the blood of the lamb sacrificed for the meal before the flight from Egypt. By sprinkling the lamb's blood with a bunch of hyssop, they ensured that the Lord would pass over their homes as he carried out the final plague upon Egypt. Jesus is himself the new Passover Lamb of the new and final

When the soldiers had **crucified** Jesus,
  they took his **clothes** and **divided** them into four **shares**,
  a share for each **soldier**.
They also took his **tunic**, but the tunic was **seamless**,
  woven in one **piece** from the top down.
So they said to one another,
  "Let's not **tear** it, but cast **lots** for it to see whose it will be,"
  in order that the passage of **Scripture** might be **fulfilled**
    that says:
      They divided my **garments** *among them,*
        and for my **vesture** *they cast* **lots**.
This is what the soldiers **did**.
Standing by the **cross** of Jesus were his **mother**
  and his mother's **sister**, **Mary** the wife of **Clopas**,
  and Mary of **Magdala**.
When Jesus **saw** his mother and the **disciple** there whom
    he **loved**
  he said to his mother, "**Woman**, behold, your **son**."
Then he said to the **disciple**,
  "Behold, your **mother**."
And from that hour the disciple took her into his **home**.

After this, aware that everything was now **finished**,
  in order that the Scripture might be **fulfilled**,
  Jesus said, "I **thirst**."
There was a **vessel** filled with common **wine**.
So they put a sponge **soaked** in wine on a sprig of **hyssop**
  and put it up to his **mouth**.
When Jesus had **taken** the wine, he said,
  "It is **finished**."
And bowing his **head**, he handed over the **spirit**.

[Here all kneel and pause for a short time.]

Now since it was **preparation** day,
  in order that the bodies might not **remain**
  on the cross on the **sabbath**, »

Tone shift: quoting scripture.

New scene. Women are much grieved.
Four women are identified: "his mother's sister" is different from "Mary the wife of Clopas." Clopas = KLOH-puhs; Magdala = MAG-duh-luh

New scene. Stress Jesus' awareness and control. Hyssop = HIS-uhp

Jesus' "spirit" is the Holy Spirit, the spirit of the new creation. Jesus' Death is the giving of the Spirit.

Passover: a passage through death to fullness of life.

Finally, Jesus himself proclaims what the evangelist has stated: "It is finished." For the third time in three verses, John uses the same word with multi-layered meaning. He announces that Jesus has died, and that in so doing, God's plan for human salvation is completed, brought to its intended goal. At this moment, Jesus "handed over the spirit." Yet again, John employs dual meaning. On one hand, he simply states that Jesus has died, returning the life-breath of God to the One who first

created his life in the flesh (see Genesis 2:7). More profoundly, the evangelist proclaims that in ending his earthly life, Jesus fulfills his promise to send "the Advocate" upon returning to the Father (John 16:1–15). John uses the Greek word *parakletos*, variously translated but indicating the Holy Spirit; at root, the word designates someone who can be counted upon to stand at the side of another.

In the following passage, Pilate's order to break Jesus' legs may reflect a known practice; if a crucified prisoner did not die within several days, the legs might be bro-

ken to hasten death. For John, however, the scene presents an opportunity for theological commentary. The blood and water flowing from the side of Jesus can be understood to symbolize the Spirit, earlier in the Gospel identified with water, and Jesus' life itself, signified by blood, given for those he loves. With few quoted words, John announces that Jesus brings to completion three Old Testament motifs: the Paschal Lamb, the Suffering Righteous One, and the Messiah (Exodus 12:46; Psalm 34:21; Zechariah 12:10).

Breaking legs assured quicker death, by asphyxiation.

Blood and water: important symbols.

With conviction.

for the sabbath day of that week was a **solemn** one,
    the Jews asked Pilate that their legs be **broken**
    and that they be taken **down**.
So the **soldiers** came and **broke** the legs of the **first**
    and then of the **other** one who was crucified with Jesus.
But when they came to Jesus and saw that he was already **dead**,
    they did **not** break **his** legs,
    but **one** soldier thrust his **lance** into his **side**,
    and immediately **blood** and **water** flowed out.
An **eyewitness** has **testified**, and his testimony is **true**;
    he **knows** that he is speaking the **truth**,
    so that you **also** may come to **believe**.
For this happened so that the **Scripture** passage might
        be **fulfilled**:
*Not a **bone** of it will be **broken**.*
And again **another** passage says:
*They will **look** upon him whom they have **pierced**.*

With tender respect for Joseph and, later, Nicodemus. Arimathea = ayr-ih-muh-THEE-uh; Nicodemus = nik-oh-DEE-muhs; myrrh = mer; aloes = AL-ohz

After this, **Joseph** of **Arimathea**,
    secretly a **disciple** of Jesus for **fear** of the **Jews**,
    asked Pilate if he could **remove** the body of Jesus.
And Pilate **permitted** it.
So he came and **took** his body.
Nicodemus, the one who had first come to him at **night**,
    also came bringing a mixture of **myrrh** and **aloes**
    weighing about one hundred **pounds**.
They took the **body** of Jesus
    and bound it with **burial** cloths along with the **spices**,
    according to the Jewish burial custom.

Slow pacing.

Now in the place where he had been crucified there was
        a **garden**,
    and in the garden a **new tomb**, in which no one had yet
        been **buried**.
So they laid Jesus **there** because of the Jewish **preparation** day;
    for the tomb was close by.

        As in the synoptic Gospel accounts, Joseph of Arimathea asks for and receives for burial the body of Jesus, but the evangelist adds a significant detail. With the burial of Jesus, John returns to the place in which he began his Passion account: a garden. Again he suggests that all that was lacking in the first garden "in the beginning" will now be created anew. The body of Jesus is laid in a new tomb, in which no one has yet been buried; from it will spring the new life of God's new creation. M.F.

HOLY SATURDAY: EASTER VIGIL

LECTIONARY #41

READING I   Genesis 1:1—2:2

A reading from the Book of Genesis

In the **beginning**, when God created the **heavens** and the **earth**,
   the earth was a formless **wasteland**, and **darkness** covered
     the **abyss**,
   while a mighty **wind** swept over the **waters**.

Then God **said**,
   "Let there be **light**," and there **was** light.
God saw how **good** the light was.
God then **separated** the light from the **darkness**.
God called the light "**day**," and the darkness he called "**night**."
Thus **evening** came, and **morning** followed—the **first** day.

Then God said,
   "Let there be a **dome** in the **middle** of the waters,
   to **separate** one body of water from the **other**."
And so it **happened**:
   God **made** the dome,
   and it separated the water **above** the dome from the water
     below it.
God called the dome "the **sky**."
Evening came, and **morning** followed—the **second** day.

Then God said,
   "Let the **water** under the sky be gathered into a single **basin**,
   so that the dry **land** may appear." **»**

Speak the first three words with all that is in you. Notice the five-part pattern of each day. Use the repeated refrains to draw your listeners deeper into the pattern of God's creative work. The *pattern* should be obvious, so it is better to *stress* the repetitions than to hide them with novel readings on each day. Their regularity, familiarity, and predictability give the passage much of its power. So don't rush them.

The declaration that creation is "good" and the accomplishment of God's command are stressed each time they recur.

Renew your energy with each "Then God said."

READING I | The readings for this greatest of liturgies begin with the story of God's first creation and come full circle with the beginning of humankind's re-creation through Christ. The First Reading comes from the beginning of the Old Testament, presenting one of the two creation narratives that are combined into one creation account in the Book of Genesis. This story most likely comes from the hand of a group of priests writing during the Babylonian exile, and the account reflects their concern with assuring the captive people that the Lord is their one source of life and their future. Thus the writer begins with God bringing life and order out of formless chaos; the Hebrew word *ruah*, here translated "mighty wind," can mean breath, wind, or spirit. The divine power that brings all material creation into being is the same force that will enliven the human creature in the second creation story (Genesis 2:7).

The story unfolds in a systematic pattern of one day following the next, with specific creatures brought to life in orderly fashion by God's mighty Word. Throughout, the writer continues to emphasize the divine power at work, and repeatedly notes that what is created is "good"; the original Hebrew word has a vast range of meanings, including "pleasing, valuable, and able to fulfill its purpose." God "blessed" the living creatures, including human beings, telling them to be fruitful. In the thinking of the

Identify each creation—"the earth . . . the sea"—with tenderness.

There is much detail here: use the words marked for emphasis to guide you in placing your stress. Every word isn't important. Here it's the energy and enthusiasm that matter most.

Here as before, it's more important to convey a sense of joy and wonder rather than overemphasizing details.

Proclaim "and he made the stars" quickly, with excitement or slowly, with amazement. Note that the purpose of each of the lights somehow serves humanity.

Each time it recurs, this refrain should convey the end of an epoch of time and creation. Speak with a sense of accomplishment, joy, and peace.

And so it **happened**:
   the water under the sky was **gathered** into its basin,
   and the dry **land** appeared.
God called the **dry land** "the **earth**,"
   and the **basin** of the **water** he called "the **sea**."
God saw how **good** it was.
Then God said,
   "Let the **earth** bring forth **vegetation**:
   every kind of **plant** that bears **seed**
   and every kind of **fruit** tree on earth
   that bears fruit with its **seed** in it."
And so it **happened**:
   the earth brought forth every kind of plant that bears **seed**
   and every kind of **fruit** tree on earth
   that bears fruit with its **seed** in it.
God saw how **good** it was.
Evening came, and morning **followed**—the **third** day.

Then God said:
   "Let there be **lights** in the dome of the sky,
   to separate **day** from **night**.
Let them mark the fixed **times**, the **days** and the **years**,
   and serve as **luminaries** in the dome of the sky,
   to shed **light** upon the earth."
And so it **happened**:
   God made the **two** great lights,
   the **greater** one to govern the **day**,
   and the **lesser** one to govern the **night**;
   and he made the **stars**.
God set them in the **dome** of the sky,
   to shed **light** upon the earth,
   to **govern** the day and the night,
   and to separate the **light** from the **darkness**.
God saw how **good** it was.
Evening came, and **morning** followed—the **fourth** day.

ancient Hebrew world, the two notions are intimately connected, for a blessing was believed to be permanent and to impart the power to give life. In their precarious situation, the priestly editors continue to reassure God's people that they do have a future—one envisioned and empowered by God from the beginning.

In this first story, God creates humankind only after providing a sustainable world for it. The writer uses the word *adam*, meaning humankind, indicating that God formed the human race as a whole, male and female, in the divine image. This is God's purpose for *adam*; this creature alone can, and is meant to, reflect the Creator in the world. The author underscores the idea that God alone is the source of life for the human creature by using a specific verb meaning "to create"; this Hebrew word (*bara*) is used only of something formed by God. God instructs this unique creature, humankind, to "have dominion" over the other creatures. To avoid misunderstanding, this statement must be understood in Old Testament context. In the view of ancient Israel, the one true King was the Lord, and any human king was his representative. Hence human rulers were expected to rule as God does,

This "day" teems with life; there is much excitement and energy in this narration.

Notice God "blesses" the creatures. End this section with calm satisfaction.

Renew energy once again with joy at the thrill of creating life.

The reading reaches a subclimax here. *All creation is good!*

A nobler, slower pacing. Humans are made in God's own likeness! Use, don't rush, the repetitions. They deepen our sense of these great truths.

Speak this as a blessing. All the beauty and good God has created is entrusted to humanity.

Then God said,
"Let the water **teem** with an **abundance** of living **creatures**,
and on the **earth** let **birds** fly beneath the **dome** of the sky."
And so it **happened**:
God created the great **sea** monsters
and all kinds of **swimming** creatures with which the
water **teems**,
and all kinds of winged **birds**.
God saw how **good** it was, and God **blessed** them, saying,
"Be **fertile**, **multiply**, and **fill** the water of the seas;
and let the birds **multiply** on the earth."
Evening came, and morning **followed**—the **fifth** day.

Then God said,
"Let the **earth** bring forth all kinds of living **creatures**:
cattle, **creeping** things, and wild **animals** of all kinds."
And so it **happened**:
God made all kinds of wild **animals**, all kinds of **cattle**,
and all kinds of **creeping** things of the earth.
God saw how **good** it was.

Then God said:
"Let us make **man** in our **image**, after our **likeness**.
Let them have **dominion** over the **fish** of the sea,
the **birds** of the air, and the **cattle**,
and over all the wild **animals**
and all the creatures that crawl on the **ground**."
God created **man** in his **image**;
in the image of **God** he created him;
male and **female** he created them.
God **blessed** them, saying:
"Be **fertile** and **multiply**;
fill the earth and **subdue** it.
Have **dominion** over the fish of the **sea**, the birds of the **air**,
and all the **living** things that move on the earth." »

ensuring just and peaceful relationships among all people and things.

After ensuring continuing life for the human creature by giving green plants and animals for food, God surveys the whole of creation and once again pronounces it "very good." Closing the orderly pattern of day-by-day creation, the author presents one chief reason for an important Jewish religious law: avoiding work on the

Sabbath, the seventh day of the week, in order to devote time to praising God and studying divine teaching. If even God "rested" from work on the Sabbath, how much more ought God's people to follow such an example?

God **also** said:

"**See**, I give you every **seed**-bearing plant all over the earth
and every **tree** that has seed-bearing **fruit** on it to be your **food**;
and to all the **animals** of the land, all the **birds** of the air,
and all the living creatures that crawl on the **ground**,
I give all the **green** plants for food."
And so it **happened**.
God looked at **everything** he had made, and he found it
very good.
Evening came, and **morning** followed—the **sixth** day.

Thus the **heavens** and the **earth** and all their array
were **completed**.
Since on the **seventh** day God was **finished**
with the work he had been doing,
he **rested** on the seventh day from all the work he
had undertaken.

[Shorter: Genesis 1:1, 26–31a]

This is the summary statement: God's creation is *very* good!

With a sense of accomplishment and pride. Pause after "completed."

"Rested" suggests more than not working; it means delighting in the "work," that is, the beloved creation God has now completed.

For meditation and context:

RESPONSORIAL PSALM   Psalm 104:1–2, 5–6, 10, 12, 13–14, 24, 35 (30)

R. Lord, send out your Spirit, and renew the face of the earth.

Bless the LORD, O my soul!
 O LORD, my God, you are great indeed!
You are clothed with majesty and glory,
 robed in light as with a cloak.

You fixed the earth upon its foundation,
 not to be moved forever;
with the ocean, as with a garment, you
 covered it;
 above the mountains the waters stood.

You send forth springs into the watercourses
 that wind among the mountains.
Beside them the birds of heaven dwell;
 from among the branches they send forth
 their song.

You water the mountains from your palace;
 the earth is replete with the fruit
 of your works.
You raise grass for the cattle,
 and vegetation for man's use,
producing bread from the earth.

How manifold are your works, O LORD!
 In wisdom you have wrought them all—
the earth is full of your creatures.
 Bless the LORD, O my soul!

Or:

TO KEEP IN MIND
Openings and Closings: differ in tone from the Scripture and require pauses, after the opening dialogue and before the closing dialogue. These formulas are prescribed, so don't vary the wording.

For meditation and context:

TO KEEP IN MIND

Names of characters: Often the first word of a reading. Lift out the names to ensure listeners don't miss who the subject is.

RESPONSORIAL PSALM   Psalm 33:4–5, 6–7, 12–13, 20 and 22 (5b)

R. The earth is full of the goodness of the Lord.

Upright is the word of the LORD,
    and all his works are trustworthy.
He loves justice and right;
    of the kindness of the LORD the earth
    is full.

By the word of the LORD the heavens
    were made;
    by the breath of his mouth all their host.
He gathers the waters of the sea as in a flask;
    in cellars he confines the deep.

Blessed the nation whose God is the LORD,
    the people he has chosen for his own
    inheritance.
From heaven the LORD looks down;
    he sees all mankind.

Our soul waits for the LORD,
    who is our help and our shield.
May your kindness, O LORD, be upon us
    who have put our hope in you.

READING II   Genesis 22:1–18

A reading from the Book of Genesis

The opening line both introduces and summarizes the entire story. Pause slightly after "Abraham." "Here I am" is eager.

God put **Abraham** to the **test**.
He called to him, "**Abraham**!"
"**Here** I am," he replied.
Then God said:

Don't give away what's coming at the end. God's voice is solemn, not stern. Emphasize the gravity of God's command by stressing "only" and "love."

    "Take your son **Isaac**, your **only** one, whom you **love**,
    and go to the land of **Moriah**.
There you shall **offer** him up as a **holocaust**
    on a **height** that I will point **out** to you."
Early the next **morning** Abraham saddled his **donkey**,
    took with him his son **Isaac** and two of his **servants** as well,
    and with the **wood** that he had cut for the **holocaust**,
    set out for the place of which God had told him.

Abraham works hard to hide his pain. Don't let this sound like a trip to the mall.

On the **third** day Abraham got **sight** of the place from afar.
Then he **said** to his servants:
    "Both of you stay here with the **donkey**,
    while the **boy** and I go on over **yonder**.
We will **worship** and then come **back** to you." »

READING II   Previous to this passage, God promised Abraham that he would be the father of a multitude, but the promise seemed empty when Abraham and Sarah remained childless. Heavenly messengers assured them that even in their advanced age, Sarah would conceive a son. This seemingly impossible event came to pass, renewing the promise, only to lead to the shock of today's Second Reading. While this story often arouses revulsion in modern hearers, it has root in ancient cultures which did practice child sacrifice to express the willingness to

return everything, even one's most precious object of love, to the god or gods from whom it came. The writer makes clear from the outset that the story recounts a testing of Abraham, a divine inquiry into the degree of Abraham's trusting faith (Genesis 15:1–6).

Several poignant details underscore the cost of following God's terrible command. Abraham is told to take "your son . . . your only one, whom you love" and offer him as a holocaust—an offering burned in its entirety to signify holding back nothing whatsoever from God. On the

way up the mountain, the child himself carries the wood upon which he is to be sacrificed. Addressing Abraham as "Father," Isaac innocently notes that they have brought wood and fire for a holocaust, but no sheep for sacrifice. His father's initial response already begins to emphasize his attitude of trust as he assures the boy that "God himself will provide" for the offering.

After arriving at the place of holocaust and preparing for the sacrifice, Abraham is prevented by a divine messenger from completing the sacrifice of his son. Unlike God's first call to Abraham, here the Lord's

This image foreshadows Jesus' carrying his own Cross. Don't waste it.

This dialogue is poignant: Isaac is sincerely curious and unaware. Abraham speaks intentionally and his words are pained and weighty.

Slowly: the scene grows tense and darker. Share one image at a time. Tying up the boy can't sound like he's buttoning his jacket.

Don't speak like you're describing a "near-miss," but as if you were relating the actual slaughter. "But" breaks the mood; pace is faster. The second "Abraham" is louder, stronger than the first.

"Here I am," has no sense of relief yet, just terror. The "Do not . . . " commands can be spoken with calm and tender compassion. Speak the words "I now know . . . " with solemnity. Pause after "beloved son."

beloved = bee-LUHV-uhd

Here the pace and mood become faster, more upbeat. The "ram" replaces Isaac. Don't rush. Yahweh-yireh = YAH-way—YEER-ay means "The Lord will see [to it]."

In a long passage like this, variety in pacing is urgent. Though it is "God" speaking, you must not adopt a monotone nor an overly slow delivery. Speak like a parent announcing good news to an anxious child—both reassuring and praising.

Thereupon Abraham took the wood for the holocaust
    and **laid** it on his son **Isaac's** shoulders,
    while he himself carried the **fire** and the **knife**.
As the two walked on **together**, Isaac **spoke** to his
    father Abraham:
    "**Father**!" Isaac said.
"**Yes**, son," he replied.
Isaac continued, "Here are the **fire** and the **wood**,
    but where is the **sheep** for the holocaust?"
"**Son**," Abraham answered,
    "God **himself** will provide the sheep for the holocaust."
Then the two **continued** going forward.

When they **came** to the place of which God had told him,
    Abraham built an **altar** there and arranged the **wood** on it.
Next he **tied** up his son **Isaac**,
    and put him on **top** of the wood on the altar.
Then he **reached** out and took the **knife** to **slaughter** his son.
But the LORD's **messenger** called to him from **heaven**,
    "**Abraham, Abraham**!"
"**Here** I am," he answered.
"Do not lay your **hand** on the boy," said the **messenger**.
"Do not do the least **thing** to him.
I **know** now how **devoted** you are to God,
    since you did not **withhold** from me your own beloved **son**."
As Abraham looked **about**,
    he spied a **ram** caught by its horns in the **thicket**.
So he went and **took** the ram
    and offered **it** up as a holocaust in **place** of his son.
Abraham **named** the site **Yahweh-yireh**;
    hence people now say, "On the mountain the LORD will **see**."

Again the LORD's messenger **called** to Abraham from heaven
    and said:
    "I **swear** by myself, declares the LORD,
    that because you **acted** as you **did**

messenger calls his name twice. In the Old Testament, calling someone by name twice indicates a closeness of relationship between the speaker and the one addressed. God first speaks to protect Isaac, then assures Abraham that his actions bespeak complete reverence for God. Abraham's trusting obedience not only would have cost his beloved son but dashed any hope of fulfilling the divine promise of countless offspring. But Abraham had told Isaac that God would provide a sacrificial offering, and his faith proves well-founded; the patriarch sees a

ram nearby, which ensures a holocaust offering. The naming of the place of offering is a wordplay that can be lost in translation; "the LORD will see" confirms Abraham's trust that God would "see to it" that an animal would be available for sacrifice.

Abraham meets his testing with the same unshakeable trust in divine promises that he has shown earlier. In response, God again assures Abraham that the two great promises will be fulfilled: God will give him innumerable descendants, and through the offspring of Abraham, man of obedient faith, all other peoples shall be blessed.

in not **withholding** from me your beloved **son**,
I will bless you **abundantly**
and make your **descendants** as **countless**
as the **stars** of the **sky** and the **sands** of the seashore;
your descendants shall take **possession**
of the gates of their **enemies**,
and in your **descendants** all the nations of the earth shall
     find **blessing**—
all this because you **obeyed** my **command**."

[Shorter: Genesis 22:1–2, 9a, 10–13, 15–18]

RESPONSORIAL PSALM   Psalm 16:5, 8, 9–10, 11 (1)

R. You are my inheritance, O Lord.

O LORD, my allotted portion and my cup,
     you it is who hold fast my lot.
I set the LORD ever before me;
     with him at my right hand I shall not
          be disturbed.

Therefore my heart is glad and my soul
          rejoices,
     my body, too, abides in confidence;
because you will not abandon my soul to the
          netherworld,
     nor will you suffer your faithful one to
          undergo corruption.

You will show me the path to life,
     fullness of joys in your presence,
     the delights at your right hand forever.

READING III   Exodus 14:15—15:1

A reading from the Book of Exodus

The LORD said to **Moses**, "**Why** are you crying out to me?
Tell the Israelites to go **forward**.
And **you**, lift up your **staff** and, with hand outstretched
          over the **sea**,
     split the sea in **two**,
          that the Israelites may pass **through** it on dry **land**.
But I will make the **Egyptians** so **obstinate**
          that they will go in **after** them. »

The fulfillment of these promises is what tonight's readings and liturgy are all about.

If you've given proper emphasis and not rushed the preceding, the final line will call us all to obedience.

For meditation and context:

TO KEEP IN MIND

Characters: To distinguish the various characters that populate a passage, try to understand their thoughts, feelings, and motivations. Use subtle variations in pitch, pacing, and emotion to communicate them. But don't confuse proclamation with theatrics. Suggest characters, don't "become" them.

Don't fear the repetitions in this text and have confidence in the power of this story to move your listeners. Be eager to tell it to people eager to hear it again. Begin with the strong voice of God.

"Pharaoh . . . army . . . chariots . . . charioteers": this will become a much repeated refrain. Use all the words each time the line recurs.

READING III   In the Second Reading, God repeated to Abraham the promise of countless descendants. According to Old Testament accounts, these descendants eventually found themselves enslaved in Egypt. There, the LORD called Moses to lead the Hebrews out of Egypt to Canaan, a new land of freedom. On the whole, the writer presents the story of the plagues upon Egypt, worked through Moses, as a battle between the deities of Egypt and the God of Israel. Repeatedly, Egypt's gods prove no match for the warrior-king of Israel, the Lord. The Third Reading continues an account of Hebrew flight from slavery, facilitated by the LORD's tenth and last victorious blow upon Egypt.

As the reading begins, the fleeing Hebrews have reached the edge of the sea, only to find themselves seemingly at the mercy of Pharaoh's army. Moses too appears doubtful that their escape will be complete, but God commands him to raise his staff and split the sea so that the Israelites may continue their journey to freedom. God's mighty power will be even more evident after the LORD himself causes the Egyptians to stubbornly pursue the escaping slaves into the seabed. Their efforts will, however, prove ineffective against the God of Israel, who will be glorified by his people's victory. Throughout the night, God's angel and a column of cloud stand guard for the Israelites. Later in the Exodus journey, this cloud will reappear, indicating the LORD's own protective, guiding presence.

Since ancient peoples believed that divine powers directly intervened in all aspects of human life, the writer states that the LORD sends the strong wind to dry up the waters before the Israelites. As the

Then I will receive **glory** through **Pharaoh** and all his **army**,
  his **chariots** and **charioteers**.
The Egyptians shall know that **I** am the Lord,
  when I receive glory through **Pharaoh**
  and his **chariots** and **charioteers**."

The **angel** of God, who had been **leading** Israel's camp,
  now **moved** and went around **behind** them.
The column of **cloud** also, leaving the **front**,
  took up its place **behind** them,
  so that it came **between** the camp of the **Egyptians**
  and that of **Israel**.
But the cloud now became **dark**, and thus the **night** passed
  without the rival camps coming any closer together all
    night long.
Then Moses **stretched** out his hand over the **sea**,
  and the LORD **swept** the sea
  with a **strong** east **wind** throughout the night
  and so **turned** it into **dry** land.
When the **water** was thus **divided**,
  the **Israelites** marched into the **midst** of the sea on **dry** land,
  with the water like a **wall** to their **right** and to their **left**.

The Egyptians **followed** in **pursuit**;
  all Pharaoh's **horses** and **chariots** and **charioteers** went
    after them
  right into the **midst** of the sea.
In the **night** watch just before **dawn**
  the LORD **cast** through the column of the fiery cloud
  upon the Egyptian force a **glance** that threw it into a **panic**;
  and he so **clogged** their chariot wheels
  that they could hardly **drive**.
With **that** the Egyptians sounded the **retreat** before Israel,
  because the LORD was fighting for them **against** the Egyptians.

Then the LORD told **Moses**, "**Stretch** out your **hand** over the **sea**,
  that the **water** may flow **back** upon the Egyptians,

"Column of cloud" and the "angel" are manifestations of God's presence and protection. The action intensifies. Build suspense.

Slow your pace to suggest the passage of time over the long night. Pause.

Speak with renewed vigor. See what you describe.

A marvelous sight.

Use a faster pace here.

Speak slower and quietly; you are aware that it was God who saved.

LORD predicted, the pursuing Egyptians follow them, until God, in the form of a cloud of fire, throws them "into a panic" and clogs their chariot wheels. At this, Pharaoh's army sounds the retreat, as the author sounds an important theme: the pursuers know they face defeat, because the God of the Hebrews, who has already proved to outrank all the gods of Egypt, fights "for them against the Egyptians." What the Egyptians fear becomes reality as God acts through Moses, and the waters turn back into the sea, bringing total defeat and destruction to Pharaoh's army. Awed by this mighty act of power, the Israelites affirm their belief in the Lord and in Moses as God's instrument. The reading ends with the opening line of a great hymn of praise and thanks for God's deliverance; this song is often described as Israel's first creed.

upon their **chariots** and their **charioteers**."
So Moses **stretched** out his hand over the sea,
    and at **dawn** the sea flowed **back** to its normal **depth**.
The Egyptians were fleeing head **on** toward the **sea**,
    when the LORD **hurled** them into its midst.
As the water flowed **back**,
    it **covered** the **chariots** and the **charioteers** of Pharaoh's
        whole **army**
    which had followed the Israelites into the sea.
Not a single **one** of them escaped.
But the **Israelites** had marched on dry **land**
    through the **midst** of the sea,
    with the water like a **wall** to their **right** and to their **left**.
Thus the LORD **saved** Israel on that day
    from the power of the **Egyptians**.
When Israel **saw** the Egyptians lying **dead** on the **seashore**
    and beheld the great **power** that the LORD
    had shown **against** the Egyptians,
    they **feared** the LORD and **believed** in him and in his
        servant Moses.

Then **Moses** and the **Israelites** sang this **song** to the LORD:
    I will **sing** to the LORD, for he is **gloriously triumphant**;
    horse and **chariot** he has cast into the **sea**.

Margin notes:

God's justice is uncompromising.

"Dawn" is the moment of liberation.

Narrate these lines without any hint of vindictiveness.

Speak with gratitude and relief.

God's power inspires a reverential fear. Use a hushed tone.

The joy of this song should ring in your voice and show on your face.

For meditation and context:

TO KEEP IN MIND
Pauses are never "dead" moments. Something is always happening during a pause. Practice will teach you how often and how long to pause. Too many pauses make a reading choppy; too few cause ideas to run into one another.

RESPONSORIAL PSALM   Exodus 15:1–2, 3–4, 5–6, 17–18 (1b)

R. Let us sing to the Lord; he has covered himself in glory.

I will sing to the LORD, for he is gloriously
        triumphant;
    horse and chariot he has cast into the sea.
My strength and my courage is the LORD,
    and he has been my savior.
He is my God, I praise him;
    the God of my father, I extol him.

The LORD is a warrior,
    LORD is his name!
Pharaoh's chariots and army he hurled into
        the sea;
    the elite of his officers were submerged
        in the Red Sea.

The flood waters covered them,
    they sank into the depths like a stone.
Your right hand, O LORD, magnificent
        in power,
    your right hand, O LORD, has shattered
        the enemy.

You brought in the people you redeemed
    and planted them on the mountain of
        your inheritance—
the place where you made your seat,
        O LORD,
    the sanctuary, LORD, which your hands
        established.
The LORD shall reign forever and ever.

Isaiah = ī-ZAY-uh

"Husband" and "Maker" are meant to express tenderness and compassion. Persuade us God can love us this much.

Use a brisk pace with "like a wife forsaken": and increase intensity on "a wife married in youth."

Contrast the regret of "For a brief moment . . . " with the joy of "but with great tenderness . . . ." The same point is made twice. Maintain your energy and conviction throughout.

The exile is compared to Noah's flood. God says: As I swore then, so I swear now never to punish you again.

These words represent the excess of love. Don't hold back.

Spoken directly to Jerusalem. Say this lovingly, as if embracing the one with whom you are reconciling.

Carnelians = kahr-NEEL-yuhnz

Carnelians are reddish quartz; carbuncles are smooth, round, deep-red garnets.

God is making a promise. Speak with reassuring strength and conviction.

READING IV　Isaiah 54:5–14

A reading from the Book of the Prophet Isaiah

The One who has become your **husband** is your **Maker**;
　his **name** is the LORD of **hosts**;
your **redeemer** is the **Holy** One of Israel,
　called **God** of all the **earth**.
The LORD calls you **back**,
　like a wife **forsaken** and grieved in **spirit**,
a wife married in **youth** and then cast **off**,
　says your God.
For a brief **moment** I **abandoned** you,
　but with great **tenderness** I will take you **back**.
In an outburst of **wrath**, for a **moment**
　I **hid** my face from you;
but with enduring **love** I take **pity** on you,
　says the LORD, your **redeemer**.
This is for me like the days of **Noah**,
　when I **swore** that the waters of Noah
　should never **again** deluge the earth;
so I have sworn not to be **angry** with you,
　or to **rebuke** you.
Though the mountains **leave** their place
　and the hills be **shaken**,
my **love** shall **never** leave you
　nor my covenant of peace be **shaken**,
　says the LORD, who has **mercy** on you.
O **afflicted** one, **storm-battered** and **unconsoled**,
　I lay your **pavements** in **carnelians**,
　and your **foundations** in **sapphires**;
I will make your **battlements** of **rubies**,
　your **gates** of **carbuncles**,
　and all your **walls** of precious **stones**.
All your **children** shall be taught by the LORD,
　and **great** shall be the **peace** of your children.

READING IV The first three readings for this sacred night have described Israel's God as one who always fulfills promises. That faithfulness was sorely tested by the Chosen People, who repeatedly strayed from God's ways. Many centuries after the Exodus, despite the urgings of numerous prophets, the people demonstrated their lack of faithfulness to the Covenant. God allowed the destruction of two Israelite kingdoms, the decimation of the people, and their return to their original state of captivity in a far-away country.

This passage from Isaiah most likely dates from Babylonian captivity, probably near its end as God continued to speak words of return and renewal through the prophets. Earlier prophets had likened the relationship between the Lord and the Chosen People to that of faithful and unfaithful spouses. When final destruction befell God's people, the event was compared to the steadfast husband, the Lord, divorcing his wife, Israel, for her repeated infidelity. As prophets like Isaiah turned toward messages of hope for the future,

they continued to describe a restored relationship with spousal language and images.

Isaiah envisions an imminent and astounding reversal of the people's current state; with boundless fidelity, the Lord, Creator, and Redeemer of Israel, will restore her as his beloved wife. God speaks like a rejected husband who, in a fit of painful loss and anger, cast off the unfaithful partner, but whose love cannot bear the finality of divorce. The Hebrew words with which God speaks of restoring Israel express both the loyalty demanded by covenant relationship ("enduring love")

In **justice** shall you be established,
> far from the fear of **oppression**,
> where destruction cannot come **near** you.

For meditation and context:

RESPONSORIAL PSALM   Psalm 30:2, 4, 5–6, 11–12, 13 (2a)

R. I will praise you, Lord, for you have rescued me.

I will extol you, O LORD, for you drew
> me clear
> and did not let my enemies rejoice over me.
O LORD, you brought me up from the
> netherworld;
> you preserved me from among those
> going down into the pit.

Sing praise to the LORD, you his faithful ones,
> and give thanks to his holy name.
For his anger lasts but a moment;
> a lifetime, his good will.
At nightfall, weeping enters in,
> but with the dawn, rejoicing.

Hear, O LORD, and have pity on me;
> O LORD, be my helper.
You changed my mourning into dancing;
> O LORD, my God, forever will I give
> you thanks.

<table><tr><td>TO KEEP IN MIND</td></tr><tr><td>**Pace:** The rate at which you read is influenced by the size of your church, the size of the congregation, and the complexity of the text. As each increases, rate decreases.</td></tr></table>

Isaiah = ī-ZAY-uh

Note the imperatives, but the tone is as if inviting hungry, homeless children to a feast.

Ignore the comma after "come."

Ask the questions sincerely as if expecting an answer.

To be nourished, it is necessary to heed and listen to the Lord. "That you may have life" is the heart of God's promise. Slower pace.

READING V   Isaiah 55:1–11

A reading from the Book of the Prophet Isaiah

Thus says the LORD:
All you who are **thirsty**,
> **come** to the **water**!
You who have no **money**,
> **come**, receive **grain** and **eat**;
come, without **paying** and without **cost**,
> drink **wine** and **milk**!
Why spend your money for what is not **bread**,
> your **wages** for what fails to **satisfy**?
Heed me, and you shall eat **well**,
> you shall **delight** in **rich** fare.
Come to me **heedfully**,
> **listen**, that you may have **life**.
I will **renew** with you the everlasting **covenant**,
> the benefits assured to **David**. »

and deeply felt tenderness ("pity"). God reminds the captive people that he has demonstrated fidelity to covenant promises in the past, as in the case of his covenant with Noah. Repeating words of covenant faithfulness and heartfelt love, God promises enduring love; Israel may turn from God, but God will never abandon his beloved Israel.

Isaiah now turns to address the devastated city, Jerusalem, speaking God's Word to her; she will be rebuilt with even greater glory than before. Most importantly, God will recreate the people and the

city that symbolizes their covenant with the Lord in "justice" and "peace." The Hebrew words used here connote wholeness and completeness, a state of being in which all live in righteous relationship to God and to one another.

READING V Chapters 40–55 of Isaiah are often called the "Book of Consolation," believed to date from near the end of the Babylonian exile. This part of the lengthy prophecy looks toward God's impending act of liberation from captivity (a captivity the people likened to their ances-

tors' time in Egypt). To designate the hopeful content of this section of Isaiah, the author uses a literary device called an *inclusio*, which forms a set of brackets for a body of material by beginning and ending with passages that have similar terms and content. This reading is the slightly truncated closing bracket of the *inclusio*, and so includes a number of themes from chapter 40: forgiveness, the way, God's renewing action, and the powerful Word of God. In style, the reading echoes the books of the Bible devoted to pursuing Wisdom (often personified as a woman); it also resembles

"Him" is David. The nation will be restored.

Renew your energy. Imagine those you are trying to persuade getting up to leave. Your words must catch and hold them.

This is not condemnation, but an earnest call for conversion.

This section explains why God can be so "generous in forgiving." God's plans are not our plans; God's methods not our methods. Slowly, with great dignity.

This is an important teaching about the efficacy of the Word of God: it accomplishes what it sets out to do! Go slowly. This is a long comparison: Just like rain and snow don't evaporate and return to the sky until after they have watered the earth, helping seed to grow and yielding bread for the hungry, the Word that goes forth from my mouth does not return without having accomplished the purpose for which I sent it. Speak with conviction and authority.

As I made him a **witness** to the peoples,
   a **leader** and commander of **nations**,
so shall you **summon** a nation you knew **not**,
   and nations that knew you not shall **run** to you,
because of the LORD, your **God**,
   the **Holy** One of Israel, who has **glorified** you.

Seek the LORD while he may be **found**,
   call him while he is **near**.
Let the scoundrel **forsake** his way,
   and the **wicked** man his **thoughts**;
let him **turn** to the LORD for **mercy**;
   to our **God**, who is **generous** in **forgiving**.
For **my** thoughts are not **your** thoughts,
   nor are **your** ways **my** ways, says the LORD.
As high as the **heavens** are above the **earth**,
   so high are **my** ways above **your** ways
   and **my** thoughts above **your** thoughts.

For just as from the **heavens**
   the **rain** and **snow** come down
and do not **return** there
   till they have **watered** the **earth**,
   making it **fertile** and **fruitful**,
giving **seed** to the one who **sows**
   and **bread** to the one who **eats**,
so shall my **word** be
   that goes forth from my mouth;
my **word** shall not return to me **void**,
   but shall do my **will**,
   achieving the end for which I **sent** it.

the exhortations of the ancient priests and the speeches of prophets.

Addressing the poor and hungry captive people, the prophet, like Lady Wisdom, calls them to a rich and fulfilling banquet. In the centuries following Isaiah, an overflowing banquet came to symbolize God's definitive act of salvation. For Isaiah, it probably carries overtones of renewing unity among partakers of the plentiful meal, since Israelite culture understood shared food as a sharing of life and mutual commitment. Through the prophet, God calls the people to listen and so have life. The Hebrew word

translated "listen" includes an appeal to listen and respond, to hear and obey. It recalls the Lord's ancient call to a Chosen People expressed in Deuteronomy 6:4–5: "Hear, O Israel! The LORD is our God, the LORD alone! . . . you shall love the LORD . . . ." Despite the people's failure to hear, obey, and love God above all, his forgiveness now offers to renew the ancient covenant, not only with David but with "you," the entire Chosen People. Through the new Exodus of a restored people, all nations will turn toward their God.

While the phrase, "seek the Lord," was often used by priests to invite worshippers to the sanctuary of the Temple, Isaiah broadens its meaning. He seems to ask the people to find God near at hand. Turning toward God's presence, however, calls for repentance, a change of heart and action. The prophet reassures the people that their ever-faithful God will meet them with forgiving mercy. The Hebrew word rendered "mercy" carries overtones of the tender love a woman bears for a child of her womb.

TO KEEP IN MIND

The opening: Establish eye contact and announce, from memory, "A reading from . . . ." Then take a pause (three full beats!) before starting the reading. The correct pronunciation is "A [uh] reading from" instead of "A [ay] reading from."

RESPONSORIAL PSALM   Isaiah 12:2–3, 4, 5–6 (3)

R. You will draw water joyfully from the springs of salvation.

God indeed is my savior;
  I am confident and unafraid.
My strength and my courage is the LORD,
  and he has been my savior.
With joy you will draw water
  at the fountain of salvation.

Give thanks to the LORD, acclaim his name;
  among the nations make known his deeds,
  proclaim how exalted is his name.

Sing praise to the LORD for his glorious
    achievement;
  let this be known throughout all the earth.
Shout with exultation, O city of Zion,
  for great in your midst
  is the Holy One of Israel!

Baruch = buh-ROOK

This is exhortation motivated by love.

You are asking: "Do you know why?"

The answer: "I'll tell you why!" Still, love is the motive.

Here is the better way: follow it and find peace! You are cajoling, exhorting, wanting to spur a change in behavior. There is a lilting cadence in these lines. Don't rush them. "Days" and "peace" can be sustained.

There is a dramatic shift in mood here. This is a poetic song of praise to Wisdom.

READING VI   Baruch 3:9–15, 32—4:4

A reading from the Book of the Prophet Baruch

Hear, O Israel, the **commandments** of **life**:
  listen, and know **prudence**!
How is it, Israel,
  that you are in the land of your **foes**,
  grown old in a **foreign** land,
defiled with the **dead**,
  accounted with those destined for the **netherworld**?
You have **forsaken** the fountain of **wisdom**!
  Had you walked in the way of **God**,
  you would have dwelt in enduring **peace**.
Learn where **prudence** is,
  where **strength**, where **understanding**;
that you may know also
  where are length of **days**, and **life**,
  where light of the **eyes**, and **peace**.
Who has **found** the place of wisdom,
  who has entered into her **treasuries**?

The One who knows **all** things knows **her**;
  he has probed her by his **knowledge**— ≫

Isaiah begins a kind of conclusion to the entire "Book of Consolation" by recalling the core reason for his confidence that return, renewal, and restoration will certainly come to pass. That reason is the power of God's Word. The Word, which carries the very presence of God, comes to earth to give new life and fruitfulness. Because it is God's own Word, it bears divine power, and will not fail to accomplish the divine will, which always ultimately desires human healing, wholeness, and deliverance.

READING VI | The Book of Baruch, purportedly written by Jeremiah's assistant, actually represents a collection of four different compositions. Set in the early days of Babylonian exile, the book is presented as the contents of a scroll read by Baruch to the exiled king and people. Most scholars believe the work was actually written much later, perhaps reaching the stage of final editing within the last two centuries BC. As a whole, the Book of Baruch follows the theology of Deuteronomy and its author, describing the repeating cycle of God's relationship with the Chosen People: the people's sin, the devastation allowed by God as punishment and call to conversion, and the people's repentance. In the first chapter, the people's admission of guilt is expressed in language typical of Deuteronomy and numerous prophets: failure to hear and obey God's voice, spoken through the Mosaic Law and the prophets.

This reading comes from a portion of the book patterned after wisdom literature, and virtually equates wisdom with the divine teaching given in the Law. The importance of the message in this section

"The One" = God. You are retelling the story of creation. Use a faster, joyous tempo.

"Dismisses light" means orders the sun to go down. "Calls it" indicates a sunrise. Maintain high energy here.

Let your voice ring with joy at God's goodness!

This is a new beat. Use a more sober tone. "Given her" indicates understanding. "Jacob" and "Israel" represent the whole people.

beloved: bee-LUHV-uhd

"She has appeared on earth" refers to Wisdom, now personified as the book of the Law.

Use a contrasting tone for those who "live" and those who "die." Pause before next line.

Imagine yourself saying, "Oh, my dear child, turn and receive . . . ." "Glory" indicates the Law. "Privileges" refers to knowing and observing the Law. You are saying: "Don't throw away the riches you've been given." End on a note of joy.
Blessed = BLES-uhd or blesd

the One who **established** the earth for all time,
    and **filled** it with four-footed **beasts**;
he who **dismisses** the light, and it **departs**,
    calls it, and it obeys him **trembling**;
before whom the **stars** at their posts
        shine and **rejoice**;
when he **calls** them, they answer, "Here we **are**!"
    shining with **joy** for their Maker.
Such is our **God**;
    no other is to be **compared** to him:
he has traced out the whole way of **understanding**,
    and has given her to **Jacob**, his **servant**,
    to **Israel**, his beloved **son**.

Since then she has **appeared** on earth,
    and **moved** among people.
She is the **book** of the **precepts** of God,
    the **law** that endures **forever**;
all who **cling** to her will **live**,
    but those will **die** who **forsake** her.
Turn, O Jacob, and **receive** her:
    walk by her **light** toward **splendor**.
Give not your glory to **another**,
    your **privileges** to an **alien** race.
Blessed are we, O Israel;
    for what **pleases** God is **known** to us!

For meditation and context:

<hr/>

RESPONSORIAL PSALM   Psalm 19:8, 9, 10, 11 (John 6:68c)

R. Lord, you have the words of everlasting life.

The law of the LORD is perfect,
    refreshing the soul;
the decree of the LORD is trustworthy,
    giving wisdom to the simple.

The precepts of the LORD are right,
    rejoicing the heart;
the command of the LORD is clear,
    enlightening the eye.

The fear of the LORD is pure,
    enduring forever;
the ordinances of the LORD are true,
    all of them just.

They are more precious than gold,
    than a heap of purest gold;
sweeter also than syrup
    or honey from the comb.

TO KEEP IN MIND

A substantial pause always follows "A reading from" and both precedes and follows "The word [Gospel] of the Lord."

---

of Baruch is evident in its language; "Hear O Israel" was the beginning of a prayer that Jews recited daily. The prayer appears in the Torah (Pentateuch). It calls the covenant people to hear and obey the Lord alone, and to love their one and only God above all else (Deuteronomy 6:4–5). The author poses a rhetorical question to the captive people, asking how it came to be that they find themselves in exile; the obvious answer follows: they have forsaken God's teaching, source of all wisdom.

The author calls the people to redis-cover wisdom so that they may endure and

once again find life and peace. Wisdom, typically personified as a feminine figure, comes from God, Creator of all things and the sole source of Wisdom, the only One who fully knows her. Still, God has given great wisdom to the covenant people in the form of the Law: "She is the book of the precepts of God." Again echoing Deuteronomy, the author stresses that those who follow her by observing God's teaching will have life, while those who leave the path of wisdom will perish.

The reading closes with an exhorta-tion to repentance, which the prophets

often expressed as a call to "turn" or "return." True repentance requires a dual action: turning from the way of evil, and turning toward God and divine wisdom given in the Mosaic Law. God's people have been given a great gift; what pleases God is the way of wisdom, revealed in the Torah.

READING VII   Ezekiel 36:16–17a, 18–28

A reading from the Book of the Prophet Ezekiel

The word of the LORD came to me, saying:
   Son of **man**, when the house of **Israel** lived in their **land**,
   they **defiled** it by their **conduct** and **deeds**.
Therefore I poured out my **fury** upon them
   because of the **blood** that they poured out on the ground,
   and because they defiled it with **idols**.
I **scattered** them among the nations,
   dispersing them over **foreign** lands;
   according to their **conduct** and **deeds** I judged them.
But when they came among the nations **wherever** they came,
   they served to **profane** my holy name,
   because it was said of them: "These are the people of the LORD,
   yet they had to **leave** their land."
So I have **relented** because of my holy name
   which the house of Israel **profaned**
   among the nations where they came.
Therefore **say** to the house of Israel: Thus says the Lord **GOD**:
   Not for **your** sakes do I act, house of Israel,
   but for the sake of my holy **name**,
   which you **profaned** among the nations to which you came.
I will prove the **holiness** of my great name, profaned among
      the nations,
   in whose midst you have **profaned** it.
Thus the nations shall **know** that **I** am the LORD, says the
      Lord **GOD**,
   when in their sight I prove my holiness through **you**.
For I will take you **away** from among the nations,
   gather you from all the foreign lands,
   and bring you **back** to your **own** land. »

"Their land" is their own land. Ezekiel's tone is blunt. Don't dilute the anger. "Fury," "scattered," "dispersing," "judged," "profane" are all strong words that convey God's wrath. Let them work.

"Because of the blood . . . " refers to worshiping false idols.

The exile is God's punishment for Israel's infidelity.

But the punishment backfired because it gave God a bad name.

Speak the taunt in the voice of the foreigners.

Pause at this new beat. Frustrated, God reluctantly adopts a new approach. Note that the words "profaned among the nations" is repeated three times.

God must restore his "good name."

God's anger slowly yields to mercy and love. Speak this as a promise.

The tone becomes more reassuring and loving here.

READING VII

Ezekiel, a prophet and priest of the Jerusalem Temple, arrived in Babylon among the first deportees from Judah, and continued to prophesy in the land of exile. The Babylonian conquest of the Kingdom of David and the destruction of both the city of Jerusalem and the Temple represented an unimaginable blow to the Chosen People, a fate they could never have envisioned. Where was all that they had relied upon? The Promised Land, Davidic kingship, and their very identity as Chosen People of the Lord seemed to have evaporated. To the remaining but captive people, Ezekiel spoke the Word of the Lord, proclaiming both the reasons for their desolation and God's promises of renewal.

In verses immediately preceding those in the Seventh Reading, God directed the prophet to address the mountains and hills of ancient Canaan. Ezekiel announced divine assurance that the land itself would be renewed, once again producing fruits of the earth, and that upon the Promised Land, both cities and people would be rebuilt. The reading begins with another statement of reasons for devastation and loss of the land: its people, the elect people of the Lord, despoiled it themselves by their conduct. They not only shed innocent blood, even blood of their own people, but repeatedly turned to idols instead of the God who chose them. They were chosen for a purpose: to make their covenant God known to all other nations and peoples by serving the Lord alone. In Hebrew, one word means both to serve and to worship, and their worship of the Lord was to include both communal ritual and a way of life. Ezekiel proclaims that their own repeated

God will purify the people. This is an important image of Baptism for tonight's liturgy.

Make eye contact with the assembly for this classic and memorable line. Speak slowly and sincerely.

Imagine saying this to a child whom you love in order to ensure the child's success and prosperity. Say the words "You shall be . . . God" like a spouse vowing fidelity.

I will sprinkle **clean water** upon you
    to **cleanse** you from all your **impurities**,
    and from all your **idols** I will cleanse you.
I will give you a **new** heart and place a new **spirit** within you,
    taking from your bodies your **stony** hearts
    and giving you **natural** hearts.
I will put my **spirit** within you and make you live by my **statutes**,
    careful to observe my **decrees**.
You shall **live** in the land I gave your **fathers**;
    you shall be my **people**, and **I** will be your **God**.

For meditation and context:

RESPONSORIAL PSALM   Psalm 42:3, 5; 43:3, 4:2

R. Like a deer that longs for running streams, my soul longs for you, my God.

A thirst is my soul for God, the living God.
    When shall I go and behold the face
        of God?

I went with the throng
    and led them in procession to the house
        of God,
amid loud cries of joy and thanksgiving,
    with the multitude keeping festival.

Send forth your light and your fidelity;
    they shall lead me on
and bring me to your holy mountain,
    to your dwelling-place.

Then will I go in to the altar of God,
    the God of my gladness and joy;
then will I give you thanks upon the harp,
    O God, my God!

> **TO KEEP IN MIND**
> As you are becoming familiar with your passage, read it directly from your Bible, **reading also what comes before and after** it to get a clear sense of its context.

Or:

For meditation and context:

RESPONSORIAL PSALM   Isaiah 12:2–3, 4bcd, 5–6 (3)

R. You will draw water joyfully from the springs of salvation.

God indeed is my savior;
    I am confident and unafraid.
My strength and my courage is the LORD,
    and he has been my savior.
With joy you will draw water
    at the fountain of salvation.

Give thanks to the LORD, acclaim his name;
    among the nations make known his deeds,
    proclaim how exalted is his name.

Sing praise to the LORD for his glorious
        achievement;
    let this be known throughout all the earth.
Shout with exultation, O city of Zion,
    for great in your midst
        is the Holy One of Israel!

> **TO KEEP IN MIND**
> **Pray the Scriptures:** Make reading these Scriptures a part of your prayer life every week, and especially during the week prior to the liturgy in which you will proclaim.

Or:

---

wandering from the ways of worship have brought divine judgment upon them.

Speaking through the prophet, God confronts the exiles with another reality: their fate has dishonored God's own name. In biblical thought, a name conveys the very essence of what is named, and represents the entire history and reputation of a person named. Nations that witnessed the fall and destruction of the Israelites questioned whether they were in fact the people of the Lord, thus profaning the "name" of the Lord. The promised restoration, therefore, will take place not for the sake of

those whom God has rightly judged, but for the sake of the Lord's own good name as the One who remains forever faithful to Israel.

God then details the renewal that will once again demonstrate that the Lord is a God of covenant faithfulness and enduring love to Israel, despite her numerous infidelities. Not only will the captive people return to a renewed land; God will cleanse them of their sin and the root of their sinfulness. The promise of a new heart and new spirit signifies that God will recreate his people at the core of their being. In ancient

Israel, the heart represented the core of a human being; a stony heart meant a person closed to God and the divine life within. Genesis 2:7 portrayed divine spirit as the very life-breath of humankind, but the people had shut their hearts to it. With the recreating gift of a new, "natural" heart, God's people will become what they were intended to be: a community breathing together with God's own life, guided by divine teaching. They will again live as the people of the Lord, who is always their God of loving fidelity.

For meditation and context:

RESPONSORIAL PSALM   Psalm 51:12–13, 14–15, 18–19 (12a)

R. Create a clean heart in me, O God.

A clean heart create for me, O God,
  and a steadfast spirit renew within me.
Cast me not out from your presence,
  and your Holy Spirit take not from me.

Give me back the joy of your salvation,
  and a willing spirit sustain in me.
I will teach transgressors your ways,
  and sinners shall return to you.

For you are not pleased with sacrifices;
  should I offer a holocaust, you would not
  accept it.
My sacrifice, O God, is a contrite spirit;
  a heart contrite and humbled, O God, you
  will not spurn.

EPISTLE   Romans 6:3–11

Paul's literary device is a rhetorical question. Let it sound like a question. Make eye contact with the assembly and speak as directly as Paul writes.

Take the time to understand Paul's point: what happened to Christ will happen to us. He died and was buried, then rose. We die and are buried in Baptism; we, too, will rise to new life.

Paul develops the idea: we were made one with Christ by sharing a death (Baptism) like his; so we also will be made one with him by experiencing Resurrection.

Don't let this sound repetitive. Sustain the energy. Contrast "died" and "live."

"We know" means that we are convinced! "Dies no more . . . death no longer has power . . . " is the same idea stated twice: the greater stress goes to the second statement.

Use the contrasts: "his death . . . his life."

A reading from the Letter of Saint Paul to the Romans

Brothers and sisters:
Are you **unaware** that we who were **baptized** into Christ **Jesus**
  were baptized into his **death**?
We were indeed **buried** with him through baptism into death,
  so that, just as Christ was **raised** from the dead
  by the glory of the **Father**,
  we **too** might live in newness of **life**.

For if we have grown into **union** with him through a **death**
    like his,
  we shall also be **united** with him in the **resurrection**.
We know that our **old** self was **crucified** with him,
  so that our **sinful** body might be done away with,
  that we might no longer be in **slavery** to sin.
For a **dead** person has been **absolved** from sin.
If, then, we have **died** with Christ,
  we believe that we shall also **live** with him.
We know that **Christ**, **raised** from the dead, dies no **more**;
  death no longer has **power** over him.
As to his **death**, he died to sin once and for **all**;
  as to his **life**, he lives for **God**. »

EPISTLE   Paul wrote the Letter to the Romans, actually more a treatise than a letter, near the end of his life, about thirty years after the Death and Resurrection of Christ. From its earliest days, the Church understood Baptism as immersion in Christ, shedding one's former way of life and taking on a way of life patterned according to his passage through death to greater life. The celebration of Christian Initiation at the Easter Vigil thus continues ancient faith and practice. Today's Epistle elaborates both the call and the effects of immersion in Christ's Death and Resurrection.

In the previous chapter of Romans, Paul stressed the depth of God's love revealed in Christ, who died for those who were still sinners. In today's reading, Paul explains that in Baptism, Christians enter into Christ's manner of dying: death as self-giving love that leads to greater life. The Apostle insists that a Christian's death be seen in relation to the Death of Christ and as a participation in Christ. In Baptism the believer is buried "with him" and grows in oneness with him "through a death like his." It is this likeness to Christ and union with him that brings transformed life, a sharing in his Resurrection.

Paul's view of Baptism calls for nothing less than a complete change of the whole person, a transformation wrought by the interaction of divine power and human choice. For anyone who embraces Baptism as a way of being "baptized into [Christ's] death," the former self or person enslaved to sin is "done away with." The "sinful body" (Greek *soma*) does not signify physical flesh alone, but the human being as a whole, with all its perceptions, attitudes,

Make eye contact with the assembly. We are "*dead* to sin and living for God in Christ Jesus"! Announce this joyfully.

For meditation and context:

TO KEEP IN MIND

Sense lines: Scripture in this book is arranged (as in the Lectionary) in sense lines, one idea per line. Typically at least a slight pause should follow each line, but good reading requires you to recognize the need for other pauses within lines.

Consequently, you **too** must think of yourselves as being **dead** to **sin**
and **living** for **God** in Christ **Jesus**.

RESPONSORIAL PSALM Psalm 118:1–2, 16–17, 22–23

R. Alleluia, alleluia, alleluia.

Give thanks to the LORD, for he is good,
for his mercy endures forever.
Let the house of Israel say,
"His mercy endures forever."

The right hand of the LORD has struck
with power;
the right hand of the LORD is exalted.
I shall not die, but live,
and declare the works of the LORD.

The stone which the builders rejected
has become the cornerstone.
By the LORD has this been done;
it is wonderful in our eyes.

GOSPEL Luke 24:1–12

A reading from the holy Gospel according to Luke

At **daybreak** on the **first day** of the **week**
the **women** who had come from **Galilee with** Jesus
took the **spices** they had **prepared**
and **went** to the **tomb**.
They found the **stone rolled away** from the **tomb**;
but when they **entered**,
they did **not** find the **body** of the **Lord Jesus**.
While they were **puzzling** over this, **behold**,
two men in **dazzling garments appeared** to them.
They were **terrified** and **bowed** their **faces** to the **ground**.
They **said** to them,
"**Why** do you **seek** the **living** one among the **dead**?
He is **not here**, but he has been **raised**.

Begin with a solemn and sober mood. The women come to do what they could not on Friday: anoint the body with spices and perfume.

The mood is shattered by the discovery of the rolled-back stone. The failure to find the body arouses fear.

The mood intensifies from puzzlement to terror.

The men want to build faith, not reprimand. Give them a soothing, persuasive voice meant to calm the women's fears.

Your energy should be greatest on "he has been raised."

---

and behaviors when it is dominated by sinful influences. One who, in Baptism, dies with Christ, is freed from that power and lives in him as a new person, "for God."

GOSPEL The Gospel according to Luke was most likely composed by a Greek-speaking Gentile Christian who addressed those of similar background about AD 85. As Luke himself states at the beginning of his narrative, he is a second or third generation Christian who firmly roots his account in the testimony of earlier Apostles and preachers.

Throughout his Gospel account, Luke emphasizes promise and fulfillment, especially the promise as articulated by prophets, those who produced earlier sacred Scriptures. Jerusalem lies at the heart of his theological geography; in this account, the events of Jesus' life aim toward their climax in his Death and Resurrection. There, and in Acts, the Good News spreads from Jerusalem to the whole world. Luke's description of the early Church indicates important ministries of women in the growth of Christian faith and life, and

today's Gospel portrays them as first witnesses to the Resurrection.

The previous chapter ends with Jesus' burial, observed by women disciples who then prepared to anoint his body after the Sabbath. They come to the tomb at daybreak, indicating a shift from the darkness of Jesus' torture and Crucifixion to the dawn of new life. Nearing the tomb, the women discover the first sign that something out of the ordinary has happened. Tombs in the ancient world were often caves or abandoned quarries used for burial, sealed with a wheel-shaped rock in

Your intensity dips as they gently remind the women, but rises again on the reference to "third day."

Much is suggested by "they remembered."

Speak excitedly and breathlessly. Take time with the list of women. Your tone suggests their integrity and reputation for reliability, making the Apostles' judgment of "nonsense" a surprise.

Surprise us with Peter's response.

Peter now believes the women's story, but what does it all mean? Your tone must indicate his simultaneous amazement and puzzlement.

Remember what he **said** to you while he was **still** in **Galilee**,
that the **Son** of **Man** must be **handed over** to **sinners**
and be **crucified**, and **rise** on the **third day**."
And they **remembered** his words.
Then they **returned** from the **tomb**
and **announced all these things** to the **eleven**
and to **all** the **others**.
The women were **Mary Magdalene**, **Joanna**,
and **Mary** the mother of **James**;
the **others** who **accompanied** them also told this
to the *apostles*,
but their **story** seemed like **nonsense**
and they did **not believe** them.
But **Peter** got up and **ran** to the tomb,
bent down, and **saw** the **burial** cloths **alone**;
then he went **home amazed** at what had **happened**.

THE 4 STEPS OF *LECTIO DIVINA* OR PRAYERFUL READING

1. *Lectio:* Read a Scripture passage aloud slowly. Notice what phrase captures your attention and be attentive to its meaning. Silent pause.

2. *Meditatio:* Read the passage aloud slowly again, reflecting on the passage, allowing God to speak to you through it. Silent pause.

3. *Oratio:* Read it aloud slowly a third time, allowing it to be your prayer or response to God's gift of insight to you. Silent pause.

4. *Contemplatio:* Read it aloud slowly a fourth time, now resting in God's word.

---

a groove before the opening. It would normally require several men to move such a stone, but the women find that it has been moved aside. On entering the tomb, they do not see the body of the "Lord Jesus." Luke's use of "Lord," a title of authority and divinity, may already signal that the power of God lies behind the inexplicable reality before them.

As the women struggle to understand, heavenly visitors, identified by shining garments, make their appearance. They deliver the astonishing message that the women seek in vain for the dead, for God has raised Jesus from death. (Luke, like many New Testament authors, uses the formulaic "divine passive"—"has been raised.") The angelic message continues, pointing out that what Jesus promised earlier has in fact occurred (Luke 9:22). Their call to "remember" means much more than a simple recall of the past. In biblical thought, to remember involves bringing to bear in the present, with deepened insight and understanding, previous words and events of salvation history. The women do remember, and so they return to other disciples to announce what they have heard:

he has been raised. The translation "announce" carries much of the meaning of the Greek word used here; the women are not merely reporting, they are making a proclamation of faith. But that faith will need to grow, even in the Eleven, for they discount the women's announcement as nonsense. Peter goes to investigate for himself, to find only burial cloths. Luke says that Peter marvels at the sight, but does not yet claim that he believes; that growth in faith will happen only through his own experience of the Risen One. M.F.

EASTER SUNDAY OF THE RESURRECTION OF THE LORD

LECTIONARY #42

READING I   Acts of the Apostles 10:34a, 37–43

A reading from the Acts of the Apostles

Peter proceeded to **speak** and said:
    "You know what has happened all over **Judea**,
    beginning in **Galilee** after the baptism
    that **John** preached,
    how God **anointed** Jesus of **Nazareth**
    with the Holy **Spirit** and **power**.
He went about doing **good**
    and **healing** all those oppressed by the **devil**,
    for **God** was with him.
We are **witnesses** of all that he did
    both in the country of the **Jews** and in **Jerusalem**.
They put him to **death** by hanging him on **a tree**.
This man God **raised** on the **third** day and granted that he
        be **visible**,
    not to **all** the people, but to **us**,
    the witnesses **chosen** by God in **advance**,
    who **ate** and **drank** with him **after** he rose from the **dead**.
He **commissioned** us to preach to the people
    and **testify** that he is the one appointed by God
    as **judge** of the **living** and the **dead**.
To him all the **prophets** bear witness,
    that everyone who **believes** in him
    will receive **forgiveness** of **sins** through his **name**."

Except for the first six words, the entire reading is spoken in the voice of Peter. Rhetorical questions are a device meant to capture listener attention. Remember that Peter is making a public address.

"Spirit" and "power" are important characteristics of Jesus' ministry.
Jesus' healing ministry and exorcisms are important signs of who he is. Don't rush any of this first paragraph.
Pause to establish eye contact with the assembly. Peter is saying: "I was there!" There is a personal, intimate quality to this entire text.

The announcement of Jesus' Crucifixion is followed immediately by the announcement of his Resurrection. Pause after "tree" and again after "This man." Use a more upbeat tone for the balance of the paragraph.

Speak the words "the witnesses chosen by God . . . " humbly. This emphasizes Peter's credibility.

The tone continues to be energetic and earnest. "Preach" and "testify" will be redundant unless you build energy from one to the other.

Today options are given for the readings. Contact your parish staff to learn which readings will be used.

READING I   In the Gospel reading for the Easter Vigil liturgy, Luke portrayed a skeptical Peter, who along with the rest of the Eleven dismissed the women's proclamation of the Resurrection. Peter then went to the tomb to see for himself. Finding only burial cloths, he was amazed, but Luke does not yet say that he believed. In Luke's second volume, Acts, Peter came to such depth of faith and conviction that despite opposition and persecution, he proclaimed Jesus as Messiah in numerous speeches to fellow Jews, beginning in Jerusalem, then throughout Judea, and further. At the time of today's reading, Peter has begun to open himself to Paul's missionary activity among Gentiles. By the end of Luke's two-volume work, through the efforts of Peter and Paul and many coworkers, the Good News of Jesus Christ will have spread throughout the Gentile world. Thus unfolds the story of the early Church, in stages outlined by Luke at the beginning of Acts. Through the Resurrected Christ, divine Spirit comes upon the disciples. In the power of this spirit, they will serve as witnesses to Christ "in Jerusalem, throughout Judea and Samaria, and to the ends of the earth" (Acts 1:8).

To what do these disciples bear witness? Peter begins his speech with reference to John the Baptist, the forerunner, and Jesus' earthly ministry. Jesus' proclamation by word and deed that God was beginning his final reign in Jesus' Person and work is an important part of Peter's speech, for although Jesus was crucified,

For meditation and context:

RESPONSORIAL PSALM   Psalm 118:1–2, 16–17, 22–23 (24)

R. This is the day the Lord has made; let us rejoice and be glad. or R. Alleluia.

Give thanks to the LORD, for he is good,
    for his mercy endures forever.
Let the house of Israel say,
    "His mercy endures forever."

"The right hand of the LORD has struck
        with power;
    the right hand of the LORD is exalted.
I shall not die, but live,
    and declare the works of the LORD.

The stone which the builders rejected
    has become the cornerstone.
By the LORD has this been done;
    it is wonderful in our eyes.

Colossians = kuh-LOSH-uhnz

This short text requires a slow reading.

"If then you were raised . . . " means "because you were raised . . . ."

The tone is firm, yet encouraging.

Tell us two things: who will appear and what will happen.

READING II   Colossians 3:1–4

A reading from the Letter of Saint Paul to the Colossians

Brothers and sisters:
If then you were **raised** with Christ, seek what is **above**,
    where Christ is seated at the right hand of **God**.
Think of what is **above**, not of what is on **earth**.
For you have **died**, and your life is **hidden** with Christ in **God**.
When Christ your life **appears**,
    then you **too** will appear with him in **glory**.

Or:

God raised him to new life. In raising him from death, God demonstrated the truth of Jesus' message. Peter emphasizes to his hearers that they are receiving the word of witnesses to the life, Death, and Resurrection of Jesus. They are witnesses in the dual sense of having firsthand experience of what they proclaim, and of giving public testimony to that experience. As Jesus was brought through death to new life, so these witnesses are transformed from fearful doubters to fearless witnesses to the Risen Christ.

READING II   **Colossians 3:1 – 4.** Although Paul did not found the community at Colossae, he was concerned about their faithful understanding and living of the Gospel of Christ as he knew it. The founder of this church, Epaphras, apparently reported to Paul that other teachers had misled some members of the Colossian church into deviant beliefs and practices. Seeking to correct the teaching of "specious arguments" (2:4) imported by these false teachers, Paul in his first chapter clarifies the reality of Christ, then reminds them of the implications of the

true identity and work of the one they follow. In the second chapter he emphasizes the meaning of their Baptism, in which they shared Christ's passage through death to a new kind of life.

Today's reading follows from this principle: those who are truly raised to a higher kind of life with Christ will surely seek "what is above," what is in Christ. For those baptized into Christ, life must be radically changed. For those who choose to die to a former way of life and share in life "with Christ in God," all is changed; life must be

Corinthians = kor-in-THEE-uhnz

This short text requires a slow reading. Listeners are expected to know the answer to the rhetorical questions. Pause before giving the next command.
You will become a batch of "unleavened," that is, uncorrupted, dough.

Be more energetic with the second "yeast" clause. Use ritardando (slowing toward the end) with the words "of sincerity and truth."

For meditation and context:

READING II   1 Corinthians 5:6b–8

A reading from the first Letter of Saint Paul to the Corinthians

Brothers and sisters:
Do you not **know** that a little **yeast** leavens **all** the dough?
Clear out the **old** yeast,
    so that you may become a **fresh** batch of dough,
        inasmuch as you are **unleavened**.
For our paschal **lamb**, **Christ**, has been **sacrificed**.
Therefore, let us **celebrate** the feast,
    not with the **old** yeast, the yeast of **malice** and **wickedness**,
        but with the **unleavened** bread of **sincerity** and **truth**.

TO KEEP IN MIND
Separating units of thought with pauses: Identify the units of thought in your text and use pauses to distinguish one from another. Running words together blurs meaning and fails to distinguish ideas. Punctuation does not always indicate clearly what words to group together or where to pause. The listener depends on you for this organization of ideas.

SEQUENCE   Victimae paschali laudes

Christians, to the Paschal Victim
    Offer your thankful praises!
A Lamb the sheep redeems;
    Christ, who only is sinless,
    Reconciles sinners to the Father.
Death and life have contended in that
    combat stupendous:
    The Prince of life, who died, reigns
    immortal.

Speak, Mary, declaring
    What you saw, wayfaring.
"The tomb of Christ, who is living,
    The glory of Jesus' resurrection;
Bright angels attesting,
    The shroud and napkin resting.
Yes, Christ my hope is arisen;
    to Galilee he goes before you."
Christ indeed from death is risen, our new
    life obtaining.
    Have mercy, victor King, ever reigning!
    Amen. Alleluia.

lived differently until Christ appears again in glory.

1 Corinthians 5:6b–8. Several major reasons for this letter to the Corinthian community arose from distressing reports that had reached Paul, now in Ephesus, just a few years after he had established this church. The news involved immoral activity and divisions within the community. In his response, the Apostle addresses one matter, then another, repeatedly returning to the touchstone of his Gospel message: Christ, crucified and raised for all, in fulfillment of the Scriptures. Like Jesus, Paul

uses the image of a leavening agent to impress upon the church the danger of allowing even one member's public immorality to affect the entire community.

Immediately before today's reading, Paul deals with the case of a man openly living with his father's wife. He counseled the church to expel this man for his own sake, but also for the sake of the whole. This situation is most likely the "old yeast" that Paul considers a threat to the entire community's life in Christ, and it is Christ who must always provide the life pattern for believers. Paul presents Christ "our

Passover lamb" for imitation; Christians must live in his transformed life, dying to the "old yeast" of immorality and leavening the community with Resurrection life.

GOSPEL | At the Easter Vigil, Luke's account of women finding the empty tomb of Jesus names Mary Magdalene as one of the group, and all four canonical Gospel accounts present her as first, or among the first, to discover that Jesus has been raised. John opens the scene by noting that Mary comes "while it was still dark," probably invoking the light/

Take us through the text by allowing us to experience the characters' various emotions: Mary's panic, the disciples' instant anxiety, Peter's confusion before the empty wrappings and folded cloth, and John's silent assent in faith.

Magdala = MAG-duh-luh.

Speak slowly here; the mood is a bit melancholy.

Your pace should quicken here; Mary is fearful and distressed.

Let Peter and John do the racing, not you. Convey their haste without rushing the lines. Say "but the other disciple . . . did not go in": in a hushed tone.

Stress Peter's activity: he enters, sees, and examines. Speak the words "saw and believed" with quiet reverence.

It's understandable that they would not yet fully "understand."

GOSPEL   John 20:1–9

A reading from the holy Gospel according to John

On the **first** day of the **week**,
   Mary of **Magdala** came to the **tomb** early in the **morning**,
   while it was still **dark**,
   and saw the **stone removed** from the **tomb**.
So she **ran** and went to Simon **Peter**
   and to the **other** disciple whom Jesus **loved**, and told them,
   "They have taken the **Lord** from the **tomb**,
   and we don't know where they **put** him."
So **Peter** and the **other** disciple went out and **came** to the tomb.
They both **ran**, but the **other** disciple ran **faster** than Peter
   and arrived at the tomb **first**;
   he **bent** down and saw the **burial** cloths there, but did not go **in**.
When Simon **Peter** arrived **after** him,
   he went **into** the tomb and **saw** the burial cloths there,
   and the cloth that had covered his **head**,
   not with the **burial** cloths but rolled up in a **separate** place.
Then the **other** disciple **also** went in,
   the one who had arrived at the tomb **first**,
   and he **saw** and **believed**.
For they did not yet **understand** the Scripture
   that he had to **rise** from the dead.

darkness symbolism he has used from the beginning of his Gospel account. Finding the sealing stone removed, Mary concludes that the body of Jesus has been taken away, and she reports her suspicion to Peter and the beloved disciple. They, in turn, hurry to investigate for themselves, but find only burial cloths; the presence of these wrappings, described in some detail, indicates that the body has not simply been stolen.

The beloved disciple, observing the neatly arranged burial cloths, "saw and believed." For John, believing is the ulti-

mate goal of any encounter with Jesus. At the end of this chapter, the evangelist states that the central purpose of his Gospel account is to elicit belief that Jesus is the Messiah and Son of God, thus sharing fullness of life in him. The beloved disciple, never named, seems to embody the ideal disciple: one whom Jesus loves, one who enjoys intimacy with Jesus, one who believes in Jesus. For John, to "believe in" Jesus implies an intimate relationship, a mutual sindwelling of Jesus and the believer. Given his relationship with Jesus, he believes, even without understanding.

AFTERNOON GOSPEL This Resurrection account, unique to Luke, reprises some of his major themes, including table fellowship and fulfillment of the Scriptures. The Gospel for the Easter Vigil recounted the women's discovery of Jesus' empty tomb and the angelic message that "he has been raised." This reading follows immediately in Luke, with two disciples who seem to be among those who discounted the women's announcement. As in several other Resurrection accounts, the pair does not immediately know who has engaged them

LECTIONARY #46

AFTERNOON GOSPEL   Luke 24:13–35

A reading from the holy Gospel according to Luke

The margin notes (read in order):

- The "day" of this occurrence is important.
- Emmaus = eh-MAY-uhs.
- Let your tone convey the irony of their failure to recognize the very one they're discussing.
- Jesus is "playing dumb" here.
- Cleopas = KLEE-oh-puhs.
- He responds with annoyance.
- Jesus coaxes further. Initially their response might sound like: "How could you not know this?" But soon they are into the story.
- We can't help but feel sorry for them and their sense of loss.
- Are they dismissing the testimony because it came from women?

That **very day**, the **first day** of the **week**,
  two of **Jesus'** **disciples** were going
  to a village seven miles from **Jerusalem** called **Emmaus**,
  and they were **conversing** about **all the things**
    that had **occurred**.
And it **happened** that while they were **conversing** and **debating**,
  Jesus himself drew **near** and **walked** with them,
  but their **eyes** were **prevented** from **recognizing** him.
He **asked** them,
  "**What** are you **discussing** as you **walk** along?"
They **stopped**, looking **downcast**.
One of them, named **Cleopas**, said to him in **reply**,
  "Are **you** the **only visitor** to **Jerusalem**
  who does **not know** of the **things**
    that have **taken place** there in these **days**?"
And he **replied** to them, "What **sort** of things?"
They **said** to him,
  "The **things** that **happened** to **Jesus** the **Nazarene**,
  who was a **prophet mighty** in **deed** and **word**
  before **God** and **all** the **people**,
  how our **chief priests** and **rulers** both **handed** him **over**
  to a **sentence** of **death** and **crucified** him.
But **we** were **hoping** that he would be the **one** to **redeem Israel**;
  and besides all **this**,
  it is **now** the **third day** since this took **place**.
Some **women** from our **group**, however, have **astounded** us:
  they were at the **tomb early** in the **morning**
  and did **not** find his **body**;
  they came **back** and **reported**

---

in conversation; it is the same Jesus they followed, but he has been transformed. Ironically, the discouraged disciples describe Jesus as "a prophet," but they fail to see that his prophetic word concerning his Death and Resurrection (9:22) has been fulfilled. Jesus himself emphasizes fulfillment of the Scriptures as he chides them for their inability or unwillingness to perceive their meaning, which he then explains, beginning with Moses.

The two disciples still do not recognize their companion on the journey, but when it seems that he will leave them, they press him to stay. As happens often in Luke, the sharing of a meal with Jesus reveals his person and mission. In a culture that viewed table fellowship as a profound statement of mutual acceptance and commitment, Jesus frequently dined with sinners and outcasts as a living image of the Kingdom of God that he proclaimed. At the

Last Supper, he stated that he would not share a meal again until the coming of the Kingdom (22:18); now at table with the downcast disciples, Jesus' prophecy is fulfilled, for the Kingdom has begun.

This meal also bears Eucharistic overtones in the use of four key words that reappear in early references to the Lord's Supper: take, bless, break, give. Writing after most, if not all, of the original disciples have died, Luke reminds his contemporaries

They just can't add two and two: the tomb was empty and angels announced his rising, yet this does not yet add up to Resurrection.

Jesus' emotion is real: frustration and some sadness.

This is a new beat; don't rush.

They plead with him to stay!

Slowly narrate this Eucharistic scene. Pause after "gave it to them."

Speak these lines with energy and awe.

Use a quickened pace here, but keep it natural and realistic.

Remember this is a story. Tell it as if for the first time, with enthusiasm and suspense.

that they had **indeed** seen a **vision** of **angels**
  who **announced** that he was **alive**.
Then **some** of those **with** us **went** to the **tomb**
  and found things **just** as the **women** had **described**,
  but **him** they did **not see**."
And he **said** to them, "Oh, how **foolish** you are!
How slow of **heart** to **believe all** that the **prophets spoke**!
Was it not **necessary** that the **Christ** should **suffer** these things
  and **enter** into his **glory**?"
Then **beginning** with **Moses** and **all** the **prophets**,
  he **interpreted** to them what referred to **him**
  in **all** the **Scriptures**.
As they **approached** the village to which they were **going**,
  he gave the **impression** that he was going on **farther**.
But they **urged** him, "**Stay** with us,
  for it is **nearly evening** and the **day** is **almost over**."
So he went in to **stay** with them.
And it **happened** that, while he was **with** them at **table**,
  he took **bread**, said the **blessing**,
  broke it, and **gave** it to them.
With **that** their **eyes** were **opened** and they **recognized** him,
  but he **vanished** from their **sight**.
Then they said to each other,
  "Were not our **hearts burning within us**
  while he **spoke** to us on the **way** and **opened** the **Scriptures**
    to us?"
So they **set out** at **once** and **returned** to **Jerusalem**
  where they found **gathered** together
  the **eleven** and those **with** them who were **saying**,
  "The **Lord** has **truly** been **raised** and has **appeared** to **Simon**!"
Then the **two recounted**
  what had taken **place** on the **way**
  and how he was made **known** to them in the **breaking** of **bread**.

of one important mode of Jesus' presence. At the close of this episode, he underscores the importance of Eucharist as a mode of meeting and recognizing Jesus, crucified and raised. Returning to the eleven, who confirm the women's announcement, the companions relate their own encounter at table with the Risen Christ. M.F.

APRIL 3, 2016

SECOND SUNDAY OF EASTER (OR SUNDAY OF DIVINE MERCY)

LECTIONARY #45

READING I   Acts 5:12–16

A reading from the Acts of the Apostles

Many **signs** and **wonders** were **done** among the **people**
    at the **hands** of the **apostles**.
They were **all together** in Solomon's **portico**.
None of the others **dared** to **join** them, but the **people**
        esteemed them.
Yet **more** than **ever**, **believers** in the **Lord**,
    great numbers of **men** and **women**, were added **to** them.
Thus they **even carried** the **sick** out into the **streets**
    and **laid** them on **cots** and **mats**
    so that when **Peter** came **by**,
    at least his **shadow** might **fall** on **one** or **another** of them.
A **large number** of **people** from the **towns**
    in the **vicinity** of **Jerusalem also** gathered,
    bringing the **sick** and those **disturbed** by **unclean spirits**,
    and they were **all cured**.

Begin with an upbeat and joyous tone.

A shadow of threat looms over the community, for some did not dare to gather for fear of the authorities.
Accent the "esteem" of the people.

The steady growth of the community is reason for rejoicing.

Relate these events with reverence, as if you had witnessed what you describe.

People gather from other parts of the region as word spreads of the marvels in Jerusalem.

READING I It is Easter Time, and if we need evidence of the difference Resurrection makes we have it here in this text. Recall how recently Peter suffered from the habit of putting his foot in his mouth; worse, recall his inflated promises to Jesus that crumbled the minute Peter sensed danger for himself. Now, he is an esteemed leader, renowned among believers and unbelievers for the power of God that flows through him. His shadow is enough to heal and his words win large numbers to the Lord. So much has changed in so little time.

On Divine Mercy Sunday these events retold in Acts demonstrate powerfully the extraordinary mercy of God. Peter's betrayal is a thing of the past and these simple fishermen have become powerful evangelists winning hearts to Christ, transforming lives, and eventually, the world. In the previous chapter of Acts, Peter and John gathered the community to pray for "signs and wonders" to accompany their proclamation of the Gospel (4:30). The first line of today's text attests that their prayer was answered. While some today may question and even dismiss the authenticity of biblical miracles, there is no question that miracles played a critical role in the spread of the Gospel. We see here what we also saw in Jesus' ministry: signs attract attention, excite the spirit, nurture the imagination, and strengthen faith.

The growth of the nascent community testifies to the teaching of the Apostles and to God's mercy in turning hearts into fertile ground for the seed of the Gospel. Already, we detect order and authority within the community that clearly relies on the Apostles for leadership, and foremost among them is Peter.

154

For meditation and context:

TO KEEP IN MIND

Ritardando: refers to the practice, common in music, of becoming gradually slower and expanding the words as you approach the end of a piece. Many readings end this way—with a decreased rate but increased intensity.

RESPONSORIAL PSALM   Psalm 118:2–4, 13–15, 22–24 (1)

R. Give thanks to the Lord for he is good, his love is everlasting. or R. Alleluia.

Let the house of Israel say,
  "His mercy endures forever."
Let the house of Aaron say,
  "His mercy endures forever."
Let those who fear the LORD say,
  "His mercy endures forever."

I was hard pressed and was falling,
  but the LORD helped me.
My strength and my courage is the LORD,
  and he has been my savior.
The joyful shout of victory
  in the tents of the just.

The stone which the builders rejected
  has become the cornerstone.
By the LORD has this been done;
  it is wonderful in our eyes.
This is the day the LORD has made;
  let us be glad and rejoice in it.

This is the first of six consecutive weeks we read from the Book of Revelation. Note that the word is singular.

The greeting conveys an intimate connection between John and his readers.

Patmos = PAT-muhs

It is Sunday and the Spirit takes hold of him.

The "voice as loud as a trumpet" is immediately recognized as bearing a divine message.
Remember that throughout you are narrating a divine vision; keep the tone regal and authoritative.
Jesus is seen symbolically as standing in the midst of the seven great Christian communities of that day.

READING II   Revelation 1:9–11a, 12–13, 17–19

A reading from the Book of Revelation

I, **John**, your **brother**, who **share** with you
  the **distress**, the **kingdom**, and the **endurance** we have
    in **Jesus**,
  found myself on the **island** called **Patmos**
  because I proclaimed **God's word** and gave **testimony** to **Jesus**.
I was **caught up** in **spirit** on the **Lord's** day
  and **heard behind** me a **voice** as **loud** as a **trumpet**, which said,
  "**Write** on a **scroll** what you **see**."
Then I **turned** to **see whose voice** it **was** that **spoke** to me,
  and when I **turned**, I saw **seven gold lampstands**
  and in the **midst** of the **lampstands** one **like** a **son** of **man**,
  wearing an **ankle-length robe**, with a **gold sash**
    around his **chest**. »

Speak with tenderness of those who brought their sick to be healed and, with conviction, tell of the wonders God worked through the Apostles. Note that some who come are "sick" while others are "disturbed by unclean spirits." But announce joyfully that the merciful grace of God reaches out with healing to *all* who present themselves.

READING II   Apocalyptic literature, like the Book of Revelation, is quite distinctive. Since readings will come from this book for another five weeks, it's

helpful to review some of the features of this unique writing. Apocalyptic literature always involves a revelation or unveiling of some hidden truth about the future. But to unveil, this writing ironically employs highly symbolic language—a kind of "code" that is difficult to decipher. Created to offer comfort and hope to people suffering persecution, apocalyptic writing assures readers that God will ultimately triumph over evil and will establish his Kingdom on earth.

For his efforts on behalf of the Gospel, John has been exiled to the island of Patmos. This trial makes him a "brother" to

all Christians who experience "distress" for the name of Jesus. But this distress does not define John or the others who suffer for Christ because they also share "the kingdom, and . . . endurance" in Christ. It is for exactly the purpose of encouraging those enduring tribulation that this book was written. The content of John's vision offers real sustenance to the persecuted, perhaps disillusioned Christians who may fear that God has forgotten them.

On the "Lord's day" John receives a vision in which he hears trumpets, symbols of divine presence. A voice orders him to

"Fell down" is both a response of fear and reverence.

The voice of the "son of man" is both powerful and compassionate.

Remember, these words are meant to comfort those in distress. Fill your voice with hope and blessing.

This is a command that has *three* elements.

When I caught **sight** of him, I **fell down** at his **feet** as though **dead**.
He **touched** me with his **right hand** and said, "Do **not** be **afraid**.
I am **the first** and **the last**, the **one** who **lives**.
Once I was **dead**, but **now** I am **alive forever** and **ever**.
I hold the **keys** to **death** and the **netherworld**.
Write down, therefore, what you have **seen**,
    and what is **happening**, and what **will happen afterwards**."

GOSPEL   John 20:19–31

A reading from the holy Gospel according to John

It's the day of the Resurrection, Sunday, and they're behind locked doors, full of fear, when Jesus comes and wishes peace. Those are a lot of details for a first sentence. Read with hushed reverence.

Jesus' entrance is unexpected and shocking. He speaks with authority and intimacy.

On the **evening** of that **first day** of the **week**,
    when the **doors** were **locked**, where the **disciples** were,
    for **fear** of the Jews,
Jesus came and **stood** in their **midst**
    and said to them, "**Peace** be with **you**."
When he had **said** this, he **showed** them his **hands** and his **side**.
The **disciples rejoiced** when they **saw** the **Lord**.

Not until they see the hands and side do they "rejoice."

Jesus subdues their rejoicing to announce his mission for them.

Don't rush the detail of his breathing on them.

Jesus said to them **again**, "**Peace** be with **you**.
As the **Father** has **sent me**, so I send **you**."
And when he had **said** this, he **breathed** on them and **said**
        to them,
    "**Receive** the **Holy Spirit**.
Whose **sins** you **forgive** are **forgiven** them,
    and whose **sins** you **retain** are **retained**."

Pause at the end of this dialogue before introducing Thomas.

Didymus = DID-ih-muhs.

They speak with awed enthusiasm.

Don't render Thomas as stubborn or narrow. Without knowing it, Thomas asks for what the others have already received.

Thomas, called **Didymus**, one of the **Twelve**,
    was not **with** them when **Jesus came**.
So the **other** disciples said to him, "We have **seen** the **Lord**."
But **he** said to them,
    "**Unless** I **see** the **mark** of the **nails** in his **hands**
    and **put** my **finger** into the **nailmarks**
    and **put** my **hand** into his **side**, I will **not believe**."

---

record the very things now being narrated. When he looks, first he sees "seven gold lampstands" symbolizing the seven major churches of his era, each in a different city, that represent the entire church of that time. In their midst is the mysterious "son of man," a title borrowed from the Book of Daniel, which Jesus frequently appropriated to himself. Here, the term suggests a divine persona who wields power and authority. This is a highly symbolic depiction of Christ in his heavenly glory, wearing a priestly "robe" and a kingly "sash".

It was believed that the presence of divinity brought certain death, so John falls at the feet of the son of man, who reassures him and identifies himself as "the first and the last," who holds "the keys to death and the netherworld"—another image of divine presence and power. The reading ends with the mysterious Christ figure urging John to write everything that will be revealed to him.

> GOSPEL   The reality of the Resurrection was a fact that had to be established among the early

Christian community and even among Jesus' closest disciples. John is establishing that fact here with his clear focus on physical details that assert its authenticity. The disciples cling to each other and to this place of safety because they've lost their anchor and fear for their safety. When Jesus appears, despite "locked" doors, he offers physical evidence that his Resurrection is more than a spiritual reality. And then he breathes on them as God first breathed on Adam, initiating a new creation of which they will be the heralds. But first he gives them peace, for the new life

Here starts a new beat. Sustain your energy and stress the presence of Thomas.

Deliver this "Peace be with you" in a solemn, unrushed manner as before.

Jesus is giving him what he already gave the others—physical proof of his Resurrection.

Try a brief pause between "My Lord . . . " and " . . . and my God."

What Jesus says of Thomas is true of all the Apostles.

Blessed = blesd or BLES-uhd

Don't lose energy on these final lines for they make an important statement of faith: eternal life comes through Jesus Christ.

TO KEEP IN MIND

Narrator: Knowing the point of view that the narrator is "rooting for" will help you more fully communicate the meaning of the text. The narrator always has a viewpoint, often speaking as a believer, not as an objective reporter. For this reason, the narrator is often the pivotal role in a passage. Using timbre, pitch, rate, and energy can help you convey the narrator's moods or meanings.

Now a **week later** his **disciples** were **again** inside
    and **Thomas was with** them.
Jesus came, although the **doors** were **locked**,
    and **stood** in their **midst** and said, "**Peace** be with **you**."
Then he said to **Thomas**, "**Put** your **finger here** and **see** my **hands**,
    and **bring** your **hand** and **put** it into my **side**,
    and **do** not be **unbelieving**, but **believe**."
Thomas **answered** and said to him, "**My Lord and my God!**"
Jesus **said** to **him**, "Have you **come** to **believe**
    because you have **seen** me?
Blessed are **those** who **have not seen** and **have believed**."

Now **Jesus** did **many other signs** in the **presence** of his **disciples**
    that are **not written** in this book.
But **these are written** that you may **come to believe**
    that **Jesus** is the **Christ**, the **Son** of **God**,
    and that **through this belief** you may have **life** in **his name**.

---

he offers must be lived and shared in peace. And in this new creation, they are to be the bearers of a wondrous privilege—the forgiveness of sins imparted through the Holy Spirit.

Significantly, Thomas is absent from the gathering and rejects the testimony of his closest friends, who insist they have seen the Lord. His doubt matches their certainty and he lays out clear terms for yielding his disbelief: physical and incontrovertible proof. When Jesus comes, again through locked doors, he calls on Thomas to make the test he earlier prescribed.

There is no report of Thomas touching hands or side; instead, he yields immediately when he but *sees* what the others saw one week before. Instead of their silence, Thomas responds with a spontaneous declaration of faith. Anticipating the generations who will believe *without* seeing, Jesus gently chides Thomas and utters a beatitude that extols the countless believers who have been satisfied to see with nothing but the eyes of faith.

The final five lines serve as an important epilogue to this narrative. This event, and many others like it, occurred to strengthen the belief of disciples then and now. That's why this was written down—so that faith in Jesus as "the Christ" and "Son of God" might become the bedrock of our corporate and individual faith. Not to resolve debates. Not to dispel doubts. Not to force belief. But to give life in his name. G.M.

THIRD SUNDAY OF EASTER

LECTIONARY #48

READING I Acts 5:27–32, 40b–41

A reading from the Acts of the Apostles

When the **captain** and the **court officers** had **brought**
    the **apostles** in
  and made them **stand** before the **Sanhedrin,**
  the **high priest questioned** them,
  "We gave you **strict orders,** did we **not,**
  to **stop teaching** in **that name?**
Yet you have **filled Jerusalem** with your **teaching**
  and want to **bring this man's blood** upon **us.**"
But **Peter** and the **apostles** said in reply,
  "We must **obey God** rather than **men.**
The **God** of our ancestors **raised Jesus,**
  though **you** had him **killed** by **hanging** him on a **tree.**
God exalted him at his **right hand** as **leader** and **savior**
  to grant **Israel repentance** and **forgiveness** of **sins.**
We are **witnesses** of these things,
  as is the **Holy Spirit** whom **God** has **given** to those who
    obey him.'"

The **Sanhedrin ordered** the **apostles**
  to **stop speaking** in the **name** of **Jesus,** and **dismissed** them.
So they **left** the **presence** of the **Sanhedrin,**
  rejoicing that they had been found **worthy**
  to **suffer dishonor** for the **sake** of the **name.**

The high priest has no patience for these righteous zealots.

His anger peaks at the thought that they are implicating him in Jesus' death.

Peter is self-confident. He was freed and ordered by an angel to preach of Jesus.

Even this setting is an opportunity to proclaim "the name" of Jesus.
"Repentance" and "forgiveness" should not be run together. They are distinct concepts.

Note that both the disciples and the Holy Spirit give witness.
Although the flogging is left out of our portion today, let that violence color the announcement of the disciples' brusque dismissal.

It is a sober rejoicing cited here; read slowly, aware of those today who still suffer and die for the sake of the "name."

READING I The Acts of the Apostles continues to tell the story of the spread of the Gospel in the days following the Resurrection and Ascension of Jesus. It would be interesting enough if it were only a story of struggle between disciples and hostile religious authorities; but this narrative includes an unseen character whose presence nonetheless is deeply felt. To keep them from preaching about Jesus, the authorities had the Apostles jailed. But an angel of God secretly released them during the night and ordered them to resume their preaching in the Temple area. Imagine the shock of the Sanhedrin when the very men they believe to be languishing in a cell are instead found doing the very thing that got them imprisoned in the first place.

The authorities puzzle over how these men escaped locked cells, but the Apostles are convinced God is directing their fate. That's why, after this second arrest, they dare to defy the Sanhedrin and insist they must "obey God rather than men." The authorities want to silence them to put an end to this fascination with Jesus, but also because the Apostles have colored the high priest's hands red with the blood of Jesus: "You had him killed." They announce their accusations and declare themselves "witnesses." Their brazen audacity so infuriates the leaders that they determine to kill the Apostles, but a wise council member advises them to take a "wait and see" posture instead.

The leaders settle for flogging the disciples before freeing them. Beaten and warned to keep silent about Jesus, the Apostles go forth rejoicing, not because they're free, nor because they narrowly escaped death, but because they were "found worthy" to suffer for the sake of

For meditation and context:

TO KEEP IN MIND

Word value: Words are your medium, like a painter's brush or a sculptor's chisel. You must understand the words before you can communicate them. Most words have a dictionary meaning (denotative) and an associational meaning (connotative). "House" and "home" both mean "dwelling," yet they communicate different feelings. Be alert to subtle differences in connotative meanings and express them.

RESPONSORIAL PSALM   Psalm 30:2, 4, 5–6, 11–12, 13 (2a)

R. I will praise you, Lord, for you have rescued me. or R. Alleluia.

I will extol you, O LORD, for you drew me clear
  and did not let my enemies rejoice over me.
O LORD, you brought me up from the netherworld;
  you preserved me from among those going down into the pit.

Sing praise to the LORD, you his faithful ones,
  and give thanks to his holy name.
For his anger lasts but a moment;
  a lifetime, his good will.
At nightfall, weeping enters in,
  but with the dawn, rejoicing.

Hear, O LORD, and have pity on me;
  O LORD, be my helper.
You changed my mourning into dancing;
  O LORD, my God, forever will I give you thanks.

This is the second of six consecutive weeks we read from Revelation.

You are narrating a cosmic vision that should evoke a sense of awe. Try to "see" in your own mind's eye all the images you relate.

"Living creatures" and "elders" symbolize all creation and the Church.

The seven words that characterize the Lamb should suggest *distinct* qualities.

The whole universe gives praise. Distinguish one location from another.

Speak this as your own prayer that fuses gratitude and awe.

Pause after "said" as if to listen to the "Amen" before you speak it. Imagine the whole Church falling to its knees in adoration.

READING II   Revelation 5:11–14

A reading from the Book of Revelation

I, **John**, **looked** and **heard** the voices of **many angels**
  who **surrounded** the **throne**
  and the **living creatures** and the **elders**.
They were **countless** in **number**, and they **cried out**
    in a **loud voice**:
      "**Worthy** is the **Lamb** that was **slain**
        to receive **power** and **riches**, **wisdom** and **strength**,
        honor and **glory** and **blessing**."
Then I heard **every creature** in **heaven** and on **earth**
    and **under** the **earth** and in the **sea**,
    everything in the **universe**, cry out:
      "To the **one** who **sits** on the **throne** and to the **Lamb**
        be **blessing** and **honor**, **glory** and **might**,
        forever and **ever**."
The **four living creatures** answered, "**Amen**,"
  and the **elders** fell **down** and **worshiped**.

Christ. That same sense of privilege should imbue your proclamation today.

READING II   Today's text from Revelation thrusts us into the heavenly throne room where a vast throng worships God and the "Lamb." Our liturgy is but a rehearsal for the eternal liturgy we will celebrate when we reach the shores of the divine Kingdom. John describes a cosmic ritual in which every form of life becomes a single chorus of praise to the God who created it all and to the Lamb who won salvation for all.

Written intentionally in a cryptic style that is intelligible to its intended audience, while remaining obscure to those who threaten the community of believers, apocalyptic writing offers hope and consolation to people suffering persecution. This wondrous vision counters the brutal realities and the dire risks Christians faced in the practice of their faith. At the center of this worship is a "Lamb," symbolizing Christ. At the time of the exodus, the blood of a lamb was used to mark the homes of the Israelites so that the plague sent against their Egyptian oppressors would "pass over" them. Similarly, the blood shed by the Lamb of God brings salvation from sin and death to the new Israel (us).

Theologians who write of the likelihood of extraterrestrial life contend that, theologically, nothing changes if life is found on other planets because Christ is Savior and Lord of the "universe," not just our small planet. John's vision seems in tune with that insight when he says that everything in the *universe* worships the lamb. Gathered to offer God unending praise are "elders" that represent the entire

GOSPEL   John 21:1–19

A reading from the holy Gospel according to John

At that time, **Jesus revealed** himself **again** to his **disciples**
    at the **Sea** of **Tiberias**.
He **revealed** himself in **this way**.
Together were **Simon Peter**, **Thomas** called **Didymus**,
    Nathanael from **Cana** in **Galilee**,
    Zebedee's sons, and **two others** of his **disciples**.
Simon Peter said to them, "I am going **fishing**."
They said to him, "**We also** will **come with** you."
So they **went out** and got into the **boat**,
    but **that night** they caught **nothing**.
When it was already **dawn**, **Jesus** was **standing** on the **shore**;
    but the **disciples** did not **realize** that it was **Jesus**.
Jesus said to them, "**Children**, have you **caught anything** to **eat**?"
They answered him, "**No**."
So he said to them, "**Cast** the **net** over the **right side** of the **boat**
    and you will **find** something."
So they **cast** it, and were **not** able to **pull** it **in**
    because of the **number** of **fish**.
So the **disciple** whom **Jesus loved** said to **Peter**, "It is the **Lord**."
When **Simon Peter heard** that it was the **Lord**,
    he **tucked in** his **garment**, for he was **lightly clad**,
    and **jumped** into the sea.
The **other** disciples **came** in the **boat**,
    for they were **not far** from **shore**, only about a **hundred yards**,
    dragging the **net** with the **fish**.
When they **climbed out** on **shore**,
    they **saw** a charcoal **fire** with **fish** on it and **bread**.
Jesus said to them, "**Bring** some of the **fish** you just **caught**."
So **Simon Peter** went over and **dragged** the **net ashore**
    full of one **hundred fifty-three large fish**.
Even though there were so **many**, the **net** was **not torn**.

The manifestations of Jesus serve to reinforce the authenticity of the Resurrection.

It is here that Jesus previously multiplied the loaves and fishes.

Try telling this story as a believer who is evangelizing others.

Speak the names with familiarity and affection.

Didymus = DID-ih-muhs

The number of disciples, seven, may represent the entire community of disciples.

Peter needs to keep busy, but their whole night is wasted.

Jesus brings the light of day.

Note the tender salutation.

That catch is surprising, as is their willingness to follow this stranger's advice.

The "disciple whom Jesus loved" is the first to recognize Jesus.

Peter "dresses" before jumping into the sea!

Emphasize the size of the catch.

Jesus has anticipated their hunger and met their need.

The number of fish is important. Their labor done, Jesus invites them to breakfast.

Church and four "living creatures" that represent all of creation.

John's message is clear: Christ is not a victim; he is a victor reigning at the right hand of God. He is the source of life and those who give themselves to him, no matter what present trials they must endure, will conquer death with him and find eternal reward in his Kingdom. To convey that hope, proclaim this as the poetry it is, giving the lines a joyful cadence that proclaims the awesome majesty of the one who is "worthy . . . to receive . . . honor and glory and blessing."

GOSPEL This narrative accomplishes several purposes: it asserts the authenticity of the Resurrection, it offers a glimpse of men set adrift by the sudden loss of their leader, it provides a rehabilitation scenario for Peter, and it establishes Peter as the undisputed leader of the emergent Church.

Contrary to the notion that Jesus' Resurrection was but a "spiritual" reality that offered the disciples a "sense" of the presence of Jesus, the New Testament takes pains to assert a physical Resurrection on which Christians soon

would base their lives and for which some would be martyred.

Losing Jesus' constant physical presence is so disorienting, that the disciples feel a need to return to what is familiar. But they labor through the night with empty nets. The dawn brings the light of the Son but, like the travelers to Emmaus, they fail to recognize him. Jesus takes advantage of his anonymity to coax them into casting their nets anew. Who could blame these professional fishermen if they took offense at his question and advice? But they readily acknowledge their failure and quickly agree

Asking might betray their lack of vision and of faith, so they demur.

Don't overlook the Eucharistic language here.

Again, John stresses the recurrence of Jesus' appearances to the disciples.

Don't overly emotionalize the dialogue. Jesus is direct; it is Peter who must deal with the repeated questions that sting, probe, and totally disarm.

First, Jesus asks if Peter's love exceeds that of the other disciples; then he questions the sincerity and depth of that love.

Finally, Peter lets down his defenses.
A proverb about the loss of independence in old age is used to speak of Peter's future death.

Note that his anticipated martyrdom will "glorify God."

Jesus' final words speak to us as well as Peter.

Jesus said to them, "**Come**, have **breakfast**."
And **none** of the **disciples dared** to ask him, "**Who are** you?"
  because they **realized** it was the **Lord**.
Jesus came over and **took** the **bread** and **gave** it to them,
  and in like **manner** the **fish**.
This was now the **third time** Jesus was **revealed** to his **disciples**
  after being **raised** from the **dead**.

When they had **finished breakfast**, Jesus said to Simon **Peter**,
  "**Simon**, son of **John**, do **you love** me more than **these**?"
Simon Peter answered him, "**Yes**, Lord, you **know** that
    I love you."
Jesus said to him, "**Feed** my **lambs**."
He then said to **Simon Peter** a **second** time,
  "**Simon**, son of **John**, do **you love** me?"
Simon Peter answered him, "**Yes**, Lord, you **know**
    that **I** love you."
Jesus said to him, "**Tend my sheep**."
Jesus said to him the **third** time,
  "**Simon**, son of **John**, do **you love** me?"
Peter was **distressed** that Jesus had said to him a **third** time,
  "Do **you love** me?" and he **said** to him,
  "**Lord**, **you know everything**; you **know** that I **love** you."
Jesus said to him, "**Feed** my **sheep**.
Amen, **amen**, I say to you, when you were **younger**,
  you used to **dress yourself** and **go** where **you** wanted;
  but when you **grow old**, you will **stretch** out your **hands**,
  and **someone else** will **dress** you
  and **lead** you where you do **not want** to go."
He said this **signifying** by what **kind** of **death** he would
    glorify God.
And when he had **said** this, he said to him, "**Follow** me."

[Shorter: John 21:1–14]

---

to try again. This time the fish catch them, seeming to dive into their nets. Their number symbolizes the universal nature of the kerygma, since 153 represented all the known species of fish.

Jesus is already roasting fish on a fire. In the very place he previously fed the multitude with fish and bread, he now feeds these disciples, and the Eucharistic implications are clear. Then Jesus gets down to his urgent business with Peter. It's likely that Peter has not yet admitted his denials openly, so the others may not know of his failing. Jesus allows him to undo his triple failure with a triple affirmation of love. He inquires about the depth of Peter's love and each time Peter affirms it Jesus orders him to "tend" and "feed" the flock. Peter's stewardship is not founded on leadership skills but on love of the Lord. Exercise of authority in the Church is to be an expression of one's love of Christ.

Don't overlook the human dynamic at work in the dialogue. Jesus' third question wounds Peter and finally elicits the acknowledgement that Jesus knows "everything"—his failure *and* his sincere love. Jesus then speaks of a future when Peter will no longer be master of his fate, an allusion to his death. In the context of this healing moment, Jesus' words are challenge and reassurance, warning and reward. Not only will Peter follow Jesus as shepherd of the flock, he will also follow him to the glory of martyrdom for the sake of his sheep. G.M.

FOURTH SUNDAY
OF EASTER

LECTIONARY #51

READING I   Acts 13:14, 43–52

A reading from the Acts of the Apostles

Paul and **Barnabas** continued on from **Perga**
 and reached **Antioch** in **Pisidia**.
On the **sabbath** they **entered** the **synagogue** and **took** their **seats**.
Many Jews and worshipers who were **converts** to **Judaism**
 followed **Paul** and **Barnabas**, who **spoke** to them
 and **urged** them to **remain faithful** to the **grace** of **God**.

On the **following sabbath** almost the **whole city** gathered
 to **hear** the **word** of the **Lord**.
When the **Jews** saw the **crowds**, they were **filled** with **jealousy**
 and with **violent abuse contradicted** what **Paul said**.
Both **Paul** and **Barnabas** spoke out **boldly** and **said**,
 "It was **necessary** that the **word** of **God** be **spoken** to **you first**,
 but since **you reject** it
 and **condemn** yourselves as **unworthy** of **eternal life**,
 we **now turn** to the **Gentiles**.
For **so** the **Lord** has **commanded** us,
 *I have made you a **light** to the **Gentiles**,*
 *that you may be an **instrument** of **salvation***
 *to the **ends** of the **earth**."*

The **Gentiles** were **delighted** when they **heard** this
 and **glorified** the **word** of the **Lord**.

Begin with energy to suggest the fiery preaching of the previous week that has brought a huge crowd to hear them again.

This is the fourth of eight consecutive weeks we read from Acts.

Perga = PER-guh
Antioch = AN-tee-ahk
Pisidia = pih-SID-ee-uh

Apparently, Jews and non-Jews have gathered to hear them.

Now as then, jealousy can make us oppose even the Gospel. Speak more with sadness than indictment.

Paul is strong in his conviction that the Word must now be proclaimed to those willing to hear it, no matter their ethnicity.

Paul quotes Isaiah 49:6. Shift your tone for the quotation.

Share this news with joy.

READING I Paul is in a synagogue where the previous week he preached to fellow Jews and converts to Judaism an impassioned and gripping sermon about the ministry and fate of Jesus. (For this background to the story, read verses 15–42 of Acts 13.) Paul's hearers were so taken with his message that they invited him to return the following week. You can use the introductory sentences to suggest the zeal Paul and Barnabas stirred in the hearts of their audience the previous week, zeal that results in "the whole city" gathering to hear them now. Throughout the Easter season, the First Readings give us a glimpse of how the seed of the Gospel was sown and took root in those early days following the Death of Jesus.

At the hands of Paul, the Gospel's intended audience quickly shifted from primarily Jewish to almost entirely Gentile, and today's story shows us an important turning point. Paul recognized that Jesus was the fulfillment of Old Testament prophecy and that his ministry had been exclusively to his own people. But under the influence of the Spirit, he also recognized that many of Jesus' own closed their hearts to his message; in that reality Paul discerned a call to take the Gospel to anyone and everyone who would hear it.

While the Gentiles are "delighted" to hear the Good News, the Jewish leaders were enraged with jealousy that the disciples were attracting crowds with their message. In both responses we see divine grace at work—Jesus embraced in one instance and fiercely resisted in the other. Then as now, grace can be resisted but not thwarted. Even when they shake dust from their feet, Paul and Barnabas rejoice, for they know whose will they are obeying.

Quicken your tempo to suggest the surging flood of opposition that begins to well up against Paul. Speak in the tone of the opponents.

Iconium = ī-KOH-nee-uhm

Don't rush the last line. Despite opposition from their own people, they are filled with joy in the Spirit.

For meditation and context:

> **TO KEEP IN MIND**
> **Pace:** The rate at which you read is influenced by the size of your church, the size of the congregation, and the complexity of the text. As each increases, rate decreases.

All who were **destined** for **eternal life** came to **believe**,
     and the **word** of the **Lord continued** to **spread**
     through the **whole region**.
The **Jews**, however, incited the **women** of **prominence**
     who were **worshipers**
     and the **leading men** of the **city**,
     stirred up a **persecution** against **Paul** and **Barnabas**,
     and **expelled** them from their **territory**.
So they shook the **dust** from their **feet** in **protest against** them,
     and went to **Iconium**.
The **disciples** were **filled** with **joy** and the **Holy Spirit**.

RESPONSORIAL PSALM   Psalm 100:1–2, 3, 5 (3c)

R. We are his people, the sheep of his flock. or R. Alleluia.

Sing joyfully to the LORD, all you lands;
     serve the LORD with gladness;
     come before him with joyful song.

Know that the LORD is God;
     he made us, his we are;
     his people, the flock he tends.

The LORD is good:
     His kindness endures forever,
     and his faithfulness, to all generations.

This is the third of six consecutive weeks we read from Revelation.

Remember you are proclaiming a vision that's meant to bring comfort. Read slowly and with reverence.

All of humanity is represented in God's throne room.

The "elder" asked John about those dressed in white and now provides his own answer.

READING II   Revelation 7:9, 14b–17

A reading from the Book of Revelation

I, John, had a **vision** of a **great multitude**,
     which **no one** could **count**,
     from **every nation**, **race**, **people** and **tongue**.
They stood before the **throne** and before the **Lamb**,
     wearing **white robes** and holding **palm branches**
          in their **hands**.

Then **one** of the **elders said** to me,
     "**These** are the **ones** who have **survived** the time
          of **great distress**; ≫

READING II Human hearts long to hear words of comfort and assurance like those proclaimed at the end of this text. During times of crisis, periodic woundedness, and daily struggle, we all need a pledge that tears will be wiped from our eyes and that one who loves us will forever shelter us. Though written to Christians enduring persecution and written in a way that hides its true meaning from the persecutors while making it available to believing readers, the Book of Revelation contains a timeless message. It asserts that those who oppose God's work will not pre-

vail, that suffering, even martyrdom, will lead to new and greater life than we could ever have imagined. And it assures those who suffer that they have not been forgotten, no matter how much circumstances might declare that falsehood.

In the heavenly throne room, a "great multitude" worships God and "the Lamb," whom readers would immediately recognize as a code name for Christ. The "elder" explains that those dressed in white are faithful believers who did not let the sword compromise their faith. They have mingled their blood with the blood of the Lamb, and

that blood has washed them clean. Forever now, they are privileged to stand in the presence of the divine Lamb where no form of deprivation or suffering will ever touch them. Declare this vision with pride and compassion for it speaks of both our history and our future.

GOSPEL Coming at the end of Jesus' sublime Good Shepherd discourse, this brief passage asserts Jesus' devotion for his sheep and his identity with the Father. Jesus' description of himself as the Good Shepherd left his listeners

they have **washed** their **robes**
and made them **white** in the **blood** of the **Lamb**.

> "For **this reason** they **stand** before **God's throne**
>   and **worship** him **day** and **night** in his **temple**.
> The one who **sits** on the **throne** will **shelter** them.
> They will **not hunger** or **thirst** anymore,
>   nor will the **sun** or **any heat strike** them.
> For the **Lamb** who is in the **center** of the **throne**
>   will **shepherd** them
>   and **lead** them to **springs** of **life-giving water**,
>   and **God** will **wipe away every tear** from their **eyes**."

Their reward is eternal joy in the shelter of the Lord.

This is Good News for all who sit before you. Let them know these assurances are also for them.

Anyone in your assembly longing for God's comfort should hear the hope embedded in this final line. Use eye contact with the assembly to be sure they hear it.

GOSPEL   John 10:27–30

A reading from the holy Gospel according to John

Jesus said:
"My **sheep hear** my **voice**;
    I **know** them, and they **follow me**.
I give them **eternal life**, and they shall **never perish**.
No one can take them out of **my hand**.
My **Father**, who has given them **to me**, is **greater** than **all**,
    and **no** one can take them out of the **Father's hand**.
The **Father** and I are **one**."

In a short reading, every word matters. This text is spoken entirely in the voice of Jesus.

Though originally spoken in response to opponents, in our liturgy the tone of the words might be softened and spoken with compassion and assurance.
"No one . . . " requires strength and conviction.

Jesus' words are reassuring. Pause before the final line that asserts that he and the one who is "greater than all" are one!

divided, with some asserting he was mad and others pointing to his "signs" of healing and deliverance as proof that he could not be a servant of Satan. Now, during the Feast of the Dedication, he is confronted by the Jewish authorities who want him to abandon his evasiveness: "If you are the Messiah, tell us plainly" (Acts 10:24).

In response, Jesus asserts that they don't believe because they are not among his sheep. His sheep, he goes on to say, are those who "hear" and "follow" him. But Jesus is not speaking of blind adherence to him based on the strength of his personality. Those who "hear" him hear the voice of the Father who speaks through him; they are those whose hearts are open, who recognize their dependence on God rather than on their observance of the Law, those who are the *anawim*, the poor of the Lord who trust in him for their safety and their salvation. His opponents won't "follow" him because their hearts as well as their ears are closed.

Jesus is protective of his sheep, not of his own reputation. No one can snatch his sheep from him because they have been entrusted to him by the Father. He concludes with a powerful assertion that there is no distance between what they see and hear from him and what comes from the Father. G.M.

FIFTH SUNDAY OF EASTER

LECTIONARY #54

READING I   Acts 14:21–27

A reading from the Acts of the Apostles

After **Paul** and **Barnabas** had proclaimed the **good news**
    to that **city**
  and made a **considerable number** of **disciples**,
    they returned to **Lystra** and to **Iconium** and to **Antioch**.
They **strengthened** the **spirits** of the **disciples**
  and **exhorted** them to **persevere** in the **faith**, saying,
  "It is **necessary** for us to undergo **many hardships**
  to **enter** the **kingdom** of **God**."
They appointed **elders** for them in **each church** and,
  with **prayer** and **fasting**, **commended** them to the **Lord**
  in whom they had **put** their **faith**.
Then they traveled through **Pisidia** and reached **Pamphylia**.
After proclaiming the word at **Perga** they went down to **Attalia**.
From there they sailed to **Antioch**,
  where they had been **commended** to the **grace** of **God**
  for the **work** they had now **accomplished**.
And when they **arrived**, they called the **church together**
  and **reported** what **God** had **done** with them
  and how he had **opened** the **door** of **faith** to the **Gentiles**.

This is the fifth of eight consecutive weeks we read from Acts.

"That city" is Derbe. Each city is a place where sisters and brothers grasped the faith you still profess.

Lystra = LIS-truh
Iconium = Ī-KOH-nee-uhm
Antioch = AN-tee-ahk

Speak with calm confidence and strength.

Note the complex sequence: (a) they appointed elders, (b) they prayed and fasted, (c) they entrusted them to God. Help us hear all three stages of the process.
Pisidia = pih-SID-ee-uh
Pamphylia = pam-FIL-ee-uh
Perga = PER-guh
Attalia = uh-TAHL-ee-uh
They were "commended" means that through prayer they were entrusted to God.

Like a family, the "church" awaits the news and gathers to hear of their success.

READING I Whether a seed in the ground, a child in the womb, or the unfolding of an idea, growth is always a mystery. Why did the fledgling Jesus movement prosper despite the opposition raised against it? How did a group of mostly uneducated disciples spread news of Jesus within a hostile Jewish environment and a threatening Roman empire? And why did people risk their lives and undergo "many hardships" for the sake of the Kingdom? Luke, the author of Acts, is as amazed as anyone and realizes there is no simple or single answer except that

God willed it and the Holy Spirit infused the process.

As you read the names of these obscure cities, keep in mind that you are telling the story of a miracle. But ground that miracle in the real places and real people through whom God made it happen. By consulting a map of Paul's missionary journeys you will get a sense of the scope of his travels and the geographical relationship of the cities. Paul and Barnabas had visited Lystra before and Paul left it barely alive: his healing of a cripple was used by enemies to persuade the people to stone him

(Acts 14:8–20). Now he's back; not for revenge but to ensure his recent converts are growing and thriving. So Paul knows of what he speaks when he says that "hardships" are necessary.

Speak of the spread of our faith with joy, realizing each city represents a place where people risked their reputations and their lives for that faith. And take pride that so many generously responded to God's generous initiative!

For meditation and context:

RESPONSORIAL PSALM   Psalm 145:8–9, 10–11, 12–13 (see 1)

R. I will praise your name for ever, my king and my God. or R. Alleluia.

The LORD is gracious and merciful,
   slow to anger and of great kindness.
The LORD is good to all
   and compassionate toward all his works.

Let all your works give you thanks, O LORD,
   and let your faithful ones bless you.
Let them discourse of the glory of your
     kingdom
   and speak of your might.

Let them make known your might to the
     children of Adam,
   and the glorious splendor of your
     kingdom.
Your kingdom is a kingdom for all ages,
   and your dominion endures through all
     generations.

This is the fourth of six consecutive weeks we read from Revelation.

Remember this is a vision, not a scene outside a bus window. Give it a sense of wonder and persuade us that what you describe is indeed possible.

"Sea" represents all that is chaotic and deadly in life.

Speak this vision with the joy you'd have if looking at a daughter adorned to meet her bridegroom.

Intensify the majesty of the moment. The "voice" speaks slowly, with great authority but also compassion.

Speak these as promises and sustain eye contact with the assembly.

READING II   Revelation 21:1–5a

A reading from the Book of Revelation

Then **I**, **John**, saw a **new heaven** and a **new earth**.
The **former** heaven and the **former** earth had **passed away**,
   and the **sea** was **no more**.
I also saw the **holy city**, a **new Jerusalem**,
   coming down out of **heaven** from **God**,
     prepared as a **bride adorned** for her **husband**.
I heard a **loud voice** from the **throne** saying,
   "**Behold**, **God's dwelling** is **with** the **human race**.
He will **dwell** with them and they will be **his people**
   and **God himself** will **always** be with them as **their God**.
He will **wipe every tear** from their **eyes**,
   and there shall be **no more death** or **mourning**, **wailing** or **pain**,
   for the **old order** has **passed away**."

The **One** who sat on the **throne** said,
   "**Behold**, I make **all things new**."

READING II   People of faith have the ability to see more than the circumstances they face. Self-help books and motivational speakers imitate the posture of faith when they speak of glasses as "half full" and of problems as "opportunities." The Book of Revelation was written not to reframe current realities like motivational speakers do, but to tell us that reality is already different from what it seems.

"Apocalyptic" writing like this was composed for people enduring great trials and persecution. But this brief text speaks to any age and any people who long for the regency of God. What John sees is the end of all that is finite, incomplete, and painful. From out of heaven, he sees a new reality descending; it is the new and glorious Jerusalem, the eternal city of everlasting peace that looks like a bride perfumed and adorned for her groom. The "voice" announces the startling reality that God is not aloof and distant, but a neighbor who lives with us. God will not be capricious and turn from us like one lover might abandon another; rather, God will be forever with us as our sovereign Lord.

Borrowing from Isaiah (Isaiah 25:8), John proclaims a time when "tears" and "mourning" and "pain" no longer describe human experience. John is painting both a future and a present reality for we already live a transformed reality defined by God's presence among us in Word and sacrament. Speak of the fullness of that new life as if you were watching it unfold before you with a heart brimming with joy.

Now that the betrayer is gone, Jesus can speak about the saving events his treachery will set in motion. Speak not with disappointment but with joy and hope.

There is a sense of urgency and immediacy in these lines.

Note the tender salutation.

Jesus asks no more than what he has been willing to give.

Obedience to his will configures us to his image and allows the world to see him in us.

TO KEEP IN MIND

Each text contains **three kinds of content:** intellectual-theological, emotional, and aesthetic. The plot and details of the story and the theological teaching behind them, comprise the intellectual-theological content. How the author or characters feel (or want us to feel) is the emotional content. Elements that make the writing pleasing—rhythm, repetition, suspense, and picturesque language—are the aesthetic content.

GOSPEL   John 13:31–33a, 34–35

A reading from the holy Gospel according to John

When **Judas** had **left** them, **Jesus** said,
    "**Now** is the **Son of Man glorified**, and **God** is **glorified in him.**
If **God** is glorified in him,
    God will **also glorify** him in **himself,**
    and **God** will **glorify** him **at once.**
My **children**, I will be with you only a **little while longer.**
I give you a **new commandment: love one another.**
As **I** have loved **you**, so **you also** should **love one another.**
This is how **all** will **know** that **you** are **my disciples**,
    if **you** have **love** for **one another.**"

GOSPEL   The dark shadow of Judas intersects the bright light of Resurrection that characterizes this Easter Season. We might wonder at the selection of this text if we didn't know that for John Jesus' Cross is as much a part of his "glory" as his Resurrection. Jesus speaks these words at the Last Supper, keenly aware of his impending Death and Judas' sinister role in that drama. But he knows more than Judas and understands that death will neither shame him nor thwart the divine purpose for which he came. It is "now," he declares, on the eve of his Death, that the Son of Man is "glorified." Jesus steels the disciples with this truth to keep their faith and hearts from shattering. Because John is teaching the mystery of the Cross, Judas has but set in motion events that will end in Jesus' glorification.

Jesus knows his time with them is short, and gives the disciples a "new commandment" that reveals the true nature of discipleship. "Love one another," he commands. We are to imitate our Master whose love had no limits. He gave everything for his disciples, even his life. Our love for each other must also be without limits.

We must die to ourselves for the love of others. In that way we will follow the pattern Christ gave us and enable the world to recognize Christ in us. The bedrock conviction of Christianity is that we do Christ's will only when our lives are cruciform. For the glory of the Cross is not only Christ's, but ours. G.M.

SIXTH SUNDAY
OF EASTER

LECTIONARY #57

READING I   Acts 15:1–2, 22–29

A reading from the Acts of the Apostles

From the start, your tone should suggest that there is tension to resolve.

Some who had come down from **Judea** were **instructing**
    the **brothers**,
    "**Unless** you are **circumcised** according to the **Mosaic practice**,
    you **cannot** be **saved**."

It was Pharisee converts who insisted on the need for circumcision.

You can be sure Paul argued vehemently, but without success. So, the decision is "kicked upstairs" to Jerusalem.

Because there arose **no little dissension** and **debate**
    by **Paul** and **Barnabas** with them,
    it was decided that **Paul**, **Barnabas**, and **some** of the **others**
    should go up to **Jerusalem** to the **apostles** and **elders**
    about this question.

The **apostles** and **elders**, in agreement with the **whole church**,
    decided to choose **representatives**
    and to send them to **Antioch with Paul** and **Barnabas**.

Left out here is the discussion in Jerusalem. It is the *Jerusalem* elders who send representatives back to Antioch.

Antioch = AN-tee-ahk

Barsabbas = bar-SAH-buhs

Silas = SĪ-luhs

The ones **chosen** were **Judas**, who was called **Barsabbas**,
    and **Silas**, **leaders** among the brothers.
This is the **letter** delivered by them:

The goal of the letter is to unburden the Gentile believers, so your tone is apologetic and pastoral.

"The **apostles** and the **elders**, your **brothers**,
    to the brothers in **Antioch**, **Syria**, and **Cilicia**
    of **Gentile** origin: **greetings**.
Since we have **heard** that some of **our number**
    who went out without **any mandate** from **us**
    have **upset** you with their **teachings**
    and **disturbed** your **peace** of **mind**,

READING I   From your Bible, take the time to read this passage in its entirety to get a better sense of the context of these events. Chapter 15 of Acts presents several of the elders of the early Church putting their heads together to discern an important point of Church discipline. The indispensable mark of the covenant was circumcision. As Gentile converts embraced Christianity, it was natural for Jewish believers to expect the new converts to submit to circumcision. But soon this requirement became a source of tension, and Paul championed the cause of

Gentiles who saw no need for total observance of the Mosaic Law.

While in his letters Paul often asserts his authority as an Apostle, here we see him acknowledging a higher authority within the Church as he and Barnabas set out for Jerusalem to consult with Peter, James, and other elders of that local church. Today's portion from Acts only reports the conclusion they reached, not the arguments offered to make their case. A sign of Jerusalem's importance among the early Christian communities are the two representatives sent with Paul and

Barnabas to testify in person regarding the decision of the Jerusalem elders.

In their letter to the Gentile converts, the elders assert that those who "disturbed [their] peace of mind" were acting on their own, without "any mandate" from the community in Jerusalem. They mention that "Judas and Silas" will come to give voice to the decision made by the elders and "the Holy Spirit." The sense of certainty regarding the guidance of the Spirit is a significant aspect of their life and discernment. Gentile converts are not completely exempted from the requirements of the Mosaic Law,

They spend much time substantiating the level of discernment that took place.

beloved = bee-LUHV-uhd

we have with **one accord** decided to choose **representatives**
and to **send** them to you along with our **beloved Barnabas**
   and **Paul**,
who have dedicated their **lives** to the **name**
   of our **Lord Jesus Christ**.
So we are sending **Judas** and **Silas**
   who will **also convey** this **same message** by **word** of **mouth**:
'It is the **decision** of the **Holy Spirit** and of **us**
not to **place** on you **any burden** beyond **these necessities**,
namely, to abstain from **meat sacrificed** to **idols**,
from **blood**, from **meats** of **strangled animals**,
   and from **unlawful marriage**.

Stress the role of the Spirit in the decision. You can list the directives rather quickly.

If you keep **free** of **these**,
   you will be doing what is **right. Farewell.'"

The role of the Law is not eliminated; "*If you . . . you will be doing what is right.*"

For meditation and context:

RESPONSORIAL PSALM   Psalm 67:2–3, 5, 6, 8 (4)

R. O God, let all the nations praise you! or R. Alleluia.

May God have pity on us and bless us;
   may he let his face shine upon us.
So may your way be known upon earth;
   among all nations, your salvation.

May the nations be glad and exult
   because you rule the peoples in equity;
   the nations on the earth you guide.

May the peoples praise you, O God;
   may all the peoples praise you!
May God bless us,
   and may all the ends of the earth fear him!

TO KEEP IN MIND

Separating units of thought with pauses: Identify the units of thought in your text and use pauses to distinguish one from another. Running words together blurs meaning and fails to distinguish ideas. Punctuation does not always indicate clearly what words to group together or where to pause. The listener depends on you for this organization of ideas.

---

for they are instructed to avoid several practices that Jews found especially repugnant. Pastoral sensitivity has won the day, while the importance of Law is sustained. Without burdening, the elders still challenge the Gentiles: observe "these necessities," they are told, and no one will tell you "you cannot be saved."

READING II   By the time this book was written, the Roman occupiers had destroyed Jerusalem, causing grief and fear among the people. That tragedy was a disorienting experience of great pro-

portions because the city and her Temple were the very heart of Israel. Losing them caused people to question their identity and even God's fidelity. In addition, Christians, including those of Jewish origin, were being persecuted for their faith and many had already shed their blood.

In the midst of this tribulation, John experiences a vision of a *new* "Jerusalem." This "holy city" is untouched by violence and glistens like a "precious stone" in the morning sun. This city is described as a beautiful bride. In fact, the verse immediately preceding today's text speaks of the

new Jerusalem as "the wife of the Lamb," an image of the Christian community finally gathered in the peace of the heavenly Kingdom.

Many of the details here will be lost on your hearers. Apocalyptic writing was meant to be obscure in order to hide its meaning from enemies and evildoers. But for the community for which it was intended, the symbols speak powerfully of a new time and an eternal city where fear will be vanquished and the beauty of the earthly Jerusalem will pale in comparison with the new city.

This is the fifth of six consecutive weeks we read from Revelation.

This is not your typical opening line, even in Scripture. Read slowly and significantly.

Here, your *tone* will communicate more than the words will!

Stress this reference to the twelve tribes of Israel.

Don't shy from these repetitions; give them a grand and regal tone.

As Israel was built on the foundation of the twelve tribes, the New Covenant is built on the foundation of the Twelve Apostles.

Give the explanation that the city needed no Temple or illumination with mounting conviction and joy.

READING II   Revelation 21:10–14, 22–23

A reading from the Book of Revelation

The **angel** took me in **spirit** to a **great**, **high mountain**
   and **showed** me the **holy city Jerusalem**
   coming **down** out of **heaven** from **God**.
It **gleamed** with the **splendor** of **God**.
Its **radiance** was like that of a **precious stone**,
   like **jasper**, **clear** as **crystal**.
It had a **massive**, **high wall**,
   with **twelve gates** where **twelve angels** were stationed
   and on which **names** were **inscribed**,
   the **names** of the **twelve tribes** of the **Israelites**.
There were **three** gates facing **east**,
   three **north**, three **south**, and three **west**.
The **wall** of the city had **twelve courses** of **stones**
      as its **foundation**,
   on which were inscribed the twelve **names**
   of the twelve **apostles** of the **Lamb**.

I saw **no temple** in the **city**
   for its **temple** is the **Lord God almighty** and the **Lamb**.
The **city** had **no need** of **sun** or **moon** to **shine** on it,
   for the **glory** of **God** gave it **light**,
   and its **lamp** was the **Lamb**.

Because of the obscurity of John's imagery, you must focus on sound, intensity, and tone color to convey his meaning. Like the background music in a film, your tone sets the mood and suggests the grandeur, joy, and peace of the city that gleams like precious stones. Whether or not they remember the details of this text, be sure your hearers remember that it was filled with images of hope and glory.

The symbols that are clear, the number "twelve," the "twelve tribes," the "twelve apostles" meld the tradition of Israel with the new covenant in Christ. The absence of a Temple in the new city is more than a nod to the destruction of the building in Jerusalem. The new Jerusalem needs no Temple to be God's dwelling; God no longer dwells in a house of stone, but in the hearts of his people.

GOSPEL   Jesus was the *first* Advocate of the disciples, teaching and mentoring them, freeing them from falsehoods, fears, and biases. On a daily basis, these men heard Jesus preach with imagination and authority. He used parables whose meanings were often obscure, but they also heard his explications and, no doubt, repeated them to friends and family. Jesus' teaching and insights were new, and fresh, and sometimes radical. His morals and maxims that declared the last first and losers winners reversed their expectations and opened their eyes to God's Kingdom.

Now Jesus is about to surrender his life and soon thereafter will return to the Father. In this discourse, set within the context of his final meal with them, Jesus offers assurance that they will lose nothing of what they've learned because another

GOSPEL   John 14:23–29

A reading from the holy Gospel according to John

Jesus said to his **disciples**:
  "Whoever **loves** me will **keep** my **word**,
  and my **Father** will **love him**,
  and we will **come** to him and **make** our **dwelling with** him.
Whoever does **not** love me does **not** keep my words;
  yet the **word** you **hear** is **not mine**
  but **that** of the **Father** who **sent** me.

"I have **told** you this while I am **with** you.
The **Advocate**, the **Holy Spirit**,
  whom the **Father** will **send** in **my name**,
  will **teach** you **everything**
  and **remind** you of **all** that I **told** you.
Peace I **leave** with you; my **peace** I **give** to you.
Not as the **world** gives do **I give** it to **you**.
Do **not** let your **hearts** be **troubled** or **afraid**.
You heard me **tell** you,
  'I am **going away** and I will come **back** to you.'
If you **loved** me,
  you would **rejoice** that I am **going** to the **Father**;
  for the **Father** is **greater** than I.
And now I have **told** you this before it **happens**,
  so that **when** it **happens** you may **believe**."

THE **4** STEPS OF *LECTIO DIVINA* OR PRAYERFUL READING

1. *Lectio:* Read a Scripture passage aloud slowly. Notice what phrase captures your attention and be attentive to its meaning. Silent pause.

2. *Meditatio:* Read the passage aloud slowly again, reflecting on the passage, allowing God to speak to you through it. Silent pause.

3. *Oratio:* Read it aloud slowly a third time, allowing it to be your prayer or response to God's gift of insight to you. Silent pause.

4. *Contemplatio:* Read it aloud slowly a fourth time, now resting in God's word.

Recall that the setting is the Last Supper. Jesus is preparing his closest friends for his farewell. Create a mood of intimacy and warmth.

Let "Whoever does not . . . " contrast with what went before.

Sending another advocate brings reassurance to teacher as well as students.

Here begins a new beat in the text. This is not the ritual speech of liturgy, so give it a more conversational tone.

This is a command, but spoken with compassion.

Keep in mind, Jesus has yet to ascend Calvary; anticipating his return to the Father helps him sustain his resolve.

This whole discourse has been a way of caring for and preparing them for the difficult hours ahead.

Advocate, "the Holy Spirit," will come to help them remember and understand all that Jesus taught them.

But first, Jesus is again the teacher, and reminds the disciples that there is no love without obedience. Jesus equates love with keeping his Word. Anyone who keeps his Words receives the Father's love and becomes a living tabernacle, a place where God can dwell. Those who do not keep his Word do not love him because by rejecting his Word they reject the Father, who is the source of all that Jesus says.

Jesus promises peace to those who heed his Word. His is the peace of the Kingdom that flows from the bosom of the Father and penetrates the heart of the believer, deepening faith and dismantling fear. He asserts that if they loved him they would not begrudge his return to the Father who "is greater than I." That comment acknowledges that he was sent by the Father and says only what was given him by the Father. He comforts and prepares them for his eventual leave-taking, but expects them to understand the necessity of his departure. This is the night before his

Death, but even now he is ministering to his friends, alerting them ahead of time so that when his hour comes they won't despair. Truly, Jesus loves his own until the end (John13:1). G.M.

THE ASCENSION OF THE LORD

LECTIONARY #58

READING I   Acts 1:1–11

A reading from the beginning of the Acts of the Apostles

In the **first** book, **Theophilus,**
    I dealt with **all** that **Jesus did** and **taught**
    until the **day** he was **taken up,**
    after giving **instructions** through the **Holy Spirit**
    to the **apostles** whom he had **chosen.**
He presented himself **alive** to them
    by **many proofs** after he had **suffered,**
    appearing to them during **forty days**
    and **speaking** about the **kingdom** of **God.**
While **meeting** with them,
    he **enjoined** them **not** to **depart** from **Jerusalem,**
    but to **wait** for "the **promise** of the **Father**
    about which you have heard me **speak;**
    for **John baptized** with **water,**
    but in a few days **you** will be **baptized** with the **Holy Spirit.**"

When they had **gathered together** they asked him,
    "**Lord,** are you at **this time** going to **restore**
    the **kingdom** to **Israel?**"
He **answered** them, "It is **not** for you to **know** the **times**
    or **seasons**
    that the **Father** has **established** by his **own authority.**
But you will receive **power** when the **Holy Spirit** comes **upon** you,
    and you will be **my witnesses** in **Jerusalem,**

Luke is inspiriting faith, so this background information is important and should be shared with purpose.

Theophilus = thee-OF-uh-luhs

He reviews how he ended his Gospel with the narrative of the Ascension, then begins Acts with that same story.

These are assertions of facts, not of faith. Jesus was *seen* after his Resurrection!

"Forty" is symbolic of an indefinite, but sacred, span of time.

Luke is quoting Jesus. Note, it is "the Father" who has promised to send the Spirit.

Their hearts still yearn for earthly power. By now, they should know better.

Jesus redirects their energy to the real purposes of the Father. Don't be abrupt, but speak with compassion.

Though they have no idea where this prophecy will take them, it fills them with hope.

Today options are given for Reading II. Contact your parish staff to find out which will be used.

READING I Luke authored two New Testament books: the Gospel account that bears his name and the Acts of the Apostles. He begins the second where he ended the first, at the Ascension. Jesus' saving activity comprises a single salvific event that includes his suffering, Death, Resurrection, *and* Ascension. His return to the Father completes the work Jesus came to accomplish, so this event is central to the story of salvation.

After establishing that Jesus had appeared *bodily* after his Resurrection, Luke shows Jesus ordering the Apostles to stay in Jerusalem to await the baptism of the "Holy Spirit." Given the threat from religious authorities, it would be natural for the disciples to return to Galilee. Instead, Jesus urges them to wait for "the promise of the Father"—the Holy Spirit. At the end of his earthly ministry, Jesus alludes to John the Baptist, the one who, with his baptism of water, initiated Jesus into his ministry.

The same Spirit who appeared as a dove at Jesus' water baptism will come to baptize the Apostles with power.

Still preoccupied with mundane concerns, the disciples ask when Jesus will restore the earthly kingdom of Israel. They don't yet understand the nature of the Kingdom Jesus established through his Death and Resurrection. He refocuses them on the day of Pentecost when the Spirit will empower them to take the Gospel message "to the ends of the earth." As he disappears, two (angelic) men are suddenly snapping them out of their stupor. The "men" pick up

throughout **Judea** and **Samaria**,
and to the **ends** of the **earth**."
When he had **said** this, as they were **looking on**,
he was **lifted up**, and a **cloud took** him from their **sight**.
While they were looking **intently** at the **sky** as he was **going**,
suddenly two men dressed in **white garments**
stood beside them.
They said, "**Men** of **Galilee**,
why are you **standing** there looking at the **sky**?
This **Jesus** who has been **taken up** from you into **heaven**
will **return** in the **same way** as you have **seen** him
going into **heaven**."

Paint the scene by reading slowly and "seeing" what you describe.

"Suddenly" breaks the mood of awed silence.

The "two men" are not harsh; they nudge the disciples to look to the future.

"Will return" has implications for us today as much as for them: Be ready!

For meditation and context:

RESPONSORIAL PSALM   Psalm 47:2–3, 6–7, 8–9 (6)

R. God mounts his throne to shouts of joy: a blare of trumpets for the Lord.
or R. Alleluia.

All you peoples, clap your hands,
    shout to God with cries of gladness,
for the LORD, the Most High, the awesome,
    is the great king over all the earth.

God mounts his throne amid shouts of joy;
    the LORD, amid trumpet blasts.
Sing praise to God, sing praise;
    sing praise to our king, sing praise.

For king of all the earth is God;
    sing hymns of praise.
God reigns over the nations,
    God sits upon his holy throne.

READING II   Ephesians 1:17–23

A reading from the Letter of Saint Paul to the Ephesians

Brothers and **sisters**:
May the **God** of our **Lord Jesus Christ**, the **Father** of **glory**,
    give you a **Spirit** of **wisdom** and **revelation**
    resulting in **knowledge** of him.
May the **eyes** of your **hearts** be **enlightened**,
    that you may know what is the **hope** that belongs to **his call**,
    what are the **riches** of **glory** »

You greet "brothers and sisters" with a prayer.

Father, Son, and Spirit are all mentioned in this prayer.

Increase your energy as you move through this part of the prayer.

---

where Jesus left off, urging the disciples to stop gazing and start moving. Their promise that Jesus "will return" means that we, like the disciples, must stand ever at the ready.

READING II **Ephesians 1:17–23.** More than a letter of encouragement for the Ephesian Christians, this text explains the role of the entire Church in God's plan for humanity. Using the language of praise, Paul illustrates how God's saving love, expressed in the ministry of Jesus, seeks the salvation of all. A Trinitarian prayer opens the text and sets a joyous

tone, for the Father will impart wisdom and revelation through the Holy Spirit.

Earlier in this chapter, beautiful language, likely from early hymns, expresses gratitude for the blessings God has bestowed on believers through Jesus. The prayer focuses on our response to those blessings—to open our hearts; to know the "hope" that is our birthright; to understand the inheritance Christ left us and the "power" he offers to those who "believe."

Having raised him from the dead, God has now placed Jesus at his right hand where he sits on a throne with "all things beneath his feet." That climactic statement

in the closing lines is the goal toward which you build as you move through the text.

Practice the long, unwieldy sentences. Present one idea at a time, while sustaining a joyful, prayerful tone. Note that the "eyes of [our] hearts" are to be enlightened about *three* things: "the hope" embedded in God's call, the "riches of glory," and "the greatness of his power." Jesus exercises his lordship over all things as "head" of his Body, the Church, meaning that we, who comprise that Body, share in his glory and dominion. Herald the Good News that the one who is Lord of all fills us at all times with his presence!

God's mercy allows us to share in Christ's exaltation. These words give Christ praise.

"Principality," "authority," "power," and "dominion" are four different ranks of angelic spirits. Don't blur them into one.

"He" is the Father; "him" and "his" refer to Christ. God made Jesus head of the Church: announce that great truth with joy.

in **his inheritance** among the **holy ones,**
and what is the **surpassing greatness** of **his power**
for us who **believe,**
in accord with the **exercise** of his **great might:**
which he **worked** in **Christ,**
raising him from the **dead**
and **seating** him at his **right hand** in the **heavens,**
far above **every principality, authority, power,** and **dominion,**
and **every name** that is **named**
not only in **this age** but **also** in the one to **come.**
And he put **all things** beneath his **feet**
and gave him as **head** over **all things** to the **church,**
which is his **body,**
the **fullness** of the **one** who **fills all things** in **every way.**

Or:

READING II   Hebrews 9:24–28; 10:19–23

A reading from the Letter to the Hebrews

Be aware from the start that you are comparing Christ's sacrifice with those of the Old Law.

Christ, not a human priest, intercedes for us in the very presence of God.

Your tone suggests the futility of this endless repetition.

Christ's one perfect sacrifice of himself requires no repetition.

This is an analogy: just as this is true, so is what follows.

Christ did not enter into a **sanctuary** made by **hands,**
a **copy** of the **true** one, but **heaven itself,**
that he might now **appear** before **God** on **our behalf.**
Not that he might offer himself **repeatedly,**
as the **high** priest enters **each year** into the **sanctuary**
with **blood** that is **not** his **own;**
if **that** were **so,** he would have had to **suffer repeatedly**
from the **foundation** of the **world.**
But **now once for all he** has **appeared** at the **end** of the **ages**
to take away **sin** by **his sacrifice.**
Just as it is **appointed** that **men** and **women die once,**
and after **this** the **judgment,** so also **Christ,**
offered once to take away the **sins** of **many,**

Hebrews 9:24–28; 10:19–23. As in our own society, the people for whom this exhortation was written were abandoning the faith at an alarming rate—not because of external dangers or persecution, but because of inward malaise. Their hearts had grown lukewarm and their willingness to endure the challenges of Christian living had diminished. This instruction aims to reverse the trend by urging hope in Christ and offering deeper insight into the faith.

The author of Hebrews, by comparing Jesus' self-sacrifice with the sacrificial practices of the old Law, exalts Christ's role in God's plan of salvation. Jewish practice

required the high priest to enter the Holy of Holies in the Temple made "by human hands" annually to offer the blood of animals, not his own, to atone for people's sins. Christ entered the "true," heavenly sanctuary, not to offer endless sacrifices, but to offer a single sacrifice of his own blood, an offering worth infinitely more than that of animals.

The author alludes to the Temple, high priest, annual sacrifices, and blood of sacrificial animals—sacred elements of a sacred tradition given by God through Moses. But Jesus entered the *heavenly* tabernacle and stands in the presence of the living God. As

we die once and then pass into eternity, so Jesus' perfect sacrifice was once-for-all, eternally valid and efficacious. When he returns, it won't be to cleanse us again of sin, but to reward us with salvation.

Through Baptism we have gained access to the house of God. Christ, our High Priest, intercedes for us. Our only response can be to live with pure hearts and clean consciences so that the "hope" that's born of faith will rekindle a blazing fire in our lukewarm hearts.

| GOSPEL | Luke's Gospel account of the Ascension is shorter |

Christ will return, not to atone again for sin, but to give us the salvation he won for us.

will appear a **second** time, **not** to take away **sin**
but to bring **salvation** to those who **eagerly await** him.

Our "confidence" is our Baptism. He's using his previous points to call for faith and confident hope.

Therefore, **brothers** and **sisters**, since through the **blood** of **Jesus**
we have **confidence** of **entrance** into the **sanctuary**
by the **new** and **living way** he opened for us through the **veil**,
that is, **his flesh**,
and since we have "a **great priest** over the **house** of **God**,"

You are challenging us to live according to our faith. Don't be timid.

let us **approach** with a **sincere heart** and in **absolute trust**,
with our hearts **sprinkled clean** from an **evil conscience**
and our **bodies washed** in **pure water**.

Speak boldly and out of your own experience of God's mercy and fidelity.

Let us hold **unwaveringly** to our **confession** that gives us **hope**,
for he who made the **promise** is **trustworthy**.

GOSPEL   Luke 24:46–53

A reading from the holy Gospel according to Luke

He reminds them that he had always preached about suffering and repentance. Among the "witnesses" of Jesus are those sitting in your assembly.

Jesus said to his **disciples**:
"**Thus** it is **written** that the **Christ** would **suffer**
and **rise** from the **dead** on the **third day**
and that **repentance**, for the **forgiveness** of **sins**,
would be **preached** in **his name**
to **all** the **nations**, **beginning** from **Jerusalem**.
You are **witnesses** of these things.
And **behold** I am sending the **promise** of my **Father** upon you;
but **stay** in the **city**
until you are **clothed** with **power** from on **high**."

As in Acts, Jesus says that the "Sprit" is the *Father's* promised gift to them.

What follows is all narration, spoken slowly. The mood is not without hope and expectation.
Blessed = blesd

Then he **led** them out as far as **Bethany**,
raised his **hands**, and **blessed** them.
As he **blessed** them he **parted** from them
and was **taken up** to **heaven**.
They did him **homage**

After they pay "homage" their hearts swell with joy!

and then returned to **Jerusalem** with **great joy**,
and they were **continually** in the **temple praising God**.

and simpler than his version in Acts. Here he repeats Jesus' injunction to remain in the city until the coming of the Spirit, but omits the disciples' question regarding the restoration of the kingdom and the appearance of the men in white who bid the disciples to get about the work of the Gospel. The most striking difference is the timeline: in Acts Jesus ascends at the end of forty days, after a series of appearances to the disciples. In the Gospel, however, the Ascension occurs on the day of the Resurrection, shortly after his appearance to the disciples gathered in Jerusalem.

In the verses prior to today's Gospel passage, Jesus opened the disciples' "minds to understand the Scripture" and then focused them on two points: the Messiah would suffer but rise again to new life and the Gospel of repentance and forgiveness would be preached to the world. The disciples need these two essential concepts: the first, to make sense of his traumatic and humiliating death, the second to understand the ministry he will now entrust to them. With this crucial knowledge, the disciples are prepared to be "witnesses" to Jesus' radical message. He

reminds them that the "promise" (Spirit) will soon come to clothe them with power.

In Acts, Jesus encourages and commissions; here he blesses and bids farewell. A slower pace will convey the sense of loss in the hearts of Jesus' friends. Use the verbs—"led," "raised," "blessed," "parted," and "was taken" to extend the moment of departure. Perhaps Jesus is manifested in his glory as he ascends, for they worship him and then return to the city with exuberant praise. G.M.

SEVENTH SUNDAY
OF EASTER

LECTIONARY #61

READING I   Acts 7:55–60

A reading from the Acts of the Apostles

Stephen, **filled** with the **Holy Spirit**,
    looked up **intently** to **heaven** and **saw** the **glory** of **God**
    and **Jesus** standing at the **right hand** of **God**,
    and **Stephen** said, "**Behold**, I see the **heavens opened**
    and the **Son** of **Man** standing at the **right hand** of **God**."
But they **cried out** in a **loud voice**,
    covered their **ears**, and **rushed** upon him **together**.
They **threw** him **out** of the city, and began to **stone** him.
The **witnesses** laid down their **cloaks**
    at the **feet** of a **young** man named **Saul**.
As they were **stoning Stephen**, he **called out**,
    "**Lord Jesus, receive my spirit**."
Then he **fell** to his **knees** and **cried out** in a **loud voice**,
    "**Lord**, do **not hold** this **sin against** them";
    and when he **said** this, he fell **asleep**.

Narrators often have a point of view. Here, yours is that of a believer who admires Stephen.

Don't gloss over the reference to the "Holy Spirit."

Convey the peaceful demeanor with which Stephen tells his vision and faces his death.

The prince of lies can't handle the truth and so erupts in violence.

Speak slowly and knowingly of "Saul."

Again, convey Stephen's serenity and peace in the face of death.

Note that his last prayer is more command than request. Speak with assurance that God will answer.

"Fell asleep" is a euphemism for death.

READING I   The early Christian writer, Tertullian, famously said, "the blood of the martyrs is the seed of the church" (*The Apology*, 50, s. 13). The spilling of blood for the sake of the Gospel began with Stephen whose faith and heroism are manifested in today's reading. This young deacon, accused of disparaging Hebrew faith and tradition, was brought to trial before the Sanhedrin and sentenced to death. A man of great faith also known to work miracles, Stephen drew the ire of synagogue leaders for proclaiming the superiority of Christ to Moses and the Temple. A nimble speaker, he further infuriated the leaders by besting them in debate. They retaliated by bribing false witnesses to accuse him of blasphemy.

In the midst of his trial, Stephen is suddenly graced with a vision of the Risen Christ standing at God's right hand. This reference to what Jesus had prophesied before them at his own trial—and claiming it has been *fulfilled*—so enrages the Sanhedrin that they lead Stephen out to stone him. That's where today's text joins the story. The first words we read refer to the inspiration of the Holy Spirit, a dominant theme in Luke.

Observing the violence is "a young man named Saul" whose name will soon change to Paul and who will spend the rest of his life regretting his participation in this and other acts of violence against the Church. Like Jesus, Stephen is falsely accused, and like him he forgives his attackers and invokes God's mercy upon them. At his trial, many observed that Stephen looked like an angel. Here, he proves his closer likeness to the Lord.

For meditation and context:

TO KEEP IN MIND

Eye contact connects you with those to whom you minister. Look at the assembly during the middle and at the end of every thought or sentence.

RESPONSORIAL PSALM Psalm 97:1–2, 6–7, 9 (1a, 9a)

R. The Lord is king, the most high over all the earth. or R. Alleluia.

The LORD is king; let the earth rejoice;
　let the many islands be glad.
Justice and judgment are the foundation of
　his throne.

The heavens proclaim his justice,
　and all peoples see his glory.
All gods are prostrate before him.

You, O LORD, are the Most High over all
　the earth,
　exalted far above all gods.

READING II   Revelation 22:12–14, 16–17, 20

A reading from the Book of Revelation

I, **John**, heard a **voice** saying to me:
　"**Behold**, I am **coming soon**.
I bring **with** me the **recompense** I will give to **each**
　according to his **deeds**.
I am the **Alpha** and the **Omega**, the **first** and the **last**,
　the **beginning** and the **end**."

Blessed are they who **wash** their **robes**
　so as to have the **right** to the **tree** of **life**
　and enter the **city** through its **gates**.

"**I, Jesus**, sent my **angel** to give you **this testimony**
　for the **churches**.
I am the **root** and **offspring** of **David**,
　the **bright morning star**."

The **Spirit** and the **bride** say, "**Come**."
Let the **hearer** say, "**Come**."
Let the **one** who **thirsts** come **forward**,
　and the **one** who **wants it** receive the **gift** of **life-giving water**.

The **one** who gives this **testimony** says, "**Yes**, I am **coming soon**."
Amen! Come, Lord Jesus!

Start slowly. You are narrating a grand vision and we need to know that "Behold" is spoken not by the visionary, but by one *within* the vision.

There is both comfort and discomfort in knowing we will receive what we deserve.

Read this as a declaration of all that Christ brings and offers us.
Blessed = BLES-uhd or blesd
Make eye contact as you speak this beatitude and blessing over your assembly.

Jesus is both immanent ("the root . . . of David") and transcendent ("the . . . morning star").

We return to the voice of John. The Church's desire to be reunited with her Lord must sound in your voice.
Beckon the hearts of your hearers!
The Lord announces his imminent return, and the Church responds in fervent prayer: "Amen! Come."

READING II You will be proclaiming the final words of the entire New Testament today and, as is common with parting words, they are emotional, inspiring, and possess a grand and eloquent quality. The themes and images of these verses echo the very beginning of the Book of Revelation. We hear Christ's voice throughout the text announcing blessings, "recompense," and "I am" statements that wrap around us like a promise of hope and healing.

Originally intended for people in turmoil, these words speak comfort to anyone experiencing distress, whether personal or global. The repetition of the personal pronoun "I" is the source of that comfort for it will come to us not through some abstract source but through Jesus himself. God is always a blend of mercy and justice, so Jesus brings "recompense . . . according to [each one's] deeds"—comfort for some, perhaps unsettling for others. In claiming a title previously used for God—"the Alpha and the Omega"—Jesus claims to be all that we need, the source of our all satisfaction and fulfillment of all our desires. He pronounces a beatitude upon those who "wash their robes," but his words may also warn that some will not.

In response, John speaks a prayer of yearning on behalf of the Spirit and the Church, Christ's "bride." Likely a liturgical refrain, this plea for Christ's return (in Greek, *Marana tha*) echoes also in our hearts. Let your voice convey your own eagerness to "come forward" and drink his "life-giving water" and then earnestly and humbly proclaim the ancient prayer of the Church: "Come, Lord Jesus!"

Pause after the opening narration to shift into a tone of prayer.

The ideas flow one from another. Don't speak like a lawyer making an argument, but let the poetry and sincerity of the prayer be manifest.

Christian unity testifies to Christ.

"Perfection" is only realized in "unity" that testifies to Jesus' divine origin.

Make eye contact as you speak this tender line.

Jesus longs for his followers to experience the fullness of his glory.

Jesus displays an intimate connection with the Father.

Take a significant pause, letting your listeners dwell in the prayer before initiating the closing dialogue.

TO KEEP IN MIND
Read all three commentaries. Suggestions in each can give you insight into your own passage.

GOSPEL   John 17:20–26

A reading from the holy Gospel according to John

Lifting up his **eyes** to **heaven**, Jesus **prayed** saying:
"**Holy Father**, I pray **not only** for **them**,
    but also for those who will **believe** in **me** through **their word**,
    so that they may **all** be **one**,
    as **you**, **Father**, are in **me** and **I** in **you**,
    that they **also** may be in **us**,
    that the **world** may **believe** that **you** sent me.
And **I** have given **them** the **glory you** gave **me**,
    so that **they** may be **one**, as **we** are **one**,
    I in **them** and **you** in **me**,
    that they may be brought to **perfection** as **one**,
    that the **world** may **know** that **you** sent me,
    and that **you loved them** even as **you loved me**.
Father, **they** are **your gift** to me.
I wish that where **I** am **they also** may be **with me**,
    that they may **see my glory** that **you** gave me,
    because **you loved me** before the **foundation** of the **world**.
Righteous Father, the **world also** does **not** know **you**,
    but **I know you**, and **they know** that **you** sent me.
I made **known** to them **your name** and **I will** make it **known**,
    that the **love** with which **you loved me**
    may be in **them** and I in **them**."

GOSPEL   Addressed entirely to God, Jesus' high priestly prayer is spoken in the presence of the disciples. In characteristic fashion, Jesus prays with eyes uplifted, addressing God as "Father." As with the closing words of the Book of Revelation that comprise today's Second Reading, this prayer prayed by Jesus in anticipation of his arrest and Passion expresses a tone of farewell that's certainly fitting for the Sunday following the Ascension. Oneness is the theme of Jesus' prayer. The oneness he shares with the Father he wishes for his disciples and for all who embrace the faith because of them.

Jesus' prayer has a free-form, stream of consciousness structure that includes some repetition. But rather than redundant, the repetition serves to underscore Jesus' desire for unity among his followers and their unity with him and the Father. Notice how each sentence begins with a petition or declaration that is elaborated in the succeeding lines. Renew your energy for each new sentence, then, in order to declare with vigor the new thought being presented.

Jesus prays for his disciples, shares with them his "glory," which in John is always connected to his Passion, and considers his followers God's gift to him. Let your tone convey Jesus' appreciation for those who have heard his words and let them root in their hearts. Jesus has made the unseen and unknown God visible and "will make" him known further though the Advocate he will send. We also share that task, making God visible in the love we manifest for one another. G.M.

PENTECOST SUNDAY: VIGIL

LECTIONARY #62

READING I   Genesis 11:1–9

A reading from the Book of Genesis

The whole **world** spoke the same **language**, using the same **words**.
While the people were **migrating** in the east,
   they came upon a valley in the land of **Shinar** and **settled** there.
They **said** to one another,
   "**Come**, let us mold **bricks** and **harden** them with **fire**."
They used bricks for **stone**, and bitumen for **mortar**.
Then they said, "**Come**, let us build ourselves a **city**
   and a **tower** with its top in the **sky**,
   and so make a **name** for ourselves;
   otherwise we shall be **scattered** all over the earth."

The LORD came down to **see** the city and the **tower**
   that the people had built.
Then the LORD said: "If **now**, while they are **one** people,
   all speaking the **same** language,
   they have started to do **this**,
   nothing will **later** stop them from doing whatever they
     presume to do.
Let us then go down there and **confuse** their language,
   so that one will not **understand** what another says."
Thus the LORD **scattered** them from there all over the **earth**,
   and they **stopped** building the city.
That is why it was called **Babel**,
   because there the LORD **confused** the speech of all the world.
It was from that **place** that he **scattered** them all over the earth.

Margin notes

As narrator, you know this innocent age is lost.

Speak with the arrogance that motivates their defiance.

Shinar = SHĪ-nahr.

bitumen = bih-TYOO-m*n.

Their plan is in direct defiance of God's order to "fill the earth" (1:28). They plan to enhance their own reputation without any help from God.

This is a new scene. Suggest the disapproval with which God views the city and tower.

God is not being vindictive, but protecting humanity from itself.

If an ancient child asked "Why do people speak different languages?", here is the reply.

Speak with conviction that what God has accomplished is just.

Today, options are given for the readings. Contact your parish staff to learn which readings will be used.

READING I — As at the Easter Vigil, on the brink of a great event (the Resurrection of the Lord; the coming of the Holy Spirit), God's people pause to reflect on their history in faith.

Genesis. This passage completes the first segment of Genesis, which provides a prehistory of the world. Here the author, writing with centuries of hindsight, portrays a sinful tendency in the human race from its earliest days. Humankind repeatedly tries to place itself on a par with God, an effort that inevitably ends badly. The First Reading combines an instance of this inclination with an etiology, a story describing the origin of a particular place, event, or situation—in this case the diversity of human languages.

At the beginning of the story, all people speak a single language. However, as they build human settlements, they decide to construct a city that reaches to the sky. Since ancient peoples believed that the gods inhabited the upper regions, their goal is to seek equality with the divine. In this oldest of Old Testament traditions, God is portrayed anthropomorphically, and so the Lord descends in order to observe human activity. Fearing that their common language aids the arrogant building project, God creates an impediment. If they cannot understand each other, humans will be thwarted in their efforts to reach the level of deity. The Lord's plan succeeds, and the

Or:

READING I   Exodus 19:3–8a, 16–20b

A reading from the Book of Exodus

Moses went up the **mountain** to **God**.
Then the LORD **called** to him and said,
    "**Thus** shall you say to the house of **Jacob**;
    tell the Israelites:
    You have seen for **yourselves** how I treated the **Egyptians**
    and how I **bore** you up on **eagle** wings
    and brought you here to **myself**.
Therefore, if you **hearken** to my voice and keep my **covenant**,
    you shall be my **special possession**,
    dearer to me than all **other** people,
    though **all** the earth is **mine**.
You shall be to me a **kingdom** of **priests**, a **holy** nation.
That is what you must tell the **Israelites**."
So Moses went and **summoned** the elders of the people.
When he set before them
    all that the LORD had **ordered** him to tell them,
    the people all answered **together**,
    "**Everything** the LORD has said, we will **do**."

On the morning of the **third** day
    there were peals of **thunder** and **lightning**,
    and a heavy **cloud** over the mountain,
    and a very loud **trumpet** blast,
    so that all the people in the camp **trembled**.
But **Moses** led the people out of the camp to meet **God**,
    and they **stationed** themselves at the **foot** of the mountain.
Mount **Sinai** was all wrapped in **smoke**,
    for the LORD came down upon it in **fire**.
The smoke **rose** from it as though from a **furnace**,
    and the whole mountain trembled **violently**.

Marginal notes (left column):

Exodus = EK-suh-duhs

With the opening narration you must intimate that Moses' ascent up the mountain is no ordinary climb; he is about to meet his God.

God recounts Israel's deliverance from slavery with incredible intimacy: God brings Israel not to the mountain, but "to *myself*"; the covenant is "*my* covenant,"' Israel is God's "special possession," the nation that is "holy."

Stress the conditions God sets.

"Kingdom of priests" refers to the nation as a whole. Among the nations, Israel is as special as are the priests among the people.

This is a solemn yet joyful statement of assent to God's conditions.

Describe the great theophany (manifestation of God's powerful presence) with a sense of awe.

Fire and smoke are common manifestations of God. Wind and fire imagery dominate Pentecost.

---

author thus accounts for the scattering of peoples with different languages over the earth.

    Exodus. This great theophany, a manifestation of divine presence, occurs after the Hebrew escape from Egyptian slavery and at the beginning of the long journey to Canaan. The setting is a mountain, a typical place to meet God because it stretches toward the realm of the divine. Moses ascends Mount Sinai to hear God's Word and will: the Lord will give the Law and enter into covenant with the people he has chosen; they must hear and obey God's

teaching as "a holy nation." The Hebrew word translated "holy" means "set apart"; God chooses Israel to be different from all other peoples because of their relationship with the Lord and their way of life, obedient to the Law.

    The people accept the responsibility with a single voice, committing themselves to hear and obey the God who delivered them from Egypt. The moment of God's arrival nears, indicated by common biblical imagery: thunder and lightning, cloud, and fire. Many dramatic signs signal God's summons for Moses to ascend. God and Moses

meet, setting the stage to reveal what it will mean for Israel to live as the People of God.

    Ezekiel. Ezekiel, prophet and priest from Jerusalem, arrived in Babylon among the first deportees and continued to proclaim the Word of the Lord among the captives. Much of his message alternates between confronting the exiles with their injustices and idolatry that led to this catastrophe, and encouraging them with God's promise of eventual restoration. Today's reading is an extended image of Israel's return to the land, enlivened anew by the

"Trumpet" may be a metaphor for a strong, driving wind.

The **trumpet** blast grew **louder** and **louder**, while Moses
    was **speaking**,
and God **answering** him with **thunder**.

Speak slowly here. There is great suspense in this line.

When the LORD came **down** to the top of Mount Sinai,
    he **summoned** Moses to the **top** of the mountain.

Or:

Ezekiel = ee-ZEE-kee-uhl

READING I   Ezekiel 37:1–14

A reading from the Book of the Prophet Ezekiel

To enhance rather than slight the unique features of this text (the refrain-like repetitions, and the extraordinary visions), you will need extra preparation time. The style and content of this writing is quite different from contemporary prose, so prepare until you are comfortable with and enjoying the rich imagery and poetic flow of the language.

Ezekiel finds himself transported into the midst of this scene of devastation.

The hand of the LORD came upon me,
    and he **led** me out in the **spirit** of the LORD
    and set me in the center of the **plain**,
    which was now **filled** with **bones**.
He made me **walk** among the bones in every direction
    so that I saw how **many** they were on the surface of the plain.
How **dry** they were!
He **asked** me:
    Son of **man**, can these bones come to **life**?
I answered, "Lord GOD, you **alone** know that."
Then he said to me:

God orders Ezekiel to prophesy. Speak these words with authority.

    Prophesy over these bones, and **say** to them:
    Dry **bones**, hear the word of the LORD!
Thus says the Lord GOD to these **bones**:
    See! I will bring **spirit** into you, that you may come to **life**.
I will put **sinews** upon you, make **flesh** grow over you,
    cover you with **skin**, and put **spirit** in you
    so that you may come to **life** and know that **I** am the LORD.
I, **Ezekiel**, **prophesied** as I had been **told**,
    and even as I was **prophesying** I heard a **noise**;
    it was a **rattling** as the bones came together, **bone** joining **bone**.

Don't over-dramatize these events; they should have an air of reality.

I saw the **sinews** and the **flesh** come upon them,
    and the **skin** cover them, but there was no **spirit** in them. ❯❯

---

power of divine spirit. In the Old Testament, of course, there is no understanding of the Holy Spirit as Third Person of the Trinity, but these writings do express the notion of divine spirit as indwelling and life-giving. The Hebrew word *ruah*, translated in this passage as "spirit," can also mean "wind" or "breath"; it is the same word used of the divine power that first breathed life into the human creature (Genesis 2:7).

In Ezekiel's vision, God's decimated people are represented by a field of scattered dry bones, devoid of that life-breath. The prophet is commanded to speak the powerful Word of God over the bones so

that they may live again, and know again their one true source of life. At God's Word, the bones begin to reconnect and take on flesh. But only after Ezekiel invokes the spirit of God does breath return to these lifeless bodies. The Lord then explains that the vision represents God's restoration of the defeated people, who will return to their land and breathe once more, enlivened by divine spirit. This vision does not yet imagine resurrection of the dead, a concept that arises only later in Israel's history. It does, however, emphasize the life-giving power of God to be revealed when the

Lord, as promised, re-creates a scattered, dying people.

Joel. This brief book of prophecy dates from the period after the exiles return from Babylon to reestablish God's people. For Joel, the prevailing interest and image is the coming day of the Lord, a time that can bring both judgment and vindication. In the first half of the book, a plague of locusts has devastated the land and its harvest, which Joel views as divine judgment. At the people's sustained cries of lament, God promises to reverse their misfortunes, and the day of the Lord becomes a time of divine favor.

These repetitions, like the repeated phrases of a song, add beauty to the text and etch its message in our memories. Don't treat them like redundancies to be gotten around as quickly as possible.

Only when they receive God's spirit do the bones come alive.

This promise should arouse hope in the listener.

The fulfillment of the promise will prove God's sovereignty.

Make sure you have given proper attention to words like: "spirit," "life," "winds," and "breathe." The last line contains two ideas: "I promised," and "I will do it." Don't run them together.

Then the LORD said to me:
Prophesy to the **spirit**, **prophesy**, son of man,
and **say** to the spirit: Thus says the Lord **GOD**:
From the four winds **come**, O spirit,
and **breathe** into these **slain** that they may come to **life**.
I prophesied as he **told** me, and the spirit **came** into them;
they came **alive** and stood **upright**, a vast **army**.
Then he said to me:
Son of **man**, these bones are the whole **house** of **Israel**.
They have been saying,
"Our bones are **dried up**,
our hope is **lost**, and we are cut **off**."
Therefore, **prophesy** and **say** to them: **Thus** says the Lord **GOD**:
O my **people**, I will open your **graves**
and have you **rise** from them,
and bring you **back** to the land of Israel.
Then you shall **know** that I am the LORD,
when I **open** your graves and have you **rise** from them,
O my **people**!
I will put my **spirit** in you that you may **live**,
and I will **settle** you upon your **land**;
thus you shall **know** that I am the LORD.
I have **promised**, and I will **do** it, says the LORD.

Or:

READING I   Joel 3:1–5

A reading from the Book of the Prophet Joel

This text forms the basis of much of Peter's Pentecost sermon (Acts 2:17–21). Prophesy = PROF-uh-sī.

Stress the variety of those who will receive the Spirit.

This is unexpected: "Even upon the servants." Stress these words appropriately.

Thus says the LORD:
I will pour out my **spirit** upon all **flesh**.
Your **sons** and **daughters** shall **prophesy**,
your **old** men shall dream **dreams**,
your **young** men shall see **visions**;
even upon the **servants** and the **handmaids**,
in those days, I will pour out my **spirit**.

At the final coming of the Lord, divine spirit will be poured out on all the people, even servants and handmaids, young and old alike. Joel's description continues with images common to apocalyptic thought which envisioned God's arrival as a cataclysmic event, with signs in the heavens that not only the earth but the entire cosmos would be changed. On the day of the Lord, those who hear the prophet's message and call upon their saving God will survive the time of judgment and enjoy divine presence.

READING II The Letter to the Romans, composed near the end of Paul's life, is actually more like a sermon or treatise than a letter. In it, he attempts to develop a somewhat systematic presentation of the meaning of Jesus and the new life he brings to those who believe. Paul's preaching must always be understood in light of his own radical conversion and the profound change of heart and life he experienced through his encounter with the Resurrected Christ.

In chapters preceding today's reading, Paul laid out his arguments to demonstrate that through the Death and Resurrection of Christ, believers can be freed from domination by sin, death, and the Law. He now turns to clarifying the transformed life possible for those who are now children of God, led by the Spirit. Even though this new life has already begun, all creation awaits its completion. Even those who have the Spirit as firstfruits look forward to the fullness of redemption. Although literally coming first, "firstfruits" also figuratively stood

There is a more sober mood here. Images are not terrifying, but awe-inspiring.

And I will work **wonders** in the **heavens** and on the **earth**,
  blood, **fire**, and columns of **smoke**;
the **sun** will be turned to **darkness**,
  and the **moon** to **blood**,
at the coming of the **day** of the LORD,
  the **great** and **terrible** day.
Then everyone shall be **rescued**
  who calls on the **name** of the LORD;
for on Mount **Zion** there shall be a **remnant**,
  as the LORD has said,
and in **Jerusalem survivors**
  whom the LORD shall **call**.

Those who call on God need not fear the "terrible day" of the Lord.

"Zion" and "Jerusalem" combine with "remnant" and "survivors" to create a sense of joyful hope.

For meditation and context:

RESPONSORIAL PSALM   Psalm 104:1–2, 24 and 35c, 27–28, 29bc–30 (see 30)

R. **Lord, send out your Spirit, and renew the face of the earth.**
or
R. **Alleluia.**

Bless the LORD, O my soul!
  O LORD, my God, you are great indeed!
You are clothed with majesty and glory,
  robed in light as with a cloak.

How manifold are your works, O LORD!
  In wisdom you have wrought them all—
the earth is full of your creatures;
  bless the LORD, O my soul! Alleluia.

Creatures all look to you
  to give them food in due time.
When you give it to them, they gather it;
  when you open your hand, they are filled
    with good things.

If you take away their breath, they perish
  and return to their dust.
When you send forth your spirit,
  they are created,
  and you renew the face of the earth.

TO KEEP IN MIND
When practicing, **read Scriptures aloud,** taking note of stress and pause suggestions. After several readings, alter the stress markings to suit your style and interpretation.

READING II   Romans 8:22–27

A reading from the Letter of Saint Paul to the Romans

Brothers and sisters:
We **know** that all **creation** is **groaning** in **labor** pains even
  until **now**;
  and not only **that**, but we **ourselves**,
  who have the **firstfruits** of the **Spirit**, **»**

The "labor pains" is unexpected. Don't rush past the image.

While we have already tasted life in the Spirit, we long for the fullness only the Kingdom can offer.

---

for the rest of the harvest to come, and when consecrated to God, they dedicated the entire harvest. The term was also used to signify a pledge for the future. Christians who have been justified through the Death and Resurrection of Christ already have the Spirit as firstfruits, but still look forward to the fullness of redemption. The word translated "bodies" means whole persons, rather than physical flesh alone. Christians who already live in the Spirit have grounds for such hope, but still cannot see its completion and so "wait with endurance."

The Spirit that already creates an intimate, familial bond with God also assists Christians in prayer. When human attempts fail, the indwelling Spirit prays within, in ways even the one praying may not recognize. But "the one who searches hearts"—an Old Testament reference to God—knows the intention of divine Spirit. For those who belong to Christ, the Spirit accomplishes what human beings cannot.

GOSPEL   Despite its brevity, this short passage from John carries great significance in his Gospel account. It is linked to an earlier reference to Jesus as living water, and one thread in a thematic strand of texts in which John indicates that various beliefs and practices of Judaism reach their fullness in Jesus. It also advances John's view that the Spirit is not given to believers until after Jesus' Death and Resurrection.

The setting for Jesus' statement is the last day of the Jewish feast of Tabernacles, on which the priests carried out an elaborate water ritual around the altar of the

we **also** groan within ourselves
 as we wait for **adoption**, the **redemption** of our **bodies**.
For in **hope** we were **saved**.
Now **hope** that **sees** is **not** hope.
For who **hopes** for what one **sees**?
But if we hope for what we do **not** see, we wait with **endurance**.

In the **same** way, the Spirit **too** comes to the aid of our **weakness**;
 for we do not know **how** to pray as we **ought**,
 but the Spirit **himself** intercedes with inexpressible **groanings**.
And the one who searches **hearts**
 knows what is the **intention** of the Spirit,
 because he **intercedes** for the **holy** ones
 according to God's **will**.

GOSPEL   John 7:37–39

A reading from the holy Gospel according to John

On the **last** and **greatest** day of the **feast**,
 Jesus stood up and **exclaimed**,
 "Let anyone who **thirsts** come to **me** and **drink**.
As Scripture says:
 Rivers of living **water** *will flow from* **within** *him* who
  believes in me."

He said this in reference to the **Spirit**
 that those who came to **believe** in him were to **receive**.
There was, of course, no Spirit **yet**,
 because **Jesus** had not yet been **glorified**.

There is a lively, colloquial feel to Paul's logic here.

The Spirit even prays within us when we don't know how to pray.

Don't rush past this beautiful image: "The one who searches hearts."

Suggest that he rose and spoke with great vigor at the words "Let anyone . . . ." Make eye contact with the assembly.

"From within him . . . " is one of those rare instances when you should stress the preposition.

Although this sounds parenthetical, sustain the energy. It's important.

Jesus' glorification was his Death and Resurrection.

Temple. Echoing parts of his self-revelation to the Samaritan woman at Jacob's well, Jesus invites those who thirst to come to him to drink. He then refers to a verse of Scripture which does not exist in this precise form in the Old Testament. However, both Isaiah and Ezekiel refer to saving waters in the future time of salvation. It is possible that John calls those who thirst for salvation to seek Jesus, who offered living water to the woman of Samaria; she is the only person in the entire Gospel to whom he identifies himself as the Messiah.

While grammatical ambiguity presents problems of translation in this text, it is clear that John associates living water and the Spirit. In a dry land where lack of water could quickly bring death to any living thing, living or flowing water provides an effective image for a continuing source of life. Speaking of the Spirit to be given to believers, John anticipates later chapters. In the lengthy Last Supper discourse, Jesus tells the disciples that he will soon be leaving them, but will send the Spirit as his abiding presence. Only John describes the Holy Spirit as the "Paraclete," a Greek term

referring to one who stands at the side of another. For the Fourth Evangelist, the Spirit is not given until after the Death and Resurrection of Jesus. In a multilayered phrase typical of John, the dying Jesus hands over the spirit; when the Risen Christ appears to the disciples, he breathes the Holy Spirit into them (John 19:30; 20:22), completing one great act of salvation for which the Father sent him. M.F.

PENTECOST SUNDAY: DAY

LECTIONARY #63

READING I   Acts 2:1–11

A reading from the Acts of the Apostles

When the **time** for **Pentecost** was **fulfilled**,
   they were **all in one place together**.
And **suddenly** there came from the sky
   a **noise** like a **strong driving wind**,
   and it **filled** the **entire house** in which they **were**.
Then there appeared to them **tongues** as of **fire**,
   which **parted** and came to **rest** on **each one of them**.
And they were **all filled** with the **Holy Spirit**
   and began to **speak** in **different tongues**,
   as the **Spirit enabled** them to **proclaim**.

Now there were **devout Jews** from **every nation** under **heaven**
   staying in **Jerusalem**.
At this **sound**, they **gathered** in a **large crowd**,
   but they were **confused**
   because **each one** heard them speaking in his **own language**.
They were **astounded**, and in **amazement** they asked,
   "Are not **all these people** who are **speaking Galileans**?
Then how does **each** of **us hear** them in his **native language**?
We are **Parthians**, **Medes**, and **Elamites**,
   inhabitants of **Mesopotamia**, **Judea** and **Cappadocia**, **»**

"Pentecost" doesn't refer to the Christian solemnity we celebrate today, but to the Jewish festival of the time. Start slowly and then surprise us with the spectacular events that suddenly unfold.

See Exodus 19:1–15 that recounts the giving of the Law and note the similarities with this event.

The "tongues" signify that each of these disciples is set apart for this new moment in God's plan of salvation.

The crowds were required to make a pilgrimage to Jerusalem for this major holiday that required abstaining from work.

You can speak with subdued amazement and astonishment as you ask the questions of the pilgrims.

Galileans = gal-ih-LEE-uhnz
Parthians = PAHR-thee-uhnz
Medes = meedz
Elamites = EE-luh-mīts
Mesopotamia = mes-uh-poh-TAY-mee-uh
Judea = joo-DEE-uh
Cappadocia = cap-uh-DOH-she-uh

Today options are given for the readings. Contact your parish staff to learn which readings will be used.

READING I   "Pentecost" was the Greek name for the Jewish "Feast of Weeks" that celebrated God's giving of the Law to Moses on Mt. Sinai. During the celebration, the Spirit's sudden arrival surprised all who had gathered: the newly reconstituted "Twelve," that included Matthias (newly elected to replace Judas), and a group of disciples numbering over one hundred that included Mary, the Mother of Jesus.

Ten days before, the Apostles bid final farewell to Jesus and received their mandate to witness to him to "the ends of the earth" (Acts 1:8). Now, his promise of "another advocate" (John 14:16) is fulfilled. The Spirit comes upon them not as a "tiny whispering sound" (1 Kings 19:12), but as a rushing, violent wind that shakes the house and makes their hearts tremble. They lose control of their tongues and utter words they do not know, manifesting God's Spirit already working within them.

The Spirit apparently drives them into the streets where "devout Jews from every nation" (Pentecost required adult Jewish men to pilgrimage to Jerusalem for the feast) hear the joyous tumult and gather to witness the unfolding marvel. They don't hear cacophonous nonsense, but real words each understands, though they can't understand each other. The barrier between them and God's Word is removed. The Spirit now allows God's Word to penetrate, like an arrow, deep into each human heart. But while they understand the Apostles, there is no mention of improved

Pontus = PON-thus

Phrygia = FRIJ-ee-uh

Libya = LIB-ee-uh

Cyrene = sī-REE-nee

Cretans = KREE-tuhns

The listing of nations has led to this closing statement: our differences don't impede us from hearing about God's mighty deeds!

For meditation and context:

TO KEEP IN MIND

Go slowly in the epistles. Paul's style is often a tangle of complex sentences; his mood can change within a single passage.

Pontus and **Asia**, **Phrygia** and **Pamphylia**,
Egypt and the districts of **Libya** near **Cyrene**,
as well as **travelers** from **Rome**,
both **Jews** and **converts** to **Judaism**, **Cretans** and **Arabs**,
yet we hear them **speaking** in our **own tongues**
of the **mighty acts** of **God**."

RESPONSORIAL PSALM   Psalm 104:1, 24, 29–30, 31, 34 (30)

R. Lord, send out your Spirit, and renew the face of the earth. or R. Alleluia.

Bless the LORD, O my soul!
  O LORD, my God, you are great indeed!
How manifold are your works, O LORD!
  The earth is full of your creatures.

If you take away their breath, they perish
  and return to their dust.
When you send forth your spirit,
   they are created,
  and you renew the face of the earth.

May the glory of the LORD endure forever;
  may the LORD be glad in his works!
Pleasing to him be my theme;
  I will be glad in the LORD.

Make this a bold declaration.

After a pause, announce this good news to your listeners.

Contrast this statement with the one that follows.

Stress "is" not "in." The repeated "if" statements suggest we have an important role in our salvation.

READING II   Romans 8:8–17

A reading from the Letter of Saint Paul to the Romans

Brothers and **sisters**:
Those who are in the **flesh cannot please God**.
But **you** are **not** in the **flesh**;
  on the **contrary**, **you** are in the **spirit**,
  if only the **Spirit** of **God dwells** in you.
Whoever does **not** have the **Spirit** of **Christ** does **not belong**
    to him.
But if Christ **is in** you,
  although the **body** is **dead** because of **sin**,
  the **spirit** is **alive** because of **righteousness**.
If the **Spirit** of the **one** who **raised Jesus** from the **dead dwells**
   in **you**,

---

communication among the language groups. That miracle awaits the work of the Spirit; the Spirit will be the common language of what must become a spirit-speaking Church.

READING II | **1 Corinthians**. Today's passage is a short excerpt from a longer, classic text of St. Paul that you'd do well to read in its entirety. This briefer text reinforces the message of the First Reading from Acts: despite our differences we are one in God's Holy Spirit. Here, as in other parts of Scripture, opposites are

held in tension, held up as equally true and good. Paul acknowledges our differences: we possess different spiritual gifts, engage in various forms of service, and are occupied in a variety of activities. All are good. But these differences don't negate our oneness because all our ministries are inspired and guided by God.

God's Spirit takes possession of us, says Paul, not for our own benefit, but for the benefit of all. Each of us serves the community. To make this point, Paul utilizes his grand analogy of the human body comprised of various parts. We have only two

sentences of that classic image to share, but if read without rushing and with full awareness of the sacred reality Paul is enunciating, his words will have great impact. Speak the first sentence one phrase at a time without over articulating or overdramatizing. The words will make their own point if you make sure they're clearly heard. Speak both sentences in an upbeat tone. This is instruction into the *joy* of the Kingdom, so sound like it. Distinctions don't matter anymore. Nationality, race, status in society—all these have taken a back seat to our new status as God's

the **one** who **raised Christ** from the **dead**
will give **life** to **your mortal bodies also**,
through his **Spirit** that **dwells** in **you**.
Consequently, **brothers** and **sisters**,
we are **not debtors** to the flesh,
to live **according** to the flesh.
For if you live according to the **flesh**, you will **die**,
but if by the **Spirit** you put to **death** the **deeds** of the **body**,
you will **live**.

For those who are **led** by the **Spirit** of **God** are **sons** of **God**.
For you did not receive a **spirit** of **slavery** to fall back into **fear**,
but you received a **spirit** of **adoption**,
through whom we cry, "**Abba**, **Father!**"
The **Spirit himself** bears **witness** with **our spirit**
that we are **children** of **God**,
and if **children**, then **heirs**,
heirs of **God** and **joint heirs** with **Christ**,
if only we **suffer** with him
so that we may **also** be **glorified** with him.

Or:

READING II   1 Corinthians 12:3b–7, 12–13

A reading from the first Letter of Saint Paul to the Corinthians

Brothers and **sisters**:
No one can say, "**Jesus** is **Lord**," **except** by the **Holy Spirit**.

There are **different kinds** of **spiritual gifts** but the **same Spirit**;
there are **different forms** of **service** but the **same Lord**;
there are **different workings** but the **same God**
who produces **all** of them in **everyone**. »

Speak these lines with authority. Paul is teaching about what leads to life and death; convey the importance of this instruction.

Your tone can suggest, "You're too smart and experienced to make this mistake."

Pause between "Abba" and "Father" giving each equal emphasis.

In the progression from "children" to "joint heirs," each time the new *term gets the emphasis: "***children*** . . .* ***heirs*** . . .* ***joint heirs.***"*
Give both "suffer" and "glorified" a positive tone; glory comes only with suffering.

Corinthians = kohr-IN-thee-uhnz
You begin with an important declaration: we can't proclaim Jesus as Lord if we don't have God's Spirit. (No evil spirit can declare Christ as Lord!)
Now the reading becomes more didactic, so speak like a teacher rather than an evangelist.

Here's the point: Our differences *are at the service of* oneness *in Christ.*

children who share *one* Baptism in Christ. And all drink from *one* fountain: the Spirit of God.

Romans. Though it may not always look like it, Christian theology insists that Christ's sacrifice changed everything. His victory over death freed us from slavery to sin. Before then, humanity was mired in selfishness and rebellion against God. But on the Cross, Christ changed all that. Yes, we remain in the flesh and fall into sin, but now the flesh is foreign to us and no longer characterizes us.

We've been made new, cast off our "old self," and embraced the "new self" that's led by the Spirit: these truths are perceived only with eyes of faith; but when perceived, they are cause for great rejoicing. If Christ is in us and we live life animated by the Spirit, we can overcome the flesh we still retain. We cease our rebellious clinging to our own will and embrace, instead, the will of God. But Paul's repeated use of "if" ("*If* Christ is in you . . . *if* by the Spirit you put to death . . . *if* only we suffer") suggests that Baptism is not determinism; in other words, we retain free will

regarding our salvation. Things are iffy because sharing Christ's Resurrection ("We may also be glorified with him") requires willingness to share his suffering ("If . . . we suffer with him . . . "). Not all embrace that calling.

If we allow ourselves to be led by the Spirit, we "put to death the deeds of the body." Refusal leads to death. The best news here is that the Spirit initiates us into a radically new relationship with God that makes us adopted children and "*heirs.*" But again an "if": if we share Christ's glory, *if* we willingly "suffer with him."

> To **each individual** the **manifestation** of the **Spirit**
> is given for some **benefit**.
>
> As a **body** is **one** though it has **many parts**,
> and **all** the **parts** of the **body**, though **many**, are **one body**,
> so also **Christ**.
> For in **one Spirit** we were **all baptized** into **one body**,
> whether **Jews** or **Greeks**, **slaves** or **free persons**,
> and we were **all** given to drink of **one Spirit**.

More instruction follows here: speak it slowly but with a sense of the joyful hope embedded in the lines.

The Spirit is the glue that binds us. Speak the differences—"Jews . . . free" in a positive tone, but speak of the oneness in the Spirit with even deeper joy.

TO KEEP IN MIND

Names of characters: Often the first word of a reading. Lift out the names to ensure listeners don't miss who the subject is.

SEQUENCE   Veni, Sancte Spiritus

Come, Holy Spirit, come!
And from your celestial home
  Shed a ray of light divine!
Come, Father of the poor!
Come, source of all our store!
  Come, within our bosoms shine.
You, of comforters the best;
You, the soul's most welcome guest;
  Sweet refreshment here below;
In our labor, rest most sweet;
Grateful coolness in the heat;
  Solace in the midst of woe.
O most blessed Light divine,
Shine within these hearts of yours,
  And our inmost being fill!

Where you are not, we have naught,
Nothing good in deed or thought,
  Nothing free from taint of ill.
Heal our wounds, our strength renew;
On our dryness pour your dew;
  Wash the stains of guilt away:
Bend the stubborn heart and will;
Melt the frozen, warm the chill;
  Guide the steps that go astray.
On the faithful, who adore
And confess you, evermore
  In your sevenfold gift descend;
Give them virtue's sure reward;
Give them your salvation, Lord;
  Give them joys that never end. Amen.
  Alleluia.

GOSPEL   John 14:15–16, 23b–26

A reading from the holy Gospel according to John

Jesus said to his disciples:
  "If you **love** me, you will **keep** my **commandments**.
and I will ask the **Father**,
  and he will give you another **Advocate** to be **with** you **always**.

"Whoever **loves me** will **keep** my **word**,
  and my **Father** will **love** him,
  and we will **come** to him and **make** our **dwelling with** him.

Imagine Jesus speaking these words directly to your assembly.

Give "Advocate" a tone that suggests one who cares and comforts.

Don't let these short sentences elicit a choppy, rote delivery. Making a "dwelling with him" is a tender image.

| GOSPEL | **John 20.** Jesus offers "peace" not once, but twice, to the disciples who have hidden themselves behind the locked doors of the house where they had gathered. Clearly, they are afraid, and not without good reason. The authorities want no more talk of Jesus and dead men make poor storytellers. Frightened men are also unlikely to talk, so their fear serves them well.

But Jesus' only acknowledgment of their fear is to offer the one antidote he has in his arsenal—the unique peace only he, and not the world, can give. No doubt, rumors of an empty tomb and men dressed in white have been surging throughout this "first day of the week," but these disciples have not let themselves fully believe or fully comprehend its meaning. When Jesus appears, he bolsters faith by showing his "hands and his side," and only then do the disciples "rejoice" at seeing him.

Much happens in this brief encounter. No sooner is Jesus recognized than he *commissions* the disciples to go forth, making them Apostles ("those sent" in his name). Then Jesus breathes on them, a gesture that conjures the creator God breathing life into Adam. As God gave life to Adam, now Jesus gives new life to these disciples. This dense moment contains one more dimension: Jesus' breathing is John's version of a Pentecost narrative.

Jesus imparts the Spirit and bestows the power to forgive sins. The Risen Lord has not only wished them peace, he has also shared the surest way to sustain it.

John 14. Situated within the Last Supper discourses, this oration prepares the disciples for Jesus' departure and schools them in the meaning of true discipleship. Jesus begins by equating love for

Disregard for his Word is of no small consequence because his Word comes from the Father.

Jesus' tone is reassuring and encouraging.

Remember that throughout Jesus is comforting friends who are about to endure the trauma of his Death.

Those who do **not** love me do **not** keep my words;
    yet the word you **hear** is **not mine**
    but that of the **Father** who **sent** me.

"I have **told** you this while I am **with** you.
The **Advocate**, the **Holy Spirit** whom the **Father**
    will **send** in **my name**,
    will teach you **everything**
    and **remind** you of **all** that I **told** you."

Or:

In this very dense excerpt, Jesus' Resurrection, Ascension, and imparting of the Spirit occur on the same day. For more background, see the Gospel commentary of the Second Sunday of Easter.
The first sentence contains much information. Don't rush through it.

The mention of Jesus shifts the gloomy mood.

Here he shows his pierced side; in Luke he shows his "hands and feet."

Jesus must console a second time.

Don't rush the word "breathed." That "breathing" is the reason this text is proclaimed today.

GOSPEL John 20:19–23

A reading from the holy Gospel according to John

On the evening of that **first day** of the **week**,
    when the **doors** were **locked**, where the **disciples** were,
    for **fear** of the Jews,
    Jesus came and **stood** in their **midst**
    and said to them, "**Peace** be **with you**."
When he had said this, he **showed** them his **hands** and his **side**.
The disciples **rejoiced** when they **saw** the **Lord**.
Jesus said to them **again**, "**Peace** be **with you**.
As the **Father** has **sent me**, so **I send you**."
And when he had said this, he **breathed** on them
    and said to them,
  "**Receive** the **Holy Spirit**.
Whose **sins** you **forgive** are **forgiven** them,
    and whose **sins** you **retain** are **retained**."

---

him with observance of the commandments. It seems almost mundane, that assertion that links love with obedience. Yet, Jesus repeats it. "Love" means keeping "my word;" and the result is that Jesus and the Father go to dwell in the faithful person's heart.

In stark contrast, Jesus speaks of those who "do not love" because they "do not keep my words." The contrast reinforces his initial assertion that love is expressed as obedience to God's Law. Of

course, that Law is a Law of love summarized in love of God and neighbor. But love can't be lived as an abstraction and the way we make it concrete is to let the Word we hear from Jesus—that is, not his Word but the Father's—imbue us and make us one with God's divine will.

Jesus, our first advocate who intercedes for us in heaven, promises "another Advocate," who will instruct us in all Jesus taught. "While I am still with you" both signals Jesus' immanent departure and the

significant role the Spirit will play within the life of the Christian community. The Spirit signifies the ongoing presence of Jesus among his followers; despite his return to the Father, Jesus will be with them, through the Spirit, until the end of time. G.M.

THE MOST
HOLY TRINITY

LECTIONARY #166

READING I   Proverbs 8:22–31

A reading from the Book of Proverbs

Thus says the **wisdom** of **God:**
"The LORD **possessed** me, the **beginning** of his **ways,**
 the **forerunner** of his **prodigies** of long **ago;**
from of **old I** was **poured forth,**
 at the **first, before** the **earth.**
When there were no **depths I** was brought **forth,**
 when there were no **fountains** or **springs** of **water;**
before the **mountains** were **settled** into place,
 before the **hills, I** was **brought forth;**
while as yet the **earth** and **fields** were not **made,**
 nor the first **clods** of the **world.**

"When the **Lord** established the **heavens I** was **there,**
 when he marked out the **vault** over the **face** of the **deep;**
when he made **firm** the skies **above,**
 when he fixed **fast** the **foundations** of the **earth;**
when he set for the **sea** its **limit,**
 so that the **waters** should not **transgress** his **command;**
then was **I beside** him as his **craftsman,**
 and **I** was his **delight** day by day,
playing before him all the while,
 playing on the surface of his **earth;**
 and **I** found **delight** in the human **race.**"

Poetry communicates with sound and rhythm as well as meaning. Think of this text as a melody of praise and rejoicing.

An even, consistent reading throughout will kill the life of this text. Sense the up and down movement of rhythm and energy. Some lines require a burst of energy to convey the joy they contain.

Wisdom lauds her own majesty and ancient origins. "I was here before *everything* else," she asserts proudly!

Here begins the second description of the creation of the universe.

Don't drone through this "when he" litany; let your energy rise like a fountain spraying with increasing force.

"Craftsman" can be interpreted as "confidant" and suggests great intimacy between the Creator God and Lady Wisdom. Note how Wisdom "delights" and "plays" before the Lord and then "plays" on earth and "delights" in human beings.

The revelation that Wisdom delights in humanity is the intriguing finale to this reading.

READING I Among the riches of the Old Testament is this poetic text that personifies Wisdom as a woman, a divine figure who existed before all things and was present at the creation, contributing beauty and order to the universe. You'll notice that the text speaks twice of the origins of the universe: once to laud Wisdom for her existence before all else ("The LORD possessed me . . . ") and the second time to emphasize her presence at the start of creation and her helpful role in the unfolding of human history, ("When the Lord established the heavens . . . ").

Theologically, the text is somewhat ambiguous, for the Christian tradition has understood Wisdom as representing both Christ and the Holy Spirit. Today's text represents an early understanding of Wisdom who, though personified as embodying human characteristics, is not really presented as a person. Over time, the ancient writers would better understand Wisdom as a manifestation of God's activity and self-communication in the world. In this description, Wisdom stands by observing God's creative activity and identifies herself as God's "craftsman", an intermediary who brings God's gifts to humanity. But later books give her a more active role in the divine work of creation.

Your chief task is to remember that this is poetry that uses many lines to make a single point: Wisdom existed before all things and was present at the creation. Every idea is stated a second time, but with some nuance. Capture the exuberance of Wisdom as she "plays" in God's creative presence.

For meditation and context:

TO KEEP IN MIND

Echoes: Some words echo words that went before. For example, "You shall be a glorious crown . . . a royal diadem" (Isaiah 62:3). Here "diadem" echoes "crown" so it needs no stress. In such cases, emphasize the new idea: royal.

RESPONSORIAL PSALM   Psalm 8:4–5, 6–7, 8–9 (2a)

R. O Lord, our God, how wonderful your name in all the earth!

When I behold your heavens, the work of
     your fingers,
  the moon and the stars which you set in
     place—
What is man that you should be mindful of
     him,
  or the son of man that you should care for
     him?

You have made him little less than the
     angels,
  and crowned him with glory and honor.
You have given him rule over the works of
     your hands,
  putting all things under his feet.

All sheep and oxen,
  yes, and the beasts of the field,
the birds of the air, the fishes of the sea,
  and whatever swims the paths of the seas.

You are presenting a logical argument that requires each step to reach its conclusion, so be sure each step is clearly presented.

Despite his use of logic, Paul's argument is infused with joy; don't leave out that aspect.

Pause before introducing this startling assertion. A trace of a smile would not be inappropriate.
Remain upbeat as you increase energy on the new word of each line.
"And hope . . ." is a statement of faith, not a legal argument. Speak from your own conviction.
The Trinitarian formula is completed with the naming of the Holy Spirit. The Spirit sustains our joy.

READING II   Romans 5:1–5

A reading from the Letter of Saint Paul to the Romans

Brothers and sisters:
Therefore, **since** we have been **justified** by **faith**,
     we have **peace** with **God** through our **Lord Jesus Christ**,
     through whom we have gained **access** by **faith**
     to this **grace** in which we **stand**,
     and we **boast** in **hope** of the **glory** of **God**.
Not **only** that, but we even **boast** of our **afflictions**,
     knowing that **affliction** produces **endurance**,
     and **endurance**, proven **character**,
     and proven **character**, **hope**,
     and **hope** does **not disappoint**,
     because the **love** of **God** has been poured **out** into our **hearts**
     through the **Holy Spirit** that has been **given** to **us**.

READING II "Not only that, . . ." says Paul, after laying out a profound truth of the faith "but we *even* boast . . . ." So we have not one, but two reasons to be grateful for the "grace in which we stand" as lectors proclaiming today. Paul uses a Trinitarian formula to rejoice over the salvation "God" accomplished "through our Lord Jesus Christ" and sustains "through the Holy Spirit."

The first piece of Good News is that Jesus restored "peace" between God and humanity. "Faith" in Jesus gives us access to that peace and also to "grace," that is,

God's own life surging within us. So faith leads to peace and grace and they open the door to "hope." United to Christ in faith we can hope to share in the "glory of God."

But there is *more* Good News. Because of faith, all life is changed. The seemingly unthinkable—boasting of our *"afflictions"*—is now as logical as expecting to share God's glory. Again, Paul utilizes a four-step progression and, in the world of faith we now inhabit, it doesn't strain credulity. "Affliction" makes us strong and gives us "endurance." Endurance builds "character" and character gives us reason

to "hope," a hope that "does not disappoint."

In a hard and cynical age, Paul's enthusing over hope might seem naïve. Suffering is to be overcome, or at best endured; how can one "boast" of suffering? Paul believes that if Christ makes a difference, he makes a difference in *all* things, stands with us in all things, and makes all things possible—even seeing *through* our pain to the glory that awaits us and *standing* in our pain with confidence that the Holy Spirit "that has been given to us" is a

Pause after the opening narration, and be sure your tone conveys compassion.

"But when he comes . . ." suggests a time when they *can* bear to hear the other "things."

What is "coming" is greater understanding of Jesus' teaching.

The Trinity works in one accord sharing the one truth that comes from the Father.

Use eye contact to ensure your assembly understands these words are also intended for them.

TO KEEP IN MIND

Word value: Words are your medium, like a painter's brush or a sculptor's chisel. You must understand the words before you can communicate them. Most words have a dictionary meaning (denotative) and an associational meaning (connotative). "House" and "home" both mean "dwelling," yet they communicate different feelings. Be alert to subtle differences in connotative meanings and express them.

GOSPEL   John 16:12–15

A reading from the holy Gospel according to John

Jesus said to his **disciples**:
"I have **much more** to tell you, but you **cannot bear** it **now**.
But when he **comes**, the **Spirit** of **truth**,
   he will **guide** you to **all truth**.
He will **not** speak on his **own**,
   but he **will speak** what he **hears**,
   and will **declare** to you the things that are **coming**.
He will **glorify** me,
   because he will **take** from what is **mine** and **declare** it to you.
Everything that the **Father** has is **mine**;
   for this **reason** I told you that he will **take** from what is **mine**
   and **declare** it to **you**."

---

consuming fire that can transform anything into a sacrifice of praise.

GOSPEL Taken from the Last Supper discourse, this brief text presents Jesus, as ever, trying to care for his disciples with careful explanations. Shortly before this reading begins (in verse 7), he has said, "I tell you the truth . . . ." But Jesus realizes they are not ready for *all* the truth, so he holds back certain things, like his impending Passion and Death. What they *can* "bear" he shares forcefully, and that truth concerns the coming of the

"Spirit of truth" who will make clear all that they have learned from Jesus.

In the verses immediately preceding this text, Jesus has shared something very counterintuitive: "It is better for you that I go. For if I do not go, the Advocate will not come to you. But if I go, I will send him to you." The Spirit will come, not to bring new revelations, but to help them understand what they've already heard or experienced.

While other sections of the farewell discourse may feel more intimate, there is no lack of care in this passage. Jesus knows the events of the next few days will be dis-

orienting for the disciples, so he prepares them to hold on to faith and to await the one who will vindicate both Jesus and their confidence in him. Jesus' self-confidence and the assurance he offers his disciples remain efficacious for each of us today who hears these words. The Spirit continues to witness to the "truth," who is Christ, God's living Word. On this Solemnity of the Most Holy Trinity, we celebrate that God, the source of truth, has revealed it to Jesus, the Son, who through the Spirit, graciously imparts it to us. G.M.

THE MOST HOLY BODY AND BLOOD OF CHRIST (CORPUS CHRISTI)

LECTIONARY #169

READING I   Genesis 14:18–20

Your task is to ensure all the details are heard: "Melchizedek," "bread and wine," "priest," "God Most High," "blessed," and so forth

Melchizedek = mel-KIZ-ih-dek

Salem = SAY-luhm

Deliver the "blessing" as if you were praying it yourself.

Blessed / blessed = BLES-uhd

Pause before announcing Abram's generous response and speak of it with admiration.

A reading from the Book of Genesis

In those days, **Melchizedek**, king of **Salem**,
      brought out **bread** and **wine**,
      and being a **priest** of **God Most High**,
   he **blessed Abram** with these **words**:
   "**Blessed** be **Abram** by **God Most High**,
      the **creator** of **heaven** and **earth**;
   and blessed be **God Most High**,
      who **delivered** your **foes** into your **hand**."
Then **Abram** gave him a **tenth** of **everything**.

For meditation and context:

RESPONSORIAL PSALM   Psalm 110:1, 2, 3, 4 (4b)

R. You are a priest for ever, in the line of Melchizedek.

The LORD said to my Lord: "Sit at my right
      hand
   till I make your enemies your footstool."

The scepter of your power the LORD will
      stretch forth from Zion:
   "Rule in the midst of your enemies."

"Yours is princely power in the day of your
      birth, in holy splendor;
   before the daystar, like the dew, I have
      begotten you."

The LORD has sworn, and he will not repent:
   "You are a priest forever, according to the
      order of Melchizedek."

TO KEEP IN MIND

Who really proclaims: "When the Scriptures are read in the Church, God himself is speaking to his people, and Christ, present in his own word, is proclaiming the gospel" (*General Instruction of the Roman Missal, 29*).

READING I   Melchizedek emerges from an unknown past to "bless" Abram (the future Abraham) and to celebrate the great victory Abram has won. (It was a victory indeed against four invader Kings that the combined forces of five local kings could not defeat.) Abram pursued the aggressor kings and recovered both his nephew Lot and all the possessions that had been taken. Melchizedek recognizes that it was God who made Abram victorious and arranges a banquet to celebrate his success. Melchizedek never reappears on the pages of the Old Testament except

for the Book of Psalms (Psalm 110:4) that proclaims, "You are a priest forever according to the order of Melchizedek." That reference links Melchizedek to King David, who also was both king and priest, and to Jesus who is our eternal King and great High Priest, as is so clearly affirmed in the Letter to the Hebrews.

Melchizedek is not a Hebrew, but the King of Salem. He is also priest of "God Most High," (*El Elyon*, in Hebrew) who ranks highest among the gods of the Canaanites and whom the Israelites identify as the same God they worship. Melchizedek

brings out simple elements of "bread and wine" and gives thanks for Abram's victory and God's mercy. In this primordial moment, the Church recognizes a prefigurement of the simple meal Jesus gave us to remember him. Abram responds to Melchizedek's gesture with his own overwhelming generosity. As we contemplate the Eucharist, we are invited to consider what we will return to the Lord for his abounding generosity.

Corinthians = kohr-IN-thee-uhnz
Paul is writing to correct abuses that infected the Corinthians' celebration of the Eucharistic meal.

Paul stresses his teaching is "from the Lord." "Handed over" immediately recalls Jesus' Death and the sacrificial nature of Eucharist. Jesus takes, blesses, breaks, and gives. He does the same in today's Gospel narrative.

To "do this in remembrance" is to makes him present among us.

This line is as poignant the second time as the first.
This sentence is spoken in Paul's voice; he points past the present to our eternal destiny with Christ.

READING II   1 Corinthians 11:23–26

A reading from the first Letter of Saint Paul to the Corinthians

Brothers and **sisters**:
I **received** from the **Lord** what I **also handed on** to **you**,
    that the **Lord Jesus**, on the night he was **handed over**,
    took bread, and, after he had given **thanks**,
    broke it and **said**, "**This** is my **body** that is for **you**.
Do this in **remembrance** of me."
In the **same** way also the **cup**, after **supper**, saying,
    "This **cup** is the **new covenant** in my **blood**.
Do this, as **often** as you **drink** it, in **remembrance** of me."
For as **often** as you **eat** this **bread** and **drink** the **cup**,
    you **proclaim** the **death** of the **Lord** until he **comes**.

The healings are another sign of the Kingdom's abundance; they're an important prelude to this story.

Don't take Luke's details for granted for they add great texture and humanity to the story.

The "deserted place" may symbolize the wilderness of our hearts.

Jesus places the responsibility on them, knowing full well they can't respond.

Now that the impossibility of the situation is well established, Jesus helps them see with Kingdom eyes.

Again, Luke's details root the story in concrete reality.

GOSPEL   Luke 9:11b–17

A reading from the holy Gospel according to Luke

Jesus spoke to the crowds about the **kingdom of God**,
    and he **healed** those who **needed** to be **cured**.
As the day was drawing to a **close**,
    the **Twelve** approached him and **said**,
    "**Dismiss** the **crowd**
so that they can go to the surrounding **villages** and **farms**
and find **lodging** and **provisions**;
    for we are in a **deserted** place here."
He said to them, "**Give** them some **food yourselves**."
They replied, "Five **loaves** and two **fish** are **all** we **have**,
    unless we **ourselves** go and **buy** food for **all** these people."
Now the men there numbered about **five thousand**.
Then he said to his disciples,
    "Have them **sit down** in groups of about **fifty**."

READING II Like Mark, Matthew, Luke, and John, Paul is an evangelist. And like them, his purpose is not to share memories of an admired but deceased teacher, but to proclaim a living Lord who is still intimately connected to his beloved followers. Imagine Paul sitting amongst new converts, perhaps in secret, sharing these sacred words that not only recall what Jesus did, but make him present among those gathered. Paul is not repeating a "formula" for them to memorize. His are words that elicit tears and sighs of gratitude. They evoke the Lord who

willingly gave himself to become food for us. He spoke these words—at the same time instructing that we repeat them often so that we would know we're not left orphaned—that our fears could be blotted out and our hunger fed, and so that we would never forget the God who became one of us so we could become like him.

All that and more is in these lines. There is no "trick" for conveying the special, sacred nature of these words. You need only to recognize what you are saying, to picture him who spoke them first, and sense the love that filled that first cup

of wine. What we do at the altar is not an obligation but a sacred trust, a privilege that binds us to the Lord who gave everything for us. Notice that Paul's final words remind us that this bread and wine are but food for the journey. Paul points us forward and declares that one day Christ will come and there will be no more need for remembering or for bread and wine; then we will feast on his eternal presence in the glory of the Father.

Slow your pace and assume a more solemn tone as you narrate, with eucharistic language, Jesus' compassionate response.

These details underscore the theme of abundance and the concrete reality of the miracle.

> **TO KEEP IN MIND**
> **Separating units of thought with pauses:** Identify the units of thought in your text and use pauses to distinguish one from another. Running words together blurs meaning and fails to distinguish ideas. Punctuation does not always indicate clearly what words to group together or where to pause. The listener depends on you for this organization of ideas.

They **did** so and made them **all sit** down.
Then taking the five **loaves** and the two **fish**,
   and looking up to **heaven**,
   he said the **blessing** over them, **broke** them,
   and **gave** them to the **disciples** to set before the **crowd**.
They all **ate** and were **satisfied**.
And when the leftover **fragments** were picked up,
   they filled **twelve** wicker **baskets**.

GOSPEL This dramatic narrative, recounted in all four Gospel accounts, heralds the abundance of God's Kingdom. It witnesses to the power of God to overcome our insufficiency and overwhelm us with plenty. Claims that Jesus facilitated sharing among the crowd miss the point; this text declares that no human effort is enough to fulfill our deepest hungers, for only God can do that. This is not a story of hungry bellies being filled; it is an enacted parable that announces God can fill what's hardest of all to fill: the human heart.

We might expect a Last Supper narrative for today's Solemnity. But perhaps this Gospel was chosen because this story presents Eucharist as the primary sign of the Kingdom's abundance. The crowd has followed Jesus and neglected their stomachs in their effort to satisfy their hungry hearts. The disciples recognize the need but don't recognize in Jesus one who can satisfy it. So they recommend the crowd go take care of themselves. Jesus challenges them to care for the crowd and to open their eyes and hearts to a fuller understanding of God's reign. Their imaginations

are too small. So Jesus calls for the few rations they have. The lesson he teaches they will learn slowly. Their contribution, no matter how large or small, will never be enough to fill stomachs or hearts. If this were a story about Christ unlocking human generosity, the message would be that we already hold within us all that we need to lift the human spirit to the level of the Kingdom. But the fact is that we don't have those resources, at least not on our own. With God in the equation, everything changes. What we offer *can* be enough, when God supplies what we cannot. G.M.

TENTH SUNDAY
IN ORDINARY TIME

LECTIONARY #90

READING I   1 Kings 17:17–24

A reading from the first Book of Kings

Elijah went to Zarephath of **Sidon** to the house of a **widow**.
The **son** of the mistress of the house fell **sick**,
      and his sickness grew more severe until he **stopped breathing**.
So she said to Elijah,
      "**Why** have you done this to **me**, O man of **God**?
Have you come to me to call attention to my **guilt**
      and to kill my **son**?"
Elijah said to her, "**Give** me your son."
Taking him from her **lap**, he **carried** the son to the upper room
      where he was staying, and put him on his **bed**.
Elijah **called out** to the LORD:
      "O LORD, my **God**,
      will you afflict **even** the **widow** with whom I am staying
      by killing her son?"
Then he stretched himself out upon the child three times
      and **called out** to the LORD:
      "O LORD, my **God**,
      let the **life breath** return to the **body** of this **child**."
The LORD **heard** the prayer of **Elijah**;
      the life breath returned to the child's body and he **revived**.
Taking the child, Elijah **brought** him down into the house
      from the upper room and **gave** him to his **mother**.

Elijah = ee-LĪ-juh
Zarephath = ZAYR-uh-fath
Sidon = SĪ-duhn

Since some necessary background is missing, share these details slowly to give us a chance to form images in our minds.
Stricken with grief (and maybe guilt for inviting this man into her home), the woman lashes out.
At this time, misfortune was often seen as punishment for sin.

Elijah acts impulsively, with no "plan" for improving the situation.

Now it is Elijah who feels guilty for bringing calamity to this home.

In Acts 20:7–12, Paul uses a similar strategy to revive a man who has fallen to his death. Be sure to emphasize the number of times he cried out.

After a pause, slowly narrate with joy and relief the reunion of mother and child.

READING I Imagine Elijah's dismay when the son of the starving widow (the woman who has been so good to him and trusted him), grows ill and dies. In her grief, the woman fears that the prophet has come to expose her sins and bring God's punishment down upon her. Elijah believes God led him to her door, so we can imagine him trying to make sense of this calamity. But before he can find an answer he takes action.

All he seems to know is that he must plead openly with the Lord. He has no plan; he's had no sudden revelation. But he has a relationship with God that's based on trust. God has led him before and so he trusts again. Then three times he stretches himself out upon the dead boy's body and begs the Lord to bring him back to life. Three times, not once, he makes this prayer before the boy revives. His faith is tested, just like hers. When, upon receiving her boy back, she confesses "indeed I know you are a man of God," she may as much be speaking for Elijah who likely was as awed by God's mercy as was she.

Sometimes we take action without any clear expectation of being able to influence events for the better. But we hear something beyond reason say, "Act." That ability to trust and to follow an instinct at the right time is a gift of the Spirit and usually the result of many years of intimate relationship with God. Elijah today is not a seer speaking for God, but a man of faith relying on God as years of prayer have trained him to do. Today, the difference between him and us is razor thin, for what he does is within the reach of all of us: in his fear and disorientation he knows where to run and what to say: "O Lord my God, help me!"

The woman's confession is almost a prayer that expresses joy and gratitude as well as awareness of Elijah's divine mission.

Elijah said to her, "**See**! Your son is **alive**."
The woman replied to Elijah,
  "Now **indeed** I know that **you** are a man of **God**.
The word of the LORD comes truly from your mouth."

For meditation and context:

RESPONSORIAL PSALM   Psalm 30:2, 4, 5–6, 11, 12, 13 (2a)

R. I will praise you, Lord, for you have rescued me.

I will extol you, O LORD, for you drew me
    clear
  and did not let my enemies rejoice over
  me.
O LORD, you brought me up from the
    netherworld;
  you preserved me from among those
  going down into the pit.

Sing praise to the LORD, you his faithful
    ones,
  and give thanks to his holy name.
For his anger lasts but a moment;
  a lifetime, his good will.
At nightfall, weeping enters in,
  but with the dawn, rejoicing.

Hear, O LORD, and have pity on me;
  O LORD, be my helper.
You changed my mourning into dancing;
  O LORD, my God, forever will I give you
    thanks.

TO KEEP IN MIND

Sense lines: Scripture in this book is arranged (as in the Lectionary) in sense lines, one idea per line. Typically at least a slight pause should follow each line, but good reading requires you to recognize the need for other pauses within lines.

READING II   Galatians 1:11–19

Galatians = guh-LAY-shuhnz

A reading from the Letter of Saint Paul to the Galatians

Imagine Paul having heard someone cite objections to his teaching and then launching into this spirited defense.

Two ways he did *not* receive the Gospel precede his assertion of how he *did* receive it.

I want you to know, brothers and sisters,
  that the **gospel** preached by **me** is not of **human origin**.
For I did not **receive** it from a human being, nor was I **taught** it,
  but it **came** through a **revelation** of **Jesus Christ**.

Let there be regret in his retelling of his former misguided passion.

His earlier effort and zeal for Judaism attest to his current efforts on behalf of Christ.

His contention that Christ chose him before his birth is very significant.

For you heard of my **former** way of life in **Judaism**,
  how I **persecuted** the church of God beyond measure
  and tried to **destroy** it, and progressed in Judaism
  beyond many of my contemporaries among my race,
  since I was even more a **zealot** for my ancestral **traditions**.
But when **God**, who from my mother's womb had set me apart
  and **called** me through his **grace**,
  was **pleased** to **reveal** his Son to me, »

READING II Paul writes to converts he himself won to the faith, disabusing them of false notions that to be saved they need to add aspects of Jewish Law, namely circumcision, to their faith in Christ. The self-appointed missionaries imposing these requirements also question Paul's authority and the validity of his Gospel message. They claim Paul was not instructed by Jesus and his teaching differs from that of the genuine Apostles. So here Paul is legitimating both his status as an Apostle and his teaching of the faith. He asserts that what he teaches is not of

"human origin" because he received it mystically, directly from Christ. Then he uses a counterintuitive argument to support his apostolic authority. He confesses his initial hatred of the Church, his efforts to "destroy it," and his zeal for "my ancestral traditions." So Paul's work for the Gospel was not his idea; it came from God who "from my mother's womb had set me apart."

As at the start of the passage, Paul notes that, after his conversion, he didn't consult with "flesh and blood," a reference to the Jerusalem elders. Instead he went off to Arabia, where he probably sought

solitude for reflection, typical of many biblical figures. Three years later, he returned, convinced of his call to preach Christ to the Gentiles. Paul ends this explanation with a final assertion of his autonomy, saying he spent but fifteen days with Peter (Cephas) and consulted only one other, James.

Don't let Paul sound smug as he cites his history and credentials. He's been unjustly attacked and is defending himself. But he grounds everything in Christ and on the mercy of God who overlooked his past to call him to life-long work for the Gospel.

Again, it's not "flesh and blood" but Christ who validates him.

Moses, Elijah, John the Baptist, and Jesus all sought the solitude of the desert to prepare for their mission.
Even as he concedes his meeting with Cephas he seems to negate its significance.

so that I might proclaim him to the **Gentiles**,
I did not **immediately** consult flesh and blood,
nor did I go up to Jerusalem
to those who were apostles before me;
rather, I went into Arabia and then returned to Damascus.

Then **after** three years I went up to Jerusalem
to confer with Cephas and remained with him for fifteen days.
But I did not see any other of the **apostles**,
only **James** the brother of the **Lord**.

GOSPEL   Luke 7:11–17

A reading from the holy Gospel according to Luke

Nain = nayn

The presence of the disciples and the crowd are important.

Notice how the news gets worse with each detail: he was her "only son" and she was a "widow."
Let us hear compassion in your tone.

The tone of "do not weep" should suggest that weeping is no longer necessary.

Jesus speaks with assurance and authority.

Imagine the tender moment when you narrate "gave him to his mother."

Speak the crowd's reaction with subdued reverence and fascination.

The last sentence is the proud declaration of a believer.

Jesus journeyed to a city called Nain,
    and his disciples and a large crowd accompanied him.
As he drew near to the gate of the city,
    a man who had **died** was being carried out,
    the **only** son of his **mother**, and she was a **widow**.
A large crowd from the city was with her.
When the Lord saw her,
    he was moved with **pity** for her and said to her,
    "Do not **weep**."
He stepped forward and **touched** the coffin;
    at this the bearers halted,
    and he said, "Young **man**, I tell you, **arise**!"
The dead man sat up and began to speak,
    and Jesus **gave** him to his **mother**.
Fear **seized** them all, and they **glorified** God, exclaiming,
    "A great **prophet** has arisen in our midst,"
    and "God has **visited** his people."
This report about him spread through the whole of Judea
    and in all the surrounding region.

GOSPEL   In both the First Reading and this Gospel, mothers who are widows lose their only son. In each, a man of God intervenes, restores the son to life, and then returns him to his mother. In both stories the great miracle is met with awe and fascination.

But the differences between the stories reveal the nature of Jesus' ministry and open a window into the Kingdom he proclaims. In Luke's story no one seeks out Jesus nor accuses him of being the cause of the calamity. Jesus recognizes the need and invites himself into the woman's sorrow.

Unlike Elijah, Jesus is a model of composure; he is centered and peaceful. He reaches out to the widow, not with a frantic "Give me your son," but with a reassuring "Do not weep." Jesus doesn't climb stairs to be alone with the boy and God and to cry out in desperation. Instead, before the eyes of the "large crowd" that's following him, Jesus takes full control of the situation.

It only takes his hand upon the "coffin" to stop the procession. On his own authority and through a power that resides in him, Jesus speaks the young man back to life. And immediately the boy sits up and begins

to speak. The crowd responds, as did the widow in 1 Kings, with the realization that the miracle worker is a "man of God." But here in Luke the crowd was seized with "fear." Luke's crowd senses the shift in human history that Jesus represents. The world is about to turn and Jesus is the one pushing it. When God visits his people things cannot remain the same. The raising of this young man announces to the village of Nain and to all who hear of his miracle that a new day has dawned. God has drawn near to humanity. Everything is about to change. G.M.

ELEVENTH SUNDAY IN ORDINARY TIME

LECTIONARY #93

READING I   2 Samuel 12:7–10, 13

Samuel = SAM-yoo-uhl

Let the opening narration suggest the strong rebuke that soon will follow.

The favors God has done for David turn here into a litany of indictment.

Nathan's question is a pained accusation, as if asking, "How could you have done such a thing?"

Uriah = yoo-RĪ-uh

Hittite = HIT-tīt

Ammonites = AM-uh-nīts

The punishment is the inevitable consequence of David's own choice. Don't speak with anger or vindictiveness.

Deliver this line simply and sincerely, and without adornment.

The final lines are sobering. Speak with authority but without emotion.

A reading from the second Book of Samuel

Nathan said to **David:**
"**Thus** says the Lord **God** of **Israel:**
    'I **anointed** you **king** of **Israel.**
I **rescued** you from the hand of **Saul.**
I **gave** you your lord's **house** and your lord's **wives** for your **own.**
I **gave** you the **house** of Israel and of **Judah.**
And if **this** were not **enough,** I could count up for you **still more.**
Why have you **spurned** the Lord and done **evil** in his sight?
You have **cut down Uriah** the **Hittite** with the **sword;**
    you **took his** wife as your **own,**
    and **him** you **killed** with the **sword** of the **Ammonites.**
Now, therefore, the **sword** shall **never depart** from your **house,**
    because **you** have **despised** me
    and have **taken** the **wife** of **Uriah** to be **your wife.'**"
Then **David** said to **Nathan,**
    "I have **sinned** against the Lord."
Nathan answered **David:**
    "The Lord on **his** part has **forgiven** your sin:
    you shall **not die.**"

READING I   David: shepherd, psalmist, warrior, king, adulterer, and murderer, and the only person in the Bible of whom God said, "a man after my own heart" (Acts 13:22). David did not earn his distinction because of righteousness. He had sins aplenty, but his saving grace was his reverence. He had great respect for God and understood fear of the Lord. Despite the great sin recounted here, he walked by the light of God and never forgot who his shepherd was. A man after God's heart is not a perfect person. When Samuel anointed David king, God told him not to judge from outward appearance, because "the Lord looks into the heart" (1 Samuel 16:7).

We will see in today's Gospel passage that it's hearts God cares about most, not our number of sins or good deeds. What distinguished David's heart was his dependency on the Lord. Like a child toward its parents, David was always aware of his need for God. But most of all, David's was a repentant heart. When confronted with his sin David didn't despair like King Saul who threw himself upon his sword. David understood the nature of his sin; he realized he had betrayed the Lord; he truly repented and accepted the consequences of his sin.

The prophet Nathan reviews for David all that the Lord has done for him. Then the Lord doesn't hold back in characterizing David's crime: "You have spurned the Lord," he says. David used "the sword of the Ammonites" to do his dirty work when he gave orders that Uriah should be put in the front lines of battle against the Ammonites and then abandoned. This he did to hide his adultery with Uriah's wife, Bathsheba. Nathan pronounces God's judgment on

For meditation and context:

RESPONSORIAL PSALM   Psalm 32:1–2, 5, 7, 11 (see 5c)

R. Lord, forgive the wrong I have done.

Blessed is the one whose fault is taken away,
    whose sin is covered.
Blessed the man to whom the LORD imputes
    not guilt,
    in whose spirit there is no guile.

I acknowledged my sin to you,
    my guilt I covered not.
I said, "I confess my faults to the LORD,"
    and you took away the guilt of my sin.

You are my shelter; from distress you will
    preserve me;
    with glad cries of freedom you will ring
    me round.

Be glad in the LORD and rejoice, you just;
    exult, all you upright of heart.

Galatians = guh-LAY-shuhnz

READING II   Galatians 2:16, 19–21

A reading from the Letter of Saint Paul to the Galatians

Paul is "making a case" here, so you need
good energy throughout.

He makes his point, then makes it again; save
your greater energy for the second iteration.

"Because . . . no one" is a definitive
pronouncement!

"Died" and "crucified" are not negative
references, but sources of joy!

This is Paul's profound confession that his
life is wholly committed to Christ. Speak it
with reverence.

Speak "I do not nullify . . . " with strength;
he means he won't declare Christ's Death
meaningless by relying on the Law instead
of Christ.

Brothers and **sisters:**
We who **know** that a person is **not justified** by **works** of the **law**
    but through **faith** in **Jesus Christ,**
    even **we** have **believed** in **Christ Jesus**
    that **we** may be **justified** by **faith** in **Christ**
    and **not** by **works** of the **law,**
    because by **works** of the **law no one** will be **justified.**
For **through** the **law I died** to the **law,**
    that I might **live** for **God.**
I have been **crucified** with **Christ;**
    yet **I live,** no longer **I,** but **Christ lives in me;**
    insofar as **I** now **live** in the **flesh,**
    I live by **faith** in the **Son** of **God**
    who has **loved me** and **given himself** up for **me.**
I do not **nullify** the **grace** of **God;**
    for if **justification** comes through the **law,**
    then Christ **died** for **nothing.**

David: his reign and those of his descendants will be marked by violence.

David realizes that these consequences are entirely his own doing. He
admits not only that he has sinned but that
he has sinned so gravely. His honest admission is met by God's merciful response:
"You shall not die."

READING II Paul is defending the primacy of Christ in our salva-
tion. Other teachers were persuading the
Galatian converts that they needed to
embrace elements of the Mosaic Law,

especially circumcision, to be saved. And
they faulted Paul for failing to teach the
Galatians the necessity of observing the
Law. Besides insisting on circumcision, they
required adherence to Jewish dietary practices. Paul recounts an incident when
Peter, while visiting Antioch, at first ate
readily with the racially diverse Christian
community. But when representatives
arrived from James in Jerusalem, who
strictly observed the dietary laws, Peter
suddenly stopped dining with the Gentiles.
Part of Paul's argument today is probably
directed at that hypocrisy.

Paul argues that Christ alone is
needed for salvation, not any aspects of
the old Law. In fact, he says it twice. First,
"a person is not justified by works of the
law, but through faith in Jesus Christ."
Then, "we may be justified by faith in Christ
and not by works of the law." Having been,
in his pre-Christian life, an exemplary follower of the Law, Paul now asserts with
authority that "by the works of the law *no
one* will be justified." "Through the law I
died to the law" is a bit enigmatic, but
probably Paul means that the new "law of

GOSPEL   Luke 7:36—8:3

A reading from the holy Gospel according to Luke

A **Pharisee** invited **Jesus** to **dine** with him,
   and he entered the **Pharisee's house** and reclined at **table**.
Now there was a **sinful woman** in the city
   who **learned** that he was at table in the house of the **Pharisee**.
Bringing an alabaster flask of **ointment**,
   she stood behind him at his feet **weeping**
   and began to **bathe** his feet with her **tears**.
Then she **wiped** them with her **hair**,
   kissed them, and **anointed** them with the **ointment**.
When the Pharisee who had invited him **saw** this
     he said to himself,
  "If **this man** were a **prophet**,
  he would **know who** and **what sort** of **woman** this is
   who is **touching** him,
  that she is a **sinner**."
Jesus said to him in reply,
  "**Simon**, I have something to **say** to **you**."
"**Tell me**, teacher," he said.
"Two people were in **debt** to a certain **creditor**;
   one **owed five hundred** days' wages and the **other owed fifty**.
Since they were **unable** to **repay** the **debt**, he **forgave** it for **both**.
Which of them will **love** him **more**?"
Simon said in reply,
  "The **one**, I suppose, whose **larger** debt was forgiven."
He said to him, "You have judged **rightly**." »

If you tell the story as an invested disciple rather than an objective narrator, you'll convey more of the power of the drama.

The opening narration is brisk, but slow your delivery with the entrance of the woman.

Be sure you provide enough time for the assembly to visualize what you're describing. Fill this moment with tenderness and compassion.

This public intimacy is remarkable.

Suggest the cynical attitude of the Pharisee and his guests.

Jesus is play-acting to some degree, not revealing his intent to instruct Simon.

Ask the question in a good-natured way, aware that the answer is obvious.

Christ" has replaced the Mosaic law, causing him to abandon it.

During his years following his conversion, Paul became so close to Christ that he claims an entirely new life: "I live, no longer I, but Christ lives in me." This is not poetry, but a profound theological commitment born of Paul's deep relationship with Christ. What he teaches is also true for all who claim Christ as Lord. We, too, have died with him in Baptism and now share his new life. And though we "live in the flesh" as we await the fullness of glory, still even in the flesh we live, through faith, in Christ.

Paul plays his trump card at the end: if we still need the Law for salvation, then "Christ died for nothing." Paul is not throwing out the commandments; he sees those laws not as the *source* of life but as means of living the new life we receive (only) through Christ.

GOSPEL   The Pharisee host recognizes in Jesus someone special, perhaps a prophet. But when he invites him to his home he neglects the usual protocols of greeting him with a kiss, washing his feet, and anointing his head with oil. Is his heart too small to risk these customs on a risky man like Jesus whose pedigree is uncertain and whose friends make poor references?

The woman, whose reputation is known, seeks no place of honor and opts to rests at Jesus' feet. From there she can see that they're unwashed and lets her tears flow freely upon them. This remarkable intimacy makes up for the host's omission, but more importantly it testifies to what is happening in the woman's heart. Although the Pharisee doesn't know it, Jesus *has* read her heart and has seen not a "sinner" but a

Jesus' goal is to extol the woman, not to shame Simon. The host might yet open his eyes.

Jesus is honoring all the things that have likely scandalized the guests.

Jesus must speak authoritatively here to rouse the rancor of the other guests.

Here, Jesus' words are soft and compassionate.

Do the table guests speak in whispers or loud enough for him to hear?

As always with Jesus, it all boils down to faith.

Speak the names of his companions with familiarity and reverence.

The Gospel is proclaimed with the assistance of these faithful women.

Then he turned to the **woman** and said to **Simon**,
"Do you **see** this woman?
When I **entered** your house, **you** did **not** give me **water** for my **feet**,
but **she** has **bathed** them with her **tears**
and **wiped** them with her **hair**.
You did **not** give me a **kiss**,
but she has **not ceased kissing** my **feet** since the time I **entered**.
You did **not anoint** my head with **oil**,
but **she anointed** my **feet** with ointment.
So I **tell** you, **her many sins** have been **forgiven**
because **she** has shown **great love**.
But the one to whom **little** is forgiven, **loves little**."
He said to **her**, "**Your** sins are **forgiven**."
The **others** at table said to themselves,
"**Who is this** who even forgives **sins**?"
But he said to the **woman**,
"Your **faith** has **saved** you; go in **peace**."

Afterward he journeyed from **one town** and **village** to **another**,
preaching and **proclaiming** the **good news** of the **kingdom**
of **God**.
Accompanying him were the **Twelve**
and some **women** who had been **cured** of **evil spirits**
and **infirmities**,
Mary, called **Magdalene**, from whom seven **demons**
had gone out,
Joanna, the wife of **Herod's** steward **Chuza**,
Susanna, and many **others** who **provided** for them out
of their **resources**.

[Shorter: Luke 7:36–50]

penitent whose faith in God's mercy brought her to this place and to his feet. She *came* contrite and full of *faith*; Jesus welcomed her tears and her touch, and convinced her she'd come to the right place. Her forgiveness births great love that she pours abundantly upon the Lord.

As Jesus teaches in the parable of the two debtors, the one forgiven more loves more. The Pharisee, in his righteousness, receives but scant forgiveness and thus the love he shows to Jesus is scant. Forgiveness breeds love. That's why among Jesus' last commands to his disciples was

the forgiveness of sins. A praxis rooted in telling people how good they already are produces tepid lovers. But recognition of God's mercy in the face of our sinfulness produces disciples like this woman.

We might conclude that sinners have an advantage over the righteous because the forgiveness of their greater sins produces greater love. But the formula is not that simple. There were many sinners in this town, but only this woman fell at Jesus' feet. We remain agents in our own destiny. With Pope Francis we must remember that "God never tires of forgiving; it is we who

tire of asking forgiveness." And lest those of us who strive to do our best lose heart, let's not forget that no matter what, each of us is sinner enough to respond to God's mercy with abundant love. G.M.

TWELFTH SUNDAY IN ORDINARY TIME

LECTIONARY #96

READING I Zechariah 12:10–11, 13:1

A reading from the Book of the Prophet Zechariah

Thus says the LORD:
    I will **pour out** on the house of **David**
    and on the inhabitants of **Jerusalem**
    a **spirit** of **grace** and **petition**;
    and they shall **look** on him whom they have **pierced**,
    and they shall **mourn** for him as one mourns
        for an **only son**,
    and they shall **grieve** over him as one **grieves**
        over a **firstborn**.

On that **day** the mourning in **Jerusalem** shall be as **great**
    as the mourning of **Hadadrimmon** in the plain
        of **Megiddo**.

On **that** day there shall be **open** to the house of **David**
    and to the **inhabitants** of Jerusalem,
    a **fountain** to **purify** from **sin** and **uncleanness**.

Zechariah = zek-uh-RĪ-uh

Remember that God is using the people's natural guilt over murdering God's "suffering servant" to bring them to repentance and healing. God will transform sin into salvation!

Refer to the slain servant with pain and regret.

These are tears of healthy guilt and regret.

Josiah, the last of Israel's good kings died here, provoking universal mourning.

God's mercy is now imaged as a purifying fountain that removes all "uncleanness." The Church sees this prophecy fulfilled in the ministry of Jesus and in Baptism.

READING I This reading presents an odd juxtaposition. It begins with an outpouring of "grace and petition" that yields to mourning and grieving. How does "grace" lead to mourning? The answer points to the mysterious nature of the will of God. God may allow certain things to occur, even awful things that clearly violate his will, but the evil done is never the end of the story because God never ceases being an agent in human affairs. Zachariah speaks of God's just servant as one rejected and pierced by the hatred and the weapons of the people.

It may seem the prophet speaks words of chastisement and doom as solemn indictment on those who have acted against God's chosen servant. But in reality, he is prophesying hope and repentance that lead to salvation. The people's hearts have been opened and suddenly they understand the calamity they perpetrated.

Sometimes it is the very awareness of our sins that leads us to God. The courage to look honestly at what we have done and those whom we've hurt is a hallmark of some support groups such as Alcoholics Anonymous. Rather than demoralizing the individual, that kind of honesty and self-awareness leads to reconciliation and healing. That's what God is saying here through Zechariah: those who opposed God's servant will look upon his wounded body and regret what they have done. Their grief will be greater than any in Israel's history, greater than their mourning over good King Josiah, who was fatally wounded at Megiddo. Guilt is not always a bad thing; it can be the voice of God calling us back to his loving embrace.

For meditation and context:

RESPONSORIAL PSALM   Psalm 63:2, 3–4, 5–6, 8–9 (2b)

R. My soul is thirsting for you, O Lord my God.

O God, you are my God whom I seek;
  for you my flesh pines and my soul thirsts
  like the earth, parched, lifeless and
  without water.

Thus have I gazed toward you in the
  sanctuary
to see your power and your glory,
for your kindness is a greater good than life;
  my lips shall glorify you.

Thus will I bless you while I live;
  lifting up my hands, I will call upon your
  name.
As with the riches of a banquet shall my soul
  be satisfied,
  and with exultant lips my mouth shall
  praise you.

You are my help,
  and in the shadow of your wings I shout
  for joy.
My soul clings fast to you;
  your right hand upholds me.

TO KEEP IN MIND

When practicing, **read Scriptures aloud,** taking note of stress and pause suggestions. After several readings, alter the stress markings to suit your style and interpretation.

READING II   Galatians 3:26–29

Galatians = guh-LAY-shuhnz

A reading from the Letter of Saint Paul to the Galatians

The tone is immediately upbeat for you share the Good News of what we are now, as opposed to what we were. And what makes the difference is "faith." Stress it.
Don't rush the word "clothed." It's an important image.
Make eye contact as you list the categories that no longer apply. Speak with authority *and* joy.
Pause briefly after "Christ Jesus." Then renew your energy for the final sentence.

Even though we are Gentiles, through Christ, we inherit God's promises to his Chosen People.

Brothers and sisters:
Through **faith** you are **all** children of **God** in **Christ Jesus.**
For **all** of you who were **baptized** into Christ
  have **clothed** yourselves with **Christ.**
There is neither **Jew** nor **Greek,**
  there is neither **slave** nor **free** person,
  there is not **male** and **female;**
  for you are **all one** in Christ **Jesus.**
And if you **belong** to **Christ,**
  then you are **Abraham's descendant,**
  heirs according to the **promise.**

 Paul is contrasting our current and former states, but only the current state is discussed in today's reading. In the verses that precede today's text, Paul discusses our *prior* state (prior to coming to faith) when we were "held in custody under (the) law," and the law served as our "disciplinarian" (Galatians 3:23, 24). Our current state is quite different: "now that faith [in Christ] has come" (Galatians 3:25), he says, we have become "children of God" and no longer need a "disciplinarian" to watch over us. His image of now being "clothed" in Christ describes a

profound reality. Jesus is not just a peripheral aspect of who we now are, he is our whole identity. We are covered in Christ; defined and transformed by him. Now, instead of our distinct identities defined by race, ethnicity, social status, and gender, we wear a common identity and that is Christ. We can stop focusing on what differentiates us and focus instead on what unites us: Jesus the Lord.

Of course, our uniqueness remains; we have not become bland and homogenized. But our differences take a back seat to our oneness in Christ. To God they make

no difference whatsoever in terms of his love for us and our eternal salvation. Now, difference is not a way of distinguishing ourselves but of serving the whole; our unique gifts don't make us better they enable us to serve the body of Christ. What's more, our oneness in Christ makes us one even with all Christ's ancestors in faith. We, too, are now children of Abraham and heirs of the promise God bestowed on him and his descendants.

GOSPEL   Luke 9:18–24

A reading from the holy Gospel according to Luke

Once when **Jesus** was praying in **solitude**,
 and the **disciples** were with him,
 he **asked** them, "Who do the **crowds** say that I **am**?"
They said in reply, "John the **Baptist**;
 others, **Elijah**;
 still **others**, 'One of the ancient **prophets** has **arisen**.'"
Then he said to them, "But who do **you** say that I am?"
Peter said in reply, "The **Christ** of **God**."
He **rebuked** them
 and **directed** them **not** to **tell** this to **anyone**.

He said, "The Son of **Man** must **suffer greatly**
 and be **rejected** by the **elders**, the chief **priests**,
  and the **scribes**,
 and be **killed** and on the **third** day be **raised**."
Then he said to **all**,
 "If **anyone** wishes to come **after me**,
  he must **deny** himself
 and take up his **cross daily** and **follow** me.
For whoever wishes to **save** his life will **lose** it,
 but whoever **loses** his life for **my** sake will **save** it."

Assume the quiet, reflective mood of prayer both in the narration and Jesus' opening questions.

The disciples are eager to respond, offering what they may consider serious or absurd speculation.
Don't overdramatize Jesus' question.
A simple reading is best.
Peter's reply is full of conviction. He shares a privileged revelation not given to his companions.
Jesus' stern warning confirms that Peter got it right!
Be aware of how unwelcome and disorienting this information is for these men. Jesus is not lamenting, only informing them.

Establish good eye contact with the assembly because these, too, are disciples who need to understand the cost of discipleship. Take note of the words marked for stress.

GOSPEL   Jesus has managed to avoid crowds and find a quiet place for prayer. Luke typically depicts Jesus at prayer prior to a significant moment in his ministry. In this narrative, two significant events occur: Peter's confession and Jesus' first prediction of his Passion. The second may be the more likely reason for Jesus' focused time of prayer.

Emerging from that prayer time, Jesus asks about the crowd's opinion of him. Whether or not he already knew what the throng was speculating, it's likely that his real interest is in the disciples' perception of who he is. In his meditation, he may have prayed about the approaching menace of his suffering and Death and sensed, perhaps, the great threat to the disciples' faith that would represent. Prior to that fateful moment, they would need a strong grasp on his identity or they might be scattered never to be regathered.

Peter's reply constitutes a bedrock moment, especially in Luke's telling of this incident. In Matthew and Mark, when Jesus predicts his Passion following Peter's confession, Peter refuses to believe Jesus' prediction and, of course, is rebuked by the Lord. Here, there is no such rejection or rebuke. Jesus can tell the disciples about the trials to come with confidence that that knowledge won't compromise their understanding of who he is. He can even require that they *daily* take up of their own crosses in order to imitate him, thus acquiring all by surrendering all. Note that Luke adds "daily" to counter the impression that disciples would soon suffer and die. G.M.

THIRTEENTH SUNDAY IN ORDINARY TIME

LECTIONARY #99

READING I   1 Kings 19:16b, 19–21

A reading from the first Book of Kings

The LORD said to **Elijah**:
"You shall anoint **Elisha**, son of **Shaphat** of **Abel-meholah**,
as **prophet** to **succeed** you."

Elijah set out and came upon **Elisha**, son of **Shaphat**,
as he was **plowing** with **twelve yoke** of **oxen**;
he was **following** the **twelfth**.
Elijah went **over** to him and **threw** his **cloak** over him.
Elisha left the oxen, **ran** after **Elijah**, and **said**,
"**Please**, let me **kiss** my **father** and **mother goodbye**,
and I will **follow** you."
Elijah answered, "**Go back!**
Have I done **anything** to you?"
Elisha left him, and taking the yoke of **oxen**, **slaughtered** them;
he used the **plowing** equipment for **fuel** to **boil** their **flesh**,
and gave it to his **people** to **eat**.
Then **Elisha left** and **followed Elijah** as his **attendant**.

God is *not* displeased. The great prophet Elijah, who fought mightily against idolatry, will eventually need a successor; Elisha will become his apprentice until that time. Practice distinguishing "Elijah" (ee-LĪ-juh) from "Elisha" (ee-LĪ-shuh).

Shaphat = SHAY-fat
Abel-meholah = AY-b*l-muh-HOH-lah
Emphasize the number of oxen.

A "cloak" represented the personality and authority of its owner.

Elisha is not denied this courtesy.

The import of this line is: "I'm not stopping you."

Elisha is leaving behind all claims to his family wealth.

And, eventually, Elijah's successor.

READING I   Today's collection of stories about the stern requirements of discipleship begins with a brief scene from the life of the prophet Elijah, and that scene unfolds from a previous episode in the prophet's life. Fleeing possible assassination at the hands of Queen Jezebel, Elijah retreats to Mt. Horeb, the same mountain where Moses encountered the Lord. God asks why he's come there and Elijah describes the danger. Immediately, God says, "Go back," and without hesitation Elijah does. God also orders Elijah to seek out Elisha and anoint him as his successor. God has graced Elijah with a divine encounter, but this experience of the Lord must be enough to sustain Elijah as he returns to his anointed ministry as God's prophet.

The dramatic gesture of Elijah casting his cloak upon the young man signifies God's call to Elisha to assume the prophetic ministry of Elijah. The youth knows wealth, for he follows "*twelve* yoke of oxen," a clear sign of a family of means. Elisha is immediately willing to leave all this behind and even offers his animals and equipment as sacrifices to the Lord. When he asks the indulgence to bid farewell to his family, Elijah asks in effect, "Who's stopping you?" Not an enthusiastic approval, but clearly a less demanding standard than what Jesus will articulate in today's Gospel.

Discipleship ultimately requires everything of us. Elijah had to be willing to lose his life, Elisha to place his family and wealth behind his call. There are times for moderation and times that brook no compromise. Through God's grace we pray to know the difference.

For meditation and context:

TO KEEP IN MIND
You'll read more naturally if you read **ideas rather than words,** and if you share **images rather than sentences.**

RESPONSORIAL PSALM   Psalm 16:1–2, 5, 7–8, 9–10, 11 (see 5a)

R. You are my inheritance, O Lord.

Keep me, O God, for in you I take refuge;
    I say to the LORD, "My Lord are you."
O LORD, my allotted portion and my cup,
    you it is who hold fast my lot.

I bless the LORD who counsels me;
    even in the night my heart exhorts me.
I set the LORD ever before me;
    with him at my right hand I shall not be
    disturbed.

Therefore my heart is glad and my soul
    rejoices,
    my body, too, abides in confidence,
because you will not abandon my soul to the
    netherworld,
    nor will you suffer your faithful one to
    undergo corruption.

You will show me the path to life,
    fullness of joys in your presence,
    the delights at your right hand forever.

Galatians = guh-LAY-shuhnz

Christian "freedom" means we don't have to save ourselves by observing the Law; we keep the Law in order to love fully. Stress only "freedom" in the second line.

The "yoke of slavery": Paul is saying, don't trade one form of slavery for another.

Speak as if to a group you taught and loved that is now backsliding. Persuade them they must hold on to the truth they learned.

God's Law requires "love," not circumcision.

Apparently, Paul is concerned about destructive behaviors among the Galatians.

Make use of the clear balances in these lines to underscore Paul's message of the opposition of "flesh" and "Spirit."

End on a note of Good News: freedom is yours in the Spirit!

READING II   Galatians 5:1, 13–18

A reading from the Letter of Saint Paul to the Galatians

Brothers and **sisters**:
For **freedom Christ** set us free;
    so stand **firm** and do not submit **again** to the yoke of **slavery**.

For **you** were called for **freedom**, brothers and sisters.
But do **not** use this **freedom**
    as an opportunity for the **flesh**;
    rather, **serve** one another through **love**.
For the **whole law** is fulfilled in **one statement**,
    namely, *You shall **love** your **neighbor** as **yourself**.*
But if you go on **biting** and **devouring** one another,
    beware that you are not **consumed** by one another.

I say, then: **live** by the **Spirit**
    and you will certainly not **gratify** the **desire** of the **flesh**.
For the **flesh** has **desires against** the **Spirit**,
    and the **Spirit** against the **flesh**;
    these are **opposed** to each other,
    so that you may **not do** what you **want**.
But if **you** are **guided** by the **Spirit**, you are **not** under the **law**.

READING II The "freedom" of the Kingdom Paul speaks of is not licentiousness or even libertarianism (understood as being able to do or say what you want without interference). In the Bible, being free is less about "freedom *from*" and more about "freedom *for*." Paul continues his argument against false teachers who insist that, for salvation, Gentile converts needed circumcision as well as Christ. Paul rails against that lie. Christ freed us from reliance on the requirements of the old Law. We are saved by faith in him, not by our works. But, he cautions, we mustn't use this freedom to indulge the "flesh," which here does not mean only inappropriate sexual desires but *everything* in our human nature that draws us away from God—jealousy, anger, selfishness, addiction, quarreling, dissensions, and so forth.

What we are freed *for* is love of God and neighbor, and we love the "neighbor" as we love ourselves. Here *"as"* means not "in the same way," but "at the same time." True love is never self-centered and never excludes the other. Only when we truly love ourselves with the love God has for us can we also love others with God's love. If we don't love ourselves, love of others may simply manifest insecurity or the desire to control and get others to love *us*. Such pure love is possible only in the *Spirit*. "Spirit" and "flesh" are not presented here as opposites, flesh being our worldly nature and Spirit our higher nature. Spirit is capitalized because it refers to God's Spirit, who helps us overcome our weaknesses in order to live in the liberating freedom of God.

GOSPEL   Luke 9:51–62

A reading from the holy Gospel according to Luke

When the days for **Jesus'** being **taken up** were **fulfilled,**
  he **resolutely** determined to **journey** to **Jerusalem,**
  and he sent **messengers** ahead of him.
On the **way** they entered a **Samaritan** village
  to **prepare** for his **reception** there,
  but they would **not welcome** him
  because the **destination** of his **journey** was **Jerusalem.**
When the disciples **James** and **John** saw this they **asked,**
  "**Lord,** do you want us to call down **fire** from **heaven**
  to **consume** them?"
Jesus **turned** and **rebuked** them, and they journeyed
  to **another** village.

As they were **proceeding** on their journey someone **said** to him,
  "I will **follow** you **wherever** you go."
Jesus **answered** him,
  "**Foxes** have **dens** and birds of the **sky** have **nests,**
  but the **Son** of **Man** has **nowhere** to rest his head."

And to **another** he said, "**Follow** me."
But **he** replied, "**Lord,** let me go **first** and bury my **father.**"
But he **answered** him, "Let the **dead** bury their **dead.**
But **you,** go and **proclaim** the **kingdom** of **God.**"
And **another** said, "**I will follow** you, Lord,
  but **first** let **me** say **farewell** to my family at **home.**"
To **him** Jesus said, "**No one** who sets a **hand** to the **plow**
  and **looks** to what was left **behind** is **fit** for the **kingdom**
  of **God.**"

The text begins on a sober note alluding to Jesus' upcoming Passion. Stress Jesus' resolute determination and his plans for the journey.

Begin upbeat, so the rejection in Samaria surprises us. Their hostility toward "Jerusalem" leads to Jesus' rejection.

The disciples' righteous anger blinds them to the ways of the Kingdom.

This potential disciple is all eagerness!

Jesus does not sugar-coat the demands of discipleship, which he himself has embraced first.

If the youth followed Jesus and then the need arose to bury his father, surely Jesus would give him leave. The point is the primacy of the call.
This disciple seems already half-turned away to go say "farewell."
Sometimes filial piety takes precedence (as with Elisha) but other times nothing can be permitted to distract us from our calling.
Don't let this be a harsh injunction, but a call to heroic fidelity.

GOSPEL   The Samaritan's inhospitality aroused the ire of James and John. The town rejected Jesus solely because his destination was Jerusalem, revealing the historically based hostility between Samaritans and Jews. But Jesus rebukes their call for violence, accepts rejection on this leg of his journey as he did at the start of his Galilean ministry, and refuses to be distracted from what awaits in Jerusalem. His resolute determination sets the stage for the difficult sayings that follow.

To the first would-be disciple, Jesus announces the radical poverty of "the Son of Man" (and his disciples!). To a second, he speaks of the dead burying the dead. Variously interpreted, this saying likely addresses the potential disciple's desire to delay till his father's eventual death, using that family obligation as an excuse to avoid following Jesus. Or, if the father had recently died, he may be seeking a year's reprieve in order to rebury the father's bones after the body has decayed. Even if the meaning is, "Let the *spiritually* dead bury their dead" the point remains that

nothing is to supersede one's commitment to the Gospel. Clearly, Jesus' blunt language gets our attention and shocks us into reflection on the requirements of discipleship.

The last saying asks all disciples to imitate Jesus in resisting distractions from the call of the Gospel. Jesus remains resolutely turned toward Jerusalem, his hand firmly on "the plow." Speak that last proverb not as criticism, but like a call to radical commitment that always stays the course. G.M.

FOURTEENTH SUNDAY IN ORDINARY TIME

LECTIONARY #102

READING I Isaiah 66:10–14c

Isaiah = ī-ZAY-uh

Don't weaken the power of Isaiah's words by holding back on these striking images.

The text consists of couplets that repeat in the second line what was said in the first. To avoid sounding redundant, increase energy from the first to the second line.
Remember, you are speaking these words as if to survivors of a great ordeal. Let them soothe and comfort.

God is promising to do the impossible, so speak with authority, but also with persuasive love.

Jerusalem is depicted as a nursing mother; in short order, God appropriates that same image.

The final lines speak of the future. Speak slowly and with great conviction that "heart" and "bodies" will be transformed by the Lord's "power."

A reading from the Book of the Prophet Isaiah

Thus says the LORD:
Rejoice with **Jerusalem** and be **glad** because of her,
   all **you** who **love** her;
exult, **exult** with her,
   all **you** who were **mourning** over her!
Oh, that you may suck **fully**
   of the **milk** of her **comfort**,
that you may **nurse** with **delight**
   at her **abundant** breasts!
   For **thus** says the LORD:
Lo, I will spread **prosperity** over **Jerusalem** like a **river**,
   and the **wealth** of the **nations** like an **overflowing torrent**.
As **nurslings**, you shall be **carried** in her **arms**,
   and **fondled** in her **lap**;
as a **mother comforts** her **child**,
   so will **I comfort you**;
   in **Jerusalem** you shall **find** your **comfort**.

When you **see** this, your heart shall **rejoice**
   and your bodies **flourish** like the **grass**;
the LORD's **power** shall be **known** to his **servants**.

READING I Today's First Reading comes from the later part of the Book of the Prophet Isaiah. Scholars believe that the preachings of three different gifted prophets appears in this book: "First Isaiah," from the period just before the destruction of Jerusalem and deportation of its leaders (chapters 1–39), "Second Isaiah," from the period of the exile in Babylon (chapters 40–55), and "Third Isaiah," who ministered after the exiles' return to Jerusalem (chapters 55–66). These last chapters of Third Isaiah are full of hopeful visions and images, like the one

in today's reading. In verses 7–9, just before this reading begins, the author describes a new, divinely-expedited birth for mother Jerusalem—a birth that unfolds quickly and without labor pains. That is where today's verses pick up.

Sensuous and bold, today's images present God endowing mother Jerusalem with all the nurturing character she needs to comfort and nourish her children. After the long ordeal of exile, the people hear joyous news of exile's end and of return to the home of their forbears. City and Temple lay in utter ruin, but the people will

rejoice because God will undo the destruction and "spread prosperity . . . like a river." Within the rebuilt walls of the devastated city the people will be comforted "as a mother comforts her child." They are urged to celebrate and be suckled by the new mother Israel.

Imagine a family grieving the loss of their family home or a community rebuilding after a tornado decimated their city. Speak these tender words to individual hearts, offering them visions of hope and newness. This is not the text of a political speech, but healing words meant for broken

For meditation and context:

RESPONSORIAL PSALM Psalm 66:1–3, 4–5, 6–7, 16, 20 (1)

R. Let all the earth cry out to God with joy.

Shout joyfully to God, all the earth;
    sing praise to the glory of his name;
    proclaim his glorious praise.
Say to God, "How tremendous are your
    deeds!"

"Let all on earth worship and sing praise to
    you,
    sing praise to your name!"
Come and see the works of God,
    his tremendous deeds among the children
    of Adam.

He changed the sea into dry land;
    through the river they passed on foot;
therefore let us rejoice in him.
    He rules by his might forever.

Hear now, all you who fear God,
    while I declare what he has done for me.
Blessed be God who refused me not
    my prayer or his kindness!

TO KEEP IN MIND

Pace: The rate at which you read is influenced by the size of your church, the size of the congregation, and the complexity of the text. As each increases, rate decreases.

READING II Galatians 6:14–18

A reading from the Letter of Saint Paul to the Galatians

Brothers and **sisters**:
May I **never boast** except in the **cross** of our **Lord Jesus Christ**,
    through which the **world** has been **crucified** to me,
    and **I** to the **world**.
For **neither** does **circumcision** mean **anything**,
    nor does **uncircumcision**,
    but only a **new creation**.
Peace and **mercy** be to all who **follow** this **rule**
    and to the **Israel** of **God**.

From now **on**, let **no one** make **troubles** for me;
    for I **bear** the **marks** of **Jesus** on my **body**.

The **grace** of our **Lord Jesus Christ** be with your **spirit**,
    brothers and **sisters**. **Amen**.

Galations = guh-LAY-shuhnz

This is the fifth consecutive week we read from Galatians. Here, Paul is both teacher and a healer, so his tone cannot be abrasive.

Pause after "boast" and then forcefully state of what one *can* boast—the Cross of Christ!

Don't stress what doesn't matter, but what does—"a new creation." Your listeners are that new creation!

This is a *prayer* for peace for all who follow Christ.

Don't let these words sound whining or bragging; Paul considers his suffering a privilege.
End with a prayer that sounds like a prayer.

---

hearts. Surely, many in your assembly need the succoring love of a mother and the reassurance found at her "abundant breasts."

 Throughout this letter, Paul has been defending his authority and the authenticity of his Gospel teaching against other teachers who insisted that his dismissal of circumcision was a wrong-minded accommodation made only to win easy converts. While these false teachers insisted that pagans had to be circumcised when they embraced the Gospel, Paul asserted nothing more

was needed for salvation than the Cross of Christ. Of course, Paul was right and it was no minor source of irritation to him that he needed to debate this point with the meddlers who followed him in Galatia and took upon themselves the mantle of teacher.

For Paul, the Gospel message is simple and unfettered: embrace the cross and salvation is yours. But his opponents insisted Paul wrongly left out requirements of the Mosaic Law. Paul is overwhelmed by the realization that in Christ we are made entirely new and become heirs of the salvation he won through his blood. He has no

patience with those who would assert that more than Christ is needed.

Because he has been making this argument throughout the letter, Paul now concludes with a request that he not be bothered again with these false assertions. And what he cites as reason to stop making "trouble" for him are the very bruises he bears on his own body for preaching the authentic Gospel of Christ. He has been beaten and stoned for his missionary work and he lets his wounds and scars speak for him and the authenticity of his ministry.

GOSPEL   Luke 10:1–12, 17–20

A reading from the holy Gospel according to Luke

At **that** time the **Lord** appointed seventy-two **others**
   whom he sent **ahead** of him in **pairs**
   to every **town** and **place** he intended to **visit**.
He **said** to them,
   "The **harvest** is **abundant** but the **laborers** are **few**;
   so ask the **master** of the **harvest**
   to send out **laborers** for his **harvest**.
Go **on** your way;
   behold, I am sending you like **lambs** among **wolves**.
Carry no **money bag**, no **sack**, no **sandals**;
   and greet **no one** along the **way**.
Into whatever **house** you enter, **first** say,
   '**Peace** to this **household**.'
If a peaceful person **lives** there,
   your **peace** will **rest** on him;
   but if **not**, it will **return** to you.
Stay in the **same house** and **eat** and **drink** what is **offered** to you,
   for the **laborer deserves** his **payment**.
Do **not** move **about** from **one** house to **another**. »

As the Twelve were sent to the tribes of Israel, the seventy-two are sent to the nations, believed to be seventy-two in number.

In all he says, the solicitousness of Jesus for his disciples is strongly apparent. "So ask . . . " is more prayer than admonition.

He warns them of the dangers ahead.

Don't overdramatize the instructions; Jesus is preparing them for their labors, not telling a story.

Jesus anticipates the frustrations they may encounter and the remedies they may be tempted to utilize.

Speak this declaration with authority.

> **TO KEEP IN MIND**
> **A substantial pause** always follows "A reading from" and both precedes and follows "The word [Gospel] of the Lord."

Paul's love for his Galatian converts will not allow disagreement to compromise his brotherly relationship with them. So, he concludes the letter with warm words of blessing, acknowledging even those who have questioned his teaching as "brothers and sisters."

GOSPEL   The joy of those who return to the nurturing arms of Jerusalem in today's First Reading becomes the joy of those who proclaim the Gospel of Christ to the nations. This joy is the fruit of a job well done, announcing to those who

would and would not hear it that the advent of God's Kingdom is among us.

This text might make us reexamine the oft quoted maxim, wrongly attributed to St. Francis of Assisi, that one should preach the Gospel at all times and, when necessary, use words. (Although this idea reflects Francis' spirit, these words cannot be found in what he left behind.) Rightly understood, the maxim conveys deep truth, but it may also obscure the truth Jesus is communicating here, that it is not we, but he, who brings the truth and the fullness of the Kingdom. In fact, the sev-

enty-two are told to *speak* words both to those who accept and those who reject their ministry, and in each case the words are the same: "the kingdom of God is at hand for you." The Gospel is the saving work of *Jesus*; it is not an idea but an event, a historical moment that perdures throughout time. Our task is to announce that event and the person at its center. And to do that, as Jesus instructed, we must use words.

Paul underscores that truth in Romans where he says that "everyone who calls on the name of the Lord will be saved" and

Whatever **town** you **enter** and they **welcome** you,
　　eat what is set **before** you,
　　cure the **sick** in it and **say** to them,
　　'The **kingdom** of **God** is **at hand** for **you**.'
Whatever town you **enter** and they do **not** receive you,
　　go out into the **streets** and **say**,
　　'The **dust** of your **town** that **clings** to our **feet**,
　　even that we **shake off against** you.'
Yet know **this**: the **kingdom** of **God** is at **hand**.
I **tell** you,
　　it will be **more** tolerable for **Sodom** on that day
　　　　than for **that** town."

The seventy-two returned **rejoicing**, and said,
　　"**Lord**, even the **demons** are **subject** to us because
　　　　of your **name**."
Jesus said, "I have observed **Satan** fall like **lightning**
　　from the **sky**.
Behold, I have given you the **power** to 'tread' upon **serpents'**
　　and **scorpions**
　　and upon the **full force** of the **enemy**
　　　　and **nothing** will **harm** you.
Nevertheless, do **not rejoice** because the **spirits** are **subject** to you,
　　but **rejoice** because your **names** are **written** in **heaven**."

[Shorter: Luke 10:1–9]

Speak without malice, but with stern warning.

Jesus' prophecy is not without compassion.

Pause briefly, then begin with renewed energy.

Jesus is downplaying their enthusiasm.

To paraphrase: "Yes," he says calmly, "you have received power . . . "

"But here is the true cause for rejoicing!"

TO KEEP IN MIND
Read all three commentaries.
Suggestions in each can give you insight into your own passage.

---

then asks, "But how can they call on him in whom they have not believed? And how can they believe in him of whom they have not heard? And how can they hear without someone to preach?" (Romans 10:14). Significantly, Jesus sends out these disciples to prepare the way for his own ministry to the towns. Through deeds and words they are to till the soil Jesus will sow with seed.

　　The instructions Jesus gives are sober and remarkably detailed. After alerting them to the dangers they will face as "lambs" among "wolves," he details what they can bring, where they can stay, what they can say and eat, and how they are to respond to inhospitable towns. Little is left to chance. They return enthusing at their power over demons, but Jesus responds by reminding them their power came from him and that it is salvation, not power, that is the only real cause of rejoicing. G.M.

FIFTEENTH SUNDAY IN ORDINARY TIME

LECTIONARY #105

READING I   Deuteronomy 30:10–14

Deuteronomy = d<u>oo</u>-ter-AH-nuh-mee or dy<u>oo</u>-ter-AH-nuh-mee

Be sure your assembly hears who the speaker is.
Let Moses speak the first sentence with solemn authority.

The balance of the text is a cold dose of reality splashed upon the people.

Don't make these analogies overly serious. Moses is clearly exaggerating to make his point: You don't have to fly to the heavens or cross the sea to get this!

There is an implied "No!" at the end of each hypothetical.

Pause before the final sentence. This is the climax of the text and the heart of his message.

A reading from the Book of Deuteronomy

Moses said to the **people**:
"If **only** you would **heed** the **voice** of the LORD, your **God**,
    and keep his **commandments** and **statutes**
    that are **written** in this **book** of the **law**,
    when you **return** to the LORD, your **God**,
    with **all** your **heart** and **all** your **soul**.

"For this **command** that I **enjoin** on you **today**
    is **not** too **mysterious** and **remote** for you.
It is **not** up in the **sky**, that you should say,
    '**Who** will **go up** in the **sky** to **get** it for us
    and **tell** us of it, that we may **carry** it **out**?'
Nor is it across the **sea**, that you should say,
    '**Who** will **cross** the **sea** to **get** it for us
    and **tell** us of it, that we may **carry** it **out**?'
No, it is something **very near** to **you**,
    already in your **mouths** and in your **hearts**;
    you have **only** to **carry it out**."

READING I   The human capacity to rationalize and make excuses often exceeds the willingness to embrace tough challenges. Moses has just placed a tough challenge before the Israelites. Defining fidelity to God as obedience to the Law of the Lord, Moses urges "keep his commandments"! But as soon as he admonishes, it seems he senses hesitation, a barely perceptible step backward in the heart that indicates the people's reluctance to exchange their ways for God's. Moses won't allow that weed even a moment to take hold.

To paraphrase his message: Don't think what I've just laid upon you is too much for you. Don't convince yourselves that these are remote rules you will need a learned rabbi to untangle. Don't think you'll have to climb a mountain of knowledge to understand what God requires or undertake a journey of education and study to be able to grasp it. This Law that comes from God comes not from without, but from within your own hearts. Each time you breathe you draw it in, with each exhale it issues from your mouth!

There is great passion and urgency in Moses' message to the people. They have come to the end of their desert wanderings and soon will enter the Promised Land. This instruction is Moses' gift of wisdom. Heed this, he exhorts, and you will walk the road that leads to life. Don't make it harder or more complicated than it is! Just listen to the echo in your heart. Moses' last sentence combines tenderness, compassion, and a parent's solicitous love into words meant to spare the child of needless pain. It could be so simple, he says, if you would only "carry it out."

For meditation and context:

RESPONSORIAL PSALM Psalm 69:14, 17, 30–31, 33–34, 36, 37 (see 33)

R. Turn to the Lord in your need, and you will live.

I pray to you, O LORD,
　for the time of your favor, O God!
In your great kindness answer me
　with your constant help.
Answer me, O LORD, for bounteous is your
　kindness;
　in your great mercy turn toward me.

I am afflicted and in pain;
　let your saving help, O God, protect me.
I will praise the name of God in song,
　and I will glorify him with thanksgiving.

"See, you lowly ones, and be glad;
　you who seek God, may your hearts
　revive!
For the LORD hears the poor,
　and his own who are in bonds he spurns
　not."

For God will save Zion
　and rebuild the cities of Judah.
The descendants of his servants shall inherit
　it,
　and those who love his name shall inhabit
　it.

or:

For meditation and context:

RESPONSORIAL PSALM Psalm 19:8, 9, 10, 11 (9a)

R. Your words, Lord, are Spirit and life.

The law of the LORD is perfect,
　refreshing the soul.
The decree of the LORD is trustworthy,
　giving wisdom to the simple.

The precepts of the LORD are right,
　rejoicing the heart.
The command of the LORD is clear,
　enlightening the eye.

The fear of the LORD is pure,
　enduring forever.
The ordinances of the LORD are true,
　all of them just.

They are more precious than gold,
　than a heap of purest gold;
sweeter also than syrup
　or honey from the comb.

READING II   Colossians 1:15–20

A reading from the Letter of Saint Paul to the Colossians

Christ Jesus is the **image** of the **invisible God**,
　the **firstborn** of **all creation**.
For in **him** were **created** all things in **heaven** and on **earth**,
　the **visible** and the **invisible**,
　whether **thrones** or **dominions** or **principalities** or **powers**;
　all things were **created through him** and **for him**.

Colossians = kuh-LOSH-uhnz

Start with strength making the first statement a declaration of your own faith.

He is leading to the assertion that even the angelic beings were created by Christ, so none can be superior to him.

READING II Christians came early to a cosmic understanding of Christ, discerning in one who was of flesh and blood the eternal Lord through whom all things were created. Yet the church in Colossae was threatened by false teachers who emphasized the role of angels in the work of salvation deemphasizing Christ's singular role.

　Though imprisoned, Paul has been enlisted to write a rebuttal to these false teachers that asserts the singularity of Christ and underscores his unique role. This Paul does in the form of the magnificent hymn that comprises today's entire text. Paul uses this song (that probably was already in use within the community at Colossae) to state that whatever angelic powers may exist none supersedes Christ, for all power to save resides solely in him. Christ, he says, is the "firstborn" of creation, and all that exits in heaven and earth was made *through* him. Even the angels, no matter what their rank—("thrones or dominions or . . . powers")—were created through him and for him.

　Twice, Paul calls Jesus "firstborn"—"of all creation" and "from the dead." Both declarations assert his primacy as the creator of all things and as the one who makes it possible for all to rise from the dead as he did. Because of its ancient use as a hymn of praise and because of the sublime truth it teaches, this text requires energy, conviction, awe, gratitude, and joy. Imagine someone denying Christ's identity or the necessity of his saving work. These words are an impassioned appeal to a faith that enlightens and sustains. After all, despite the joy, the text concludes by reminding us that the work of salvation was accomplished through the shedding of

Rejoice in this assertion; rather than arguing the point, celebrate Christ's dominion over all things.

His "body, the church" is sitting right in front of you. Speak to them.

The New Revised Standard Version reads: "For in Christ all the fullness of God was pleased to dwell, and through him God was pleased to reconcile to himself all things, whether on earth or in heaven, by making peace through the blood of his Cross."

Slow down for the final line that introduces the sobering reminder that what Christ did he did at great cost.

He is **before** all things,
  and in **him** all things **hold together**.
He is the **head** of the **body**, the **church**.
He is the **beginning**, the **firstborn** from the **dead**,
  that in **all** things he himself might be **preeminent**.
For in **him** all the **fullness** was pleased to **dwell**,
  and **through** him to **reconcile** all things for **him**,
  making **peace** by the **blood** of his **cross**
  through him, whether those on **earth** or those in **heaven**.

GOSPEL   Luke 10:25–37

A reading from the holy Gospel according to Luke

There was a scholar of the **law** who stood up to **test** him and said,
  "**Teacher**, what must I **do** to inherit **eternal life**?"
Jesus **said** to him, "What is **written** in the **law**?
How do **you** read it?"
He said in reply,
  "*You shall love the Lord, your God,*
  with all your heart,
  with all your being,
  with all your strength,
  and with all your mind,
  and your neighbor as yourself."
He **replied** to him, "You have answered **correctly**;
  do this and you will **live**."

But because he wished to **justify** himself, he said to **Jesus**,
  "And **who** is my **neighbor**?"
Jesus replied,
  "A **man** fell **victim** to **robbers**
  as he went down from **Jerusalem** to **Jericho**.
They **stripped** and **beat** him and went **off leaving** him **half-dead**. ❯❯

Let your tone signal that the man's motivation is insincere.

Jesus is aware of the lawyer's insincerity.

The man is learned and gives the "right" answer.

Jesus seems content to leave it at that and move on.

But the lawyer is determined to hear more from Jesus.

Now we see that Jesus had more to say all along. He dives into the story with energy.

Christ's blood—a sobering note at the end of a jubilant anthem. Because the translation of the final sentence of the text is rather obscure, the margin notes provide an alternative translation.

GOSPEL   The lawyer's lack of sincerity, signaled by his intent to "test" Jesus, elicits a polite response but no effort from Jesus to engage him. We get the impression that, if the lawyer did not ask his follow up question, the Lord might have simply walked on to attend to other business. It's the lawyer's desire to "justify himself" that casts a net into which Jesus willingly steps.

The legal expert has already demonstrated a clear grasp of the Mosaic Law, quoting a composite of Leviticus (19:18), Deuteronomy (6:5), and Joshua (22:5) to answer Jesus' question about the teaching of the law. But Jesus will now take him much further in his understanding by demonstrating that the "neighbor" he seeks can even be one he despises as an enemy. Because cultural and religious history had turned Jews and Samaritans into bitter opponents, Jesus casts a Samaritan as hero of his story in order to demonstrate the primacy of love.

Jesus intentionally scripts the story to include a "priest" and "Levite" and places them in a context that contrasts the demands of love with the legalism that infected the religion of the day like a cancer. Many Levites who served as Temple assistants in the Jerusalem Temple, lived in Jericho, about seventeen miles away. The road between was known to be dangerous; in fact, one stretch was called the "way of blood" because of frequent robberies and killings.

Jesus' narration should not betray a negative attitude toward "priest" or "Levite."

Note the extensive detail Jesus provides. The Samaritan is going to extraordinary lengths.

"The next day" starts a new beat. Begin with renewed energy.

Jesus' question requires insight and conversion.

The lawyer doesn't hesitate to name the virtue that distinguished the Samaritan as "neighbor." Pause briefly after "The one . . . ." Then, with sincerity, share the rest of his response.

Picture Jesus looking directly into the eyes of the lawyer. Jesus' words are a call to deep conversion.

A **priest** happened to be going down that road,
　　but when he **saw** him, he **passed by** on the **opposite** side.
Likewise a **Levite** came to the place,
　　and when **he saw** him, **he passed by** on the **opposite** side.
But a **Samaritan** traveler who came upon him
　　was moved with **compassion** at the sight.
He **approached** the victim,
　　poured oil and **wine** over his **wounds** and **bandaged** them.
Then he **lifted** him up on his own **animal**,
　　took him to an **inn**, and **cared** for him.
The **next** day he took out **two** silver **coins**
　　and **gave** them to the **innkeeper** with the instruction,
　　'Take **care** of him.
If you **spend more** than what I have **given** you,
　　I shall **repay** you on my way **back**.'
Which of these three, in **your** opinion,
　　was **neighbor** to the robbers' victim?"
He answered, "The **one** who **treated** him with **mercy**."
Jesus said to him, "**Go** and **do likewise**."

The priest and Levite observe the strict requirements of the Law, staying away from the victim in order to avoid ritual impurity on their way to serve in the Temple. But Jesus seeks to show a better way and his role model is a social outcast—a Samaritan who goes well beyond even reasonable expectations to care for the victim. He washes and anoints the man and then bandages him, probably with torn strips of his own clothing. He leaves a large amount of money for his care and promises more if that is not enough.

Now Jesus asks the lawyer to answer his own question about which one was the neighbor. While some commentators sense an unwillingness to let the word "Samaritan" cross his lips, the lawyer actually speaks something far more important: he names the virtue that makes one neighbor; namely, "mercy." Mercy is the attribute of God that makes us like him. Only with a merciful heart can we love our neighbor as ourselves. Whether the lawyer will "go and do likewise" we do not know. But that he now understands what's needed to *be* a neighbor is clear indeed. G.M.

SIXTEENTH SUNDAY IN ORDINARY TIME

LECTIONARY #108

READING I Genesis 18:1–10a

A reading from the Book of Genesis

The LORD appeared to **Abraham** by the **terebinth** of **Mamre**,
    as he sat in the **entrance** of his **tent**,
    while the day was growing **hot**.
Looking **up**, Abraham saw **three men standing** nearby.
When he **saw** them, he **ran** from the entrance of the tent
        to **greet** them;
    and **bowing** to the ground, he said:
    "**Sir**, if I may ask you this **favor**,
    please do not go on **past** your servant.
Let some **water** be brought, that you may **bathe** your **feet**,
    and then **rest** yourselves under the **tree**.
Now that you have come this **close** to your **servant**,
    let me **bring** you a little **food**, that you may **refresh** yourselves;
    and **afterward** you may go on your **way**."
The **men** replied, "**Very well**, **do** as you have **said**."

Abraham **hastened** into the tent and told **Sarah**,
    "**Quick**, three measures of fine **flour**! **Knead** it
        and **make rolls**."
He **ran** to the **herd**, picked out a **tender**, **choice steer**,
    and gave it to a **servant**, who quickly **prepared** it.
Then Abraham got some curds and **milk**,
    as well as the **steer** that had been prepared, »

Wait till all are settled, then announce that the "Lord" appeared to Abraham.
Terebinth = TAYR-uh-binth
Mamre = MAHM-ray

Narrate from Abraham's point of view: At first, he has no idea who the three are, but then senses the presence of divinity.

Note that he addresses the visitors in the singular.

He indicates that he will make little fuss, but then goes overboard.

"Do as you have said," should convey pleasure and gratitude.

His instructions to Sarah should convey a desire to serve rather than to impress his guests.

Slow the pace here to indicate his ability to focus on and be present to the guests.

READING I Abraham hurries and fusses over his visitors. In the Gospel, Martha does the same. Yet she receives a corrective, while Abraham receives the promise of a son. The difference is that Abraham was fully focused on his visitors. In a sense, Abraham plays both Mary and Martha in this story because after a level of preparations that would have been judged excessive, even in that culture, he stands by his visitors as they dine in order to be attentive to every need and every question.

The identity of the guests is ambiguous, compounded by the shifts in language between singular and plural. But Abraham's response to the guests signals his awareness that he is hosting *divine* visitors. Despite his age, he "runs" to greet them and instead of the simple meal he offers ("water . . . a little food") he prepares a feast. Sarah is told to knead "three measures" (half a bushel!) of flour while the servants slaughter and prepare a tender calf. Highlight all those extravagant details.

But more than providing for the physical needs of the travelers, Abraham opens himself to hear the word they have to speak. The better part of hospitality is attentiveness to the guest and what *they* have to offer. Busyness that prevents real focus on the other is not true hospitality.

God promised descendants to Abraham, but in his old age he's lost hope that they will come through his wife, Sarah. The divine messenger is clear: God's promise will be fulfilled through Sarah and her role in God's plan will be forever secured.

and **set** these before the three men;
and he **waited** on them under the **tree** while they **ate**.

They **asked** Abraham, "**Where** is your wife **Sarah**?"
He replied, "**There** in the **tent**."
One of them said, "I will **surely return** to you
    about **this** time next **year**,
and **Sarah** will then have a **son**."

Don't rush this question.

This is the great promise that will be fulfilled in Isaac.

For meditation and context:

RESPONSORIAL PSALM   Psalm 15:2–3, 3–4, 5 (1a)

R. He who does justice will live in the presence of the Lord.

One who walks blamelessly and does justice;
    who thinks the truth in his heart
    and slanders not with his tongue.
Who harms not his fellow man,
    nor takes up a reproach against his
        neighbor;
by whom the reprobate is despised,
    while he honors those who fear the LORD.

Who lends not his money at usury
    and accepts no bribe against the innocent.
One who does these things
    shall never be disturbed.

> **TO KEEP IN MIND**
> **Read all four Scriptures** for your assigned Sunday. Because all were chosen for this day, it is important to look at them together.

READING II   Colossians 1:24–28

A reading from the Letter of Saint Paul to the Colossians

Brothers and **sisters**:
Now I **rejoice** in my sufferings for **your** sake,
    and in my **flesh** I am filling **up**
    what is **lacking** in the **afflictions** of **Christ**
    on behalf of his **body**, which is the **church**,
    of which **I** am a **minister**
    in accordance with God's **stewardship given** to me
    to bring to **completion** for you the **word** of **God**,
    the **mystery** hidden from **ages** and from generations **past**.

Colossians = kuh-LOSH-uhnz

Read slowly because you are saying something surprising—that he "rejoices" in "suffering."

It will take a homilist's insight to clarify the meaning of this assertion, but if you don't ensure that they hear it, there won't be anything for him to clarify.

Paul is asserting his rightful role as Apostle and servant of the Gospel.

Speak with joy of this mystery that has now been made known.

READING II Catholic Christianity espouses a unique understanding of suffering that enables us to see it as a participation in the suffering of Christ. From that perspective, suffering itself is "redeemed" because instead of being something totally negative, it becomes, as St. John Paul II observed, a way that all of us can share in the Christ's redemptive suffering (*On the Christian Meaning of Human Suffering* [*Salvifici Doloris*, 30]). On Calvary, Christ offered up not just his suffering of that moment but the suffering he *continues* to endure throughout time in his "body," which is *us*, the Church. When we willingly share in his suffering, we participate in the Paschal Mystery, that one-time, supreme act of salvation which is his suffering, Death, and Resurrection.

Languishing in jail, Paul is enduring suffering even as he writes, but he claims to rejoice in it because he knows that he shares in Christ's own suffering for the sake of "the Church." He became a "servant" of the Church in order to preach the "word" of God that up till then had been a "mystery," hidden but now revealed to those ("the saints") who have embraced the Gospel. This oneness that believers share with Christ is itself a light to the nations. That Christ and Christians form one Body is a glorious "mystery" and this mystery is a source of "hope" for the Gentiles. Paul concludes, asserting that the Gospel admonishes "*everyone*" and teaches "*everyone*" so that "*everyone*" may be perfected in Christ. The repeated word need be stressed only the last time, but the entire sentence is spoken with a voice full of hope!

What has been "made known" to the Gentiles is the reality of Christ's oneness with his body, the Church.

But **now** it has been **manifested** to his **holy ones**,
    to whom **God** chose to make **known** the **riches** of the **glory**
        of this **mystery** among the **Gentiles**;
    it is **Christ** in **you**, the **hope** for **glory**.
It is **he** whom we **proclaim**,
    admonishing everyone and **teaching everyone**
        with **all wisdom**,
    that we may **present everyone perfect** in **Christ**.

Through you, Paul is proclaiming Christ anew! Stress the verbs "admonishing" and "teaching" and save the stress on "everyone" until the end.

GOSPEL   Luke 10:38–42

A reading from the holy Gospel according to Luke

Jesus entered a **village**
    where a **woman** whose name was **Martha welcomed** him.
She had a **sister** named **Mary**
    who sat **beside** the **Lord** at his feet **listening** to him speak.
Martha, **burdened** with much **serving**, came to him and **said**,
    "**Lord**, do you not **care**
    that my **sister** has left me by **myself** to do the serving?
Tell her to **help** me."
The Lord said to her in **reply**,
    "**Martha**, **Martha**, you are **anxious** and **worried**
        about **many** things.
There is need of **only one** thing.
Mary has chosen the **better** part
    and it will **not** be **taken** from her."

You're telling a story and the setting and character names are important. Don't rush.

Let your tone convey the unusual nature of Mary's choice and stress her *listening*.

Martha is "burdened." Your tone should convey the negative judgment Jesus will make about her state of mind and heart.

She speaks to him familiarly, like a member of the family.

Remarkably, she tells Jesus what to do. Jesus seems mildly amused by her consternation.

Though he loves her, Jesus is clear with Martha about what is the *better* part.

GOSPEL   Jesus often made a home in Bethany at the residence of Mary, Martha, and their brother Lazarus. Jesus is friend as well as rabbi to these siblings. Martha assumes the role of host and head of household when it is she who "welcomes" Jesus. Luke wants to make a statement regarding the requirements of discipleship and for him, the first step is to listen. Jesus is not about to the reject the meal Martha is busy preparing but he does reject the anxiety and worry that her work causes her. Has she—as many disciples still do today—made "doing for Christ" more important than what he seeks to do for her? He came for rest and nourishment but he brought much more than he will receive. While she prepares a meal, he shares his Word of life, and in her busyness she is going to miss it.

Mary, on the other hand, has remarkably assumed the posture of a disciple, sitting at the feet of the Lord and "listening" to what he is saying. Mary breaks a double taboo—leaving the kitchen where she "belonged" and sitting at a rabbi's feet, a place reserved for men, not women. Yet it is this posture that Jesus affirms. Jesus clearly loves both these women and his repetition of Martha's name signals his warm affection. It's not her work, but her disquiet that he chastises. Discipleship requires focus, a wakeful attentiveness than can be achieved only by a peaceful heart. Mary has found it at Jesus' feet. He challenges Martha to find it also, even as she cuts and stirs. Ecclesiastes says there is a time for everything—to prepare a meal and, when Jesus speaks, a time to listen. G.M.

SEVENTEENTH SUNDAY IN ORDINARY TIME

LECTIONARY #111

READING I   Genesis 18:20–32

A reading from the Book of Genesis

In **those** days, the LORD said:
"The **outcry** against **Sodom** and **Gomorrah** is so **great**,
    and their **sin** so **grave**,
  that I must go **down** and **see** whether or not their **actions**
    fully **correspond** to the **cry** against them that **comes** to me.
I mean to find **out**."

While **Abraham's visitors** walked on **farther** toward **Sodom**,
  the LORD remained **standing** before **Abraham**.
Then **Abraham** drew **nearer** and said:
  "Will you sweep away the **innocent** with the **guilty**?
Suppose there were fifty **innocent** people in the city;
  would you **wipe out** the place, **rather** than **spare** it
  for the **sake** of the **fifty innocent people** within it?
Far be it from **you** to do such a thing,
  to make the **innocent** die with the **guilty**
  so that the **innocent** and the **guilty** would be treated **alike**!
Should not the **judge** of all the **world** act with **justice**?"
The LORD **replied**,
  "If I find **fifty** innocent people in the city of Sodom,
  I will **spare** the **whole place** for **their** sake."

The outcry comes from the victims of injustice. As defender of the weak and the poor, God must respond. Speak with strength, not vindictiveness.

God will "go down" to verify if the "outcry" is justified.

"Abraham's visitors" are the three (divine) visitors Abraham hosted in his tent who announced he'd have a son within the year.

Abraham is alarmed at what might happen and immediately intervenes!
His tone is bold at the start.

Abraham speaks to God as if God were an earthly king worried about his reputation. He also appeals to God's sense of Justice.

Abraham becomes more apologetic and deferential as he pushes for greater indulgence.

READING I Though we may find his negotiating prowess charming and entertaining, it is not Abraham's skill at bargaining that's being highlighted here but his concern for others and, more importantly, God's inclination to mercy. Abraham has just entertained three visitors in whom he has recognized the eternal God. Now, as they depart, God ponders whether to share with Abraham the purpose of the three visitors' journey to Sodom and Gomorrah. God concludes that, since Abraham has been chosen to be the father of nations, he needs to know the

consequence of sin in order to teach his future offspring to do what is right and just in God's eyes.

Sodom and Gomorrah were indeed sinful and became examples within the Bible of corrupt and immoral cities. Isaiah, Ezekiel and Jeremiah ascribe their destruction to rampant injustice (Isaiah 1:1–10; 3:9), mistreatment of the poor (Ezekiel 16:46–51), and overall corruption (Jeremiah 23:14). But the Genesis story (in the chapter following that in which we find today's reading, chapter 19), depicts the sin as the disregard for one of the culture's most

sacred values, hospitality, and that disregard is graphically demonstrated by the effort of some of the men in the city to commit homosexual rape against the divine visitors.

As soon as Abraham becomes aware of the cities' impending doom, he begins his intercession. The dialogue with God is mostly one sided with Abraham appealing to God's mercy, insisting God could never let the just be swept away with the guilty. God is immediately persuaded to spare "the whole place" for the sake of the few even when the number of the few becomes

Abraham is clever, but not insincere.

Quicken your pace in order to sneak in one more request.

Imagine a conversation with your employer asking for a larger and larger raise and the finessing you would need to do to keep pushing for more.
God's tone can remain consistent throughout—even and without overt emotion.
Read at a brisk pace without belaboring the exchange between Abraham and God.

Carefully set up the final request, then spring the surprisingly small number of ten.

Pause after he replied and solemnly announce the Lord's final response.

For meditation and context:

Abraham spoke up **again**:
"**See** how **I** am **presuming** to speak to my Lord,
though I am but **dust** and **ashes**!
What if there are five **less** than **fifty** innocent people?
Will you destroy the **whole city** because of those **five**?"
He answered, "I will **not** destroy it, if I find **forty-five** there."
But Abraham **persisted**, saying "What if only **forty** are
found there?"
He replied, "I will **forbear** doing it for the **sake** of the **forty**."
Then Abraham said, "Let **not** my Lord grow **impatient** if I go on.
What if only **thirty** are found there?"
He replied, "I will **forbear doing** it if I can find but **thirty** there."
Still Abraham went **on**,
"Since I have thus **dared** to speak to my **Lord**,
what if there are no more than **twenty**?"
The LORD answered, "I will **not destroy** it, for the **sake**
of the **twenty**."
But he **still** persisted:
"**Please**, let **not** my Lord grow **angry** if I **speak** up this **last** time.
What if there are at **least ten** there?"
He replied, "For the **sake** of those **ten**, I will **not destroy** it."

RESPONSORIAL PSALM   Psalm 138:1–2, 2–3, 6–7, 7–8 (3a)

R. Lord, on the day I called for help, you answered me.

I will give thanks to you, O LORD, with all
my heart,
for you have heard the words of my
mouth;
in the presence of the angels I will sing
your praise;
I will worship at your holy temple
and give thanks to your name.

Because of your kindness and your truth;
for you have made great above all things
your name and your promise.
When I called you answered me;
you built up strength within me.

The LORD is exalted, yet the lowly he sees,
and the proud he knows from afar.
Though I walk amid distress, you preserve
me;
against the anger of my enemies you raise
your hand.

Your right hand saves me.
The LORD will complete what he has done
for me;
your kindness, O LORD, endures forever;
forsake not the work of your hands.

---

smaller and smaller. Abraham, depicted as having a unique face-to-face relationship with God that allows for the prodding and persuading he accomplishes here, is consummately diplomatic and self-deprecating as he persuades the Lord to settle for an increasingly smaller number of righteous. Don't let the Lord's replies sound like grudging consent but like the willing extension of divine mercy. Abraham is apparently as aware of the people's sinfulness as God is and possesses a heart as open and generous as God's in asking

mercy for a people that has fallen so short of God's expectations.

READING II Every crucifix you see depicts a small handwritten note at the top bearing the letters "INRI" (initials for the Latin inscription *Iesus Nazarènus, Rex Iudaeorum,* or Jesus the Nazarene, King of the Jews.) Paul's argument here invites us to imagine another note with a different set of letters, "IOU," nailed to the cross. Sin, he tells us, puts us under a legal bond, one that we could never repay ourselves. The weight of that

enormous debt incurred by our sins would crush us. That's why Jesus took it upon himself, so it could be nailed to the cross with him. Now, we are free of debt. Even new sins we commit are paid for because Christ's generous act of self-giving has forever erased all past and future debt.

All this is true because of our participation in the Death and Resurrection of Christ through our Baptism. We were buried in the waters of Baptism and rose through those waters to new life in him because we placed our faith in the God who raised Christ from the dead. God's

READING II   Colossians 2:12–14

Colossians = kuh-LOSH-uhnz

Begin slowly and continue slowly or this text will become a blur. Remember, you are announcing Good News.
Your *faith* in the power of God who raised Christ brought about your own resurrection.

Despite our sinfulness, God reached out to save us.

God raised us to life together with Christ.

Don't rush the powerful image of our debt being nailed to the cross.

A reading from the Letter of Saint Paul to the Colossians

Brothers and **sisters**:
You were **buried** with him in **baptism**,
    in which you were also **raised** with him
    through **faith** in the **power** of **God**,
    who **raised** him from the **dead**.
And even when you were **dead**
    in **transgressions** and the **uncircumcision** of your **flesh**,
    he **brought** you to **life** along **with** him,
    having **forgiven** us all our **transgressions**;
    obliterating the bond **against** us, with its **legal** claims,
    which was **opposed** to us,
    he also **removed** it from our **midst**, **nailing** it to the **cross**.

GOSPEL   Luke 11:1–13

Be sure to highlight that Jesus is in prayer.

Moved by Jesus' ability to pray, they ask for instruction.

Keep the prayer upbeat. Each intercession stands alone, so end one before beginning the next.

Pause briefly before beginning the following narration.

A reading from the holy Gospel according to Luke

Jesus was **praying** in a certain **place**, and when he had **finished**,
    one of his **disciples** said to him,
    "**Lord**, **teach** us to **pray** just as **John** taught **his** disciples."
He said to them, "When you **pray**, say:
    Father, **hallowed** be your **name**,
        your **kingdom come**.
        Give us each day our **daily bread**
        and **forgive** us **our sins**
        for **we ourselves** forgive **everyone** in **debt** to **us**,
        and do **not subject** us to the **final test**."

great love and mercy are manifested in the fact that God did all this for us, not because we had become worthy or earned God's favor. No, indeed. God acted decisively on our behalf when we still bore the stain of sin, when our likeness to the creator was twisted and contorted by sin, and when the world was marked by rebellion. It was then, when we could not act on our own behalf that God acted for us.

Such Good News should be shared with joy. The text is a bit obscure and can't easily be grasped at first hearing. Your listeners may not clearly remember what you say, but they always remember how you make them feel. So be sure you make them feel the joyful nature of this good news.

GOSPEL   Jesus' formula for efficacious prayer is rather simple: don't multiply words but be persistent. Luke's version of the Lord's Prayer is shorter than Matthew's. Here, Jesus' prayer simply addresses God as "Father" and names God as the one who sustains us each and every day, forgives us of our sins, and keeps us from "the final test." Though Matthew's rendering of the Our Father is longer, it lacks the teaching we find here on the importance of perseverance and the efficacy of prayer.

Many debate the role of prayer and wonder if it "changes God's mind" or simply disposes the pray-er to accept whatever God's will turns out to be. Here, it is clear that Jesus encourages the believer to pray and to pray insistently. His parable presents a neighbor who disregards the bounds of common courtesy in order to gain his goal. Jesus tells a story with clear and compelling details of a sleeping neighbor whose door is already closed and secured, whose

Tell the story with energy and without overemphasizing the details.

His request is made with clear expectation of a positive response.

He is tired and annoyed. His attitude says, "How could you even *think* I would get out of bed at this hour?"

Like a teacher asserting a point of which you are certain.

Don't rush this classic saying of Jesus. Address each phrase to a different section of the assembly.

Experience may seem to contradict this strong declaration. Speak with conviction.

Speak the examples at a good pace; the point is the father's willingness to satisfy his child, not the specific details.

Consistent with his emphasis on the Spirit, Luke substitutes "Holy Spirit" for Matthew's "good gifts."

And he said to them, "Suppose one of you has a **friend**
    to whom he goes at **midnight** and says,
    '**Friend, lend** me three loaves of **bread**,
    for a **friend** of mine has **arrived** at my **house** from a **journey**
    and I have **nothing** to **offer** him,'
    and he says in reply from **within**,
    'Do **not bother** me; the door has **already** been **locked**
    and my **children** and **I** are already in **bed**.
I **cannot** get **up** to give you **anything**.'
I **tell** you,
    if he does **not** get up to give the visitor the loaves
    because of their **friendship**,
    he **will** get up to give him **whatever** he needs
    because of his **persistence**.

"And I **tell** you, **ask** and you will **receive**;
    seek and you will **find**;
    knock and the door will be **opened** to you.
For **everyone** who **asks**, **receives**;
    and the one who **seeks**, **finds**;
    and to the one who **knocks**, the **door** will be **opened**.
What **father among** you would hand his **son** a **snake**
    when he **asks** for a **fish**?
Or **hand** him a **scorpion** when he **asks** for an **egg**?
If **you** then, who are **wicked**,
    know **how** to give **good** gifts to your **children**,
    how much more will the **Father** in **heaven**
    give the **Holy Spirit** to those who **ask** him?"

bed is warm and filled with his children who are sleeping beside him. He doesn't want his or his family's rest disturbed and says, essentially, "Go away and leave me alone." But despite the late hour and the obvious inconvenience, Jesus counsels perseverance because while "friendship" may not assure a positive response from the neighbor, persistence will.

    The story invites us to imagine God as that neighbor who overcomes reluctance and lethargy because of the urgency and tenacity of our intercession. The final section states and restates God's willingness to respond to persistent prayer. The classic "ask . . . seek . . . knock" saying is so beloved because it is so compelling and reassuring. Jesus declares that those who ask receive and those who seek find. He doesn't hedge or equivocate. It's a promise. Knock and the door *will* be opened. There is nothing to finesse. For those who might still doubt, Jesus goes further offering examples he hopes will erase uncertainty. What "father," he asks, would disappoint his child? Despite their being "wicked," human parents follow the human instinct to care for their children. How much more then, will the all-good God do for those who ask him? This much: he will give them "the Holy Spirit." G.M.

EIGHTEENTH SUNDAY IN ORDINARY TIME

LECTIONARY #114

READING I   Ecclesiastes 1:2; 2:21–23

A reading from the Book of Ecclesiastes

> **Vanity** of **vanities**, says **Qoheleth**,
>   **vanity** of **vanities**! **All** things are **vanity**!
>
> Here is one who has **labored** with **wisdom** and **knowledge**
>   and **skill**,
>   and **yet** to **another** who has **not labored** over it,
>   he must **leave property**.
> This **also** is vanity and a **great misfortune**.
> For **what profit comes** to **man** from all the **toil** and **anxiety**
>   of **heart**
>   with which he has **labored** under the **sun**?
> **All** his days **sorrow** and **grief** are his occupation;
>   even at **night** his mind is **not** at **rest**.
> This **also** is **vanity**.

Ecclesiastes = ih-klee-zee-AS-teez

Qoheleth = koh-HEL-uhth

Ecclesiastes = ih-klee-zee-AS-teez

Qoheleth = koh-HEL-uhth
This classic refrain will also end the book.
Speak the second iteration slower than the first. And increase your intensity further on "*All* is vanity."
The attitude underlying these lines is cynical and pessimistic. Don't hide that fact.

Avoid anger, but make this blunt statement without equivocation.

You or someone you know has made similar assertions. Convey the frustration that leads to such declarations.

It's all so futile!

Don't overstate the final line. But, after a slight pause, speak it with conviction.

READING I   "Ecclesiastes" is the Greek translation of the Hebrew name of this book, *Qoheleth*, which means a gatherer of students or "collector" of wisdom. The singularly pessimistic perspective of the book seems foreign to everything else said in the Bible. While an occasional ray of sunlight breaks through the author's gloom, the book's overall message reeks of skepticism and argues against finding any lasting value in the things of human life—not money, nor fame, nor pleasures, nor the possessions we strive so hard to acquire.

Like the mid-twentieth-century European absurdist playwrights, the author sees life as futile and pointless. Death awaits us all and death, it was believed at that time, led to Sheol, a neutral place of neither punishment nor reward. It's no wonder this is the only appearance of Ecclesiastes in the Sunday Lectionary!

Ecclesiastes balances the sometimes overly positive and self-assured attitudes expressed elsewhere in the Wisdom literature, but what's important to remember is that it is written by a person of faith. There is no denying the truth that nothing in life

endures; we can't take our wealth or fame with us nor our favorite possessions. Jesus will say the same in today's Gospel. It's a sobering point, but it reminds us that life, as good as it can be, is ultimately a stepping stone into eternity—and to new, *abundant*, life!

READING II   The chief difference between today's message from Ecclesiastes and this text from Paul is that Paul offers a clear alternative to the things of this world that he says lead to futility and meaninglessness. Like Qoheleth,

TO KEEP IN MIND

Build: refers to increasing vocal intensity as you work toward a climactic point in the text. It calls for intensified emotional energy, which can be communicated by an increase or decrease in volume, or by speaking faster or slower. The point is to show more passion, greater urgency, or concern.

Colossians = kuh-LOSH-uhnz

"If" sets up an "if/then" clause: "if" you were raised, "then" seek . . . .

Contrast "above" and "on earth."
Having "died" in Christ is a positive thing spoken with gratitude!

Speak with authority and urgency. "Earthly" things are like a cancer sure to kill the life of our spirit.

Make eye contact on this very direct injunction.
Don't ignore the clothing imagery used here.

RESPONSORIAL PSALM Psalm 90:3–4, 5–6, 12–13, 14, 17 (95:8)

R. If today you hear his voice, harden not your hearts.

You turn man back to dust,
  saying, "Return, O children of men."
For a thousand years in your sight
  are as yesterday, now that it is past,
  or as a watch of the night.

You make an end of them in their sleep;
  the next morning they are like the
    changing grass,
which at dawn springs up anew,
  but by evening wilts and fades.

Teach us to number our days aright,
  that we may gain wisdom of heart.
Return, O LORD! How long?
  Have pity on your servants!

Fill us at daybreak with your kindness,
  that we may shout for joy and gladness all
    our days.
And may the gracious care of the LORD our
    God be ours;
  prosper the work of our hands for us!
  Prosper the work of our hands!

READING II Colossians 3:1–5, 9–11

A reading from the Letter of Saint Paul to the Colossians

Brothers and **sisters**:
If you were **raised** with **Christ**, **seek** what is **above**,
  where **Christ** is **seated** at the **right hand** of **God**.
Think of what is **above**, **not** of what is on **earth**.
For **you** have **died**,
  and your **life** is **hidden** with **Christ** in **God**.
When **Christ** your **life appears**,
  then **you too** will **appear** with him in **glory**.

Put to **death**, then, the **parts** of you that are **earthly**:
  immorality, **impurity**, **passion**, **evil desire**,
  and the **greed** that is **idolatry**.
Stop **lying** to one another,
  since you have taken off the **old** self with its **practices**
  and have put on the **new** self,
  which is being **renewed**, for **knowledge**,
  in the **image** of its **creator**. »

Paul tells us worldly things don't sustain us and don't endure. In Baptism we experienced the saving death of Christ that he died once for all on Calvary. But Baptism also gave us a share in his Resurrection and calls us to raise our eyes heavenward where we find the things of everlasting life rather than the corrupt things of this world that lead to destruction.

Our new life in Christ is "hidden" from the world that doesn't understand us and from the devil who would take it from us. Sometimes, it's even hidden from ourselves when we lose heart or when God's love

seems distant. But our new life resides in Christ and when he is revealed in glory, so shall we be. It only makes sense, then, to "put to death," those earthly things that lead to death—"immorality, impurity, passion, evil desire . . . ." Paul calls for a radical rejection of these inclinations that come from our sinful nature. Like a cancer, they are to be removed. He uses clothing imagery to remind us of what we have "taken off" and "put on."

The passage ends with a joyful declaration that differences have been removed; it's our oneness in Christ that makes us dis-

tinct, not our differences in color or nationalities. Proclaim that message with eye contact and delight. And don't rush the climactic final line!

GOSPEL Echoes of Ecclesiastes can be heard in this Gospel text, but their impact is quite different here. First Jesus refuses to arbitrate the quarrel between brothers, a quarrel born of "greed" that has become a wedge between siblings who should value their love and oneness above their possessions. Jesus draws an object lesson from this fracture

As good as this diversity is, it no longer matters in light of our oneness.

Oneness trumps diversity because our oneness is Christ!

Here there is not **Greek** and **Jew**,
  circumcision and **uncircumcision**,
  barbarian, **Scythian**, **slave**, **free**;
  but **Christ** is **all** and **in all**.

GOSPEL   Luke 12:13–21

A reading from the holy Gospel according to Luke

Someone in the **crowd** said to **Jesus**,
  "**Teacher**, tell my **brother** to **share** the **inheritance** with me."
He **replied** to him,
  "**Friend**, **who** appointed **me** as your **judge** and **arbitrator**?"
Then he said to the **crowd**,
  "Take **care** to **guard against all greed**,
  for though **one** may be **rich**,
  one's **life** does not consist of **possessions**."

The petitioner is speaking over the crowd seeking to get Jesus' attention.

Jesus' salutation, "Friend," should soften the impact of his refusal to be drawn in.

Lift your voice for Jesus' address to the crowd.

Then he told them a **parable**.
"There was a **rich** man whose **land** produced a **bountiful harvest**.
He **asked** himself, '**What** shall I **do**,
  for I do **not** have **space** to **store** my **harvest**?'
And he said, '**This** is what I shall do:
  I shall **tear down** my **barns** and build **larger** ones.
There I shall **store all** my **grain** and **other goods**
  and I shall **say** to myself, "**Now** as for **you**,
  you have so **many** good things stored up for **many years**,
  rest, **eat**, **drink**, **be merry**!" '
But **God** said to him,
  'You **fool**, **this night** your **life** will be **demanded** of you;
  and the things you have **prepared**, to **whom** will they **belong**?'
Thus will it be for **all** who store up treasure for **themselves**
  but are **not rich** in **what matters** to **God**."

Though he's still addressing the crowd, Jesus can assume a quieter storytelling tone. Subtly differentiate between the "rich man," God, and Jesus' narrator voice.

He's pleased with his solution!

His pride is the result of hard and honest work. Nonetheless, he's deluding himself.

God's voice shatters his smug complacency.

With good eye contact, direct these blunt words to your assembly.

and warns that "possessions" don't substitute for the real stuff of life.

    Jesus' parable could have been taken right out of Qoheleth's playbook. His lead character has a problem any landowner would envy: Where shall I put all this bounty? His tone should suggest the enviable nature of his situation as he imagines building his "larger" barns, safely storing his abundant harvest, and sees himself kicking back in self-congratulatory delight. In the midst of the rich man's revelry, Jesus

introduces a jarring, somber note as God's voice chides him for his foolishness in thinking that his worldly goods could provide lasting security and for forgetting where true security lies.

    Jesus' final line might seem most appropriate for those who sleep in on Sundays and seldom darken the church doors. But even those in church can lapse into righteous conviction that their attendance and their "envelope" ensure (perhaps require!) God's rewards. Blindness to

"what matters to God" can occur within as well as outside the walls of the church. A blunt delivery that reveals what's at stake will serve this text far better than any attempt to soften its tone. G.M.

NINETEENTH SUNDAY IN ORDINARY TIME

LECTIONARY #117

READING I   Wisdom 18:6–9

A reading from the Book of Wisdom

> The **night** of the **passover** was known **beforehand** to our **fathers**,
>   that, with **sure knowledge** of the **oaths** in which they
>   put their **faith**,
>   they might have **courage**.
> Your people **awaited** the **salvation** of the **just**
>   and the **destruction** of their **foes**.
> For when you **punished** our **adversaries**,
>   in this you **glorified** us whom you had **summoned**.
> For in **secret** the **holy children** of the **good**
>   were offering **sacrifice**
>   and putting into **effect** with one **accord** the **divine institution**.

Begin with a tone of gratitude and prayer.

The people, despite their slavery, could rejoice in their knowledge that God would save them.

The single act of passing through the sea saved the Israelites and destroyed their enemies. Speak with a sense of awe and gratitude.

They prepared for their time of deliverance "in secret" by offering sacrifice and waiting in faith.

For meditation and context:

TO KEEP IN MIND
As you are becoming familiar with your passage, read it directly from your Bible, **reading also what comes before and after it** to get a clear sense of its context.

RESPONSORIAL PSALM   Psalm 33:1, 12, 18–19, 20–22 (12b)

R. Blessed the people the Lord has chosen to be his own.

Exult, you just, in the LORD;
    praise from the upright is fitting.
Blessed the nation whose God is the LORD,
    the people he has chosen for his own
        inheritance.

See, the eyes of the LORD are upon those
        who fear him,
    upon those who hope for his kindness,
to deliver them from death
    and preserve them in spite of famine.

Our soul waits for the LORD,
    who is our help and our shield.
May your kindness, O LORD, be upon us
    who have put our hope in you.

READING I   Each Sunday's First Reading sets the stage for the Gospel by introducing the theme that lies at the center of the Gospel text. Today, preparedness is that theme. In the Gospel, the message is sobering, but the Wisdom text celebrates Israel's readiness for God's decisive action in the Exodus.

For centuries Israelites languished in Egypt as slaves of their Egyptian masters. All the while, however, they clung to the promises or "oaths" God made to their ancestors. Despite the passage of so much time and despite circumstances that made fulfillment seem impossible, the people "put their faith" in God believing he would be faithful and they would not be disappointed.

This faith enabled them to endure hardships. Moses enters the history of the Jewish people as an unlikely hero: he has lived in the royal court as a prince of Egypt and has no credential other than his assertion that God sent him to deliver Israel from slavery.

But because of the faith they had cultivated during their long years of waiting, the people recognized God's messenger in Moses and responded on that fateful night when God sent the plague to each Egyptian home to bring death to each firstborn. But the homes of the Israelites were "passed over." In this way God "punished [their] adversaries" and simultaneously "glorified" the Israelites whom God had "summoned." A single act—passing through the waters of the Red Sea—punished one people and set the other free.

You are not simply reciting information here. You are addressing God and remembering God's acts of mercy demonstrated in the foreknowledge given the Chosen

READING II   Hebrews 11:1–2, 8–19

A reading from the Letter to the Hebrews

Use the greeting to secure everyone's attention, then declare confidently this classic explanation of what faith is.

Brothers and **sisters:**
Faith is the **realization** of what is **hoped** for
    and **evidence** of things **not seen.**
Because of it the **ancients** were well **attested.**

"Attested" means "commended" or "given approval." Read this line slowly and deliberately.

By **faith** Abraham **obeyed** when he was **called** to go **out** to a place
    that he was to **receive** as an **inheritance;**
    he **went out, not knowing where** he was to go.

Stress "by faith" each time it recurs.

By **faith** he sojourned in the **promised** land as
        in a foreign **country,**
    dwelling in **tents** with **Isaac** and **Jacob,**
        heirs of the **same promise;**
    for he was looking **forward** to the city with **foundations,**
        whose **architect** and **maker** is **God.**

Abraham left his home and willingly lived simply to achieve God's will.

By **faith** he received **power** to **generate,**
    even though he was **past** the **normal** age
    —and Sarah **herself** was **sterile**—
    for he thought that the one who had **made** the promise
        was **trustworthy.**
So it was that there came **forth** from **one** man,
    himself as **good** as **dead,**
    descendants as **numerous** as the **stars** in the **sky**
    and as **countless** as the **sands** on the **seashore.**

"As good as dead" is a colorful exaggeration. Speak it with some playfulness.

All these **died** in **faith.**
They did **not receive** what had been **promised**
    but **saw** it and **greeted** it from **afar**
    and **acknowledged** themselves to be **strangers** and **aliens**
        on **earth,**
    for those who **speak thus show** that they are **seeking**
        a **homeland.**

They died still holding on to faith despite not having seen its complete fulfillment. Speak with admiration.

People and in their dramatic rescue through the waters of the sea. Such love is remembered with gratitude.

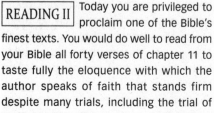

Today you are privileged to proclaim one of the Bible's finest texts. You would do well to read from your Bible all forty verses of chapter 11 to taste fully the eloquence with which the author speaks of faith that stands firm despite many trials, including the trial of God's seeming silence. The author's heroes clung to faith over decades and generations; they left their homeland and dwelled

in tents in foreign lands, they hung on to the promise of "descendants as numerous as the stars in the sky" and most significantly, they died without seeing the complete fulfillment of God's promises.

Had they not persevered, these ancestors would not have become the patriarchs and matriarchs of the nation they eventually came to be. Faith enabled them to "see" with their mind's eye and with their hearts what God had promised but was not yet. Hebrews holds up these men and women, not because what they did was historically important for the evolution of

the nation, but because they modeled what is necessary in the life of every believer. Faith has always been and always will be the "evidence of things not seen." Facts and things we can see before our eyes don't require faith. Faith is about the "not yet," the "hoped for," the "promise" and the "dream." And lest we conclude that dreamers are asleep and living a fantasy, not life, the author of Hebrews offers this eloquent homily to persuade us otherwise.

For you as reader, the challenge of this text is its length and its multiple biblical allusions. While essential, reading slowly is

If they had been **thinking** of the land from which they had **come**,
   they would have had **opportunity** to **return**.
But **now** they desire a **better** homeland, a **heavenly** one.
Therefore, God is **not ashamed** to be called their **God**,
   for he has **prepared** a **city** for them.

By **faith** Abraham, when put to the **test**, offered up **Isaac**,
   and he who had **received** the **promises** was ready
      to **offer** his **only son**,
of whom it was said,
   "Through **Isaac** descendants shall **bear** your **name**."
He reasoned that **God** was able to **raise** even from the **dead**,
   and he received **Isaac back** as a **symbol**.

[Shorter: Hebrews 11:1–2, 8–12]

GOSPEL   Luke 12:32–48

A reading from the holy Gospel according to Luke

Jesus said to his **disciples**:
   "Do not be **afraid** any **longer**, little **flock**,
   for your **Father** is **pleased** to give you the **kingdom**.
Sell your belongings and give **alms**.
Provide **money** bags for yourselves that do **not** wear **out**,
   an **inexhaustible treasure** in **heaven**
      that no **thief** can reach nor **moth destroy**.
For where your **treasure** is, **there also** will your **heart** be.

"**Gird** your **loins** and **light** your **lamps**
   and be like **servants** who await their master's **return**
      from a **wedding**,
   ready to open **immediately** when he **comes** and **knocks**.
Blessed are those **servants**
   whom the master finds **vigilant** on his arrival.
Amen, I say to you, he will **gird** himself,
   have them **recline** at **table**, and **proceed** to **wait** on **them**.
And should he **come** in the **second** or **third** watch ❯❯

Let your voice suggest that you, too, desire that "better homeland."

This is the climactic example of Abraham's exemplary faith. Speak with awareness of how remarkable a demonstration of faith this was.

Abraham's faith was so strong that he trusted God would find a way to undo what he was asked to do. Use ritardando on the final phrase.

The challenging directives that follow are shared in the context of God's unfailing love and the dismissal of fear.

While these are imperatives, the tone should be one of gentle persuasion.

Take a substantial pause after sharing this profound truth.
Renew your energy and deliver these instructions with upbeat vitality.

Blessed = BLES-uhd or blesd

Jesus offers one of his stunning reversals in the image of the master waiting on his own servants.

not enough to convey this message. You must speak of these characters with knowledge and affection and full awareness of their significant contribution to salvation history. The refrain, "by faith," repeated four times, moves you through the text, connecting each successive section to what went before. In our excerpt, the elucidation of the role of faith climaxes in Abraham's willingness to sacrifice the very son through whom God's promises were to be fulfilled. He reasoned, we are told, that God could raise Isaac from the dead. And though Isaac did not really die, his "return" from the death Abraham was willing to inflict upon him, makes him a "symbol" of Jesus' Resurrection.

GOSPEL   Using multiple scenarios that portray the difference between prepared, faithful servants and self-serving, unfaithful servants, Jesus teaches us about the need for preparedness, and that need is foremost, not only in the lives of church leaders but in the life of every disciple.

Jesus addresses his listeners in tender words—"little flock"—that reveal his pas-toral approach and his constant love for them. Given what follows, his initial instructions can be seen as strategies for preparedness. His first is "Do not be afraid" Scripture's most commonly repeated phrase and, among the Gospels, repeated most often in Luke. Release from fear makes radical living possible, so Jesus endorses selling possessions and storing up treasures in heaven rather than where thief and moth can generate fear of losing them. The classic "where your treasure is . . . " is an invitation to make Christ and

Blessed = BLES-uhd or blesd

Remember, Jesus' analogies are predicated by his cultural context.

Eye contact is imperative on this line.

Peter's question is honest and direct. Jesus' response is another story.

This is the third time Jesus pronounces as "blessed" those "servants" who are found ready.

While these images may seem extreme and untastefully violent, recent history within the Church provides ample evidence of serious abuse of power.

While authoritative, there can also be regret heard in your delivery of this servant's fate.

Again, eye contact is a must for this familiar but powerful saying.

and find them **prepared** in this way,
blessed are those servants.
Be **sure** of **this**:
if the **master** of the house had **known** the hour
when the **thief** was coming,
he would **not** have let his house be broken **into**.
You also must be prepared, for at an **hour** you do **not expect**,
the **Son** of **Man** will **come**."

Then **Peter** said,
"**Lord**, is this parable meant for **us** or for **everyone**?"
And the Lord **replied**,
"**Who**, **then**, is the **faithful** and **prudent steward**
whom the **master** will put in **charge** of his **servants**
to distribute the **food allowance** at the **proper time**?
Blessed is that servant whom his **master** on **arrival** finds **doing** so.
Truly, I **say** to you, the **master** will put the servant
in charge of **all** his property.
But if **that servant** says to himself,
'My master is **delayed** in coming,'
and begins to **beat** the menservants and the maidservants,
to **eat** and **drink** and get **drunk**,
then that servant's **master** will **come**
on an **unexpected day** and at an **unknown hour**
and will **punish** the servant **severely**
and assign him a **place** with the **unfaithful**.
That servant who **knew** his master's will
but did **not** make **preparations nor act** in **accord** with his **will**
shall be beaten **severely**;
and the **servant** who was **ignorant** of his master's will
but **acted** in a way **deserving** of a **severe** beating
shall be beaten **only lightly**.
Much will be **required** of the **person entrusted** with much,
and still **more** will be demanded of the person **entrusted**
with **more**."

[Shorter: Luke 12:35–40]

his Gospel our only treasure so that our hearts will always be with his.

In Jesus' day, weddings were protracted affairs that could last a week or more. The master's return, then, was truly uncertain. Jesus offers both tender and alarming images of the master's response to servants who are either faithful and vigilant or profligate and self-indulgent. The faithful see a master willing to don an apron and wait on them, but those who did not wait in readiness are met with severe punishment.

Peter asks if this lesson on preparedness is meant for all or just the leaders. Jesus seems to ignore his inquiry, but actually gives a clear response: vigilance is expected of all to the degree that matches their understanding. That awareness and readiness is expected of all who follow Christ is seen in Jesus' lavish praise of the servant the master finds already doing his duty. He is the one who will be put in charge because he saw and responded to need without waiting for instructions. This is the critical difference between harsh and lenient judgment: those who know and do

not act should expect severity because much is required of those entrusted with much. But even those given less are not entirely exempt of responsibility. While more is demanded of the privileged, readiness is expected of all. G.M.

TWENTIETH SUNDAY IN ORDINARY TIME

LECTIONARY #120

READING I   Jeremiah 38:4–6, 8–10

A reading from the book of the prophet Jeremiah

In those days, the **princes** said to the **king**:
"**Jeremiah** ought to be put to **death**;
  he is **demoralizing** the **soldiers** who are **left** in this **city**,
  and all the **people**, by **speaking** such things to them;
  he is **not interested** in the **welfare** of our **people**,
  but in their **ruin**."
King **Zedekiah** answered: "**He** is in **your** power";
  for the **king** could do **nothing** with them.
And so they **took Jeremiah**
  and **threw** him into the **cistern** of Prince **Malchiah**,
  which was in the **quarters** of the **guard**,
  letting him down with ropes.
There was **no water** in the **cistern**, only **mud**,
  and **Jeremiah sank** into the **mud**.

Ebed-melech, a court official,
  went there from the **palace** and said to him:
"**My lord king**,
  these **men** have been at **fault**
  in all they have **done** to the **prophet Jeremiah**,
  casting him into the cistern.
He will **die** of **famine** on the **spot**,
  for there is **no more food** in the **city**." »

Their anger and hostility should be immediately apparent.

Their self-interest persuades them they are doing the right thing.

Zedekiah sounds like Pilate in abrogating responsibility.

Use the details to suggest the horror of being lowered into this sure death trap.

Pause before starting this new beat that brings hope back into the story.

His tone is confident; these are the words of a truly righteous man.

READING I   Following God's will often guarantees resistance. Today's Gospel reminds us that even neighbors and family members will oppose us when God's searing truth issues from our lips and falls upon ears that don't want to hear it. Such was the fate of Jeremiah. The unpopular message he was given to herald was that deportation and exile were inevitable and that resistance to the Babylonian invaders would prove futile. The people had turned to false gods and the coming chastisement was the result of their blatant idolatry.

God had fortified Jeremiah for his difficult task, assuring him, "they will fight against you, but not prevail over you" (Jeremiah 1:19). While his life was never taken, the prophet endured much suffering. In this reading, King Zedekiah is persuaded to take action against the prophet in order to keep his dire warnings from causing the troops to lose heart. Jeremiah has been calling for surrender to Babylon in order to save the city and king. But Zedekiah won't trust Jeremiah, fearing for his own fate if he is taken prisoner.

The king's officials would kill Jeremiah in order to silence him and it takes the intervention of the eunuch Ebed-melech to persuade the king to reverse his earlier order. Because of his faith, Ebed-melech is later told by Jeremiah that he will survive the fall of Jerusalem to the Babylonians.

This is a tale of anger and planned retribution, of corrupt motives and criminal injustice suddenly overturned by the efforts of an honest man who risks his own life for the sake of another. Let your delivery match the drama of the story.

Now, Zedekiah speaks with greater confidence and authority for he knows he's doing the right thing.

Then the **king** ordered **Ebed-melech** the **Cushite**
  to take three men along with him,
  and **draw** the **prophet Jeremiah** out of the **cistern**
    before he should **die**.

For meditation and context:

RESPONSORIAL PSALM   Psalm 40:2, 3, 4, 18 (14b)

R. Lord, come to my aid!

I have waited, waited for the LORD,
    and he stooped toward me.

The LORD heard my cry.
He drew me out of the pit of destruction,
    out of the mud of the swamp;
he set my feet upon a crag;
    he made firm my steps.

And he put a new song into my mouth,
    a hymn to our God.
Many shall look on in awe
    and trust in the LORD.

Though I am afflicted and poor,
    yet the LORD thinks of me.
You are my help and my deliverer;
    O my God, hold not back!

TO KEEP IN MIND

Go slowly in the epistles. Paul's style is often a tangle of complex sentences; his mood can change within a single passage.

READING II   Hebrews 12:1–4

A reading from the letter to the Hebrews

Pause briefly after the salutation.

If you have statues or stained glass depicting the communion of saints, you might want to throw a glance in that direction as you speak this line.
The key words in these lines are "persevere" and "Jesus."

Stress Jesus' willingness to suffer for us.

"So that you may not grow weary . . ." should be spoken with great sincerity.

A fast delivery will obscure the meaning of the final sentence. Read slowly, with awareness of the great cost of discipleship.

Brothers and **sisters**:
Since we are **surrounded** by so great a **cloud** of **witnesses**,
    let us **rid** ourselves of **every burden** and **sin** that **clings** to us
    and **persevere** in running the **race** that lies **before** us
    while keeping our **eyes fixed** on Jesus,
      the **leader** and **perfecter** of **faith**.
For the **sake** of the **joy** that lay **before** him
    he **endured** the **cross**, **despising** its **shame**,
    and has taken his **seat** at the **right** of the **throne** of **God**.
Consider how he **endured** such **opposition** from **sinners**,
    in order that you may not **grow weary** and **lose heart**.
In **your struggle** against **sin**
    you have not yet **resisted** to the **point** of **shedding blood**.

READING II In the Cathedral of Our Lady of the Angels in Los Angeles hang massive tapestries depicting saints from various eras and all parts of the world. The saints stand side by side, facing forward toward the altar, as if they were part of the liturgical assembly, offering worship at every liturgy. It is a powerful depiction of the "cloud of witnesses" that the author of Hebrews says "surround" us at every moment.

Because we have so many role models, we are encouraged to do what they did: "persevere in running the race that lies before us." To run swiftly and far, we are told to lay aside the burden of sin that weighs us down and holds us back. The saints took Jesus as their role model because he willingly endured the "cross" for the sake of the "joy" that lay *beyond* the grave where he now reigns in glory.

The author understands that although Christian faith brings eternal reward, it never promises to spare us suffering and trial. But in our suffering, we won't endure anything Jesus hasn't already endured on our behalf. He blazed the trail so we could take our strength from him. Aware that martyrs had given their all for their faith, the writer of Hebrews reminds his readers that they have not "*yet*" reached the point of shedding their blood. At that time, martyrdom was a distinct possibility, and in this century that is witnessing more shedding of Christian blood than any of the previous twenty, it remains a sobering reality.

GOSPEL The cost of discipleship echoes in all three of today's readings. Jesus is keenly aware of the price he will pay and is in "anguish" (under stress) awaiting the "baptism" of his

GOSPEL   Luke 12:49–53

A reading from the holy Gospel according to Luke

Jesus said to his **disciples**:
   "I have **come** to set the **earth** on **fire**,
   and how I **wish** it were **already blazing**!
There is a **baptism** with which I **must** be **baptized**,
   and how **great** is my **anguish** until it is **accomplished**!
Do you **think** that I have **come** to establish **peace** on the **earth**?
No, I tell you, but rather **division**.
From now **on** a **household** of **five** will be **divided**,
   three against **two** and **two** against **three**;
   a **father** will be **divided** against his **son**
   and a **son** against his **father**,
   a **mother** against her **daughter**
   and a **daughter** against her **mother**,
   a **mother-in-law** against her **daughter-in-law**
   and a **daughter-in-law** against her **mother-in-law**."

Pause after the introduction and speak with authority.

He longs for the fire to blaze because it is a purifying fire.
He is referring to his own death.

It would be naiveté to think so!

Speak with regret as you list the relationships that will be marred by dissension and division. The list is intentionally somewhat exhaustive to convince us no relationships are exempt from the possibility of division.

> **TO KEEP IN MIND**
> **Separating units of thought with pauses:** Identify the units of thought in your text and use pauses to distinguish one from another. Running words together blurs meaning and fails to distinguish ideas. Punctuation does not always indicate clearly what words to group together or where to pause. The listener depends on you for wthis organization of ideas.

death. He came to proclaim the Kingdom of his Father and he knows that some will embrace that message while others will reject it. Jesus' message will set people against one another because it won't be possible to remain neutral in the face of one who has been set ablaze with the Gospel. Others will either stoke the fire or douse the blaze.

Jesus makes no apology for the turmoil he brings. In fact, he lays out a challenge, asking: "Do you think that I have come to establish peace on the earth?" One could not expect to navigate the length of the Colorado River without experiencing the turbulence of its rapids; they are an inevitable part of the experience. Just so, says Jesus, is the "division" and controversy that accompany the proclamation of the Gospel. They go hand in hand.

Jesus understands and alerts his followers that the road on which he will lead them won't be easy. Division will come, not because Jesus wants it, but because oil and water don't mix, because evil won't keep company with good, because dark is dismissed even by the smallest flame. It can't be any other way. That's why those who should be clinging to each other will instead build walls. G.M.

THE ASSUMPTION OF THE BLESSED VIRGIN MARY: VIGIL

LECTIONARY #621

READING I 1 Chronicles 15:3–4, 15–16; 16:1–2

A reading from the first Book of Chronicles

David assembled all **Israel** in **Jerusalem** to bring the **ark** of the LORD
    to the place that he had **prepared** for it.
David also called together the sons of **Aaron** and the **Levites**.

The **Levites** bore the ark of God on their **shoulders** with **poles**,
    as **Moses** had **ordained** according to the word of the LORD.

David commanded the **chiefs** of the **Levites**
    to appoint their **kinsmen** as **chanters**,
    to play on musical **instruments**, **harps**, **lyres**, and **cymbals**,
    to make a loud **sound** of **rejoicing**.

They **brought** in the ark of God and set it within the **tent**
    which David had **pitched** for it.
Then they offered up burnt **offerings** and **peace** offerings to God.
When David had **finished** offering up the burnt offerings and
      peace offerings,
    he **blessed** the people in the **name** of the LORD.

Chronicles = KRAH-nih-k*ls

Since the "ark" can be seen as a metaphor for Mary, speak of it with great care and reverence.
David has amassed a large and solemn assembly. The details of the careful handling of the ark are important; don't rush past them.

The joy of the festival is amplified by the presence of singers and musicians. Your tone should suggest the joyful, epic nature of this celebration.

A hushed tone will help you convey the solemn and dramatic nature of this special moment.
"Burnt offerings" required the offering of an entire animal. "peace offerings" required that only the fat be offered on the altar.
Establish eye contact and speak with great dignity of David blessing the people in God's name.

READING I   The First and Second Books of Chronicles cover about 400 years in Israel's history, from the death of King Saul and early rise of King David (about 1000 BC) to the Babylonian exile (597–538 BC). The Chronicler devotes much time and attention to the reign of King David. In fact, most of First Chronicles focuses on David, Israel's greatest king, according to the author of Chronicles.

One of David's decisions, made early in his forty-year reign and reflected in today's reading, was to bring the Ark of the Covenant back to Jerusalem. David recap-tured the Ark from the Philistines in a battle, and recognized the importance of restoring the Ark to its rightful place in Jerusalem. For the ancient Israelites, the Ark of the Covenant represented the Lord's presence in their midst. It was a powerful sign and symbol of the covenantal relationship between God and Israel. According to Jewish tradition, the Ark contained the stone tablets upon which the Ten Commandments were written, Aaron's rod, and a jar of manna preserved from the days of the Israelites' forty-year Exodus journey in the desert.

The sacrificial ritual of burnt offerings and peace offerings to God at the installation of the Ark were an expression of Israel's purity laws. The people were keenly aware of the tension between the sacred and the profane, and took pains to be clean and holy in God's presence. The ritual of presenting these sacrificial offerings was not only an acknowledgment of their sin and separation from God, but also a desire for union and intimacy with God.

Over time, the Christian tradition came to associate Mary with the Ark of the Covenant. Just as the Ark carried items

For meditation and context:

TO KEEP IN MIND

Pace: The rate at which you read is influenced by the size of your church, the size of the congregation, and the complexity of the text. As each increases, rate decreases.

RESPONSORIAL PSALM   Psalm 132:6–7, 9–10, 13–14 (8)

R. Lord, go up to the place of your rest, you and the ark of your holiness.

Behold, we heard of it in Ephrathah;
    we found it in the fields of Jaar.
Let us enter into his dwelling,
    let us worship at his footstool.

May your priests be clothed with justice;
    let your faithful ones shout merrily for joy.
For the sake of David your servant,
    reject not the plea of your anointed.

For the LORD has chosen Zion;
    he prefers her for his dwelling.
"Zion is my resting place forever;
    in her will I dwell, for I prefer her."

Corinthians = kohr-IN-thee-uhnz

This text is pure celebration disguised as progressive reasoning. Paul uses logic to celebrate the great truth of Christianity: death, our most fearsome foe, will one day meet its death!
Read carefully, for what we anticipate is not yet here.

Take joy in announcing the ultimate victory of life over death! Increase your intensity from the first to the second question.

First you share the logic: "sting . . . sin"; "power . . . law."
Then, the gratitude that in Christ that formula has been shattered.

READING II   1 Corinthians 15:54b–57

A reading from the first Letter of Saint Paul to the Corinthians

Brothers and sisters:
When that which is **mortal** clothes itself with **immortality**,
    then the **word** that is **written** shall come **about**:

> *Death is swallowed up in **victory**.*
> ***Where**, O death, is your **victory**?*
> ***Where**, O death, is your **sting**?*

The **sting** of **death** is sin,
    and the **power** of sin is the **law**.
But thanks be to **God** who gives **us** the victory
    through our **Lord** Jesus **Christ**.

---

representing the Lord's historic presence with Israel, Mary carried in her womb the divine presence of Christ. Mary, a woman without sin, brought forth into the world her son, who is the perfect union between the human and the divine.

READING II The Second Reading for both Assumption Masses (vigil and day), are taken from First Corinthians 15. In this chapter, Paul addresses Christ's Resurrection from the dead. Among the letters of Paul in the New Testament, 1 Corinthians 15 is Paul's most

sustained discussion on the meaning of the Resurrection and its implications for all who profess faith in Christ.

Today's brief reading is taken from Paul's concluding remarks in chapter 15 concerning the resurrection of the body on the last day. Paul quotes Hosea, a prophet active in the northern kingdom of Israel in the eighth century BC: "Death is swallowed up in victory. Where, O death, is your victory? Where, O death, is your sting?" For Paul, faith in Christ results in the ultimate victory of life over death. Within Christian tradition, the Assumption of Mary into

heaven is a powerful affirmation of Christ's victory over death.

GOSPEL This brief Gospel reading is taken from Luke's travel narrative, 9:51—19:44. These ten chapters narrate Jesus' journey from Galilee to the city of Jerusalem in Judea. On the journey, Jesus interacts with three different groups of people: his disciples, his opponents, and the crowds. He teaches his disciples about what true discipleship entails; he confronts his opponents (mostly the Pharisees) for abusing their power and privilege; and he

Proclaim the introductory lines as if addressing the large crowd that surrounds Jesus.

Do as the woman did and raise *your* voice.

Blessed / blessed = BLES-uhd or blesd

The woman's voice is full of admiration!

Drop your voice to announce Jesus' response, then speak it with appreciation for the people who submit their wills to God's, among whom, Mary is our best model.

TO KEEP IN MIND

Tell the story: Make the story yours, then share it with your listeners. Use the language; don't throw away any good words. Settings give context; don't rush the description. Characters must be believable; understand their motivation. Dialogue reveals character; distinguish one character from another with your voice.

GOSPEL   Luke 11:27–28

A reading from the holy Gospel according to Luke

While **Jesus** was **speaking**,
   a **woman** from the **crowd called** out and said to him,
   "Blessed is the **womb** that **carried** you
   and the **breasts** at which you **nursed**."
He replied,
   "**Rather**, **blessed** are those
   who **hear** the word of God and **observe** it."

---

challenges the crowds to accept his invitation to follow him. Today's reading is a brief lesson to the crowds.

This text can be easily misunderstood as Jesus dismissing the respect due to his mother. Part of the potential misreading can be traced to the common translation of the Greek word, *menoun*. In his quick retort to the woman, Jesus says, "Rather (*menoun*), blessed are those who hear the word of God and observe it." *Menoun* could also be translated as "more truly." While both translations accurately connote the negative aspect present in the original

Greek, "more truly" softens the impact and more likely reflects Luke's intention here.

But in fact, the brief exchange between Jesus and a woman from the crowd speaks more to Luke's larger theological aims in his Gospel account than to the relationship between Mary and Jesus. In Luke's view, Jesus revealed that "family" in the Kingdom of God is more clearly associated with those who hear and obey the Word of God than with strict biological relationships. Luke presents a similar idea earlier in his Gospel account when Jesus, engulfed in a crowd listening to his teach-

ing, is told that "his mother and his brothers" have come to see him. Jesus responds that "his mother and his brothers" are hearers and doers of the Word (Luke 8:19–21). Of course, Luke's audiences will remember his account of Jesus' conception and infancy, in which Mary is, in fact, the paramount example of one who hears and obeys God's Word. D.S.

THE ASSUMPTION OF THE BLESSED VIRGIN MARY: DAY

LECTIONARY #622

READING I Revelation 11:19a; 12:1–6a, 10ab

A reading from the Book of Revelation

God's **temple** in heaven was **opened**,
and the **ark** of his **covenant** could be seen in the temple.

A great **sign** appeared in the sky, a **woman** clothed with the **sun**,
with the **moon** under her **feet**,
and on her **head** a **crown** of twelve **stars**.
She was with **child** and **wailed** aloud in **pain** as she labored to
give **birth**.
Then **another** sign appeared in the sky;
it was a huge red **dragon**, with seven **heads** and ten **horns**,
and on its heads were seven **diadems**.
Its **tail** swept away a third of the **stars** in the sky
and **hurled** them down to the **earth**.
Then the dragon **stood** before the woman about to give **birth**,
to **devour** her child when she gave birth.
She gave birth to a **son**, a **male** child,
destined to **rule** all the nations with an iron **rod**.
Her child was caught up to **God** and his **throne**.
The woman herself **fled** into the **desert**
where she had a place prepared by **God**. »

You are narrating a vision filled with powerful imagery that requires a grand and solemn tone worthy of the cosmic events described here.

Speak in a positive tone of the "sign," for it refers to the woman chosen by God.
All the symbols are significant, so be sure to stress each one.
That she is pregnant and in childbirth is surprising information; be sure you don't make it sound ordinary or insignificant.
Announce "another sign" with a negative tone, for now you are introducing the archenemy who seeks the lives of the woman and her child.
This is indeed a powerful adversary!

Avoid cheap dramatics, but be sure to convey the destructive horror that threatens mother and child.
Despite the circumstances, convey a sense of peace as you announce the child's birth.

The peace is short-lived; with energy and quickened tempo speak of these efforts to secure safety.

READING I The Book of Revelation is widely regarded as the Bible's finest piece of apocalyptic literature. Earlier versions of apocalyptic literature are seen in some writings of the Old Testament, such as the Book of Daniel, chapters 7–12 and the Book of Zechariah, chapter 14. This literary form flourished in the Middle East for about 400 years, from 200 BC–AD 200. Apocalyptic literature was written during times of crisis with the aim of bringing comfort and hope to those experiencing religious and political persecution. These texts are full of images, symbols, and num-

bers that function as a kind of coded language understood by the author and the people the text was written for, but not by their persecutors.

Most scholars date the writing of the Book of Revelation to the later stages of the reign of Domitian, AD 81–96. Under this emperor, the early Christians in the Roman Empire faced severe persecution. Although the author of Revelation is unknown, many early Church Fathers believed that the Apostle John wrote this text while in exile on the island of Patmos, as stated in the opening verses, John 1:1–9.

In today's reading, we hear a part of John's description of his dramatic vision. In it the "ark of his covenant" is connected with a woman and her newborn son under attack by evil forces, the "huge red dragon." The original recipients of this book would have likely decoded the images of the woman and her son as Mary and the infant Jesus. The hope offered in this apocalyptic vision was the assurance of God's saving presence against evil forces seeking to destroy his plan for salvation.

Just as God was present to the ancient Israelites in both the Temple and the Ark,

Then I heard a loud **voice** in heaven say:
   "Now have **salvation** and **power** come,
      and the **Kingdom** of our **God**
      and the **authority** of his **Anointed** One."

For meditation and context:

TO KEEP IN MIND
Dialogue imitates real conversation, so it often moves faster than the rest of the passage.

RESPONSORIAL PSALM   Psalm 45:10, 11, 12, 16 (10bc)

R. The queen stands at your right hand, arrayed in gold.

The queen takes her place at your right hand
   in gold of Ophir.

Hear, O daughter, and see; turn your ear,
   forget your people and your father's house.

So shall the king desire your beauty;
   for he is your lord.

They are borne in with gladness and joy;
   they enter the palace of the king.

READING II   1 Corinthians 15:20–27

Corinthians = kohr-IN-thee-uhnz

First, Paul establishes the premise: Christ rose from the dead, the first of many to follow.

Paul utilizes progressive reasoning to make his point. Like a teacher, lead your listeners from one point to the next.

What follows the colon is an explanation of how things must progress in "proper order."

Paul shares a profound, mystical truth. Speak slowly of this weighty subject.

All pretenders to Christ's throne will be "destroyed." Don't shy from making full use of this strong language.

Speak the final line as if you were warning death to be on alert!

A reading from the first Letter of Saint Paul to the Corinthians

Brothers and sisters:
Christ has been **raised** from the **dead**,
   the **firstfruits** of those who have fallen **asleep**.
For since **death** came through **man**,
   the **resurrection** of the dead came **also** through man.
For just as in **Adam** all **die**,
   so too in **Christ** shall all be brought to **life**,
   but **each** one in proper **order**:
   Christ the **firstfruits**;
   then, at his **coming**, those who **belong** to Christ;
   then comes the **end**,
   when he hands over the Kingdom to his God and **Father**,
   when he has **destroyed** every **sovereignty**
   and every **authority** and **power**.
For he must reign until he has put all his **enemies** under his **feet**.
The **last** enemy to be destroyed is **death**,
   for "he subjected **everything** under his feet."

---

so, too, God prepared a safe haven for Mary and her newborn Son, Jesus. Christians could be comforted knowing that even the forces of evil would not prevail against the power of God's Kingdom or the authority of God's Son.

READING II Paul's most extensive treatment of the theology of the Resurrection of Christ is found in 1 Corinthians 15. Part of what prompts Paul to address the Resurrection in such detail is that some in the Corinthian congregation denied the reality (and perhaps even the

necessity) of the Resurrection. Believers in Christ who did not agree with Paul and who subsequently promoted their own version of the Gospel message were a constant problem for Paul. It was not uncommon for a new and different version of the Good News to develop in Christian congregations after Paul's departure. This most certainly happened in the city of Corinth (see, for example, 2 Corinthians 11:3–6) and in the churches in the province of Galatia (see, for instance, Galatians 1:6–10).

Paul's theology of the Resurrection in 1 Corinthians 15 falls into three parts: a

summary of the basic kerygma (preaching) of the early Church on the Resurrection (verses.1–11), a defense of the reality of Christ's Resurrection (verses 12–34), and an explanation of what existence would be after the final resurrection of the dead (verses 35–58). Today's reading is part of the larger overall defense that Paul launches against those who deny the resurrection of the dead (1 Corinthians 15:12–34). It picks up on the argument that Paul was making about the reality and the effects of Jesus' Resurrection from the dead. According to Paul, God's Resurrection

GOSPEL   Luke 1:39–56

A reading from the holy Gospel according to Luke

Mary set out
　　and traveled to the **hill** country in **haste**
　　to a town of **Judah**,
　　where she entered the house of **Zechariah**
　　and greeted **Elizabeth**.
When Elizabeth **heard** Mary's greeting,
　　the infant **leaped** in her **womb**,
　　and **Elizabeth**, **filled** with the Holy **Spirit**,
　　cried out in a loud voice and said,
　　"**Blessed** are you among **women**,
　　and blessed is the **fruit** of your **womb**.
And how does this **happen** to me,
　　that the mother of my **Lord** should come to me?
For at the moment the **sound** of your greeting reached my **ears**,
　　the **infant** in my womb leaped for **joy**.
Blessed are you who **believed**
　　that what was **spoken** to you by the Lord
　　would be **fulfilled**." »

You want to create a sense of "haste" without blurring the words or meaning.

Zechariah = zek-uh-RĪ-uh

The role of the Spirit, as in all of Luke's Gospel account, is important here.

Express these familiar lines with joy! Elizabeth speaks with prescience of Mary as "mother of [her] Lord."

Blessed / blessed = BLES-uhd
Elizabeth lauds Mary for her trust in God.

Mary's great Magnificat *comprises the balance of the text.*

of Jesus is not simply Christ's victory over death. It is, in fact, just the beginning of the universal victory over death. As the "first-fruits," Jesus' Resurrection begins the "proper order" of the eschaton (the end-time). So much of what fueled Paul's zealous and relentless preaching of the Gospel was his firm conviction about the imminent return of Christ and the consummation of the age, the end-time. The mark of the end-time and the final victory is accomplished when Christ has destroyed the "last enemy": death. In the Assumption of Mary,

we see the continuation of Christ's victory over death.

GOSPEL　Scholars date the writing of the Gospel according to Luke toward the end of the first century, around AD 85. With the birth of Jesus occurring before the death of Herod the Great in 4 BC, that would make the composition of Luke's infancy narrative (1:5—2:52), which includes the dialogue between Mary and Elizabeth in today's reading, about one hundred years after the events it is reporting. In this regard, it is interesting to note

that in the prologue to Luke's Gospel account (1:1–4), Luke tells us that he relied on "eyewitnesses from the beginning" and "ministers of the word" in the writing of his "narrative."

The encounter between Mary and Elizabeth provides Luke with an important opportunity to advance one of his theological objectives in composing his infancy narrative. Elizabeth's reaction to Mary made clear that the relationship between John and Jesus was established from the very beginning. John was the forerunner to Jesus, the Messiah. Furthermore, Elizabeth's

These are words of praise and gratitude, so speak them with joy!

Remember, this is a poetic text meant to be sung. Share the images one at a time.

blessed: blesd

Lift out the significant contrasts of "mighty" and "lowly" and "hungry" and "rich."

If you "see" the images and the characters she names you won't rush this beautiful text.

Conclude the Canticle and then pause. The closing narration tells us Mary remained with Elizabeth until the birth of John.

TO KEEP IN MIND

The opening: Establish eye contact and announce, from memory, "A reading from . . . ." Then take a pause (three full beats!) before starting the reading. The correct pronunciation is "A [uh] reading from" instead of "A [ay] reading from."

And Mary said:

"My **soul** proclaims the **greatness** of the Lord;
   my spirit **rejoices** in God my **Savior**
   for he has with **favor** on his lowly servant.
From this day all generations will call me **blessed**:
   the Almighty has done **great** things for me
   and **holy** is his **Name**.
He has **mercy** on those who **fear** him
   in **every** generation.
He has shown the **strength** of his arm,
   and has **scattered** the proud in their **conceit**.
He has cast down the **mighty** from their **thrones**,
   and has **lifted** up the **lowly**.
He has filled the **hungry** with **good** things,
   and the **rich** he has sent away **empty**.
He has come to the **help** of his servant **Israel**
   for he has **remembered** his promise of **mercy**,
   the promise he made to our **fathers**,
   to **Abraham** and his children for **ever**."

Mary **remained** with her about three **months**
   and then **returned** to her **home**.

---

exuberant praise of Mary allowed Luke to present some of her defining characteristics: both she and the fruit of her womb were blessed in a special and unique way; Mary would be known henceforth as the "mother of my Lord"; and Mary never wavered in her trust of the Lord.

The Gospel reading concludes with Mary's hymn of praise to the Lord, often referred to as the *Magnificat*. Here again, numerous themes that are developed in the Gospel according to Luke are present in Mary's canticle: rejoicing in the Lord, the poor and marginalized receiving divine preference, the abundance of God's mercy, the reversal of fortunes for the rich and the poor, and the fulfillment of God's historic promises to Israel.

Over time, the words spoken in the *Magnificat* would form the basis for a theology of Mary. Luke's attention to Mary in his Gospel account (especially in the infancy narrative) and in Acts (in the early formation of the Church in Jerusalem) certainly helped give rise to the development of Mariology in the later Church. The Gospel reading for today informs us of the divine grace enveloping and sustaining Mary throughout her life. It was in God's presence throughout Mary's life, and at the moment of her death, that we ground our theology for the celebration of the Assumption of the Blessed Virgin Mary. D.S.

TWENTY-FIRST SUNDAY IN ORDINARY TIME

LECTIONARY #123

READING I   Isaiah 66:18–21

A reading from the Book of the Prophet Isaiah

Thus says the LORD:
I know their **works** and their **thoughts**,
and I **come** to gather **nations** of **every language**;
   they shall **come** and **see** my **glory**.
I will set a **sign** among them;
   from **them** I will send **fugitives** to the **nations**:
   to **Tarshish**, **Put** and **Lud**, **Mosoch**, **Tubal** and **Javan**,
   to the **distant coastlands**
   that have never **heard** of my **fame**, or **seen** my **glory**;
   and they shall **proclaim** my **glory** among the **nations**.
They shall bring **all** your **brothers** and **sisters** from all the **nations**
   as an **offering** to the LORD,
   on **horses** and in **chariots**, in **carts**, upon **mules**
     and **dromedaries**,
   to **Jerusalem**, my **holy mountain**, says the LORD,
   just as the **Israelites** bring **their offering**
   to the **house** of the LORD in **clean vessels**.
Some of these I will take as **priests** and **Levites**, says the LORD.

Isaiah = ī-ZAY-uh

Immediately, the tone is lofty and authoritative but with underlying tenderness and comfort.

Speak of the "sign" as something truly rare and unexpected!

Tarshish = TAHR-shish
Put = POOT
Lud = LUHD
Tubal = TOO-buhl
Javan = JAY-vuhn

You are not describing an ordinary event, but something marvelous and undreamed of: foreigners going to extraordinary lengths to return Jewish refugees to their homeland.

The return of scattered Israelites will be an offering of worship to God.

This news is remarkable. Announce it with joy and wonder.

READING I This reading and today's Gospel both announce a vision of salvation that's extended to the ends of the earth. Through Isaiah, prophesying here at the end of the exile, God announces that the Gentile nations will come to know the Lord and experience his "glory" and merciful love. God will accomplish this wonder through a startling plan: the nations of the earth will receive "fugitives" from Jerusalem, that is, exiles who have returned home from Babylon, who will serve as missionaries in the Gentile lands. These fugitives are the "sign" God promises to "set" among them to give witness to God's strong, saving arm and his mercy.

Although the nations mentioned were only from the European and African continents, the implication is that all the earth will receive the grace of coming to know the Lord, an idea that was initially revolutionary but which later grew steadily throughout the Old Testament. In response to God's mercy, the foreigners will bring back to Jerusalem "all your brothers," (that is, the Jews who, for various reason had been scattered among the nations). No effort will be spared and every means utilized—horses and chariots, carts, mules, and camels—to bring Israelites back to their homes.

The seemingly unextraordinary assertion of the final sentence is actually a startling announcement: God will choose from among the *Gentile* pilgrims, priests, and Levites to minister among his people. God's goodness knows no bounds!

READING II Powerful leaders often show the least deference to and come down hardest on those under them whom they trust most. Ironically, that

For meditation and context:

TO KEEP IN MIND

Read all three commentaries.
Suggestions in each can give you
insight into your own passage.

RESPONSORIAL PSALM   Psalm 117:1, 2 (Mark 16:15)

R. Go out to all the world and tell the Good News. or Alleluia.

Praise the LORD, all you nations;
   glorify him, all you peoples!

For steadfast is his kindness toward us,
   and the fidelity of the LORD endures
   forever.

READING II   Hebrews 12:5–7, 11–13

A reading from the Letter to the Hebrews

Brothers and **sisters**,
You have **forgotten** the **exhortation** addressed to you as **children**:
"My **son**, do not **disdain** the **discipline** of the **Lord**
     or lose **heart** when **reproved** by him;
   for whom the **Lord loves**, he **disciplines**;
     he **scourges** every **son** he **acknowledges**."
Endure your **trials** as "**discipline**";
   God treats you as **sons**.
For what "**son**" is there whom his **father** does **not discipline**?
At the time,
   all discipline seems a **cause** not for **joy** but for **pain**,
   yet **later** it brings the **peaceful fruit** of **righteousness**
to those who are **trained** by it.

So **strengthen** your **drooping hands** and your **weak knees**.
Make **straight paths** for your **feet**,
   that what is **lame** may **not** be **disjointed** but **healed**.

This text is a "spoken homily" meant to rouse and encourage. Be sure your tone communicates that.

Imagine a grandparent speaking to a teenager who thinks his or her parents are too strict. Helps the teen see things from the other side.

This is an appeal to common sense. Speak with conviction.

Adopt a slower pace here to explain that time lends perspective.

Make eye contact and encourage, like a coach at halftime.

He's saying: "Walk the straight and narrow so that the joints already bruised will heal rather than break!" Again, you're trying to encourage.

---

can sometimes be a sign of the leader's confidence in those who often go long stretches between kudos, relying on their knowledge that the boss really does respect them. The author of Hebrews believes the same is true of "fathers" and of the God who is our Father. Like earthly mentors, God shows interest in us by expecting from us the best we can deliver, by pointing out our foibles, and chastising us when that's what's needed to get us back on track.

The author is also aware that giving oneself to Christ is no guarantee of an easy life. On the contrary, enduring "trials" is an inevitable part of the Christian path; any mature disciple will know that and won't seek an alternate route. Writing because he fears his readers may be losing their Christian faith, the author writes what he dubs a "message of encouragement" with a goal of rekindling the fire of their faith. Ironically, their waning zeal didn't result from outside persecution but from their own malaise. They had grown tired of resisting the temptations of their age in order to live like Christ.

The author gives you several strong phrases with which to rouse your assembly out of any weariness from which they suffer: "My son, do not disdain. . . . Strengthen your drooping hands. . . . Make straight paths for your feet." Even hardship can bring joy for it reminds us that God uses every means to refine and purify us.

GOSPEL   Earlier in his Gospel, Luke tells another parable of a master who's gone to bed and bolted the door (Luke 11: 5–8). In that story the persistent neighbor manages to rouse his friend

GOSPEL   Luke 13:22–30

A reading from the holy Gospel according to Luke

Jesus passed through **towns** and **villages**,
    teaching as he went and **making** his **way** to **Jerusalem**.
Someone **asked** him,
    "**Lord**, will **only a few people** be **saved**?"
He **answered** them,
"**Strive** to **enter** through the **narrow** gate,
    for **many**, I tell you, will **attempt** to **enter**
    but will not be **strong** enough.
After the **master** of the **house** has **arisen** and **locked** the door,
    then will you stand **outside knocking** and **saying**,
    '**Lord**, **open** the **door** for us.'
He will **say** to you in **reply**,
    'I do **not know where** you are **from**.'
And **you** will **say**,
    'We **ate** and **drank** in your **company** and you **taught**
        in our **streets**.'
Then **he** will **say** to you,
    'I do **not know where** you are **from**.
Depart from me, **all you evildoers**!'
And there will be **wailing** and **grinding** of **teeth**
    when you see **Abraham**, **Isaac**, **and Jacob**
    and **all** the **prophets** in the **kingdom of God**
    and **you yourselves** cast **out**.
And people will come from the **east** and the **west**
    and from the **north** and the **south**
    and will **recline** at **table** in the **kingdom** of **God**.
For **behold**, some are **last** who will be **first**,
    and some are **first** who will be **last**."

The opening narration should convey Jesus' great concern for the people.

This question is not dispassionate.
Rather than responding with bad news, Jesus' reply offers the way that leads to salvation.

This is one of Jesus' "hard sayings." There is no way to lessen the difficult teaching conveyed here. To do so would be a disservice to your assembly.

This reply will be repeated; keep it grave each time. It has the weight of saying, "I don't know who you are."

Though the parable suggests the choice is God's, we know it is we who say no, not God.

This is a dire image of exclusion from the banquet. Its stark imagery is intentional!

Those coming from the four winds are the Gentiles who precede those first invited.

---

to get the bread he needs. But here, the master denies even knowing those who stand outside desperately knocking. This is why proof-texting is seldom a good idea. Rarely does one text tell the whole story and often another text tells a very different tale. The story here is that the narrow gate that leads to salvation won't remain open forever. God overflows with mercy, but God respects our freedom and won't force mercy upon us.

The master's refusal to open the door isn't a metaphor for God's exhausted patience, but of our diminished capacity to accept God's mercy. At some point, we become incapable of asking. We shut our eyes and close our hearts, and the love God still seeks to give us can't find a home in us. No amount of knocking will be of any use because the door we knock on is our own; only we hold the key, but at that point, we're warned, we won't make use of it.

The words "I do not know where you are from" don't imply that God makes an issue of our place of origin; rather, they suggest the choices we make can change us into someone unrecognizable. Some will not find a home in the Kingdom because they've already made a home somewhere else.

Jesus speaks the truth with great regret that Gentiles who were last to hear the Gospel will enter the Kingdom ahead of those (the Jews) who were invited first. It will take effort on your part as reader to communicate the *great* effort it takes to make choices that lead to the Kingdom. G.M.

TWENTY-SECOND SUNDAY IN ORDINARY TIME

Sirach = SEER-ak

The salutation should set your tone!

These first two sentences give commands: "conduct . . . humble yourself"! The goal is to persuade.

Maintain a slow pace and serene tone throughout. After each pair of lines, pause and breathe to renew your energy and then share the new idea.

Pause and sustain eye contact before announcing, "The word of the Lord."

For meditation and context:

TO KEEP IN MIND

Pray the Scriptures: Make reading these Scriptures a part of your prayer life every week, and especially during the week prior to the liturgy in which you will proclaim.

LECTIONARY #126

READING I   Sirach 3:17–18, 20, 28–29

A reading from the Book of Sirach

My **child**, conduct your affairs with **humility**,
   and you will be **loved more** than a **giver** of **gifts**.
Humble yourself the **more**, the **greater** you **are**,
   and you will find **favor** with **God**.
What is **too sublime** for you, **seek not**,
   into **things** beyond your **strength search not**.
The **mind** of a **sage** appreciates **proverbs**,
   and an **attentive ear** is the **joy** of the **wise**.
Water quenches a **flaming fire**,
   and **alms atone** for **sins**.

RESPONSORIAL PSALM   Psalm 68:4–5, 6–7, 10–11 (see 11b)

R. God, in your goodness, you have made a home for the poor.

The just rejoice and exult before God;
   they are glad and rejoice.
Sing to God, chant praise to his name;
   whose name is the LORD.

The father of orphans and the defender of widows
   is God in his holy dwelling.
God gives a home to the forsaken;
   he leads forth prisoners to prosperity.

A bountiful rain you showered down, O God,
   upon your inheritance;
   you restored the land when it languished;
your flock settled in it;
   in your goodness, O God, you provided it
   for the needy.

READING I   Written nearly 200 years before Jesus by a teacher named Ben Sira, (the Greek form of the name is "Sirach") this book was accepted as canonical by the Church even though it never became a formal part of the Jewish Bible. Protestants also exclude it from their collection of Scripture. But it is easy to see why the Church found divine inspiration at the core of this writing, and it's not difficult to imagine Jesus having read these verses that find echoes in his own sayings.

That humility leads to favor in the sight of God and that those who are greatest should be servants of all are certainly familiar themes in Christian teaching. One who glories in his or her own good work can't at the same time give glory to God. In making his points, Sirach employs the same humility he endorses. His style is simple and humble, comprised of two-line epigrams or wise sayings that all speak of the benefits of humility both in the conduct of secular "affairs" and in the service of the Lord.

Maxims like these are meant to stand alone, not dependent on what precedes or follows. As such, you must let each have its say before moving on to the next. Rushing will destroy the gentle rhythm of these lines. But simple and unadorned verses of similar length and structure can lure you, unwittingly, into a sing-song cadence. Avoid that trap. The reading begins with two imperative sentences that encourage model behavior; they are followed by declarative sentences that make a clear statement and end with a full stop. Imagine a wise elder sharing this advice with a beloved pupil.

READING II   Hebrews 12:18–19, 22–24a

A reading from the Letter to the Hebrews

Brothers and **sisters**:
You have **not** approached that which could be **touched**
     and a **blazing fire** and **gloomy darkness**
     and **storm** and a **trumpet** blast
     and a **voice speaking words** such that **those** who **heard**
     begged that **no message** be further **addressed** to them.
No, you have **approached Mount Zion**
     and the **city** of the **living God**, the **heavenly Jerusalem**,
     and countless **angels** in festal **gathering**,
     and the **assembly** of the **firstborn enrolled** in **heaven**,
     and **God** the **judge** of **all**,
     and the **spirits** of the **just** made **perfect**,
     and **Jesus**, the **mediator** of a new **covenant**,
     and the **sprinkled blood** that speaks more **eloquently**
          than that of **Abel**.

GOSPEL   Luke 14:1, 7–14

A reading from the holy Gospel according to Luke

On a **sabbath Jesus** went to **dine**
     at the home of one of the leading **Pharisees**,
     and the **people** there were **observing** him **carefully**.

He told a **parable** to those who had been **invited**,
     noticing how they were choosing the **places** of **honor**
          at the **table**.
"When you are **invited** by someone to a **wedding banquet**,
     do not **recline** at table in the **place** of **honor**. »

Margin notes

Pause after the salutation, then, as if with a shake of the head, speak of those things that are *not* part of our experience in Christ. Your tone says, "Yes these were fearful things, but they don't exist any longer!"
God's voice was so terrifying that the people wanted to shut it out!

Your tone should communicate the very different climate of the new covenant.

Name each segment of the citizenry of the new Jerusalem with pride and delight. Each is more assurance of the safety and goodness of this Holy City.

Slow your pace at the end of the first sentence to draw attention to the watching eyes of the Pharisees.

Don't assume a judgmental tone here.

To hold their attention, Jesus' tone would need to avoid harshness and remain upbeat. The lesson will be clearer if the tone is not judgmental.

READING II Imagine a young person on the eve of a major life event that is both thrilling and daunting, like a wedding. A groom or bride might be intimidated by the anticipated pageantry, by the commitment, and by the unfolding relationship that lies ahead. A wise parent or friend might speak to them much as the author of Hebrews speaks today.

Asking them to consider a similarly thrilling but *more* daunting experience—going to college, entering the military, starting a job—the friend or parent might say, "This is nothing *like* that. You had *reason* to fear and even feel alone, but this is just the *opposite*. You have the embrace of someone who *loves* you, the support of *family*, the experience of *knowing* this person with whom you'll now be one."

Making the same point, the author of Hebrews contrasts the old covenant made in the midst of the thunder and fire of Mt. Sinai, a sight that filled the people with fear of God and made them want to shut their ears to block God's fearful voice, with the new covenant made under wholly different circumstance. In the new covenant, we stand with Christ at Mt. Zion in the company of innumerable angels and saints. Rather than fear, this setting fills us with peace, for we see those who went before us assembled in "festal gathering." Though we stand before "God the judge of all," we are not alone but in the company of "Jesus, the mediator of a new covenant" who intercedes for us and turns what might be fearful into an experience of safety, solace, and communion! It is a hopeful message to be spoken in hope-filled joy!

The host would find this awkward, to say the least.

Jesus' tone says, "Here is a better way!"

Take time with this important saying.

Now Jesus is in full teacher mode. His concern is for the neglected poor, but also for the rich who need to learn this lesson in order to rise with the "righteous."

blessed = blesd

Offer this assurance with great conviction.

> **TO KEEP IN MIND**
> **Build:** refers to increasing vocal intensity as you work toward a climactic point in the text. It calls for intensified emotional energy, which can be communicated by an increase or decrease in volume, or by speaking faster or slower. The point is to show more passion, greater urgency, or concern.

A more **distinguished** guest than you may have been
    invited by him,
  and the **host** who invited **both** of you may **approach you**
    and **say,**
    '**Give** your **place** to **this man**,'
  and then you would **proceed** with **embarrassment**
  to take the **lowest** place.
Rather, when you are **invited**,
  go and **take** the **lowest place**
  so that when the **host comes** to **you** he may say,
  'My **friend, move up** to a **higher** position.'
Then you will **enjoy** the **esteem** of your **companions** at the **table**.
For **every one** who **exalts** himself will be **humbled**,
  but the one who **humbles** himself will be **exalted**."
Then he **said** to the **host** who **invited** him,
  "When you hold a **lunch** or a **dinner**,
  do **not** invite your **friends** or your **brothers**
  or your **relatives** or your **wealthy neighbors**,
  in case they may **invite** you **back** and you have **repayment**.
Rather, when you hold a **banquet**,
  invite the **poor**, the **crippled**, the **lame**, the **blind**;
  blessed indeed will you be because of **their inability**
    to **repay you**.
For **you** will be **repaid** at the **resurrection** of the **righteous**."

GOSPEL The wisdom of Ben Sira recommended humility as a means of winning favor with God. Here, Jesus teaches that humility is the route to "esteem" even among neighbors and colleagues. Only Luke records this Sabbath banquet where, he says, Jesus was being closely scrutinized. Obviously, the convention of place cards had not yet come into fashion, so one who was self-aggrandizing ran the risk of overestimating his importance and choosing a place reserved for someone more important. At first glance, it seems Jesus is offering Emily Post-style advice on etiquette meant to ward off the likelihood of being "embarrassed." To avoid such a plight, Jesus advises taking the lowest place so the host can invite you higher, making you the envy of all.

Such advice might be expected in a book on winning friends and influencing people, but not in a teaching on the spiritual disposition worthy of God's Kingdom. But the second half of the text puts the first in proper perspective, for it reveals, as occurs often in Luke, Jesus' concern for the poor and his attitude toward the rich. We see Jesus' advice is not given as a means to an end, a manipulative strategy to gain in a roundabout way the praise and admiration of others. He counsels, counter-culturally, doing for those who *can't* do back for us. This time, he predicts no earthly honor or affirmation, but an eternal reward, visible only to eyes of faith, that will come at the eternal banquet that celebrates "the resurrection of the righteous." G.M.

TWENTY-THIRD SUNDAY IN ORDINARY TIME

LECTIONARY #129

READING I   Wisdom 9:13–18b

Since these questions will be out of context and unexpected, pause between them to let your listeners ponder.

Don't sound harsh; this is a reflection on the human condition, not a condemnation.

The text is saying that our humanity is limited in its ability to grasp the greater truths.

Express both joy and gratitude that God has given us at least a degree of understanding.

End on a note of humble gratitude.

A reading from the Book of Wisdom

Who can **know** God's **counsel**,
  or who can **conceive** what the Lord **intends**?
For the **deliberations** of **mortals** are **timid**,
  and **unsure** are our **plans**.
For the **corruptible body burdens** the **soul**
  and the **earthen shelter** weighs down the **mind**
    that has **many concerns**.
And **scarce** do we **guess** the things on **earth**,
  and what is within our **grasp** we find with **difficulty**;
  but when **things** are in **heaven**, **who** can **search** them out?
Or **who** ever **knew** your **counsel**, except **you** had given **wisdom**
  and **sent** your **holy spirit** from on **high**?
And **thus** were the **paths** of those on **earth** made **straight**.

READING I | There are two opposing theological ways of speaking about God, the "cataphatic" and the "apophatic." The cataphatic attempts to assert what is true about God—God is being, justice, love—while the apophatic approach, convinced that anything we say is incomplete and falls short of the reality of God, insists that, therefore, we can only say what God is *not*. While the historical books of the Old Testament try to make affirmative statements about who God is based on Israel's *experience* of God, the Wisdom literature understands that those efforts ultimately fail because God transcends every category humans have ever devised or ever will.

That's the simple point of this text. It seeks to remind us humans of the great limitations under which we labor. It is hard enough for us to understand human affairs—"scarce do we guess the things on earth"—so seeking to probe those of heaven becomes the sheerest folly. Often, the best way to teach is through questions that make the student consider the issue and come to his or her own conclusion. The author of Wisdom poses four questions in this brief text demonstrating deft pedagogy. "Who can know . . . who can conceive . . . " can be asked not in a confrontational way, but as if by a teacher who trusts students' ability to reason and understand.

The final question is put to God in acknowledgment that whatever understanding we have about God was given to us *by* God. End the reading with gratitude that God's mercy has led us to walk "straight paths."

For meditation and context:

RESPONSORIAL PSALM　Psalm 90:3–4, 5–6, 12–13, 14, 17 (1)

R. In every age, O Lord, you have been our refuge.

You turn man back to dust,
　saying, "Return, O children of men."
For a thousand years in your sight
　are as yesterday, now that it is past,
　or as a watch of the night.

You make an end of them in their sleep;
　the next morning they are like the
　　changing grass,
which at dawn springs up anew,
　but by evening wilts and fades.

Teach us to number our days aright,
　that we may gain wisdom of heart.
Return, O Lord! How long?
　Have pity on your servants!

Fill us at daybreak with your kindness,
　that we may shout for joy and gladness all
　　our days.
And may the gracious care of the Lord our
　　God be ours;
　prosper the work of our hands for us!
　Prosper the work of our hands!

READING II　Philemon 9–10, 12–17

A reading from the Letter of Saint Paul to Philemon

Philemon = fi-LEE-muhn

Paul does not refrain from using every persuasive angle: I am *old* and a *prisoner.*
Onesimus = oh-NES-uh-muhs

Stress Paul's designation of Onesimus as his "child."

Paul continues to pour it on: Onesimus is his very "*heart*"!

He's saying, I overcame my own desires in order to do the right thing (suggesting, perhaps, that Philemon now also do the right thing).

Paul grows more serious and philosophical here. Slow your pace.

Onesimus' conversion should impact Philemon even more than Paul.

beloved = bee-LUHVD

Paul clinches his argument with an appeal to Philemon's esteem for their relationship.

I, Paul, an **old** man,
　and now also a **prisoner** for **Christ Jesus**,
　urge you on behalf of my **child Onesimus**,
　whose **father** I have **become** in my **imprisonment**;
　I am **sending him**, that is, my own **heart**, **back** to you.
I should have **liked** to **retain** him for **myself**,
　so that he might **serve** me on your **behalf**
　in my **imprisonment** for the **gospel**,
　but I did not want to do **anything** without your **consent**,
　so that the **good** you **do** might not be **forced** but **voluntary**.
Perhaps **this** is why he was **away** from you for a while,
　that you might have him **back forever**,
　no longer as a **slave**
　but **more** than a **slave**, **a brother**,
　beloved especially to **me**, but even **more** so to **you**,
　as a **man** and in the **Lord**.
So **if you** regard **me** as a **partner**, **welcome him** as you would **me**.

READING II　From prison, Paul writes to a leader of the Christian community in Colossae about a runaway slave whom Paul has met and converted to Christianity. The scandal of a disciple of Christ owning a slave is mitigated by the expectation of Christ's imminent return, making social change seem unnecessary. While Christians may have been powerless to change the society, they were not powerless to change their own attitudes and influence those of others.

That's precisely what Paul does here. His encounter with Onesimus has resulted in the development of a father-son bond between them. Paul would gladly keep the young man with him as an aid in his imprisonment and as a brother in his apostolic ministry, but he wants to leave Philemon free to make such a choice rather than compel it. He sends the boy back, however, different than he found him and he wants Philemon to be very much aware of it.

Onesimus has become a brother in the Lord; he is newly minted and it seems Paul finds it inconceivable that Philemon would overlook that fact and treat him as any less than a brother. Paul has come to love this young man, but he believes that Philemon will love him even more when he is able to recognize in him not the "slave" he knew before, but the "man . . . in the Lord" he has become.

Speak with urgency and passion about the need to see Onesimus for who he really is. Paul's revolutionary attitude toward Onesimus set the stage for the evolution of new viewpoints about a person's dignity in Christ.

GOSPEL　Today's First Reading speaks of God's inscrutabil-

GOSPEL   Luke 14:25–33

A reading from the holy Gospel according to Luke

Great **crowds** were traveling with **Jesus**,
    and he **turned** and **addressed** them,
        "If **anyone** comes to me without **hating** his **father** and **mother**,
        wife and **children**, **brothers** and **sisters**,
        and even his **own life**,
        he **cannot** be my **disciple**.
Whoever does **not** carry his **own cross** and **come after me**
        cannot be my **disciple**.
Which of you **wishing** to construct a **tower**
        does not **first** sit down and **calculate** the **cost**
        to see if there is **enough** for its **completion**?
Otherwise, after laying the **foundation**
        and finding himself **unable** to **finish** the **work**
        the onlookers should **laugh** at him and **say**,
        '**This** one **began** to **build** but did not have the **resources**
            to **finish**.'
Or what **king marching** into **battle** would not **first sit down**
        and **decide** whether with **ten** thousand troops
        he can **successfully** oppose **another king**
        advancing upon him with **twenty** thousand troops?
But if **not**, while he is **still** far **away**,
        he will **send** a **delegation** to ask for **peace** terms.
In the **same way**,
        anyone of you who **does not renounce all** his **possessions**
        cannot be my **disciple**."

Lift your voice to suggest his address to the large crowd.

Notice, it's not only family, but even ourselves we must be willing to renounce.

The urgent energy lessens for this section.

Offer the second example, "Or what king . . ." immediately, without taking a pause.

Contrast "*ten*" and "*twenty*" thousand.

Pause here before declaring, with sustained eye contact, the final admonition.

ity. This text, most of which contains material unique to Luke, demonstrates that inscrutability. While the language is concrete and replete with everyday images relating to construction and warfare, the message of total detachment seems everything but human or commonplace. Although Jesus constantly presents the Kingdom with prosaic images that ground it in human experience, there remains something about the Kingdom that clearly transcends all our categories.

The text begins and ends with statements of total dedication and extreme detachment. A disciple is to come to Jesus "hating his father and mother" and "renounce all his possessions." In between are lessons on the folly of undertaking an enterprise without sufficient forethought. Doing so, Jesus tells us, brings either humiliation or destruction. But Jesus surely wants disciples, so his words can't be meant to discourage the genuine and sincere. Perhaps Jesus experienced too often the cloying praise of the faint-hearted; perhaps, as with the rich young man whom Jesus loved but who nonetheless went off after hearing just such a hard saying as found here, Jesus wants would-be disciples to understand the consuming dedication required of those who undertake to follow him.

Following Christ not only requires placing him ahead of all other values and concerns, it also demands a willingness to carry our cross and suffer with him. The old Law required allegiance and care for one's father; Jesus says the Kingdom of our heavenly father takes precedence over all things, even our parents of flesh and blood. G.M.

TWENTY-FOURTH SUNDAY IN ORDINARY TIME

LECTIONARY #132

READING I   Exodus 32:7–11, 13–14

A reading from the Book of Exodus

The LORD said to Moses,
"Go down at **once** to your **people**,
    whom you brought **out** of the land of **Egypt**,
    for they have become **depraved**.
They have soon turned **aside** from the way I pointed **out** to them,
    making for themselves a **molten calf** and **worshiping** it,
    sacrificing to it and crying out,
    '**This** is your God, O **Israel**,
    who brought you **out** of the land of **Egypt**!'
I see how **stiff-necked** this people is," continued the LORD
        to Moses.
"Let me **alone**, then,
    that my **wrath** may blaze up **against** them to **consume** them.
Then I will make of you a **great nation**."

But Moses **implored** the LORD, his God, saying,
"**Why**, O LORD, should your **wrath** blaze up
        against your **own people**,
    whom **you** brought out of the land of Egypt
    with such **great power** and with so **strong** a **hand**?
Remember your **servants Abraham**, **Isaac**, and **Israel**,
    and how you **swore** to them by your **own self**, saying,
    'I will make your **descendants** as **numerous** as the **stars**
        in the **sky**;

Note that God and Moses will take turns, like exasperated parents, labeling the Israelites "your people."
Stress that it is the Lord who speaks.

Don't hold back expressing God's anger and frustration.

God's disappointment is over their repeated infidelity and for mistaking a human object for the eternal God.

Rather than rage, these words can sound like an angry person hoping to be "held back" from taking retribution.

Moses' voice should be a blend of humility and confidence in God's merciful love.

Recall the patriarchs with tenderness and repeat God's promise with the assurance with which God first pronounced it.

READING I There are two sections to this reading and both are important for conveying its full message. First is the idolatry. Nothing in the Old Testament was as persistent or as hard to eradicate as this grave sin. Consistently God's people allowed this cancer to grow to the point that God was forced to intervene, like a scalpel-wielding surgeon, to excise this deadly tumor. We tend today to think idolatry is a thing of the ancient past when people built idols of stone and metal and set them up for worship. Given the presence of many statues in our churches, it may seem odd that God would become so passionate about this weakness. But God's passion is focused on infidelity, a deep down lack of trust in the God who numerous times had demonstrated unconditional love and loyalty.

The second section includes Moses' intercession and God's change of mind. Some of the power and beauty of the Old Testament is found in the human emotions and motives it ascribes to God. That God would be susceptible to intercession that "reminds" him of his saving actions in the past and of his promises to the patriarchs portrays God with such immanence that he appears almost human. In folksy fashion Moses says, in effect, "You've already invested so much in this people; you're on record with promises of ancestors and land; you can't renege on that now."

And, remarkably, God is persuaded. But not out of fear of appearing a liar or of bruising his reputation; no, God relents because it's in God's nature to do so. Ours is a God of mercy.

READING II St. Paul seldom hesitates to draw lessons from the cir-

Take a substantial pause before announcing God's change of heart.

and **all** this **land** that I **promised,**
    I will **give** your **descendants** as their **perpetual heritage.'"**
So the LORD **relented** in the **punishment**
    he had **threatened** to **inflict** on his **people.**

For meditation and context:

RESPONSORIAL PSALM   Psalm 51:3–4, 12–13, 17, 19 (Luke 15:18)

R. I will rise and go to my father.

Have mercy on me, O God, in your goodness;
    in the greatness of your compassion wipe
        out my offense.
Thoroughly wash me from my guilt
    and of my sin cleanse me.

A clean heart create for me, O God,
    and a steadfast spirit renew within me.
Cast me not out from your presence,
    and your Holy Spirit take not from me.

O Lord, open my lips,
    and my mouth shall proclaim your praise.
My sacrifice, O God, is a contrite spirit;
    a heart contrite and humbled, O God, you
        will not spurn.

TO KEEP IN MIND
Pauses are never "dead" moments. Something is always happening during a pause. Practice will teach you how often and how long to pause. Too many pauses make a reading choppy; too few cause ideas to run into one another.

Beloved = bee-LUHV-uhd

Be aware of where you are headed; Paul is not expressing generic gratitude but thanks for God's inexplicable mercy!

He's not bragging, but confessing his earlier ignorance and arrogance.

Don't speak of his "ignorance" as an excuse; Paul is nothing but grateful here.

This is a grand and solemn truth best spoken with heartfelt simplicity.

Connect his thoughts: (a) I was chosen (b) because as a great sinner (c) I'm an example of God's mercy!

READING II   1 Timothy 1:12–17

A reading from the first Letter of Saint Paul to Timothy

Beloved:
I am **grateful** to him who has **strengthened** me, **Christ Jesus**
    our **Lord,**
    because he **considered** me **trustworthy**
    in **appointing** me to the **ministry.**
I was once a **blasphemer** and a **persecutor** and **arrogant,**
    but I have been **mercifully treated**
    because I **acted** out of **ignorance** in my **unbelief.**
Indeed, the **grace** of our **Lord** has been **abundant,**
    along with the **faith** and **love** that are in **Christ Jesus.**
This saying is **trustworthy** and deserves **full acceptance:**
    Christ Jesus came into the **world** to **save sinners.**
Of these **I** am the **foremost. »**

cumstances of his own life. And when those circumstances are far from flattering, he's no less inclined to shed light on them if he thinks they will prove useful for others in their efforts to better understand the Gospel or to deal with the problematic circumstances of their own lives.

You probably know already that Paul's first contact with followers of Christ was as their persecutor. He had excelled in his studies of the old Law and was convinced that the Jesus movement presented a threat to true religion and that this sect must be wiped out. With great zeal he pur-

sued this goal, persecuting and even putting to death some of Jesus' followers. One of the great ironies of Christian history is that this would-be destroyer of the faith became one of its greatest and most effective promoters.

Hiding nothing, Paul willingly admits his past. And he's grateful that God chose him for "the ministry" despite having been its most ardent opponent. Paul is incapable of seeing a glass half empty. Even in these circumstances that might have sent another person hiding in shame, he finds God's grace at work. And from these cir-

cumstances of his life he derives a theological truth that he declares with great assurance: Jesus came for people like him. Sinners are so mired in the muck of their lives that they are hopelessly stuck and need a savior to extract them from the mess of their own making.

Paul is happy to serve as an "example" of God's mercy. In his ministry, he could go about saying, in so many words, "Look at me and what I did. Yet Christ chose me to bring his Good News to the nations. If God could show such mercy to one like me, why

Paul ends with a moment of deep prayer. Don't list God's attributes like grocery items. Each reveals a profound dimension of the mystery of God.

But for **that reason** I was **mercifully treated**,
　　so that in **me**, as the **foremost**,
　　　　Christ Jesus might **display** all his **patience** as an **example**
　　　　for those who would come to **believe** in him for **everlasting life**.
To the **king** of **ages**, **incorruptible**, **invisible**, the **only God**,
　　honor and **glory forever** and **ever. Amen.**

GOSPEL Luke 15:1–32

A reading from the holy Gospel according to Luke

The makeup of the crowd attracted to Jesus disturbs the Pharisees who find reason to grumble.

They don't bother whispering; they want him to hear their displeasure.

Imagine Jesus moving among the crowd, catching one person's eye and then another. These stories should be animated and upbeat.

The tone throughout says, "This is obvious; everyone (even you!) would behave this way!"

Here Jesus speaks for God and the ways of God's Kingdom—sure to anger his critics.

Note Luke's use of a female image to present God's love for sinners.

Tax collectors and **sinners** were all drawing **near** to **listen**
　　　　to **Jesus**,
　　but the **Pharisees** and **scribes** began to **complain**, saying,
　　"**This** man **welcomes sinners** and **eats** with them."
So to **them** he addressed this **parable**.
"**What man** among you having a **hundred** sheep
　　　　and losing **one** of them
　　would not **leave** the **ninety-nine** in the desert
　　and go after the **lost one** until he **finds** it?
And when he **does** find it,
　　he **sets** it on his **shoulders** with **great joy**
　　and, upon his arrival **home**,
　　he **calls** together his **friends** and **neighbors** and **says** to them,
　　'**Rejoice** with me because I have **found** my **lost sheep**.'
I tell you, in **just** the **same way**
　　there will be **more joy** in **heaven** over **one sinner** who **repents**
　　than over **ninety-nine righteous people**
　　who have **no need** of **repentance**.

"Or **what woman** having **ten coins** and **losing one**
　　would not **light** a **lamp** and **sweep** the **house**,
　　searching carefully until she **finds** it?
And when she **does** find it,
　　she **calls** together her **friends** and **neighbors**
　　and **says** to them,

---

would you question that he could be merciful to you?"

　　Keep Paul's gratitude and fervor in mind as you read. Paul always has an objective: here it is to convince his hearers that nothing can separate them from the love of God. And you are his mouthpiece.

 GOSPEL Because the Pharisees are scandalized by Jesus' popularity among "tax collectors and sinners," Jesus weaves a collection of stories about

God's mercy and the need for human cooperation with God's grace. Jesus' first two stories are less challenging to the sensibilities of his opponents. In each case, an item of value is lost and the owner goes to great lengths to recover it. The "hero" of his first story is anyone in the crowd, presumably even the Pharisees, willing to imagine the scenario he lays out. Like the "sheep" of the first story, the lost "coin" of the second is recovered, bringing great joy to its owner and her neighbors. These narratives are

"easy" in the sense that even the Pharisees will readily concede that no one wants to lose something of value, not even God. But apparently these two stories don't sufficiently communicate the depth of Jesus' concern for the lost, nor of God's mercy toward sinners who repent.

　　So Jesus launches into his best story and in doing so introduces a great deal of complexity, both about the dynamic of forgiveness and reconciliation, and about the response of those who have been less prof-

As above, emphasize the *public* rejoicing.

Pause before launching into the story of the prodigal as if deciding that more needs to be said about forgiveness and repentance.

Suggest the father's dismay as he accedes to his son's demands.

Don't rush this mention of his dissolution. Take note of the strong words "squandered" and "life of dissipation."

Your tone should reveal how great an indignity it was for a Jew to feed a Gentile's pigs.

This seems less a conversion than a move for self-preservation. But still it requires humility and trust.

This time he is just rehearsing. The sincerity will come later.

The character of the father is revealed in this initiative toward the son.

Now, give the son's confession the sound of sincerity.

'**Rejoice** with me because I have **found** the **coin** that I **lost**.'
In **just** the **same way**, I **tell you**,
　　there will be **rejoicing** among the **angels** of **God**
　　over **one sinner** who **repents**."

Then he said,
　　"A man had **two sons**, and the **younger** son said to his **father**,
　　'**Father give** me the **share** of your **estate** that should **come**
　　　　to me.'
So the **father divided** the **property between** them.
After a few **days**, the younger son **collected** all his **belongings**
　　and **set** off to a **distant country**
　　where he **squandered** his inheritance on a **life** of **dissipation**.
When he had **freely** spent **everything**,
　　a **severe famine** struck that **country**,
　　and he **found** himself in dire **need**.
So he **hired** himself **out** to one of the local **citizens**
　　who sent him to his **farm** to tend the **swine**.
And he **longed** to **eat** his **fill** of the **pods** on which the **swine** fed,
　　but **nobody gave** him any.
Coming to his **senses** he **thought**,
　　'How **many** of my father's hired **workers**
　　have **more** than **enough** food to eat,
　　but here am **I**, **dying** from **hunger**.
I shall **get up** and **go** to my **father** and I shall **say** to him,
　　"**Father**, I have **sinned** against **heaven** and **against you**.
I no longer **deserve** to be **called your son**;
　　treat me as you would **treat one** of your **hired workers**."'
So he **got up** and **went back** to his **father**.
While he was **still** a **long way off**,
　　his **father** caught **sight** of him,
　　and was **filled** with **compassion**.
He **ran** to his son, embraced him and **kissed** him.
His son **said** to him,
　　'**Father**, I have **sinned** against **heaven** and **against you**;
　　I no longer **deserve** to be called **your son**.' ≫

ligate in their sinning and who resent the extravagance of the Father's mercy. The story of the prodigal needs no rehearsing. Jesus makes the boy self-absorbed and self-indulgent: he wants what he wants and he wants it now. Given his character, his fate is predictable. But the depths to which he sinks probably shock his listeners, for the boy is reduced to feeding pigs and even envies the husks on which they fill their bellies. At this low ebb, the boy comes to his senses and realizes that even as a servant

he'd live better back home than here. So he rehearses his plea to his father and begins his return journey.

All the while, he has had no contact with his father. He knows not if his father pines for him or has cursed his memory. Neither does he know if, upon his return, he will be relegated among the "hired hands" or his father's "servants." He doesn't seem to care. Home is calling and he sets out. Now the father reenters the story and we learn that the older man did

not wait for the son's arrival, but rushed toward him instead; he also didn't let him complete his rehearsed speech but immediately summoned his servant to dress the boy and prepare a celebration.

A fourth act unfolds that reintroduces the elder brother brooding about the fuss being made over his undeserving sibling. The father spends little time reassuring the elder son—"you are here with me always; everything I have is yours." According to the father, nothing more need be said. But

The father's voice is filled with excitement and breathless joy.	But his **father** ordered his **servants**,
	   '**Quickly** bring the **finest robe** and put it **on** him;
	   put a **ring** on his **finger** and **sandals** on his **feet**.
	Take the **fattened calf** and **slaughter** it.
	Then let us **celebrate** with a **feast**,
	   because this **son** of **mine** was **dead**, and has **come** to **life** again;
	   he was **lost**, and has been **found**.'
	Then the **celebration began**.

"Now the older son" introduces a dark cloud that temporarily blocks the sun of the joyful celebration.	Now the **older** son had been **out** in the **field**
	   and, on his way **back**, as he **neared** the **house**,
	   he heard the **sound** of **music** and **dancing**.
	He **called** one of the **servants** and **asked** what this might **mean**.
	The servant said to him,

The "servant" shares the father's joy over the younger son's return.	'Your **brother** has **returned**
	   and your **father** has **slaughtered** the **fattened calf**
	   because he has him **back safe** and **sound**.'

Pause briefly before reintroducing the father.	He became **angry**,
	   and when he **refused** to enter the house,
	   his **father came out** and **pleaded** with him.
	He said to his father in reply,
	   '**Look, all** these **years I served you**
	   and not **once** did I disobey **your orders**;
	   yet you **never** gave me **even** a **young goat** to **feast** on
	      with **my friends**.

The son feels wronged and entitled to his anger.	But when **your** son **returns**,
	   who **swallowed** up **your property** with **prostitutes**,
	   for **him** you **slaughter** the fattened **calf**.'

The father's tone needs to convey sincere compassion.	He **said** to him,
	   '**My son**, **you** are here with me **always**;
	   everything I have is **yours**.
	But **now** we **must celebrate** and **rejoice**,
	   because your **brother** was **dead** and has **come** to **life** again;

Use ritardando (slowing gradually toward the end) on this final line.	he was **lost** and has been **found**.'" [Shorter: Luke 15:1–10]

the fact that one of his sons had been lost—hopelessly, irredeemably, heart-wrenchingly lost—and that this son is now found *must* be celebrated. There is no other choice. While much reflection on this story centers on the Father's mercy and the elder son's parsimonious heart, the post-debauchery behavior of the prodigal is often overlooked.

Without the boy's awareness of the state he'd sunk to, without his humility to admit his errors and ask forgiveness, without his determination to make the long journey back home, the father's love could not have reached him. We can count on the father of this story being a truthful rendering of God, our Father. But the heart of the matter lies in whether we can count on ourselves to resemble the portrait of the prodigal rendered in this story. Life not only changes our circumstances, it also changes us. And sometimes we change to a point where there may be no turning back. All are offered forgiveness, but not all embrace it. The story of the prodigal reminds us we can always return home, and that if we choose, sadly and tragically, we can remain in the far country. G.M.

TWENTY-FIFTH SUNDAY IN ORDINARY TIME

LECTIONARY #135

READING I   Amos 8:4–7

A reading from the Book of the Prophet Amos

Make eye contact. The prophet's goal is to get people to hear God's warning!

Convey the impatience of the greedy who want to get back to making money.

Ephah = EE-fah (a unit of dry measure)

Shekel = SHEK-*l (a unit of weight)

Their plots become increasingly sinister and heartless.

Pause, then announce God's solemn promise. The threat here is greater than in the opening line.

> **Hear this**, you who **trample** upon the **needy**
>   and **destroy** the **poor** of the **land**!
> "**When** will the **new moon** be **over**," you ask,
>   "that we may **sell** our **grain**,
>   and the **sabbath**, that we may **display** the **wheat**?
> We will **diminish** the **ephah**,
>   **add** to the **shekel**,
>   and **fix** our **scales** for **cheating**!
> We will **buy** the **lowly** for **silver**,
>   and the **poor** for a **pair** of **sandals**;
>   even the **refuse** of the **wheat** we will **sell**!"
> The Lord has **sworn** by the **pride** of **Jacob**:
>   **Never** will I **forget** a **thing** they have **done**!

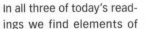

READING I In all three of today's readings we find elements of the conviction that spirituality does not consist only in one's personal relationship with God, necessary as that is, but also in concrete and just relationships with our neighbors.

The prophet Amos prophesied in the northern kingdom of Israel at a time of great economic growth. Despite the prosperity, greed among some of the wealthy was unabated and Amos challenges their blatant self-indulgence and its attendant hypocrisy. Seasonal and weekly festivals, like the new moon and Sabbath that afforded the poor a brief respite from their labor, were seen by the rich as obstacles to moneymaking. They longed for the holy time to end so they could return to their greed-driven enterprises of tampering and cheating. In the reading, they even brag of selling debtors into slavery for the price of a "pair of sandals." The text verbalizes the secret thoughts of the greedy who think they can conspire with impunity. Be sure your tone conveys the unscrupulous and evil nature of their scheming.

But Amos declares that God is neither unaware nor unconcerned about the plight of the poor.

The ominous closing line reveals that God is taking note and is ready for action to vindicate the weak and helpless. This text comprises a social oracle that begins and ends with solemn words of warning that require solemn delivery. It is important that they be heard as warning because God desires nothing more than repentance and conversion. Perhaps greed will turn to compassion in some hearts that hear these words today.

For meditation and context:

RESPONSORIAL PSALM   Psalm 113:1–2, 4–6, 7–8 (see 1a, 7b)

R. Praise the Lord who lifts up the poor. or Alleluia.

Praise, you servants of the LORD,
   praise the name of the LORD.
Blessed be the name of the LORD
   both now and forever.

High above all nations is the LORD;
   above the heavens is his glory.
Who is like the LORD, our God, who is
     enthroned on high
   and looks upon the heavens
     and the earth below?

He raises up the lowly from the dust;
   from the dunghill he lifts up the poor
to seat them with princes,
   with the princes of his own people.

READING II   1 Timothy 2:1–8

Beloved = bee-LUHV-uhd

A reading from the first Letter of Saint Paul to Timothy

With urgency, you are giving instructions. Speak with authority.

Beloved:
First of all, I **ask** that **supplications**, **prayers**,
   petitions, and **thanksgivings** be offered for **everyone**,
   for **kings** and for **all** in **authority**,
   that we may lead a **quiet** and **tranquil** life
   in all **devotion** and **dignity**.

Don't rush the benefits of praying for our leaders.

God expects us to pray. Speak in a gentler tone.

This is **good** and **pleasing** to **God** our **savior**,
   who wills **everyone** to be **saved**
   and to come to **knowledge** of the **truth**.
     For there is **one God**.
     There is also **one mediator** between **God** and **men**,
     the **man Christ Jesus**,
     who **gave** himself as **ransom** for **all**.

This is the instruction of a loving teacher.

This was the **testimony** at the **proper time**.
For **this** I was **appointed preacher** and **apostle**
   —I am **speaking** the **truth**, I am **not lying**—,
   teacher of the **Gentiles** in **faith** and **truth**.

God gave him this responsibility that all might be saved.

End softly and humbly, calling for prayer that is characterized by the peace you pray for.

It is my **wish**, then, that in **every place** the men should **pray**,
   lifting up holy hands, without **anger** or **argument**.

READING II   Paul is tapping the wisdom that Jesus demonstrated when he advised the Pharisees to "repay to Caesar what belongs to Caesar" (Luke 20:25). But of course, that advice didn't include worship of the emperor, which was expected of subjects and citizens of the Roman Empire. *Praying* for the emperor and other officials, however, laid a blanket of protection over the early Christians and guarded them from close scrutiny. So, Paul's advice is practical as well as altruistic. The practice of praying for kings was ancient, begun after the Persian king,

Cyrus, ended the exile and allowed Jews to return to Jerusalem to rebuild the city and Temple.

But Paul is calling for more than prudent self-interest; he is calling for selfless prayer that ultimately contributes to the *common* good. Paul understands that God is Lord, not only of Christians and Jews, but of all people, and that he desires all, even pagans, to be saved. God also desires justice and peace to prevail among all people. One way to ensure that is to pray for leaders, no matter their stripe. Assure your lis-

teners, as Paul does, that God finds such prayer "good and pleasing."

The God of *all* is manifested in the one *savior*, who died and rose to *save* all people. Paul insists this message came to him from Christ and was entrusted to him to proclaim to the *nations*. Because he was not among the original Twelve Apostles, Paul asserts his apostolic authority ("I am not lying") to assure his readers of the legitimacy of his claims. Take your cue from the word "urge" at the beginning. The goal is persuasion and that requires faith in your heart and conviction in your voice.

GOSPEL   Luke 16:1–13

A reading from the holy Gospel according to Luke

> *Jesus* said to his **disciples**,
>> "A **rich** man had a **steward**
>> who was **reported** to him for **squandering** his **property**.
>
> He **summoned** him and said,
>> 'What is this I **hear** about you?
>
> **Prepare** a full **account** of your **stewardship**,
>> because you can **no longer** be my **steward**.'
>
> The **steward** said to himself, '**What** shall I **do**,
>> **now** that my **master** is taking the **position** of **steward**
>>> **away** from me?
>
> I am **not strong** enough to **dig** and I am **ashamed** to **beg**.
> I **know** what I shall **do so** that,
>> when I am **removed** from the **stewardship**,
>> they may **welcome** me into their **homes**.'
>
> He called in his master's **debtors one** by **one**.
> To the **first** he said,
>> '**How much** do you **owe** my master?'
>
> He replied, '**One hundred measures** of **olive** oil.'
> He said to him, '**Here** is your **promissory** note.
> **Sit down** and quickly **write** one for **fifty**.'
> Then to **another** the steward said, 'And **you**,
>> **how much** do **you owe**?'
>
> He replied, '**One hundred kors** of **wheat**.'
> The steward **said** to him, '**Here** is **your** promissory note;
>> **write** one for **eighty**.' **»**

Jesus is in full teacher mode; start briskly.

The rich man's inquiry is stern.

The manager remains calm, resorting to logic rather than panic.

Your tone implies he has taken full charge of the situation.

He makes every effort to sound magnanimous.

Pause before citing the master's commendation.

This text offers a glimpse of the liturgical practice of the early Church that prayed much as we do today by first naming those for whom we pray (those in "authority") and then asking for a specific blessing ("that we may lead a . . . tranquil life").

GOSPEL   Jesus was sometimes dismayed that disciples lacked the will, determination, and resources to work as effectively for the Kingdom as nonbelievers worked for their interests in the world. To inspire that kind of initiative Jesus tells this parable.

We don't expect "antiheroes" in the Gospel. Typically, Jesus' exemplary characters are likable and inspiring and it's easy to see how imitating them ennobles us. But in this case, we are told to imitate one whose behavior appears to be shockingly wrong. Resourcefulness can be admirable, but what of these tactics? Some scholars reason that the steward is wisely deducting only his own commission, owed him for negotiating the master's business. Others contend that he is reducing the unjust and usurious interest owed to the master.

Whether the steward is slicing off the master's profits or deducting his own, the master, initially outraged that the servant had played fast and loose with his resources, now commends him for acting "prudently."

Through his maneuvering, the steward banks a great deal of goodwill for later when he will need it. Jesus encourages us to emulate that initiative, becoming as proactive with resources for eternal life as we are with the wealth we have in this world. Of course, it is the steward's prudence, not his dishonesty, which Jesus praises. But

Your tone comments on the master's attitude, helping us understand that prudence is being praised, not dishonesty.

Jesus draws a lesson from his story.

Make eye contact. This teaching counters the notion that we can cheat "just a little bit."

Slow the pace here. For some, this will be a "hard saying," difficult to accept.

The last sentence is a solemn pronouncement spoken with authority.

TO KEEP IN MIND
Stress: identifies words that are more important or expressive than others and require more stress. Use your judgment about the amount of stress so as to avoid an artificial delivery.

And the master **commended** that dishonest steward
    for acting **prudently**.

"For the **children** of **this world**
    are more **prudent** in **dealing** with their **own generation**
    than are the **children** of **light**.
I **tell** you, make **friends** for **yourselves** with **dishonest wealth**,
    so that when it **fails**, you will be **welcomed**
        into **eternal dwellings**.
The **person** who is **trustworthy** in **very small** matters
    is also **trustworthy** in **great ones**;
    and the **person** who is **dishonest** in **very small** matters
    is also **dishonest** in **great ones**.
If, therefore, you are **not trustworthy** with **dishonest wealth**,
    who will **trust** you with **true** wealth?
If you are **not trustworthy** with what **belongs** to **another**,
    who will **give** you what is **yours**?
No servant can serve **two** masters.
He will **either hate** one and **love** the **other**,
    or be **devoted** to one and **despise** the other.
You cannot serve both God and mammon."

[Shorter: Luke 16:10–13]

---

don't fear the jolt this parable may initially give your assembly. Becoming unsettled can make hearts more receptive to the three moral pronouncements that follow the parable.

In the first, "Make friends . . . with dishonest wealth," perhaps a better translation of the Greek for "dishonest wealth" would be simply "worldly resources," which can often lead one to dishonesty. Worldly resources in themselves are not con-

demned, but should be used wisely, not clung to, with the understanding that all earthly goods will pass away, and if we have been able to see where our salvation ultimately lies and let go of the immediate and worldly, we will be "welcomed into eternal dwellings." Second, if "you are not trustworthy with dishonest wealth" reminds us that our behavior here on earth influences our eternity. Finally, "God and mammon" is a blunt dose of truth meant to

convince us that we must own our possessions, not let *them* possess *us*. Only if money is used with a view to our heavenly destiny (and that destiny requires sharing with the less fortunate) can we be sure it has not become an idol that has usurped God's rightful place at the center of our lives. G.M.

TWENTY-SIXTH SUNDAY IN ORDINARY TIME

LECTIONARY #138

READING I   Amos 6:1a, 4–7

Even this opening narration should signal the harsh judgment to follow.

Your tone must tell us that this "complacency" is ill-gotten and ungodly.

Your energy and disapproval grow with each item added to this list.

They drink wine by the bowlful!

This is where their focus *should* be. Pause before the final sentence.

Speak slowly. This is not God's vengeance, but the sad consequence of their choices!

For meditation and context:

A reading from the Book of the Prophet Amos

Thus says the LORD, the **God** of **hosts**:
Woe to the **complacent** in **Zion**!
Lying upon **beds** of **ivory**,
    stretched **comfortably** on their **couches**,
they eat **lambs** taken from the **flock**,
    and **calves** from the **stall**!
Improvising to the **music** of the **harp**,
    like **David**, they **devise** their own **accompaniment**.
They **drink wine** from **bowls**
    and **anoint** themselves with the **best oils**;
    yet they are **not** made **ill** by the **collapse** of **Joseph**!
Therefore, **now** they shall be the **first** to go into **exile**,
    and their **wanton revelry** shall be **done away** with.

TO KEEP IN MIND
Read all three commentaries. Suggestions in each can give you insight into your own passage.

RESPONSORIAL PSALM   Psalm 146:7, 8–9, 9–10 (1b)

R. **Praise the Lord, my soul!** or
R. **Alleluia.**

Blessed is he who keeps faith forever,
    secures justice for the oppressed,
    gives food to the hungry.
The LORD sets captives free.

The LORD gives sight to the blind;
    the LORD raises up those who were bowed
    down.
The LORD loves the just;
    the LORD protects strangers.

The fatherless and the widow he sustains,
    but the way of the wicked he thwarts.
The LORD shall reign forever;
    your God, O Zion, through all
        generations. Alleluia.

READING I   As would the southern kingdom 135 years later at the hands of the Babylonians, the land of Israel in the north was overcome by pagan invaders and its citizens taken into exile in 721 BC. The prophet Amos anticipates this destruction and sees it as the result of the nation's indifference to the needy. Although he was from the southern kingdom, Amos denounces the excesses of the rich elite of the northern kingdom who delight in prosperity that benefits only them, while the poor get poorer.

This text precedes last week's equally threatening passage and rails mercilessly against the indulgent lifestyle of the wealthy who luxuriate in excess, oblivious to the crying need that surrounds them. Because theirs is a chosen blindness, it places an onerous load of guilt upon them. The rich feign religious observance, but their rituals become nothing more than excuses for more opulent living—"lambs" and "calves" fed on milk rather than grazed on grass were intended for ritual sacrifice, not for the consumption of the wealthy. Amos is blunt and forceful in his critique.

He understands that love of God never ignores the needs of one's neighbors and that prayer and sacrifice don't substitute for righteous living that includes sharing resources with the needy.

Your proclamation must indicate that Amos speaks for a God who cares about injustice and won't stand idly by as it happens. Sadly, Amos announces, the time for change is passed and the people's fate is sealed. There is no way to soften that hard truth!

READING II　1 Timothy 6:11–16

A reading from the first Letter of Saint Paul to Timothy

But **you**, **man** of **God**, pursue **righteousness**,
　　devotion, **faith**, **love**, **patience** and **gentleness**.
Compete **well** for the **faith**.
Lay hold of **eternal life**, to which you were **called**
　　when you made the **noble confession** in the presence
　　　of **many witnesses**.
I charge you before **God**, who gives **life** to **all** things,
　　and before **Christ Jesus**,
　　who gave **testimony** under **Pontius Pilate**
　　　for the **noble confession**,
　　to **keep** the **commandment** without **stain** or **reproach**
　　until the **appearance** of our **Lord Jesus Christ**
　　that the **blessed** and **only** ruler
　　will make **manifest** at the **proper** time,
　　the **King** of **kings** and **Lord** of **lords**,
　　who **alone** has **immortality**, who dwells
　　　in **unapproachable light**,
　　and whom **no** human being has **seen** or **can see**.
To **him** be **honor** and **eternal power**. **Amen**.

Catch your listeners' attention immediately with the unexpected salutation, then slowly list the virtues we are to pursue.

What's at stake is our "eternal life." Be sure to make this sound important.

"I charge you" is fraternal encouragement, not scolding.

"The commandment" refers to *all* commandments.

The two titles are similar, but increase your energy from the first to the second.
Beloved = bee-LUHV-uhd

Speak the last line from memory.

GOSPEL　Luke 16:19–31

A reading from the holy Gospel according to Luke

Jesus said to the **Pharisees**:
"There was a **rich man** who dressed in **purple garments**
　　and **fine linen**
　　and dined **sumptuously** each day.
And lying at his door was a **poor man** named **Lazarus**,
　　covered with **sores**,

Unique to Luke, this parable, addressed to the Pharisees, calls us all to repentance in due season.

Luke's concern for the contrast between rich and poor is manifested in his language. Contrast "purple garments and fine linen" with the more pungent language that refers to Lazarus ("sores," "scraps," "dogs," and "licked").

READING II　The passage begins with a contrast: "But you . . . ," it states, indicating a contrast with what went before. In the verses just prior, Paul exhorts authentic teaching shared without hope of financial reward. The "man of God," an Old Testament title applied to Moses and the prophets, is expected to behave in ways different from the culture, Paul insists. He addresses the litany of virtues in the first sentence to Timothy as an elder, but today they are also proposed to all members of your assembly.

Leadership is both a privilege and a burden that must be taken seriously. While few would question that truth, Paul asserts the same is true of discipleship. The same snares that can trap a leader and cause his downfall can detour and trip any believer. Paul employs strong imperatives both when reminding Timothy of his Baptism celebrated in the "presence of many witnesses," and when urging the young leader to "compete well," letting no resistance or obstacles prevent him from staying in the race to the finish line. Use the imperatives "pursue," "compete," "lay hold of," to impress upon your assembly the importance of these exhortations.

"Keep the commandment" charges Timothy, and each of us, not to mind any one *particular* injunction, but to surrender ourselves to the *entirety* of God's Law until the Lord returns in glory. Seamlessly, the text transitions to prayer that you must pray slowly and with great sincerity. First your words describe the mighty and awesome God, and then they call us to a response of humble praise.

Contrast the serene fate of Lazarus with the rich man's torment.

who would **gladly** have eaten his fill of the **scraps**
  that **fell** from the rich man's **table**.
Dogs even used to **come** and **lick** his **sores**.
When the **poor man died**,
  he was carried away by **angels** to the **bosom** of **Abraham**.
The **rich man also died** and was **buried**,
  and from the **netherworld**, where he was in **torment**,
  he **raised** his **eyes** and saw **Abraham** far **off**
  and **Lazarus** at his **side**.
And he **cried** out, 'Father **Abraham**, have **pity** on me.

He has no compunction about asking to be waited upon.

Send Lazarus to **dip** the tip of his **finger** in **water** and **cool**
   my **tongue**,
  for I am **suffering torment** in these **flames**.'
Abraham replied,
  '**My child**, **remember** that you received
  what was **good** during your **lifetime**
  while **Lazarus** likewise **received** what was **bad**;
  but **now he** is **comforted** here, whereas **you** are **tormented**.

Keep Abraham's response temperate, without a trace of vindictiveness. He calls him "child," a kindness that makes the irreversible fate all the more chilling.

This "chasm" is of our making, not God's.

Moreover, between **us** and **you** a **great chasm** is established
  to **prevent anyone** from **crossing** who might **wish** to go
  from **our side** to **yours** or from **your side** to **ours**.'
He said, 'Then I **beg** you, **father**,
  send him to my **father's house**, for I have **five brothers**,
  so that he may **warn** them,
  lest they **too come** to this **place** of **torment**.'

His concern for his brothers seems genuine, but he wants them "warned" rather than relying on their consciences to lead them to just and merciful living.

But **Abraham replied**, 'They have **Moses** and the **prophets**.
Let them **listen** to **them**.'
He said, 'Oh **no**, father **Abraham**,
  but if **someone** from the **dead** goes to them, they will **repent**.'

He grows more urgent in his naiveté. He sets up the irony of Abraham's final comment.

Then **Abraham** said, 'If they will **not** listen to **Moses**
   and the **prophets**,
  neither will they be **persuaded** if someone should **rise**
   from the **dead**.'"

Here is the heart of the message; this hard truth can't be diluted.

GOSPEL The message of this Gospel text, like that of today's First Reading, is neither easy nor welcome. In both, we're told it is possible to run out of time and that there is no reversing the fate that follows the sounding of the bell. The demon Screwtape, of C.S. Lewis' invention, advises his younger protégé that the best way to deceive humans is to persuade them there is *always* plenty of time. It is a lie we all want to believe, hence its persuasive power. But the difficult truth Jesus proclaims through today's parable cautions us to keep an eye on the clock.

Talk of God's mercy can give the impression that everything depends on God: God never *tires* of forgiving us; you can stake your life on that! What is sometimes overlooked is the need to *ask* forgiveness and *accept* God's mercy. Jesus' parable presents a rich man even more hardened in self-centeredness after death than he was in life. He knows the right language, calling out to "*Father* Abraham" and asks for "pity" but he expresses no remorse and is just as eager to *use* Lazarus in the "netherworld" as he was in life. For him, others exist to be at his service. When his

request for relief isn't honored, he again asks to use Lazarus, this time as a messenger, to warn his brothers. Abraham understands these brothers share the rich man's spiritual DNA and would no more respond to Lazarus returned from the dead than did the rich man himself when Lazarus daily begged at his doorstep.

We're meant to find ourselves in the rich man, not Lazarus, so make him reasonable, not sinister. The tone is sincere and temperate throughout. Only the outcome is dire. G.M.

TWENTY-SEVENTH SUNDAY IN ORDINARY TIME

LECTIONARY #141

READING I   Habakkuk 1:2–3; 2:2–4

Habakkuk = huh-BAK-kuhk or HAB-uh-kuhk

Are these the words of a single intercessor or of several praying about different sets of circumstances?

Fix a concrete situation of desperate need in your mind to lend passion and energy to these concerns.

Pause to allow time to transition to the more solemn tone of this section where the prophet quotes God.

This is a promise that faith will not be disappointed.

See with the eyes of faith, not those of the body!

Faith is always the mark of those who find favor with God and who can endure without losing heart.

A reading from the Book of the Prophet Habakkuk

How long, O LORD? I cry for **help**
  but you do not **listen**!
I cry out to you, "**Violence!**"
  but you do **not intervene**.
Why do you let me see **ruin**;
  why must I look at **misery**?
Destruction and **violence** are before me;
  there is **strife**, and **clamorous discord**.
Then the LORD **answered** me and said:
  Write down the **vision clearly** upon the **tablets**,
  so that one can **read** it **readily**.
For the **vision** still has its **time**,
  presses **on** to **fulfillment**, and will **not disappoint**;
if it **delays**, **wait** for it,
  it will **surely come**, it will **not** be **late**.
The **rash one** has **no integrity**;
  but the **just one**, because of his **faith**, shall **live**.

READING I   Who is the speaker? A father whose child is dying of cancer? A wife awaiting the return of her husband from war? An elderly person who's read one too many headlines about school or workplace shootings? A young person afraid of growing up in a world where terror breaks out at any moment? Our speaker is a prophet of God who lives within a privileged relationship with the Lord and who is entrusted with vision and insight beyond the reach of the rest of us. Yet this prophet wrestles with the same ancient question that plagues so many:

Why does evil occur right before God's eyes? Why does God not prevent or at least erase the evil done? If such questions seem out of place in Scripture, you better look more closely at God's Word that never shies from earnest expressions of human emotion, even anger, bitterness, and despair. If God won't or can't do anything about evil, then spare me having to look at it, says the prophet.

Habakkuk's doubts regarding God's justice and rule of the earth sprang from the desperate circumstances of his time. Judah languished amidst such religious dis-

solution and political peril that Habakkuk wondered whether God was really in charge. When the Lord responds, it's not with a solution, but a promise. Habakkuk is to record the splendid vision of deliverance and restoration he has seen. Writing down a vision, it was believed, would help make it come true. Over and over (six times!) God promises the vision will be fulfilled. But it will take faith and patience to reach that day and only the "just," not the "rash," will get there.

For meditation and context:

RESPONSORIAL PSALM   Psalm 95:1–2, 6–7, 8–9 (8)

R. If today you hear his voice, harden not your hearts.

Come, let us sing joyfully to the LORD;
  let us acclaim the Rock of our salvation.
Let us come into his presence with
  thanksgiving;
  let us joyfully sing psalms to him.

Come, let us bow down in worship;
  let us kneel before the LORD who made
    us.
For he is our God,
  and we are the people he shepherds, the
    flock he guides.

Oh, that today you would hear his voice:
  "Harden not your hearts as at Meribah,
    as in the day of Massah in the desert,
  where your fathers tempted me;
    they tested me though they had seen my
      works."

READING II   2 Timothy 1:6–8, 13–14

Beloved = bee-LUHV-uhd

The salutation is tender but the message is strong and challenging.

Set afire what is already within you—that you received in Holy Orders! "Power," "love," and "self-control" are three *distinct* qualities. Differentiate them.

These words comprise a spiritual pep-talk from someone whose own life circumstances are dark and painful.

Recall the suffering you've endured in life that could embolden you to invite others to not fear suffering.

Even today, millions suffer daily for the faith. How might they encourage others to safeguard it?

A reading from the second Letter of Saint Paul to Timothy

Beloved:
I **remind** you to **stir** into **flame**
    the **gift** of **God** that you have through the **imposition**
      of my **hands**.
For **God** did not give us a **spirit** of **cowardice**
    but rather of **power** and **love** and **self-control**.
So do **not** be **ashamed** of your **testimony** to our **Lord**,
    nor of me, a **prisoner** for **his sake**;
    but **bear your** share of **hardship** for the **gospel**
    with the **strength** that comes from **God**.

Take as your **norm** the **sound words** that you **heard** from **me**,
    in the **faith** and **love** that are in **Christ Jesus**.
Guard this **rich trust** with the **help** of the **Holy Spirit**
    that **dwells within** us.

READING II Attributed to Paul who writes from prison, these words urge the reader not to let the sufferings of Christ, nor those being endured by Paul, become a source of scandal or embarrassment. The world expects success to look like success and be accompanied by fame, wealth, and adulation. Paul knows well that the Gospel does not bring such things. But he also knows the wearying effects of enduring hardships. So he encourages Timothy, a bishop whom Paul himself ordained, to find again the faith that first flamed within him when he was bap-

tized so he can remember the sweet taste of that for which he may have to endure bitter trials.

In fact, Paul assures Timothy he will have to bear his "share of hardship for the gospel." Like Jesus, Paul asks for nothing he has not been willing to give himself. Only the endurance of suffering can embolden one to the point of inviting others to embrace it. What circumstances in your life could give you that audacity? Paul trusts in the goodness of God and reminds Timothy that God has given us his Spirit, who burns within us not with fear but with "power"!

That same Spirit endows us with "love" and "self-control" so we can proceed down life's path with confidence and peace. All Timothy has learned from Paul remains true and reliable. Now he must "guard" that "rich trust" to ensure it remains pure and true even to our day, as we must guard it for those who follow us.

GOSPEL Jesus taught by example. Though he often spoke of faith, it was how he lived it that touched the disciples. He demonstrated that it was necessary to have faith to cast out demons,

Speak their request slowly, stressing both "increase" and "faith."

Don't scold; Jesus is giving a lesson on the power of faith.

Speak with the expectation that you will be believed!

Your tone asks, "Who would make such a ridiculous offer?"

These are not harshly stated orders but expected interaction between master and servants.

Of course not!

The Gospel is not endorsing self-abusive humility, but a healthy awareness that doing one's duty is not extraordinary.

GOSPEL　Luke 17:5–10

A reading from the holy Gospel according to Luke

The **apostles** said to the **Lord**, "Increase our **faith**."
The **Lord replied**,
　　"If you have **faith** the size of a **mustard seed**,
　　you would **say** to this **mulberry** tree,
　　'**Be uprooted** and **planted** in the **sea**,' and it would **obey** you.

"**Who** among you would **say** to your **servant**
　　who has **just** come in from **plowing** or **tending sheep**
　　　in the field,
　　'**Come here immediately** and **take** your **place** at **table**'?
Would he **not rather say** to him,
　　'**Prepare** something for **me** to **eat**.
Put on your **apron** and **wait** on me while I **eat** and **drink**.
You may **eat** and **drink** when I am **finished**'?
Is he **grateful** to that **servant** because he **did** what
　　　was **commanded**?
So should it **be** with **you**.
When you have **done all** you have been **commanded**,
　　say, 'We are **unprofitable servants;**
　　we have **done** what we were **obliged** to do.'"

THE 4 STEPS OF *LECTIO DIVINA* **OR PRAYERFUL READING**

1. *Lectio:* Read a Scripture passage aloud slowly. Notice what phrase captures your attention and be attentive to its meaning. Silent pause.

2. *Meditatio:* Read the passage aloud slowly again, reflecting on the passage, allowing God to speak to you through it. Silent pause.

3. *Oratio:* Read it aloud slowly a third time, allowing it to be your prayer or response to God's gift of insight to you. Silent pause.

4. *Contemplatio:* Read it aloud slowly a fourth time, now resting in God's word.

---

to be forgiven, to experience the healing of limbs and spirit. On a daily basis, the disciples saw the fruit of faith manifested in the life and ministry of Jesus. And so they blurted out, 'Lord, "*increase* our faith.'" If faith is who Jesus was, they wanted faith; if faith enabled Jesus to do what he did, they wanted faith; if faith was the pathway to salvation and eternity with their Lord, they wanted faith. So they ask the only one they know who can give it to them. Ironically, such a request could only come from those already imbued with substantial faith.

In reply, Jesus says that "faith the size of a mustard seed" is all that's needed to do the impossible. Using an obvious exaggeration, Jesus tells the disciples that causes can be much smaller than the results they engender. But Jesus doesn't stop there. In further response to their request for greater faith, he illustrates the concrete form faith takes. And that form is service. His no-nonsense example presents a master who expects servants to do their work without having to thank them for simply doing their duty. Discipleship is its own reward. Those who enter the vineyard can't

stand around waiting to be crowned with laurel. Faith changes us into servants who do what's necessary—love, give witness, repent, forgive—no matter how hard the task. And they do it expecting nothing in return. G.M.

TWENTY-EIGHTH SUNDAY IN ORDINARY TIME

LECTIONARY #144

READING I   2 Kings 5:14–17

A reading from the second Book of Kings

Naaman went down and **plunged** into the **Jordan seven times**
   at the **word** of **Elisha**, the **man** of **God.**
His **flesh** became **again** like the **flesh** of a little **child,**
   and he was **clean** of his **leprosy.**

Naaman returned with his whole **retinue** to the **man** of **God.**
On his **arrival** he **stood** before **Elisha** and **said,**
   "**Now I know** that there is **no God** in **all** the **earth,**
   except in **Israel.**
Please accept a **gift** from your **servant.**"

Elisha replied, "**As** the Lord **lives** whom I **serve,** I will **not
   take** it,"
and **despite Naaman's urging,** he **still refused.**
Naaman said: "If you will **not accept,**
   please let me, your **servant,** have **two mule-loads** of **earth,**
   for I will **no longer** offer **holocaust** or **sacrifice**
   to **any other god** except to the Lord."

Naaman = NAY-uh-muhn
Elisha = ee-LĪ-shuh

Take time describing this ritual action; then, pause before announcing his cleansing.

Narrate with the attitude of rejoicing and gratitude that must have filled Naaman's heart.

This is a remarkable (and risky) profession of faith for this pagan official.

No hint of rudeness or superiority, just confidence that he has done his duty.

Take time with these details. Show a connection between his desire for the soil and his determination to worship only the God of Israel.

 READING I The introduction to this book speaks of three kinds of content found in all literary texts: intellectual, emotional, and aesthetic. Identifying each is critical, and today's First Reading demonstrates the importance of identifying the *intellectual* content. You won't be able to do that without reading what comes before this passage in 2 Kings 5. There you will learn that Naaman, army commander and foreign dignitary, has come to Israel in the hope of curing his leprosy. But his hopes are dashed when Elisha simply sends word to him to bathe in the Jordan rather than making some grand spectacle of healing. Angry and disappointed, he prepares to leave, but is persuaded by his servants that he has nothing to lose in following Elisha's instructions.

Our passage recounts the miracle that follows. The words "plunged," "seven times," and "little child" help create a sense of the remarkable healing. But something more important follows; Namaan, in the grip of gratitude, embraces the God of Israel as earth's *only* god and promises to worship no other. Back home, duty will bind him to worship his nation's god, yet he boldly makes this declaration. Because of the belief that gods could be worshipped only in their own land, he even asks for soil to take with him on which he will erect an altar to worship the Lord. The remarkable faith of this foreigner sets the stage for the faith-filled Samaritan of the Gospel.

Elisha's refusal of gifts for his service reflects no rancor, but his awareness that he did only what God required, so any reward will come from the Lord. Both men are bold exemplars of faith lived and spoken with conviction.

For meditation and context:

RESPONSORIAL PSALM   Psalm 98:1, 2–3, 3–4 (see 2b)

R. The Lord has revealed to the nations his saving power.

Sing to the LORD a new song,
    for he has done wondrous deeds;
his right hand has won victory for him,
    his holy arm.

The LORD has made his salvation known:
    in the sight of the nations he has revealed
      his justice.
He has remembered his kindness and his
    faithfulness
      toward the house of Israel.

All the ends of the earth have seen
    the salvation by our God.
Sing joyfully to the LORD, all you lands:
    break into song; sing praise.

Beloved = bee-LUHV-uhd

A slight pause after "remember" and moving slowly through the sentence will highlight this important opening.
Paul is imprisoned for his faith.

Contrast the freedom enjoyed by God's Word to go where it will.

This is a joyful declaration: he suffers willingly for the good of others!

Be sure to balance "died"/"live" and "persevere"/"reign."

READING II   2 Timothy 2:8–13

A reading from the second Letter of Saint Paul to Timothy

Beloved:
Remember Jesus Christ, **raised** from the **dead**,
    a **descendant** of **David**:
    such is my **gospel**, for which I am **suffering**,
      even to the point of **chains**, like a **criminal**.
But the **word** of **God** is **not chained**.
Therefore, I bear with **everything** for the **sake** of **those**
    who are **chosen**,
    so that **they too** may **obtain** the **salvation** that is
      in **Christ Jesus**,
    together with **eternal glory**.
This **saying** is **trustworthy**:
    If we have **died** with him
      we shall also **live** with him;
    if we **persevere**
      we shall also **reign** with him.

READING II   Paul's key word appears at the beginning: "remember." That's what liturgy is—an act of ritual remembrance of the saving acts of God in Christ. Paul is not theorizing but speaking from the heart about his own lived experience of faith. He has preached this "gospel" and is now suffering for it, writing from a prison cell. A clever play on words asserts that God's word won't be subverted; the "word of God" *will* be preached! Paul suffers willingly because he trusts that his suffering will be for the benefit of those who have come to know Christ.

Paul then quotes words not his own that likely were part of a liturgical hymn already in use. Note his assertion that the words are "trustworthy," confirming that they offer reliable teaching. Using synonymous parallelism, Paul makes a *single* point with *two* similar statements: those who "have died" will "live; those who "persevere" will "reign." Then, using another parallel construct, he makes a disconcerting pronouncement: "If we deny him he will deny us" and "if we are unfaithful he remains faithful." Those statements may appear contradictory—how can Christ

"deny" us and "remain faithful" at the same time? But the text contrasts our infidelity to Christ with Christ's fidelity to himself and God, not to *us*. It's not promising Christ won't let anything bad happen to us. Rather, it's saying that Christ must be true to himself, and that means he *must* judge our unfaithfulness. It's in his nature to do so. Even God can't pretend sin never happened; either we repent or Christ must judge us.

GOSPEL   Jesus is headed toward Jerusalem and the destiny

Note the suggestions for placing stress. Paul says that Christ remains faithful to himself and God; his righteousness requires that he judge our unfaithfulness.

But if **we deny him**
he will deny us.
If we are **unfaithful**
he remains **faithful**,
for he **cannot deny himself**.

GOSPEL Luke 17:11–19

A reading from the holy Gospel according to Luke

Let your tone suggest the serious nature of his journey.

Samaria = suh-MAYR-ee-uh

The Law required this distance. Raise your volume.

"When he saw them" should suggest his immediate compassion.

The priests had to authenticate cures of leprosy.

Is their reaction marked by joy, awe, gratitude?

We should hear the joy of the healed Samaritan in this narration.

Remember, Jesus admires the Samaritan. He regrets that the others did not come to claim a greater healing.

Make these words sincere and full of assurance.

As **Jesus** continued his **journey** to **Jerusalem**,
he traveled through **Samaria** and **Galilee**.
As he was entering a **village**, **ten lepers** met him.
They **stood** at a **distance** from him and **raised** their **voices**, saying,
"**Jesus**, **Master**! Have **pity** on us!"
And when he **saw** them, he said,
"**Go show** yourselves to the **priests**."
As they were **going** they were **cleansed**.
And one of them, **realizing** he had been **healed**,
returned, **glorifying God** in a loud **voice**;
and he **fell** at the **feet** of **Jesus** and **thanked** him.
He was a **Samaritan**.
Jesus **said** in **reply**,
"**Ten** were **cleansed**, were they **not**?
Where are the **other nine**?
Has **none** but this **foreigner** returned to give **thanks** to **God**?"
Then he **said** to him, "**Stand up** and **go**;
your **faith** has **saved** you."

that awaits him there, yet he never fails to respond to the needs of others. This healing story is unique to Luke, but the evangelist's interest seems to lie less on the healing miracle and more on the virtue for which the Samaritan leper is commended. Often, Jesus touches those he heals, but this time he forgoes ritual and outward sign and simply orders that the Samaritans show themselves to the priests. Lacking Naaman's reluctance, the ten follow Jesus' command and suddenly discover they were healed "as they were going."

The ten had demonstrated faith by calling out to Jesus and addressing him as "master." But Jesus gave them nothing on which to hang their faith. There is no verbal exchange or overt show of compassion, so Jesus' words of instruction must clearly signal that he *has* recognized their need and decided to grant what they seek. That only one returns genuinely disappoints Jesus. His question, "Has none but this foreigner returned . . . ?" cannot suggest contempt for the Samaritan. Rather, your tone should convey Jesus' admiration for this foreigner's exemplary faith. Jesus expected their return because he wasn't finished with them. Their return would have bolstered the faith of the crowds who witnessed the earlier encounter. But Jesus' intent goes deeper. The nine settled for too little for had they returned, they too would have received the far greater gift he gives the Samaritan: the promise of salvation. G.M.

TWENTY-NINTH SUNDAY IN ORDINARY TIME

LECTIONARY #147

READING I   Exodus 17:8–13

A reading from the Book of Exodus

In those days, **Amalek** came and waged **war** against **Israel**.
Moses, therefore, said to **Joshua**,
  "Pick out certain **men**,
  and **tomorrow** go out and **engage Amalek** in **battle**.
I will be standing on top of the **hill**
  with the **staff** of **God** in my **hand**."
So **Joshua did** as **Moses told** him:
  he **engaged Amalek** in battle
  after **Moses** had **climbed** to the top of the hill
    with **Aaron** and **Hur**.
As long as **Moses** kept his **hands** raised **up**,
  Israel had the **better** of the fight,
  but when he let his **hands rest**,
  Amalek had the **better** of the fight.
Moses' hands, however, grew **tired**;
  so they put a **rock** in **place** for him to **sit** on.
Meanwhile Aaron and **Hur supported** his **hands**,
  one on **one** side and **one** on the **other**,
  so that his **hands** remained **steady** till **sunset**.
And **Joshua mowed** down **Amalek** and his **people**
  with the **edge** of the **sword**.

Amalek = AM-uh-lek

Moses takes decisive action to rebuff Amalek's attack. He is determined and strong.
His "staff" represents God's powerful presence.
Your sober tone announces the beginning of battle.

Aaron = AYR-uhn
Hur = her
A shift in tone can signal the differing impact that the upraised and resting hands had on the battle.

Speak with urgency: they aren't simply making him comfortable but ensuring Israel's victory!

Connect the "steady" hands with the consequence that follows. This is God's victory: speak with gratitude, not disdain.

READING I Wielding the staff he previously used to split the Red Sea and to call its destructive waters back down upon Pharaoh's army, Moses intercedes for his people as they engage in battle against the Amalekites who are trying to deny the Israelites the land God promised them. Noticing that Israel had the better of the fight whenever Moses' arms were upraised, Aaron and Hur help him sustain that posture through the long hours of battle. But this cause and effect relationship points to God's mercy, not some sorcery that Moses uses to control God. God remains ever free, but invites us to intercede, that he might manifest his mercy. And that's exactly what we see here: Moses, the nation's leader, not on his own but with the help of assistants, asks God's help, and God concretely manifests it by giving Israel the victory.

The language is graphic and concrete. Use the references to Moses' weariness, the stone he was given to sit upon, the men holding up each of his arms, and the defeat of Amalek to convey that Moses is doing all he can to support Joshua whom he has sent into battle. We find here a happy confluence of images: the physical battle of metal meeting metal and a spiritual battle as Moses prays to support the men who give their lives to protect the Promised Land. The words that describe that effort ("his hands remained steady till sunset") support today's Gospel message regarding the need for *constant* prayer, so give them due stress. The final line conveys a biblical perspective on the consequences of opposing God's will.

For meditation and context:

TO KEEP IN MIND

When practicing, **read Scriptures aloud,** taking note of stress and pause suggestions. After several readings, alter the stress markings to suit your style and interpretation.

Beloved = bee-LUHV-uhd

This is more an earnest plea than an instruction.

Speak confidently of the reliability of Scripture.

This is a classic and bold declaration!

Conjure different images as you speak the words "teaching . . . refutation" to help you distinguish one from another.

Take a breath before starting this section and speak with solemn authority.

Use the imperatives to boldly invite your assembly to take on these important tasks. Within it are hearts that need to be convinced, reprimanded, or encouraged. Your heartfelt proclamation can help open their hearts to instruction.

RESPONSORIAL PSALM   Psalm 121:1–2, 3–4, 5–6, 7–8 (see 2)

R. Our help is from the Lord, who made heaven and earth.

I lift up my eyes toward the mountains;
   whence shall help come to me?
My help is from the LORD,
   who made heaven and earth.

May he not suffer your foot to slip;
   may he slumber not who guards you:
indeed he neither slumbers nor sleeps,
   the guardian of Israel.

The LORD is your guardian; the LORD is your
      shade;
   he is beside you at your right hand.
The sun shall not harm you by day,
   nor the moon by night.

The LORD will guard you from all evil;
   he will guard your life.
The LORD will guard your coming and your
      going,
   both now and forever.

READING II   2 Timothy 3:14—4:2

A reading from the second Letter of Saint Paul to Timothy

Beloved:
Remain **faithful** to what you have **learned** and **believed**,
   because you **know** from **whom** you **learned** it,
   and that from **infancy** you have known the **sacred Scriptures**,
   which are **capable** of giving you **wisdom** for **salvation**
   through **faith** in **Christ Jesus**.
All Scripture is **inspired** by **God**
   and is **useful** for **teaching**, for **refutation**, for **correction**,
   and for **training** in **righteousness**,
   so that **one** who **belongs** to **God** may be **competent**,
   equipped for **every good work**.

I **charge** you in the presence of **God** and of **Christ Jesus**,
   who will **judge** the **living** and the **dead**,
   and by his **appearing** and his kingly **power**:
   proclaim the **word**;
   be **persistent** whether it is **convenient** or **inconvenient**;
   convince, **reprimand**, **encourage** through **all patience**
      and **teaching**.

READING II   This text that speaks lovingly, knowingly, and wisely of the role God's Word can (and should) play in our lives. Addressed by Paul to his protégé, Timothy, it speaks just as powerfully today to anyone who remains open to God's Word and desires that it become the fuel that drives their hearts. Only one who loves God's Word, who has put that Word to use and learned from it could speak with such conviction of its usefulness for "teaching, for refutation, for correction." Add to the above that Paul writes from prison anticipating death, and the text takes on

the tone and urgency of a dying man's final wish. Timothy learned the faith from Paul himself and was privileged to be weaned on God's Word "from infancy." Don't rush the words that name the effectiveness of Scripture—each is distinct and adds new information about the Word's significance and our need for its wisdom. All that you say is premised on the conviction that "all Scripture is inspired."

   The final lines take on a serious tone as Paul solemnly charges Timothy to "proclaim" the Word. Paul willingly suffered for that awesome task and asks Timothy to be

as committed, even as willing to suffer when it is "inconvenient" to preach. You end with another list that calls us to do the hard work of the Gospel. Each verb names a distinct opportunity to make a difference by sharing, patiently, God's powerful Word.

GOSPEL   There is an easy link between this Gospel story and today's other readings. But how does the theme of persistence jibe with Jesus' other pronouncements regarding the need for simplicity in prayer and his admonition to avoid babbling like pagans who think

GOSPEL   Luke 18:1–8

A reading from the holy Gospel according to Luke

Jesus told his **disciples** a **parable**
  about the **necessity** for them to **pray always**
    without becoming **weary**.
He **said**, "There was a **judge** in a certain **town**
  who **neither feared God** nor **respected** any **human being**.
And a **widow** in that town used to **come** to him and **say**,
  '**Render** a **just decision** for me against my **adversary**.'
For a **long time** the judge was **unwilling**, but **eventually**
    he thought,
  'While it is **true** that I neither **fear God** nor **respect**
    any **human being**,
  because this **widow** keeps **bothering** me
  I shall **deliver** a just **decision** for her
  lest she finally **come** and **strike** me.'"
The **Lord** said, "**Pay attention** to what the **dishonest judge says**.
Will not **God** then secure the **rights** of his **chosen** ones
  who **call out** to him **day** and **night**?
Will he be **slow** to **answer** them?
I **tell** you, he will **see to it** that **justice** is **done** for them **speedily**.
But when the **Son** of **Man comes**, will he find **faith** on **earth**?"

Let the opening narration itself be a consoling teaching about God's mercy.

Begin with the robust confidence of the selfish judge.

Your tone is of an all-knowing narrator who anticipates where the story is going.

There is no fear in his tone, only the desire to be rid of this nagging widow.

The brief narration serves as a pointer to the lesson about to follow.

Jesus' tone suggests that the right response is obvious!

His final question underscores the fact that persistent faith, not endless verbiage in prayer, is the point of Jesus' parable.

---

they will be heard because of their many words (Matthew 6:7). The fit is seamless if we realize that Jesus is calling for persistence in faith, not multiplication of words. We must return to God again and again, not with long discourses, but with simple faith that in humility of heart and in plain language, places our needs before him with confidence in his merciful love.

Twice we are told that the judge of Jesus' parable neither fears God nor respects human beings, yet somehow he offers a point of reference for God's relationship with us. Keep in mind that parables seek a single reference point and don't mirror in every detail the real-life circumstances Jesus is addressing. In this case, Jesus teaches by contrast. If this uncaring and unjust judge rules favorably because of persistence, how much more will the all-merciful God respond to the manifest faith of earnest and humble believers?

Luke's audience anticipates the imminent return of Christ while enduring persecution. Jesus' parable gives them reason to hang on in hope. Jesus' questions regarding God's demeanor are consoling: God *will* be faithful! But his last question is full of challenge, as much, if not more so, today as when Jesus spoke it. If not here and in our hearts, where will the Risen Christ find faith on the earth? G.M.

THIRTIETH SUNDAY IN ORDINARY TIME

LECTIONARY #150

READING I Sirach 35:12–14, 16–18

Sirach = SI-ruhk; SEER-ak

Begin with authority and sweep the assembly as you declare this consoling truth.

Contrast what God does and does not do!

Fix concrete images of "orphan" and "widow" in your mind so you are not speaking of abstractions but of real people.

In the following lines you are stating and restating a single idea—that earnest prayers accomplish their goal. Speak with conviction and with enough energy to persuade

The final line offers assurance that whenever it comes, God's mercy is never too late.

A reading from the Book of Sirach

The LORD is a **God** of **justice**,
    who knows **no favorites**.
Though not **unduly partial** toward the **weak**,
    yet he **hears** the **cry** of the **oppressed**.
The LORD is **not deaf** to the **wail** of the **orphan**,
    nor to the **widow** when she **pours** out her **complaint**.
The **one** who **serves God willingly** is **heard**;
    his **petition** reaches the **heavens**.
The **prayer** of the **lowly pierces** the clouds;
    it does **not rest** till it **reaches** its **goal**,
nor will it **withdraw** till the **Most High responds**,
    judges justly and **affirms** the **right**,
and the LORD will **not delay**.

READING I Continuing last week's focus on prayer, we shift from stressing the need for persistence to looking at the inner *disposition* that best attunes us and allows our prayers to rise to God. Quite simply, Sirach teaches that our God, who is so merciful and just, is seeking those very qualities within his people. It is not favoritism toward the "weak" that causes God to be attentive to their prayers, but his passion for justice and concern for his children's deepest needs and attitudes.

God's attention is fixed in a special way both on those who suffer injustice and those who do justice. As the rest of the chapter from which this passage is taken makes clear, the doing of justice is the offering most pleasing to God. And in this reading, note the active, efficacious nature of prayer that emanates from "humble" hearts and from the one who "serves God willingly." Their prayer reaches "the heavens" and does not "rest till it reaches its goal." Share that news with conviction and joy. Your proclamation should convey to your assembly that this text is intended to encourage those with adequate resources as well as those in difficult financial circumstances. We all share in the impartial love of our merciful God and in his expectations for humility and just behavior.

For meditation and context:

TO KEEP IN MIND

Context: Who is speaking in this text? What are the circumstances?

RESPONSORIAL PSALM Psalm 34:2–3, 17–18, 19, 23 (7a)

R. The Lord hears the cry of the poor.

I will bless the LORD at all times;
  his praise shall be ever in my mouth.
Let my soul glory in the LORD;
  the lowly will hear me and be glad.

The LORD confronts the evildoers,
  to destroy remembrance of them from the
  earth.
When the just cry out, the LORD hears them,
  and from all their distress he rescues them.

The LORD is close to the brokenhearted;
  and those who are crushed in spirit he
  saves.
The LORD redeems the lives of his servants;
  no one incurs guilt who takes refuge in
  him.

Beloved = bee-LUHV-uhd

Paul is preparing for death. "Libation" is wine poured out as a sacrificial offering. "Departure" is a euphemism for his death. His tone is confident and resigned.

Paul is keenly aware that he did all this only with Christ's help, so he speaks with gratitude.

Because he understands God's merciful love, he knows God will bless all those who remain faithful. Again, the timbre of the lines is gratitude.

Paul was wounded by this disloyalty, but his prayer for them is sincere.

This is why he can be generous and forgiving: Christ did not abandon him!

To the very end, Paul's trust will be unwavering.
Pause before the final line, then speak it as a prayer.

READING II 2 Timothy 4:6–8, 16–18

A reading from the second Letter of Saint Paul to Timothy

Beloved:
I am **already** being **poured out** like a **libation**,
  and the time of my **departure** is at **hand**.
I have **competed well**; I have **finished** the **race**;
  I have **kept** the **faith**.
From now on the **crown** of **righteousness** awaits me,
  which the **Lord**, the **just judge**,
  will **award** to me on that day, and **not only** to **me**,
  but to all who have **longed** for his **appearance**.

At my **first** defense **no one appeared** on my **behalf**,
  but **everyone deserted** me.
May it **not** be held **against** them!
But the **Lord stood by** me and **gave** me **strength**,
  so that **through** me the **proclamation** might be **completed**
  and all the **Gentiles** might **hear** it.
And I was **rescued** from the **lion's mouth**.
The **Lord** will **rescue** me from **every evil threat**
  and will bring me **safe** to his **heavenly kingdom**.
To him be **glory forever** and **ever. Amen.**

| READING II | Imagine a beloved elder—a former teacher, an uncle or grandparent, a pastoral or political figure—sitting down as death tightens its hold to write you a final letter of encouragement and instruction. Paul has reached such a point in his life. He's writing from prison, anticipating death, and addressing a younger man whom he has mentored and who will persevere in proclaiming the Gospel after Paul's death. There is a tender, personal quality to the writing as Paul uses athletic imagery to assess his ministry, concluding that he has "finished the race"

and "kept the faith" despite the many trials and afflictions that were his recompense for accepting Christ's mandate to bring the Gospel to the Gentiles.

Because his reward in this life was struggle and pain, Paul anticipates a "crown of righteousness" from the hands of his "just" Lord. But that reward also will be given to "all" whose hearts long for Christ. The text then jumps ahead to verses where Paul, abandoned and lonely, speaks of his reliance on the Lord despite the failure of his companions to remain loyal. Again, the language is personal and heartfelt, but

don't make it sound maudlin or self-indulgent. Paul's self-pity is always tempered by his confidence in the Lord. He boasts of the "strength" he received, the "proclamation" completed through him, and his deliverance from "the lion's mouth" in order to glorify his merciful Lord. He concludes with confident hope that he will be rescued, not from physical danger, but for eternal life. And for that he sings Christ's praises!

The introductory sentence sets the necessary context for Jesus' teaching.

Show no bias toward either character.

Note that the Pharisee is speaking "to himself."

Don't give the Pharisee an overly obnoxious tone; he thinks he's just telling the truth.

Read slowly, one phrase at a time, to suggest the tax collector's tentative approach.

His words are few, but heartfelt.

Pause before relating Jesus' assessment of the situation. He's turning an outcast into a role model and a pillar of society into a failure. Stress the contrasts as if trying to convince a skeptical crowd.

TO KEEP IN MIND

Sense lines: Scripture in this book is arranged (as in the Lectionary) in sense lines, one idea per line. Typically at least a slight pause should follow each line, but good reading requires you to recognize the need for other pauses within lines.

GOSPEL   Luke 18:9–14

A reading from the holy Gospel according to Luke

Jesus addressed this **parable**
　　to those who were **convinced** of their **own righteousness**
　　and **despised everyone else**.
"Two **people** went up to the **temple** area to **pray**;
　　one was a **Pharisee** and the **other** was a **tax collector**.
The **Pharisee** took up his position and spoke this prayer
　　　to himself,
　　'**O God**, **I thank you** that I am **not** like the **rest** of **humanity**—
　　greedy, **dishonest**, **adulterous**—or even like this **tax collector**.
I fast **twice** a week, and I pay **tithes** on my **whole income**.'
But the **tax collector** stood off at **a distance**
　　and would not even **raise** his **eyes** to **heaven**
　　but **beat** his **breast** and **prayed**,
　　'**O God**, be **merciful** to me a **sinner**.'
I **tell** you, the **latter** went home **justified**, **not** the **former**;
　　for whoever **exalts** himself will be **humbled**,
　　and the one who **humbles** himself will be **exalted**."

GOSPEL │ What's the difference between Paul's litany of accomplishments (I fought the good fight; I finished the race; I kept the faith) and the self-righteousness of this Pharisee? Luke gives it away in his introduction: Jesus is speaking to and about those who laud themselves while *despising* everyone else. It's not the sense of accomplishment that reeks, but the sense of superiority. The Pharisee is not grateful, like Paul, for what God has given him, but for the ways he outshines his neighbors and especially the despised tax-collector. Unlike Paul, he doesn't realize that his condition results from God's grace and mercy; instead, he believes it is his own accomplishment. How tragic that Jesus' judgment on this man is that all his effort—laudatory as it seems—is done in vain.

The tax-collector does not even raise his head for it is weighed down by the burden of his sins. Looking to where God resides in his heart and beating on its door, he simply begs for mercy. He offers no excuses and never entertains the thought that at least he's better than some others. All that he leaves to God, offering only his sincere contrition. In this drama, both God and penitent play necessary roles. But the Pharisee mistakes God's role as that of a passive listener who hears performance reports and assigns gold stars. The publican recognizes God's true role—to welcome and love every honest and contrite heart, to generously dispense mercy, and to justify us in a way we could never merit on our own. G.M.

THIRTY-FIRST SUNDAY IN ORDINARY TIME

LECTIONARY #153

READING I   Wisdom 11:22—12:2

A reading from the Book of Wisdom

> **Before** the LORD the whole **universe** is as a **grain**
>   from a **balance**
> or a **drop** of morning **dew** come down upon the **earth.**
> But **you** have **mercy** on **all,** because you can **do all things;**
>   and you **overlook** people's **sins** that they may **repent.**
> For you **love all** things that **are**
>   and **loathe nothing** that you have **made;**
>   for what you **hated,** you would not have **fashioned.**
> And how could a thing **remain,** unless **you willed** it;
>   or be **preserved,** had it not been **called forth** by **you?**
> But you **spare** all things, because they are **yours,**
>   **O** LORD and **lover** of **souls,**
>   for your **imperishable spirit** is in **all** things!
> Therefore you **rebuke offenders little** by **little,**
>   **warn** them and **remind** them of the **sins**
>   they are **committing,**
>   that they may **abandon** their **wickedness** and **believe**
>   in **you, O** LORD!

You are telling God about the wonder of all his creation!

"But you . . . " conveys human amazement that God, so powerful, is willing to be so merciful.
God "overlooks" for a purpose—that we might repent!
Some ancient cultures believed God created both good *and* evil.

These rhetorical questions are meant to convey awe that God made and sustains all things in creation.

God not only loves creation, but God's "imperishable spirit" is *in* all things.

God does not shy from pointing out our shortcomings, but God's "rebuke" is a gift that leads to salvation.

Sustain eye contact through this final sentence. It is more a prayer than a declaration.

| READING I | You are setting the stage for Zacchaeus, whose conversion in today's Gospel seems instantaneous, but more likely occurred "little by little," as we hear in this text from Wisdom. While reviewing the events of Israel's deliverance from Egyptian slavery, the author digresses with this reflection on God's mercy. Compared with God, the "whole universe" is like a tiny weight used on the most sensitive scales or like a single drop of morning dew. The Bible's starting point is always the greatness of God who, nonetheless, deigns to love and care for us frail creatures like a mother loves the child of her womb. In God's eyes, existence equals goodness because everything God made is good. That goodness precedes any action or accomplishment on our part. We don't earn worthiness, it is bestowed on us as an essential aspect of our existence.

These are not the words of a theologian and less those of a lawyer. They are the words of a mother looking at the marvel of the child she has birthed and of a father overwhelmed by his love even for an errant or rebellious child. Don't read as if you were telling God something he doesn't know. Rather, you are marveling at and rejoicing over human goodness—a goodness you yourself share. The final sentence describes the ideal parent or teacher who, motivated by love, never ceases coaxing children to repentance by inviting them, "little by little," to face the sins that dull their senses and keep them from experiencing the fullness of God's love. We are invited to turn from sin in order to taste the sweetness of God's mercy.

For meditation and context:

RESPONSORIAL PSALM   Psalm 145:1–2, 8–9, 10–11, 13, 14 (see 1)

R. I will praise your name for ever, my king and my God.

I will extol you, O my God and King;
    and I will bless your name forever and
        ever.
Every day will I bless you;
    and I will praise your name forever and
        ever.
The LORD is gracious and merciful,
    slow to anger and of great kindness.
The LORD is good to all
    and compassionate toward all his works.

Let all your works give you thanks, O LORD,
    and let your faithful ones bless you.
Let them discourse of the glory of your
        kingdom
    and speak of your might.

The LORD is faithful in all his words
    and holy in all his works.
The LORD lifts up all who are falling
    and raises up all who are bowed down.

Thessalonians = thes-uh-LOH-nee-uhnz

Pause after the salutation.

Give this the quality of an earnest prayer for your own assembly.

Each phrase conveys a new idea; take your time so you don't blur one into another.

Pause and take a breath before starting the second sentence. This is the "business" at hand that must now be addressed!

He's urging them not to be easily thrown off by rumors and lies.

"The day of the Lord" is no small matter to get wrong; correcting this misinformation is essential.

READING II   2 Thessalonians 1:11—2:2

A reading from the second Letter of Saint Paul to the Thessalonians

Brothers and **sisters**:
We **always pray** for you,
    that our **God** may make you **worthy** of his **calling**
    and powerfully bring to **fulfillment every** good **purpose**
    and **every effort** of **faith**,
    that the **name** of our **Lord** Jesus may be **glorified** in **you**,
    and **you** in **him**,
    in accord with the **grace** of our **God** and **Lord Jesus Christ**.

We **ask** you, **brothers** and **sisters**,
    with regard to the **coming** of our **Lord Jesus Christ**
    and our **assembling** with him,
    not to be **shaken** out of your **minds** suddenly, or to be **alarmed**
    either by a "**spirit**," or by an **oral statement**,
    or by a **letter allegedly** from **us**
    to the **effect** that the **day** of the **Lord** is at **hand**.

READING II Two long sentences comprise this short reading and they don't seem to have much connection to each other. The first is both the assurance of prayers and a prayer in itself while the second is a no-nonsense instruction about not being misled by false teaching. Because of his paternal concern for the various Christian communities, especially those he himself helped establish like this one at Thessalonica, Paul seeks to sustain those communities through constant prayer. So he begins with that assurance, establishing his fatherly connection to and responsibility for them.

Then he quickly addresses a serious matter that has caused great unrest in the community. A letter, probably forged but purporting to be from Paul, has been circulated that claims the "end times" are already upon them. This news has shaken them "out of their minds" and caused great unrest. Paul's goal is to protect them from this lie and to assure them that the end is not yet upon them. He disputes the legitimacy of whatever seemingly spirit-induced utterance or "spirit" they have heard, of any assumed authoritative pronouncement or "oral statement" that is gaining currency, and of the *letter* claiming to be in his hand that he now discredits. As he had to do in several of the communities he founded, Paul confronts the false teachings with all the zeal of the consummate evangelist he was and all the urgency of a protective parent.

There is no indication of Jesus' intent to encounter Zacchaeus.

Here is a rich man not used to being deprived of what he wants.

His unorthodox solution becomes the doorway to his salvation.

Jesus brings urgency into the situation, perhaps sensing an opportunity that must not be squandered.

Zacchaeus immediately responds with joy to Jesus' self-invitation.

Does Zacchaeus fear that the crowd will dissuade Jesus from entering his home? He doesn't risk it and takes remarkable action right there and then.

The Old Testament prescribes this level of restitution (see 2 Samuel 12:6) so Zacchaeus seems aware of the Law.

All three final lines are classic. Don't rush them and sustain eye contact on the last line assuring your assembly this applies to them.

GOSPEL　Luke 19:1–10

A reading from the holy Gospel according to Luke

At that **time**, **Jesus** came to **Jericho** and intended
　　to pass **through** the town.
Now a **man** there named **Zacchaeus**,
　who was a chief **tax** collector and also a **wealthy** man,
　was seeking to **see who Jesus was**;
　but he could **not see** him because of the **crowd**,
　for he was **short** in **stature**.
So he **ran** ahead and **climbed** a **sycamore** tree in order to **see Jesus**,
　who was about to **pass** that **way**.
When he **reached** the place, **Jesus looked** up and said,
　"Zacchaeus, come down **quickly**,
　for **today** I **must stay** at your **house**."
And he **came** down **quickly** and received him with **joy**.
When they **all saw** this, they began to **grumble**, saying,
　"He has **gone** to **stay** at the **house** of a **sinner**."
But **Zacchaeus stood** there and said to the **Lord**,
　"Behold, **half** of my **possessions**, **Lord**, I shall **give** to the **poor**,
　and if I have **extorted anything** from **anyone**
　I shall **repay** it **four times over**."
And **Jesus** said to him,
　"Today salvation has come to this **house**
　because **this** man **too** is a **descendant** of **Abraham**.
For the **Son** of **Man** has come to **seek**
　and to **save** what was **lost**."

GOSPEL　Familiar and beloved, the story of Zacchaeus should shake us to our core. What if he hadn't climbed that tree? Would Jesus have found him some other way? Who was the seeker and who the pursued? Was Jesus already looking for this tax collector or did the outcast's bold gesture win Jesus' attention and therefore Zacchaeus' salvation? So much rested on that decision to climb a tree. What if he hadn't been too short to see? What if he'd been satisfied with simply hearing Jesus' voice? Luke tells us he wanted to see "who Jesus was" and that

takes more than a cursory look. From the vantage point of the tree, Zacchaeus had time as well as sight lines to look on Jesus and size him up. By the time Jesus invites himself into the short man's home, Zacchaeus has made his decision about this teacher, and he wastes no time responding to Jesus' request to give him a place to rest.

But Zacchaeus' joy is soon the town's gossip as they marvel that the teacher doesn't know this man's reputation. And then there's a miracle: unbeckoned and unprodded, Zacchaeus offers restitution for

all his thieving. How did this happen? What brought him "little by little" to the point where he could so easily give away half his fortune? "Salvation" came to his house that day, but its journey likely started long before with tugs at his heart and pangs in his conscience. Was it perhaps because the "lover of souls" had been working long and silently to bring him to repentance and because Zacchaeus yielded to those dimly felt promptings that this is a story of salvation? G.M.

ALL SAINTS

LECTIONARY #667

READING I Revelation 7:2–4, 9–14

A reading from the Book of Revelation

I, **John**, saw another **angel** come up from the East,
  holding the **seal** of the living **God**.
He cried out in a loud **voice** to the four angels
  who were given power to **damage** the **land** and the **sea**,
  "Do **not** damage the land or the sea or the trees
  until we put the **seal** on the foreheads of the **servants**
    of our God."
I heard the **number** of those who had been marked with the seal,
  one **hundred** and forty-four **thousand** marked
  from every **tribe** of the children of **Israel**.

After this I had a vision of a great **multitude**,
  which no one could **count**,
  from every **nation**, **race**, **people**, and **tongue**.
They stood before the **throne** and before the **Lamb**,
  wearing white **robes** and holding **palm** branches in
    their hands.
They cried out in a loud **voice**:

  "**Salvation** comes from our **God**, who is seated on the **throne**,
  and from the **Lamb**." »

READING I — This reading from the Book of Revelation combines two separate visions reported by John in chapter seven: 7:1–8, the vision of the "one hundred forty-four thousand" marked with the seal, and 7:9–17, the vision of the triumph of the elect. These visions are placed between the breaking of the sixth and seven seals that secure "the scroll" in heaven, hiding it from human view. The scroll, which can be opened only by the Lamb (the Resurrected Christ), reveals God's plan for salvation.

In the first vision, John speaks of the "hundred and forty-four thousand," literally the square of twelve (represented by the twelve tribes of Israel) times one-thousand. This large number symbolized the depth of God's fidelity to his promises to Israel. Each believer "marked" with the seal will be protected by God from the coming wrath at the end of time.

In the second vision, John sees "a great multitude" of people standing "before the throne" (where God sits) and "before the Lamb" (Christ). The emphasis on the diversity of peoples standing before the throne and the Lamb ("from every nation, race, people, and tongue") signals the universal dimension of God's plan to save all people who profess faith in Christ, especially those who are martyred for the faith.

It is easy to see why the Church selects this passage to be read each year as the First Reading for the Solemnity of All Saints. Here we find biblical grounding for our belief that God rewards all the faithful who die in right relationship with him.

All of heaven joins the exuberant hymn of praise.

Give us a sense that the cry of praise filled the heavens.

The "elder" knows the answer to his own question. His tone is gentle and wise.

The elder speaks with pride and admiration of those who survived persecution and trial.

That these multitudes entered the heavenly sanctuary, not through their own merit, but because of the work of the Lamb, should fill us with expectant hope.

For meditation and context:

TO KEEP IN MIND

The opening: Establish eye contact and announce, from memory, "A reading from . . . ." Then take a pause (three full beats!) before starting the reading. The correct pronunciation is "A [uh] reading from" instead of "A [ay] reading from."

All the **angels** stood around the throne
   and around the **elders** and the four living **creatures**.
They **prostrated** themselves before the throne,
   worshiped God, and exclaimed:

  "**Amen. Blessing** and **glory**, **wisdom** and **thanksgiving**,
    honor, **power**, and **might**
  be to our God **forever** and **ever. Amen**."

Then one of the **elders** spoke up and said to me,
   "Who are these wearing white **robes**, and where did they
    come from?"
I said to him, "My **lord**, **you** are the one who knows."
He said to me,
   "These are the ones who have **survived** the time
    of great distress;
   they have **washed** their robes
   and made them **white** in the **Blood** of the **Lamb**."

RESPONSORIAL PSALM   Psalm 24:1bc–2, 3–4ab, 5–6 (6)

R. Lord, this is the people that longs to see your face.

The Lord's are the earth and its fullness;
  the world and those who dwell in it.
For he founded it upon the seas
  and established it upon the rivers.

Who can ascend the mountain of the Lord?
  or who may stand in his holy place?
One whose hands are sinless, whose heart
  is clean,
  who desires not what is vain.

He shall receive a blessing from the Lord,
  a reward from God his savior.
Such is the race that seeks him,
  that seeks the face of the God of Jacob.

READING II   The three Letters of John and the Gospel according to John share a similar style, vocabulary, and theology. This has led scholars to group these texts together and label them the "Johannine writings." Tradition attributes John, one of the Twelve Apostles, as the author of these writings. Scholars debate whether the letters were written before the Gospel account, or vice versa. There is, however, a general consensus that all of these writings are dated toward the end of the first century.

An important theme that runs through the First Letter of John is the idea that believers in Jesus as the Son of God are "children of God." This common faith unites all believers as family. What also binds believers together is the world's resistance and opposition to this faith: "the world does not know us." In this way, Christians stand in solidarity with Christ, who was likewise rejected by the world.

As children of God, we wait in hope for the future revelation at the Second Coming of Christ. It is in this hope that we find our purity. John assures all who believe in

Christ of the reward that awaits us at the end-time: "we shall be like him, for we shall see him as he is."

GOSPEL   The Beatitudes (Matthew 5:1–12) are the opening remarks from Jesus' Sermon on the Mount (Matthew 5:1—7:29). Here Jesus offers a prescription for sainthood. In defining the characteristics of those who enter the Kingdom of Heaven, Jesus both comforts and challenges all those who wish to follow him and be counted among his disciples.

READING II   1 John 3:1–3

A reading from the first Letter of Saint John

Beloved:
See what **love** the Father has **bestowed** on us
    that we may be called the **children** of God.
Yet so we **are**.
The reason the **world** does not know us
    is that it did not know **him**.
Beloved, we **are** God's children **now**;
    what we **shall** be has not yet been **revealed**.
We **do** know that **when** it is revealed we shall be **like** him,
    for we shall see him as he **is**.
Everyone who has this hope based on **him** makes himself **pure**,
    as **he** is pure.

Beloved = bee-LUHV-uhd

The passage is full of wonder at the love of God who makes us his beloved children. Focus on that love before you begin.

Look at the assembly as you make this solemn affirmation.

Regret tinges this admission that the world rejected Christ.

Pause briefly after "beloved" before continuing. While some things are *unknown*, John confidently asserts that "At least we know *this* much."

This hope we have requires action on our part—to purify ourselves of all that pollutes the mind and heart.

TO KEEP IN MIND

Word value: Words are your medium, like a painter's brush or a sculptor's chisel. You must understand the words before you can communicate them. Most words have a dictionary meaning (denotative) and an associational meaning (connotative). "House" and "home" both mean "dwelling," yet they communicate different feelings. Be alert to subtle differences in connotative meanings and express them.

Writing to a largely Jewish-Christian community, Matthew is careful to present Jesus in a portrait appealing to his audience —as the new Moses—and the context for the Sermon on the Mount illustrates this well.

At the beginning of his public ministry in Galilee, even before Jesus performs any mighty deeds, Matthew presents Jesus as the giver of the new Law. A full three chapters (Matthew 5–7) are devoted to presenting Jesus not only supporting the Mosaic Law ("You have heard that it was said . . . ") but also fulfilling that Law ("But I say to you . . . "). Even the setting of the Sermon (on a mountain, teachings being delivered, believers assembled) likely conjured up images for Matthew's community of Moses delivering the Law at Mt. Sinai.

The Beatitudes offer insights into the proper disposition needed for entry into the Kingdom. For Jesus, the call to discipleship was not solely rooted in a reward in the afterlife. Jesus challenged his followers to build the Kingdom of Heaven on earth: be meek and merciful, be clean of heart, and seek peace. He also offered comfort to those suffering in this life: those poor in spirit and those mourning, those persecuted and suffering for the faith.

For Jesus, disciples took many different paths on the road to sainthood. But each path was to be realized in this life on earth. Whether meek or mourning, a peacemaker or one persecuted, Jesus called on all of his followers to "rejoice and be glad." Our saints are models of the faith who live with confidence and conviction that their "reward will be great in heaven." D.S.

Beloved = bee-LUHV-uhd

There are many effective ways to proclaim this familiar Gospel text. You can pause after each "blessed"; or prior to each "for they . . ."; or you might forgo pauses and deliver each Beatitude like a dart flying toward the bull's-eye. What is critical is that you keep a clear image of what (or better, whom) each Beatitude names. Have someone in mind for each of the eight "blesseds" and let their unique goodness color the way you proclaim.

These statements are meant to comfort those who live the Beatitudes and those who think they can't.

The message of these provocative statements is counter-cultural. How would your delivery be affected if some in your assembly got up and left in the middle of your speaking?

Leave time for silence between the Beatitudes so each can sink in. Don't shy from emphasizing the word "blessed" each time it recurs.

Speak the final beatitude with awareness that some in your pews have indeed been insulted and slandered for the sake of the Kingdom.

Although the passage ends with an imperative, let your tone make it an invitation to dream God's Kingdom dream.

GOSPEL   Matthew 5:1–12a

A reading from the holy Gospel according to Matthew

When Jesus saw the **crowds**, he went up the **mountain**,
   and after he had **sat** down, his **disciples** came to him.
He began to **teach** them, saying:

   "**Blessed** are the **poor** in **spirit**,
      for theirs is the Kingdom of **heaven**.
   Blessed are they who **mourn**,
      for they will be **comforted**.
   Blessed are the **meek**,
      for they will inherit the **land**.
   Blessed are they who **hunger** and **thirst** for **righteousness**,
      for they will be **satisfied**.
   Blessed are the **merciful**,
      for they will be shown **mercy**.
   Blessed are the clean of **heart**,
      for they will see **God**.
   Blessed are the **peacemakers**,
      for they will be called **children** of God.
   Blessed are they who are **persecuted** for the sake
         of **righteousness**,
      for theirs is the Kingdom of **heaven**.
   Blessed are **you** when they **insult** you and **persecute** you
      and utter every kind of **evil** against you **falsely** because
         of **me**.
   Rejoice and be **glad**,
      for your **reward** will be **great** in **heaven**."

TO KEEP IN MIND
The closing: Pause (three beats!) after ending the text. Then, with sustained eye contact, announce from memory, "The word [Gospel] of the Lord." Always pronounce "the" as "thuh" except before words beginning with a vowel, as in "thee Acts of the Apostles." Maintain eye contact while the assembly

THE COMMEMORATION OF ALL THE FAITHFUL DEPARTED (ALL SOULS' DAY)

LECTIONARY #668

READING I   Wisdom 3:1–9

A reading from the Book of Wisdom

> The **souls** of the **just** are in the **hand** of **God**,
>   and **no torment** shall **touch** them.
> They **seemed**, in the **view** of the **foolish**, to be **dead**;
>   and their **passing away** was thought an **affliction**
>   and their **going forth** from us, utter **destruction**.
> But **they** are in **peace**.
> For if before **men**, indeed, they be **punished**,
>   yet is their **hope** full of **immortality**;
> **chastised** a **little**, they shall be **greatly blessed**,
>   because **God tried** them
>   and found them **worthy** of himself.
> As **gold** in the **furnace**, he **proved** them,
>   and as **sacrificial offerings** he **took** them to **himself**.
> In the **time** of their **visitation** they shall **shine**,
>   and shall **dart** about as **sparks** through **stubble**;
> they shall **judge nations** and **rule** over **peoples**,
>   and the LORD shall be their **King forever**.
> Those who **trust** in him shall **understand truth**,
>   and the **faithful** shall **abide** with him in **love**:
> because **grace** and **mercy** are with his **holy ones**,
>   and his **care** is with his **elect**.

Left margin notes:

The melodic opening line is the foundation for all that follows. Speak with joyful confidence.

Let your tone convey that here appearances don't match the reality.

This is another line to be delivered with utter conviction.

The purification that may come after death is not to be feared but welcomed as God's gift that prepares one for final judgment. Speak with authority.

blessed = blesd

The energy builds and the tempo quickens a bit as you offer the lovely image of souls shining like sparks.

The final sentence can be delivered at a slower pace, emphasizing the words "grace" and "mercy" that await God's elect.

The readings given here are suggestions. Any reading from the Lectionary for the Commemoration of All the Faithful Departed (#668) or the Masses for the Dead (#1011–1015) may be used. Ask your parish staff which readings to prepare.

READING I   The Book of Wisdom belongs to Israel's Wisdom traditions and is one of the final books written in the Old Testament. Scholars date the writing of this book to about one hundred years before the birth of Jesus. In it, the author, who is a Jewish sage, addresses a variety of topics, such as the importance of justice, the depth of God's mercy, and the folly of idolatry. In today's reading, the author focuses on suffering and death, offering his perspective on the suffering and death of the righteous.

Your proclamation will begin with a comforting image: "The souls of the just are in the hand of God, and no torment shall touch them." The author then offers two contrasting perspectives on the destiny of the righteous who suffer and die. For those without faith, the suffering and death of the righteous simply amounts to "utter destruction," a death with no meaning or consequence. But for those with faith, guided by wisdom, they see the righteous finally at "peace" in their death. The just who suffer and die receive "immortality" and are "greatly blessed" by God.

For the faithless, there is little rhyme or reason to the life and death of the just. But for those who live by faith, God is fully present and in control, even in what appears to be a dismal ending. In fact, according to this Jewish sage, it was God

For meditation and context:

TO KEEP IN MIND

Sense lines: Scripture in this book is arranged (as in the Lectionary) in sense lines, one idea per line. Typically at least a slight pause should follow each line, but good reading requires you to recognize the need for other pauses within lines.

RESPONSORIAL PSALM   Psalm 27:1, 4, 7, 8b, 9a, 13–14 (1a) (13)

R. The Lord is my light and my salvation. or I believe that I shall see the good things of the Lord in the land of the living.

The Lord is my light and my salvation;
   whom should I fear?
The Lord is my life's refuge;
   of whom should I afraid?

One thing I ask of the Lord;
   this I seek:
To dwell in the house of the Lord
   all the days of my life,
that I may gaze on the loveliness of the Lord
   and contemplate his temple.

Hear, O Lord, the sound of my call;
   have pity on me and answer me.
Your presence, O Lord, I seek.
   Hide not your face from me.

I believe that I shall see the bounty of the
   Lord
   in the land of the living.
Wait for the Lord with courage;
   be stouthearted and wait for the Lord!

READING II   Romans 5:5–11

A reading from the Letter of Saint Paul to the Romans

Brothers and **sisters**:
Hope does **not disappoint**,
   because the **love** of **God** has been **poured out** into our **hearts**
   through the **Holy Spirit** that has been **given** to us.
For **Christ**, while we were **still helpless**,
   died at the appointed time for the **ungodly**.
Indeed, only with **difficulty** does one **die** for a **just person**,
   though **perhaps** for a **good person**
   one might **even find courage** to **die**.
But **God proves** his **love** for us
   in that while we were **still sinners Christ died** for us.
How much more then, since we are **now justified** by his **Blood**,
   will we be **saved** through **him** from the **wrath**.
Indeed, if, while we were **enemies**,
   we were **reconciled** to God through the **death** of his **Son**,
   how much more, once **reconciled**,
   will we be **saved** by his **life**.

This is a bold statement to share with people who have lost loved ones. Speak from the knowledge of God's love within your own heart.

This is a bedrock Christian conviction: Christ died for us not when we were deserving, but when we were steeped in sin.

Even if one might die for a "good" person, the fact is Christ died for the undeserving—us.

If God showered mercy on us during our time of alienation, how can he not shower even more on us now that Christ has "reconciled" us?

End as joyfully as you began. The purpose of the text is not to argue a point, but to comfort with the truth of God's merciful love.

who "chastised" the righteous in order to test them so as to find them "worthy of himself." Through their suffering, death, and trust in the Lord, the just come to know the truth and love of God. In this way, they enter immortality as God's "elect." They are honored and revered by all as God's "holy ones."

READING II   **Romans 5:5–11.** This reading, extracted from Paul's longer teaching about the virtues of faith, hope, and love (5:1–11), leads us through a careful argument designed to give reas-

surance about the future destiny of the faithful Christian. We disciples of Jesus Christ have a firm hope for the future that will not disappoint us, Paul explains, because Christ gave himself up to death for us, and this death set in motion a process of redemption.

With Christ's death, the Holy Spirit was given to us, through which God's love was "poured out into our hearts," enabling us to live as disciples. And beyond that, Christ's death released us from sin. To help us more fully appreciate how difficult such a sacrifice would be, Paul proposes the

two scenarios of dying for a just person and a good person, and then emphasizes that Christ gave himself for us when we were "still sinners."

Paul then adds yet more layers to his argument about the implications of this extraordinary act of sacrificial love, using two "if/then" statements. First, since even *now* we are "justified by his Blood," then in the future, at the Last Judgment, "how much more . . . will we be saved through him from the wrath." Second, if, in our unworthiness God was willing to be reconciled to us through "the *death* of his Son,"

Not only **that**,
> but we **also boast** of **God** through our **Lord Jesus Christ**,
> through **whom** we have now **received reconciliation**.

Or:

READING II   Romans 6:3–9

A reading from the Letter of Saint Paul to the Romans

Brothers and **sisters**:
Are you **unaware** that **we** who were **baptized** into **Christ Jesus**
> were **baptized** into his **death**?
We were indeed **buried** with him through **baptism** into **death**,
> so **that**, just as **Christ** was **raised** from the **dead**
> by the **glory** of the **Father**,
> we **too** might **live** in **newness of life**.

For if we have **grown** into **union** with him through a **death**
> like his,
> we shall also be **united** with him in the **resurrection**.
We know that our **old** self was **crucified** with him,
> so that our **sinful body** might be **done away** with,
> that we might **no longer** be in **slavery** to **sin**.
For a **dead** person has been **absolved** from sin.
If, then, we have **died** with **Christ**,
> we **believe** that we shall also **live** with him.
We know that **Christ**, **raised** from the **dead**, **dies** no **more**;
> **death** no longer has **power** over **him**.

Paul jolts us to attention with a rhetorical question: Don't you know that by being baptized in Christ you were baptized (initiated) into this death?
The joyful consequence of that dying in Christ is heralded here: We were "buried" like Christ so we could rise like him to "newness of life"!

"A death like his" refers to our Baptism. Paul is repeating his point to ensure we get it. Be sure your tone is gentle and reassuring.

"If then we have" is a repetition. But let your energetic tone keep it from sounding redundant.
The last two lines make the same assertion twice, so give greater stress to the second iteration. "We know" means "We are convinced!"

then after being reconciled how much more efficacious will our salvation be through Christ's resurrected *life* at the end of time?

Step by step, Paul has built a convincing explanation of the dynamics of Christian salvation, from Christ's sacrificial death on the Cross (granting our reconciliation) through his return and resurrection of the dead at the end (sealing our redemption). One of the more pressing points that Paul is asserting in this section of Romans is that God's love and mercy are directed to all people. Christ died for both the "ungodly"

and the "just." The death of God's Son has "reconciled" all believers with God.

Romans 6:3–9. One of the interesting features of Paul's Letter to the Romans is that Paul himself did not establish the community of believers in Rome. In fact, Paul had yet to meet the Christians in Rome when he wrote this letter to them. So in a very real sense, this letter was intended to introduce Paul and his Gospel message to the Christian community in Rome.

Then, as now, Christian life began with Baptism. In the water bath, one was cleansed of all previous sin, joined to the

person of Jesus Christ, and so invited into his Death and Resurrection. In this reading, Paul explains the mysterious dynamics of Christianity's distinctive claim: that disciples follow Christ into eternal life.

Paul's initial question, "Are you unaware . . . ?" invites his readers into awareness through the poetic explanation that will follow. They have experienced the ritual; now he wants them to understand its deep significance. As Christ trusted completely in his Father, giving himself up to death, so those who are baptized give themselves up also, sharing spiritually in

Pause after the introductory phrase to shift to the compassionate and reassuring tone of Jesus.

Jesus' assertion that none be "lost" means we must weigh the evidence of our own experience against the infinite mercy of God.

Stress "this" here as in the previous sentence. God wants what we want—for everyone who has known Christ to share God's eternal life.

Make eye contact and, from memory, share the hope-filled final line.

TO KEEP IN MIND

Separating units of thought with pauses: Identify the units of thought in your text and use pauses to distinguish one from another. Running words together blurs meaning and fails to distinguish ideas. Punctuation does not always indicate clearly what words to group together or where to pause. The listener depends on you for this organization of ideas.

GOSPEL   John 6:37–40

A reading from the holy Gospel according to John

Jesus said to the **crowds:**
"**Everything** that the **Father gives** me will **come** to me,
  and I will **not reject anyone** who **comes** to me,
  because I **came** down from **heaven** not to do my **own will**
  but the **will** of the one who **sent** me.
And **this** is the **will** of the **one** who **sent** me,
  that I should not **lose anything** of what he **gave** me,
  but that I should **raise** it on the **last day.**
For **this is** the **will** of my **Father,**
  that **everyone** who **sees** the **Son** and **believes** in him
  may have **eternal life,**
  and I shall **raise** him on the **last day.**"

THE 4 STEPS OF *LECTIO DIVINA* OR PRAYERFUL READING

1. *Lectio:* Read a Scripture passage aloud slowly. Notice what phrase captures your attention and be attentive to its meaning. Silent pause.

2. *Meditatio:* Read the passage aloud slowly again, reflecting on the passage, allowing God to speak to you through it. Silent pause.

3. *Oratio:* Read it aloud slowly a third time, allowing it to be your prayer or response to God's gift of insight to you. Silent pause.

4. *Contemplatio:* Read it aloud slowly a fourth time, now resting in God's word.

Christ's death and burial through Baptism, trusting that they will also share in his rising, in "newness of life." Although Baptism occurs but once, Christians continue to reflect on their experience of dying and rising, using it as a pattern for their lives so that gradually they will have "grown into union with him through a death like his." In the process of that growing into union, old selves are "done away with," the Christians are "no longer . . . in slavery to sin," and as "Christ, raised from the dead, dies no more," disciples will be "united with him in resurrection."

GOSPEL   Today's reading is an excerpt from Jesus' bread of life discourse in the Gospel according to John—one of five major discourses in John, all of which speak to his identity as the Word incarnate. This brief passage deepens our Commemoration of All the Faithful Departed, since it focuses on Jesus' understanding of his mission—working with the Father for human salvation.

In these words, Jesus reveals three important insights about his work with the Father. First, the Father "gives" Jesus followers, and he (Jesus) "will not reject anyone who comes to me." Unconditional acceptance is "the will of the one who sent [him]." Second, Jesus "will not lose" anyone sent to him by the Father. All believers are valued. And third, each one who believes in the Son will have "eternal life"; the Son will "raise him on the last day." Such a powerful testimony of God's desire for our salvation and Christ's effort on our behalf should strengthen our trust. D.S.

THIRTY-SECOND SUNDAY IN ORDINARY TIME

LECTIONARY #156

READING I   2 Maccabees 7:1–2, 9–14

A reading from the second Book of Maccabees

It **happened** that **seven brothers** with their **mother** were **arrested**
and **tortured** with **whips** and **scourges** by the **king**,
to **force** them to eat **pork** in **violation** of **God's law**.
One of the brothers, **speaking** for the **others**, said:
"**What** do you **expect** to **achieve** by **questioning** us?
We are **ready** to **die** rather than **transgress** the **laws**
of our **ancestors**."

At the point of **death** he said:
"You **accursed fiend**, you are **depriving** us of this **present life**,
but the **King** of the **world** will **raise** us up to **live again forever**.
It is for **his** laws that we are **dying**."

After him the **third** suffered their cruel **sport**.
He put out his tongue **at once** when told to do so,
and **bravely** held out his **hands**, as he spoke these noble **words**:
"It was from **Heaven** that I received these;
for the **sake** of his **laws** I **disdain** them;
from **him** I **hope** to **receive** them **again**."
Even the **king** and his **attendants marveled**
at the young man's **courage**,
because he regarded his **sufferings** as **nothing**. »

Maccabees = MAK-uh-beez

The opening words belie the gruesome nature of what follows, so begin with a weighty tone.
Don't rush past the violent language: "tortured"; "whips"; "scourges."
They have considered their decision and this brother speaks it for the rest.

The identification of this as the "second" brother is left out. "He" substitutes for "the second brother."
He mocks their ignorance.

The cruelty of the persecutors is reinforced by the use of the word "sport."

He makes three statements: Where he got them, his willingness to sacrifice them, and his conviction that they will be restored.

Convey the wonder of the king at the young man's courage.

READING I Our First Reading presents a remarkable story of brothers who willingly sacrifice their lives rather than defy God's Law that forbade the eating of pork. While intriguing in its depiction of heroic fidelity, the story's most important feature is each brother's profession of faith in a life beyond this one. The final Sundays of the year focus on our eternal destiny, a theme picked up in today's Gospel, and invite us to ponder and prepare for that new life. Jewish thought didn't embrace this belief till late in Israel's history so this conviction is rarely professed in

the Old Testament. Not until the Book of Daniel and the Second Book of Maccabees, written approximately 150 years before Christ, does belief in the afterlife take concrete form. The Lectionary's interest in this reading derives more from that articulation than from the heroism demonstrated by this zealous family.

Today's excerpt tells only half the story, for the lives of *seven* brothers and their *mother* are taken by the Seleucid Greeks who have occupied Israel. In the Bible story, you'll find details of savagery left out of today's portion, but there is heroism enough

left for you to recount, a heroism made possible by the invincible conviction of this family that they will be reunited in the eternal realm of God's mercy.

Present each martyr as the noble figure he is even when speaking condemnation like "You accursed fiend" and "for you, there will be no resurrection." Those are not words of vengeance, but acts of faith that acknowledge God's mercy on those who are faithful and God's judgment on those who mock God. Each brother has his moment of unwavering faith that should wound and convict us with its fierce

Remember, you are speaking of four murders. Don't lose the weighty tone needed to relate this remarkable story.

His courage is rooted in his faith that he will rise again. His final comment reflects the conviction that evildoers would *not* rise from the dead.

After he had **died**,
> they **tortured** and **maltreated** the **fourth** brother
>   in the **same** way.
When **he** was **near death**, he said,
> "It is my **choice** to **die** at the **hands** of **men**
> with the **hope God** gives of being **raised up** by him;
> but for **you**, there will be **no resurrection** to **life**."

For meditation and context:

RESPONSORIAL PSALM   Psalm 17:1, 5–6, 8, 15 (15b)

R. Lord, when your glory appears, my joy will be full.

Hear, O LORD, a just suit;
> attend to my outcry;
> hearken to my prayer from lips without
>   deceit.

My steps have been steadfast in your paths,
> my feet have not faltered.
I call upon you, for you will answer me, O
>   God;
> incline your ear to me; hear my word.

Keep me as the apple of your eye,
> hide me in the shadow of your wings.
But I in justice shall behold your face;
> on waking I shall be content in your
>   presence.

> **TO KEEP IN MIND**
> **Pray the Scriptures:** Make reading these Scriptures a part of your prayer life every week, and especially during the week prior to the liturgy in which you will proclaim.

Thessalonians = thes-uh-LOH-nee-uhnz

READING II   2 Thessalonians 2:16—3:5

**A reading from the second Letter of Saint Paul
    to the Thessalonians**

You begin with a prayer comprised of several phrases that communicate separate thoughts. Don't run them together.

"Good hope" refers to Christ's return at the end of time.

Brothers and **sisters**:
May our **Lord Jesus Christ himself** and **God** our **Father**,
> who has **loved** us and **given** us **everlasting encouragement**
> and **good hope** through his **grace**,
>   **encourage** your **hearts** and **strengthen** them
>   in every **good deed** and **word**.

passion and certitude. Strive for a delivery that invites us to their level of belief. The first brother speaks for all, asserting their willingness to die. The second, not clearly identified in the text, is the fiercest, while the third presents the most reasoned and poignant rationale for his willingness to die. The fourth emphasizes his "choice" while warning his torturers of their dire destiny.

READING II   Behind every biblical text there is always a context that illuminates the words we proclaim. Today's straightforward text was

addressed to Christians who had been instructed to anticipate the return of Christ during their lifetime. When that did not occur, they had to set about the far more difficult task of *being* the Body of Christ, living lives in this world that proclaimed the lordship of Jesus and enabled his "word" to "speed forward and be glorified." This week and next, we read exhortations from this letter regarding how to live faithfully that Christian life.

Paul starts with prayer, so your delivery must convey the prayerful nature of the opening lines. Scripture is forever reminding

us that everything depends on prayer because prayer establishes our relationship with God. The opening benediction demonstrates that prayer is not a listing of wants and needs but an exchange of "love" and a dialogue of "hearts" that strengthens us for "every good deed and word." After praying *for* us, Paul *asks* for prayer that all he and his companions do will further the work of the Gospel. Note that he does not shy from naming the forces of evil, both human and in the realm of spirit, that assemble against God's people. That "not all have faith" is a warning to shun naiveté and to live soberly,

Invite your assembly to join the prayer Paul requests for the spread of the Gospel.

Don't make light of this sobering truth that there are those who work against the Gospel.

God's faithfulness is a source of comfort!

These words are also true of your assembly. Speak them sincerely.

With strong eye contact, you end with another prayer directed at your listeners.

Finally, **brothers** and **sisters**, **pray** for us,
    so that the **word** of the **Lord** may speed **forward** and be **glorified**,
    as it did among **you**,
    and that we may be **delivered** from **perverse** and **wicked people**,
    for **not all** have **faith**.
But the Lord **is faithful**;
    he will **strengthen** you and **guard** you from the **evil one**.
We are **confident** of **you** in the **Lord** that what **we instruct you**,
    you are **doing** and will **continue** to do.
May the **Lord direct your hearts** to the **love** of **God**
    and to the **endurance** of **Christ**.

GOSPEL   Luke 20:27–38

A reading from the holy Gospel according to Luke

The parenthetical comment is the most important information in the opening sentence. There is no need to signal their ulterior motives.

Their first statement sets the parameters for the legal question.

"Now" signals the complications that make the situation seemingly difficult to resolve.

With self-satisfaction, the Pharisee suggests he's presented a nut too hard to crack!

Stress "seven" as if to remind Jesus not to ignore the details of the story.
Jesus is not argumentative for his teaching is as much for the crowd as for the leaders.
His words paint a heavenly realm of serenity and joy.

Some **Sadducees**, those who **deny** that there is a **resurrection**,
    came **forward** and put this **question** to Jesus, saying,
    "**Teacher**, **Moses** wrote for us,
    *If someone's **brother** dies leaving a **wife** but **no child**,*
    *his **brother** must **take** the wife*
    *and raise up **descendants** for his brother.*
Now there were **seven** brothers;
    the **first** married a **woman** but **died childless**.
Then the **second** and the **third** married her,
    and likewise all the **seven died childless**.
Finally the **woman also** died.
Now at the **resurrection** whose **wife** will **that woman be**?
For **all seven** had been **married** to her."
Jesus said to them,
    "The **children** of **this age marry** and **remarry**;
    but those who are **deemed worthy** to **attain** to the **coming age**
    and to the **resurrection** of the **dead**
    neither marry nor are **given** in **marriage**. ≫

conscious of the opposition we inevitably face when we give our lives to Christ.

We often speak of "God's work" because it is God who does the work, not us. That is why failure should never daunt us. Often, what looks like failure is just a step on the journey, led by God, toward the expansion of his Kingdom. That's why Paul reminds us that "the Lord is faithful." It is Christ we follow and Christ who will win the day. Our task is to show up and put our gifts and our lives at God's disposal.

This immensely pastoral text ends as it began, with a prayer. The prayer, which

you must deliver with sincerity and sustained eye contact, asks that hearts remain focused on God's love for them. In good times and in bad, it is that love that sustains us. When we forget it, we lose our way.

GOSPEL This episode, related also and perhaps more clearly in Matthew (22:23–33), demonstrates the tenuous nature of belief in life after death even in Jesus' own day. The Pharisees set out to mock this belief by positing a preposterous scenario which they believe will

undermine belief in resurrection. But they have chosen the wrong target, for Jesus has no trouble besting their efforts to stump him.

After citing the Law of levirate marriage (see Deuteronomy 25:5–10) that was established to ensure a man who married but died childless was not left without heirs, they set out to trap Jesus with a tale that's sure to amuse the crowd while forcing Jesus into a choice that will pit him against one side or the other. They're playing a game they've played before and lost; this time they seem to think their trap is

This final teaching requires a higher level of energy. Jesus is using the Law they espouse to prove their contention wrong, but again, avoid an argumentative tone and strive, instead, to communicate the love of God that keeps us eternally alive.

TO KEEP IN MIND

Tell the story: Make the story yours, then share it with your listeners. Use the language; don't throw away any good words. Settings give context; don't rush the description. Characters must be believable; understand their motivation. Dialogue reveals character; distinguish one character from another with your voice.

They can no longer **die**,
　　for they are **like angels**;
　　and they are the **children** of **God**
　　because **they** are the **ones** who will **rise**.
That the **dead will rise**
　　even **Moses** made known in the **passage** about the **bush**,
　　when he called out '**Lord**,'
　　the **God** of **Abraham**, the **God** of **Isaac**, and the **God** of **Jacob**;
　　and he is not **God** of the **dead**, but of the **living**,
　　for to **him all** are **alive**."

[Shorter: Luke 20:27, 34–38]

THE 4 STEPS OF *LECTIO DIVINA* OR PRAYERFUL READING

1. *Lectio:* Read a Scripture passage aloud slowly. Notice what phrase captures your attention and be attentive to its meaning. Silent pause.

2. *Meditatio:* Read the passage aloud slowly again, reflecting on the passage, allowing God to speak to you through it. Silent pause.

3. *Oratio:* Read it aloud slowly a third time, allowing it to be your prayer or response to God's gift of insight to you. Silent pause.

4. *Contemplatio:* Read it aloud slowly a fourth time, now resting in God's word.

foolproof! But Jesus easily brushes aside their simplistic logic asserting that while marriage is the way of "this age" those found worthy of the resurrection will not be defined or bound by such labels. That heavenly life will transcend our categories; there, death will be no more and we will be simply "children of God" enjoying an angelic existence.

Then Jesus cites their own Law that they know well and cannot ignore (Deuteronomy 3:6). How could Moses refer to God as the God of Abraham, Isaac, and Jacob if those patriarchs are no longer living? The declaration that the Lord is "not God of the dead, but of the living" is the truth Jesus came to proclaim both through his life and teaching, but most of all through his own Resurrection from the dead.

Left out of our pericope is the assessment of "some" of the Pharisees that Jesus "answered well." Sometimes, truth overcomes even intentional blindness. G.M.

THIRTY-THIRD SUNDAY IN ORDINARY TIME

LECTIONARY #159

READING I Malachi 3:19–20a

A reading from the Book of the Prophet Malachi

Lo, the day is **coming**, **blazing** like an **oven**,
     when all the **proud** and all **evildoers** will be **stubble**,
and the **day** that is **coming** will set them on **fire**,
     leaving them **neither root nor branch**,
     says the LORD of **hosts**.
But for **you** who **fear** my **name**, there will **arise**
     the **sun** of **justice** with its **healing rays.**

RESPONSORIAL PSALM Psalm 98:5–6, 7–8, 9 (see 9)

R. The Lord comes to rule the earth with justice.

Sing praise to the LORD with the harp,
     with the harp and melodious song.
With trumpets and the sound of the horn
     sing joyfully before the King, the LORD.

Let the sea and what fills it resound,
     the world and those who dwell in it;
let the rivers clap their hands,
     the mountains shout with them for joy.

Before the LORD, for he comes,
     for he comes to rule the earth;
he will rule the world with justice
     and the peoples with equity.

Malachi = MAL-uh-kī

Be sure all are attentive before you begin.
Pause after speaking the exclamation "Lo"
and then continue with high energy.

These are hard truths spoken without malice,
but with conviction.
Holding back on this stern message deprives
listeners of an important truth.
"But . . . " is spoken with strength, but in a
comforting tone. God's fire can both destroy
and heal.

     For meditation and context:

TO KEEP IN MIND

The closing: Pause (three beats!)
after ending the text. Then, with
sustained eye contact, announce
from memory, "The word [Gospel]
of the Lord." Always pronounce
"the" as "thuh" except before words
beginning with a vowel, as in "thee
Acts of the Apostles." Maintain eye
contact while the assembly makes
its response.

READING I Eschatology, the study of the end-times, is an important concern of the final weeks of the liturgical year. It's appropriate that as we approach the end of the year, we contemplate the end of time in order to remind ourselves that Christ will in fact return and no one knows when that day will be. One of Satan's best tricks, C. S. Lewis wrote, is to convince us that we have plenty of time. But only God knows how much time we actually have; therefore, vigilance is a hallmark of Christian living.

Malachi's words are meant to trouble the comfortable who have grown lax and disillusioned. After the exile and the rebuilding of the Temple, the people have become lukewarm in their faith. Danger threatens from without and yet the people don't place their trust in God. So the prophet sounds the alarm to warn the people that the day of the Lord, fierce and "blazing like an oven" will reduce evildoers to "stubble." Stories and films that depict the end in apocalyptic terms take their lead from this text. It's meant to rouse and it does its job well. The language itself

(through the use of short words like "fire," "root," and "branch") contributes to the sense of urgency. Let your tone convey that much is at stake!

But the final sentence offers hope to those who "fear [God's] name." For them (us), the sun will shine with healing rays for the fire of God's love both purifies and heals.

READING II Paul is capable of soaring to lofty heights and then coming down to earth to deal with the most prosaic matters. In doing so, he teaches us that even minor matters can

READING II 2 Thessalonians 3:7–12

**A reading from the second Letter of Saint Paul
    to the Thessalonians**

Brothers and **sisters:**
You **know** how one must **imitate** us.
For we did **not act** in a **disorderly** way **among** you,
    nor did we eat **food** received **free** from **anyone**.
On the **contrary**, in **toil** and **drudgery**, **night** and **day**
    we **worked**, so as not to **burden any** of you.
Not that we do not **have** the **right**.
Rather, we wanted to **present** ourselves as a **model** for you,
    so that you might **imitate** us.
In **fact**, when we were **with** you,
    we **instructed** you that if **anyone** was **unwilling** to work,
    neither should that one **eat**.
We hear that some **are conducting** themselves among you
        in a **disorderly** way,
    by not keeping **busy** but **minding** the **business of others**.
Such people we **instruct** and **urge** in the **Lord Jesus Christ**
        to **work quietly**
    and to **eat** their **own food**.

GOSPEL Luke 21:5–19

A reading from the holy Gospel according to Luke

While **some** people were speaking about
    how the **temple** was adorned with **costly stones**
        and **votive offerings**,
    Jesus said, "**All** that you **see** here—
    the days will **come** when there will **not** be **left**
    a **stone** upon **another stone** that will not be **thrown down**."

Thessalonians = thes-uh-LOH-nee-uhnz

Paul is all teacher today correcting and laying down the law. His tone immediately calls his listeners to attention!

Paul is just stating facts, not self-aggrandizing.

At his own expense, Paul offered a "model for [them]."

Paul is concerned about the disruption caused by the slackers in the community.

Paul claims the authority of Christ to order everyone to do their fair share.

Let the grand description of the Temple contrast with the fate Jesus predicts in the following lines.

Jesus takes no joy in this prediction.

---

disrupt the Body of Christ in the way a torn nail or a bruised toe can preoccupy us even when the rest of our body is feeling well. Today, Paul is addressing freeloaders who are taking advantage of the openness and generosity of the Christian community. Such behavior is seldom tolerated long and the dysfunction in Thessalonica has reached Paul's ears.

In typical fashion, Paul is unafraid to point to himself as a model for them to follow. This is not arrogance, but an indication of how carefully he lived his life. Paul was a teacher who understood that one teaches better through actions than through words. So whenever he lived among fellow Christians he was scrupulous to offer an example worthy of their imitation. Candidly, he reminds them that he never took advantage while living among them and, instead, worked "night and day" to make his own living.

Like a parent, Paul doesn't miss the chance to point out that he *could* have asked for deference and special treatment; but he eschewed such privilege in order to teach them. And his teaching was clear and stern: no work means no food! But some prefer being busybodies to keeping busy. So to them Paul says, hush up, get to work, and pack your own lunch!

GOSPEL Throughout his ministry, Jesus repeated that his Kingdom was not of this earth. Though he was concerned about the day to day life of his followers and for the kind of discipleship one had to embrace to enter God's Kingdom, Jesus never stopped directing focus to an eschatological future whose advent even he was not privileged to know.

Their eager curiosity alerts Jesus to how easily they might be fooled, so he responds with urgency, counseling caution.

Let your tone encourage composure.

These apocalyptic signs, dire as they are, will be preceded by even more painful personal struggles with governments and families.

Even in times of such distress we can give witness to our faith.

Jesus' tone suggests the sorrow with which his listeners would receive such unsettling news.

Slow down on the last two lines. Jesus, Shepherd of the sheep, speaks authoritatively of his care for those who cling to the sheepfold.

Then they **asked** him,
"**Teacher**, **when** will this **happen**?
And what **sign** will there be when **all** these things
    are **about** to **happen**?"
He **answered**,
"**See** that you not be **deceived**,
   for **many** will come in my **name**, saying,
   '**I** am **he**,' and 'The **time** has **come**.'
Do **not** **follow** them!
When you hear of **wars** and **insurrections**,
   do **not** be **terrified**; for such things **must** happen **first**,
   but it will not **immediately** be the **end**."
Then he said to them,
"**Nation** will **rise** against **nation**, and **kingdom** against **kingdom**.
There will be **powerful earthquakes**, **famines**, and **plagues**
   from **place** to **place**;
   and **awesome sights** and **mighty signs** will come from **the sky**.

"**Before** all this **happens**, **however**,
   they will **seize** and **persecute** you,
   they will **hand you over** to the **synagogues** and to **prisons**,
   and they will have you **led** before **kings** and **governors**
   because of **my name**.
It will **lead** to your giving **testimony**.
Remember, you are **not** to **prepare** your defense **beforehand**,
   for I **myself** shall **give** you a **wisdom** in **speaking**
   that **all** your **adversaries** will be **powerless** to **resist** or **refute**.
You will even be **handed over** by **parents**, **brothers**,
    relatives and **friends**,
   and they will put **some** of you to **death**.
You will be **hated** by **all** because of **my name**,
   but not a **hair** on your **head** will be **destroyed**.
By your **perseverance** you will **secure** your **lives**."

Whenever the end may come, it is undeniable that each day draws us closer. And just as illness and handicaps in our younger years help us anticipate old age and life's end, so too, wars, natural disasters, and great signs in the sky help us anticipate the day when the life of the planet will cease and all existence will be forever transformed. Jesus is drawn into discussing the end after gazing on the Temple and anticipating its imminent demise. Such awareness is healthy and necessary for all mature believers.

Realizing that fascination with end-times will attract charlatans who hope to profit from fears and uncertainty, Jesus warns of con men who will claim his identity. He also names some of the signs of the times that will bring terror and distress upon the earth. Most significant is the persecution some will suffer for the "name" of Jesus. Regarding this, Jesus counsels calm, for all they will need and need to say will be provided. Most startling is the prophecy that believers will be betrayed by family members and meet death at the hands of those they loved. It's a grim and ominous picture of what the future holds, but with the warning comes a promise that "perseverance" brings salvation. G.M.

OUR LORD JESUS CHRIST, KING OF THE UNIVERSE

LECTIONARY #162

READING I   2 Samuel 5:1–3

Hebron = HEB-ruhn

With the first line, set a tone of regal solemnity.

A reading from the second Book of Samuel

In those days, **all** the **tribes** of **Israel** came to **David**
     in **Hebron** and said:
     "**Here** we **are**, **your bone** and **your flesh**.
In days **past**, when **Saul** was our **king**,
     it was **you** who led the **Israelites out** and brought them **back**.
And the LORD said to you,
     'You shall **shepherd** my **people Israel**
     and shall be **commander** of Israel.'"
When all the **elders** of **Israel came** to **David** in **Hebron**,
     King David made an **agreement** with them there
          before the LORD,
     and they **anointed** him **king** of **Israel**.

Although Saul was king, it was David who led the armies and won many victories.

It was God's will that David be king. Speak "shepherd" and "commander" with great reverence.

They negotiate a covenant and then formally anoint him king.

TO KEEP IN MIND
As you are becoming familiar with your passage, read it directly from your Bible, **reading also what comes before and after** it to get a clear sense of its context.

RESPONSORIAL PSALM   Psalm 122:1–2, 3–4, 4–5 (see 1)

R. Let us go rejoicing to the house of the Lord.

I rejoiced because they said to me,
     "We will go up to the house of the LORD."
And now we have set foot
     within your gates, O Jerusalem.

Jerusalem, built as a city
     with compact unity.
To it the tribes go up,
     the tribes of the LORD.

According to the decree for Israel,
     to give thanks to the name of the LORD.
In it are set up judgment seats,
     seats for the house of David.

READING I Jesus was often called "Son of David." David was Israel's king, both by God's choice and the people's. As David's "son," Jesus can claim the title and throne of his forbearer, and when Jesus takes that throne, it will be forever.

This reading celebrates Christ's kingship by looking back at his ancestry and linking him with David, who was Israel's greatest king, a man after God's own heart. David ruled a united kingdom and remained Israel's model of the ideal king throughout her history. By conjuring the image of David, the shepherd boy who became a mighty warrior, the liturgy reminds us that Jesus' kingly identity is also multivalent. Like his ancestor, Jesus is shepherd and "commander" of Israel, who avoids breaking the bruised reed but who assumes his throne as King of Kings.

There is a tender relationship between the would-be king and the tribes of Israel that suggests the oneness between God and his people. The tribes characterize themselves as "your bone and your flesh," as if they were his progeny rather than his subjects. In David, who represented God's authority on earth, the nation finds both a father and a powerful leader. Of course, David was but a man who possessed tragic flaws. But in him we see the foreshadowing of a distant descendant who will also combine compassion and dominion and will ascend a cruciform throne that becomes the seat of life.

READING II (See also the Fifteenth Sunday in Ordinary Time for further commentary on this text.) It is almost impossible to read this passage without seeing cosmic images of stars being born and comets hurtling through

READING II   Colossians 1:12–20

A reading from the Letter of Saint Paul to the Colossians

Brothers and **sisters:**
Let us give **thanks** to the **Father,**
    who has made you **fit** to **share**
    in the **inheritance** of the **holy ones** in **light.**
He **delivered us** from the **power** of **darkness**
    and **transferred us** to the **kingdom** of his **beloved Son,**
    in whom we have **redemption,** the **forgiveness** of **sins.**

        He is the **image** of the **invisible God,**
            the **firstborn** of **all creation.**
        For in **him** were **created** all things in **heaven** and on **earth,**
            the **visible** and the **invisible,**
            whether **thrones** or **dominions** or **principalities** or **powers;**
            all things were **created through him** and **for him.**
        He is **before all** things,
            and **in** him **all things** hold **together.**
        He is the **head** of the **body,** the **church.**
        He is the **beginning,** the **firstborn** from the **dead,**
            that in **all** things he **himself** might be **preeminent.**
        For in **him** all the **fullness** was **pleased** to **dwell,**
            and **through** him to **reconcile** all **things** for him,
            making **peace** by the **blood** of his **cross**
            through him, whether those on **earth** or those in **heaven.**

Sidebar notes (left column):

Call your assembly to prayerful thanks that, in Christ, God made us worthy of salvation.

Because he loves us, God always takes the initiative. Proclaim this joyfully.

beloved = bee-LUHV-uhd

The ancient Christological hymn begins here.

Here are four categories of angels; distinguish each from the others.

Take joy and pride in naming these attributes of Christ, your Savior.

Employ a slower and more considered delivery here.

"The blood of his cross" helps set the stage for today's ironic Gospel.

---

space. Christ is presented as the eternal Word through whom God created the world. The text jumps from images of Jesus accomplishing the work of salvation by winning forgiveness of our sins to grand images of the eternal Christ, "the firstborn of all creation," bringing all things, "visible and invisible," into existence and reigning over the angelic powers of heaven.

The structure of this passage is that of a liturgical hymn, in use at the time of this writing, which sings of Christ as "firstborn" of both *creation* and our *salvation*. He preceded all things and all things are held together by him. This primacy is discussed for good reason. False teachers had infected the faith of believers in Colossae persuading them that Christ's role was inferior to that of angels. From prison, Paul tackles this falsehood by asserting that through Christ even the angelic beings—"thrones . . . dominions . . . powers"—were created.

Christ's supremacy is further underscored by the repetition (six times) of the phrase "all things" that tells us in no subtle way that, as firstborn of creation, he is lord of *everything*! His parallel role as firstborn of the dead names him Savior, something he accomplished "through the blood of his cross." Let your joyous proclamation announce that in him is the "fullness" of God, because he is God!

GOSPEL   Jesus' teaching, so full of ironic insight, continues on this day as he teaches from the throne of his Cross. The Gospel texts of the other liturgical years, taken from Matthew and John, present Jesus in control, whether sparring with Pilate or speaking of his Second Coming. But here we have a nearly mute Jesus who is mocked by "rulers," "sol-

GOSPEL   Luke 23:35–43

A reading from the holy Gospel according to Luke

The rulers **sneered** at Jesus and said,
    "He **saved others**, let him **save himself**
    if he is the **chosen** one, the **Christ** of **God**."
Even the **soldiers** jeered at him.
As they **approached** to offer him **wine** they called out,
    "If **you** are **King** of the **Jews**, **save** yourself."
Above him there was an **inscription** that read,
    "**This** is the **King** of the **Jews**."

Now **one** of the **criminals** hanging there **reviled** Jesus, saying,
    "Are **you** not the **Christ**?
Save yourself and **us**."
The **other**, however, **rebuking** him, said in **reply**,
    "Have **you** no **fear** of **God**,
    for you are **subject** to the **same condemnation**?
And **indeed**, **we** have been **condemned justly**,
    for the **sentence** we **received corresponds** to our **crimes**,
    but **this** man has done **nothing** criminal."
Then he said,
    "**Jesus**, **remember** me when you **come** into your **kingdom**."
He **replied** to him,
    "**Amen**, I **say** to **you**,
    today you will be with **me** in **Paradise**."

Notice that only the leaders and soldiers mock Jesus, not the crowd.

They spit their words at him in mocking insult.

You might echo the voice of Pilate who required this sign.

Does he turn his anger and self-hatred on the helpless man beside him?

His life of crime has not withered all his faith. It would seem he's inviting his fellow thief to a like conversion.

In the original Greek, the verb for "remember" suggests the thief repeated the phrase multiple times.

Jesus demonstrates his sovereignty in determining the man's fate. Speak the line slowly and simply.

diers," and even a condemned "criminal." Jesus' cruciform throne places him above the jeering crowd, but he speaks no words to defend or save himself, only words promising salvation to one who is as much outcast as he is. So, even here Jesus does in fact demonstrate his kingship, for his pain and seeming helplessness are no impediment to pronouncing a sentence of life for the so-called "good thief" at his side.

Jesus' companions in death are two condemned strangers, one who echoes the jeers of the leaders and one who senses the mysterious grace that emanates from the man wearing a thorny crown. The angry thief demands that Jesus intervene and save his earthly life. But the other, recognizing his own guilt and the fitting punishment it garnered, focuses beyond and begs Jesus to "remember" him in his Kingdom. His remarkable honesty and stunning faith make this thief an unlikely role model. He recognized and confessed his sins and then repented and asked forgiveness. For this, he was canonized on the cross by the Lord himself. Despite his guilt, this thief called Jesus by name. We too, sinners all, can confidently approach our King, call him by name, and say, "Jesus, remember me." G.M.